THE NEW INTERNATIONAL

WEBSTER'S
VEST POCKET
DICTIONARY

**TRIDENT
PRESS
INTERNATIONAL**

Published by
Trident Press International
2005 EDITION

Cover Design Copyright • Trident Press International
Copyright © 2005 Trident Press International

ISBN 1582792127

All Rights Reserved

Printed in Colombia by Cargraphics S.A.

a, A *indefinite article* used before a word beginning with a consonant; — *adj.* for each, first in order

aard´vark *n.* an African mammal that feeds on ants and temites

aard´wolf *n.* a mammal of the hyena family that feeds on termites

a•ba´ *n.* a sleeveless Arab robe

a•back´ *adv.* pressed backward; to the rear —**taken aback** caught by surprise, disconcerted

ab´a•cus *n.* an ancient device inc performing calculations by the use of rows of beads on rods

a•baft´ *adv.* toward the stern of a ship —*prep.* further back than

ab•a•lo´ne *n.* an edible shellfish lined with mother-of-pearl

a•ban´don *n.* spontaneity; unrestrained enthusiasm —*vt.* to give up; forsake; to give in to emotion —**a•ban´don•ment** *n.*

a•ban´doned *adj.* forsaken; unrestrained; lacking modesty, shameless

a•base´ *vt.* degrade; dishonor

a•base´ment *n.* humiliation, shame

a•bash´ *vt.* to make confused; to embarrass —**a•bash´ed•ly** *adv.*

a•bash´ment *n.* confusion, disorientation, embarrassment

a•bate´ *vi., vt.* to lessen; to re duce —**a•bat´a•ble** *adj*

abate´ment *n.* a lessening; mitigation —**a•bat´or** *n.*

ab´a•tis *n.* a defensive barricade

a•bat•jour´ *n.* a device for deflecting sunlight; a skylight

ab•at•toir *n.* a slaughterhouse

ab•ax´i•al *adj.* facing away from the axis

ab´ba•cy *n.* the office or jurisdiction of an abbot

ab´bess *n.* the director of a nunnery

ab´bey *n.* a monastery or nunnery

ab´bot *n.* the director of a monestary

ab´bot•cy, ab´bot•ship *n.* the office and trappings of an abbot

ab•bre´vi•ate *vt.* to shorten

ab•bre´vi•a´tion *n.* a short ened form

ABC´s *n.* the basics; rudimentary elements; beginning knowledge

ab´di•cate *vi., vt.* to formally renounce a responsibility; to give up a throne —**ab´di•ca´tion** *n.*

ab•do´men *n.* the lower portion of the human trunk, from the diaphragm to the pelvic girdle

ab•dom´i•nal *adj.* pertaining to the abdomen —**ab•dom´i•nal•ly** *adv.*

ab•du´cent *adj.* of a muscle that pulls away from the body

ab•duct´ *vt.* to kidnap; to carry away

ab•duc´tion *n.* a kidnapping; the abducting of a person by force

ab•duc´tor *n.* a muscle that pulls away from the axis of the body

a•beam´ *adj., adv.* at right angles to the keel of a ship

a•be•ce•dar´ian *adj.* primary, rudimentry —*n.* a beginning student.

abed' *adj.* in bed

ab·er'rance, ab·er'ran·cy *n.* deviation from the right or usual course

ab·er'rant *adj.* abnormal —*n.* a strange or abnormal person —**ab·er'rant·ly** *adv.*

ab·er·ra'tion *n.* an abnormality; a deviation; delusion, derangement —**ab·er·ra'tion·al** *adj.*

abet' *vt.* assist or support in wrongdoing —**a·bet'ment** *n.*

a·bet'tor, a·bet'ter *n.* one who assists; an accessory or collaborator

a·bey'ance *n.* a temporary state of suspension; a hiatus

a·bey'ant *adj.* in a dormant state

ab·hor' *vt.* to loathe

ab·hor'rence *n.* a strong aversion.

ab·hor'rent *adj.* detestable; causing disgust —**ab·hor'·rent·ly** *adv.*

a·bid'ance *n.* continuance

a·bide' *vi.* to stay in a place; to remain unchanging —*vt.* to wait for; to endure; to submit to

a·bid'ing *adj.* continuing, steadfast —**a·bid'ing·ly** *adv.*

a·bil'i·ty *n.* power, faculty; competence; endowed with skill

a·bi·o·gen'e·sis *n.* the theory that life may be created from inorganic matter —**a·bi·o·ge·net'ic** *adj.*

a·bi·og'e·nist *n.* one who believes in the spontaneous generation of life

a·bi·ot'ic *adj.* regarding inorganic matter; not organic; not living

ab·ject', ab'ject *adj.*

wretched; beyond all hope; without self esteem —**ab'·ject'ly** *adv.*

ab·jec'tion *n.* a degrading condition.

ab·jure' *vt.* renounce under oath; recant or retract; abstain from —**ab·ju·ra'tion** *n.*

ab·la'tion *n.* a wearing away; surgical excision of tissue —**ab·late** *vt., vi.*

ab'la·tive *adj.* in grammar, expressing separation or removal from source, as *freedom from fear*

a·blaze' *adj., adv.* on fire; aroused to passion or excitement; fervent

a'ble *adj.* possessing adequate ability; qualified — **a'bly** *adv.*

a'ble·bod'ied *adj.* sound of body; physically capable

abloom' *adj.* in bloom; flowering.

ab'lu·ent *adj.* used for cleaning —*n.* a cleansing agent

ab·lu'tion *n.* the act of washing; a bath; a ceremonial washing during a religious ceremony

a'bly *adv.* in a competent mariner; proficiently

ab'ne·gate *vt.* to give up, as a privilege or desire —**ab'ne·ga·tor** *n.*

ab·ne·ga'tion *n.* rejection or renunciation; self-denial; disavowal

ab·nor'mal *adj.* unnatural; differing from the normal or average

ab·nor·mal'i·ty *n.* an aberration; an oddity or anomaly; a malforma-tion or peculiarity

ab·nor'mal·ly *adv.* to an unusual degree; exceedingly, exceptionally.

ab·nor´mi·ty n. a monstrosity or perversion.

a·board´ adv. onto a conveyance; in agreement, as to support for a common cause —**all aboard** a warning to passengers that the vehicle is about to depart

a·bode´ n. a dwelling; a place of habitation or residence

a·bol´ish vt. to put an end to; to invalidate —**a·bol´ish·ment** n.

ab·o·li´tion n. the act of terminating or eliminating

ab·o·li´tion·ist n. one who wishes to abolish something

a·bom´i·na·ble adj. hateful; horrible; offensive —**a·bom´in·a·bly** adv.

a·bom·i·na´tion n. extreme disgust or abhorrence; that arousing feelings of disgust

ab·o·rig´i·nal adj. native or indigenous —n. a native inhabitant

ab·o·rig´ine n. a native or earliest known inhabitant of a region

ab·o·rig´i·nes pl. n. first in habitants: the flora and fauna of an area

a·bort´ vi. to bring forth young before full development; to terminate prematurely —vt to cause an early, unsuccessful conclusion

a·bor´tion n. a miscarriage; a failure to evolve normally; the product of failure, a monstrosity; a failed attempt —**a·bor´tion·ist** n.

a·bor´tive adj. useless; vain or futile

a·bound´ vi. to be plentiful

a·bout´ adv. almost or approximately; in another direction —prep. in or around

an area; particular to or associated with: an air about her; approximating: departing about noon; in regard to: a book about money management .

a·bout´·face n. a turn to the rear; an abrupt reversal

a·bove´ adv. over; overhead; higher in rank —adj. foregoing or preceding —n. something before or over —prep rising over or higher: the moon above the lake —**above all** having precedence; most important

ab·ove´board adj., adv. candid, forthright; with nothing concealed

a·brade´ vt. to scrape or wear away

a·bra´sion n. the act or result of a wearing away; an injury from contact with a rough surface

a·bra´sive adj. wearing; capable of eroding; disagreeable or offensive —n. a material which abrades, as sandpaper or emery —**a·bra´sive·ly** adv. —**a·bra´sive·ness** n.

a·breast´ adv. side by side

a·bridge´ vt. to shorten; to condense, by reducing to fewer words; to lessen or de prive, as of civil rights

a·bridg´ment n. that which has been shortened; an abstract

a·broad´ adv. away; in a foreign land; widely circulated

ab·ro·gate´ vt. to repeal or annul; to abolish —**ab´ro·ga´tion** n.

a·brupt´ adj. sudden; unexpected —**ab·rupt´ly** adv.

ab´scess n. a collection of pus in a body cavity

3

ab•scis´sa n. in a graph, the distance of a reference point from the Y-axis, parallel to the X-axis

ab•scis´sion n. severance or removal; in speaking, an abrupt pause for dramatic effect

ab•scond´ vi. to leave quickly and secretly

ab´sence n. a deficiency or inadequacy; truancy; lack or want

ab´sent adj. not present; lacking; inattentive —**ab•sent´** vt. to remain away — **ab´sent•ly** adv.

ab´sen•tee´ n. one who is absent —adj. of one not present: absentee landlord; of action by one absent: an absentee vote

ab´sen•tee´ism n. the state of being absent; the frequency of absence

ab´sent•mind´ed adj. preoccupied; unmindful of immediate demands; forgetful — **ab´sent•mind´ed•ly** adv. — **ab´sent•mind´ed•ness** n.

ab´sinthe n. wormwood; an anise flavored liqueur

ab´so•lute adj. complete; perfect; without reservation; unadulterated; not dependent on an arbitrary standard —n. that which is perfect

absolute zero n. 459.6° F. below zero; the temperature at which a substance would be wholly deprived of heat

ab´so•lu´tion n. exoneration; vindication; forgiveness; the ceremonial remission of sin

ab´so•lut•ism n. despotism; a principle that grants a ruler unlimited powers — **ab•so•lu•tis´tic** adj.

ab•solve´ vt. to acquit of guilt or complicity; to free from an obligation; to pardon or remit from sin —**ab•solv´a•ble** adj. —**ab•solv´er** n.

ab•sorb´ vt. to engross completely; to assimilate; to occupy entirely —**ab•sorb´a•ble** adj.

ab•sor´bent adj. disposed to absorb —n. a substance that absorbs —**ab•sorb´en•cy** n.

ab•sorb´ing adj. stimulating or enticing —**ab•sorb´ing•ly** adv.

ab•sorp´tion n. the process of absorbing; concentration or preoccupation —**ab•sorp´tive** adj.

ab•stain´ vi. to forbear; to avoid or shun voluntarily

ab•ste´mi•ous adj. avoiding excess; temperate —**ab•ste´mi•ous•ly** adv.

ab•sten´tion n. temperance, foregoing —**ab•sten´tious** adj.

ab´sti•nence n. the practice of avoiding something, such as intoxicating drink —**ab´sti•nent** adj.

ab´stract adj. apart from the absolute or concrete; theoretical; difficult to understand; impersonal; of a style of art —n. an abridgment; a summary; a non-specific idea or term —**ab•stract´** vt. to take from; to condense; to form a notion of: an abstract concept —adj. general; theoretical; considered apart from the specific —**ab•strac´tion•al** adj.

abstract art a school of art that makes use of designs based on relationships rather than representation of objects

ab•stract´ed adj. disassociated or apart; obscure; preoccupied —**ab•stract´ed•ly** adv.

ab•strac´tion n. preoccupation; an ideal —**ab•strac´tive** adj.

ab•struse´ adj. difficult to comprehend **ab•struse´ly** adv.

ab•surd´ adj. Irrational; preposterous; ridiculous **ab•surd´ly** adv.

ab•surd´i•ty n. that which is preposterous or ridiculous

a•bun´dance n. a quantity in excess of need; plenty

a•bun´dant adj. bountiful; more than enough —**a•bun´dant•ly** adv.

a•buse´ n. improper use; misapplication; cruel treatment —vt. to use incorrectly; to harm by improper use; to injure by mistreating

a•bu´sive adj. characterized by abuse; serving to abuse **a•bu´sive•ly** adv. **a•bu´sive•ness** n.

a•but´ n. to touch; border; form a line of contact —vt. to border on

a•but´ment vi. a supporting element of a structure; a buttress

a•bys´mal adj. bottomless; extreme —**a•bys´mal•ly** adv.

a•byss´ n. a bottomless gulf; a chasm; a tremendous depth

ac•a•deme´, ac´a•deme n. a place of learning; an academy; a scholarly environment

ac´a•dem´ia n. the academic world; institutions of learning collectively

ac´a•dem´ic adj. scholarly; of

traditional learning; theoretical or hypothetical —n. a scholar; member of a learned society —**ac•a•dem´i•cal** n. —**ac•a•dem´i•cal•ly** adv.

a•cad´e•my n. a preparatory school; a society of scholars

a•cap•pel´la adj. vocal music without instrumental accompaniment

ac•cede´ vi. to come into an office; to agree to —**ac•ced´ence** n.

ac•cel´er•ate vi. to move more rapidly; to hurry —vt. to increase the speed of; to hasten the natural course of: to *accelerate growth*

ac•cel´er•a•tion n. a hastening; the rate of increase in speed

ac•cel´er•a´tor n. a device that controls speed; that which increases speed, flow etc.

ac´cent n. voice stress in the pronunciation of a word; a mark (´)to indicate vocal stress; a manner of speaking which differs from place to place —vt. to stress; to speak or produce with an accent

ac•cen´tu•ate vt. to stress; to emphasize —**ac•cen´tu•a•tion** n.

ac•cept´ vt. to take what is offered; to agree to; to embrace as true; to take in as a member —**ac•cept´ance** n.

ac•cept´a•ble adj. satisfactory; worthy of acceptance; adequate, although not entirely pleasing: *an acceptable level of error* —**ac•cept´a•bil´i•ty** n. —**ac•cept´a•bly** adv.

ac•cept´ed *adj.* generally believed

ac´cess *n.* an approach or passage; permission to enter; a means of obtaining — *vt.* to gain the use of, as a computer program or data

ac•ces´si•ble *adj.* easily reached; easily influenced; allowing access; attainable —**ac´ces´si•bil´i•ty** *n.*

ac´ces´so•ry, ac•ces´sa•ry *adj.* added; aiding, contributing; supplemental —*n.* an accomplice; a thing added —**ac•ces´so•rize** *vt.*

ac´ci•dent *n.* an unexpected occurrence; a misadventure; an unintentional act

ac•ci•den´tal *adj.* happening by chance; fortuitous; incidental —**ac´ci´den´tal•ly** *adv.*

ac•claim´ *vt.* to applaud; to receive with approval; to approve by proclamation —*vi.* to applaud or shout —*n.* enthusiastic applause

ac´cla•ma´tion *n.* applause; general approval

ac´cli´mate, ac•cli´ma•tize´ *vi., vt.* to grow accustomed

ac´clam´a•to´ry *adj.* expressing joy and adulation

ac•cliv´i•ty *n.* an upward slope

ac´co•lade´ *n* any honor or award; words of praise

ac•com´mo•date´ *vi.* to become adjusted —*vt.* to supply food or lodging; to adapt; to be suitable for —**ac•com´mo•da•tive** *adj.*

ac•com´mo•da´tion *n* an adaptation; a reconciliation; a convenience; board or lodging; assistance; a willingness to provice assistance

ac•com´pa•nist *n.* one who plays or sings to enhance a performance of another —**ac•com´pa•ni•ment** *n.*

ac•com´pa•ny *vt.* to go with; to escort; to play or sing with another; to supplement; to occur at the same time: *cold   accompanied by fever*

ac•com´plice *n.* an associate in crime; a knowing confederate

ac•com´plish *vt.* to perform; to fulfill, as an obligation; to complete

ac•com´plished *adj.* completed; fulfilled; proficient; refined

ac•com´plish•ment *n.* something completed; a worthly attainment

ac•cord´ *n.* agreement; spontaneous desire —*vi.* be in agreement; harmonize —*vt.* to grant; bring into harmony —**of one´s own accord** freely done, without urging —**according to** as per direction or plan; as reported

ac•cord´ance *n.* conformity; accord; harmony

ac•cord´ing•ly *adv.* as a result

ac•cost´ *vt.* to confront

ac•count´ *n.* a computation; a report; a record of transactions —*vi.* to provide a reason; to be responsible —*vt.* to impute —**give a good account** to do well —**on account** on credit —**on no account** under no circumstance —**take into account** bear in mind

ac•count´a•ble *adj.* having liability; responsible; able to be explained —**ac•count•a•bil´i•ty** *n.*

ac•count´an•cy *n.* the office and duties of an accountant

ac´count´ant *n.* one experienced in keeping accounts; one records or audits financial records —**public accountant** an accountant whose services are available to the public —**certified public accountant** (*US*) an accountant sanctioned by a state examining body

ac•count´ing *n.* a settlement; a statement of the finances of an organization; the profession of recording financial transactions

ac•cred´it *vt.* to certify; to send with credentials

ac•cre´tion *n.* a growth; an accumulation or addition, as of a sedimentary deposit

ac•cru´al *n.* an increase or accumulation; something that increases

ac•crue´ *vi.* to increase; to be added to, as interest

ac•cu´mu•late *vt.* to pile up; to gather —*vi.* to increase — **ac•cu´mu•la•tor** *n.*

ac•cu´mu•la´tion *n.* a collection; a growth or increase

ac•cu´mu•la•tive *adj.* tending to increase —**ac•cu´mu•la•tive•ly** *adv.*

ac´cu•ra•cy *n.* a measure of precision; correctness; exactness

ac´cu•rate *adj.* very exact; precise; capable of precise measurement; within set limits —**ac´cu•rate•ly** *adv.*

ac•curs´ed, **ac•curst´** *adj.* under a curse; deserving a curse

ac•cu•sa´tion, **ac•cu´sal** *n.* the act of accusing or being accused

ac•cuse´ *vi.* to verbalize charges —*vt.* bring a charge against —**ac•cus´ing•ly** *adv.*

ac•cused´ *n.* a person or persons charged with a crime

ac•cus´tom *vt.* to make or become familiar through use; to adapt to

ac•cus´tomed *adj.* habitual or usual; customary; characteristic

ace *n.* a single spot on a playing card or die; one who excels, an expert; in tennis, a point won on the serve — *vt.* to score an ace

ac´er•bate *vt.* to make harsh or bitter; intensify; to annoy

a•cer´bic, **a•cerb´** *adj.* sour tasting; harsh in manner or language —**a•cer´bi•ty** *n.*

ac´e•tate *n.* a fiber used in the making of textiles

a•ce´tic *adj.* sour; having the sourness of vinegar; containing acetic acid or vinegar —**a•ce´ti•fy** *vi.*, *vt.*

acetic acid *n.* a colorless sour acid; the chief component of vinegar

ac´e•tone *n.* a colorless, flammable liquid ketone used as a solvent

a•cet´y•lene *n.* a colorless, flammable gas used as a fuel in welding

a•ce´tyl•sal•i•cyl´ic acid *n.* aspirin

ache *vi.* to hurt; to suffer throbbing pain; to suffer loss; to feel sympathy —*n.* a dull protracted pain — **ach´i•ness** *n.* —**ach´y** *adj.*

a•chieve´ *vi.* reach an objective —*vt.* to accomplish; to complete successfully — **a•chiev´a•ble** *adj.*

a•chieve´ment *n.* the act of

accomplishing; a notable act; an accomplishment

ac´id *adj.* sour and sharp; caustic or sarcastic —*n.* a sour substance

a•cid´ic *adj.* having the properties of acid

a•cid´i•fy *vi.* to turn acid —*vt.* to transform into acid

a•cid´i•ty *n.* sourness and tartness; degree of acid strength

acid test a test of quality, veracity, etc.; a severe test

ac•knowl´edge *vt.* to admit or confess; to certify; show appreciation; confirm receipt of —**ac•knowl´edge•a•ble** *adj.*

ac•knowl´edge•ment, ac• knowl´edge•ment *n.* recognition of responsibility; a response; appreciation; confirmation of receipt

ac´me *n.* the highest point; zenith

ac´ne *n.* a skin affliction

a´corn *n.* fruit of the oak tree

a•cous´tic, acous´ti•cal *adj.* pertaining to sound or the sense of hearing —**a•cous´ti•cal•ly** *adv.*

a•cous´tics *pl. n.* the study of sound; the sound quality in a place

ac•quaint´ *vt.* to make aware of; to inform; to introduce — **be acquainted with** familiar, but not well known

ac•quaint´ance *n.* knowledge; familiarity; an associate; one known to another

ac´qui•esce´ *vi.* to comply without enthusiasm; to accept as inevitable —**ac´qui• es´cence** *n.* —**ac´qui•es´ cent** *adj.*

ac•quire´ *vt.* to obtain or gain

ac´qui•si´tion *n.* a thing

gained; an appropriation

ac•quis´i•tive *adj.* prone to acquire —**ac•quis´i•tive•ly** *adv.*—**ac•quis´i•tive•ness** *n.*

ac•quit´ *vt.* to pronounce innocent; to discharge a trust; to behave or act: *he acquitted himself well*

ac•quit´tal *n.* a discharge of duty; in law, a finding of not guilty, or being set free by judgment of a court

ac•quit´tance *n.* a settlement of liability; proof of such settlement

a´cre *n.* a *land* measure equal to 4,840 square yards

a´cre•age *n.* property; a single parcel of land

ac´rid *adj.* sharp in taste or smell; pungent —**ac´rid•ly** *adv.*—**ac´rid•ness** *n.*

ac•ri•mo´ni•ous *adj.* sarcastic; caustic; acerbic

ac´ri•mo•ny *n.* sharp or bitter speech or temperament

ac´ro•bat *n.* a trapeze artist, gymnast, or tumbler —**ac´ ro•bat´ic** *adj.*

ac´ro•bat´ics *n.* gymnastics

ac´ro•nym *n.* a word formed from the initial letters of a name such as *NASA* for *National Aeronautics and Space Administration*

ac•ro•pho´bi•a *n.* a fear of heights —**ac•ro•pho´bic** *adj.*

a•cross´ *adv.* from one side to the other; on the opposite side —*prep.* at the other side; from one side to the other; upon: *I came across the papers yesterday*

a•cros´tic *n.* a written message whose initial letters form a word or another message

a•cryl´ic *adj.* of or made from

acrylic resin —n. a transparent resin; an acrylic substance such as paint or fiber

act vi. to behave oneself; to perform a function or produce an effect: *acid acts on metal* —vt. to play on the stage; to behave in a certain way —**act as** to serve temporarily —**act on** follow an order —**act up** to be troublesome —**get into the act** join in —**put on an act** to pretend

act′ing adj. standing in for another; operating —n. a stage performance; an affectation

ac′tion n. putting forth energy; decisiveness: *a man of action:* the result of activity; a manner of movement; moving parts; a thing done; a law suit —**ac′tions** pl. n. one's behavior or conduct

ac′tion·a·ble adj. forming the basis for a lawsuit —**ac′tion·a·bly** adv.

ac′ti·vate vt. to make active; to purify by aeration —**ac′ti·va′tion** n.

ac′tive adj. energetic, lively; operative: *an active volcano;* taking part: *an active member,* —**ac′tive·ly** adv. —**ac′tive·ness** n.

ac·tiv′i·ty n. lively movement; a planned undertaking; a transaction

ac′tiv·ism n. involvement in social issues —**ac′tiv·ist** n.

ac′tu·al adj. existing in fact — n. a thing that is real —**ac′tu·al·i·ty** n.

ac′tu·al·ise (Brit.), **ac′tu·al·ize** (US) vt. to make real; portray realistically

ac′tu·al·ly adv. truly; as a matter of fact

ac′tu·ar·y n. one who calculates risk as for insurers —**ac·tu·ar′i·al** adj.

ac′tu·ate vt. to impel; put in motion; cause to act —**ac′tu·a′tion** n.

a·cu′i·ty n. insight; discernment in reasoning or perception

a·cu′men n. insight; quick to understand; intelligence; sagacity

ac·u·punc′ture n. an Oriental treatment for pain or illness using fine needles —**ac′u·punc·tur·ist** n.

a·cute′ adj. pointed, sharp; keen of mind; serious, as an acute illness; intense, as pain —**a·cute′ly** adv.

acute angle n. an angle of less than 90°

ad n. an advertisement

ad′age n. a proverb or maxim

ad′a·mant adj. unyielding; resolute in belief —**ad′a·mant·ly** adv.

a·dapt′ n. to grow adjusted to —vt. to make suitable; to accommodate —**adapt′a·ble** adj. —**a·dapt·a·bil′i·ty** n.

ad·ap·ta′tion n. something modified; the process of modifying

a·dapt′er, a·dap′tor n. a device for modifying for a different use; a connecting device

a·dap′tive adj. capable of being modified —**a·dap′tive·ly** adv.

add vi. to increase; to perform addition; —vt. to increase; to total numbers; to speak or write more —**add up** to total; seem reasonable

add′end n., pl. **ad·den′da** a

number added to an existing number, called the *augend*

ad•den´dum *n.* an addition; a thing to be added, such as an appendix

ad´dict *n.* one given to illegal drugs or alcohol —**ad•dict´** *vt.* to be devoted to: *addicted to work;* to be .dependent on: *addicted to drugs*

ad•dic´tion *n.* psychological or physiological dependence; a compulsion

ad•dict´ed *adj.* predisposed to

ad•dic´tive *adj.* habit-forming

ad•di´tion *n.* the process of summing numbers; something added; an increase — **ad•di´tion•al** *adj., n.*

ad´di•tive *n.* an ingredient that alters flavor, performance, etc. —*adj.* tending to increase

ad´dle *vt.* to become confused —*vt.* to cause, to be; to muddle: *addled by strong drink* —*adj.* confused, incoherent

ad´dle•brained´ *adj.* confused; flustered; also **ad´dle•pat´ed**

ad•dress´ *vt.* to speak or write to; to direct to: *address a letter,* to attend to: *address a problem* —*n.* a speech; one's bearing or manner; a specific location

ad•dress´a•ble *adj.* approachable; able to locate, as computer data

ad•dress•ee´ *n.* one addressed

ad•duce´ *vt.* to cite as an example or proof —**ad´duc´i•ble** *adj.*

ad•duct´ *vt.* to pull toward the axis of the body —**ad•duc´tion** *n.*

ad•duc´tor *n.* of a muscle that pulls toward the median axis of the body

ad´e•noid *n.* glandular tissue at the upper part of the throat —*adj.* glandular

a•dept´ *adj.* extremely skilled; proficient —**ad´ept´** *n.* a person who is highly skilled; an expert —**a•dept´ly** *adv.* — **a•dept´ness** *n.*

ad´e•quate *adj* barely sufficient; suitable for immediate need —**ad´e•qua•cy** *n.* —**ad´ e•quate•ly** *adv.*

ad•here´ *vi.* to stick; to follow closely; to follow faithfully — **ad•her´ence** *n.*

ad•he´sion *n.* sticking or being stuck; a close attachment

ad•he´sive *adj.* tending to stick; gummed —*n.* that which causes adhesion — **ad•he´sive•ness** *n.*

adhesive tape material coated with adhesive, for securing or binding

ad hoc´ relating to a particular thing

ad hoc committee a committee formed for a particular purpose

ad in•fi•ni´tum to infinity; forever; unlimited

ad´i•pose *adj.* pertaining to fat

ad•ja´cence ad•ja´cen•cy *n.* the state of being near or neighboring

ad•ja´cent *adj.* near or join-ing; neighboring

ad•jec•ti´val, ad´jec•ti•val *adj.* like an adjective

ad´jec•tive *n.* a word that modifies a noun; a phrase used as an adjective —*adj.* pertaining to or functioning as an adjective

ad•join´ *vt.* to be close; to touch; to unite —*vi.* to be close or in contact

ad•journ´ vi., vt. to end; postpone; to move to another place —**ad•journ´meat** n.

ad•judge´ vt. to order by law; to decide judicially

ad•ju´di•cate vi. to perform the function of a judge —vt. to decide judicially —**ad•ju´di•ca´tion** n. —**ad•ju´di•ca•tive** adj.

ad´junct adj. supplementary; additional —n. something added; one assigned as a subordinate; a nonessential quality

ad•jure´ vt. to charge under oath; to appeal intently —**ad•jur´a•to´ry** adj. —**ad•jur´er,** **ad•ju´ror** n.

ad•just´ vi. to adapt or conform —vt. to arrange so as to fit; to reconcile differences —**ad•just´a•ble** adj.

ad•just´ment n. the process of adjusting; amount of settlement: *an insurance adjustment;* an allowance for wear

ad´ju•tant n. an assistant who carries out the directives of a superior

ad lib´ adj. created spontaneously: *ad lib remarks* —adv. spontaneously —vi., vt. to improvise —n.

ad•min´is•ter vi. to perform managerial duties; to assist —vt. to manage; to dispense, as justice; to conduct, as a swearing in or test; to provide assistance

ad•min´is•trate vt. to administer

ad•min´is•tra´tion n. the act of administering; power or party in office; term of office; settlement of an estate —**ad•min´is•tra´tive** adj. —**ad•min´is•tra•tive•ly** adv.

ad´mi•ra•ble adj. deserving admiration —**ad´mi•ra•bly** adv.

ad•mi´ral•ty n. the jurisdiction of an admiral; the branch of the , juiciary responsible for maritime affairs

ad•mi•ra´tion n. appreciation, as of something rare or beautiful; that which causes appreciation, approval, etc.

ad•mire´ vt. to regard with wonder; to esteem; to respect —vi. to express admiration —**ad´mi•ra•bly** adv.

ad•mis´si•ble adj. worthy of consideration; allowable —**ad•mis´si•bil´i•ty** n. —**ad•mis´si•bly** adv.

ad•mis´sion n. the act of admitting; the price paid for entrance; the right to enter; confession

ad•mit´ vt. to allow to enter; to be the means to enter; to allow membership, as to a club or society; to accede to or acknowledge —vi. to afford entrance

ad•mit´tance n. right or permission to enter; the act of admitting; admission or entrance

ad•mit´ted adj. accepted as valid; confessed; acclaimed; acknowledged

ad•mit´ted•ly adv. confessedly

ad•mix´ture n. a combination; a blending of ingredients; an additional ingredient

ad•mon´ish vt. to counsel; offer a mild rebuke; instruct —**ad•mon´ish•ment** n.

ad´mo•ni´tion n. a mild rebuke; a warning —**ad•mon´i•to´ry** adj.

a•do´ n. unnecessary activity; bustle; commotion

a•do´be adj. made from sun-dried brick —n. a sun-dried brick; a building made from such bricks; the earth or clay of which such building blocks are made

ad•o•les´cence n. the period of growth from childhood to maturity

ad•o•les´cent adj. characteristic of youth; youthful; lacking maturity —n. a youth

a•dopt´ vt. to raise as one's own; to take up and follow; adopt a change; to enact, as a law —**a•dop´tion** n. — **a•dop´tive** adj.

a•dor´a•ble adj. delightful; enchanting —**a•dor´a•bly** adv.

ad´o•ra´tion n. worship or reverence; deep affection or esteem

a•dore´ vi., vt. to cherish; to be especially fond of — **a•dor´ing•ly** adv.

a•dorn´ vt. to decorate or embellish; to beautify — **a•dorn´ment** n.

ad•re´nal adj. near the kidneys; of the adrenal glands —n. an adrenal gland

adrenal gland either of two small glands located above the kidneys

ad•ren´al•in, ad•ren´al•ine n. a stimulant secreted by the adrenal glands

a•drift´ adj., adv. wandering; lacking direction or purpose

a•droit´ adj. clever or resourceful; expert —**a•droit´ly** adv.

ad•sorb´ vt. to retain gas or liquid on the surface — **ad•sorp´tion** n.

ad•u•la´tion n. base flattery; extravagant praise **ad´u•late** vt. —**ad´u•la•to•ry** adj.

a•dult´ adj. fully developed; full-grown; mature in manner; of or for a mature person —n. a fully grown person or animal; one who has attained legal majority

a•dul´ter•ant n. a substance that tends to contaminate

a•dul´ter•ate´ adj. impure; contaminated —vt. to make impure; to lessen the value of —**a•dul´ter•a´tion** n.

a•dul´ter•ous adj. characterized by or relating to adultery —**a•dul´ter•ous•ly** adv.

a•dul´ter•y n. sexual unfaithfulness by one who is married

ad va•lo•rem in proportion to value

ad•vance´ adj. before due: an advance payment; before the rest: an advance party —n. progress; an improvement; a prepayment —vi. to make progress; to rise —vt. to move forward; to offer or promote; to pay before due

ad•vanced´ adj. ahead of: an advanced student; late in time: the advanced stage of a project

ad•vance•ment n. furtherance: the advancement of science

ad•van´tage n. a favorable circumstance; superiority; a gain or benefit —vt. to benefit; to be of service to —**take advantage of** put to good use; to exploit

ad´van•ta´geous adj. providing advantage; beneficial — **ad´van•ta´geous•ly** adv.

ad´vent n. a coming, as of an

important event

ad•ven´ture n. an exciting undertaking; a speculative venture —vi. to venture; to take risks —vt. to place at risk —**ad•ven´tur•er** n.

ad•ven´ture•some adj. inclined to risky or hazardous activities

ad•ven´tur•ous adj. inclined to take risks; characterized by risk; hazardous —**ad•ven´tur•ous•ly** adv.

ad´verb n. a word that qualifies a verb, adjective, or other adverb, as to define time, place, manner, degree, etc. —**ad•verb´i•al** adj.

ad´ver•sar´y n. an opponent; one openly antagonistic —**ad•ver•sar´i•al** adj.

ad•verse´, ad•verse´ adj. acting against; unfavorable; moving in opposition —**ad•verse´ly** adv.

ad•ver´si•ty n. a state of hardship; difficult circumstances; misfortune

ad´ver•tise´ vi. to proclaim publicly; to request publicly such as for employment —vt. to give public notice of; to proclaim the advantage of —**ad•ver•tis•er** n.

ad•ver•tise´ment n. public notice in the media to sell, announce an event, etc.

ad´ver•tis•ing n. any method of publicizing; the business of publicizing

ad•vice´ n. counsel or guidance

ad•vis´a•ble adj. deserving of recommendation; opportune —**ad•vis´a•bil´i•ty** n. —**ad•vis´a•bly** adv.

ad•vise´ vi. offer advice —vt. give advice; recommend; to

inform —**ad•vis´er, ad•vi•sor** n.

ad•vised´ adj. deliberately considered; informed —**ad•vise´ment** n.

ad•vis´ed•ly adv. with forethought; carefully; prudently

ad•vi´so•ry adj. having power to advise; offered as advice —n. a recommendation; information

ad´vo•ca•cy n. pleading of a cause; support for a cause

ad´vo•cate n. one who pleads or argues a cause; a supporter; a lawyer —vt. to support or defend; to promote a cause; to argue in favor —**ad•voc´a•to•ry** adj.

adze, adz n. a cutting tool similar to an axe

ae´gis n. protective power; sponsorship or patronage

aer´ate vt. oxygenate; charge with gas; to purify by exposure to air —**aer•a´tion** n.

aer´i•al adj. of or like air; performed in the air or by aircraft; growing in the air; insubstantial or spiritual —n. (Brit.) a device for receiving radio or television signals

aer´i•al•ist n. an aerial acrobat

aer•ie n. the nest of a bird; any dwelling at a high elevation

aer´o•dy•nam´ics n. the study of bodies moving in the air

aer´o•nau´tics pl. n. the study of the design and operation of aircraft —**aer•o•nau´tic, aer•o•nau´ti•cal** adj.

aer´o•plane (Brit.) n. a fixed-wing aircraft

aer´o•sol adj. pertaining to a substance dispensed as a

fine spray —n. a suspension of fine particles; a substance under pressure released as a fine spray

aerosol bomb container holding a liquid released as spray or foam

aer′o•space adj. of the near outer space; of the science of space flight —n.

aerospace industry the business of designing and manufacturing space craft

aes′thete n. a connoisseur of beauty, fine art, etc.; one devoted to refinement and pretentious in appreciation of art and culture

aes•thet′ic, aes•thet′i•cal adj. prizing the artistic; characterized by taste — **aes•thet′i•cal•ly** adv.

aes′thet′ics n. the study of beauty and art, and the feelings they evoke

a•far′ adv. remotely; from a distance

af•fa•ble adj. pleasant; friendly —**af•fa•bil′i•ty** n. — **af•fa•bly** adv.

af•fair′ n. a bit of business; a social gathering; a minor dispute; a small matter; a romantic liaison .

af•fect′ vt. to influence; to arouse, emotion; be partial to; make a pretense of.—n. an emotion

af′fec•ta′tion n. an elaborate pretense; an artificial manner

af•fect′ed adj. acted upon, as by a drug; influenced emotionally; feigned to impress others; acting in an unnatural manner

af•fec′tion n. kind feelings for another; a fondness; love

af•fec′tion•ate adj. expressing fondness; loving —**af•fec′tion•ate•ly** adv.

af′fi•da′vit n. a written statement made under oath and notarized

af•fil′i•ate vt. to take in as a member; to join or associate with —vi. to become allied — n. one allied with another as a member, partner, etc. — **af•fil′i•a′tion** n.

af•fin′i•ty n. any natural attraction; a close relationship; a spiritual attraction between persons; the force by which chemical elements form compounds; a resemblance that suggests common origin

af•firm′ vt. to declare to be true; to ratify, as a statute —vi. to make a formal declaration —**af′fir•ma′tion** n.

af•firm′a•tive adj. positive; supportive —n. expressing confirmation

affirmative action a program for correcting past discrimination

af•fix′ vt. to attach or fasten; to add, as a signature; to attribute blame or responsibility —**af′fix** n. something added

af•fla′tus n. articulation of divine knowledge; any creative impulse

af•flict′ vt. to oppress; to cause distress —**af•flic′tive** adj. —**af•flic′tive•ly** adv.

af′flic′tion n. a state of distress; that which causes suffering; a misfortune; a calamity

af•flu•ence n. wealth; abundance; a rich supply

af′flu•ent adj. prosperous,

generously supplied —*n.* a wealthy person; a stream or *river* that flows into another —**af′flu•ent•ly** *adv.*

af•ford′ *vt.* to be able to meet expenses; to undergo without inconvenience: *we can afford to go*; to confer or grant: *afford one pleasure* — **af•ford•a•bil′i•ty** *n.* —**af•ford′a•ble** *adj.*

af•front′ *n.* an intentional insult —*vt.* to insult; treat with arrogance

a•fi•cio•na′do *n.* an enthusiastic *fan*

a•field′ *adv.* off the *usual* path; of endeavors which have gone astray

a•fire′ *adj., adv.* on fire; of one who exhibits great enthusiasm

a•float′ *adj., adv.* resting on the surface; drifting; of a financial state: *they barely remain afloat*

a•foot′ *adj., adv.* on foot; walking; progressing: *something is afoot*

a•fore′men•tioned *adj.* stated earlier; referred to previously

a•fore′said *adj.* said before

a•fore′ thought *adj.* premeditated

a•foul′ *adj., adv.* entangled — **run afoul of** get into difficulty with

a•fraid′ *adj.* filled with fear or apprehension; anxious; regretful: *I'm afraid there's been a mistake*

a•fresh′ *adv.* once again; anew

aft *adj.* of the stern of a vessel —*adv.* toward the rear; astern

af′ter *adj.* subsequent; succeeding in time or place

—*adv.* at a later time —*prep.* later than; in succession: *time after time*; in pursuit of: *searching after knowledge*; concerning: *inquire after* — *conj.* following: *after dinner, we talked*

aft′er•burn′er *n.* a device in a jet engine that ignites unburned gas

af′ter•ef•fect *n.* a symptom which follows the initial effects

af′ter•glow *n.* the glow after a light source has disappeared; a pleasant feeling after an enjoyable experience

af′ter-hours′ *adj.* following the business day; of an establishment open past the legal closing time

af′ter•im•age *n.* the impression remaining after stimulus is gone

af′ter•life *n.* life after death

af′ter•math *n.* the consequence or result of an action

af′ter•noon *n.* part of the day between noon and sunset

af′ter•shock *n.* tremors that follow in the wake of an earthquake

af′ter•taste *n.* a taste remaining in the mouth after eating

af′ter•thought *n.* a notion occurring after a decision or action

af′ter•ward, af′ter•wards *adv.* subsequently; in the time following

a•gain′ *adv.* one more; at another time; repeated; furthermore

a•gainst′ *prep.* pressing upon; in comparison to; in opposition to

15

a·gape´ *adj.*, *adv.* open-mouthed; anything left open, as a door

a´gar *n.* a substance obtained from seaweed and used as a culture medium or a food product

ag´ate *n.* a type of quartz; a child's marble; in printing, 5 $1/2$ point type

age *n.* a stage of life; a time in history; the condition of being old —*vi.* to ripen or mature —*vt.* to cause to grow old —**of age** old enough to be legally responsible

a´ged *adj.* advanced in years; characteristic of old age —*n.* elderly persons —**aged´** *adj.* at the age of; brought to a desired state by time, as an *aged steak* —**ag´ed·ly** *adv.*

age´ism *n.* discrimination based on age; undue preoccupation with age

age´less *adj.* not changed by age; not limited by time; eternal —**age´less·ness** *n.*

a´gen·cy *n.* an active force; the means for doing something; the business of acting for others; the office of an agent; a division of a governmental department

a·gen´da *n.*, *pl.* a·gen´da or a·gen´dum a catalogue of aims; a schedule of duties, events, etc.

a´gent *n.* person or thing that serves to change; one who acts for another; an authorized representative

ag·glom´er·ate´ *adj.* densely clustered; gathered into a mass —*n.* things thrown to·gether; fused volcanic rock —*vi.*, *vt.* to form into a mass —**ag· glom·er·a´tion** *n.*

ag·glu´ti·nate *adj.* joined together —*vi.*, *vt.* to join; to farm a term by combining words; to mass together by adhesion —**ag·glu´ti·nant** *adj.*

ag·glu·ti·na´tion *n.* a mass; a combination which forms a new word

ag·gran´dize *vt.* make great; to make seem greater —**ag·gran´dize·ment** *n.* —**ag· gran´diz·er** *n.*

ag´gra·vate´ *vt.* to make worse; to exasperate or annoy —**ag´gra·va´tion** *n.*

ag´gre·gate´ *adj.* gathered together; forming a cluster; of mineral fragments —*n.* a collection; an entire amount; a mixture of mineral fragments —*vt.* to collect into a mass; to amount to —**ag´ gre·gate·ly** *adv.* **ag´gre· ga´tion** *n.*

ag·gres´sion *n.* an act of hostility; the instinct to act forcefully; assertiveness

ag·gres´sive *adj.* disposed to hostile or belligerent action; bold and assertive —**ag· gres´sive·ly** *adv.* —**ag·gres´ sive·ness** *n.* —**ag·gres´sor** *n.*

ag·grieve´ *vt.* to cause sorrow; to distress

a·ghast´ *adj.* horrified; astonished

ag´ile *adj.* exhibiting quickness and dexterity; mentally alert —**ag´ile·ly** *adv.* —**ag´ ile·ness, a·gil´i·ty** *n.*

ag´i·tate´ *vi.* to stir interest by incessant discussion —*vt.* to stir up; to perturb; to move sharply and irregularly —**ag´i·ta´tion** *n.*

a·glow´ *adj.*, *adv.* glowing

ag·nos´tic *adj.* claiming

inability to prove the existence of God; skeptical —*n.* one who embraces agnosticism; a doubter or questioner

ag•nos´ti•cism *n.* the doctrine that man lacks any valid knowledge; the theory that origins must remain unknown; the belief that the existence of God cannot be proved

a•gog´ *adj., adv.* excited; agitated; in a state of impatient curiosity

a•gon´ic *adj.* forming no angle —**agonic line** an imaginary line where magnetic north and true north coincide

ag´o•nize *vi.* sustain extreme distress; struggle over —*vt.* to torture; to cause torment —**ag´o•niz•ing** *adj.* —**ag´o•niz•ing•ly** *adv.*

ag´o•ny *n.* suffering caused by pain; an intense emotion; a violent effort

ag•o•ra•pho´bi•a *n.* fear of open spaces

a•grar´i•an *adj.* pertaining to distribution of lands; relating to agricultural interests —*n.* an advocate for equitable distribution of farm land or farm income

a•gree´ *vi.* to be like minded; to consent; to correspond; to come to terms —*vt.* to acknowledge

a•gree´a•ble *adj.* pleasurable; amiable; in accord with — **a•gree´a•bly** *adv.*

a•greed´ *adj.* brought into harmony; resolved by consent

a•gree´ment *n.* an understanding between parties; a contract

ag´ri•bus´i•ness *n.* an enterprise associated with agriculture, such as food processing or farm machinery

ag´ri•cul´ture *n.* the business that deals with land and livestock cultivation —**ag•ri•cul´tur•al** *adj.*

ag•ri•cul´tur•al•ist, ag•ri•cul´tur•ist *n.* one who studies or is engaged in the business of agriculture

a•gron´o•my, ag•ro•nom´ics *n.* the application of science to the raising of crops — **a•gron´o•mist** *n.*

a•ground´ *adj., adv.* on . the shore; stranded —**run aground** of a vessel which beaches in shallow water

a´gue *n.* chills and fever

ah *interj.* an exclamation of surprise

a•ha´ *interj.* an exclamation of triumph, derision, etc.

a•head´ *adv.* in advance; at the front; before due —**get ahead** to improve one's lot

a•hem´ *interj.* a sound made in the throat to gain attention

aid *n.* assistance; one who assists —*vi., vt.* to provide assistance to

aide *n.* a confidential assistant

AIDS *Acquired Immune Deficiency Syndrome .n.* a viral disease that attacks the body's immune system

ail *vi.* be in poor health —*vt.* to affect with pain or distress —**ail´ing** *adj.*

ail´ment *n.* a slight illness

aim *vi.* have a purpose; to point, as a firearm —*vt.* to direct toward: *aim your remarks at the jury* —*n.* an act of pointing; an intention

aim·less adj. without purpose —**aim·less·ly** adv.

air n. the atmosphere; a light breeze; a tune; a characteristic manner; an affectation —vt. to ventilate; to announce abroad: air one's feelings —**up in the air** undecided

air bag a device to protect the occupants of an automobile

air·borne adj. carried by air; flying

air brake n. a brake operated by compressed air

air cham·ber n. a compartment filled with air as in a hydraulic system

air con·di·tion·ing regulation of the temperature and humidity of inside air —**air·con·di·tioned** adj.

air·craft n. a flying machine

aircraft carrier a ship that functions as a base for airplanes

air·drop n. supplies delivered by parachute from an aircraft —vt. to discharge by parachute from an aircraft

air express n. shipment by air

air·frame n. the structural framework of an aircraft

air·freight n. freight shipped by airplane

air gun n. a weapon or tool operating on compressed air

air·hole, air hole n. a hole made by air or by which air is allowed to escape; a breathing hole in ice

air·ing n. exposure to air to freshen or dry; a stroll outdoors; a public debate; a broadcast

air·lift n. the movement of

supplies by air —vt., vi.

air line n. a tube, hose, etc. for supplying air

air·line n. an organization operating aircraft for passengers and cargo: the routes which aircraft travel

air·lock n. a chamber with controlled air pressure, providing a link between a vessel and it's surrounding environment

air·mail n. mail carried by airplane —at.

air·plane (US) n. a fixed-wing aircraft

air pocket n. a vertical air current

air·port n. a base for aircraft

air pres·sure n. pressure of the atmosphere

air pump n. a device for compressing, moving, or removeing air

air·speed n. speed measured in relation to the surrounding air

air·space n. the area above a nation, subject to its jurisdiction

air·strip n. an airport: a stretch of ground used to land aircraft

air·tight adj. not allowing air in or out; complete, with no weakness: an airtight alibi

air·waves n. pl. the medium traveled by radio and television signals

air·worthy adj. of an aircraft which is in proper condition for flight

air·y adj. open to the atmosphere; breezy; porous

aisle n. a narrow passageway between rows of seats, people, etc.

a·jar adj., adv. partly open

a•kin´ *adj., adv.* related by blood; similar in some fashion

à la after the manner of

al´a•bas´ter *n.* a variety of gypstim used for statuary, vases, etc. —*adj.* smooth and white

à la carte according to the menu; items priced individually

à•la•ri•ty *n.* willingness; readiness; liveliness —**a•lac´ri•tous** *adj.*

à la mode´ according to the fashion; in food service, usually denoting a dish served with ice cream

a•larm´ *n.* a warning; a device which alerts; a sudden fright —*vt.* to warn of danger; to frighten

a•larm´ing *adj.* causing fright or apprehension —**alarm´ing•ly** *adv.*

a•larm´ist *n.* one easily alarmed; one who excites others without cause

a•las´ *interj.* an expression of disappointment or sorrow

al´ba•core *n.* a tunny; a salt water food fish of the tuna family

al´ba•tross´ *n.* sea bird of the South Seas; a symbol of affliction

al•be´it *conj.* although; even though; notwithstanding

al•bi´no *n.* a person, animal, or plant lacking natural pigmentation

al´bum *n.* a blank book, as for photographs or stamps; a sound recording

a•lbu´men *n.* a type of protein such as found in eggs and milk —**al•bu´mi•nous** *adj.*

al´che•my *n.* an ancient art dedicated to unlocking mysteries such as universal healing or eternal youth

al´co•hol *n.* a clear liquid used as a solvent or intoxicant; a beverage containing alcohol

al•co•hol´ic *adj.* containing alcohol; caused by alcohol or alcoholism —*n.* one suffering from alcoholism

al´co•hol•ism *n.* the habitual and excessive consumption of alcohol

al´cove *n.* a recess connected to a large room; a secluded retreat

ale *n.* a type of beer

ale´house *n.* a place where beer is sold for consumption on premises

a•lert´ *adj.* ready for action; bright; lively —*n.* a warning signal; preparedness —*vt.* to prepare; to warn —**on the alert** prepared; watchful —**a•lert´ness** *n.*

al•fres´co, al fres´co *adj.* occuring out of doors —*adv.* in the open air

al´gae *pl. n.,* sing. **al´ga** a simple organism that lives in water

al´ge•bra *n.* a mathematical system of highly formalized rules and symbols —**al•ge•bra´ic, al•ge•brai´cal** *adj.* —**al•ge•bra´i•cal•ly** *adv.*

al´go•rithm *n.* a systematic method of problem solving; a set of computer instructions

a´li•as *n.* an assumed name

al´i•bi *n.* a defensive plea; an excuse

a´li•en *adj.* foreign; owing allegiance to another country; unfamiliar; inconsistent; *alien to his nature* —*n.* one not a citizen of the country; a stranger

al·ien·a·ble *adj.* that can be legally transferred, such as property

al·ien·ate *vt.* to antagonize; to transfer property or title

al·ien·a·tion *n.* a feeling of not belonging; indifference

a·light *adj., adv.* lighted, as a fire —*vi.* to dismount; to land or perch

a·lign *vt.* to arrange into a line; to adjust; to identify with —*vi.* to come into line —**a·lign·ment** *n.*

a·like *adj.* matching in some way; equivalent —*adv.* in like manner

al·i·ment *n.* food; something that provides nourishment —**al·i·men·tal** *adj.*

al·i·men·ta·ry *adj.* pertaining to food or nutrition; supplying nutrition

alimentary canal the path traveled by food through the body

al·i·mo·ny *n.* an allowance paid after a dissolved marriage

a·line *vi.* to come into line —*vt.* to arrange in a line; to come into agreement with —**a·line·ment** *n.*

alive *adj.* functioning; alert; in existence; animated —**alive with** abounding

al·ka·li *n.* a soluble substance that neutralizes acids —**al·ka·line** *adj.* —**al·ka·lin·i·ty** *n.*

ai·ka·loid *n.* an alkaline substance

all *adj.* entire; greatest possible: *in all respects;* primarily; *all neck and legs* —*n.* entirety —*pron.* everyone or

each one; everything —*adv.* entirely; exclusively —**above all** most important —**after all** nevertheless —**all but** almost —**all in** tired —**all in all** all together; all things considered —**all out** without constraint —**at all** under any condition; in any way

al·lay *vt.* to calm; reduce in intensity, alleviate

al·le·ga·tion *n.* an assertion made without proof

al·lege *vt.* to attest; to assert; to plead in support or denial

al·leg·ed *adj.* asserted; not proven —**al·leg·ed·ly** *adv.*

al·le·giance *n.* loyalty; an obligation of loyalty

al·le·gor·ic, al·le·gor·i·cal *adj.* pertaining to allegory —**al·le·gor·i·cal·ly** *adv.*

al·le·go·ry *n.* use of people or animals to represent abstract concepts; symbols employed in literature; any symbolic representation

al·ler·gen *n.* a substance capable of producing an allergic reaction

al·ler·gic *adj.* caused by an allergy; susceptible to; having an aversion

al·ler·gist *n.* one who diagnoses and treats allergies

al·ler·gy *n.* un usual sensitivity to a substances

al·le·vi·ate *vt.* to relieve; to lessen —**al·le·vi·a·tion** *n.*

al·le·vi·a·tive, al·le·vi·a·to·ry *adj.* tending to relieve, as in severity

al·ley *n.* a narrow street or passageway —**al·ley·way** *n.*

al·li·ance *n.* a formal agreement between countries or persons; a union by treaty, marriage, etc.

al·lied´ *adj.* closely related; affiliated, as by treaty

al·li·ga´tor *n.* an American or Chinese reptile, similar to the crocodile with a shorter, wider snout

al·lit·er·a´tion *n.* a series of words beginning with the same consonant sound: *"Peter Piper picked a peck..." —* **al·lit´er·a·ate** *vi., vt.* **—al·lit´er·a·tive** *adj.* **—al·lit´er·a·tive·ly** *adv.*

al·lo·cate *vt.* to allot or assign a share; to designate for a particular purpose

al·lo·ca´tion *n.* a thing or amount set aside

al·lot´ *vt.* to apportion to; to distribute by lot **—al·lot´ment** *n.*

all´-out´ *adj.* wholehearted, concentrated

al·low´ *vt.* permit to have, happen, do, etc.; to acknowledge as true; to provide for: *allow extra money for incidentals —***allow for** consider a condition: *allow for his inexperience —***al·low´a·ble** *adj.*

al·low´ance *n.* that allowed; amount budgeted for a purpose; a discount; a variance to be reckoned: *make allowance for*

al´loy *n.* a mixture of metals; anything that lessens value or purity *—vt.* to combine metals; to make metal less pure by mixing

all´·time´ *adj.* unparalleled

al·lude´ *vt.* to refer to casually or indirectly

al·lure´ *vt.* tempt; attract *—vi.* be subtly attractive *—n.* appeal; the ability to attract; a quality that attracts

al·lur´ing *adj.* appealing; attractive; seductive **—al·lur´ing·ly** *adv.*

al·lu´sion *n.* a casual or indirect reference **—al·lu´sive** *adj.*

al·lu´vi·um *n.* soil deposited by moving water **—al·lu´vi·al** *adj.*

al´ly *n.* persons or groups unified for a common purpose *—vt.* to unite *—vi.* to form an alliance; to become united

al´ma·nac *n.* a yearly publication with information about weather, astronomical data, etc.

al´mond *adj.* of the taste, color, etc. of an almond *—n.* the fruit of the almond tree or the tree itself

al´most, al·most´ *adj., adv.* close to; very nearly

alms *n., sing. & pl.* a donation

a·lone´ *adj., adv.* unaccompanied; detached; excluding all others; unique, without equal

a·long´ *adv.* tracing the length of; progressing beside; advanced in distance or time *—prep.* following the path of **—all along** the entire time; from the beginning **—get along** to persevere; to live in harmony

a·loof´ *adj.* distant; reserved *—adv.* apart **—a·loof´ness** *n.*

a·loud´ *adv.* audibly; out loud

al´pha·bet´ *n.* the symbols of a written language

al´pha·bet´ic, al´pha·bet´i·cal *adj.* of a written language; arranged in order **—al´pha·bet·ize** *vt.*

al´pha·nu·mer´ic *adj.* data comprising both letters and numbers

al·read´y *adv.* by this time or a time referred to

al´tar *n.* a place for sacred offerings; the focus of a place of worship

al´ter *vt.* to modify; to adjust fit; to spay —*vi.* to undergo change —**al´ter·a·ble** *adj.* —**al·ter·a´tion** *n.*

al·ter·cate´ *vi.* to quarrel; to argue bitterly —**al´ter·ca´tion** *n.*

al´ter·nate *adj.* every other; following by turns —*vt.* to use in turn —*vi.* to occur by turns —*n.* a substitute —**al´ter·nate·ly** *adv.*

al´ter·na´tion *n.* a changing back and forth

al·ter´na·tive *adj.* providing a choice —*n.* a choice; one of the options; something that must be decided —**al·ter´na·tive·ly** *adv.*

al·though´ *conj.* even though

al·tim´e·ter *n.* an instrument for measuring altitude

al´ti·tude´ *n.* elevation from a reference point; the angle of a celestial body in relation to the horizon

al´to *n.* the musical range between tenor and mezzo soprano

al´to·geth´er *adv.* in all; all things being considered

al´tru·ism *n.* unselfish regard for others —**al´tru·ist** *n.* —**al·tru·is´tic** *adj* —**al·tru·is´ti·cal·ly** *adv.*

a·lum´na *n.,* *pl.* **a·lum´nae** a female who has attended a school

a·lum´nus *n.* *pl.* **a·lum´ni** a person, who has attended a school

al´ways *adv.* for all time; every time

a·mal´gam *n.* a mixture

a·mal´ga·mate *vt.* to combine with mercury; to unite or integrate —*vi.* to become combined; to mix with another metal

a·man·u·en´sis *n.* *pl.* **a·man´u·en´ses** one employed to copy manuscripts; a secretary

a·mass´ *vt.* to accumulate— **a·mas´a·ble** *adj.*

am·a·teur *adj.* done by one lacking professional skill — *n.* one who participates for pleasure only, not profit; one who lacks skill

am·a·teur´ish *adj.* lacking professional skill —**am·a·teur´ish·ly** *adv.*

a·maze´ *vt.* to fill with wonder; to astonish —**a·maz´ed·ly** *adv.* —**a·maze´ment** *n.*

am·bas´sa·dor *n.* a diplomat —**am·bas·sa·do´ri·al** *adj.*

am´bi·ance, am´bi·ence *n.* the character of a place; atmosphere

am·bi·dex´trous *adj.* able to use both hands well; skillful, dexterous

am´bi·ent *adj.* encompassing; of the surrounding area

am·big´u·ous *adj.* not clear; vague; open to misinterpretation —**am·bi·gu´i·ty** *n.*

am·bi´tion *n.* a firm aspiration; a desired goal; passion or energy

am·bi´tious *adj.* marked by aspiration; desirous; eager; appearing difficult —**am·bi´tious·ly** *adv.*

am·biv´a·lent *adj.* of contradictory emotions; unsure — **am·biv´a·lence** *n.* —**am·biv´a·lent·ly** *adv.*

am′bu•lance n. a vehicle for transporting the sick or injured

am′bu•lant adj. moving about

am′bu•late vi. to walk or move —**am•bu•la′tive** adj.

am′bu•la•to′ry adj. able to walk; able to move about

am′bus•cade′ n. an ambush; a hiding place —vt. to attack suddenly from hiding

am′bush n. a surprise attack; those hiding in wait; a deception or trap —vt. to lie in wait; to attack

a•mel′io•rate′ vi., vt. to make or become better; to improve -a•mel′io•rant n. —**a•mel′io•ra•tive** adj.

a•men′a•ble adj. agreeable; responsive to authority; open to criticism —**a•me′na•bly** adv.

a•mend′ vt. to improve; to change; to free of error —vi. to improve —**a•mend′a•ble** adj.

a•mend′a•to•ry adj. serving to correct or improve

a•mend′ment n. a correction; a removal of error; an addition which alters

a•mends′ pl. n. compensation for a wrong; an apology

a•men′i•ty n. a pleasant quality; something that makes more comfortable

A•mer•i•ca′na n. things typically American; papers, antiques, etc. associated with American history and customs

A•mer′i•can•ism n. a manner or custom peculiar to the people of the US; a fondness for or loyalty to the US and its institutions

am′e•thyst n. bluish-violet

type of quartz; a bluish-violet color

a′mi•a•ble adj. friendly; good-natured —**a•mi•a•bil′i•ty** n. **am′i•ca•ble** adj. agreeable; congenial —**am•i•ca•bil′i•ty** n. —**am′i•ca•bly** adv.

a•mid′, a•midst′ prep. among; in the middle of

a•mi′no ac′id anorganic acid; part of the protein molecule

a•miss′ adj. out of order; improper, faulty —adv. wrongly; in an improper way —**take amiss** to be offended

am′i•ty n. friendly relations; good will

am′me•ter n. an instrument for measuring an electric current

am′mu•ni′tion n. a projectile; an explosive used as a weapon; information used to attack or defend

am•ne′si•a n. loss of memory —**am•ne′si•ac** n., adj.

am′nes•ty n. an official pardon —vt. grant a pardon to

am′ni•on n. the membranous sac surrounding a fetus

a•moe′ba n. a one-celled protozoan —**a•moe′bic** adj.

a•mong′, a•mongst′ prep. in the midst of; included within an array

a•mor′al adj. without concern of ethical distinction; lacking a sense of right or wrong —**a•mo•ral′i•ty** n.

am′o•rous adj. loving; passionate; suggesting desire; connected with love —**am′o•rous•ly** adv.

a•mor′phous adj. lacking definite form; unorganized —**a•mor′phism** n.

am′or•tise (Brit.), **am′or•tize** (US) vt. to discharge a debt

23

by regular payments —**am**′**or·tis·a·ble**, **am·or′tiz·able** *adj.*—**am·or·ti·sa′tiom, am·or·ti·za′tion** *n.*

a·mount′ *n.* a total; a quantity; the entire value or effect —*vi.* add up to; be equal to

am·per′age, am·per·age *n.* the strength of an electrical current

am′pere *n.* standard unit for measuring an electric current

am′per·sand *n.* a symbol (&) representing the word *and*

am·phet′a·mine *n.* a stimulant used as a medication

am·phib′ian *n.* an animal or craft that functions in water or on land

am·phib′i·ous *adj.* living or operating in water and on land —**am·phi′i·ous·ly** *adv.*

am′phi·the·a′ter *n.* a structure with seats rising from a central arena

am′ple *adj.* large in capacity or size; more than enough; sufficient —**am′ple·ness** *n.* **am′ply** *adv.*

am·pli·fi′er *n.* a device that reinforces electrical impulses

am′pli·fy *vt.* increase or expand —**am′pli·fi·ca′tion** *n.*

am′pli·tude′ *n.* extent, largeness, fullness

am′pul, am′pule *n.* a vial of medication, often for injection

am′pu·tate′ *vt.* to surgically remove —**am′pu·ta′tion** *n.*

a·muck′ *adj.* in a frenzy; crazed —*adv.* in a barbarous manner

am′u·let *n.* a magical charm

a·muse′ *vt.* to occupy pleasantly; to induce a smile or laughter

a·mus′ing *adj.* entertaining; causing laughter —**a·mus′iag·ly** *adv.*

a·muse′ment *n.* a diversion; that which brings pleasure; a feeling of enjoyment

amusement park a recreational area with rides, refreshments, etc.

an *adj. indef. art.* each or any: an article before words beginning with a vowel sound

a·nach′ro·nism *n.* something out of its proper order — **a·nach·ro·nis′tic, a·nach′ro·nous** *adj.*

an·aer′obe *n.* a microorganism that exists without oxygen —**an·aer·o′bic** *adj.*

an·aes·the′si·a (*Brit.*) *n.* loss of sensation or sensitivity

an·aes·the′si·ol·o·gy (*Brit.*) *n.* the study of anaesthesia and its effects —**an·aes·the·si·ol′o·gist** (*Brit.*) *n.*

an′aes·thet′ic (*Brit.*) *adj.* pertaining to or producing anaesthesia: making insensitive —*n.* an agent that produces a loss of feeling — **an′aes·thet′i·cal·ly** *adv.*

an·aes′the·tise (*Brit.*) *vt.* to render insensitive to pain

an′a·gram′ *n.* a word or phrase made by rearranging the letters of another word or phrase

an·al·ge′si·a *n.* a deadening of pain without loss of consciousness

an·al·ge′sic *n.* medicine that relieves pain — *adj.* causing analgesia

an′a·log (*US*) *adj.* of data represented by a continuous variable

an´a•logue (*Brit.*) *adj.* of data represented by a continuous variable

a•nal´o•gous *adj.* similar in certain ways —**a•nal´o•gous•ly** *adv.*

a•nal´o•gy *n.* a partial similarity; a comparison based on similarity

a•nal´y•sis *n.* the division of a thing into parts for examination

an´a•lyst *n.* one skilled in examination or study; a psychoanalyst

an´a•lyt´ic, an•a•lyt´i•cal *adj.* pertaining to analysis; expert in analysis —**an•a•lyt´i•cal•ly** *adv.*

ana•lyt´ics *n.* the branch of logic concerned with analysis

an´a•lyse (*Brit.*), **an´a•lyze** (*US*) *vt,* to break down for study; to make analysis; to psychoanalyze

an•a•phy•lac´tic *adj.* of a severe reaction to a usually harmless substance —**an•a•phy•la´ti•cal•ly** *adv.*

an•a•phy•lax´is *n.* abnormal sensitivity; anaphylactic shock

anaphylactic shock severe reaction caused by exposure to a usually harmless substance

an•ar´chic, an•ar´chi•cal *adj.* promoting anarchy; lacking order—**an•ar´chi•cal•ly** *adv.*

an´arch•y *n.* the absence of governmental authority —**an´arch•ist** *n.* —**an•ar•chis´tic** *adj.*

a•nath´e•ma *n.* an ecclesiastical ban; a denunciation; a person condemned; anything greatly disliked

a•nat´o•mist *n.* a specialist in or student of anatomy

a•nat´o•mise (*Brit.*), **a•nat´o•mize** (*US*) *vt.* dissect for study; to study in great detail —**a•nat´o•mi•sa´tion, a•nat´o•mi•za´tion** *n.*

a•nat´o•my *n.* the study of animal or plant structure; the structure of an organism; dissection for study; any detailed study — **an•a•tom´ic, an•a•tom´i•cal** *adj.* —**an•a•tom´i•cal•ly** *adv.*

an´ces•tor *n.* a forefather; one from whom descended; a forerunner —**an•ces´tral** *adj.* —**an•ces´tral•ly** *adv.* — **an´ces•try** *n.*

an´chor *n.* a device to hold a ship or boat in place; any device that secures in place —*vt.* to hold in place; to fix firmly —*vi.* to lie at anchor; to be fixed in place

an´chor•age *n.* a place where ships lie at anchor; a fee for anchoring

an´cho•rite *n.* a religious recluse

an´chor•per´son *n.* the primary reporter for a newscast

an´cient *adj.* very old; antiquated —*n.* one from the distant past; a very old person —**an´cient•ness** *n.*

an´cil•la•ry *adj.* secondary; auxiliary

and *conj.* as well as; added to; to: try and do *better*

and´i•ron *n.* a metal support for wood in a fireplace

an•drog´y•nous *adj.* bearing both male and female characteristics; unisex: of a style not distinctly male or female —**an•drog´y•nous•ly** *adv.* — **an•drog´y•ny** *n.*

an´droid *n.* an automaton that resembles a human

an´ec·dot·al *adj.* consisting of anecdotes —**an´ec·dot·al·ly** *adv.*

an´ec·dote *n.* a short amusing story

a·ne´mi·a *n.* a deficiency of red blood corpuscles or hemoglobin

a·ne´mic *adj.* afflicted with anemia; listless; lacking vitality —**a·ne´mi·cal·ly** *adv.*

an·e·mom´e·ter *n.* a device for measuring the force of wind

an´er·oid *adj.* not using fluid, as *an aneroid barometer*

an·es·the´si·a (US) *n.* loss of sensation; loss of sensitivity to pain

an·es·the´si·ol·o·gy (US) *n.* the study of anesthesia and its effects —**an·es·the·si·ol´o·gist** (US) *n.*

an·es·thet´ic (US) *adj.* pertaining to or producing anesthesia; making insensitive to pain —*n.* an agent that produces loss of feeling

an·es´the·tist (US) *n.* one who administers anesthetics

an·es´the·tize (US) *vt.* to render insensitive to pain

an·eu´rysm, an´eu·rism *n.* swelling at a weak point in an artery

a·new´ *adv.* again; freshly

an´gel *n.* a supernatural being; a guiding influence; a backer

an´ger *n.* strong displeasure; ire; wrath —*vt.* to make irate; to provoke —*vi.* to become angry

an·gi´na pec´to·ris a heart condition marked by severe pain in the chest

an´gle *n.* an ulterior motive; stratagem; point of view; fishing tackle; the intersection of two lines or planes —*vi.* to obtain by cunning; to fish with a hook and line —**an´gu·lar** *adj.* —**an·gu·lar´i·ty** *n.*

an´gler *n.* a fisherman; one who schemes to achieve an end

An´gli·cise (Brit.), **An´gli·cize** (US) *vi.* to become like the English —*vt.* to appropriate an English style

an´gling *n.* the skill of fishing with special hooked lures

An·glo´phile *n.* a devotee of England and its institutions

an·gos·tu´ra bark the bark of a tree used as a tonic or flavoring

an´gry *adj.* showing displeasure; threatening; indicating anger —**an´gri·ly** *adv.* —**an´gri·ness** *n.*

angst *n.* a feeling of apprehension

ang´strom, ang´strom u´nit a factor for the measure of wavelength; a hundred millionth of a centimeter

an´guish *n.* severe misery —*vi., vt.* to experience or cause distress

an´gu·lar *adj.* like an angle; gaunt; lacking grace —**an´gu·lar·ly** *adv.*

an·hy´drous *adj.* of a chemical compound which contains no water

an·i·mad·ver·sion *n.* severe criticism

an·i·mad·vert´ *vi.* to comment; to censure

an´i·mal *n.* a living creature; creatures of the earth, separate from man; a brutal person —*adj.* pertaining to animals; like an animal

an´i•mate *adj.* living; lively — *vt.* make lifelike; stimulate

an´i•mated *adj.* spirited; lively; vivacious

an´i•ma´tion *n.* the process of imparting life or spirit; being alive; the making of cartoons

an´i•mism *n.* the belief in a soul; the belief that inanimate objects possess a spirit —**an´i•mis´tic** *adj.*

an´i•mos´i•ty *n.* a strong feeling of hostility; hatred

an´i•mus *n.* animosity; an animating energy or purpose

an´ise *n.* aromatic seeds used for flavoring and medicine

an´i•seed *n.* anise seed; the seed of the anise plant

an´kle *n.* the joint connecting the foot and the leg

an´nals *pl. n.* a chronological record; any historical account; a periodical that reports discoveries, etc.

an•neal´ *vt.* to process in order to make less brittle; to strengthen by trial, as determination

an´ne•lid *adj.* pertaining to a group of segmented invertebrates, as earthworms, leeches, etc. —*n.*

an•nex´ *n.* something added; an auxiliary building —**an•nex´** *vt.* to add; to incorporate into —**an´nex•a´tion** *n.*

an•ni´hi•late *vt.* to destroy; to defeat —**an•ni´hi•la´tor** *n.*

an•ni´hi•la´tion *n.* total destruction

an´ni•ver´sa•ry *n.* a date occurring at the same time each year; the celebration of a past event

an´no•tate´ *vt.* to provide a

commentary —**an•no•ta´tion** *n.* —**an´no•ta•tive** *adj.*

an•nounce´ *vt.* to proclaim; to make known; to report the appearance of —**an•nounce´ment** *n.* —**an•nounc´er** *n.*

an•noy´ *vt.* to bother; to irritate —*vi.* to be bothersome —**an•noy´ance** *n.* —**an•noy´ing** *adj.*

an´nu•al *adj.* yearly; occuring every year —*n.* a publication that comes out once a year; a plant that lives only one season —**an´nu•al•ize** *vt.* —**an´nu•al•ly** *adv.*

an•nu´i•ty *n.* an annual allowance; the receipt or payment of a stipend; periodic payment for future return

an•nul´ *vt.* to make or declare invalid; to revoke —**an•nul´ment** *n.*

an´nu•lar *adj.* formed like a ring; marked by rings —**an•nu•lar´i•ty** *n.* —**an´nu•late, an´nu•lat•ed** *adj.*

an•nun´ci•ate *vt.* to announce —**an•nun´ci•a•tor** *n.*

an•nun•ci•a´tion *n.* a proclamation; the act of announcing

an´o•dyne´ *adj.* soothing; having power to eliminate pain —*n.* medication that eases pain; anything that soothes or comforts

a•noint´ *vt.* to sprinkle or rub with oil or ointment; to consecrate

a•nom´a•ly *n.* deviation from a norm; a peculiarity; one who is peculiar —**a•nom•a•lis´tic, a•nom´a•lous** *adj.* —**a•nom•a•lis´ti•cal•ly** *adv.*

an•o´mic *adj.* socially unstable —*n.* one alienated from normal society

27

a·non´y·mous *adj.* lacking the name of the donor or author; lacking distinctive characteristics —**an·o·nym´i·ty** *n.* —**a·non´y·mous·ly** *adv.*

an·oth´er *adj., pron.* one other; different

an´ser·ine *adj.* of or like a goose; foolish or silly

an´swer *n.* response to a question; an action in kind; retaliation; a solution —*vt.* to respond; to prove sufficient; to be accountable; to correspond —*vt.* to act in response; to be sufficient; to correspond —**an´swer·er** *n.*

an´swer·able *adj.* accountable; able to be responded to —**an´swer·a·bly** *adv.*

ant *n.* a small communal insect

ant·ac´id *adj.* correcting acidity —*n.* an alkali; a remedy for acidity

an·tag´o·nism *n.* animosity; mutual hostility or opposition

an·tag´o·nist *n.* an adversary; one who or that which opposes —**an·tag·o·nis´tic** *adj.* —**an·tag·o·nis´ti·cal·ly** *adv.*

an·tag´o·nize´ *vt.* to oppose; to counteract

an´te *n.* initial stake in poker; a prize or reward; an inducement —*vt.* to bet before a hand is dealt; to pay one's share —*vi.* to pay up

an´te·ce´dent *adj.* going before, preceding —*n.* anything that logically precedes; a noun or pronoun to which a relative pronoun refers—**an·te·ce´dence, an·te·ce´den·cy** *n.*

an´te·cham·ber *n.* a room which serves as an entranceway

an´te·date *vt.* to backdate; to occur earlier than

an·te·di·lu´vi·an *adj.* before the Biblical flood; antiquated —*n.* anything that lived before the Biblical flood; anything very old

an´te·lope´ *n.* a graceful quadruped allied to the deer

an´te·me·rid´i·an *adj.* before noon

an·ten´na *n., pl.* **an·ten´nae, an·ten´nas** sensory organs of an insect; a device for transmission or reception of radio or television signals

an´te·pe´nult *n.* third syllable from the end of a word

an´te·pe·nul´ti·mate *adj.* the third from the end of anything

an·te´ri·or *adj.* toward or at the front; earlier in time

an´te·room *n.* a waiting room; an antechamber

an´them *n.* a hymn; triumphal music —**national anthem** the official song of a nation

an´ther *n.* part of the stamen in a flower that holds pollen

an·thol´o·gise (*Brit.*), **an·thol´o·gize** (*US*) *vi.* to compile or publish an anthology —*vt.* to include in an anthology —**an·thol´o·gis·er, an·thol´o·gist, an·thol´o·giz·er** *n.*

an·thol´o·gy *n.* a collection of literary selections; an assortment or catalog of comments

an·tho·zo´an *n.* a class of marine creatures that includes corals and sea anemones —**an·tho·zo´ic** *adj.*

an´thra·cite´ *n.* a hard coal

an´thrax *n.* an infectious disease

an´thro•poid *adj.* similar to a human; pertaining to man, apes, and monkeys —*n.* any of the larger apes —**an´thro•poid´al** *adj.*

an•thro•pol´o•gy *n.* study of the customs and culture of man —**an•thro•po•log´ic, an•thro•po•log´i•cal** *adj.* —**an•thro•pol´o•gist** *n.*

an•thro•po•mor´phic *adj.* having human form or characteristics

an•thro•po•mor´phism *n.* endowing a spirit, natural phenomena, etc. with human attributes

an•thro•po•mor´phise (*Brit.*), **an•thro•po•mor´phize** (*US*) —*vt., vi.* to attribute human qualities to things that are not human

an´ti- *prefix* against or opposed to

an•ti•bi•ot´ic *adj.* preventing bacterial growth —*n.* a substance that destroys microorganisms

an´ti•bod´y *n.* a protein in the body that neutralizes harmful matter

an´tic *adj.* bizarre; incongruous —*n.* a caper or prank; a ridiculous act

an•tic´i•pate *vt.* to expect; foresee; be prepared for; to act so as to forestall; to take too hastily —*vi.* consider prematurely —**an•tic´i•pa´tion** *n.* —**antic´i•pa•tive** *adj.* —**antic´i•pa•to•ry** *adj.*

an´ti•cli´max *n.* a reduction in effectiveness —**an´ti•cli•mac´tic** *adj.* —**an´ti•cli•mac´ti•cal•ly** *adv.*

an•ti•cli´nal, an•ti•clin´ic *adj.*

a downward incline on two sides, as an upward arch of rock stratum

an•ti•cline *n.* a rock stratum forming an upward bend

an´ti•dote´ *n.* a substance used to counteract a poison —**anti•dot´al** *adj.* —**anti•dot´al•ly** *adv.*

an´ti•freeze *n.* a liquid cooling agent

an´ti•gen, an•ti•gene´ *n.* a substance that provokes development of antibodies —**an•ti•gen´ic** *adj.* —**an•ti•gen´i•cal•ly** *adv.*

an´ti•he´ro *n.* an unlikely champion; one who does not possess the usual qualities attributed to a hero

an•ti•his´ta•mine´ *n.* a drug used to treat cold and allergy syptoms

an•ti•ma•cas´sar *n.* a covering for the backs and arms of chairs

an•ti•mag•net´ic *adj.* resistant to the influence of a magnetic field

an´ti•mat´ter *n.* charged particles that are in opposition to matter

an´ti•mo•ny *n.* a metallic element used in alloys and pigments

antipas´to *n.* an appetizer of delicacies

an•tip´a•thy *n.* a strong or deep-seated aversion —**an´tip•a•thet´ic** *adj.* —**an•tip•a•thet´i•cal•ly** *adv.*

an´ti•phon *n.* a verse chanted in response; passages arranged for alternate chanting —**an´ti•phon´ic, an´ti•phon´i•cal** *adj.* —**an•tiph´o•nal•ly** *adv.*

an´ti•pode *n.* exact opposite

an·tip´o·des *pl. n.* anything at the opposite extreme

an·ti·py·ret´ic *adj.* preventive of fever —*n.* a medicine to relieve fever

an·ti·quar´i·an *adj.* of antiquity or the collection of antiquities —*n.* a collector or dealer in antiquities

an´ti·quate *vt.* to make old or obsolete; to make appear old

anti·quat·ed *adj.* old-fashioned; out of date; no longer useful

an·tique´ *adj.* old; made much earlier; of an ancient style —*n.* a relic; an object valued because of age; an ancient style —*vt.* to make resemble an antique

an·tiq´ui·ty *n.* ancient history; an ancient relic

an·ti·sep´sis *n.* the destruction of harmful bacteria

an·ti·sep´tic *adj.* thoroughly clean; able to destroy harmful bacteria —*n.* a substance that destroys harmful microorganisms

an·ti·so´cial *adj.* adverse to social contact; opposed to social order; disruptive — **an·ti·so´cial·ly** *adv.*

an·tith´e·sis *n., pl.* **an·tith´e·ses** opposing thoughts or expressions; the direct opposite

an·ti·thet´ic, an·ti·thet´i·cal *adj.* being in opposition — **an·ti·thet´i·cal·ly** *adv.*

an·ti·tox´in *n.* an antibody; a preparation that acts against disease

an·ti·trust´ *adj.* opposition to practices in restraint of trade; pertaining to the regulation of trusts, monopolies, etc.

an·ti·ven´in *n.* antitoxin which protects against snake bite or venom

an´to·nym *n.* a word opposite in meaning to another word —**an·to·nym´ic, an·ton´y·mous** *adj.*

an´trum *n., pl.* **an´tra** a cavity, especially in a bone; a sinus cavity

a´nus *n.* the opening at the lower end of the alimentary canal

an´vil *n.* a heavy metal block used as a base for forming metals; a fixed base, as the lower contact of a telegraph key

anx·i·e·ty *n.* a feeling of uneasiness; a cause for anxiety; eagerness; a state marked by tension or dread

anx´ious *adj.* apprehensive over an uncertainty; impatient for fulfillment —**anx´ious·ly** *adv.*

an´y *adj.* one or some, without preference —*pron.* one or more of several —*adv.* at all

an´y·bod·y *pron.* any person —*n.* a person of importance

an´y·how *adv.* in any way whatever; in any case

an´y·more *adv.* at this time

an´y·one *pron.* any person

an´y·thing *adv.* at all; in any way —*n., pron.* a thing of any kind

an´y·way *adv.* in any event; nevertheless

an´y·where *adv.* in any place

a·or´ta *n.* the large artery from the heart that carries blood to all of the body except the lungs

a·part´ *adj.* separated; disassociated —*adv.* separately; independently —**apart from**

with the exception of

a•part´heid *n.* the policy of racial discrimination in South Africa

a•part´ment (*US*) *n.* a room or rooms serving as living quarters

ap´a•thy *n.* a lack of emotion; unconcern; lacking interest —**apa•thet´ic, ap´a•thet´i•cal** *adj.*

ape *n.* a large tailless primate, such as a gorilla; one who imitates; one who is rude or clumsy —*vt.* to imitate — **ape´like** *adj.* —**go ape** to show great emotion

a•per•ri•tif´ *n.* a beverage, often wine, served before a meal

ap´er•ture´ *n.* an opening; a hole or slit

a´pex *n.* a climax; the highest point

a•pha´sia *n.* loss of ability to speak or understand language —**a•pha´si•ac, a•pha´sic** *adj., n.*

a•phe´li•on *n.* the point in an orbit farthest from the sun

aph´o•rism *n.* a wise saying; an adage —**aph•o•ris´tic, aph•o•ris´ti•cal** *adj.*

aph•ro•dis´iac *adj.* intensifying sexual desire —*n.* a substance reputed to intensify sexual desire

a•pi´an *adj.* pertaining to bees

a´pi•ar´y *n.* a place where bees are kept

a•piece *adv.* for each; to each

a•plomb *n.* self-confidence; assurance

a•poc´a•lypse´ *n.* the symbolic destruction of evil; a prophetic revelation; total destruction —**a•poc•a•lyp´tic, a•poc•a•lyp´ti•cal** *adj.*

a•poc´ry•pha *pl. n.* writings of questionable authenticity

a•poc´ry•phal *adj.* not genuine; of dubious origin; fictitious

ap´o•gee *n.* the highest point in an orbit —**ap•o•ge´al, ap•o•ge´an** *adj.*

a•po•lit´i•cal *adj.* uninterested in politics; of no political importance

a•pol´ogist *n.* one speaking in defense of a person or cause

a•pol´ogy *n.* a formal argument or defense; an expression of regret —**a•pol•o•get´ic** *adj.* —**a•pol´o•gise, a•pol´o•gize** *vi.*

ap•o•plec´tic *n.* one subject to attacks of apoplexy —**ap•o•plec´tic, ap•o•plec´ti•cal** *adj.* showing the symptoms of apoplexy

ap´o•plex•y *n.* a fit of anger; sudden disorder of the nervous system: a stroke

a•pos´ta•sy *n.* abandonment of one's beliefs or principles

a•pos´tate *n.* one guilty of apostasy —*adj.*

a•pos´ta•tize *vi.* to abandon one's beliefs or principles

a•pos´tle *n.* one of those sent by Christ to preach; a missionary; an adherent — **a•pos´tle•ship** *n.*

a•pos´to•late *n.* the office, duties, etc. of an apostle

ap•os•tol´ic, ap•os•tol´i•cal *adj.* pertaining to an apostle; in accordance with the practice of the apostles; of the line of succession from the Apostles; papal

a•pos´tro•phe´ *n.* a mark (´) to show omission, form a possessive, and certain plurals

a•poth´e•car•y n. one who prepares medications — **apothecaries´ measure** the system of measure used to prepare prescription medicine — **apothecaries´ weight** the system of weights used to prepare prescription medicine

ap´o•thegm n. a terse saying; a maxim

a•pothe•o´sis n. the exaltation of a person to divine honors; deification — **a•po´the´o•size** vt.

ap•pal´, ap•pall´ vt. to horrify; to stun — **ap•pal´ling, ap•pall´ing** adj. — **ap•pal´ling•ly, ap•pall´ing•ly** adv.

ap´pa•ra´tus n. a device designed for a particular use

ap•par´el n. clothing

ap•par´ent adj. evident; seeming to be — **ap•par´ent•ly** adv.

ap•pa•ri´tion n. a strange manifestation

ap•peal´ vi. to request aid; to be looked on favorably; to plead for rehearing — vt. request hearing in a higher court — n. a request for aid; a favorable quality; a petition to a higher power **ap•peal´a•ble** adj. — **ap•peal´ing•ly** adv.

ap•pear´ vi. come into view; seem to be; to be published; to present oneself as ordered by law

ap•pear´ance n. a semblance; one's demeanor; publication; attendance, as in court

ap•pease´ vt. to calm; to satisfy — **ap•pease´ment** n. — **ap•peas´a•ble** adj.

ap•pel´lant adj. regarding appeals — n. one who appeals

ap•pel•la´tion n. a name or title — **ap•pel´la•tive** adj., n. — **ap•pel´la•tive•ly** adv.

ap•pend´ vt. to add; to attach

ap•pen´dage n. an addition; a subsidiary part — **ap•pen´dic´u•lar** adj.

ap•pend´ant adj. attached; allied in a subordinate position

ap•pen•dec´to•my n. removal of the appendix

ap•pen•di•ci´tis n. inflammation of the vermiform appendix

ap•pen´dix n., pl. **ap•pen´dix•es** or **ap•pen´di•ces** supplementary material; an outgrowth

ap´per•tain´ vi. be relevant; to relate

ap´pe•tite´ n. a desire for food or drink; any compelling desire

ap´pe•tiz´er n. a small amount of food served before a meal; a sample that stimulates

ap´pe•tiz´ing adj. stimulating the appetite; tantalizingly attractive

ap•plaud´ vi., vt. express approval; commend or praise — **ap•plaud´a•ble** adj. — **ap•plaud´a•bly, ap•plaud´ing•ly** adv. — **ap•plaud´er** n.

ap•plause´ n. approval shown by clapping of hands

ap´ple n. the fruit of the apple tree; the apple tree; various exotic fruits or trees — **apple of one's eye** cherished

ap´ple•jack n. brandy distilled from apple cider

ap´ple•sauce n. a dish of cooked, spiced and pureed apples; that which is nonsense or not believed

ap•pli´ance n. a device designed for a special purpose

ap´pli•ca•ble adj pertinent; appropriate —**ap´pli•ca•bil´i•ty, ap´pli•ca•ble•ness** n. —**ap´pli•ca•bly** adv.

ap´pli•cant n. candidate for a job

ap•pli•ca´tion n. something applied, as medication; a formal request; the act of putting in effect; close and consistent attention

ap•pli´ca•to•ry adj. that can be used; practical

ap´pli•ca•tor n. a device for applying a substance to a surface

ap•plied´ adj. put into practice; of something practical

ap•pli•que´ n. an ornament —vt. to decorate by applying

ap•ply´ vi. to request; to be relevant —vt. to spread on; to use; to devote to a particular use

ap•point´ vt. to name or select

ap•point•ee´ n. one selected

ap•point´ment n. a scheduled meeting; a position

ap•por´tion vt. to distribute —**ap•por´tion•ment** n.

ap•pose´ vt. arrange side by side or opposite —**ap•pos´i•tive** adj.

ap´po•site adj. pertinent; fit

ap•po•si´tion n. in immediate connection —**ap•po•si´tion•al** adj. —**air po•si´tion•al•ly** adv.

ap•praise´ vt. set a value for; to estimate worth

ap•pre´ci•a•ble adj. sufficient to be noticed; apparent; discernible

ap•pre´ci•ate vt. show gratitude; to recognize and understand; increase in value

ap•pre´ci•a´tion n. recognition; the amount of increase

ap•pre´ci•a•tive adj. showing appreciation

ap•pre•hend´ vt. to capture; grasp mentally; to await with dread —vi. to comprehend —**ap´pre•hen´sion** n.

ap•pre•hen´si•ble adj. able to be understood —**ap•pre•hen´si•bly** adv.

ap•pre•hen´sive adj. troubled; possessing understanding —**ap•pre•hen´sive•ly** adv.

ap•pren´tice n. one learning a trade; a beginner —vt. to accept as an apprentice —**ap•pren´tice•ship** n.

ap•prise´, ap•prize´ vt. to notify or make aware

ap•proach´ vi. draw near —vt. come near; be similar —n. means of access; a technique **ap•proach•a•bil´i•ty** n —**ap•proach´a•ble** adj.

ap´pro•ba´tion n. approval; high regard —**ap•pro´ba•tive, ap•pro´ba•to•ry** adj.

ap•pro´pri•ate´ adj. suitable; proper —vt. to take; set apart for a particular use —**ap•pro´pri•ate•ly** adv. —**ap•pro´pri•ate•ness** n.

ap•prov´al n. consent; official sanction; a favorable opinion —**on approval** merchandise to be tested without obligation to buy

ap•prove´ vi. express approval —vt. give consent; to view favorably —**ap•prov´ing•ly** adv.

ap•prox´i•mate adj. similar; close —vt. to come near —**ap•prox´i•mate•ly** adv. —**ap•prox´i•ma´tion** n.

ap•pur´te•nance n. an adjunct —**ap•pur´te•nant** adj.

a′pron n. a protective covering; the front of a stage

ap′ro·pos′ adj. appropriate — adv. with respect to; regarding

apse n. an extended portion of a building

apt adj. appropriate; likely, probable; competent, talented —**apt′ly** adv. —**apt′ness** n.

ap′ti·tude n. a natural gift; quickness of understanding

a′qua adj. light blue—green — n. a blue green color

aq′ua·cul·ture n. cultivation of fish or plants in water

a·quar′ium n. a fish tank; a building for exhibiting sea life

aq′ua·tint n. an etching for tints or washes; the copper plate used; a wash print

aq′ua vi′tae n. alcohol; distilled spirits

aq′ue·duct′ n. a conduit for water

a′que·ous adj. watery; formed by or containing water

aq′ui·line adj. like an eagle; curved like an eagle's beak

ar·a·besque′ n. an intricate scrollwork design; a ballet position

Ar′a·bic adj. of the language and culture of Arabia —n. any of the Middle Eastern languages

Arabic numerals the figures 0, 1, 2, 3, 4, 5, 6, 7, 8, 9

ar′a·ble adj. able to be cultivated; suitable for cultivation

a·rach′nid n. a class of insects that includes spiders and scorpions

Ar·a·ma′ic n. an ancient Semitic language

ar′bi·ter n. one qualified to judge

ar′bi·trar·y adj. discretionary; capricious; autocratic —**ar′bi·trar′i·ly** adv. —**ar′bi·trar′i·ness** n.

ar′bi·trate vi., vt. to settle by submitting to a third party —**ar′bi·tra′tive** adj.

ar′bi·tra′tion n referral of dispute to a disinterested party

ar′bi·tra′tor n. a judge

ar′bor n. a place shaded by low trees or vines

ar·bo′re·al adj pertaining to trees

ar·bo·res′cent adj. branching —**ar·bo·res′cence** n.

ar·bo·re′tum n. a botanical garden

ar′bor·vi′tae n. an evergreen shrub

arc n. a section of a curve

ar·cade′ n. a row of shops

ar·cane′ adj. secret; mysterious

arch adj. most distinguished; crafty —n. a curved supporting structure —vi. to be curved like an arch —vt. to form into a curve

ar′chae·ol·o·gy (Brit.) n. the study of places and artifacts of the past —**ar·chae·o·log′i·cal** adj —**ar·chae·ol′o·gist** n.

ar·cha′ic adj ancient; old-fashioned

arch′an·gel n. a high ranking angel

ar′cha·ism n an obsolete expression; an antiquated style —**ar·cha·is′tic** adj.

arch′bish′op n. a church official

arch·bish·op′ric n. the office of an archbishop

arch•dea´con n. a lay church official —**arch•dea´con•ate** n.

arch´di´o•cese n. the jurisdiction of an archbishop

arch•en´e•my n. a chief adversary

ar´che•ol´o•gy (US) n. var. of *archaeology* —**ar´che•o•log´i•cal** adj. —**ar•che•ol´o•gist** n.

ar´cher•y n. the art of shooting with bow and arrow

ar´che•type n. a standard pattern, model —**ar´che•typ•al, ar•che•typ´ic** adj.— **ar•che•typ´i•cal•ly** adv.

arch´fiend´ n. a principal demon

ar´chi•pel´a•go n. a sea with many small islands; a ain of islands

ar´chi•tect´ n. one who designs structures; a planner *architect of peace* —**ar•chi•tec´tur•al** adj. —**ar´chi•tec´ture** n.

ar´chive, ar´chives n. a place where records are collected and stored —**arch•chi´val** adj.

arch´way n. passage under an arch

arc lamp, arc light a high intensity light

arc´tic adj. of the polar regions

ar´dent adj. passionate; en thusiastic; zealous —**ar´- dent•ly** adv.

ar´dor n. passion; enthusiasm

ar´du•ous adj laborious; strenuous —**ar´du•ous•ly** adv.

a´re•a n. a section of land; the extent or scope of anything

area code (US) a three digit telephone prefix that identi fies locality

a´re•a•way´ n. an open space in or around a building; a passageway

a•re´na n. an area for sporting events; a sphere of conflict

ar´gent adj like ailver; gray- white —n. silver; a silvery quality or color

ar•gen´tine adj. silvery —n. a silver-white metal of tin and zinc

ar´gil n. white clay; potter's earth

ar´gon n. an inert gas

ar´got n. words peculiar to a group, trade, etc.

ar•gue vi. to dispute —vt. attempt to prove —**ar´gu•a•ble** adj. —**ar´gu•a•bly** adv.

ar´gu•ment n. reason offered as proof; the art of reasoning; a discussion or debate; —**ar•gu•men•ta´tion** n.

ar•gu•men´ta•tive adj. disposed to argue; characterized by argument; open to question —**ar•gu•men´ta• tive•ly** adv.

ar´gyle, ar´gyll n. a design of diamonds overlaid with a contrasting design; hosiery with such a design

a•ri´a n. a melody, an elegant solo

ar´id adj. dry, parched; desolate, barren; dull, un- interesting

a•rise´ vi. to rise; to ascend upward; to emanate from something

ar•is•toc´ra•cy n. government by the privileged; nobility, the upper class

a•ris´to•crat´ n. member of the aristocracy —**a•ris´to• crat´ic** adj. —**a•ris•to•crat´ i•cal•ly** adv.

a•rith´me•tic´ n. calculating

by numbers —**ar•ith•met´ic, ar•ith•met´i•cal** adj. —**ar´ith•met´i•cal•ly** adv.

arithmetic mean the middle value of a group of numbers

arithmetic progression a sequence of values which differ from the previous by a constant quantity

ark n. a flat-bottomed boat or scow

ark of the covenant chest containing sacred tablets of the Hebrews

arm n. an upper limb; part of a garment covering the arm; part of a chair; a thing that looks or functions like an arm; a weapon —vi. prepare for conflict —vt. provide with weapons; provide that needed for an encounter; *armed with information* —**an arm and a leg** a high price —**arm's length** precluding intimacy or conspiracy

ar•ma´da n. a fleet of warships

Ar´ma•ged´don n. a decisive battle

ar´ma•ment n. weapons and equipment of a military in-stallation; forces equipped for battle; the act of equipping for war

ar´ma•ture n. a piece of iron connecting poles of a magnet; a core which revolves through a magnetic field; arms or armor; protective devises, as an animal's shell

arm´chair n. a chair with sides

ar•mis•tice n. a truce; a temporary cessation of hostilities

ar•moire´ a large storage cabinet

ar´mor n. protective covering;

the vehicles of war —vt. to don armor —**ar´mored** adj.

ar´mor•er n. a manufacturer of arms; a custodian of small arms

ar´mor•y n. place where arms are manufactured or stored

ar´my n. body of soldiers; a large number

a•ro´ma n. an agreeable odor; a distinctive quality —**ar´o•mat´ic, ar´o•mat´i•cal** adj.

ar•ound´ adv. so as to surround; in. the opposite direction; from place to place; in proximity —prep. encircling; on the other side of; in proximity —**come around** recover consciousness; be persuaded

ar•ouse´ vt. to awaken; to stir up, excite —**a•rous´al** n.

ar•peg´gi•o n. sounding of the notes of a chord in rapid succession

ar•raign´ vt. to accuse; summon to face charges —**ar•raign´ment** n.

ar•range´ vt. put in order; come to terms; orchestrate a musical composition

ar•range´ment n. that arranged; the way in which something is ordered; a musical adaptation

ar´rant adj. notoriously wicked —**ar´rant•ly** adv.

ar•ray´ n. an orderly display; fine garments; an impressive gathering —vt. to gather in order; to adorn

ar•rear´, arrears´ n. being behind; that which is behind —**in arrears** behind in making payment —**ar•rear´age** n.

ar•rest´ n. capture —vt. to slow or stop; to capture and detain —**ar•rest´er, ar•res´ tor** n.

ar•rest´ing adj. attracting attention; noteworthy — **ar•rest´ing•ly** adv.

ar•rive´ vi. to reach a destination; attain success — **ar•riv´al** n.

ar´ro•gant adj. overbearing; insolent; marked by pride or vanity —**ar´ro•gance** n. — **ar´ro•gant•ly** adv.

ar´row n. a pointed shaft; a drawing in the shape of an arrow

ar´row•root n. a nutritious starch used in food preparation

ar•roy´o n. a steep-sided dry gulch; a stream

ar´se•nal n. a place where arms and munitions are made or stored

ar´son n. setting of fire with criminal intent —**ar´son•ist** n.

art n. skill; any craft requiring skill; creative work —**arts** pl. n. the humanities

ar•te´ri•al adj. pertaining to the vessels that carry blood from the heart; corresponding to an artery: *an arterial highway*

ar´ter•y n. a vessel that carries blood from the heart; any main channel, as of communication

art´ful adj. crafty or cunning; ingenious or resourceful — **art´ful•ly** adv. —**art´ful• ness** n.

ar•thri´tis n. painful inflammation of a joint —**ar•thrit´ ic** adj.

ar´thro•pod n. an invertebrate with segmented limbs and body, such as an insect,

spider, or crab —**ar•throp´ o•dous, ar•throp´o•dal** adj.

ar´ti•choke´ n. an edible plant resembling the thistle

ar´ti•cle n. a written piece; a clause in a document; a distinct item

ar•tic´u•lar adj. pertaining to the joints —**ar•tic´u•lar•ly** adv.

artic´u•late adj. clearly spoken —vi. speak clearly; to be jointed —vt. to speak clearly; to form with joints —**ar•tic´ u•late•ly** adv. —**ar•tic´u• la´tion** n.

ar´ti•fact´ n. an article fashioned by humans, especially a relic

ar´ti•fice n. a clever scheme

ar•ti•fi´cial adj. not natural; imitation; affected —**ar•ti• fi•ci•al´i•ty** n. **ar•ti•fi´cial• ly** adv

ar•til´ler•y n. ordnance, cannon; the branch of military using ordnance

ar´ti•san n. a craftsman; one skilled

art´ist n. one skilled, esp. with a sense of style — **ar•tist•ry** n.

ar•tiste´ n. a skillful performer

ar•tis´tic, ar•tis´ti•cal adj. pertaining to arts; pleasing; receptive to art —**ar•tis´ti• cal•ly** adv.

art´less adj. without deception; natural; innocent; rough; unskilled; lacking taste —**art´less•ly** adv. — **art´less•ness** n.

art´y adj. affected; ostentatious —**art´i•ness** n.

as adv. equally: *this car is as fast as the other*, for example: *to quote, as a verse*;

—*conj.* equal to: such *a plan as this cannot fail;* at the same time; in proportion: *the light grows brighter as we get nearer,* in the manner that: *do as you are told;* because: *as it was raining, we drove slowly*

as•cend´ *vi.* to move or slope upward; to move lower to higher —*vt.* to move upward; to succeed, as to a throne — **as•cend´a•ble, as•cend´i•ble** *adj.* —**as•cent´** *n.*

as•cend´ant, as•cend´ent *adj.* rising; commanding —*n.* a position of prominence — **as•cend´an•cy, ascend´en•cy** *n.*

as´cer•tain´ *vt.* make certain —**as•cer•tain´a•ble** *adj.* — **as•cer•tain´a•bly** *adv.* —**as•cer•tain´ment** *n.*

as•cet´ic *adj.* austere; *n.* one who leads a life of austerity —**as•cet´i•cal•ly** *adv.* —**as•cet´i•cism** *n.*

as•cribe´ *vt.* to impute; to attribute as coming from or caused by

a•scor´bic ac´id *n.* vitamin C

as´cot *n.* a type of necktie

a•sex´u•al *adj.* having no distinct sexual organs —**a•sex•u•al´i•ty** *n.* —**a•sex´u•al•ly** *adv.*

ash *n.* the residue left from burning; a tough, elastic tree or its wood

a•shamed´ *adj.* shame engendered by a failing; impeded by embarrassment — **a•sham´ed•ly** *adj.*

ash´en *adj.* pale in color; pertaining to the wood of the ash tree

a•shore´ *adv.* on the shore; aground

ash´y *adj.* like ashes; ash colored; covered with ashes

a•side´ *adv.* to one side; apart

as´i•nine *adj.* stupid or silly — **as´i•nine•ly** *adv.* —**as•i•nin´i•ty** *n.*

ask *vi.* make inquiries —*vt.* to question; inquire about; make a request; state a price

a•skance´ a•skant´ *adv.* with suspicion; with a sideways glance

a•skew´ *adj., adv.* out of line; to one side

a•slant´ *adj.* slanting; tilted — *adv.* in a *slanting* position — *prep.* across at an angle

a•sleep´ *adj.* dormant; sleeping; dead —*adv.* into a state of rest

a•so´cial *adj.* avoiding social contact; self-centered

asp *n.* the European viper

as•par´a•gus *n.* a plant with tender, edible shoots

as´pect *n.* appearance; a particular viewpoint

as•per´i•ty *n.* roughness; harshness

as•perse´ *vt.* to accuse falsely; to slander —**as•per´sion** *n.*

as´phalt´ *n.* a material used for paving —**as•phal´tum** *n.* **as•phyx´i•ate** *vt.* to suffocate —**as•phyx´i•a´tion** *n.*

as´pic *n.* a gelatin garnish or mold

as´pir•ant *adj.* aspiring —*n.* one who tries; a candidate

as´pi•ra´tion *n.* extreme desire; a thing desired

aspire´ *vi.* to long for or seek after

as´pi•rin *n.* acetylsalicylic acid; a remedy for headache or fever

ass *n.* a beast of burden; a stubborn or foolish person

as•sail´ vt. to attack violently —**as•sail´a•ble** adj. —**as•sail´ant** n.

as•sas´si•nate vt. to murder; to attack by slander or inuendo— **as•sas´sin, as•sas•si•na´tion** n.

as•sault´ n. an attack —vi., vt. make an attack —n.

as•say´ n. a testing —vt. to analyze

as•sem´blage n. a gathering

as•sem´ble vi., vt. gather together; to put together —**as•sem´bly** n.

assembly line workers and machines arranged so as to permit efficient fabrication of products

as•sent´ n. agreement; consent —vi. to agree —**as•sent´er, as•sen´tor** n. —**as•sent´ing•ly** adv.

as•sert´ vt. to declare; to state with conviction —**as•sert´a•ble, as•sert´i•ble** adj. —**as•ser´tion** n.

as•ser´tive adj. authoritative; insistent —**as•ser´tive•ly** adv. —**as•ser´tive•ness** n.

as•sess´ vt. to set a value; to impose, as a fine or tax; to evaluate —**as•sess´a•ble** adj. —**as•sess´ment** n. —**as•ses´sor** n.

as´set n. property that has value; anything useful or appealing

as•sev´er•ate vt. to declare emphatically

as•sid´u•ous adj. painstaking; diligent —**as•sid´u•ous•ly** adv.

as•sign´ vt. to designate; appoint; to ascribe —**assign´a•ble** adj. —**as•signment** n.

as•sig•na´tion n. an appointment; an illicit meeting

as•sim´i•late vi. to be absorbed; to become like —vt. to absorb and digest; adapt or conform —**as•sim•i•la´tion** n.

as•sist´ n. the act of helping —vi. to aid —vt. to help; work as a helper —**as•sis´tance** n. —**as•sis´tant** n.

as•so´ci•ate adj. joined with others; linked —n. a coworker; a thing linked —vt. to unite; to bring into relationship; associate poetry with romance —vi. to be in company with —**as•so´ci•a•tion** n.

as´so•nance n. resemblance in sound; an approximation

as•sort´ vi. to fall into like groups —vt. to classify; to divide into groups

as•sort´ed adj. consisting of variety; diverse; sorted or classified

as•sort´ment n. a collection

as•suage´ vt. to alleviate; to calm; to satisfy

as•sume´ vt. to undertake; to take for granted —**as•sum´a•ble** adj. —**as•sum´a•bly** adv.

as•sump´tion n. act of assuming; supposition —**as•sump´tive** adj.

as•sur´ance n. confidence; conviction; an encouraging statement

as•sure´ vt. to convey confidence; to guarantee —**as•sur´ance** n.

as•sured´ adj. undoubted; sure; confident

as´ter•isk n. a star-like character (*) used to mark references

asth´ma n. a respiratory ailment

asth·mat´ic n. one suffering from asthma —**asth·mat´ic, asth·mat´i·cal** adj. affected with asthma **asth·mat´i·cal·ly** adv.

a·stig´ma·tism´ n. a visual defect —**a·stig·mat´ic** adj.

a·stir´ adj., adv. moving about

as·ton´ish vt. to stun, amaze —**as·ton´ish·ing** adj.

as·ton´ish·ment n. surprise; amazement; a thing causing surprise

a·stound´ vt. to overcome with amazement —**as·tound´ing** adj. —**as·tound´ing·ly** adv.

as´tral adj. of the stars

a·stray´ adj., adv. off the correct path; straying into error or evil

a·stride´ adj., adv. with one leg on each side

as·trin´gent adj. stern; severe; disposed to draw together organic tissue —**as·trin´gen·cy** n. —**as·trin´gent·ly** adv.

as´tro·dome n. an enclosed field for sporting events; a structure for making celestial observations

as´tro·labe n. an old navigational instrument

as·trol´o·gy n. the belief that the stars can influence human affairs —**as·trol´o·ger** n. —**as·tro·log´ic, as·tro·log´i·cal** adj. —**as·tro·log´i·cal·ly** adv.

as´tro·naut´ n. a space traveler

as·tro·nau´tics pl. n. the science of space travel

as·tro·nom´ic, as·tro·nom´i·cal adj. pertaining to astronomy; numerous —**as·tro·nom´i·cal·ly** adv.

as·tron´o·my n. the study of

stars, planets, etc. —**as·tron´o·mer** n.

as´tro·phys´ics n. study of the physical properties of stars,planets,etc.—**as·tro·phys´i·cist** n.

as·tute´ adj. exhibiting a keen mind; shrewd —**as·tute´ly** adv.

a·sun´der adj. disconnected — adv. in pieces

a·sy´lum n. sanctuary; home for the sick

a·sym´me·try n. lack of proportion

a·sym·met´ric, a·sym·met´ri·cal adj. disproportionate —**a·sym·met´ri·cal·ly** adv.

at prep. in the exact location; on or near; toward; in the condition of: two people at odds

at´a·vism n. retrogression to an earlier state —**at´a·vist** n. —**at·a·vis´tic** adj. —**at·a·vis´ti·cal·ly** adj.

a·tax´i·a n. failure to control muscular movement — **a·tax´ic** adj., n.

at´el·ier n. an artist's studio

a´the·ism n. denial that gods exist —**a´the·ist** n. —**a·the·is´tic, a´the·is´ti·cal** adj. —**a·the·is´ti·cal·ly** adv.

ath´lete n. one trained in athletics —**ath·let´ic** adj. —**ath·let´i·cal·ly** adv.

ath·let´ics pl. n. sporting contests, gymnastics, etc. collectively

a·thwart´ adv. from side to side —prep. across; in opposition to

a·tilt´ adj., adv. tilted upward

at´las n. a book of maps

atmosphere´ n. air surrounding the earth; the mood of an environment;

40

decor —**at•mos•pher´ic, at•mos•pher´i•cal** adj. —**at•mos•pher´i•cal•ly** adv.

at•mos•pher´ics n. broadcast interference

a´toll n. a coral island and its reef, enclosing a lagoon

at´om n. a tiny particle; smallest combinable particle of an element —**a•tom´ic** adj. —**a•tom´i•cal•ly** adv.

atomic clock a precise instrument for the measurement of time

atomic energy energy liberated by the fission or fusion of atoms

atomic number the number which serves to identify an element

atomic weight the weight of an atom of an element relative to that of an atom of carbon

at´om•ize´ vt. to separate into atoms; to make liquid into a fine spray —**at´om•iz•er** n.

a•to•nal´i•ty n. lack of tonal quality —**a•ton´al, a•ton•al•is´tic** adj. —**a•ton´al•ly** adv.

a•tone´ vi. to make amends —**a•ton´a•ble, a•tone´a•ble** adj.

a•tone´ment n. reparation for wrong

a´top´ adj., adv. on or at the top

a´tri•um n. an entrance hall; an open area in a building; one of the chambers of the human heart

a•tro´cious adj. cruel, wicked; offensive, tasteless —**a•tro´clouts•ly** adv. —**a•troc´i•ty** n.

at´ro•phy n. a wasting away of body tissue —vi., vt. to waste away —**a•troph´ic** adj.

at•tach´ vi. to adhere —vt. to fasten on; to take by legal means —**at•tach´a•ble** adj. —**at•tach´ment** n.

at•ta•ché´ n. a person assigned to a diplomatic mission

attaché case n. a briefcase; a flat case with a hingd lid

at•tack´ n. any hostile action —vt. to strike out against; to assault; to take up vigorously —**at•tack´er** n.

at•tain´ vi. to arrive —vt. to gain; to achieve —**at•tain´a•ble** adj. —**at•tain´ment** n.

at•tain´der n. loss of civil rights by a person sentenced for a crime

at•tar´ n. a fragrant oil extracted from flower petals

at•tempt´ n. a try —vt. to try; make an effort —**at•tempt´a•ble** adj. —**at•tempt´er** n.

at•tend´ vi. to heed; give care —vt. to minister to; to accompany; be present

at•tend´ance n. one's presence; the record of one's presence over time; collectively, those who attend

at•tend´ant adj. present; waiting upon; following as a consequence —n. one who waits upon; a servant; an accompaniment

at•ten´tion n. concentration; alertness; notice; attentiveness

at•ten´tive adj. considerate, thoughtful —**at•ten´tive•ly** adv.

at•ten´u•ate vt., vi. make or become thin or fine; to reduce or become lessened —**at•ten´u•a•ble** adj. —**at•ten•u•a´tion** n.

at•test´ vt. to testify; to certify under oath

41

at´tic *n.* an area directly beneath the roof and above the last full floor of a building

at•tire´ *n.* clothing —*vt.* to dress

at´ti•tude´ *n.* the bearing of a person; position in relation to a plane surface; state of mind; disposition

at•tor´ney *(US)* *n.* a lawyer

at•tract´ *vt.* to draw or be drawn towards; to entice — **at•trac´tion** *n.*

at•tract´ive *adj.* possessing power to entice —**at•tract´ive•ly** *adv.* —**at•tract´ive•ness** *n.*

at´tri•bute´ *n.* a quality or characteristic —**at•tri´bute** *vt.* to impute —**at•trib´ut•a•ble** *adj.*

at•tri´tion *n.* a wearing away; loss of workers, as by retirement

at•tune´ *vt.* to adjust; to bring into conformity with

a•typ´i•c, a•typ´i•cal *adj.* not characteristic; inconsistent with the norm

au´burn *adj., n.* reddish-brown color

auc´tion *n.* a sale by bid —*vt.* to sell by bid —**auc•tion•eer´** *n.*

au•cou•rant´ *adj.* up to date; fashionable

au•da´cious *adj.* bold, daring; shameless —**au•da´cious•ly** *adv.* —**au•da´cious•ness, au•dac´i•ty** *n.*

au´di•ble *adj.* able to be heard —**au´di•ble•ness** *n.* — **au´di•bly** *adv.*

au´di•ence *n.* a formal interview; those who attend a show, etc.

au´di•o *adj.* involving sound waves —*n.* sound

audio frequency sound waves within the range of human hearing

au´di•o•phile´ *n.* one interested in high-fidelity sound

au´di•o•vis´u•al *adj.* embracing both sound and sight — *n.* material that incorporates sound and sight

au´dit *n.* a verification of finances —*vt.* to examine; to attend college classes as a listener

au•di´tion *n.* a tryout —*vi., vt.* to try out, as for a job

au´dit•or *n.* one who examines accounts; one who attends a class without credit

au´di•to´ri•um *n.* a meeting room

au´di•to•ry *adj.* pertaining to hearing

au´ger *n.* a boring tool

aug•ment´ *vi., vt.* to increase; supplement **aug•men•ta´tion** *n.* —**aug•men´tive** *adj.*

au grat´in *adj.* cooked with cheese or bread crumbs

au´gur *vi., vt.* to predict; be an omen

au´gu•ry *n.* the art of divination; an omen

au•gust´ *adj.* inspiring reverence; imposing

au na•tu•rel´ *adj.* of ungarnished food; nude

aunt *n.* the sister of one's parent or the wife of one's uncle; a title of affection

au´ra *n.* an invisible field or quality; a gentle breeze

au´ral *adj.* pertaining to the hearing

au´re•ate *adj.* the color of gold

au´ri•cle *n.* one of two atriums of the heart; the outer ear

au•ric´u•lar *adj.* relating to hearing

au·rif′er·ous adj. containing gold

au·ro′ra n. the dawn; a luminous display in the polar night sky

aus·cul·tate vt. to examine by listening —**aus·cul·ta′tion** n.

aus′pice n. an omen; patronage

aus·pi′cious adj. favorable; fortunate —**aus·pi′cious·ly** adv. —**aus·pi′cious·ness** n.

aus·tere′ adj. stern; plain in decor —**aus·ter′i·ty** n.

au·then′tic adj. genuine; official —**au·then′ti·cal·ly** adv. —**au·then·tic′i·ty** n.

au·then′ti·cate vt. to verify; prove genuine —**au·then′ti·cation** n. —**au·then′ti·ca·tor** n.

au′thor n. one who originates —**au′thor·ship** n.

au·thor·i·tar′i·an adj. autocratic; strict —n. an advocate of authority

au·thor′i·ta·tive adj. with authority—**au·thor′i·ta·tive·ly** adv.

au·thor·i·ty n. power to command; one invested with power

au′tho·rise′ (Brit.), **au′thor·ize′** (US) vt. to approve; to permit —**au′thor·ised**, **au′thor·ized** adj.

au·to·bi·og′ra·phy n. one's life story —**au′to·bi·o·graph′i·cal** adj. —**au′to·bi·o·graph′i·cal·ly** adv.

au·toc′ra·cy n. absolute rule; a dictatorship; rule of a dictator; a state governed by an absolute ruler

au′to·crat′ n. an absolute ruler —**au·to·crat′ic** adj. —**au·to·crat′i·cal·ly** adv.

au′to·graph′ n. signature — vt. to sign

au′to·mate vt. to operate by automation

au·to·mat′ic adj. involuntary; self-operating —**au·to·mat′i·cal·ly** adv.

au·to·ma′tion n. automatic operation

au·tom′a·ton n. a robot; a machine controlled by a computer; one who moves mechanically

au′to·mo·bile (US) n. a passenger vehicle; a car

au·to·nom′ic adj. involuntary; acting unconsciously —**au·to·nom′i·cal·ly** adv.

autonomic nervous system that which controls involuntary actions of the body

au·ton′o·mous adj. independent; acting without supervision or control —**au·ton′o·mous·ly** adv.

au·ton′o·my n. self government; functioning of a group apart from its parent organization

au′to·pi′lot n. a device to maintain an aircraft's course and attitude

au·top′sy n. medical examination of a dead body

au′tumn n. the season between summer and winter; (US) fall —**au·tum′nal** adj.

aux·il′ia·ry adj. helping; supplementary

a·vail′ vi. to assist or aid —vt. to be of value —n. benefit

a·vail′a·ble adj. at one's disposal; obtainable —**a·vail′a·bil′i·ty** n.

av′a·lanche′ n. a mass of snow or earth falling from a height; anything in an abnormal quantity

a•vant-garde´ *adj.* reflecting recent trends —*n.* those who promote new or unconventional techniques

av´a•rice *n.* greed; a passion for wealth —**av•a•ri´cious** *adj.* —**av•a•ri´cious•ly** *adv.*

av´a•tar *n.* the incarnation of a Hindu god; physical phenomenon

a•venge´ *vt.* to exact punishment for a wrong

av´e•nue *n.* a wide street; an approach; a means of access

a•ver´ *vt.* to declare to be true

av´er•age *adj. of* a median value; not exceptional —*n.* the value of several elements divided by the number of elements —*vt.* to find or fix an average value

a•verse´ *adj.* opposed; reluctant —**a•verse´ly** *adv.*

a•ver´sion *n.* a dislike; profound distaste; that which is distasteful —**a•ver´sive** *adj.*

a•vert´ *vt.* to turn away, to ward off —**avert´a•ble, a•vert´i•ble** *adj.*

a´vi•ar´y *n.* a place for keeping birds

a´vi•a´tion *n.* the development and operation *of* aircraft —**a´vi•a•tor** *n.*

avid´ *adj.* eager; enthusiastic —**av´id•ly** *adv.*

av•o•ca´tion *n.* a hobby; a sideline —**avo•ca´tion•al** *adj.*

a•void´ *vt. to* shun; keep from happening —**a•void´a•ble** *adj.* —**a•void´a•bly** *adv.* —**a•void´ance** *n.*

av´oir•du•pois´ *n.* the system of weights of the United States

a•vow´ *vt.* declare openly; confess —**a•vow´a•ble** *adj.*

a´vow´al *n.* acknowledgment; open admission

a´vowed´ *adj.* readily acknowledged; openly declared —**avow´ed•ly** *adv.*

a•vun´cu•lar *adj. of* an uncle

a•wait´ *vt.*, watch for; to be ready for

a•wake´ *adj.* not sleeping; alert —*vi.* to wake; become aware —*vt.* arouse; to make aware

a•wak´en *vi.*, *vt.* to awake

a•wak´en•ing *adj.* stimulating; exciting —*n.* a rekindling

a•ward´ *n.* a judgment; a prize —*vt.* to grant by judgement

a•ware´ *adj.* familiar with; conscious —**a•ware´ness** *n.*

a•wash´ *adj.*, *adv.* at water level; overflowing; inundated: *awash in job applications*

a•way´ *adj.* at a distance —*adv.* distant; to the side; diligently: *working away;* removed from one's keeping; immediately: *fire away* —*interj.* begone

awe *n.* wonder or fear —*vt.* to fill with wonder

awe´some *adj.* overwhelming; inciting awe

awe´struck *adj.* stunned; impressed

aw´ful *adj.* inspiring fear; dreadful; formidable

aw´ful•ly *adv.* in a dreadful manner; exceedingly: *awfully bright*

a•while´ *adv.* for a time

awk´ward *adj.* clumsy; inconvenient; embarrassing —**awk´ward•ly** *adv.* —**awk´ward•ness** *n.*

awl *n.* a pointed tool

awn *n.* a bristlelike part of grasses

awn´ing n. a structural projection to ward off sun and rain

awry´ adj., adv. not straight

ax, axe n. a tool for chopping wood

ax´i•al adj. along an axis

ax´i•ol•o•gy n. the study of values

ax´i•om n. an adage —**ax´i•o•mat´ic** adj. —**ax•i•o•mat´i•cal•ly** adv.

ax´is n., pl. **ax´es** a line around which an object rotates

ax´le n. a shaft for a wheel

az´i•muth n. the arc between the horizon and a star

a•zo´ic adj. referring to the time on earth before the appearance of life

az´ure adj. sky-blue —n.

b, B n. second letter of the alphabet; second-rate, as a B-movie

bab´ble n. a rippling sound; incoherent noises —vi. to prattle foolishly —vt. to disclose carelessly

babe n. an infant; one lacking in experience or knowledge

ba´bel n. a bedlam of sounds

ba´by adj. childish; small —n. an infant; the youngest or smallest; one who acts like a child —vt. to handle gingerly —**ba´by•ish** adj.

baby doll a short woman's nightgown

baby food puréed food for an infant

baby grand a small grand piano

baby´s-breath a plant having small white or pink flowers

ba´by•sit´ vi., vt. to care for children —**ba´by-sit•ter** n.

bac´ca•lau´re•ate n. a bachelor's degree; a farewell address

bac•cha•nal´ adj. drunken revelry —n. a reveler; a riotous feast —**bac•cha•na´lia** n. —**bac•cha•na´lian** adj.

back adj. in the rear; isolated; of an earlier time —adv. toward the rear; to a bygone place or condition —n. the hindmost part; the spine of a body; the far side; the part of an object not normally used: back of a knife; the spine of a book —vi., vt. to move or cause to move backward; support or assist

back´bit´er vt. one who speaks ill of another

back´bone n. the spinal column; the main support: backbone of the country; courage; spunk

back burner a place of low priority

back´drop n. a background

back´er n. a supporter; one who provides financial help or encouragement; an apologist

back´fire n. a fire set to halt a forest fire; premature explosion in an engine; backward explosion in a gun —vi. to set a backfire; the explosive sound of a backfire; achieve an opposite result

back´gam´mon n. a board game for two players, often involving wagers

back´ground n. that in the rear; part of a picture or scene behind the main object; secondary; peripheral; one's experience; sound to enhance a performance; a description of prior events

back´hand *adj.* not straight-forward or sincere —*adv.* with a backhand stroke —*n.* a movement made with the hand turned backward

back´hand•ed *adj.* with the hand turned backward; insincere; ironic; turned in an opposite direction

back´ing *n.* support; a group of supporters; the act of moving backward; material added for strength

back´lash´ *n.* a sharp recoil; a reaction

back´log´ *n.* a reserve; orders to be filled or processed

back´-ped•al *vi.* to retreat

back seat *n.* a seat in the rear; a position of secondary importance

back´side *n.* the back part; the posterior or rump

back´slap *vi.* insincere friendliness —*vt.* to be overly friendly

back´slide *vi.* to return to old ways

back´spin *n.* reverse rotation; a rebounded effect or result

back´stage´ *adj.* situated offstage —*adv.* behind or to the side of the stage —*n.* the rear or sides of a stage, as wings or dressing rooms

back´stairs´ *n.* stairs at the back of a dwelling —*adj.* underhanded; indirect

back´stop *n.* a screen on a playing field to confine the game projectile —*vi.* to sustain or reinforce

back´stretch *n.* the part of a racecourse farthest from the spectators

back talk *n.* an insolent or argumentative response

back´track *vi.* to retrace one's steps; to retreat from an earlier opinion

back´up *n.* support; an accumulation: something held in readiness

back´ward *adj.* reversed; bashful; retarded —*adv.* in the direction of the back; toward time past; in reverse order —**back´wards** *adv.* —**back´ward•ness** *n.*

back´wa•ter *n.* a place judged to be backward or undeveloped

back´woods *adj.* undeveloped; culturally deprived —*n.* a sparsely settled area; an area which is not culturally advanced

ba´con *n.* cured meat from the back or side of a hog

bac•te´ri•a *n. pl.*, sing. **bac•te´ri•um** microorganisms that cause disease, fermentation, etc. —**bac•te´ri•al** *adj.*

bac•te´ri•cide *n.* a substance which destroys bacteria

bad *adj.* not satisfactory; unacceptable; evil; naughty; unlucky; offensive; incorrect; detrimental; unfortunate; improper; concerned: *to feel bad about* —**not bad, not half bad, not so bad** rather good —*n.* that which is bad; collectively, those who are bad

badge *n.* a symbol of authority

badg´er *n.* a burrowing mammal —*vt.* to tease or pester

bad´i•nage *n.* playful banter

bad´ly *adv.* incorrectly; offensively; detrimentally; with intense desire

baf´fle *vt.* to confound; to obstruct or impede —**baf´fle•ment** *n.* —**baf´fling** *adj.*

bag *n.* a sack, purse, suitcase, etc.; the amount a bag contains —*vi.* to bulge or hang loosely —*vt.* place in a bag; to attain, as by hunting —**in the bag** certain —**left holding the bag** charged with responsibility or blame —**bag and baggage** completely; with all one's possessions

bag·a·telle´ *n.* a trifle

ba´gel *n.* a hard roll shaped like a doughnut

bag´gage *n.* luggage; a lascivious woman; a useless idea or practice

bag´gy *adj.* loose; ill-fitting

bag´man *n.* one who collects or distributes illegal money

ba·guet´, ba·guette´ *n.* a crystal cut to a narrow; rectangular shaped

bail *n.* security to insure one's appearance in court —*vt.* to free one on security; to remove water —**bail´ment** *n.* —**bail´or** *n.*

bail´iff *n.* an officer of the court

bail´i·wick *n.* the office of a bailiff; one's place or sphere of influence

bail out parachute from an airplane; post bond; distance oneself from unpleasantness

bails´man *n.* one who posts bail

bait *n.* an enticement —*vt.* to lure or entice; to tease or provoke

bake *vi.* to become firm and dry from heat —*vt.* to cook or harden with dry heat

bak´er *n.* one who makes and sells baked products —**baker's dozen** thirteen, giving extra to avoid penalty for short count

bak´er·y *n.* a place for making or selling baked goods

baking powder a baking soda mixture used as a leavening agent

baking soda (*US*) sodium bicarbonate; a compound used in cooking, cleaning, as an antacid, etc.

bak´sheesh, bak´shish *n.* a gratuity; a bribe

bal·a·lai´ka *n.* a three-stringed musical instrument of Russian origin

bal´ance *n.* a device for weighing; an amount owed; a state of equilibrium; an amount left; a state of harmony —*vi.* to be equal —*vt.* to compare; to compensate; to reconcile; as financial records

balance of payments the difference between payments and receipts for trade between nations

balance of power a comparison of the relative strength of nations

balance of trade a comparison of the value of imports and exports

balance sheet a statement of financial condition

bal´co·ny *n.* a platform outside an upper window; an upper level of seats in a theater

bald *adj.* without hair or natural covering; unadorned

bal´der·dash *n.* nonsense

bald´faced *adj.* audacious, brazen; obvious, as *a baldfaced lie*

bale *n.* a large bundle —*vt.* to tie or wrap —**bal´er** *n.*

ba·leen´ *n.* whalebone

bale´ful *adj.* noxious; harmful

balk *vi.* to refuse to proceed or take part

balk´y *adj.* prone to stop suddenly; reluctant to participate

ball *n.* a sphere; a game that uses a round object for throwing, hitting, etc.; a formal dance —**on the ball** qualified; alert

bal´lad *n.* a sentimental song; a song or poem that tells a story —**bal•lad•eer´** *n.*

bal•lis´tics *n.* the study of the motion of projectiles **bal•lis´tic** *adj.*

bal•loon´ *n.* a bag inflated so as to float in the air; a small inflated toy or decoration; a final payment on an installment loan

bal´lot *n.* a paper vote; a vote cast; a list of those running for office

ball´point pen´ a pen that distributes ink by use of a ball bearing

ball´room *n.* a large room for parties and dancing

bal´ly•hoo *n.* boisterous patter; an overblown promotion

balm *n.* an ointment for healing or soothing; anything soothing

balm´y *adj.* aromatic; soothing; slightly mad; very foolish —**balm´i•ness** *n.*

ba•lo´ney, bo•lo´gna *n.* a large, mild sausage; idle or nonsensical talk

bal´sa *n.* a tree of tropical America; the light wood from the balsa tree

bal´sam *n.* a fragrance; a tree which exudes balsam; an aromatic ointment; a soothing or healing agent

bal´us•ter *n.* one of the small pillars which support a hand rail

bal´us•trade *n.* a hand rail and its supporting balusters

bam•boo´ *n.* a hollow-stemmed grass

bam•boo´zle *vi.* to practice trickery —*vt.* to deceive

ban *n.* a prohibition; an ecclesiastical sentence of interdiction —*vt.* to forbid or prohibit; to impose a ban

ba´nal *adj.* commonplace; trite —**ba•nal´i•ty** *n.* —**ba•nal´ly** *adv.*

band *n.* a flat strip of material; a broad contrasting stripe; a range of frequencies: *a broadcast band;* a group of persons —*vi.* to associate —*vt.* to encircle or join with a strip of material; to unite

band´age *n.* cloth to bind a wound —*vt.* to bind or cover with a cloth

ban•dan´a, ban•dan´na *n.* a large, brightly colored handkerchief

ban´dit *n.* a robber, thief; one who steals or defrauds

band´lead•er, band´mas•ter *n.* the leader of a group of musicians

ban•do•leer´, band´do•lier´ a broad belt with loops for cartridges

band saw a motor driven saw

band shell (*US*) a bandstand for outdoor concerts

band´stand *n.* an outdoor stage for musicians or other entertainers

band´wag•on *n.* a decorated wagon that carries a band in a parade —**climb on the bandwagon** change to an apparently winning position

48

ban´dy *adj.* curved or bowed —*vt.* to exchange quips; to pass along

ban´dy·leg´ged *adj.* bowlegged

bane *n.* a cause of distress or destruction; a deadly poison

bang *n.* a sudden loud noise; enthusiasm —*vt.* to strike loudly —*vi.* to make a loud noise; to strike noisily

ban´ish *vt.* to exile; to dismiss or drive away —**ban´ish·ment** *n.*

ban´is·ter, ban´nis·ter *n.* a handrail along a staircase

ban´jo *n.* a stringed instrument with a long narrow neck and circular sound box

bank *n.* a mound or heap; the edge of a body of water; the sloping of a curve or turn; a financial institution; a supply held in reserve; like elements stored together —*vi.* to incline an airplane; to trade at a bank —*vt.* form a slope; rebound at an angle, as in billiards; to deposit in a bank —**bank on** have faith in —**bank´a·ble** *adj.*

bank account an account with a bank; funds available to the holder of such an account

bank book a record of the transactions of a bank account

bank´er *n.* the owner or manager of a bank; a bank executive; one who holds stakes in a game of chance

bank note a promissory note issued by a bank

bank´roll (*US*) *n.* the money which one possesses —*vt.* to back financially —**bank´roll·er** *n.*

bank´rupt *adj.* insolvent; unable to pay debts; wanting: *morally bankrupt* —*n.* one unable to honor debts —*vt.* to cause to default

ban´ner *n.* a flag; a large display of greeting, advertisement, etc.; a newspaper headline

ban´quet *n.* a feast; a formal dinner

ban·quette´ *n.* a bench for seating along a wall, as in a restaurant

ban´shee *n.* in Gaelic folklore, a spirit whose wailing predicts death

ban´tam *n.* a small domestic fowl

ban´tam·weight *n.* a boxer who weighs from 113 to 118 pounds

ban´ter *n.* light-hearted jesting —*vt.* to exchange jibes —*vt.* to tease —**ban´ter·ing·ly** *adv.*

bap´tism *n.* purification rite of the Christian Church; an initiatory rite or experience —**bap·tis´mal** *adj.*

bap´tise (*Brit.*), **bap´tize** (*US*) *vt.* to consecrate by a ceremony

bar[1] *n.* an oblong piece of rigid material; anything that blocks access; the legal profession; a stripe to denote rank; a division in a musical score —*vt.* to close off; to exclude

bar[2] *n.* (*Brit.*) a room in a public house or club where drink is sold

bar[3] *n.* (*US*) an establishment where beverages and food are sold

barb *n.* a sharp spine; a sharp retort

bar·bar·i·an *adj.* uncivilized—
n. an uncultured person—
bar·bar·ic *adj.* —**bar·bar·i·cal·ly** *adv.*

bar'bar·ism *n.* a savage state

bar'bar·i·ty *n.* brutal or crude conduct; vulgarity

bar'ba·rous *adj.* lacking in culture; crude; brutal —**bar'ba·rous·ly** *adv.* —**bar'ba·rous·ness** *n.*

bar'be·cue' *n.* an outdoor celebration; food cooked over an open fire —*vt.* to roast over a charcoal fire; to baste with a tangy sauce

barbed *adj.* having pointed ends; sharp or piercing

barbed wire fencing with sharp pieces at regular intervals

bar'ber *n.* one who trims the hair, beard, etc. —*vt.* to trim the hair

bard *n.* a poet

bare *adj.* lacking clothing or covering; stark, plain; meager —*vt.* to uncover, expose —**bare'ness** *n.*

bare'back *adj.* an animal without a saddle —*adv.* without a saddle

bare'faced *adj.* with nothing concealed; impudent; obvious: *a barefaced lie*

bare'hand'ed *adj.* without benefit of a tool or weapon other than hands

bare'ly *adv.* only just; scarcely

bar'gain *n.* an understanding; a good price —*vi.* to negotiate

barge *n.* a boat carrying freight on inland waters —*vi.* to act clumsily

bar'i·tone' *n.* musical range between bass and tenor

bark *n.* the covering of a tree; sound made by a dog —*vt.* to make the sound of a dog

bark'keep *n.* one who operates a bar; a bartender

bark'er *n.* one whose patter is intended to attract patrons

barn *n.* a farm building

bar'na·cle *n.* a type of crustacean

barn'storm *vi.* to tour rural areas, as for politicking

ba·rom'e·ter *n.* an instrument that measures atmospheric pressure; anything that predicts change —**bar·o·met'ric** *adj.*

bar'on *n.* in British peerage, the rank above a baronet and below a viscount; one having great power

bar'on·age, bar'o·ny *n.* the sphere of influence, of a baron

ba·roque' *adj.* characteristic of the style of 16th and 17th century Europe; pertaining to that period —*n.* the baroque form; anything characteristic of the baroque style

bar'racks *pl. n.* buildings for housing soldiers, workers, etc.

bar·ra·cu'da a large, voracious fish found in tropical seas

bar·rage' *n.* heavy artillary fire; anything overwhelming

barred *adj.* blocked or decorated with bars; banned; not allowed

bar'rel *n.* a cylindrical storage container; any cylinder —**over a barrel** at the mercy of another

bar'ren *adj.* incapable of reproducing; unproductive;

desolate —**bar´ren•ly** *adv.*
bar´ren•ness *n.*

bar•rette´ (US) *n.* a small appliance for keeping hair in place

bar´ri•cade´ *n.* a barrier or blockade —*vt.* to create a barrier

bar´ri•er *n.* an obstruction

bar´ris•ter *n.* an attorney

bar•tend´er *n.* one who mixes and serves beverages at a tavern

bar´ter *n.* the exchange of goods or services —*vi., vt.* to trade

ba´sal *adj.* fundamental

ba•salt´ *n.* a dark volcanic rock

base *adj.* humble; cowardly; corrupt —*n.* a foundation; a starting place —*vt.* to form or place on a foundation; to establish a basis for

base´born *adj.* illegitimate; born of lower class parents; common

base´less *adj.* with no foundation; groundless; gratuitous

base´line *n.* a point of reference

base´ment *n.* a foundation or floor below the main floor of a building

bash *n.* a shattering blow —*vt.* to strike with a heavy blow

bash´ful *adj.* timid; shy —**bash•ful•ly** *adv.* —**bash´ful•ness** *n.*

ba´sic *adj.* fundamental; forming a basis —**ba´si•cal•ly** *adv.*

ba´sil *n.* an aromatic plant of the mint family or its leaves

ba•sil´i•ca *n.* an ancient Roman building; a church built after the Roman style

ba´sin *n.* a wide, shallow container; an area drained by a body of water

ba´sis *n.* a fundament principle; an essential quality or ingredient

bask *vi.* to relax in warmth; to revel in the glow of a pleasant situation

bas´ket *n.* a container made of woven material

bas-re•lief´ *n.* a sculpture of raised subjects from a flat background

bass[1] *adj.* of the lowest musical range —*n.* the lowest voice in music; an instrument in that range

bass[2] *n.* a food or game fish

bas´si•net´ *n.* a basket for a baby; a container for baby clothes, etc.

bas•soon´ *n.* a double-reed bass wind instrument —**bas•soon´ist** *n.*

bass´wood *n.* the linden tree; the wood of the linden tree

bas´tard *adj.* born out of wedlock; unusual or irregular; of inferior quality —*n.* an illegitimate child; a hybrid plant or animal; that, which deviates from the usual —**bas´tard•ize** *vt.* —**bas•tard•i•za´tion** *n.*

baste *vt.* to sew with loose stitches; to moisten food while cooking

bas´ti•on *n.* a strongly defended position

bat *n.* a cudgel; a stick for striking a ball; a nocturnal flying mammal —*vi.* to take a turn at bat —*vt.* to strike with a bat

batch *n.* a quantity processed at one time, a number of things

bath n. the act of cleansing; liquid for bathing; a room set aside for bathing; natural springs claimed to have healing power **—take a bath** suffer a financial loss

bathe vi. wash; take a bath; go into water; be covered with liquid—vt. to immerse in liquid; to wash; cover, as though with liquid: *bathed in moonlight*

bath′robe (US) n. a loose, casual garment, usually closed at the front with a belt

ba·tik′, bat·tik′ n. a process for dying fabric to obtain a complex, multicolored design; the fabric

ba·tiste′ n. a fine, sheer fabric

bat·on′ n. a short staff

bat·tal′ion n. a large group

bat′ten n. a narrow strip of wood; a strip used to stiffen a theater flat or hold a strip of lights **—**vt. to strengthen or secure with battens

bat′ter n. a′ mixture used to coat other food **—**vt. subject to blows; to damage by beating or use

bat′ter·y n. a number of things used together; the illegal touching of a person; a device for storing an electrical charge

bat′ting n. material for stuffing pillows, comforters, etc.

bat′ty adj. a little crazy; odd

bau′ble n. a worthless trinket

bawd n. the operator of a brothel

bawd′y adj. racy; indecent; vulgar **—bawd′i·ly** adv. **— bawd′i·ness** n.

bawl n. a loud outcry **—**vi. sob noisily; to bellow **—bawl out**

to berate

bay adj. reddish-brown **—**n. a reddish-brown horse; a wide inlet of the sea; a compartment for storage; the laurel which provides bay leaf for seasoning food; the cry of a dog in pursuit **—**vi. to cry out as a hound in pursuit **— at bay** cornered; held off

bay′ou n. a marshy inlet; a creek flowing through a delta

bay window a set of windows that project outside a building

ba·zaar′ n. a market or fair

beach n. a sandy shore; a place for sunbathing or swimming **—**vi., vt. to strand a boat

bea′con n. a warning signal

bead n. a small decorative ornament; a drop of liquid; the front sight of a rifle **—**vi. to gather in drops **—**vt. to decorate with beads **—draw a bead** take careful aim

beak n. a bird's bill

beak′er n. a container with a lip for pouring

beam n. a large section of wood or metal; part of a balance; a shaft of light **—**vi., vt. to shine, radiate

bean n. a leguminous plant, it's pod, or seeds; the head **—**vt. to hit on the head, as by something thrown

bear vi. to suffer a burden; to be productive; to have reference to **—**vt. to possess; to endure; to produce offspring; to assume a burden **—bear down** exert pressure **—bear in mind** remain conscious of **—bear out/bear witness** confirm or support

— **bear up** maintain strength or attitude —**bear′a•ble** *adj.*
— **bear′a•bly** *adv.*

bear *n.* a large animal with shaggy hair; an ill-tempered person; one who expects a decline in price

beard *n.* facial hair —*vt.* to defy boldly — **beard′ed** *adj.*

bear′ing *n.* manner; a machine part; a compass heading; relevance

bear′ish *adj.* rough; surly; inclined to sell in anticipation of a decline — **bear′ish•ly** *adv.*

beast *n.* an animal other than a human; animal qualities; one who is savage or brutal —**beast′li•ness** *n.* —**beast′ly** *adj.*

beat *adj.* exhausted — *n.* a blow; a repeated fluctuation; area covered by a policeman or watchman —*vt.* to strike repeatedly; to sound by striking; to shape by hammering; to mix by stirring; to best another —*vi.* to pulsate

be•a•tif′ic *adj.* making happy; showing pleasure —**be•a•tif′i•cal•ly** *adv.*

be•at′i•fi•ca′tion *n.* a condition of blessedness —**be•at′i•fy** *vt.*

be•at′i•tude′ *n.* perfect happiness

beau *n.* an escort; a sweetheart

beau•ti′cian *n.* one skilled in the arts of hairdressing, manicure, etc.

beau′ti•ful *adj.* pleasing to the senses

beau′ti•fy′ *vt.* to make beautiful —**beau′ti•fi•ca′tion** *n.*

beau′ty *n.* anything that by its quality pleases the senses —**beau′te•ous** *adj.*

beaux-arts′ *n.* fine arts

bea′ver *n.* a large aquatic rodent; a high hat made from beaver fur

be′bop *n.* improvisational jazz

be•calm′ *vt.* to induce tranquility; to cease moving

be•cause′ *conj.* for the reason that

beck′on *vi., vt.* to summon — *n.* a summoning gesture

be•cloud′ *vt.* to obscure

be•come′ *vi.* to come to be; to change into —*vt.* to suit

be•com′ing *adj.* attractive; suitable

bed *n.* a place where one sleeps; a base or foundation; a specially prepared area: *flower bed, road bed* —**marriage bed** lying together for the purpose of procreation

be•daz′zle *vt.* to blind; to impress

bed′ding *n.* linens for a bed; litter for an animal's bed; a foundation

be•deck′ *vt.* to adorn; to decorate

be•dev′il *vt.* to harass or torment; to bewitch —**be•dev′il•ment** *n.*

bed′lam *n.* great confusion

be•drag′gle *vi., vt.* to soil or soak

bed′rid•den *adj.* confined to bed

bed′rock *n.* solid rock be-neath the surface material

bed′room *n.* a room for sleeping

bedroom community a residential area for those who work elsewhere

bed′sore *n.* an ulcer on the body

bed′spread *n.* a bed covering

53

bed´stead *n.* the framework which supports springs, mattress, etc.

bed´time *n.* the time for going to bed

bee *n.* an insect that produces honey; a social gathering

bee´bread *n.* food for bees

beech *n.* a tree with smooth, ash-gray bark that produces an edible nut; the wood of the beech

beef *n.* an adult ox, cow, steer, etc. or its flesh; muscle; a complaint

beef´y *adj.* large or muscular —**beef´i•ness** *n.*

bee´hive *n.* a nesting place for a colony of honey bees; a busy place

bee´line *n.* the shortest distance —**make a beeline for** go directly and quickly

beer *n.* an alcoholic beverage fermented from malts and hops; a beverage made from roots

bees´wax *n.* a substance secreted by honey bees

beet *n.* a fleshy root vegetable

be•fall´ *vi.* to come about; to occur —*vt.* to happen to

be•fore´ *adj.* preceding in time or place —*conj.* sooner than; rather than —*prep.* ahead of; in front of; in advance of

be•foul´ *vt.* to contaminate or pollute

be•friend´ *vt.* to accept as a friend; to assist

be•fud´dle *vt.* to confuse

beg *vi., vt.* to ask for alms; to plead

beg´gar *n.* one who begs; one impoverished —*vt.* to seem inadequate: *beggar the question;* to impoverish

beg´gar•ly *adj.* like a beggar; poverty-stricken; squalid

be•gin´ *vi., vt.* start; come into being

be•gin´ner *n.* a novice; one starting

be•gin´ning *n.* onset; a starting time or place; the first part

be•grudge´ *vt.* to envy another; give reluctantly —**be•grudg´ing•ly** *adv.*

be•guile´ *vt.* to deceive; to defraud; to charm —**be•guil´ing•ly** *adv.*

be•have´ *vi., vt.* to conduct oneself well —**be•hav´ior** *(US),* **be•hav´iour** *(Brit.) n.* —**be•hav´ior•al, be•hav´iour•al** *adj.*

be•he´moth *n.* a huge beast

be•hest´ *n.* a decree; a command

be•hind´ *adv.* toward the rear; in the past; in arrears —*prep.* at the far side of; following; not revealed

be•hold´ *vt.* to view

beige *adj.* light brownish-gray —*n.* the color of natural wool; a fabric of undyed, unbleached wool

be´ing *n.* that exists; conscious existence; essential nature of a thing

be•la´bor *vt.* to denounce at length; to needlessly prolong an argument

be•lat´ed *adj.* past the proper time —**be•lat´ed•ly** *adv.*

belch *vi.* to expel gas through the mouth; to expel violently

be•lea´guer *vt.* to harrass or annoy; to besiege

bel´fry *n.* a bell tower

be•lie´ *vt.* misrepresent; prove false

belief´ *n.* faith; trust; an expectation

believe´ vi. to have trust —vt. to accept as true; to expect —**be•liev´a•ble** adj. —**be•liev´a•bly** adv.

be•lit´tle vt. to disparage

bell n. a metallic instrument, struck to emit a tone; anything bell-shaped; a flared end

bel´la•don´na n. deadly nightshade; a poisonous herb

bell´boy n. a hotel porter

belle n. a pretty female

bel´li•cose´ adj. hostile; aggressive —**bel´li•cose•ly** adv.

bel•lig´er•ent adj. warlike; at war —n. one engaged in war —**bel•lig´erence, bel•lig´er•en•cy** n.; **bel•lig´er•ent•ly** adv.

bel´low vi., vt. to cry out —n. a loud cry

bel´lows pl. n. a device for producing a stream of air

bel´ly n. the abdomen; the stomach; any similar protrusion

bel´ly•ache n. a pain in the stomach; vi. to complain

belly´but•ton n. the navel

belly dance a dance marked by gyrations of the hips and abdomen

bel´ly•ful n. all that the stomach can hold; all that one can endure

belly laugh boisterous laughter

be•long´ vi. to be part of

be•long´ings pl. n. all that one owns

be•lov´ed adj. cherished —n. one who is loved

be•low´ adv. in a lower place —prep. farther down; inferior

belt n. a band worn around the waist; a band connecting wheels in a machine; a moving line that transports from one place to another; a geographic zone; a blow —vt. to encircle or secure with a belt; to strike —**below the belt** unfair

belt´way (US) n. a roadway around a city

be•moan´ vi., vt. to express sorrow; mourn

be•muse´ vt. to absorb or preoccupy —**be•mus´ed•ly** adv.

bench n. a long hard seat; a work table; the office of a judge; judges collectively

bench mark, bench´mark n. a surveyor´s marker; a reference point

bend vi. to turn; to yield; bow —vt. to curve or incline; to subdue —n. a curved part— **bend´a•ble** adj.

be•neath´ adj., adv. below; in a lower position —prep. below or under; subordinate; unbefitting: it is beneath her dignity

ben´e•dic´tion n. an invocation of blessing —**ben•e•dic´-to•ry** adj.

ben´e•fac´tion n. the act of helping; the help given — **ben•e•fac´tor** n.

be•nef´i•cence n. active goodness; a charitable act —**be•nef´i•cent** adj. —**be•nef´i•cent•ly** adv.

ben´e•fi´cial adj. advantageous; profitable —**ben•efi•cial•ly** adv.

ben´e•fi´ci•ar•y n. ont who holds or receives a benefit or inheritance

ben´e•fit n. a thing that helps; an activity to aid a cause; payments received for retirement, illness, etc. —vt. to help —vt. to aid

be•nev′o•lence n. a bent to do good; a charitable act —**be•ne′vo•lent** adj. —**be•nev′o•lent•ly** adv.

be•nign′ adj. kindly; medically harmless —**be•nign′ly** adv.

bent adj. curved or warped; deformed; resolved —n. a tendency; an inclination; an innate talent

be•numb′ vt. to daze or stun; to deaden or paralyze

bequeath′ vt. to pass on, especially after death —**be•queath′al** n.

be•quest′ n. a thing passed on

be•rate′ vt. to reprimand or scold

be•reave′ vt. to deprive of by death —**be•reave′ment** n.

be•ret′ n. a flat soft cap

ber′ry n. a small juicy fruit

ber•serk′ adj., adv. violent, rampaging; out of control

ber•serk′er n. an early Norse warrior notable for savagery in battle

berth n. a sleeping place; a position in a ship's crew; room for ships to clear at sea; space to anchor

be•seech′ vt. to implore; to beg —**be•seech′ing•ly** adv.

be•set′ adj. troubled; beleaguered —vt. to torment; to decorate

be•side′ prep. adjacent to; alongside

be•sides′ adv. furthermore; else; in addition —prep.

be•siege′ vt. to lay siege to; to overwhelm, as with information

be•smirch′ vt. to defame; bring dishonor upon

best adj. finest —adv. to the highest degree —vt. to defeat

bes′tial adj. of a beast; savage; brutal —**bes•ti•al′i•ty** n.

be•stir′ vt. to stir to action

be•stow′ vt. togive—**be•stow′al** n.

best′sell′er n. that which outsells all others; that selling extremely well —**best′-sell′ing** adj.

bet vi., vt. to wager —n. the stake in a wager —**bet′tor, bet′ter** n.

be•ta•tron′ n. an electron accelerator

be•tray′ vt. to be disloyal; to lead astray —**be•tray′al** n.

be•troth′ vt. to commit to marry —**be•troth′al** n.

be•throthed′ adj. engaged to be married —n. the person to whom one is engaged

bet′ter adj. more suitable; improved; recovering —adv. in a more suitable fashion —n. one in a superior position —vt. to improve; to outdo —**bet′ter•ment** n.

be•tween′ adv. in an intermediate position —prep. of that which separates or connects

bev′el adj. biased; sloping —n. a sloping surface; an angle; a tool for measuring angles —vi. to slant —vt. to cut at an angle

bev′er•age n. a liquid for drinking

bev′y n. a group

be•wail′ vt. to lament

be•ware′ vi., vt. to be on one's guard

be•wil′der vt. to confound; to astonish —**be•wil′der•ing•ly** adv. —**be•wil′der•ment** n.

be•witch′ vt. to enchant or charm; to captivate —**be•witch′ing** adj. —**be•witch′ing•ly** adv.

be·yond' *adv.* farther away — *prep.* surpassing

bi·an'nu·al *adj.* twice each year

bi'as *n.* prejudice; partiality — *vt.* to influence

bible *n.* a writing sanctioned or approved —**bib'li·cal** *adj.*

bib·li·og'ra·phy *n.* a list of information sources —**bib·li·og'ra·pher** *n.*

bib'li·o·phile *n.* a collector of books

bi·cam'er·al *adj.* having two legislative bodies

bicarbonate of soda (*Brit.*) sodium bicarbonate; a compound used in cooking, cleaning, etc.

bi·cen·ten'ni·al *adj.* occurring once in two hundred years —*n.* a two hundred year anniversary —**bi·cen·ten'a·ry** *adj., n.*

bi'ceps *n.* a muscle having two points of connection

bick'er *n.* a petty quarrel —*vi.* to quarrel

bi·cus'pid *n.* a tooth with a two-pointed crown

bi'cy·cle *n.* a two-wheeled vehicle propelled by the rider —*vi., vt.* to ride a bicycle —**bi'cy·clist** *n.*

bid *n.* an amount offered; an attempt —*vt.* to request; make an offer; to declare openly —**bid'der** *n.*

bid'dy *n.* a hen; a gossip

bi·en'ni·al *adj.* lasting two years; every two years —*n.* a plant that lives two years

bi'fo·cals *pl. n.* corrective lenses for both near and distant vision

bi'fur·cate *vi., vt.* to split in two —**bi'fur·cate, bi'fur·cat·ed** *adj.* forked; having

two branches —**bi·fur·ca'tion** *n.*

big *adj.* large; important; massive; substantial; generous

big'a·mist *n.* one having two or more spouses —**big'a·mous** *adj.*—**big'a·my** *n.*

big'heart·ed *adj.* generous —**big'heart·ed·ly** *adv.*

big'ot *n.* intolerant person —**big'ot·ed** *adj.*—**big'ot·ry** *n.*

bi'jou *n.* an ornament or bauble; a piece of jewelry; a trinket

bike *n.* a bicycle; a motorcycle

bi·ki'ni *n.* a brief bathing suit

bi·lat'er·al *adj.* reciprocal; involving two parties —**bi·lat'er·al·ly** *adv.*

bile *n.* a digestive fluid secreted in the liver; bitterness or hostility

bi·lin'gual *adj.* able to converse in two languages

bil'ious *adj.* of bile or ailments of the liver; ill-tempered —**bil'ious·ly** *adv.* —**bil'ious·ness** *n.*

bilk *vt.* to cheat or swindle; to defraud —**bilk'er** *n.*

bill *n.* an invoice; (*US*) paper money; a draft *of* a law; a bird's jaw; a beak —*vt.* to tender an invoice

bill'board *n.* a large outdoor sign

bil'lion (*US*) *n.* one thousand million

bil of fare a restaurant menu

bill of lading a shipping document

bill of sale a document attesting to the transfer of property

bil'low *n.* a large wave; a surging mass —*vi., vt.* to surge —**bil'low·y** *adj.*

bi•month•ly adj., adv. every two months

bin n. a receptacle for storage

bi•na•ry adj. comprised of two parts; of a numbering system in base two

binary star a double star

bind —vt. to make fast; to fasten together; to obligate —vi. to tie; to be obligatory —n. a difficult situation

bind´er n. one who binds books; something that joins; a temporary agreement

bind´ing adj obligatory, re quired —n. something used to join

bi•no´mi•al adj. of a two part equation —n. a mathematical equation

bi´o•as•tro•nau´tics n. the study of life in a weightless environment

bi´o•chem´is•try n. biological or physiological chemistry

bi•o•de•grad´a•ble adj. readily decomposed through bacterial action

bi•o•e•col´o•gy n. the study of the interrelationship of animals and plants to their environment

bi•og´ra•phy n. the story of a person's life —**bi•og´ra•pher** n. —**bi•o•graph´ic, bi•o•graph´i•cal** adj.

biological clock the natural cycles in the life of an organism

biological warfare the use of microorganisms as a weapon of war

bi•ol´o•gy n. the science that deals with life forms —**bi•ol´o•gist** n. —**bi•o•log´i•cal** adj. —**bi•o•log´i•cal•ly** ad u.

bi•op•sy n. the removal of tissue for laboratory analysis

bi´o•sphere n. all life on earth; the earth area which supports life

bi´o•tin n. a B vitamin

bi•par´ti•san adj. consisting of two parties —**bi•par´ti•san•ship** n.

bi•par´tite adj. having two parts

bi´ped´ n. any creature with two feet

bi•po´lar adj. having two poles; of opposing doctrines, natures, etc.

birch´bark n. the bark of the birch tree; a canoe made from the bark —adj. resembling the birch

birch beer a beverage flavored with oil of birch

bird n. a feathered animal

bird of prey a bird that hunts

birth n. the act of coming into life; background or lineage

birth´mark n. an impression on the skin evident at birth; a blemish

birth´right n. rights by virtue of being born into a family or country

birth´stone n. a gem associated with a particular birth month

bi•sect vt divide into two parts —**bi•sec´tion** n.

bi•sex´u•al adj. of both sexes

bish´op n. a ranking member of the clergy; a chess piece

bish´op•ric n. the office of a bishop

bisque n. a thick, creamed soup

bit n. a small scrap; a boring tool; a minor part; a mouthpiece

bitch n. a female dog —vi. complain

bite n. taking by the teeth; the

amount taken; damage made by teeth; a stinging — vi. to grip; to hurt; have a sharp taste; to take bait — vt. seize with the teeth; sting

bit´ter adj. acrid tasting; cruel or harsh; resentful — **bit´ter•ly** adv. —**bit´ter•ness** n.

bit´ters n. a flavoring or tonic made from bitter herbs

bit´ter•sweet adj. a flavor both bitter and sweet; pleasure accompanied by pain or sadness

bi•week´ly adj., adv. occurring once every two weeks

bi•year´ly adj., adv. occurring once every two years

bi•zarre´ adj. extremely unusual

blab vi., vt. to chatter; to reveal —**blab´ber** n., vi.

black n. the absence of color; the opposite of white — **black´en** vi., vt.

black-and-blue adj. bruised

black and white written; not in full color; clearly expressed

black art sorcery; witchcraft

black´ball´ vt. to ostracize

black´board´ n. a surface for drawing or writing with chalk

black eye discoloration around the eye; a blemish to one's reputation

black´guard n. a villain, scoundrel

black´-heart´ed adj. wicked, sinister

black hole a collapsed star

black light ultraviolet light

black´list n. those exclude —vt. to deliberately exclude

black magic sorcery, witchcraft

black´mail´ n. extortion —vt. to extort payment by threat

black market illegal trade

black´-mar´ket vt. to trade on the black market —adj.

black´out´ n. a loss of power; a temporary loss of consciousness

black sheep one who is different; an outcast

black´smith n. a worker in iron

black tie formal; a formal affair

black´top (US) n. a road surface —vt. to surface with asphalt

bladder n. an internal body pouch; anything resembling such a pouch

blade n. a plant leaf; a broad, flat surface; a cutting part

blame n. condemnation; accountability —vt. charge with responsibility; condemn or rebuke —**blam´a•ble** adj. —**blame´ful** adj.

blame´less adj. innocent; irreproachable —**blameless•ly** adv. —**blame´less•ness** n.

blanch vi. to whiten —vt. make white; bleach; immerse food briefly in boiling water

bland adj. soothing, mild; insipid

blan´dish vt. persuade by flattery

blank adj. empty, vacant —n. a void; emptiness; a form — **draw a blank** unable to remember or accomplish

blan´ket adj. encompassing —n. a bed covering; a thing that covers —vt. to cover; to canvass

blank verse unrhymed poetry

blare n. a harsh noise —vi., vt.

to sound loudly

blar´ney n. flattering speech

bla•se´ adj. indifferent, unconcerned

blas´pheme´ vt. to speak or act irreverently —vi. to utter blasphemy

blas´phe•my n. profane or irreverent expression —**blas´phe•mous** adj.

blast n. sudden rush; a harsh sound; an explosion —vi. make a harsh sound; to set off an explosive —vt. to explode; to denounce

blast furnace a furnace for separating impurities from metallic ore

blas´tant adj. offensively noisy; obvious —**bla´tant•ly** adv.

blaze n. a burst of light —vi. to burn

bla´zer n. a sports jacket

bleach n. a cleaner —vi. to grow white —vt. to remove color; to make white

bleach´ers pl. n. bench seating

bleak adj. desolate; dreary; gloomy

blear´y adj. blurred or indistinct —**blear´i•ly** adv. —**blear´i•ness** n.

bleat n. the cry of an animal —vi. vt.

bleed vi. to lose vital fluid; to run together, as dye —vt. to draw fluid or gas; print off a page; to impoverish

blem´ish n. a defect —vt. to deface

blend n. a mixture —vi. vt. to mix; make a gradual transition

bless vt. to consecrate; to favor —**bless´ed•ness** n.

bless´ed adj. consecrated; blissful; rewarded

bless´ing n. an invocation, grace; divine sanction; good fortune

blight n. a plant disease; anything that damages —vt. to destroy

blimp n. an airship

blind adj. sightless; unseen — n. that obscures or conceals —vt. to deprive of sight; to dazzle

blind´fold n. that restricting sight —vt. to cover the eyes of; to mislead

blinding adj. swift; faster than the eye —**blind´ing•ly** adv.

blind spot an area of restricted vision; a prejudice

blink vi., vt. to flicker the eyelids; flash on and off, as a light

biink´er n. a flashing light; (US) an automobile turn signal

blintz, blintze n. a filled pancake

bliss, n. happiness; ecstasy, rapture —**bliss´ful** adj. —**bliss´ful•ly** adv.

blis´ter n. a bulging sac; a transparent covering for merchandise —vi., vt. to form a blister

blithe adj. gay; lighthearted; vivacious —**blithe´ly** adv.

bliz´zard n. a violent snowstorm

bloat vi., vt. to swell

blob n. a clump of indefinite shape

bloc n. a political alliance

block n. a large chunk; a system of pulleys; a related group; a barrier —vt. to hinder or restrict; form a rough plan —**block´age** n.

block´ade´ n. a barrier —vt. to

60

set up a barrier

block´bust•er adj. extravagant —n. an extravagant work; an investor who uses deception to buy property at reduced prices

block´head n. a stupid person —**block´head•ed•ness** n.

block letter a plain character, without serifs or embellishment

blond adj. of fair skin; a light finish

blonde n. a blond female

blood n. a vital body fluid; heritage; kinship —**new blood** a new member or members

blood bank a reserve of blood

blood bath a massacre; wholesale replacement of executives

blood brother a male sibling; one bound by an oath or ceremony

blood count analysis of blood

blood´curd•ling adj. frightening; ghastly

blood´ed adj. pedigreed; of known stock

blood´hound n. a dog used to track; one relentless in pursuit

blood´less adj. lacking blood; without bloodshed, peaceful; indifferent

blood´let•ting n. bloodshed; a replacement of many employees

blood money payment for an illegal deed; gain from suffering

blood pressure a measure of the force of blood in the arteries

blood relation, blood relative one related by birth

bloodshed n. carnage;

slaughter

blood´stained adj. soiled by blood; guilty of shedding blood

blood´suck•er n. a parasite; one who takes —**blood´suck•ing** adj.

blood´thirst•y adj. barbarous; inclined to murder; ruthless —**blood´thirst•i•ly** adv.

blood vessel any of the arteries, veins, or capillaries

blood´y adj. bleeding or containing blood; bloodstained; murderous —**blood´i•ly** adv. —**blood´i•ness** n.

bloom n. a flower; a healthy glow —vi. to flower; to glow

bloope´r n. a mistake; a silly blunder

blos´som n. a flower —vi. to develop

blot n. a flaw; dishonor; a spot —vt. to stain; to dishonor; to get rid of

blotch n. a stain —vt. to blemish

blotch´y adj. discolored; blemished

blouse n. a loose shirt

blow n. a sharp rap; a setback; a blast of air; a windstorm —vi. to move air; to be carried on air; to be stormy —vt. to expel air; to propel by air; to waste; to fail; to leave —**blow up** to explode; to form by blowing; enlarge a photograph

blow´out n. the bursting of a tire; a large party or celebration

blow´torch n. a tool that produces an intense flame

blow•up n. an explosion; an enlarged photograph

blub´ber n. whale fat; excess fat —vi. to weep

bludg´eon n. a heavy club — vt. to strike with a club; to bully

blue adj. blu in color; despondent —n. the color of a clear sky —vt. to make blue in color

blue baby a child born with a heart or respiratory defect

blue´bell n. any of a variety of plants with blue bell-shaped flowers

blue blood, blue´blood n. an aristocrat; high society — **blue´-blood•ed** adj.

blue chip, blue´chip adj. of a stable company; of anything preceived as stable —**blue´-chip** adj.

blue collar an industrial worker

blue´grass adj. of a type of mountain music —n.

blue jeans, blue•jeans n. a type of trouser made from blue denim

blue laws laws prohibiting transaction of business on Sunday

blue´nose n. one who imposes a moral code on others

blue-pen´cil vt. to edit or correct

blue´print n. an engineer's drawing; any detailed plan of action

blue ribbon first prize

blue-sky´ adj. of no intrinsic value; a wish or dream

blue streak fast, lively or animated

bluff adj. abrupt in manner — n. a steep bank; a deception —vt. to mislead by feigning; to deceive

blun´der n. a mistake —vi. make a foolish error; move clumsily

blunt adj. not sharp; plainspoken; slow-witted —vt. to dull; reduce effectiveness — **blunt´ness** n.

blur n. anything hazy —vt., vi. make or become indistinct —**blur´ry** adj.

blurb n. a brief announcement; a comment on a book cover or jacket

blurt vt. say without thinking

blush n. a sudden reddening; a reddish color —vi., vt. to become red —**blush´er** n. — **blush´ing•ly** adv.

blus´ter n. arrogant speech — vi. to blow in gusts; to act arrogant or bullying —**blus´ter•ing•ly** adv. —**blus´ter•ous, blus´ter•y** adj.

bo´a n. a large snake; a long scarf

boar n. a mature male pig

board n. a plank; a panel; meals provided; a group that regulates —vt. supply with meals; to get on

board´er n. a lodger; a paying guest

board foot a measure of lumber

boarding house an establishment that provides rooms and meals

boarding school a school that provides a residence and meals

board´walk n. a wooden walkway

boast vi., vt. to brag — **boast´ful** adj. —**boast´ful•ly** adv.

boat n. a vessel of inland seas —**boat´ing** adj., n.

bob´bin n. a spool for thread or yarn

bobby pin (US) a metal hair pin

bob´sled n. a long sled

bock　beer a dark German beer

bod´ice n. the upper part of a dress

bod´i•ly adj. physical; of the body —adv. totally, entirely

bod´y n. physical structure; a main part; a person; a group; density

body politic society; those united

bog n. a small swamp or marsh

bo´gus adj. of doubtful authenticity

bo•he´mi•an n. one who is unconventional, as an artist or writer

boil vi. to bubble; to cook in boiling liquid; to churn; seethe with rage —vt. heat to boiling; to process in boiling liquid

boil´er n. a tank producing steam; a tank for heating and storing water

boiling point the temperature at which a liquid boils; conditions which cause one to lose control

bois´ter•ous adj. noisy; rowdy —bois´ter•ous•ly adv.

bold adj. daring; forceful; impudent —**bold´ly** adv. — **bold´ness** n.

bold´-faced, bold´faced adj. impudent; brazen

bo•le´ro n. a Spanish dance; a short jacket

bol´lix vt. to bungle; to mismanage

bol´ster n. a long pillow —v. to prop up; to reinforce

bolt n. a bar for securing; a threaded fastener; a roll of cloth; a sudden start –vi. to spring; to break away—vt.

to secure with a bar; to eat hurriedly; to break away

bomb n. a casing filled with explosives; a failure —vi. to fail utterly —vt. to attack with bombs

bom•bas´tic adj. high-sounding but meaningless — **bom•bas´t** n. —**bom•bas´ti•cal•ly** adv.

bomb´shell n. a bomb; a sudden shock; a rude awakening

bo´na fide adj. genuine; sincere; in good faith

bo•nan´za n. a rich source; a profitable venture

bon´bon n. a small candy

bond n. a formal obligation; that which binds —vt. protect by bond; place in bonded storage; tie or join

bond´age n. servitude, enslavement

bond´ed adj. secured by a bond; in bonded storage; bound by fetters

bonds´man n. one who furnishes a bond for a fee

bone n. hard tissue forming the skeleton—vt. to remove bones

bon´er n. a silly mistake; a blooper

bon´fire n. a large outdoor fire

bon´net n. a females hat

bo´nus n. an extra payment; any extra benefit

bon´y adj. of bones; skinny; emaciated; with many bones, as a fish —**bon´i•ness** n.

boob n. one who is foolish; an oaf

booby trap a device designed to be set off by an unsuspecting victim

book *n.* pages bound together with a cover; part of a lengthly work; a body of information

book´case *n.* a freestanding set of shelves for books, artifacts, etc.

book´end *n.* a device to keep a row of books in place

book´ie *n.* a bookmaker

book´ish *adj.* scholarly; given to studying —**book´ish•ly** *adv.*—**book´ish•ness** *n.*

book´keep•ing *n.* recording of financial dealings —**book´keeper** *n.*

book´let *n.* a small book

book´mak•er *n.* one who accepts wagers —**book´mak•ing** *n.*

book´mark *n.* a device to keep the reader's place in a book

book´mo•bile´ *n.* a mobile library

book´plate *n.* a label in or on a book

book review a verbal or written commentary about a book

book´worm *n.* one who spends considerable time reading or studying

boom *n.* a deep sound; an upturn —*vi.* to make a deep sound

boo´me•rang *n.* a bent stick that returns when thrown; a thing that acts differently than planned

boon *n.* good fortune

boon´dog•gle *n.* a pointless project; a no-win situation

boor *n.* one who is vulgar or unrefined —**boor´ish** *adj.* —**boor´ish•ly** *adv.*—**book´ish•ness** *n.*

boost *n.* assistance; an increase —*vt.* push upward; to increase; promote

boot *n.* a covering for the foot —*vt.* to kick; to dismiss from a job

booth *n.* a stall for displaying goods; partially isolated seating

boot´leg´ *adj.* illegal —*vi.*, *vt.* to sell illegally **boot´leg•ger** *n.*

boo´ty *n.* loot; spoils of war

booze *n.* an alcholic beverage —**booz´er** *n.*—**booz´y** *adj.*

bor´der *n.* a boundary; margin —*vt.* to extend along the boundary

bor´der•line *adj.* marginal; of questionable value —*n.* an edge or line

bore *n.* a round hole; a dull person —*vt.* make a hole; to make weary

bore´dom *n.* lack of interest; listlessness

bor´ing *adj.* uninteresting, tiresome —**bor´ing•ly** *adv.*

bor´ough *n.* in Britain and some US states, an incorporated town

bor´row *vi.*, *vt.* to take with agreement to return; to adopt, as an idea

bos´om *n.* the breast; closeness

boss *n.* supervisor; one in charge —*vi.*, *vt.* to supervise

boss´y *adj.* like a boss; domineering —**boss´i•ness** *n.*

boss´ism *n.* control of a political district by an autocratic leader

bot´a•ny *n.* the study of plants —**bo•tan´i•cal** *adj.*— **bot´a•nist** *n.*

botch *n.* shoddy work —*vt.* bungle; do a shoddy job — **botched** *adj.*—**botch´y** *adj.*

both´er *n.* a cause of

irritation; vexation —*vi.* be concerned with; fuss over — *vt.* to trouble; inconvenience —**both´er•some** *adj.*

bot´tle *n.* a glass container; the amount a bottle holds — *vt.* to put into bottles — **bot´tler** *n.*

bot´tle•neck´ *n.* an obstruction

bot´tom *adj.* of the lowest point —*n.* the lowest part; seat of a chair

bouf•fant´ *adj.* puffed out

bough *n.* the branch of a tree

boul´der *n.* a large rock or stone

bou´le•vard´ *n.* a broad paved street

bounce *n.* a rebound; capacity to rebound; zest, spirit —*vi.* to rebound; to spring; to return a check for lack of funds —*vt.* to throw and cause to rebound; to eject an undesirable; to dismiss —**bounc´er** *n.*

bound *adj.* obligated; determined; tied or restricted —*n.* a leap —*vi.* to leap; to border on —*vt.* to cause a leap or bounce; to mark a border

bound´a•ry *n.* a border or limit

bound´less *adj.* without end; unlimited —**bound´less•ly** *adv.*—**bound´less•ness** *n.*

boun´te•ous *adj.* plentiful — **boun´ti•ful** *adj.* —**boun´ti•ful•ly** *adv.*

boun´ty *n.* a profusion; a reward

bou•quet´ *n.* cut flowers; fragrance

bour´bon *n.* a whiskey —*adj.* made from or with bourbon

bour•geois *adj.* of the middle class; conventional —*n.*

bour•geol•sie´ *n.* the middle class

bout *n.* a struggle; an occurrence

bou•tique´ *n.* a small specialty shop

bou•ton•niere´ *n.* a lapel flower

bo´vine *adj.* of oxen or cows

bow *n.* a bending; the front of a ship; a curve; a device for shooting arrows; a decorative knot —*vi., vt.* to bend the body in greeting; to yield

bow´el *n.* an intestine —*pl.* **bow´els** the intestines; the inside of anything perceived as deep and dark

bowl *n.* a deep dish for food; anything similar —*vt.* play at bowling

bowl´er *n.* one who bowls; a derby

bowl´ing *n.* a game of tenpins

box *n.* a squarish container

box´car (*US*) *n.* a rail freight car

box´er *n.* a prizefighter

box office location where tickets are sold, as for a sporting event

box score detailed statistics

box seat premium seats

boy *n.* a male youth —**boy´hood** *n.* —**boy´ish** *adj.* — **boy´ish•ly** *adv.*

boy´cott´ *n.* a refusal to deal with —*vt.* to avoid dealings with

bra *n.* a brassiere; top of a swimsuit

brace *n.* a support or fastener; a pair of marks { } to connect elements; a pair —*vt.* to support; to fit with braces; to steady oneself

brace´let *n.* jewelry for the wrist

brack´et n. an angled support; a pair of marks [ ] to enclose words; a group of associated elements —vt. to support or enclose; to group associated elements

brack´ish adj. slightly salty; disagreeable in taste

brad n. a small finishing nail

brag vi., of to boast —n. a boast; a thing boasted about; a boaster

brag·ga·do´ci·o n. bravado; a swaggering manner

brag´gart, brag´ger n. one who boasts; a blowhard

braid (US) n. interwoven hair; a band of woven material —vt. to interweave; to trim with braid

braille n. writing for the blind

brain n. the center of thought; mental ability; a bright person

brain´child n. that produced by one's own creative powers

brain´less adj. lacking common sense; mindless

brain´pow•er n. the ability to think; intellect

brain´storm n. inspiration —vi. take part in a session designed to generate ideas — **brain´storm•er** n.

brain´wash vt. to indoctrinate

brain´y adj. extremely intelligent; quick-witted —**brain´i•ness** n.

braise vt. to simmer in liquid

brake n. a device for slowing or stopping —vi., vt. to slow or stop

bran n. the outer husk of grain

branch n. an extension —vi. to extend from the main part

brand n. a burning stick; a

mark of ownership, stigma, etc.; a trademark —vt. to mark with a brand

bran´dish vt. to wave menacingly

brand´-new adj. recently introduced or acquired; not used

bran´dy n. an alcoholic beverage

brash adj. impetuous; insolent —brashly adv. — **brash´ness** n.

brass n. an alloy of copper; things made from the alloy; boldness, impudence; high-ranking persons —adj. of or made from brass

brass´y adj. brazen; impudent —brass´i•ly adv. —brass´i•ness n.

brat n. a badly behaved child —brat´ty adj.

bra•va´do n. false courage; bluster

brave adj. courageous; bold —vt. to face courageously — **brave´ly** adv.

brav´er•y n. courage

bra•vu´ra n. a showy display; ostentation

brawl n. a noisy quarrel to quarrel noisily

brawn n. muscle; muscular strength —brawn´i•ness n. —brawn´y adj.

bray n. the harsh cry of a donkey; any similar noise

bra´zen adj. like brass; bold, impudent —bra´ zen•ly adv. —bra´zen•ness n.

bra´zier n. a coal heater or cooker; a worker in brass

breach n. a break; violation of a contract; a disagreement —vt. to break through; violate agreement

bread n. a baked or fried food

made from grain; food in general; money

bread and butter essentials; primary, as a product line

bread line a distribution of free food; those waiting for free food

breadth n. width

bread´win•ner n. the one who works to support others

break n. a breach; an interval of rest; luck or opportunity; a sudden move —vi. to come apart; become inoperable; sever; to happen suddenly; run away —vt. part by force; to ruin; cause to fail; to violate a contract —**break´a•ble** adj.

break´age n. things broken; an allowance for things broken

break´down n. failure to work; a separation into parts for analysis

break´er n. a wave that strikes shore

breakfast n. the first meal of the day to eat breakfast

break´-in adj. of a period of trial —n. unauthorized entry, as to rob

breaking point maximum stress that can be tolerated

break´neck adj. of travel at high speed; dangerous

break´through´ n. a notable finding

break´up n. a tearing down or disintegration; a separation

break´wa•ter n. a harbor barrier to shield against the impact of waves

breast n. the front of the chest

breast´plate n. a piece of armor to protect the chest

breath n. air taken into the lungs; the act of breathing; a

light breeze; a whisper

breathe vi., vt. to take air into the lungs; to whisper —**not breathe a word** promise to keep a secret

breath´er n. a break; a brief rest

breath´tak•ing adj. exciting; awe-inspiring

breeches pl. n. tapered trousers ending just below the knee

breed n. a group of common ancestry; a particular type —vi. to originate; to reproduce —vt. to bring forth young; to rear —**breed´er** n.

breed´ing n. the production of offspring; good manners, courtesy

breeze n. a gentle wind; easily done —vi. move quickly — **breez´i•ly** adv. —**breez´y** adj.

breeze´way n. an enclosed passageway between buildings

breth´ren pl. n. brothers

brev´i•ty n. the quality of being brief

brew vt. make beer, coffee, etc; formulate a plan

bribe n. payment to influence —vi. to pay illegally —**brib´er•y** n.

brick n. a building block; a reliable person —vt. to build with brick —**hit the bricks** go on strike

brick´bat n. a harsh comment; an aspersion

brid´al adj. of a bride or wedding

bride n. a married woman

bride´groom n. a married man

brides´maid n. a bride's attendant

bridge *n.* a span over an obstacle; any similar structure or link

bridge´work *n.* dentures

bri´dle *n.* a harness; any restraint —*vi.* take offense —*vt.* control

brief *adj.* momentary; concise —*n.* a summary —**brief´ly** *adv.*

brief´case *n.* hand luggage

brief´ing *n.* a short summary of a situation; a set of instructions

brig *n.* a brigantine; a ship's jail

bri•gade´ *n.* an organized group

brig´an•tine *n.* a two-masted ship

bright *adj.* full of color; quick-witted; lively; auspicious; encouraging —**bright´ly** *adv.* —**bright´ness** *n.*

bright´en *vi.*, *vt.* to make bright, as by polishing

bril´liant *adj.* full of light; dazzling; ingenious; talented —*n.* a fine gem —**bril´liance** *n.* —**bril´liant•ly** *adv.*

brim *n.* the lip of a container; a projection, as on a hat —*vt.*, *vi.* to fill or be full —**brim´ful** *adj.*

brim´stone *n.* sulphur

brine *n.* a salt solution; the sea —**bri´i•ness** *n.* —**brin´y** *adj.*

bring *vt.* to convey; to influence —**bring about** cause to happen

brink *n.* an edge or limit

bri´oche *n.* a light, rich bread

brisk *adj.* quick; active; stimulating —**brisk´ly** *adv.* —**brisk´ness** *n.*

bris´tle *n.* short, stiff hair —*vi.* become tense; take

offense —**bris´tly** *adj.* —**bris´tli•ness** *n.*

brittle *adj.* easily broken; fragile; unbending —**brit´-tle•ness** *n.*

broach *vt.* to bring up for discussion

broad *adj.* wide in scope; open, obvious; general — **broad´en** *vi.*, *vt.* —**broad´ly** *adv.* —**broad´ness** *n.*

broad´cast´ *adj.* of radio or television —*vi.*, *vt.* to make widely known

broad´cloth´ *n.* a fine, smooth cloth

broad´-mind´ed *adj.* open to the unconventional — **broad´-mind•ed•ly** *adv.* —**broad´-mind• ed•ness** *n.*

bro•cade´ *n.* a heavy fabric covered with a´raised design

bro•chure´ *n.* a booklet or folder

brogue *n.* a type of accent

broil *vt.* to cook by direct exposure to intense heat — **broil´er** *n.*

bro´ken *adj.* in pieces; out of order; imperfect; ill or dispirited

bro´ker *n.* one who trades for others

bro´ker•age *n.* the office of a broker; fees charged by a broker

bron´co *n.* a horse of the west

bronze *n.* an alloy of copper and tin

brooch *n.* a large decorative pin

brood *adj.* of a breeding animal —*n.* offspring hatched at one time; all the children in a family —*vi.*, *vt.* to sit eggs; to meditate morbidly; to pine or grieve

brook *n.* a small stream

broom *n.* a bundle of stiff fibers

broth *n.* a clear, thin soup

broth´el *n.* a place of prostitution

broth´er *n.* a male sibling; a close friend; a fellow member —**broth´er•hood** *n.*

brot´her-in-law *n.* brother by marriage

brow *n.* the forehead; the projecting top of a steep bank

brow´beat *vt.* to intimidate; to harangue —**brow´beat•er** *n.*

brown´-bag *(US) vi., vt.* to carry lunch; to bring liquor to a restaurant —**brown-bag´ger** *n.*

brown´out *n.* a dimming of lights

brown´stone *n.* a row house fronted with brown stone

browse *vi., vt.* to feed on shoots or leaves; to examine casually

bruise *n.* a slight injury —*vt.* to wound without breaking the skin; to damage one's ego, etc.

bruis´er *n.* a large, strong man

brunch *n.* an elaborate late breakfast

brunet, bru•nette´ *adj.* having dark hair or eyes —*n.*

brunt *n.* the main shock or impact

brush *n.* bristles attached to a handle; a dense growth; a light touch; a brief encounter —*vi., vt.* to use a brush; to touch lightly

brusque *adj.* abrupt; discourteous; curt — **brusque´ly** *adv.*

brutal *adj.* extremely cruel — **bru•tal´i•ty** *n.*

bru´tal•ise *(Brit.),* **bru´tal•ize** *(US) vt.* degrade or demean —**bru•tal•i•sa´tion, bru´tal•i•za´tion** *n.*

brute *adj.* unreasoning; savage —*n.* a beast; a barbarian; a monster

brut´ish *adj.* bestial; savage —**brut´ish•ly** *adv.* —**brut´ish•ness** *n.*

bub´ble *n.* a tiny ball of trapped gas —*vi., vt.* to make or form bubbles — **bub´bly** *adj.*

buc•ca•neer´ *n.* a pirate

buck *n.* a male animal —*vi., vt.* to move in an effort to throw a rider

buck´et *n.* a container for carrying water, coal, etc.

buck´le *n.* a device for joining ends of a strap; a decoration similar to a buckle —*vi., vt.* join with a buckle; to bend under heat or pressure

buck´ram *n.* a coarse cloth

buck´shot *n.* heavy shot

buck up encourage or cheer

bu•col´ic *adj.* of a country or farm setting —**bu•col´i•cal•ly** *adv.*

bud *n.* a small growth preceding a leaf or flower —**nip in the bud** end in the early stages —**bud´like** *adj.*

bud´dy *n.* a close friend; a comrade

buddy system pairing for protection

budge *vi.* to move a little

budg´et *n.* a projection of need —*vi., vt.* to plan for future needs —**bud´get•ar•y** *adj.* —**bud´get•er** *n.*

buff *vt.* to shine, polish; to burnish —**in the buff** naked

buf´fet *n.* a blow —*vt.* to strike

buf•fet′ a sideboard for storage and serving food; an informal meal

buff′er n. something that polishes; padding to protect against contact

buf•foon′ n. a clown or jester; a fool —**buf•foon′ish** adj.

bug n. an insect; a disease-causing microorganism; an annoying defect; a device for eavesdropping　—vt. to eavesdrop; to annoy

bug′a•boo n. a gremlin; something causing difficulty, fear, or anxiety

bug′-eyed adj. amazed; astonished

bug′gy adj. infested with bugs; eccentric, crazy —n. a light carnage

bu′gle n. a hunting or military horn —vi., vt. to signal with a bugle

build n. one's physical form —vi. to put up a building; to Increase —vt. to construct; cause to grow

build′ing n. a structure with sidewalks and a roof

build′up n. promotion; puffery; a gradual increase

built′-in adj. installed as a part of a structure

built′-up adj. covered by buildings

bulb n. a tuberous root; anything similar

bul′bous adj. round; shaped like a bulb; rotund, corpulent

bulge n. a swelling; a projection —vi., vt. to swell; project

bulk adj. of the aggregate; not broken down —n. the main part —vi., vt. to enlarge, expand

bulk′head n. a wall of a ship

bulk′y adj. of significant size; awkward or difficult — **bulkiness** n.

bull n. the adult male of some animals; a speculator

bull′doz′er n. an earth-moving machine; one who aggressively promotes —**bull′doze** vt.

bul′le•tin n. a brief statement; a timely report; a newsletter

bul′let-proof adj. safe from bullets; of an unbreakable agreement

bull′frog′ n. a large North American frog

bull′head′ed adj. stubborn; obstinate —**bull′head•ed•ly** adv. —**bull′head•ed•ness** n.

bull′horn n. a hand-held amplifier

bul′lion n. bulk gold or silver

bull′ock n. a steer; a castrated bull

bull′pen n. waiting area for a baseball team; any waiting or holding area; those available to be used

bull's′eye n. the center of a target; the achtevcment of a goal

bul′ly n. one who intimidates the weak —vi., vt. to intimidate

bul′wark n. a fortification; the side of a ship above the deck

bum adj. of inferior quality; worthless —n. a tramp; a loafer; one addicted to a pursuit to live by begging —vt. to get by freeloading

bum′mer n. a bad experience; a washout

bump n. a blow; a bulge or swelling —vi., vt. to hit or collide with

bump′er adj. remarkably

large —n. a guard to protect against contact

bump'kin n. an unrefined person

bump'tious adj. arrogantly conceited —**bump'tious•ly** adv.

bump'y adj. marked by bulges; rough; irregular — **travel a bumpy road** undertake a difficult task

bun n. a small bread roll

bunch n. a cluster of like things —vi., vt. to gather together

bun'dle n. things bound together —vt. make in bundles; dress warmly

bung n. a stopper in a barrel or cask

bun'ga•low' n. a small house

bun'gee, bungee cord n. an elastic cord used to secure cargo

bun'gle vi., vt. make or work clumsily —n. an imperfect deed —**bun gling•ly** adv.

bun'ion n. inflammation on the toe

bunk n. a bed attached to a wall; any sleeping place; meaningless information — vi. to rest or stay

bunk'er n. a fortified position

bunk'house n. sleeping quarters

bunk mate, bunk'mate n. one who shares living and sleeping space

bun'ny n. a rabbit

bunt vi., vt. to hit a baseball lightly —n.—**bunt'er** n.

bun'ting n. cloth for flags; a decorative banner; a baby's wrap

buoy n. a channel marker — vt. keep afloat; encourage — **buoy'ant** adj.

bur'den n. a heavy load; a responsibility —vt. to weigh down —**bur'den•some** adj.

bu•reau (US) n. a chest of drawers; an office, department, or agency

bu•reauc'ra•cy n. governing through departments with limited jurisdiction or authority —**bu'reau•crat** n.

bu•reau•crat'ic adj. to act strictly according to rules — **bu•reau•crat'i•cal•ly** adv.

bu•reau'cra•tise (Brit.), **bu•reau'cra•tize** (US) vi., vt. make into a bureaucracy — **bu•reau•cra•ti•sa'tion, bu•reau•cra•ti•za'tion** n.

burg n. a small town or village

bur'geon vi. to grow rapidly or profusely; to flourish

burg'er n. a ground food patty; a sandwich made with such a patty

bur'gla•ry n. a breaking in to rob —**bur'glar** n. —**bur'glar•ize** vi.

bur'i•al n. the act of burying

bur'lap (US) n. a coarse cloth for sacks and upholstry backing

bur•lesque' n. broad comedy; satire; theatrical entertainment —vt. to imitate with mockery or satire

bur'ly adj. strong and muscular —**bur'li•ness** n.

burn n. an injury by fire —vi. be on fire; emit light or heat; injured by fire; heated by emotion —vt. set on fire; consume by fire —**burnt** adj.

bur'nish n. a smooth luster — vt. to polish —**bur'nish•er** n. **bur•noose', bur'nous'** n. a long hooded cloak

burp n. belch

bur'ro n. a donkey

71

bur′row n. a hole that shelters
—vi., vt. to dig or hide —
bur′row•er n.

bur′sar n. the comptroller of a
college or university

bur′sa•ry n. a treasury

burst n. a sudden action —vi.
vt. to break or cause to
break suddenly

bur′y vt. place in the ground;
to cover; to remove from
mind; to completely absorb
oneself

burying ground an ancient
cemetary

bus n. a vehicle for a large
number of passengers; an
omnibus; (Brit.) a large,
double-decker vehicle

bus′boy n. a restaurant
worker

bush n. a low woody plant; a
low wooded area —**beat
around the bush** to talk
without commitment —
bush′i•ness n. —**bush′y** adj.

bushed adj. tired; fatigued

bush′el n. a dry measure of 4
pecks

bush′ing n. a sleeve for reducing friction between machine parts

bush′whack vi., vt. to ambush

busi′ness n. commerce; buying and selling; one's occupation; any matter for concern —**got the business**
subjected to rough treat-
ment —**mean business** be
resolute

busi′ness•like adj. professional

buss n. a kiss —vi., vt. kiss
playfully

bust n. a sculpture of the upper body; the chest; a failure; a severe downturn —vi.,
vt. break; make or become

bankrupt

bus′tle n. brisk activity —vi.
to move briskly —**bus′
tling•ly** adv.

bus′y adj. active; occupied —
bus′i•ly adv.

bus′y•bod•y n. a meddler

bus′y•work n. useless activity

butch′er n. one who sells
meat; a murderer —vt. process meat; massacre; do
sloppy work —**butch′er•y** n.

but′ler n. a manservant

butler's pantry a station between kitchen and dining
room

but′ter n. an edible fat; a
spread used like butter —
but′ter•y adj.

but′ter•ball n. a chubby person

but′ter•fat n. fat from milk

but′ter•fin•gered adj. clumsy

but′ter•fly adj. of or like a
butterfly —n. an insect with
colorful wings

but′ter•milk n. the liquid
remains from churning
butter

but′ter•scotch n. a flavoring
of brown sugar and butter
—adj.

but′ton n. a small fastener; a
thing resembling a button —
vi., vt. fasten with buttons —
button down finalize —**button up** don't speak —**on the
button** precise

but′ton-down adj. of a collar
with buttoned tips; conservative

but′ton•hole n. a slit to receive a button —vt. compel
one to listen

but′tress n. a structure that
reinforces; reinforcement —
vt. to reinforce —**flying buttress** an arched buttress

connected to a wall

bux´om *adj..* full-figured —
bux´om•ly *adv.* **—bux´om•
ness** *n.*

buy *n.* a purchase; a bargain
—*vt.* obtain for money; accept as valid

buy off to bribe

buy time to stall

buzz *n.* a droning; a low
murmur; a telephone call
—*vi.* make a droning sound;
talk excitedly —*vt.* speak
rapidly; make a telephone
call; signal with a buzzer

by *prep.* proximity in space or
time; at the hand of;
through the medium of —
adv. near

by´-and-by´ *n.* a time in the
future

bye law *(Brit.)* the rules governing an association or organization

by´gone *adj.* past **—let bygones be bygones** forgive a
past indiscretion

by´law *(US)* *n.* the rules governing an association or organization

by´-line *n.* an attribution; a
naming of the author

by´pass´ *n.* an alternative
route —*vt.* to detour; to cir-
cumvent

by´-path *n.* a route seldom
taken

by´-play *n.* peripheral events

by´-prod´uct *n.* material accumulated during process-
ing; a secondary product

by´stand•er *n.* one who is
present, but not involved

byte *n.* a set of binary digits; a
computer word

by´way *n.* a side road

c, C *n.* third letter of the

alphabet; third-rate; a symbol for 100

cab *n.* a taxicab; an area for
the operator of heavy
equipment

ca•bal´ *n.* plotters; a secret
plot

cab´a•la, cab•ba´la *n.* mystical
teachings; a mystical or
esoteric doctrine **—cab•a•lis´
tic** *adj.*

ca•ba´na *n.* a bathhouse

cab•a•ret´ *n.* a nightclub

cabi´n *n.* a small house; a
room on a boat or plane

cabin boy an apprentice sea-
man

cab´i•net *n.* an article of furniture; a body of advisors

cab´i•net•mak•er *n.* a craftsman in wood **—cab´i•net•ry**
n.

cabin fever anxiety or boredom from living in a con-
fined space

ca´ble *n.* a heavy rope; a bundle of insulated conductors;
a cablegram; cable television
—*vt.* connect with cable; to
send a cablegram

cable car a vehicle drawn by
cable

ca´ble•gram *n.* a message carried by undersea cable

cable television transmission
of television signals by cable

ca´ble•vi•sion *n.* cable television

ca•boo´dle *n.* a batch or group

ca•boose´ *(US)* *n.* last car on a
train

cab•ri•o•let´ *n.* a small carriage

cab´stand *n.* a place where
taxicabs or carriages to wait
for fares

ca•ca´o *n.* a tropical tree or
its seeds, used to make

chocolate products

cache n. a place for storing; material stored; computer memory that stores data for quick retrieval

ca•chet´ n. a mark of authenticity

ca•coph´o•ny n. dissonance; a harsh noise —**ca•coph´o•nous** adj. —**ca•coph´o•nous•ly** adv.

cac´tus n., pl. **cac´ti, cac´tus•es** a desert plant with spiney leaves

cad n. a nasty person; a rogue

ca•dav´er (US) n. a dead body

ca•dav´er•ous adj. pale, gaunt

ca´dente, ca´den•cy n. a rhythmic sound; a measured beat —**ca´denced, ca´dent** adj.

ca•den´za n. a musical flourish

ca•det´ n. a military student

cadge vi., vt. to beg; acquire by begging; to freeload —**cadg´er** n.

ca´dre n. staff; key personnel

ca•du´ce•us n. emblem of the medical profession —**ca•du´ce•an** adj.

cae•sar´e•an, caesrean section n. delivering a baby by surgery

ca•fe´, ca•fé´ n. a coffeehouse

café au lait a beverage of equal parts dark coffee and scalded milk

caf•e•te´ri•a n. a limited service restaurant; (US) a facility where employee meals are served

caf•feine´ n. a stimulant in tea and coffee —**ca´fein•at•ed** adj.

caf´tan n. a long, loose robe or dress

cage n. a place of confinement

—vt. put in confinement

ca´gey adj. cunning; shrewd, clever —**ca´gi•ly** adv. —**cag´i•ness** n.

cai´man, cay´man n.a Central or South American crocodile

cais´son n. an ammunition chest; a wagon for carrying ammunition

caisson disease a condition suffered by divers who surface too quickly

ca•jole´ vi., vt. to appeal repeatedly; wheedle by flattery —**ca•jol´er•y** n. —**ca•jol´er** n. —**ca•jol´ing•ly** adv.

cake n. a sweet pastry; something formed into a patty or block —vi., vt. to harden; form a crust —**icing on the cake** an unexpected bonus —**piece of cake** easy to do

cake´walk n. a strutting dance; a thing easily accomplished

ca•lam´i•ty n. extreme misfortune; tragedy —**ca•lam´i•tous** adj. —**ca•lam´i•tous•ly** adv.

cal´ci•fy vi., vt. to turn to stone or stone-like —**cal•ci•fi•ca´tion** n.

cal´ci•mine n. a white liquid used to cover plastered walls

cal´ci•um n. a mineral essential to the growth of bones; teeth, etc.

cal´cu•late´ vt. use mathematics; estimate —**cal´cu•la´tion** n. —**cal´cu•la•tor** n.

cal´cu•lat•ed adj. computed or reckoned; deliberate

cal´cu•lat•ing adj. scheming; shrewd or crafty —**cal´cu•lat•ing•ly** adv.

cal´cu•lous adj. relating to or

having a stony deposit

cal•cu•lus *n.*, *pl.* **cal•cu•li**, **cal•cu•lus•es** a stone-like deposit; a system of computation

cal´dron , **caul´dron** *n.* a large kettle

cal´en•dar *n.* a system of recording a year; a list of appointments

calf *n.*, *pl.* **calves** the young of certain animals; a cured hide; the back of the leg below the knee

cal´i•ber *n.* the diameter of a cylinder; the quality of a person

cal´i•brate *vt.* to regulate or adjust —**cal•i•bra´tion** *n.*

cal´i•co´ *n.* a printed cotton cloth

cal´i•per *n.* a device for measuring thickness or diameter

ca´liph, **ca´lif** *n.* an Islamic leader

cali´ph•ate *n.* land ruled by a caliph

cal´is•then´ics *pl. n.* exercises

cal•lig´ra•phy *n.* artistic writing; embellished writing —**cal•li•graph´ic** *adj.*

call´ing *n.* ones profession

calling card a card that identifies a caller; a business card

cal•li´o•pe´ *n.* a steam-powered instrument similar to the pipe organ

cal´lous *adj.* heartless; indifferent —**cal´lous•ly** *adv.* —**cal´lous•ness** *n.*

cal´low *adj.* young and inexperienced; immature —**cal´low•ness** *n.*

cal´lus *n.* thickened skin

calm *adj.* still; tranquil; composed —*n.* stillness; tranquility —*vi.*, *vt.* to soothe or pacify —**calm´ly** *adv.*

calm´a•tive *n.* a sedative

cal´o•rie *n.* a measure of heat; the large calorie, used to measure the energy produced by food —**ca•lor´ic** *adj.* —**ca•lor´i•cal•ly** *adv.*

cal•o•rif´ic *adj.* producing heat; high in calories —**cal•o•rif´i•cal•ly** *adv.*

ca•lum´ni•ate *vi.* , *vt.*; to spread rumors —**ca•lum•ni•a´tion** *n.*

ca•lum´ni•ous *adj.* slanderous —**ca•lum´ni•ous•ly** *adv.*

cal´um•ny *n.* slander; defamation

calve *vi.*, *vt.* to give birth to a calf

ca•lyp´so *n.* the music of Trinidad

ca•ma•ra´de•rie *n.* good fellowship

cam´ber *n.* arching; curvature

cam´bric *n.* a fine linen fabric

cam´cord•er *n.* a video camera

cam´el *n.* a common beast of burden in the deserts of Asia and Africa

cam´e•o´ *n.* a shell or gem carved in relief; a brief appearance

cam´er•a *n.* a device for recording visual images —**cam´er•a•man** *n.*

cam´er•a lu•ci´da *n.* an optical device for projecting an image

cam´ou•flage´ *n.* protection through deceptive use of color and form; a device to conceal or deceive

camp *n.* a temporary living area; something flamboyant or outdated —*vi.*, *vt.* to live outdoors —**camp´er** *n.* —**camp´site** *n.*

cam•paign´ n. an undertaking to achieve an objective —vi. to participate in such an undertaking

cam•pa•ni´le n. a bell tower

cam•pa•nol´o•gy n. the art of designing and making bells —**cam•pa•nol´o•gist** n.

camp´fire n. an outdoor fire

cam´pus adj. of a school or its surroundings —n. the grounds or buildings of a complex

ca•nal´ n. an artificial waterway; a waterway made navigable; a duct or channel —vt. to build a canal

can´a•pe n. an appetizer of bread spread with meat, cheese, etc.

ca•nard´ n. a misleading tale; a hoax

can´cel vt. to invalidate; rescind; delete —**can•cel•la´tion** n.

can´cer n. a malignant growth; any infectious evil — **can´cer•ous** adj.

can•de•la´brum n., pl. **can•de•la´bra** a large, branching candle holder

can´did adj straightforward, honest; impartial —**can´did•ly** adv.

can´di•date n. a nominee

can´died adj coated with sugar

can´dle n. a wax cylinder with a wick burned for light —vt. to examine in front of a bright light —**burn the candle at both ends** to work or play too hard —**not hold a candle to** to be inferior

can´dle•light adj. lighted by candles; of soft light —n. subdued light

can´dle•pow•er n. a measure

of intensity of light

can´dle•stick n. a candle; a candle holder; a candelabrum

can´dor n. frankness or honesty

can´dy (US) n. a confection of sugar and flavoring —vt. glaze with sugar

candy striper a hospital volunteer

cane n. the stem of a woody plant; the plant; rattan used in weaving; a walking stick; a rod for flogging —vt. to beat with a cane

cane´brake n. a stand of sugar cane

cane´sugar sugar from cane

ca´nine´ adj. of or like a dog —n. a dog; a sharp-pointed tooth

can´is•ter n. a small container

can´ker n. an ulcerous sore; something that corrupts — vi., vt. to infect or corrupt —**can´ker•ous** adj.

canned adj. (US) of processed food in metal containers; recorded; prepared ahead; contrived

can´ner n. one involved in the processing and packaging of food

can´ner•y n. an industrial plant where raw food is processed

can´ni•bal n.any creature that eats its own kind

can´ni•bal•ise (Brit.), **can´ni•bal´ize** (US) vt., vt. devour one's kind; remove parts for use elsewhere

can´ny adj. cautious, watchful; shrewd —**can´ni•ly** adv.

ca•noe´ n. a light, narrow boat —vi., vt. to travel or carry by canoe

can´on *n.* church law; an established principle, a standard

ca·non´ic, ca·non´i·cal *adj.* about church law; accepted —**ca·non´i·cal·ly** *adv.*

can´on·ist *n.* an authority in canon law —**can·on·is´tic** *adj.*

can´on·ize *vt.* to sanctify or consecrate; to glorify, venerate

canon law rules governing a church

can´o·py *n.* a protective covering; anything similar —*vt.* to create an overhead covering

cant *n.* a sloping surface; terminology of a particular group; insincere speech —*vi., vt.* to slope or cause to slope; to speak in a jargon

can´ta·loupe´ *n.* a variety of melon

can·tan´ker·ous *adj.* quarrelsome, disagreeable

caf·e·te´ri·a *n.* a limited service restaurant; *(US)* a facility where employee meals are served

can·teen´ *n.* a container for drinking water; a place serving food; *(Brit.)* a cutlery collection

can´ti·cle *n.* a hymn

can´ti·lev·er *n.* a projection anchored by a wall

can´tor *n.* a choir leader; a leader in prayer or scripture reading

can´vas *n.* a heavy cloth for sails, tents, etc.; an oil painting

can´vass *vi., vt.* to seek out opinions, votes, etc. —**can´vass·er** *n.*

can´yon *n.* a narrow gorge

cap *n.* covering for the head; any cover —*vt.* place a top on; to cover

ca´pa·ble *adj.* having skill —**ca·pa·bil´i·ty** *n.* —**ca´pa·bly** *adv.*

ca·pa´cious *adj.* spacious; massive; having much space —**ca·pa´cious·ly** *adv.* —**ca·pa´cious·ness** *n.*

ca·pac´i·ty *n.* ability to hold; having aptitude; properly qualified

cape *n.* a sleeveless outer garment, a cloak; a point of land

caper *n.* a playful leap; a silly action —*vi.* to leap playfully; to frolic

cap·il·lar´y *adj.* like a hair; of hair-like blood vessels —*n.* tiny blood vessels

cap·il·lar´i·ty *n.* the action of a liquid and a solid that encloses it

cap´i·tal *adj.* punishable by death; most significant; first-rate —*n.* a seat of government; assets; an uppercase letter; the top of a column

cap´i·tal·ise (*Brit.*), **cap´i·tal·ize** (*US*) *vt.* to write in uppercase letters; to finance; exploit for profit —**cap·i·tal·i·sa´tion, cap·i·tal·i·za´tion** *n.*

cap´i·tal·ism *n.* a system of private ownership —**cap·i·tal·ist** *n.* —**cap·i·tal·is´tic** *adj.*

capital punishment a death penalty

Capitol home of the US Congress —**capitol** home of a state legislature

capit´u·late´ *vi.* to surrender —**ca·pit·u·la´tion** *n.*

ca·pote´ *n.* a long, hooded cloak

ca·price´ *n.* an impetuous action; tending to be unpredictable —**ca·pri´cious** *adj.* —**ca·pri´cious·ly** *adv.* —**ca·pri´cious·ness** *n.*

cap´size *vt.* to upend — **cap´siz·a·ble** *adj.*

cap´stan *n.* a device for hoisting anchor; a spindle for magnetic tape

cap´sule´ *n.* a small container, such as for a seed or for medicine; a closed compartment in a spacecraft — **cap´su·lar** *adj.*

cap´sul·ize *vt.* to summarize; to furnish in abbreviated form

cap´tain *n.* a military officer; a group leader: *captain of the team*

cap´tion *n.* a heading; descriptive matter

cap´tious *adj.* critical; fond of finding fault —**cap´tious·ly** *adv.* —**cap´tious·ness** *n.*

cap´ti·vate´ *vt.* to attract; to fascinate or bewitch

cap´tive *adj.* held prisoner; restricted; fascinated —*n.* a prisoner — **cap´tiv´i·ty** *n.* — **cap´tor** *n.*

captive audience listeners held by charisma; those who cannot leave, as at a business meeting

cap´ture *n.* taking or being taken; that .taken —*vt.* take — and hold; to captivate — **cap´tor, cap´tur·er,** *n.*

car *n.* an automobile; an area for passengers, as of an elevator; *(US)* a railway passenger vehicle

ca·rafe´ *n.* a beverage container

car´a·mel *n.* burnt sugar flavoring; a candy; the color of burnt sugar —**car´a·mel·ize** *vi., vt.*

car´at *n.* a unit of weight for gems

car´a·van *n.* a company of travelers; a file of vehicles or pack animals; *(Brit.)* a mobile home.

car·a·van´sa·ry *n.* an inn; a haven for caravans

car´a·vel *n.* a small, 15th century sailing ship

car´a·way *n.* a flavoring seed; the herb that produces such seeds

car´bine *n.* a light rifle

car·bo·hy´drate *n.* an organic compound; the main source of energy in food

car´bon *n.* a nonmetallic element present in all organic compounds

car´bo·nate *vt.* to infuse with carbon dioxide —**car·bon·a´tion** *n.*

carbon dating determining age by measuring carbon 14 —**car´bon·date** *vt.*

car·bon di·ox·ide *n.* gas released by respiration and absorbed by plants

carbon 14 a radioactive isotope of carbon used to date relics

car´bon·ize *vt.* to convert to carbon; to coat or combine with carbon

car·bon mon·ox·ide *n.* a colorless, odorless, poisonous gas

carbon copy an exact duplicate

car·bon tet·ra·chlo·ride *n.* a colorless solvent used as cleaning fluid

car´bun·cle *n.* red gemstone;

a skin eruption similar to a boil

car´bu•re•tor n. a device for mixing air and gas for an engine

car´cass n. a dead animal; the human body

car•cin´o•gen n. a cancer-causing substance —**car•cin•o•gen´ic** adj.

car•ci•no´ma n. a cancerous growth

car•ci•no•ma•to´sis n. the spread of a carcinoma throughout the body

card n. a stiff paper; a witty or amusing person —**business card** a card that identifies the holder —**credit card** an authorization to purchase on credit —**playing card** cards for playing games —**trading card** cards depicting personalities, events, etc.

car´da•mom n. a spice

card´board n. a stiff paper — adj. of or like cardboard

card-carrying adj. of a member; one espousing a cause

car´di•ac´ adj. of the heart

car´di•gan n. a buttoned sweater

car´di•nal adj. primary; foremost

cardinal number a number that designates quantity

car•di•ol´o•gy n. the study of the heart, its function, and diseases

car•di•ol´o•gist n. one who specializes in diseases of the heart

card shark an expert at cards

card table a table designed for card playing; a table with folding legs

care n.concern; acting with caution; responsibility —vi., vt. feel concern —**couldn't**

care less of no concern

ca•reen´ vt. to lean; to swerve

ca•reer´ n. one's progress; a line of work —**ca•reer´ist** n.

care´free adj. without concern or worry; lighthearted

care´ful adj. cautious; attentive to detail; frugal —**care´ful•ly** adv. —**care´ful•ness** n.

care´giv•er n. one charged with the health and well-being of another

care´less adj. reckless, lacking caution; inattentive —**care´less•ly** adv. —**care´less•ness** n.

ca•ress´ vt. to touch lightly; to stroke lovingly —n. expression of affection; gentle touching —**ca•ress´ing•ly** adv. —**ca•ress´ive** adj.

car´et n. a proofreader's mark (^)

care´tak•er n. one who maintains or preserves; a temporarily selection

care´worn adj. weary; showing the effects of a burden

car´fare n. the price of a ride

car´go n. freight

car´i•ca•ture n. an exaggerated likeness; something inferior —vt. to ridicule; create a distorted likeness

car´ies n. the decay of teeth

car´il•lon n. a set of bells used to make music —**car•il•lon•neur´** n.

car´load n. the amount that can be carried by a vehicle

car´mine n.deep red

car´nage n. a massacre; the remains of a slaughter

car´nal adj. of the flesh; of worldly pleasures; temporal

car´ni•val n. merrymaking; a

local festival; (*US*) *a* traveling show

car·ni·vore *n.* any creature that consumes the flesh of another

car·niv·o·rous *adj.* flesh-eating

car·ol *n.* a song of joy —*vi.* to sing

car·o·tene, car·o·tin *n.* a substance that converts *to* vitamin A

ca·rot·e·noid *adj.* of a pigment in the yellow to red range —*n.*

ca·rot·id *adj.* of the two main arteries of the neck —*n.*

ca·rouse´ *n.* drunken revelry —*vi.* engage in drunken revelry

car·ou·sel´, car·rou·sel´ *n.* a merry-go-round; a revolving device that feeds a continuous stream

carp *vi.* to find fault; to complain

car·pen·ter *n.* a worker in wood—*vi.* work with wood —**car·pen·try** *n.*

car·pet *n.* thick covering for a floor

car·pet·bag *n.* a type of luggage made from carpeting

carpetbagger one who moves to an area to profit from local conditions

car pool a group who share rides —**car pool** *vi.*

car·port *n.* an open structure for protecting an automobile

car·riage *n.* one's bearing; a horse-drawn vehicle —**baby carriage** a transport for the very young

car·riage *n.* (*Brit.*) a railway passenger vehicle

car·ri·er *n.* anything that transports; one infected by

disease without symptoms —**common carrier** a company that transfers goods

car·ri·on *n.* decaying flesh

car·ry *n.* to convey from one place to another; to support or sustian

carried away caught up in events

carry on operate or manage; remain firm in adversity; behave childishly

car·ry·o·ver *n.* something left from a previous time

car·ry-out, car·ry·out *adj.* of food to be eaten off the premises

cart *n.* a small wheeled conveyance that is pulled or pushed —*vt.* to transport by cart —**cart´er** *n.*

cart off to take away

cart´age *n.* the act of transporting; a charge for transporting

carte blanche full authority

car·tel´ *n.* a business alliance; any coalition for a common cause

car·tog´ra·phy *n.* the art of making maps

car·ton *n.* a cardboard box

car·toon *n.* a caricature; a line drawing —*vi., vt.* to make or draw cartoons —**animated cartoon** a set of drawings that create the image of movement

car·tridge *n.* a small carrier for material such as film or tape

cart´wheel *n.* an acrobatic maneuver that involves turning the body perpendicular to the ground

carve *vt.* to fashion or divide by cutting —**carve up** to divide; to share

carv´ing n. a figure made by cutting

cas·cade´ n. a succession of steep waterfalls; a number of devices connected in series —vi., vt.

case n. an instance: in any case; a legal action; a container —**just in case** for contingency —**on his/her case** critical, faultfinding

case study an analysis

case´work·er n. a social worker

cash n. money at hand; currency; liquid assets —vt. convert to cash —**petty cash** money kept on hand for incidentals —**cash´a·ble** adj.

cash-and-carry terms of a sale: no credit and no delivery

cash´book n. a record of cash transactions; a cash journal

cash box storage for cash receipts, petty cash, etc.

cash crop produce grown to sell

cash discount a rebate for cash

cash´ew n. an edible nut or its tree

cashi·er´ n. one responsible for the receipt and disbursement of cash

cash´mere n. a type of fine wool

cash reg·is·ter n. a machine for recording sales and storing cash

cas´ing n. framework; the outer covering of sausage

cask n. a barrel

cas´ket n. a small chest; a coffin

cas´se·role n. an earthenware pot; the slow baking of food; food cooked and served in a single dish

cas·sette n. a small case for film, magnetic tape, etc.

cas´sock n. a clergyman's robe

cast n. theact of throwing or projecting, as an object or a glance; a thing formed in a mold; the actors in a theatrical production; the appearance of a thing —vi., vt. throw; to select performers

cast´a·way n. a person or thing abandoned

caste n. social position or status

cas´ti·gate´ vt. to criticize severely —**cas´ti·ga´tion** n. — **cas´ti·ga·tor** n.

cast´ing n. that formed in a mold

cast iron an alloy of iron

cas´tle n. a fortification

cast´off adj. discarded —n. discarded material, a remnant

castor oil oil of the castor bean, used as lubricant and medication

cas´trate vt. to remove testicles; to spay; to make ineffectual

cas´u·al adj. without plan; haphazard; careless —**cas´u·al·ly** adv.

cas´u·al·ty n. a serious accident; one harmed in an accident or incident

cat·a·bol´ic adj. of conversion of tissue to energy —**ca·tab´o·lism** n.

cat´a·clysm n. major disturbance —**cat·a·clys´mal** adj.

cat´a·comb´ n. an underground cemetery

cat´a·lep·sy n. a condition marked by rigidity and a

trancelike state —**cat·a·lep·tic** *adj.*

cat·a·log´, cat·a·logue´ *n.* a book of merchandise; any listing of related material —*vi., vt.* to list or classify

ca·tal´y·sis *n.* change in rate of a chemical reaction with an additive

cat·a·lyst *n.* a substance that alters a chemical reaction; any thing that brings conclusion or resolution—**cat·a·lyt´ic** *adj.*

cat·a·ma·ran´ *n.* a sailboat with twin hulls

cat·a·mount *n.*a wildcat

cat·a·pult *n.*a seige weapon; a device for launching aircraft —*vi., vt.*

cat·a·ract´ *n.* a large watetfall; a disease of the eye

ca·tarrh´ *n.*inflammation of a mucous membrane

ca·tas´tro·phe *n.* a great disaster, a complete failure —**cat·a·stroph´ic** *adj.* —**cat·a·stroph´i·cal·ly** *adv.*

cat burglar a stealthy thief

cat´call *n.*a sound of disapproval —*vi., vt.* to jeer

catch *n.* a prize; that captured; a drawback; a fastener —*vt.* to take hold; take unawares; overtake

catch´all *n.* a place where things are kept or left; a useless item —**catchall phrase** meaningless drivel

catch´ing *ndj* contagious

catch on understand, comprehend;tu become popular

catch phrase a slogan or motto

catch´y *adj* attention-getting; easily remembered

cat·e·chise (*Brit.*), **cat·e·chize** (*US*) *vt.* to teach by

questioning —**cat·e·chi·sa´tion, cat·e·chi·za´tion** *n.*

cat·e·chism *n.* questions for teaching fundamentals —**cat·e·chist** *n.*

cat·e·chu´men *n.* one being instructed in fundamentals

cat·e·gor´ical *adj.* without qualification; absolute —**cat·e·gor·i·cal·ly** *adv.*

cat·e·go·rize *n.* to classify or type; to arrange —**cat·e·go·ri·za´tion** *n.*

cat·e·go´ry *n.* a classification

cabe·na´tion *n.* formed in succession; a continuity—**nate·nate** *n.*

ca´ter *vi.* to provide food; to indulge —**ca´ter·er** *n.*

cat´er·waul *n.* a wail, as of a rutting cat; discordant screeching —*vi.*

cat´gut *n.* tough line, as used for stringing musical instruments

ca·thar´sis *n.* a cleansing or purgation —**cathar´tic** *adj.*

ca·the´dral *n.* a large church

cathedral ceiling a vaulted dome

cath´e·ter *n.* a slender tube for internal examination, passing fluid, etc. —**cath´e·ter·ize** *vt.*

cath´ode·ray tube a vacuum tube that displays images

cath´o·lic *adj.* broad in scope or taste —**ca·thol´i·cise** (*Brit.*), **ca·thol´i·cize** (*US*) *vi., vt*

cat´nap *n.* a light sleep —*vt.* to doze

cat´nip *n.* a type of mint

cat-o-´-nine´tails *n.* a whip

cat´tle *n.*livestock

cat´ty *adj.* catlike, cunning; malicious, vindictive, spiteful

catty-corner, **catty-cornered** *adj.* diagonal —*adv.* at a diagonal

cat´walk *n.* a narrow walkway

cau´cus *n.* a closed conference; a faction within a political party

cau´dal *adj.* of or like a tail; near the tail —**cau´dal•ly** *adv.*

cau´date *adj.* having a tail

caul *n.* membrane covering a fetus

caul´dron *n.* a large kettle

caulk *n.* a malleable scaler —*v.* to apply a sealer

caus´al *adj.* of cause and effect —**caus´al•ly** *adv.* —**cau•sal´i•ty** *n.*

cau•sa´tion *n.* the act of causing

cause *n.* an agent of change; an objective —*n.* to make happen

cause´way *n.* an elevated road

caus´tic *adj.* corrosive; biting or sarcastic —**caus´ti•cal•ly** *adv.*

cau´ter•ise (*Brit.*), **cau´ter•ize** (*US*) *vt.* to destroy or seal by burning

cau´tion *n.* discretion; prudence; a warning —*vt.* to warn; to admonish —**cau´tion•ary** *adj.* —**cau´tious** *adj.* —**cau´tious•ly** *adv.*

cav´al•cade´ *n.* a procession; a series

cav´a•lier´ *adj.* casual; non chalant; hauty —*n.* an armed horseman, a gentleman —**cav•a•lier´ly** *adv.*

cav´al•ry *n.* mounted soldiers

cave *n.* a hollow under the earth

ca´ve•at *n.* a formal notice

cave´-in *n.* a place where the surface gives way

cave man prehistoric man; a rough or crude individual

cav´ern *n.* a hollow in the earth, a large cave —**cav´ern•ous** *adj.*

cav´i•ar *n.* the eggs of a fish: roe

cav´il *n.* a trivial abjection —*vi* to quibble —**cav´il•er** *n.*

cav´i•ty *n.* a hole or hollow place

ca•vort´ *vi.* to frolic; to prance

caw *n.* the call of a crow —*vi.*

cay *n.* an offshore island or reef

cay•enne´ *n.* a hot red pepper

CD *n.* a compact disc

cease *vi.*, *at.* to stop —**ces´sa´tion** *n.*

cease-fire a temporary cessation

cease´less *adj.* without end; never stopping —**cease´lesaly** *adv.*

cede *n.* to surrender

ce•dil´la *n.* a mark under the letter c(ç) to indicate an s sound

ceiling *n.* the top of a room; an upper limit —**hit the ceiling** to grow excited; to lose one's temper

cel´e•brant *n.* one who celebrates

cel´e•brate´ *vt.* to commemorate; to praise publicly; make known —**cel•e•bra´tion** *n.*—**cel´e•bra´tive** *adj.* —**cel´e•bra•to´ry** *adj.*

cel´e•brat•ed *adj.* widely praised

ce•leb´ri•ty *n.* one who is famous

ce´ler´i•ty *n.* quickness; dispatch

ce•les´tial *adj.* of the sky or heavenly bodies —**ce•les´tial•ly** *adv.*

celestial navigation laying a course by sighting on the stars

cel'i•ba•cy n. sexual abstinence; being unmarried

cel'i•bate adj. practicing celibacy —n. one who practices celibacy

cell n. a small plain room; the fundamental component of organisms; basic unit of a storage battery

cel'lar n. an underground area —**in the cellar** of the lowest ranking

cell division the means by which cells reproduce

cel'lo n. a stringed instrument of the violin family — **cel'list** n.

cel'lo•phane n. a thin, transparent material made from cellulose

cell phone, cellular phone (US) a mobile telephone

cel'lu•lar adj. like a cell; consisting of cells

cel'lule n. a small cell

cel'lu•lite n. fatty deposits

cel'lu•lose n. a complex carbohydrate from cell walls of plants, used many products

Cel'si•us adj. of a thermometer on which the freezing point of water is 0° and the boiling point is 100°

ce•ment' n. a building material; an adhesive —vt. to join with cement; to unite firmly

cem'e•ter•y n. a place of burial

ce'no•bite n. a member of a religious order living communally

cen'o•taph n. a monument; an empty tomb

cen'ser n. an incense holder

cen'sor n. one authorized to examine for objectionable material —vt. to judge what is suitable —**cen'sor•a•ble** adj. —**cen'sor•ship** n.

cen•so'ri•ous adj. expressing censure; faultfinding —**cen•so'ri•ous•ly** adv. —**cen•so'ri•ous•ness** n.

cen'sur•a•ble adj. open to reproach; at fault

cen'sure n. disapproval; an official rebuke —vt. express disapproval

cen'sus n. a count of population

cen'taur n. a mythical creature, half man and half horse

cen•te•nar'i•an n. one who has lived to the age of 100 years

cen•ten'ni•al adj. of 100 years —n. a one-hundredth anniversary

cen'ter (US) n. the middle point or part; a hub —vi. to focus —vt. to place on or at a point of focus

cen'ter•board n. a panel that descends below the keel of a sailing vessel —**retractable centerboard**-a centerboard that can be raised

centered (US) adj. focused; concentrated; self-confident; at the center

center of gravity (US) the point at which weight is concentrated

cen'ter•piece n. a dominating decoration or display

cen•tes'i•mal adj. of a hundredth part

cen'ti•grade' adj. divided into one hundred degrees; of the Celsius thermometer

cen'ti•gram n. one hundredth part of a gram

cen´ti•me´ter n. one hundredth part of a meter

cen´tral adj at or near the center, significant; of a single origin —**cen•tral´i•ty** n. —**cen´tral•ly** adv.

central heating a heating plant that serves an entire building

cen´tral•ism n. a concentration of power at one place — **cen´tral•ise** (Brit.), **cen´tral•ize** (US) vi., vt.

central nervous system the brain and spinal cord of the body

central processing unit (CPU) the chip that controls a computer

cen´tre (Brit.) n. the middle point; a hub —vi. to concentrate —vt. to place on or at a point of focus

centred (Brit.) adj. focused; self-confident; at the centre

centre of gravity (Brit.) the point at which weight is concentrated

cen´trif´u•gal adj. moving away from a center — **cen•trif´u•gal•ly** adv.

centrifugal force tendency of anything revolving to move outward

cen´tri•fuge n. a device that forces matter outward

cen•trip´e•tal adj. moving toward a center

cen•tu´ri•on n. in ancient Rome, a commander of one hundred men

cen´tu•ry n. one hundred years; a group of one hundred

ce•phal´ic adj. of the head

ce•ram´ic adj. made from baked clay —**ce•ram´ist** n. —**ce•ram´ics** n.

ce´re•al n. a grain used as food; food prepared from grain —adj.

cer´e•bral adj. of brawn or intellect

cerebral palsy a disorder from damage to the central nervous system

cer´e•brum n. the front of the brain

cer´e•ment n. a shroud; a burial garment

cer•e•mo´ni•al adj. of a ritual; stately —n. a formal system of ritual —**cer•e•mo´ni•al•ly** adv.

cer•e•mo´ni•ous adj. with great formality; devoted to ritual or ceremony —**cer•e•mo´ni•ous•ly** adv.

cer´e•mo´ny n. a formal rite or ritual; a formality

ce•rise´ adj. bright red

cer´tain adj. definite; reliable; inevitable; of an indefinite quality —**cer´tain•ly** adv. —**cer´tain•ty** n.

cer•tif´i•cate n. an official document

certificate of deposit a document confirming the deposit of funds

cer•ti•fi•ca´tion n. affirmation

cer´ti•fied adj. authorized; approved; vouched for

certified public accountant an accountant recognized as having knowledge of his trade

cer´ti•fy vt. to make known; to declare in writing — **cer´ti•fi•a•bie** adj. —**cer´ti•fi•a•bly** adv.

cer´ti•tude n. conviction; confidence

ce•ru´le•an adj. of an azure hlue color

cer´vi•cal adj. of the cervix

cer´vix n. the neck; a neck—like part

ces•sa´tion n. an ending or stopping

ces´sion n. a surrender or renunciation; a waiver

cess´pool n. a large receptical for effluence; a place that is corrupted

chad n. bits of paper from tape or cards used in computer processing

chafe n. irritation or wear from friction —*vi.* to rub; become irritated —*vt.* to irritate; to annoy—**chafe at the bit** show impatience

chaff n. the waste from threshing; anything worthless

chaf´ing dish´ n. a warming dish

cha•grin´ n. embarrassment —*vt.* to embarrass

chain n. a set of links; any set of connected elements; a thing that binds —*vt.* to bind or restrain

chain gang a prison work party

chain letter a letter containing material to be passed on to others

chain lightning lightning having many branches; a person seen to move quickly in many directions

chain reaction a series of events

chain saw a portable power saw

chain store a group of retail outlets

chair n. a place for sitting; a position of authority —*vt.* to preside over

chair´lift n. a conveyance for transporting skiers up a hill

chair´man, chair´person n. one who officiates, as over a meeting

chaise longue, chaise lounge n. a chair with support for the legs and back

cha•let´ n. a style of Swiss house

chal´ice n. a goblet

chalk n. type of limestone; a marker for a blackboard — *vt.* to write with chalk — **chalk´y** adj.

chalk´board n. a slate; a surface for writing with chalk

chal´lenge n. a difficult task; invitation to compete; a questioning —*vt.* to invite to compete; call into question —**chal´lenge•a•ble** adj.

chal´leng•ing adj. difficult, formidable; intriguing, fascinating

cham´ber n. a bedroom; a meeting room; a board; an enclosed space

cham´ber•maid n. one who cleans

chamber music light music for performance by a small musical group

chamber of commerce an organization that promotes business

champ n. a champion —*vt.* to chew —**champ at the bit** be impatient

cham•pagne´ n. sparkling wine; the yellowish color of the wine

cham´pi•on n. supporter of a cause; one with attributes of a winner —*vt.* to fight for; to support

chance adj. fortuitous; unplanned —n. a random or unexpected occurrence; a wager; an opportunity

—*vi.* occur accidentally —*vt.* risk —**chanc'i•ness** *n.* —**chanc'y** *adj.*

chan'cel•ler•y *n.* office of chancellor

chan'cel•lor *n.* president of a university; a prime minister

chan'de•lier' *n.* an elaborate hanging light fixture

change *n.* alteration; a substitution; transformation; coins —*vt.* make different; exchange; transform

change'a•ble *adj.* temporary; adaptable; unstable, flighty, or fickle —**change•a•bil'i•ty, change'a•ble•ness** *n.* —**change'a•bly** *adv.*

change'less *adj.* constant; permanent

change of heart a shift in thinking

change of pace something dissimilar; a respite from the usual

change'o•ver *n.* passing to another; a transformation; an altenng

chang'er *n.* one who changes; that which changes records, disks, etc.

chan'nel *n.* a bed for naturally flowing water; a passageway for liquid; a band or route for communications —*vt.* wear into ruts; send through a conduit; to direct

chan'nel•ing *n.* the concept of being a conduit for a spiritual force

chant *n.* a primitive musical form; a rhythmic recitation —*vi.,vt.*

cha'os *n.* extreme confusion —**cha•ot'ic** *adj.* —**cha•ot'i•cal•ly** *adv.*

chap *n.* a man or boy —*vi., vt.* to roughen the skin

chap•ar'ral *n.* a thicket

cha•pa'ti *n.* Indian skillet bread

cha•peau' *n., pl.* **cha•peaus', cha•peaux'** a hat

chap'el *n.* a small room set aside for worship; a small church

chap'er•on' *n.* one who oversees —*vt.* to overseer or supervise

chap'lain *n.* a clergyman

chap'let *n.* prayer beads

chaps *n.* leg protectors

chap'ter *n.* a part of a book; a distinct period; branch of a lodge

char *vt.* scorch; to charcoal

char'ac•ter *n.* a written or printed symbol; a distinctive quality; moral strength; a person in a story, an odd person —**character actor** one who specializes in portraying unusual persons —**character assassination** slander

char•ac•ter•is'tic *adj.* typical; distinguishing —*n.* a distinctive style —**char•ac•ter• is'ti•cal•ly** *adv.*

char'ac•ter•ize *vt.* to depict, typify

cha•rade' *n.* a game of acting out; a thinly disguised deception; a sham

char'broil *vt.* to broil over charcoal; to barbecue —**char'broiled** *adj.*

char'coal' *n.* charred wood used as fuel; a stick for sketching —*vt.* to charbroil; to sketch with charcoal

charge *n.* asking price; a financial obligation; an assigned duty; one under another's care; a call to attack;

mild excitement—*vt.* set a price; incur financial obligation; command; hold liable; accuse; attack —**charge´a•ble** *adj.* —**charge account** permission to purchase on credit

char•gé d'af•faires´ *n.* a diplomat

char´i•ot *n.* a two-wheeled, horse-drawn vehicle; the family car —*vi.*, *vt.* to ride in a chariot

cha•ris´ma *n.* leadership quality; charm, appeal

char´is•mat´ic *adj.* having charisma; of a religious group —*n.* one reputed to have divine powers

char´i•ta•ble *adj.* generous; forgiving —**char´i•ta•bly** *adv.*

char´i•ty *n.* almsgiving; an institution for aiding those in need

char´la•tan *n.* a fake; one who claims falsely

charley horse a muscle cramp

charm *n.* something having magical power; that attracts or pleases —*vt.* to please

charmed fortunate, lucky — **live a charmed life** experience good fortune

charm´ing *adj.* captivating; appealing —**charm´ing•ly** *adv.*

chart *n.* a map; a graphic representation —*vt.* make a map or graph

char´ter *n.* permit that grants right or authority —*vt.* establish by charter; lease

charter member one who joins at the beginning

char•treuse´ *n.* a pale green color; a liqueur —*adj*

char´y *adj.* cautious

chase *n.* pursuit —*vt.* pursue; drive away —*vi.* follow in pursuit

chasm *n.* a narrow gorge or ravine; any sharp division — **chas´mal** *adj.*

chaste *adj.* virtuous, pure in thought or conduct — **chaste´ly** *adv.* —**chaste´ nets, chas´ti•ty** *n.*

chas´ten *n.* to correct by punishing

chas´tise´ *vt.* punish, scold sharply —**chas´tise´ment** *n.*

chas´ti•ty *n.* purity; innocence

chat *n.* casual conversation — *vi.* to converse —**chat´ty** *adj.*

cha•teau´ *n.* a country house

chat´tel *n.* personal property

chat´ter *n.* foolish talk to speak foolishly; to click rapidly

chat´ter•box *n.* a constant talker

chauf´feur *n.* a hired driver; one who drives —*vt.* to drive for another

chau´vin•ism *n.* fanatical patriotism; irrational belief in one's superiority —**chau´vin•ist** *n.* —**chau•vin•is´tic** *adj.*

cheap *adj.* inexpensive; of lit-tle value

cheap´en *vt.* to depreciate; to debase

cheap shot an underhanded remark

cheap•skate *n.* a tightwad; a miser

cheat *n.* a swindle; a fraud — *vi.*, *vt.* to defraud; be dishonest

check *n.* a slowing; an examination; an invoice; a negotiable instrument; a pattern of squares —*vt.* to slow forward progress; to examine

check·er·board *adj.* of a pattern of squares —*n.* a game board of squares used to play checkers and chess

checking account (*US*) money that can be transferred by check

check´list *n.* a reference list

check´mate *n.* a winning move in chess; an action that thwarts

check´´-out, check´out *n.* a tally of purchases; the time a place must be vacated; verification

check´point *n.* a location for inspection or verification

check´room *n.* a place for temporary storage of coats

check´up *n.* an examination

ched´dar *n.* a type of cheese

cheek *n.* the side of the face; impertinence, rudeness

cheek´bone *n.* a bone at the side of the face near the top of the cheek

cheek´y *adj.* brazen, bold; impertinent

cheer *n.* a good mood; a source of pleasure; encouragement —*vi., vt.* to gladden; to sound approval—**cheer´ful** *adj.* **cheer´ful·ly** *adv.* —**cheer´ful·ness** *n.*

cheer´lead·er *n.* one who leads the cheering for a team; one seen as overzealous in promoting

cheer´less *adj.* dreary, dismal; barren —**cheer´less·ly** *adv.*

cheer´y *adj.* happy; lighthearted; jaunty—**cheer´i·ness** *n.*

cheese *n.* a food made from milk

cheese´cake *n.* a pie-like dessert; picture of a scantily clad person

cheese´cloth *n.* a loosely woven cotton cloth

chees´y *adj.* of or like cheese; lacking quality

chef *n.* a cook; the director of a kitchen staff

chem´i·cal *adj.* of chemistry —*n.* a substance involved in a chemical process —**chem´i·cal·ly** *adv.*

chemical warfare the use of chemicals an enemy

che·mise´ *n.* a type of dress or an undergarment for women

chem´is·try *n.* the study of the properties of matter —**chem´ist** *n.*

chem·o·ther´a·py *n.* treatment of illness by the use of chemicals

cheque *n.* (*Brit.*) an invoice; a negotiable paper; a design of squares

cher´ish *vt.* to hold dear; to protect

cher·oot´ *n.* a type of cigar

cher·vil *n.* an herb used for flavoring

chess *n.* a board game for two

chest *n.* the upper part of the front of a body; a box; a cabinet

chest´nut *n.* an edible nut or its tree; a reddish-brown horse —*adj.* a brownish color —**pull chestnuts out of the fire** recover from a difficult situation

chest of drawers furniture with drawers for storage

chest´y *adj.* having a large chest; buxom

chev´ron *n.* uniform insignia

chew *vt., vi.* gnnd with the teeth; to consider —**chew**

out to scold; upbraid — **chew the fat, chew the rag** to talk; converse

chew´y adj. of food that is tough or difficult to chew — **chew´i•ness** n.

chic adj. stylish; smartly dressed —n. refinement in style or manner

chi•can´ery n. deception; trickery

chi´chi adj. elegant; of an overdone style; of a haughty manner

chick n. a young bird

chick´en n. a domestic fowl; a coward —adj. fearful, timid; overly strict —**chicken out** back down —**no spring chicken** not young

chicken feed an inconsequential amount; insignificant

chick´en•heart´ed adj. fearful; fainthearted

chicken pox a childhood disease

chicken wire a light fencing

chic´le n. substance in chewing gum

chic´o•ry n. a flowering plant, its edible leaves, or its root

chide vt., vt. to scold quietly —**chid´ing•ly** adv.

chief adj. significant —n. a leader

chief executive, chief executive officer the highest ranking administrator of an organization

chief justice head of a judicial body

chief´ly adj. of or like a chief —adv. especially, mainly, primarily

chief of staff the leading director of an organization

chief of state a head of government

chief´tain n. a chief

chif•fon´ n. a lightweight cloth

chif•fo•nier´ n. a chest of drawers

child n., pl. **chil´dren** an infant; offspring —**child´s play** easy

child´bear•ing n. carrying an unborn child; giving birth — adj.

child´birth n. bringing forth a baby

child´hood n. infancy to puberty; a time of growth and development

child´ish adj. acting like a child; immature; silly — **child´ish•ly** adv. —**child´ish•ness** n.

child´less adj. having no offspring

child´like adj. exhibiting attributes of a child; innocent; adolescent

chil´i n. a type of pepper

chill adj. slight cold —n. coldness; shivering caused by illness —vt. to make cold

chill´er n. that shocks or frightens

chill´y adj. of a cold, uncomfortable environment; discourteous or unfriendly — **chill´i•ness** n.

chill´ing adj. frightening; causing concern — **chill´ing•ly** adv.

chime n. a bell; the sound of bells —vi., vt. sound in harmony —**chime in** to interrupt or take part

chi•me´ra n. an imaginary monster; a wild fancy — **chi•mer´i•cal** adj.

chim´ney n. a vent for smoke

chimney sweep one who cleans chimneys

chin n. the front of the lower jaw —vi. to idly chat or gossip

chi´na n. procelain; fine dinnerware

china cabinet, china closet a cupboard

chine n. a backbone or spine

chink n. a crack or slit —vt. to fill in a crack —**a chink in one's armor** a weakness

chi´no n. a cotton cloth —**chinos** casual slacks made from the cloth

chi•noi•se•rie´ n. an oriental style

chintz´y add. cheap; gawdy, vulgar; of poor quality

chip n. a small piece; a thin slice; a game piece —vi., vt. to break off —**a chip off the old block** a son who is like his father —**chip in** to contribute —**have a chip on one's shoulder** be testy —**in the chips** wealthy

chipped beef thinly sliced-dried beef

chip´per adj. light-hearted; cheerful

chi´rop•o•dist n. a podiatrist; a specialist in disorders of the foot —**chi•rop´o•dy** n.

chi´ro•prac´tor n. one who treats disorders by manipulation

chis´el n. a tool for shaping wood —vt. cut with a chisel; to cheat; obtain by deception —**chis´el•er** n.

chit n. a bill; a marker or IOU

chit´chat n. idle, meaningless, talk

chiv´al•ry n. qualities attributed to a knight —**chiv´al´rous** adj. —**chiv´al•rous•ly** adv.

chive n. a flavoring herb

chlo´ri•nate vt. purify with chlorine —**chlo•rin•a´tion** n.

chlo´rine n. a chemical for water purification, cleaning, etc.

chock n. a stopper or wedge; a guide for lines on the deck of a ship

chock-full adj. filled to the brim

choc´o•late n. flavoring from cacao beans —adj. flavored with cacao

choice adj. preferred; superior —n. the right of choosing; a thing chosen; an alternative; a favored part

choir n. a group of singers; part of a church set aside for singers

choir´boy n. a choir member; one perceived as being pious

choke n. the sounds of one choking; a device that alters air flow —vi. to have difficulty breathing; have difficulty performing —vt. to throttle or strangle; to obstruct or restrict —**choke back** to suppress, as tears

choke´ber•ry n. a bitter fruit reputed to cause choking, or its bush

choke´bore n. a shotgun bore that maintains a tight pattern of shot

choke´cher•ry n. a chokeberry

choke collar a dog collar that tightens as strain is put on the leash; a leather collar with metal studs

choke chain leash for a choke collar

choke down to eat with difficulty

chok´er n. one who throttles; a closely fitting necklace

choke up to block or clog; overcome by emotion

chol´er n. a state of irritation; anger or rage —**chol´er·ic** adj.

cho´line n. a B vitamin

choose vi., vt. to select; to prefer

choos´y adj. selective; fastidious

chop n. a cut of meat; a sharp blow to cut into small pieces

chop´per n. a helicopter

chop´py adj. marked by quick starts and stops or moves; discordant

chop´sticks n. rods used in the orient to manipulate food

chop su´ey a quasi-oriental dish

cho´ral adj. of a performance by a choir or chorus, or the music

cho·rale´ n. a choir or chorus; musical work for a choir or chorus

chord n. a set of musical tones; anything harmonious; a straight line joining two points on an arc

chore n. a small task; a difficult job

cho·re´a n. a nervous disorder

cho´re·o·graph vi., vt. to create and direct a dance; to carefully plan and direct any activity

cho´re·og´ra·phy n. creation and direction of dances —**cho·re·og´ra·pher** n.

chor´tle n. a quiet laugh; a chuckle —vi., vt. to chuckle or snicker

chorus n. a group of singers or dancers; a group acting in accord; a refrain —vi., vt. to perform in unison

chos´en adj. selected; favored

chow n. a breed of dog; food —**chow time** meal time

chow´der n. a soup; a hodgepodge —**chowderhead** an addled thinker

chow mein´ a quasi-oriental stew

chris´ten vt. name; bring into service —**chris´ten·ing** n.

chris´ten·dom n. the time of Christianity; area populated by Christians; the known world

Christian adj. of the followers of. Christ —n. a follower of Jesus —**Christian name** one's given name

Chris·ti·an´i·ty n. the Christian religion; Christians generally

chro·mat´ic adj. of colors; of a musical progression

chro´ma·tin n. the substance in cells that forms chromosomes

chrome n. chromium for plating —vt. to plate with chromium

chro´mi·um n. a metallic element

chro´mo·some´ n. a strand of DNA

chron´ic adj. recurring; habitual

chron´i·cle n. an ordered record; a detailed report —vt. record or narrate — **chron´i·cler** n.

chro·nol´o·gy n. an ordered record of events —**chron·o·log´ic** adj. —**chron·o·log´i·cal·ly** adv.

chro·nom´e·ter n. a device for measuring time with great accuracy

chro·nom´e·try n. the study

of accurate measure of time

chub´by *adj.* round and plump

chuck *n.* a device for securing a tool; a shim —*vt.* to throw; to discard

chuck´le *n.* a quiet laugh —*vi.* to laugh quietly

chuck´le·head *n.* a foolish person

chum *n.* a friend or associate; bits of fish used as bait —*vi.* hang about together; to attract game fish with bait — **chum´mi·ness** *n.*

chump *n.* one who is gullible; a victim; a stupid or foolish person

chunk *n.* a lump; a substantial amount —*vt.* to cut or form lumps

chunk´y *adj.* stocky; containing solid bits —**chunk´i·ness** *n.*

church *n.* a place of worship; group of worshippers — **church´go·er** *n.*

church´ly *adj.* pious; worshipful; of a church or its offices

church´war·den *n.* a long clay pipe

church´y *adj.* of one preoccupied with religion or affairs of a church

church´yard *n.* the grounds about a church; a burial ground

churl *n.* a bumpkin; a curmudgeon

churl´ish *adj.* crude, vulgar; grouchy, surly —**churl´ish·ly** *adv.*

churn *n.* a device for making cream into butter —*vi., vt.* to make butter; to agitate — **churn´er** *n.*

chute *n.* an inclined trough

chut´ney *n.* spicy fruit relish

chutz´pah, chutz´pa *n.* brazenness; audacity; insolence

cic´a·trix *n., pl.* **cic´a·tri·ces, cic´a·trix·es** a scar

cic´a·trise (*Brit.*), **cic´a·trize** (*US*) *vi., vt.* to heal by forming a scar

ci´der *n.* juice from apples

ci·gar´ *n.* a roll of smoking tobacco

cig´a·ret´, cig´a·rette´ *n.* finely cut cured tobacco rolled in paper

cil´i·a *n. pl.,* sing. **cil´i·um** small hair-like projections

cinch *n.* a wide belt; an easy task —*vt.* to secure with a cinch

cinc´ture *n.* a belt or sash; that encircles —*vt.* to bind or encircle

cin´der *n.* rock-like material formed by great heat; material burned that has not turned to ash

cinder block a concrete block

cin´e·ma *n.* a movie theater; making of films; motion-picture industry

cin·e·ma·tog´ra·pher *n.* operator of a motion-picture camera; one who produces or directs films

cin·e·ma·tog´ra·phy *n.* the art of motion picture photography

cin·e·rar´i·um *n.* a place where the ashes of cremated bodies are kept

cin´na·bar *n.* mercuric sulphide, the source of mercury; bright red

ci´pher *n.* zero; a thing of no value; a secret code; an encoded message

cir´ca *prep.* about, approximate

93

cir•ca•di'an *adj.* of twenty-four hour biological rhythms

cir'cle *n.* a round figure; a group of people; extent of influence; a cycle —*vi.* to revolve; move in a circle —*vt.* to move around; to surround

cir'clet *n.* a small circle

cir'cuit *n.* a continuous route; journey in exercise of a calling; course of electricity —**cir'cuit•ry** *n.*

circuit board *n.* insulated board containing elements of a circuit

circuit breaker a device that interrupts an electrical circuit

circuit court a traveling judiciary

cir•cu'i•taus *adj.* roundabout or devious —**cir•cu'i•tous•ly** *adv.*

cir•cu•lar *adj.* round; of that moving in a circle; circuitous —*n.* a widely distributed advertisement

cir'cu•late' *vi., vt.* to move freely; move on a predetermined course —**cir'cu•la•to'ry** *adv.*

cir•cum'fer•ence *n.* boundary of a circle —**cir•cum•fer•en'tial** *adj.*

cir•cum•lo•cu'tion *n.* an evasive, lengthly means of expression

cir•cum•nav'i•gate *vt.* travel around —**cir•cum•navi•ga'tion** *n.*

cir'cum•scribe *vt.* to circle; define limits of —**cir•cum•scrip•tion** *n.*

cir•cum•spect *adj.* cautious; prudent—**cir•cum•spec'tion** *n.*

cir'cum•stance *n.* happening

cir'cum•stan'tial *adj.* of little importance; inconclusive

cir'cum•vent *vt.* to bypass; avoid by craft —**cis•cum•ven'tion** *n.*

cir'cus *n.* a traveling show; frantic activity or disorder

cis'tern *n.* a storage tank; a container for rain water; a reservoir

cit'a•del *n.* a stronghold; a refuge

ci•ta'tion *n.* quotation; a summons to appear; a commendation

cite *vt.* to quote; summon before a court of law —**cit'a•ble** *adj.*

cit'ied *adj.* of or like a city

cit'i•fy *vt.* to build up; become like a city or city person —**cit'i•fied** *adj.*

cit'i•zen *n.* one entitled to protection of the state; an inhabitant

cit'i•zen•ry *n.* citizens collectively

cit'ric *adj.* pertaining to citrus fruit or the acid of the fruit

cit•ron•el'la *n.* a pungent oil

cit'rus *n.* oranges, lemons, limes, etc. or their trees —*adj.*

cit'y (US) *n.* an incorporated area

cit'y (Brit.) *n.* urban area with a cathedral or named by royal warrant

city council governing body of a city

city hail the seat of city government —**can't fight city hall** the futility of opposing established authority

city manager administrator of a city

city planning the process of regulating growth and

change in a city

cit´y•scape n. view of a city skyline

city slicker one suave or urbane

civ´ic adj. of a city or its citizens

civ´ic-mind´ed adj. in the best interests of a city or its citizens

civics n. the study of the rights and duties of citizenship

civ´il adj. of citizens; civilized; formally polite; pertaining to rights of individuals —**civ´il•ly** adv.

civil defense a program for training volunteers to pro-tect and aid in the event of attack or disaster

civil disobedience opposition to government by noncompliance

civil engineer one who specializes incommunity services, such as roads and bridges

ci•vil´ian n. one not associated with the military, law enforcement, etc. —adj. of civilians or civil life

ci•vil´i•ty n. courteous behavior

civ•i•li•sa´tion (Brit.), **civi•li•za´tion** (US) n. the culture of a people; protection of a civilized state

civ´i•lise (Brit.),**civ´i•lize**(US) vi.,vt. to convert from a savage state —**civ´i•lised, civ´i•lized** adj.

civil law the rights of individuals

civil liberty the right to act without undo interference by government

civil war war within a nation

clab´ber n. thick sour milk — vi., vt. to curdle

clad adj. clothed; covered by metal

clad´ding n. a layer of metal; the process for covering with metal

claim vt. demand as a right; state as fact —n. a demand; basis for a demand; a thing demanded; an assertion — **claim´ant, claim´er** n.

clair•voy´ant ad,. of ability to sense that not apparant —n. —**clair•voy´ance** n.

cla´mant adj. crying out noisily; insistent —**cla´mant•ly** adv.

clam´ber vi. to climb

clam´my adj. unpleasantly cold and damp —**clam´mi•ness** n.

clam´or n. loud outcry —vi. demand insistantly —**clam´or•ous** adj.

clamp n. a device used to join or hold —vt. to join with a clamp

clamp´down n. enforcement of restrictions —**clamp down** grow restrictive; forbid or prohibit

clan n. a family; a tribe; a group with common interests —**clan´nish** adj.

clan•des´tine adj. secret, hidden —**clan•des´tine•ly** adv.

clang n. a metallic sound —vi.

clang´or n. persistent clanging —vi. to make noise — **clang´or•ous** adj.

clap n. a sharp sound; a blow —vi., vt. make a sharp sound; applaud

clap´board n. wood siding — vt. to apply wood siding

clap´trap n. idle words

clar´et n. a dry red wine

clar'i•fy vi., vt. to make or become clear —**clar•i•fi•ca'titan** n.

clar'i•net' n. a woodwind instrument —**clar•i•net'ist** n.

clar'i•on adj. clear, distinct —n. a medieval trumpet; the sound made —vt. proclaim distinctly

clar'i•ty n. the quality of being clear

clash n. a harsh noise; a conflict —vi. to come into conflict

clasp n. a fastener; an embrace —vt. to fasten; to embrace

class n. a distinct type; social rank; quality —vt. to grade or rank

class action suit legal action on behalf of a group of people

clas'sic adj. of the highest order; famous; traditional; uncomplicated —n. a work that is famous or traditional —**clas'si•cal** adj.

clas'si•cism n. qualities associated with ancient Greece or Rome; classical scholarship —**clas'si•cist** n.

clas'si•fied adj. arranged in suitable categories; secret

clas'si•fy vt. arrange according to a system; restrict use or distribution —**clas'si•fi•ca'tion** n.

class'ism n. awareness of difference in station; discrimination

class'mate n. one in the same class in school; a contemporary

class'room n. a room for teaching

class'y adj. of fine manners or style; elegant; splendid

clat'ter n. noise; a hubbub —vi. rattle or reverberate

clause n. part of a sentence; a section of a document —**claus'al** adj.

claus•tro•pho'bi•a n. fear of confined spaces —**claus•tro•pho'bic** adj.

cla•vier', **cla•vier'** n. a stringed instrument with a keyboard

claw n. a curved appendage for grasping; anything like a claw

clay n. earth that is malleable when moistened; a material used for pottery, modeling, etc.

clay'more n. a broadsword

clay pigeon a target for shooting; one open to attack

clean adj. free of contamination; pure, undefiled; distinct, readable; smooth or well proportioned; flawless —adv. neatly; entirely —vi. be cleansed —vt. wash or scrub; disinfect; prepare for eating

clean'-cut adj. clear, precise; of a pleasing appearance

clean'ly adj. kept clean —adv. in a clean manner —**clean'li•ness** n.

cleanse vt. make clean; free from sin

clean-shaven without facial hair

clean'up n. the process of cleaning; the ridding of corruption, vice, etc.

clear adj. bright, unclouded; distinct, unmistakable; calm, untroubled; unencumbered by debt —adv. obviously, completely —vt. set or make free; wipe clean; absolve; jump over —**clear the**

air discuss freely —**clear up** explain —**in the clear** absolved of guilt

clear′ance n. exoneration; official sanction; the space between

clear′-cut adj. without ambiguity; denuded of trees —vt.

clear headed adj. discerning; reasonable, sensible

clearing n. an area devoid of trees

clear′ing•house n. a facility for processing information or negotiable instruments

clear′-sight•ed adj. shrewd; keenly perceptive

cleat n. a small projection on furniture or footwear; a device for securing lines

cleave vi., vt. to split; to separate

clem′en•cy n. leniency, mercy

clench n. a rigid hold —vt. make a fist; grit one's teeth

cler′gy n. those ordained for religious service

cler′i•cal adj of a clerk or member of the clergy

clerk n. an office worker; a counter person, as in a hotel or store

clev′er adj. skillful; intelligent; witty —**clev′er•ly** adv. —**clev′er•ness** n.

cli•ché′ n. a trite phrase

cli′ent n. a customer; one dependent on another

cli•en•tele′ n. clients as a group

cliff n. a high, steep face of rock

cliff′-hang•er, cliff′hang•er n. a story full of suspense

cli′mate n. prevailing weather; any condition that influences

cli•ma•tol′o•gy n. the study of

climate —**cli•ma•tol′o•gist** n.

cli′max′ n. a final or significant element; a turning point or crisis

climb n. scaling; advancement or improvement —vi., vt. mount by using hands and feet; an ascension —**climb′a•ble** adj.

clinch n. a fastening; a hug —vt. to fasten; to conclude —**clinch′er** n.

cling vi. hold fast, adhere; remain near, be emotionally attached —**cling′y** adj.

clinging vine one inclined to dependence on others

cling′stone adj. of a fruit with pulp firmly attached to the pit —n.

clin′ic n. a place for medical treatment; an infirmary or dispensary; an intensive learning session

clin′i•cal adj. of a clinic; sterile; scientific or objective

clinical thermometer a thermometer to measure body temperature

clip n.a thing cut; a fast pace; a sharp blow; a fastener —vi. cut off; move rapidly —vt. cut or cut off; shorten, as of speech; strike with a sharp blow; to cheat; to fasten

clip joint concern that overcharges

clip′per n. one who cuts or trims; a tool for cutting; a sailing ship

clip′ping n. act of cutting; that cut

clique n. a small exclusive group —**cli′quey, cli′quish** adj.

cloak n. a long cape; that

which covers or conceals —
vt. to cover or conceal; to
camouflage

cloak´-and-dag´ger *adj.* of
secret activities

cloak´room *n.* a place for
coats

clob´ber *vt.* hit forcefully; to
win

clock *n.* a device for marking
time —*vt.* to measure time,
output, distance, etc.

clock´work *n.* workings of a
clock—**like clockwork** according to plan

clod *n.* a lump of earth; a dull
or stupid person —**clod´dish**
adj.

clod´hop•per *n.* a country
bumpkin; a heavy shoe

clog *vi.* become obstructed —
vt. obstruct or impede —*n.*
an obstruction; a shoe with
a wooden sole

clois´ter *n.* a covered walk; a
place of seclusion —*vt.* to
seclude ur protect —**clois´
tered** *adj.*

close *adj.* nearby; similar;
confining; restrictive; limited
—**close´ly** *adv.*

close *n.* an enduig, coucltision
—*vi., vt.* of to conclude; to
shut, to connect

close by near; beside

close call, close shave a near
miss; a narrow escape

closed shop a company that
hires only union members

close´fist•ed *adj.* stingy, miserly

close´out *n.* selling discontin-
ued items or to liquidate a
business —*vi., vt.* to sell out
a business

close quarters a crowded
space

clos´et (*US*) *n.* a storage area

—*vt* to store; to consult pri-
vately

close´up an intimate or near
view

clos´ing *adj.* of a final stage —
n. the ending or finalization

closing costs expense of fi-
nalizing a contract

clo´sure *n.* a conclusion; that
closes

clot *n.* a soft mass —*vi.* to coagulate

cloth *n.* a fabric

clothe *vt.* cover; furnish with
clothing —**clothes** *n.* wearing apparel

clothes´horse *n.* one who is
inordinately fond of clothes

clothes peg (*Brit.*), **clothes´
pin** (*US*) *n.* a device for securing clothing to a line for
drying

clothes tree an upright post
with hooks for hanging hats
and coats

cloth´ier *n.* one who manu-
factures or sells clothes

cloth´ing *n.* wearing apparel

clo´ture *n.* a parliamentary
maneuver for closing debate

cloud *n.* a mist of water; a
mass of smoke, dust, etc.;
anything resembling a
cloud, shade or gloom — *vi.,
vt.* to obscure —**have one's
head in the clouds** day-
dream —**living under a
cloud** suspected; depressed
—**cloudy** *adj.*

cloud´burst a sudden heavy
rain

cloud´less *adj.* clear, sunny

cloud nine a state of bliss

clout *n.* a blow; power or influence —*vt.* to strike

clove *n.* a fragrant spice;
segment of a bulb, as garlic

clo´ven *adj.* split; cleft

clo´ver·leaf n. a complex highway interchange

clown n. one who uses broad humor, acts like a foul, is clumsy or incompetent —vi. to perform or act like a fool —**clown´ish** adj.

cloy vi., vt. make unpleasant by excess, as very rich or sweet —**cloy´ing·ly** adv.

club n. a heavy stick; a group organized for common purpose —vt. to strike with a club

club´foot´ n. a congenital deformity

club´house n. meeting place or facilities used by members

cluck n. the sound of a hen; a foolish person

clue n. information —**clue in** to inform or provide with information

clum´sy adj. awkward; poorly fashioned —**clum´si·ness** n.

clus´ter n. a bunch —vi., vt. to come together —**clus´ter·y** adj.

clutch n. a device that grabs and holds —vt. grasp and hold closely

clut´ter n. disarray —vt. to scatter

coach (US) n., passenger compartment; a trainer —vt. to teach

coach (Brit.) n. a large vehicle for passengers —vt. to teach or train

co·ag´u·late vi., vt. change to a thick soft mass —**co·ag·u·la´tion** n.

coal n. a combustible; an ember

co·a·lesce´ n. unite or merge

co·a·li´tion n. a temporary union

coarse adj. rough; vulgar or obscene —**coarse´ly** adv. —**coarse´ness** n.

coars´en vt. to make rough

coast n. land by the sea —vi. move by force of gravity; slack off

coast´er n. a sled; a mat

coast guard a naval force

coast´line n. land along shore

coat n. an outer garment; protective covering; a layer: a coat of paint

coat´dress n. a long buttoned frock

coat´ing n. a rover or layer, material for making coats

coat of arms a family emblem; armonial bearings

coat´rack n. a post or row of hooks for hanging hats and coats

coat´room n. a place for coats

coat´tail n. the bottom of a coat —**on someone´s coattails** profit from the success of another

co·au´thor n one who writes or ensiles in collaboration with another

coax vt. to cajole —vt. persuade by wheedling —**coax´ing·ly** adv.

co·ax´i·al adj. having common axis

coaxial cable cable used to transmit telephone, television, etc. signals

cob n. the core on which kernels of corn grow, a male swan

co´balt n. a metalic element

cobalt blue dark blue

cob´ble vt. to repair shoes

cob´bler n. one who makes or repairs shoes; a fruit pie

cob´ble-stone n. paving stone

COBOL *n.* acronym for Common Business *Oriented Language*, a computer programming language

cob'web' *n.* a spider web

co'ca *n.* a tropical plant; the source for cocaine

co'caine' *n.* a narcotic

coc'cyx *n.* the end of the spine

co•chair' *n.* one who shares the duties of a chairperson —*vi.*

cock *n.* a male bird; a device for regulating flow; striking part of a gun; pile of hay; a jaunty angle —*vt.* to set; set at a jaunty angle

cock-a-leek'ie *n.* a Scottish soup

cock'a•ma•mie *adj.* fictional; fabricated; ridiculous

cock-and-bull story a fabrication

cocked hat a three-cornered hat **knock into a cocked hat** to spoil; reveal as false

cock'eyed *adj.* out of alignment; ridiculous; faulty reasoning

cock'ney *n.* a rhyming dialect; speaker of the dialect —*adj.* of the dialect or those who speak it

cock'sure *adj.* self-confident

cock'tail' *n.* beverage or food served before or at the start of a meal

cock'y *adj.* overconfident; flamboyant

co'coa' *n.* a powder from cacao beans; a beverage; a brown color

cocoa butter fat from cacao seeds

co'co•nut *n.* fruit of a coconut palm

coconut milk the thin liquid

from the center of the coconut

coconut oil oil from coconut meat

coconut palm a tropical tree that produces coconuts

co•coon' *n.* a protective cover

cod *n.* a *type* of food fish

co'da *n.* a musical phrase

cod'dle *vt.* to overindulge; pamper or treat gently; cook by poaching

code *n.* arrangement of a body of law; a system of symbols or signs —*vt.* translate into symbols

co'deine *n.* a derivative of opium

codg'er *n.* an old man

cod'i•cil *n.* an addendum

cod'i•fy *vt.* to arrange —**cod'i•fi•ca'tion** *n.*

cod'-liv•er oil *n.* oil from the liver of codfish, rich in vitamins A and D

co'ed' *adj.* coeducational —*n.* a female student

co•ed'it *vt.* jointly prepare for publication —**co•ed'i•tor** *n.*

co•ed•u•ca'tion•al *adj.* of an institution for male and female students

co•erce' *vt.* to force; to compel

co•er'cion *n.* use of threats or force to compel —**co•er'cive** *adj.*

co•ex•ist' *n.* exist at the same time; live in harmony —**co•ex•is'tence** *n.* —**co•ex•is'tent** *adj.*

cof'fee *n.* a beverage from seeds of a tropical plant; the plant; informal gathering; light brown color

coffee beans seeds of a coffee plant

coffee break a brief rest period

cof•fee•cake *n.* a bread-like pastry

cof´fee•house *n.* a café

cof´fee•pot *n.* a utensil for making and serving coffee

coffee shop a coffee house; a shop that sells exotic coffee and utensils

coffee table a low table

cof´fer *n.* a strongbox; a re-inforced shelter; a cofferdam

cof´fer•dam *n.* a barrier to hold back water for construction or repairs taking place below water level

cof´fin *n.* a box for burial

cog *n.* gear tooth; minor functionary

co´gent *adj.* forceful or compelling

cog´i•tate´ *vi.* consider carefully

cog´nac *n.* a brandy

cog´nate´ *adj. of* common ancestry

cog•ni´tion *n.* mental processes —**cog´ni•tive** *adj.*

cog•ni•zance *n.* knowledge; awareness —**cog´ni•sant** *adj.*

cog´no´men *n.* a family name

cog´wheel *n.* a toothed wheel

co•hab´it *vi.* to live together— **co•hab´i•tant** *n.* —**co•hab•i• ta´tion** *n.*

co´here´ *vi.* to hold together naturally or logically —**co• her´ence** *n.*

co•her´ent *adj.* congruous; logically connected —**co´ her´ent•ly** *adv.*

co•he´sive *adj.* sticking —**co• he´sion** *n.*—**co•he´sive• ness** *n.*

co´hort *n.* a colleague or friend; a contemporary

coif *vt.* to style hair —*n.* coif-fure

coif•fure´ *n.* a hair style

coin *n.* a metal piece with monetary value to mint coins; to make or invent — **coin´er** *n.*

coin´age *n.* the process of minting; the money system of a country

co´in•cide´ *vi.* to correspond exactly; be in accord

co•in´ci•dence *n.* a coinciding; a chance event —**co•in´ ci•dent** *adj.*

co•in•ci•den´tal *adj.* characterized by chance; accidental

co•i´tus, co•i´tion *n.* sexual intercourse —**co´i•tal** *adj.*

col´an•der *n.* a perforated drain

cold *adj.* lacking heat or warmth; unfeeling or un-friendly —*n.* absence of heat; a viral infection —**go in cold** without preparation —**have cold feet** be reticent —**have down cold** know thoroughly —**in the cold** left out —**turn a cold shoulder** scorn or ignore

cold´blood´ed *adj.* unfeeling, callous —**cold´blood´ed•ly** *adv.*

cold chisel a steel tool for cutting

cold cream a cosmetic skin cleanser

cold cuts processed meats

cold front a cold air mass

cold´heart´ed *adj.* unresponsive; lacking compassion — **cold´heart´ed•ly** *adv.* — **cold´heart´ed•ness** *n.*

cold pack a cool, wet compress; a chemical ice pack used in first aid

cold snap sudden cold weather

cold sore a viral infection

about the mouth following a cold, fever, etc.

cold storage a refrigerated area

cold turkey suddenly, without preparation

cold war unfriendly relations between countries without fighting

cole´slaw n. shredded cabbage salad

col´ic n. persistent discomfort experienced by an infant

col´i•se´um n. an arena

co•li´tis n. Infection of the intestine

col•lab´o•rate´ vi. work together: cooperate —**col•lab´o•ra•tive** adj.

col•lage´ v. an artistic composalon constntcted of odd bits of material

col•lapse´ vi. to break down suddenly; fold into a compact unit —**col•laps´i•ble** adj.

col´lar n. the neck of a garment; a band worn around the neck

col´lards, collard greens n. a green leafy vegetable

col´late vt. gather together In order

col•lat´er•al adj. similar; pledged as a guarantee —n. that pledged as a guarantee —**col•lat´er•al•ly** adv.

col•lat´er•al•ize vt. pledge as security; to guarantee

col•league´ n. an associate

col•lect´ vi., vt. gather together; secure payment —**col•lec´tion** n.

col•lect´ed adj. gathered, accumulated; calm and composed

col•lect´ive adj. consolidated; of a venture in which

people work for common good —n. a group; a cooperative organization

collective bargaining negotiations

col´lege n. an institution of learning; an association

col•le´gi•an n. a student at a college —**col•le´gi•ate** adj.

col•lide´ vt. come together violently

col•li´sion n. a coming together; a clash of opinions

col´lo•cate vt. to arrange; categorize

col•lo´qui•al adj. used informally —**col•lo´qui•al•ly** adv.

col•lo´qui•al•ism n. a word or phrase used informally

col´lo•quy n. a formal discussion

col•lu´sion n. a conspiracy. a plot —**col•lu´sive** adj.

co´lon n. a punctuation mark (:); the large intestine

colo´nel n. a military officer

co•lo´ni•al adj. of an outpost

co•lo´ni•al•ism n. a policy of settling new lands —**co´lo´ni•al•ist** adj., n.

col´o•nist n. one who founds or lives to a colony —**col´o•nise´** (Brit.), **col´o•nize´** (US) vt.

col•on•nade´ n. a series of columns

col´o•phon n. a printed emblem

col´or (US) n. the sensation created by varying light waves; any substance used to dye or tint —vi., tit. to give or change color

col•or•a´tion n. shades and tones

col•or•blind (US) adj. incapable of distinguishing colors; without racial prejudice

col´ored (US) adj. having color; of a non-caucasian; biased

col´or•fast (US) adj. of a cloth that will not bleed or fade when washed

col´or•ful (US) adj. bright; picturesque; quaint or unusual —**col´or•ful•ly** adv.

col´or•ing (US) n. applying color

col´or•ize (US) vt. add color

col´or•less (US) adj. bland; uninteresting

col´ors (US) n. a banner or flag

co•los´sal adj. amazingly large

co•los´sus n. an extremely large structure or statue

co•los´to•my n. creation of an opening for disposal of body waste

col´our (Brit.) n. the sensation created by varying light waves; any substance used to dye or tint —vt., vt. to give or change color

col´our•blind (Brit.) adj. incapable of distinguishing colors, without racial prejudice

col´oured adj. (Brit.) having color; of a non-caucasian race; biased

col´our•ful adj. (Brit.) bright; picturesque; quaint or unusual —**col´our•ful•ly** adv.

col´oriz•ing n. (Brit.) applying color

col´our•ise´ vt. (Brit.) add color

col´our•less adj. (Brit.) bland; uninteresting

col´ours (Brit.) n. a banner or flag

colt n. a young horse, donkey, etc.

col´umn n. a support; a vertical section of a printed page

col´um•nist n. a writer of commentary

co´ma n. a state of deep sleep

com´bat n. armed conflict, a battle; a struggle —**com•bat´** vt. fight against; contend

com•ba´tive adj. inclined to fight

com´bi•na•tion n. a blending or merging —**com•bi•na´tion•al** adj.

com´bine n. a machine for harvesting; an association — **com•bine´** vi.,vt. to join forces; unite

com´bo n. an instrumental ensemble

com•bus´ti•ble adj. easily ignited; excitable —n. material easily ignited —**com•bus•ti•bil´i•ty** n.

com•bus´tion n. burning

comeback n. return to a previous state, as in politics; a sharp retort

come´di•an n. one who writes or performs comedy

co•me´dic adj. pertaining to comedy

come´down n. a reversal of fortune

com´e•dy n. an attempt to amuse

comedy of errors mistakes more humorous than tragic

come´ly adj. attractive; pleasing in appearance — **come´li•ness** n.

come´on n. an enticement

co•mes´ti•ble n. food

come•up´pance n. a humbling penalty that is deserved; retaliation

com´fort n. contentment; relief —vt. relieve; aid or assist

com´forta•ble adj. at ease; free of pain — **com´fort•a•bly** adv.

com´fort•er n. one who

consoles; *(US)* a heavy bed covering

com'ic *adj.* funny —*n.* a comedian

com'i•cal *adj.* amusing, hu-morous; facetious **-corn'i•cal•ly** *adv.*

comic book illustrated stories

comic opera a humorous work in the style of grand opera

comic relief a humorous incident

comic strip a series of cartoons

com'ing *adj* drawing near; promising —**have it coming** deserve

coming-out' *n.* a debut

com'ma *n.* a punctuation mark (,)

com•mand' *n.* authority to lead; an order; ability to use well —*vt.* to order

com•man•deer' *vt.* to take charge

com•mand'er *n.* one in charge

commander in chief senior officer

com•mand'ing *adj.* having authority; impressive; compelling

commanding officer one who is in charge of a military unit or post

com•mand'ment *n.* a regulation

com•man'do *n.* a warrior

command post temporary headquarters

com•mem'o•rate *vt.* to honor —**com•mem'o•ra'tion** *n.*— **com•mem'o•ra•tive** *adj.,* *n.*

com•mence' *vi., vt.* to begin

com•mence'ment *n.* a beginning; a school graduation ceremony

com•mend' *vt.* praise; entrust

com•mend'a•ble *adj.* worthy of praise; admirable

com•men•da'tion *n.* a medal

com•men'su•ra•ble *adj.* to the same degree; proportionate

com•men'su•rate *adj.* equivalent or comparable; corresponding

com'ment *n.* a remark —*vi.* speak or write about — **com'men•tar'y** *n.*

com'men•ta•tor *n.* one who reports

com'merce *n.* the buying and selling of goods and services

com•mer'cial *adj.* of commerce; undertaken for profit —*n.* paid advertising; *(Brit.)* a traveling salesman —**com•mer'cial•ly** *adv.*

commercial art advertising art and design

com•mer'cial•ize *vt.* operate for profit —**com•mer'cial•i•za'tion** *n.*

com•min'gle *vi., vt.* to mix together; combine

com•mis'er•ate *vi., vt.* express sorrow or pity —**com•mis•er•a'tion** *n.*

com•mis•sar'y *n.* a store or cafeteria

com•mis'sion *n.* a group given authority; duties authorized; a fee —*vt.* to grant authority

com•mis'sion•er *n.* an authority; head of a government department

com•mit' *vt.* to do; to give for safekeeping; to bind or obligate

com•mit'ment *n.* a pledge or promise; dedication

com•mit'tee *n.* a group appointed for a special purpose

com•mo'di•ous *adj.* spacious —**com•mo'di•ous•ness** *n.*

com•mod´i•ty *n.* anything traded

com´mon *adj.* ordinary; widespread; shared —*n.* a public square —**com•mon•al´i•ty** *n.*

common carrier a company that transports passengers or freight

common denominator a multiple shared by a set of fractions; shared feature or trait

common ground agreement

common law tradition or usage

com´mon•place *adj.* ordinary —*n.* anything ordinary or trite

com´mon•sense *adj.* sound, rational

common sense reasonable judgement

common touch empathy for the average citizen

com´mon•weal *n.* public welfare

com´mon•wealth *n.* the people of a state, nation, etc.; a government

com•mo´tion *n.* a disturbance

com•mu•nal•ize *vt.* to form a commune; transfer property to a commune

com´mu•nal *n.* a grodp formed to share labor and its rewards; a cooperative —**com•mu´nal** *adj.*

com•mune´ *vi.* to converse; be in harmony with

com•mu•ni•ca•ble *adj.* infectious or contagious

com•mu´ni•cate´ *vi.* share information; be understood —*vt.* convey information; to transmit illness

com•mun´ion *n.* close fellowship; a group comprising a fellowship

com´mu•nism *n.* a theoretical classless society marked by common ownership of property —**com´mu•nist** *n.* —**com´mu•nis´tic** *adj.*

com•mu•ni´ty *n.* society; members of a political unit; those who share a common interest

community collage an educational institution

community property property held in common

community service voluntary work; work assigned as punishment

com´mu•nise *vt.* place in control of the community at large

com•mu•ta´tion *n.* a substitution; traveling to and from work

com•mute´ *vi.* to travel to and from work; make an exchange —*vt.* to substitute —**com•mut´er** *n.*

com´pact´ *adj.* taking little space; light —*n.* a covenant; a small car

com•pact´ *adj.* dense *vt.* to pack tightly -**com•pact´ness** *n.*

compact disk *n.* a digital storage device

com•pan´ion *n.* one *who* accompanies; a friend; an attendant

com•pan•ion•a•ble *adj.* cordial, congenial

companion piece part of a set

com•pan´ion•way *n.* a hall or stairway aboard ship

com´pa•ny *n.* an assembly or association; a guest; ,companionship

company store a retail establishment operated for employees

company union a bargaining unit that is unaffiliated or controlled by an employer

com·pa·ra·ble adj. similar

com·par·a·tive adj. relative to others; corresponding

com·pare´ vt. to contrast; to resemble —**com·par´i·son** n.

com·pas´sion n. concern for another; pity; sympathy -**com·pas´sion·ate** adj.

com·pat´i·ble adj. able to exist or work together —**com·pat·i·bil´i·ty** n.

com·pa·tri·ot n. a colleague

com·peer´ n. a comrade or friend; a peer; one's equal

com·pel´ vt. bring about by force

com·pel´ling adj. forceful; impressive

com·pen´di·ous adj. summarized

com·pen´di·um n. an abridgment

com·pen·sate´ vt. to offset; to pay —**com·pen·sa´tion** n. —**com·pen´sa·to·ry** adj.

com·pete´ vi. to work against

com·pe·tence, com·pe·ten·cy n. adequate qualification; fitness

com·pe·tent adj. qualified; suitable, adequate —**com·pe·tent·ly** adv.

com·pe·ti´tion n. rivalry; a rival

com·pet·i·tive adj. disposed to rivalry —**com·pet´i·tive·ness** n.

com·pet´i·tor n. one who competes

com·pile´ vt. to arrange in order —**com·pi·la´tion** n.

com·pla´cence, com·pla·cen·cy n. contentment; self-satisfaction; apathy —**com·pla´cent** adj.

com·plain´ vt. express dissatisfaction —**com·plain´er** n.

com·plaint´ n. an expression of dissatisfaction

com·plai´sant adj. accommodating; obliging -**com·plai´sance** n.

com·plect´ed adj. of skin coloring

com´ple·ment n. that which completes —vt. to make complete

com·ple·men´ta·ry adj. of a part that completes; corresponding

com·plete´ adj. lacking nothing —vt. conclude; accomplish successfully —**com·ple´tion** n.

com·plex´ adj. complicated -**com´plex** n. a group of related elements —**com·plex´i·ty** n.

com·plex´ion n. appearance of the skin; the general nature of a thing

com·pli´ance n. a tendency to yield; conformity —**com·pli´ant** adj.

com´pli·cate´ vt., vi. make difficult

com´pli·cat·ed adj. intricate, tangled; difficult to understand —**com·pli·ca´tion** n.

com·plic´i·ty n. involvement

com´pli·ment n. praise; courtesy —vt. to praise

com·ply´ vi. to act on a request

com·po´nent n. an integral part

com·port´ment n. conduct

com·pose´ vt. to form; put in order; to create; to calm oneself; to arrange elements for printing

com·posed´ adj. calm, deliberate

com•pos´er *n.* one who creates

com•pos´ite *adj.* made up of several —*n.* a material made by combining

com´po•si´tion *n.* forming or combining; placement; a thing formed

com•pos´i•tor *n.* one who sets type

com´post *n.* decomposed matter; potting soil —*vt.* to make compost

com•po´sure *n.* tranquillity, self-control

com´pote *n.* marinated fruit; a stemmed serving dish

com•pound´ *adj.* made up of two or more elements —*n.* a mixture —**com•pound´** *vt.* to combine; to increase by Adding to

com´pre•hend´ *vt.* understand; to include —**com´pre•hen´sion** *n.*

com´pre•hen´sive *adj.* broad in scope —*n.* a graphic layout —**com´pre•hen´sive•ly** *adv.*

com´press *n.* a pad applied to a wound —**com•press´** *vt.* press together, squeeze; make compact —**com•press´i•ble** *adj.*

com•prise´ *vt.* to include; consist of

com´pro•mise *n.* a settlement —*vt.* settle by concession; expose to difficulty ur danger

comp•trol´ler *n.* the overseer of financial affairs of an organization

com•pul´sion *n.* driving force; irrational impulse —**com•pul´sive** *adj.*

com•pul´so•ry *adj.* obligatory

com•punc´tion *n.* doubt from fear of wrongdoing

com•pute´ *vt.* to calculate - **com•put´a•ble** *adj.*-**com•pu•ta´tion** *n.*

com•put´er *n.* an electronic device for processing data

com•put•er•ese´ *n.* terminology used by those involved with computers

computer graphics artwork produced with the and of a computer

com•put´er•ise (*Brit.*), **com•put´er•ize** (*US*) *vt.* operate with the aid of a computer —**com•put•er•i•sa´tion, com•put•er•iza´tion** *n.*

com´rade *n.* a friend or companion —**com´rade•ship** *n.*

con *adv.* against; of an opposing view -*n.* an opposing; a swindle; a convict —*vt.* to swindle; to trick

con•cat´e•nate *vt.* to join; to link together —**con•cat•e•na´tion** *n.*

con´cave´ *adj.* curved like the inner surface of a sphere

con•ceal´ *vt.* to cover; keep secret —**con•ceal´ment** *n.*

con•cede´ *vt.* acknowledge; to grant

con•ceit´ *n.* an overly high opinion of oneself —**con•ceit´ed** *adj.*

con•ceiv´a•ble *adj.* able to tie believed or understood

con•ceive´ *vt.* to understand

con´cen•trate´ *n.* a substance made dense or intense —*vt.* increase density or intensity; focus one's attention

con•cen´tric *adj.* having a common center

con´cept *n.* a theory; a broad understanding

con•cep´tion *n.* a beginning

con•cep´tu•al *adj.* theoretical or abstract

con·cep´tu·al·ize *vt.* to form a theory —**con·cep´tu·al·i·za´tion** *n.*

con·cern´ *n.* a matter of interest; a feeling of anxiety; a business firm —*vt.* to show interest; to cause anxiety — **con·cerned´** *adj.*

con·cert *n.* mutual agreement; a program of music — **con·cert´** *vt.* to resolve by mutual agreement

con·cert´ed *adj.* harmoniously; unified —**con·cert´ed·ly** *adv.*

con·cer´to *n.* a music arranged for orchestra and a solo instrument

con·ces´sion *n.* a conceding; a thing conceded; a business venture

con·ces´sion·aire´ *n.* one who operates a business

conch *n.* a large marine mollusk

con·cil´i·ate´ *vt.* to appease, placate —**con·cil´i·a·to·ry** *adj.*

con·cise´ *adj.* succinct; brief and to the point —**con·cise´ly** *adv.*

con´clave *n.* a large gathering; a secret meeting

con·clude´ *vt.* end; deduce by reasoning —**con·clu´sion** *n.*

con·clu´sive *adj.* final; convincing —**con·clu´sive·ly** *adv.*

con·coct´ *vt.* make or devise —**con·coc´tion** *n.*

con·com´i·tant *adj.* associated with; connected —**con·com´i·tance** *n.*

con´cord *n.* harmony or agreement; a treaty

con·cord´ance *n.* an agreement; an index of leading words in a text

con·cor´dant *adj.* harmonious

con´course *n,* a broad walkway

con·crete´ *adj.* solid; precise —*n.* a building material — *vi., vt.* to solidify —**con·crete´ly** *adv.*

con·cre´tion *n.* a hardened mass

con·cu´pis·cence *n.* intense desire; lustfulness —**con·cu´pis·cent** *adj.*

con·cur´ *vi.* to correspond or coincide; to agree —**con·cur´rence, con·cur´ren·cy** *n.*

con·cur´rent *adj.* in agreement; occurring together; convergent

con·cus´sion *n.* a shock; injury caused by an impact

con·demn´ *vt.* to disapprove; to find guilty; punish; declare unfit for use —**con´dem·na´tion** *n.*

con·den·sa´tion *n.* compaction; collected moisture; an abridgement

con·dense´ *vt.* make dense; to compress; abridge or summarize

condensed milk thick, sweet milk

con·de·scend´ *vi.* to lower oneself; to he patronizing — **con·de·scen´sion** *n.*

con·de·scend´ing *adj.* patronizing

con·dign´ *adj.* suitable

con´di·ment *n.* a seasoning or relish

con·di´tion *n.* a requirement; a circumstance; a thing that modifies —*vt.* to modify or influence

con·di´tion·al *adj.* contingent

con·di´tioned *adj.* in a proper state

con·dole´ *vi.* to sympathize; to

console; to comfort

con·do′lence n. sympathy

con′do·min′i·um[1] (Brit.) n. territory governed by two or more nations

con′do·min′i·um[2] (US) n. apartment individually owned; a building which houses such an apartment

con·done′ vt. foregive; disregard without protest

con′dor n. a large vulture

con·du′cive adj. contributing or leading to —**con·du′cive·ness** n.

con′duct n. the way one acts —**con·duct′** vt. to lead; to behave in a certain manner; to convey

con·duc′tor n. a leader; a guide; one in charge; material which transmits heat or electricity

con·duct′ance n. the ability to transmit electricity —**con·duc′tive** adj.

con·duc′tion n. conveyance

con′dult n. a channel

cone n. a geometric solid with a circular base that rises to a point

con′fab n. a discussion —vi.

con·fab·u·la′tion n. a conversation or informal discussion

con·fec′tion n. a sweet edible

con·fec′tion·er·y n. a shop where confections are made or sold

con·fed′er·a·cy n. an alliance —**con·fed′er·a′tion** n.

con·fed′er·ate n. an associate or accomplice —vt. to unite

con·fer′ vi. to meet for discussion —vt. to grant, as an honorary degree

con′fer·ence n. a formal meeting

conference call a telephone connection for more than two persons

con·fess′ vt. to acknowlege

con·fes′sion n. an admission of guilt

con·fes′sor n. one who confesses; a priest who hears confessions

con·fet′ti n. bits of colored paper tossed in the air during festivities

con′fi·dant n. a trusted friend

con·fide′ vi., vt. to share a secret

con′fi·dence n. trust or faith; self-assurance; something confided

confidence game a swindle

con′fi·dent adj. self-assured

con′fi·den′tial adj. secret —**con·fi·den·ti·al′i·ty** n.

con·fid′ing adj. trusting

con·fig′ure vt. set up or arrange

con·fig·u·ra′tion n. arrangement; structure

con′fine n. an enclosure -**con·fine′** vt. restrict; shut in

con·firm′ vt. prove; validate —**con·fir·ma′tion** n.

con·firmed′ adj. resolved; proved

con′fis·cate vt. seize by authority —**con·fis′ca·to·ry** adj.

con′fla·gra′tion n. a large fire

con′flict n. a clash of ideas or interests; open warfare -**con·flict′** vi.

conflict of interest moral obligation at variance with personal interest

con′flu·ence n. a flowing together

con·form′ vi. adapt; follow custom or tradition —**con·form′i·ty** n.

con·found' *vt.* confuse, bewilder

con·fra·ter'ni·ty *n.* a brotherhood

con·front' *vt.* come face to face —**con·fron·ta'tion** *n.*

con·fuse' *vt.* bewilder; to mistake; to mingle indiscrimately

con·fu'sion *n.* bewilderment; a state of chaos or disorder

con·fute' *vt.* to prove in error

con·geal' *vi., vt.* thicken or solidify

con·gen'ial *adj.* friendly; compatible —**con·ge·ni·al'i·ty** *n.*

con·gen'i·tal *adj.* existing at birth; hereditary —**con·gen'i·tal·ly** *adv.*

con·gest' *vt.* clog or obstruct; to overcrowd —**con·ges'tive** *adj.*

con·ges'ted *adj.* overcrowded

con·glom'er·ate *adj.* gathered in a mass —*n.* an agglomeration; a diversified corporation —*vi., vt.*

con·grat'u·late *vt.* to express joy

con·grat·u·la'tions *n.* an expression of pleasure at good fortune

con·gre·gate *vt.* to assemble —**con·gre·ga'tion** *n.*

con'gress *n.* a coming together; a formal assembly

con·gru'ence *n.* a state of agreement; harmony —**con'gru·ent** *adj.*

con·gru'ous *adj.* appropriate; suitable or fitting

con'i·cal *adj.* shaped like a cone

co'ni·fer *n.* evergreen tree or shrub —**co·nif'er·ous** *adj.*

con·jec'tur·al *adj.* based on speculation

con·jec'ture *n.* speculation; judgement based on scant information —*vt.* to speculate

con·join' *vi., vt.* to unite or connect

con·ju'gal *adj.* of or pertaining to marriage —**con·ju·gal'i·ty** *n.*

con'ju·gate *adj.* joined together —*vt.* to join —**con'ju·ga'tion** *n.*

con·junc'tion *n.* a joining; a word that connects

con·junc'tive *adj.* connective

con·junc·ti·vi'tis *n.* an inflammation of the eyelid

con'jure *vi, vt.* summon a spirit

conk *n.* a blow —*vt.* to strike —**conk out** to suddenly fail or quit

con man a confidence man; swindler

con·nect' *vi.* become linked —*vt.* link together **con·nec'tor** *n.*

con·nect'ed *adj.* linked; joined in order; having important contacts

con·nec'tive *adj.* serving to link —*n.* a bond; that joins or links

con·nec'tion *n.* a joining; a part that joins; a relationship

con·nip'tion *n.* a fit; a frenzy; excitement or rage

con·niv'ance *n.* secret involvement

con·nive' *vi.* cooperate secretly in wrongdoing —**con·niv'er** *n.*

con'nois·seur' *n,* an expert; a person of discriminating taste

con·no·ta'tion *n.* an implied meaning; an insinuation

con•note´ vt. to suggest or imply

con•nu´bi•al adj. of marriage

con´quer vi., vt. to overcome —**con´quer•or** n —**con´quest** n.

con•san´guine, con•san•guin´e•ous adj. of common ancestry

con´science n. sense of right and wrong

con•sci•en´tious adj. guided by conscience; thorough —**con•sci•en´tious•ness** n.

con´scious adj. awake; aware —**con´scious•ly** adv.

con´script n. one drafted —**con•script´** vt. draft into the military

con´se•crate´ vt. set apart as sacred; dedicate to a worthy cause —**con´se•cra´tion** n.

con•sec´u•tive adj. in logical order —**con•sec´u•tive•ly** adv.

con•sen´su•al adj. mutually consenting —**con•sen´su•al•ly** adv.

con•sen´sus n. general agreement

con•sent´ n. permission —vi. grant

con´se•quence n. that logically follows; relative significance

con´se•quent adj. following as a result —n. anything that follows

con•se•quen´tial adj. having significance, that creates or is an effect

con´se•quent•ly adv. as a result

con•serv´an•cy n. a group devoted to preservation of natural resources

con•ser•va´tion n. the protection of natural resources

conservation of energy the principal that energy may be converted, but is never diminished

con•serv´a•tism n. moderation; opposition to change

con•serv´a•tive adj. cautious; reserved or moderate —n. one reserved or moderate

con•serv´a•to•ry n. a greenhouse; a school of music or drama

con•serve´ n. fruit preserve — vt. to guard against damage or waste

con•sid´er vt. carefully contemplate; bear in mind; be respectful; to deem, believe

con•sid´er•a•ble adj. large, extensive; substantial

con•sid´er•ate adj. having regard

con•sid´er•a´tion n. careful contemplation; payment for services

con•sid´ered adj. given careful thought; deliberate

con•sign´ vt. to give over to another

con•sign´ment n. goods transferred to another for sale or safekeeping

con•sist´ vi. to be made up of

con•sist´ence, con•sist´en•cy n. uniformity; texture

con•sist´ent adj. constant; unwavering; harmonious

con•sis´to•ry n. a church council

con•sole´ vt. comfort —**con•sol´a•ble** adj. —**con´so•la´tion** n.

con•sol´i•date´ vi., vt. to combine

con•som•mé´ n. a clear broth

con´so•nance n. harmony; a pleasant blending of sound

con´sort n. a spouse or associate —**con•sort´** vi., vt. to associate with

con•sor´ti•um n. an alliance

con•spic´u•ous adj. obvious, apparent; notable

con•spir´a•cy n. a secret plan

con•spir´a•to´ri•al adj. inclined to scheming or collusion; conspiring

con•spire´ vi. to plot secretly; to work together, as of circumstances

con´sta•ble n. an officer of the law

con•sta´bu•lar•y n. the jurisdiction of a peace officer; law officers

con´stant adj. unchanging; continual; steadfast —**con´stan•cy** n.

con•ster•na´tion n. a state of confusion and distress

con•stit´u•en•cy n. a district; a body of supporters —**con•stit´u•ent** adj.

con´sti•tute´ vt. to found, establish; to make up, be the parts of

con´sti•tu´tion n. basic structure —**con•sti•tu•tion•al´i•ty** n.

con•strain´ vt. confine; restrain; to compel —**con•straint´** n.

con•strict´ vt. make smaller

con•struct´ vt. to build; piece together —**con•struc´tion** n.

con•struc´tive adj. helpful or useful

con•strue´ vt. interpret or deduce; to understand

con´sul n. a member of the diplomatic corps —**con´su•lar** adj.

con´su•late n. the offices of a consul

con•sult´ vi. to exchange

views —vt. to refer for advice or information

con•sult´ant n. one hired to analyze and advise

con•sul•ta´tion n. a meeting to inform and plan

con•sult´ing adj. advisory

con•sum´a•ble adj. subject to being expended or dissipated —n. material used up or spent by use

con•sume´ vt. to make use of; deplete, devour, or destroy

consumer goods possessions that satisfy the needs of individuals

con•sum´er•ism n. a passion for acquisition; advocacy of consumer spending; protection from false advertising or shoddy merchandise

con´sum•mate adj. perfect; skillful —vt. to complete or perfect

con•sump´tion n. use; amount used; a weeding by disease —**con•sump´tive** adj.

con´tact n. touch; interaction; one connected —vt. to touch; speak to

con•ta´gion n. the spread of disease

con•ta´gious adj. spread by contact

con•tain´ vt. to hold; have capacity; keep within limits —**con•tain´er** n.

con•tain´er•ize vt. place in standardized containers for shipment

con•tain´ment n. confinement

con•tam´i•nate´ vt. to pollute; make impure —**con•tam´i•nant** n.

con•temn´ vt. view with contempt

con´tem•plate vt. study or

ponder; to consider —**con´tem•pla´tion** n.

con•tem´pla•tive adj. thoughtful; reflective

con•tem´po•rar´y adj. current —n. a peer —**con•tem´po•ra´ne•ous** adj.

con•tempt´ n. disdain; disrespect —**con•tempt´i•ble** adj.

con•temp´tu•ous adj. disdainful

con•tend´ vi. compete; dispute —vt. claim to be true —**con•tend´er** n.

con•tent´ adj. satisfied —n. satisfaction —**con´tent** n. all within

con•tent´ed adj satisfied —**con•tent´ed•ly** adv.

con•ten´tion n. an argument or dispute; an assertion

con•ten´tious adj. quarrelsome

con•ter´mi•nous adj. neighboring; adjoining

con´test n. competition —**con•test´** vt. to dispute; compete

con•tes´tant n. one who disputes, as a will; one who competes

con´text n. setting; background

con•tig´u•ous adj. touching; adjacent —**con•tig´u•ous•ly** adv.

con•ti´nence n. moderation; self-restraint —**con´ti•nent** adj.

con´ti•nent n. a major land mass

continental drift the gradual shifting of land mass

con•tin´gence n. contact; adjacency

con•tin´gen•cy n. possibility or liklihood; that happens by chance

con•tin´gent adj. by chance; unpredictable —n. a contingency; a representative group

con•tin´u•al adj. repeated

con•tin´u•a´tion n. restarting after a pause; a thing added, an extension

con•tin´ue vi. to endure, remain —vt. persist; remain; to resume after interruption —**con•tin´u•ance** n.

con•tin•u´i•ty n. being continuous

con•tin´u•ous adj. unbroken; connected; without interruption

con•tort´ vt. to twist; distort —**con•tort´ed** adj. twisted; misshapen; deformed

con•tor´tion n. abnormal twisting

con´tra•band´ adj. of prohibited goods —n. illegal merchandise

con´tract n. an agreement —vi., vt enter into agreement —**con•tract´** vt. to acquire; to shorten

con•trac´tu•al adj. pertaining to or implying agreement

con•trac´tor n. party to a contract

con´tra•dict´ vt. to oppose; be inconsistent —**con´tra•dic´tion** n.

con´trail n. a condensed vapor trail

con•trap´tion n. a contrivance; a makeshift device

con•tra•ri´e•ty n; dissension or opposition; inconsistency

con´trar•y adj. opposing; disagreeable —**con´trar•i•ness** n.

con´trast n. difference —**con•trast´** vi. show difference —vt. to set off

con•tra•vene' *vt.* to oppose; to contradict; to interfere or infringe upon

con•tri'bute *vi.*, *at.* give; submit for publication **-con'tri•bu'tion** *n.*

con•trite' *adj.* feeling regret —**con•trite'mess, con•tri'tion** *n.*

con•triv'ance *n.* a thing created

con•trive' *vt.* to devise or scheme

con•trol' *n.* power or authority, a device that regulates —*vt.* regulate or restrain —**con•trol'la•ble** *adj.*

con•trol'ler *n.* an executive responsible for financial control; a device that regulates

con•tro•ver'sial *adj.* subject to debate or disagreement

con'tro•ver•sy *n.* a dispute

con'tro•vert *vt.* to dispute; to contradict —**con•tro•vert'i•ble** *adj.*

con•tu•ma'cious *adj.* disobedient

con•tu•me•ly *n.* rudeness; insolence

con•tuse' *vt.* to injure; to bruise

con•tu'sion *n.* a bruise

co•nun'drum *n.* an enigma; a puzzle

con•va•lesce' *vi.* to recover; to regain health —**con•va•les'cence** *n.*

con•va•les'cent *adj.* regaining health —*n.* one who is recovering

con•vene' *vi.*, *vt.* to assemble

con•ven'ient *adj.* accessible; suited —**con•ven'ience** *n.*

con'vent *n.* a religious community

con•ven'tion *n.* a gathering; that generally accepted

con•ven'tion•al *adj.* customary; adhering to tradition; not unusual

con•verge' *vi.* to approach a common point; to grow closer —**con•ver'gence** *n.* —**con•ver'gent** *adj.*

con•ver'sant *adj.* familiar or knowledgeable —**con•ver'sance** *n.*

con•ver•sa'tion *n.* verbal exchange

con•verse' *vi.* to speak familiarly —**con'verse** *adj.* reversed; transposed -*n.* interchanged; opposite

con•ver'sion *n.* a change —**con•vert'** *vt.*

con•vert'i•ble *adj.* fitted for change —*n.* a thing designed for change

con•vey' *vt.* transport; make known

con•vey'ance *n.* a means for moving passengers or freight; transfer of property; a deed

conveyor belt a band that moves goods, as in a manufacturing plant

con•vict' *n.* one found guilty of a crime; one serving a sentence —**con•vict'** *vt.* find guilty, condemn

con•vince' *vt.* to persuade

con•viv'i•al *adj.* congenial; gregarious —**con•viv•i•al'i•ty** *n.*

con•vo•ca'tion *n.* a congregation; a formal gathering

con•voke' *vt.* call a meeting

con•vo•lute' *vt.* form in a spiral; to twist or intertwine

con'vo•lut'ed *adj.* complicated; intricate or twisted

con'voy *n.* (*Brit.*) a company of travelers; a file of vehicles

con•vulse´ of. to shake violently

convul´sion n. uncontollable muscle spasms; a severe disturbance —**con•vul´sive** adj.

cook n. one who prepares food —vi. act as cook; be changed by exposure to heat —vt. to prepare food for eating —**cook the books** to prepare false financial records —**cook up** to devise or concoct

cook´book n. a book of instrucnans for the prepnrn lion of food

cook´er n. a device designed for a particular type of cooking —**pressure cooker** a put that cooks using steam pressure; a job where one works under extreme pressure

cook´e•ry n. art of food preparation

cook´ie (US) n. a small cake-like confection

cookie cutter a device for shaping cookies —**cookie-cutter** a project that has been precisely planned

cook´ware n. containers and implements for processing food

cool adj. more cold than hot; calm, collected; indifferent; discourteous —**cool´ly** adv. —**cool´ness** n.

cool box (Brit.) a cold storage unit

cool´er¹ (Brit.) n. a detention cell

cool´er² (US) n. a cold storage unit; a wine cocktail

cool-head´ed adj. disposed to remain calm or composed

coop n. a small cage —vt. to confine -**flew the coop** escaped

coop´er n. one who makes barrels

coop´er•age n. the making of barrels; barrels and casks collectively; the charge for making barrels

co•op´er•ate´ vi. to work together; to comply —**co•op´er•a´tion** n.

co•op´er•a•tive adj. working with others; of a communal organization —n. an association operated for the benefit of its members

cop n. a law officer —vt. to seize; to steal —**cop out** to give up

co•pa•cet´ic adj. fine, acceptable; peaceful

cope vi. to face and deal with

cop´i•er n. one who imitates; a duplicating machine

coping saw a hand saw with a very thin blade to cut decorative pieces

co´pi•ous adj. abundant; abounding in thoughts or words

cop´y n. reproduction; a manuscript; text —vt. to imitate; reproduce

cop´y•cat n. one who imitates

cord n.a light rope (US) anything like a rope, as an electrical cord; a measure of cut firewood

cord´age n. rope; an amount of wood

cor´date´ adj. heart-shaped

cor´dial adj. friendly —**cor•dial´i•ty** n. —**cor´dial•ly** adv.

cord´ite n. an explosive

cord´less adj. battery-operated; requiring no cord

core n. the innermost part

—*vt.* remove the inner part from fruit

cork *n.* bark of the cork tree; anything made of or like cork —*vt.* to stop a bottle

cork´age *n.* a charge for serving

cork´board *n.* a wall panel

corn *n.* (*Brit.*) wheat or oats; (*US*) the edible seed of the corn plant; a hard seed, as a *peppercorn*; trite humor: a painful growth on the foot —*vt.* to preserve with salt

corn bread bread made of cornmeal

cor´ner *n.* an angle formed by two lines or surfaces -*adj.* at or near a corner —*vt.* to trap —**around the corner** in the near future —**cut corners** compromise quality, etc. —**turn the corner** survive a crisis

cor´nerstone *n.* a basic element; a foundation stone

cor•net´ *n.* a brass wind instrument; paper or pastry formed into a cone and filled with a confection

corn flour (*Brit.*) *n.* a starch extracted from corn, used in cooking

cor´nice *n.* projected molding at the top of a building or a window

corn meal ground corn

corn´row *n.* a hairstyle pattern

corn´starch (*US*) *n.* a starch extracted from corn, used in cooking

cor´nu•co´pi•a *n.* a horn filled with fruits, etc.; a conical container

corn´y *adj.* trite; hackneyed

cor•o•nar•y *adj.* regarding arteries for blood feedin the

heart muscle; pertaining to the heart —*n.* coronary artery; coronary thrombosis

coronary bypass shunting of blood around a damaged artery

coronary occlusion coronary thrombosis

coronary thrombosis obstruction of a coronary artery

cor´o•na´tion *n.* a ceremony for the crowning of a monarch

cor´o•ner *n.* a public official who inquires into any unnatural death

cor•o•net´ *n.* a small crown

cor´po•ral *adj.* of the body -*n.* a non-commissioned officer

cor´po•rate *adj.* of a corporation

corporate raider one who seeks to gain control of a corporation

cor´po•ra´tion *n.* a legal entity authorized to act as one individual

cor•po´re•al *adj.* material; tangible

corps *pl. n.* people acting together

corpse (*Brit.*) *n.* a dead body

cor´pu•lent *adj.* excessively fat —**cor´pu•lence** *n.*

cor´pus *n, pl.* **cor´por•a** the main part of a fleshly structure; a comprehensive collection of writing

cor´pus de•lic´ti substantial proof of a crime; body of a murder victim

cor•ral´ *n.* an enclosure for livestock —*vt.* to surround and capture

cor•rect´ *adj.* accurate; proper, suitable —*vt.* to

make right; to adjust

cor•rec´tion n. the process of making right; an amount adjusted

cor´re•late´ vt. establish a relationship —**cor´re•la´tion** n.

cor•rel´a´tive adj. related, corresponding

cor•re•spond´ vi. be similar; conform; communicate by letter —**cor•re•spon´dence** n.

correspondence school instruction by mail

cor´ri•dor n. a long passageway

cor´ri•gi•ble adj. able to be reformed

cor•rob´o•rate´ vt. to support or strengthen —**cor•rob´o•ra´tive** adj.

cor•rode´ vt. destroy gradually —**cor•ro´sion** n. —**corro´sive** adj.

cor•rupt´ adj. immoral; altered —vt. pervert, debase; alter, contaminate —**cor•rupt´i•ble** adj. —**cor•rupt´tion, cor•rupt´ness** n.

cor•rup´tive adj. tending to corrupt

cor•sage´ n. a small flower arrangement worn on a dress or the wrist

cor´sair n. a buccaneer, a pirate

cor•tege´, cor•tége´ n. attendants

cor´tex n. outer layer of an organ

cor•us•cate´ vi. to give off flashes; to sparkle, glitter —**cor•us•ca´tion** n.

co´sign vi., vt. share responsibility —**co•sig´na•to•ry** adj.

cos•met´ic adj. improving

appearance; superficial improvement —n. a preparation to improve one's appearance —**cos•met´i•cal•ly** adv.

cos•me•tol´o•gy n. the art of selecting and applying cosmetics

cos´mic adj. of the universe; of immense proportions

cosmic dust minute space particles

cos•mog´o•ny n. theories of creation

cos•mog´ra•phy n. study of the configuration of the universe —**cos•mog´ra•pher** n.

cos•mol´o•gy n. study of the nature of the universe —**cos•mol´o•ger** n.

cos´mo•naut n. an astronaut

cos´mo•pol´i•tan adj. common to the entire world; worldly —n. an urbane or sophisticated person

cos´mos n. universal order

cost n. price; value of a thing; expense of producing or obtaining

cost´-ef•fec´tive adj. worth the expenditure

cost´ly adj. expensive; splendid —**cost´li•ness** n.

cost of living expense of necessities

cos´tume n. typical mode of dress; appropriate clothing

costume jewelry fake jewelry

cot n. a small, folding bed

co´te•rie n. a close circle of friends

co•til´lion It a forrnal dance

cot´tage n. a simple house

cottage industry a small business

cot´ton n. soft hairs from a tropical plant, used for thread or cloth

cotton candy (US), **cotton floss** (Brit.) a confection of spun sugar

cot·ton·seed n. seed from the cotton plant, a source of cooking oil

cot'ton·tail n. a rabbit

couch n. (US) a sofa —vt. to recline; to express in a particular way

cough n. clearing of the lungs —vi. to expel air suddenly and noisily

coun'cil n. an officially elected or appointed group —coun'ci·lor n.

coun'sel n. advice; guidance; a legal adviser —vi., vt. to give advice

count vi., vt. number in order

count'down n. the final check or preparation before an event

coun'te·nance n. appearance —vt. express approval

count'er adj. opposing —adv. —vi., vt. to react or respond

count'er n. a device for counting; a flat working surface

coun'ter·act vt. to mitigate — **coun·ter·ac'tive** adj.

coun'ter·at·tack n. a move to blunt an attack —vi., vt. retaliation

coun'ter·bal'ance n. an element that counteracts another

coun'ter·claim n. an opposing assertion

coun'ter·cul·ture n. a lifestyle that opposes traditional values

coun'ter·feit adj. forged; fraudulent —n. an imitation —vt. copy with intent to defraud; to fake —vi. to practice deception

coun'ter·mand vt. to cancel or reverse a previous order

coun'ter·meas·ure n. an action in opposition to another

coun'ter·pane n. a bedspread

coun'ter·part n. an opposite member; a complement

coun'ter·point n. a thing that interacts with another; a musical form

coun·ter·pro·duc'tive adj. opposite of that intended; detrimental

coun·ter·rev·o·lu'tion n. opposition to reform

coun'ter·sign' n. authentication; a secret sign or signal —vt. authenticate by signing

coun'ter·weight n. a balance

coun'tess n. a woman of noble birth

count'less adj. innumerable

coun·tri·fied adj. characteristic of a farmer or small-town dweller

coun'try n. area of a nation or state; a rural area —adj. of a rural area

country club a facility for socializing, sports, etc.

coun'try·man a. another citizen

country music a musical style indigenous to the southern U.S.

country rock combination of country music with rock and roll

coun'try·side n. view of a rural area

coun'ty n. an administrative subdivision

county fair a festival featuring products from a county

county seat location of the government of a county

coup n. a splendid achievement

coup d´etat overthrow of a government

cou•pé´ n. (Brit.) a half compartment at the end of a railway car

coupe n. a two-door automobile

cou´ple n. a pair; two united socially; something that links —vt. to link —**coup´ler** n. —**coup´ling** n.

cou´pon n. entitlement to a benefit; a form of transmittal

cour´age n. ability to face danger or adversity with confidence

cou•ra´geous adj. brave; fearless —**cou•ra´geous•ly** adv.

cour´i•er n. a messenger

course n. direction or route; method of action; a program of study —vi., vt. to race; move swiftly; dash

court n. an open area; play area for certain games; a forum of justice; royal households —vt. to supplicate or flatter for benefit

cour•te•ous adj. considerate; well-mannered —**cour´te•ous•ly** adv.

cour´te•san n. a prostitute; mistress

cour´te•sy n. politeness; an act of consideration

court´house n. home of a court

court´ly adj. dignified; elegant —**court´li•ness** n.

court of appeals a court for review of the decisions of a lower court

court of law a judicial forum

court´room n. room in which legal proceedings are conducted

court´ship n. process to gain the approval of another; a wooing

court´yard n. an open space in the center of a large building

cous´in n. a relative of the same generation who is not a sibling

cou•ture´ n. the designing of women's clothing; high-fashion clothing —**cou•tu´rier** n.

cove n. a small sheltered bay; a recess in a wall

cov´en n. an assembly of witches

cov•e•nant n. a binding agreement; a formal contract

cov´er n. thing that shields or shelters —vt. to place over

cov´er•all n. a loose outer garment that covers the entire body

cover charge fixed charge at a restaurant or night club

cov´er•ing n. a thing used to protect or shield

cov´er•let n. a light bed covering

cov´ert adj. hidden; disguised

cov´er-up it. action designed to hide

cov´et vi., vt. desire longingly —**cov´et•ous** adj. —**cov´e•tous•ly** adv.

cov´ey n. a small flock of birds

cow n. an adult female mammal

cow´ard n. one who lacks courage

cow´boy n. worker on a cattle ranch

cow´catch•er n. a bumper on a locomotive to fend off obstacles

cow college a college of agriculture

cow´er vi. to shrink back

cow´hand n. a cowboy

cow´hide´ n. leather from a cow

cowl n. a hood or hooded garment; a similar covering

cow´lick n. an unruly shock of hair

cowl´ing n. covering for an engine

cow´punch•er n. a cowboy

co•work´er, co-work´er n. an associate at work

cox´swain n. the helmsman of a small boat or racing shell

coy adj. shy, demur; affecting shyness; evasive —**coy´ly** adv.

coz´en vi., vt. to deceive

coz´y adj. comfortable —n. cover for a teapot —**cosy up** attempt to get in good graces —**play it cozy** act cautiously or secretively

crab n. an edible crustacean; an ill-tempered person —vi. to fish for crabs; complain

crab´by adj. grouchy; ill-humored

crack adj. first-rate —n. a sharp sound; a fracture; a sharp blow; a type of cocaine —vi., vt. produce a sharp sound; strike; split; to break down mentally —**crack the whip** press for greater output, demand strict adherence to rules

crack´down n. strict enforcement or punishment —vi. enforce strictly or punish severely

crack´er n. a thin crisp wafer; (US) a country boy — **crack´ers** (Brit.) mentally deranged

crack´er•jack adj. outstanding

crack´head n. user of crack cocaine

crack´house n. a place where crack cocaine is processed

crack´le n. the finely cracked surface of some pottery —vi. a series of snapping or cracking noises —vt. produce fine cracks on pottery

crack´pot adj. insane; eccentric —n. one who is strange or eccentric

crack´-up n. a vehicular accident; a mental breakdown

cra´dle n. a baby's bed; place of early development; a device for supporting a heavy object

craft n. art or trade; skill in deception; ships —vt. to form with skill

crafts´man n. a skilled worker; an artisan —**crafts´-man•ship** n.

craft´y adj. clever; scheming —**craft´i•ly** adv. —**craft´i•ness** n.

crag n. a rough projecting rock

crag´gy adj. rough and steep; irregular —**crag´gi•ness** n.

cram vt. compress or compact

cramp n. sudden involuntary muscular contraction —vt. to restrict

cramped adj. confined; restraining

crane n. a large wading bird; a machine for raising heavy objects

cra´ni•al adj. of the cranium

cranial nerve n. nerve at the stem of the brain

cra´ni•um n. the skull

crank n. an arm for transferring motion; an eccentric or complaining person —vi., vt. turn a handle

crank´case n. an oil reservoir

crank´shaft n. a rod that drives a crank for transfernng movement

crank´y adj. irritable; ill-tempered; testy —**crank´i•ness** n.

cran´ny n. a small opening

crap n. excrement; junk, trash; foolishness; anything useless

crap out to lose at craps; to drop out due to exhaustion, fear, etc.

crap´py adj. of inferior quality

craps pl. n. a game of dice

crap´shoot n. a risky venture

crap´u•lence n. excessive eating or drinking —**crap´u•lent** adj.

crap´u•lous adj. inclined to excessive eating or drinking; suffering from such excess —**crap´u•lous•ly** adv.

crash n. a sudden loud noise; a collision; sudden financial collapse —vi. make a loud noise; collide; fail suddenly; bed down temporarily —vt. to cause a noise or collision; to attend without invitation

crash helmet n. protective headgear

crash´-land vi., vt. end or set down in an unconventional manner

crash pad temporary living quarters

crass adj. crude; vulgar; tasteless

crate n. a box made of wood —vt. to pack

cra´ter n. a bowl-shaped depression

cra•vat´ n. a scarf worn at the neck

crave vi., vt. to long for — **crav´ing** n.

cra´ven adj. cowardly

craw n. the crop of a bird; an animal's stomach —**stick in one's craw** to displease; irritate

craw´dad, **craw´fish** n. crayfish

crawl n. slow movement; swimming stroke —vi. to move on hands and knees; move slowly or feebly

crawl space (US) space under a house for access to wiring, plumbing, etc.

cray´fish n. a small freshwater crustacean similar to a shrimp

cray´on n. colored wax for drawing

craze n. a fad —vi., vt. anger; enrage

cra´zy adj. insane; foolish; overly enthusiastic —n. one crazed

creak´y adj. squeaky —**creak´i•ly** adv. —**creak´i•ness** n.

cream n. a rich component of milk; that made from cream; the color of cream; the consistency of whipped cream; the best part —adj. containing or like cream —vt. remove cream from milk; to blend

cream cheese a soft cheese

cream´er n. a pitcher for serving cream; a nondairy product used to lighten and flavor coffee

cream puff a light filled pastry

cream sauce a smooth light sauce

cream soda a vanilla flavored drink

cream´y adj. containing cream; of the consistency of heavy cream

crease n. a mark made by folding —vt. to make or form creases in

cre•ate' vt. to originate; produce through artistic endeavor

cre•a'tion n. the act of creating, that which is created —**cre•a'tor** n.

cre•a'tion•ism n. belief in the Biblical account of the creation

cre•a'tive adj. displaying or rousing imagination or inventiveness

cre•a•tiv'i•ty n. inventiveness

crea'ture n. a living being

creature comforts those things that provide contentment for the body

cre'dence n. acceptance as true

cre•den'tial n. that attesting to one's knowledge or authority

cre•den'za n. a sideboard

credibility gap incongruity between what is said and what is done

cred'i•ble adj. plausible; believable

cred'it n. trust; approval or praise —vt. believe in; assign an attribute

credit card a line of credit for the purchase of goods or services

credit line the credit one is allowed

credit rating assessment ability and prospect for repaying obligations

cre'do n. a creed

cre•du'li•ty n. tendency to believe

cre•d'u•lous adj. inclined to believe

creed n. a statement of beliefs

creek n. (US) a stream; (Brit.) a small inlet of the sea —**up the creek** in a difficult predicament

creel n. a fisherman's bag

creep vi. move along the ground; move slowly with great stealth

creep'y adj. apprehensive; uneasy —**creep'i•ly** adv. — **creep'i•ness** n.

cre'mate' vt. to incinerate

cre•ma•to'ri•um, cre'ma•to• ry n. a place where the dead are cremated

cre'o•sote n. a wood preservative

crêpe n. a thin crinkled cloth; a thin pancake

crepe paper a thin crinkled paper

cres•cen'do adj., adv. gradu-ally increasing —n. a gradual increase

crest n. a decorative plume; a device over a coat of arms; the highest point —**crest'ed** adj.

crest'fall•en adj. saddened; shamed; disheartened

cre•ta'ceous adj. of chalk or a chalk-like substance

cre'tin n. a buffoon; one suffering from cretinism

cre'tin•ism n. a disease marked by deformity and retardation

cre•vasse' n. a deep fissure, chasm

crev'ice n. a narrow crack

crew n. a group working together

crew cut a close-cropped hair style

crew'el n. a type of embroidery

crib n. a bed for a small child; a small building or bin for storage —*vi.*, *vt.* to cheat or steal

crib·bage *n.* a card game

crick *n.* stiffness of the back or neck

crime *n.* an act in violation of the law; a disgraceful act

crim·i·nal *adj.* in the nature of a crime —*n.* one convicted of crime —**crim·i·nal·i·ty** *n.*

criminal code the body of law that deals with criminal offenses

criminal court a court that tries criminal cases

criminal law law that deals with crime and punishment for crime

crim·i·nol·o·gy *n.* study or methodical investigation of crime —**crim·i·nol·o·gist** *n.*

crimp *n.* a pleat or fold —*vt.* crumple or crinkle; form into wrinkles

crim·son *adj.*, *n.* deep red

cringe *vi.* to cower or shrink

crin·kle *vt.*, *vi.* form in wrinkles; to rustle, as paper —**crin·kly** *adj.*

crin·o·line *n.* a petticoat; a stiff cloth

crip·ple *n.* one deprived —*vt.* lose use of a limb; impair —**crip·pler** *n.*

cri·sis *n.*, *pl.* **cri·ses** a decisive or turning point; a traumatic event

crisp *adj.* brittle; clean and fresh; invigorating —*vi.*, *vt.* to make crisp —**burned to a crisp** blackened so as to be inedible; severely sunburned —**crisp·ness** *n.*

crisp·y *adj.* brittle —**crisp·i·ness** *n.*

cri·te·ri·on *n.* a basis for judging

crit·ic *n.* a reviewer of movies,

art, etc.; one who tends to faultfinding

crit·i·cal *adj.* tending to find fault; marked by careful analysis; dangerous; decisive —**crit·i·cal·ly** *adv.*

crit·i·cise (*Brit.*), **crit·i·cize** (*US*) *vi.*, *vt.* to evaluate; to find fault —**crit·i·ciam** *n.*

cri·tique *n.* a careful analysis

crit·ter *n.* a creature; a small animal

croak *n.* a deep, rough voice —*vi.*, *vt.* utter a deep, rough sound; to die

crock *n.* an earthenware pot; misleading or incorrect information

crock·er·y *n.* pottery

croc·o·dile *n.* a large amphibious reptile

crocodile tears insincerity

crois·sant *n.* a light breakfast roll

crone *n.* an old woman; a hag

cro·ny *n.* a close friend

cro·ny·ism *n.* favoring friends or supporters

crook *n.* a device with a curved end; one living by dishonest means —*vi.*, *vt.* to bend

crook·ed *adj.* bent; dishonest

croon *vi.*, *vt.* sing in a low, soft tone

crop *n.* agricultural products; amount harvested; a thing cut short —*vt.* to trim; cut or clip —**crop up** appear suddenly or unexpectedly

crop duster a small airplane that sprays insecticide or fungicide

crop·per *n.* one who farms on shares, a sharecropper; a bad experience; a failed venture

crop rotation changing crops

each year to avoid depleting the soil

cro•quet´ *n.* a lawn game

cro•quette´ *n.* a deep-fried cake of chopped meat or seafood

cross *adj.* angry; cranky —*n.* an intersecting horizontal and vertical line; a burden, affliction; a hybrid —*vt.* intersect; travel or reach over; oppose —**cross a palm** pay a bribe

cross´beam *n.* a structural member

cross´bow *n.* a medieval weapon

cross´breed *n.* a hybrid —*vi.*, *vt.* to produce a hybrid —**cross´bred** *adj.*

cross´check *vi., vt.* to verify

cross´-coun•try *adj., adv.* across a land; through rugged country

cross´cur•rent *n.* a flow of water across the main current; influence contrary to the main thrust

cross-ex•am•i•na´tion *n.* a careful questioning, especially to refute

cross´-eyed *adj.* marked by uncoordinated eye movements

cross´-fer•ti•li•za´tion *n.* breeding with a different line

cross´hatch•ing *n.* a pattern of crossing parallel lines

cross´ing *n.* a place for moving from one side to the other; place where two ways cross: an intersection

cross´ly *adv.* in a grouchy manner

cross´-pol´li•nate *vi., vt.* to transfer pollen from one species to another

cross´-ref•er•ence *n.* tribute

to another source —*vt.* refer to another mention; prepare a reference to other sources

cross´road *n.* intersection of roads; an important time or incident

crotch *n.* an intersection; the area where the legs meet at the trunk

crotch´et *n.* odd or whimsical notion

crouch *vi.* to bend low with limbs drawn close; to cower in fear

crou´pi•er *n.* one who operates a casino gambling table

crou´ton *n.* a small piece of crisp bread garnish for soup or salad

crow´bar *n.* a metal prying tool

crowd *n.* a group gathered in one place; people with something in common —*vi.*, *vt.* squeeze or push —**city hall crowd** local politicians

crown *n.* a symbol of sovereignty; power or office of a monarch; symbol of distinction —*vt.* confer with a crown; be the highest part; bring to successful completion

crow's´-feet *n.* a pattern of lines around the corner of the eyes

crow's´-nest *n.* a high platform

cru´cial *adj.* extremely :uplift-cant; decisive —**cru´cial•ly** *adv.*

cru´ci•fy´ *vt.* put to death on a cross; to treat cruelly

crud *n.* gunk; a worthless or nasty thing

crude *adj.* unrefined or raw; lacking manners or tact —**crude´ly** *adv.*

cru´el *adj.* inclined to inflict; barbarous; pleasure taken in suffering; heartless — **cru´el·ly** *adv.*

cru´et *n.* a narrow mouth jar

cruise *n.* a pleasure voyage — *vi.* travel about for pleasure

crul´ler *n.* a cake fried in melted fat

crumb *n.* a piece or fragment

crum´ble *vi., vt.* to break into fragments; collapse or disintegrate

crum´bly *adj.* easily broken to small pieces; consisting of fragments; dilapidated, fallen in

crum´my *adj.* cheap; shoddy; shabby

crum´pet *n.* a small batter cake baked on a griddle

crum´ple *vi., vt.* to crush; collapse

crunch *n.* a difficult situation — *vi., vt.* to grind with a crackling sound

cru·sade´ *n.* a broad campaign — *vi.* participate in a campaign

crush *n.* a crowding; passing infatuation; fruit drink — *vt.* to press so as to bruise or break; to crowd; to subdue

crust *n.* a hard surface; insolence — *vi., vt.* cover with a crisp surface

crust´y *adj.* brusque, uncivil — **crust´i·ness** *n.*

crutch *n.* an aid or support

crux *n.* a decisive factor; the heart of a matter

cry *n.* a scream or shout; weeping — *vi.* scream or shout; weep — *vt.* to plead or beg — **a far cry** very different than expected

cry´ba·by *n.* one who complains

cry·o·gen´ics *pl. n.* the science of creation and effects of low temperature — **cry·o·gen´ic** *adj.*

crypt *n.* an underground chamber

crypt·a·nal´y·sis *n.* the science of deciphering codes

cryp´tic *adj.* enigmatic; having hidden meaning

cryp´to·gram *n.* a coded message

cryp´to·graph *n.* a means for writing or deciphering coded messages — **cryp·tog´ra·pher** *n,*

crys´tal *adj.* of glass or certain minerals; tranparent — *n.* a high-quality glass; geometric particles of a mineral; glass covering a watch

crystal-clear easily understood

crys´tal·line *adj.* like or of crystal

crys´tal·ize *vi., vt.* form or cause to form a crystal; bring to permanent form — **crys·tal·li·za´tion** *n.*

cub´by·hole *n.* a small compartment

cube *n.* a solid form with six square faces; the third power of a number — *vt.* to raise to the third power — **cu´bic** *adj.*

cube steak beef tenderized by a pattern of cross cuts

cu·bi·cle *n.* a small enclosure

cub´ism *n.* an abstract art syle using geometric patterns — **cub´ist** *n.*

cuck´old *n.* a man whose wife has been unfaithful — **cuck´old·ry** *n.*

cud *n.* food regurgitated from the stomach of a ruminating animal

cud´dle *n.* an embrace —*vi.,
vt.* to embrace

cud´dly *adj.* affectionate; lov-
able; appealing —**cud´dle•
some** *adj.*

cudg´el *n.* a heavy stick; a
club

cue *n.* a signal or hint —*vt.* to
signal

cue ball an unmarked ball
struck with the cue in pool
or billiards

cuff *n.* a slap; the end of a
sleeve; (US) turned up material at the end of a trouser
leg —*vt.* to slap

cui•sine´ *n.* a particular style
of food

cul´-de-sac´ *n.* a street with
a single outlet and a turn-
about at the end

cu´li•nar´y *adj.* of cooking

cull *n.* something selected for
removal —*vt.* to select

cul´mi•nate´ *vi., vt.* to come
or bring to completion —**cul•
mi•na´tion** *n.*

cul´pa•ble *adj.* deserving
blame —**cul•pa•bil´i•ty** *n.* —
cul´pa•bly *adv.*

cul´prit *n.* one accused or
guilty

cult *n.* a extremist group considered to be or obsessive in
their beliefs

cul´ti•vate´ *vt.* to tend crops;
to promote or nurture

cul´tu•ral *adj.* of a particular
culture

cul´ture *n.* the characteristics
of a society; enlightenment,
refinement

cultured pearl a pearl grown
from an implanted irritant

culture shock disorientation
from exposure to the unfamiliar

cul´vert *n.* a conduit or drain

passing under a road, path,
etc.

cum´ber•some *adj.* unwieldy;
difficult to maneuver; bulky;
awkward

cu´mu•late *vi., vt.* to collect;
to accumulate —**cu´mu•la•
tive** *adj.*

cu•mu•lo•nim´bus *n.* a cloud
structure associated with
storms

cu´mu•lus *n.* a tall cloud
structure with a dark, flat,
moisture-laden base —**cu´
mu•lous** *adj.*

cu•ne´i•form *adj.* wedge-
shaped, as of certain ancient
writing —*n.*

can´ning *adj.* sly, crafty —*n.*
skillful at deceiving

cup *n.* an open container for
serving beverages; a measure of 8 ounces

cup´board *n.* storage for dinnerware

cup´cake (US) *n.* a small cake

cup´ful *adj.* amount a cup
can hold

cu•pid´i•ty *n.* avarice; greed

cu´po•la *n.* a domed ceiling; a
small domed structure on a
roof

cur *n.* a dog; a vile person

cu´rate *n.* a clergyman who
assists

cu´ra•tor *n.* a custodian

curb *n.* a checking; hindrance;
(US) a curbstone —*vt.* to
subdue; check

curd *n.* coagulated milk

cur´dle *vi., vt.* to turn into
curd; to coagulate

cu´ra•tor *n.* an overseer

cure *n.* an agent that restores
health —*vt.* effect recovery;
preserve food —**cur´a•tive**
adj., n.

cure´-all *n.* universal remedy

cur´few n. a time limit

cu´ri·os´i·ty n. a desire to learn; a rare or unusual artifact

cu´ri·ous adj. eager to learn; inquisitive; unusual

cur´li·cue n. an ornate curve

curl´y adj. having waves or ringlets; inclined to curl — **curl´i·ness** n.

cur´mudg´eon n. an ill-tempered or disparaging person

cur´ren·cy n. paper money

cur´rent adj. of the present — n. a general tendency or movement

current account (Brit.) deposit of funds for transfer by cheque

cur·ric´u·lum n. a course of study; studies offered by a school

cur´ry n. a piquant blend of spices; a dish or sauce prepared with curry — vt. to groom a horse

cur´sive adj. connected handwriting

cur´so·ry adj. hastily done; casual

curt adj. short, concise; brusque

cur´tail´ vt. cut short; reduce; to lessen — **cur´tail´ment** n.

cur´tain n. hanging material; something that covers or obscures — vt. to cover, as with a curtain

curtain call a performer's return to the stage to acknowledge applause

curtain raiser a brief entertainment before the main show

curt´sy n. a bow — vi. to make a bow

cur·va´ceous adj. of an attractive figure

cur·va´ture n. a curved part

curve n. a smooth deviation — vi., vt. to deviate from the straight

cush´y adj. easy, as a cushy job

cusp n. a projection; intersection of two lines — **cus´pi·date** adj.

cus´pid n. a tooth with a single point

cuss n. a person or animal — vi., vt. to curse

cus´tard n. a thick, creamy dessert

cus·to´di·an n. a caretaker — **cus·to´di·al** adj.

cus´to·dy n. care and protection

cus´tom adj. made to order — n. common practice; tradition

cus´tom·ar·y adj. usual; according to custom — **cus´tom·ar´i·ly** adv.

cus´tom-built´ adj. made to order

cus´tom·er n. a patron

cus´tom·house n. a clearing house for imports and exports

cus´tom·ize vt. alter to suit

cus´tom-made adj. custombuilt

cut n. incision; reduction; a sharp, derogatory comment — vi. use a sharp instrument; to disparage; move quickly; to penetrate; reduce or trim; offend with a remark; pass across or through; discontinue or stop — **a cut above** significantly better — **cut and dried** a foregone conclusion; routine — **cut loose** act with abandon — **cut no ice** of no influence — **cut out for** suited to —**cut through** get to the point

cu•ta´ne•ous adj. relating to the skin

cut´back´ n. a reduction

cu´ti•cle n. outer layer of skin: the epidermis; skin around the nails

cut´ler•y n. utensils for cutting

cut´let n. a slice of meat from the rib or leg; a chopped meat patty

cut´off´ adj. of a limit —n. a shortcut; a device for shutting off flow

cut´-rate adj. reduced in price; of questionable quality

cut´throat adj. murderous; unmerciful; relentless —n. a murderer

cutting adj. sharp or piercing —n. the act of slicing; a thing cut off

cutting board a surface for cutting

cutting edge the latest innovation

cut´up n. a joker

cu•vée´ n. a particular blend of wine

cy´cle n. time for a series of events; a bicycle or motorcycle —vi. occur by turns; pass through one occurrence; ride a bicycle, etc.

cy´clic, cy´cli•cal adj. occurring in cycles

cy´clist n. a bicycle, etc. rider

cy´clone´ n. a violent, rotating windstorm; a device that separates by whirling

cy´clo•tron´ n. a particle accelerator

cyn´ic n. one who denies the sincerity of others —**cyn´i•cal** adj.

cy•tol´o•gy n. study of cells

csar n. formerly, a male monarch; one having great power

d, D fourth letter of the alphabet; 500 in Roman numerals

dab n. a small quantity —vi., vt. pat lightly

dab´ble vi. to engage in superficially

daf´fy adj. silly, ridiculous

daft adj. insane; foolish

dai´ly adj. each day —adv. every day

daily double a wager

dain´ty adj. delicate; fragile —**dain´ti•ly** adv. —**dain´ti•ness** n.

dair´y n. place for processing milk

dairy cattle cows cultivated for milk

daisy chain connected series

dal´li•ance n. flirtation

dal´ly vi. to flirt or trifle; waste time

dam n. a barrier; an obstruction —vt. to hold back; to obstruct

dam´age n. breakage; injury causing loss of value —vt. to mar or injure

dam´ages n. compensation

dam´ask n. linen fabric; rose color —adj. of damask linen; rose colored

dame n. a matron

damp adj. slightly moist —n. humidity; moisture —vt. to moisten; slow a fire by reducing air supply; to check sound waves —**damp´ish** adj. —**damp´ly** adv.

damp´en vt. to moisten; check or deaden; to lessen enthusiasm —vi. become moist

damp´er n. a valve for controlling flow

dance n. graceful, rhythmic movement —vi., vt, move to music

danc·er·cise n, rhythmic exercise set to music

dan´der n. temper; anger

dan´di·fy vt. to dress like a dude

dan´dy adj. first-rate —n. a man overly attentive to appearance

dan´ger n. a cause of injury or pain

dan´ger·ous adj. perilous; liable to injure or harm —**dan´ger·ous·ly** adv. —**dan´ger·ous·ness** n.

dan´gle vi., vt. to hang loosely

dank adj. disagreeably damp; clammy —**dank´ness** n.

dap´per adj. stylish; smartly dressed; alert, active

dare n. a challenge —vt. be bold —vt. to have courage; to challenge —**dar´ing** adj. —**dar´ing·ly** adv.

dare´dev·il adj. bold and adventurous —n, one who takes chances; —**dare´dev·il·ry, dare´dev·il·try** n.

dark adj. lacking light; dismal, gloomy; sinister; unenlightened —n, a lack of light; night —**dark´ish** n.

dark´en vi., vt. to become or make dark; become obscure or confusing —**dark´en·er** n.

dark horse unexpectedly successful

dart n. a pointed missile; sudden movement —vi., vt, move suddenly and rapidly

dash n. a hasty move; mark (-) of punctuation; a small amount —vi. to rush; to smash —vt. to thrust or smash violently; act hastily

dash´board n. panel at the front an automobile

dash´ing adj. adventurous, gallant; jaunty; stylishly elegant —**dash´ing·ly** adv.

das´tard n. a malicious or cowardly person —**das´tard·ly** adv.

da´ta n. pl., sing. **dat´um** information; facts or figures

da´ta·base n. a collection of related data

data processing n. the manipulation of data, especially by a computer

date n, a point in time; an appointment; an escort; fruit of a palm —vi. exist from a particular time; become obsolete; to escort —vt. mark the date of; arrange a meeting with

date´book n. an appointment book

dat´ed adj. marked with a date; from a previous time; out of style

daub vi., vt. apply crudely

daugh´ter n. female offspring

daugh´ter-in-law n. a son's wife

daunt vt. discourage

daunt´less adj. daring; heroic; not to be discouraged

dav´en·port n. (Brit.) a type of desk; (US) a sofa

daw´dle vi., vt. to waste time

dawn a. the start of day; a beginning —vi. to begin

day n. daylight hours, sunrise to sunset; a 24-hour span; an era

day´bed n. a lounge used for a bed

day´book n. a daily journal

day´break n. dawn

day camp a camp that does not provide overnight accommodations

day care tending of children; a facility where children are tended

day´dream n. a fantasy —vi. to be lost to reverie

day´light n. sunlight

day nursery day care facility

day one the start of a venture

day room a recreation room

day shift the working hours from early morning until late afternoon

day´time n. sunrise to sunset

day´-to-day´ adj. regular; routine

daze n. a stupor; bewilderment —vt. to stun; bewilder —daz´ed•ly adv.

daz´zle vi., vt. to blind temporarily; to amaze —daz´zling•ly adv.

dea´con, dea´con•ess n. a lay officer in a church; a minister's assistant

de•ac´ti•vate vt. make inoperable or ineffective; to release from service

dead adj. lacking life; lacking vitality or brilliance; dispassionate; numb; ancient or out of date; no longer useful; absolute; dead on; exhausted —dead´ness n.

dead´beat adj. an idler; one who doesn't repay debts

dead´bolt n. a latch

dead center at the exact center

dead´en vt. anesthetize; to reduce

dead´end a road without an outlet; an unprofitable venture —dead´-end´ adj. lacking means for continuation or advancement

dead´fall n. a snare; a fallen tree and the debris it carries

dead´head n. operating without cargo or passengers; dull or stupid person —vi. travel without cargo

dead heat a tie or stalemate

dead letter undeliverable mail

dead´line n. time established for completion

dead´lock n. a stalemate

dead´ly adj. apt to cause injury or death; lethal; extremely effective —dead´li•ness n.

dead´pan adj., adv. without expression —n. a blank look

dead reckoning estimating position based on experience

dead ringer a precise match

dead´wood n. something useless

deaf adj. unable to hear; unwilling to be persuaded —deaf´ness n.

deaf´en vt. make deaf; overwhelm with sound —deaf´en•ing adj.

deal n. an agreement; a business transaction; distribution —vi. take action; do business —vt. to distribute —deal´er n.

deal´er•ship n. a business authorized to market a product

dean n. an officer in a school or college; one senior or preeminent

dear adj. cherished; expensive —n. a loved one —adv. with affection; at great cost —dear´ly adv.

dearth n. a lack or scarcity

death n. the termination of life

death benefit insurance payment on the death of a policyholder

death certificate the official record of a person's death

death´less *adj.* undying; enduring —**death´less•ly** *adv.*

death´like *adj.* gaunt; pale

death´ly *adj.* ghastly; deathlike —*adv.* to a deadly extent

death´trap *n.* an unsafe place

death´watch *n.* attendance at the bedside of a dying person

de•ba´cle *n.* the total dissolution of order; a rout

de•bar´ *vt.* to exclude; prohibit or restrict —**de•bar´ment** *n.*

de•bark´ *vi., vt.* leave a ship or aircraft; disembark

de•base´ *vt.* lower in worth or purity; adulterate —**de•base´ment** *n.*

de•bate´ *n.* an airing of opposing views; a formal argument —*vi., vt.* discuss openly; engage in formal argumentation; consider or contemplate —**de•bat´a•ble** *adj.*

de•bauch´ *vt.* to corrupt or debase —**de•bauch´er** *n.*

de•bauch´er•y *n.* revelry; intemperance; excessive indulgence

de•ben´ture *n.* a promissory note

de•bil•i•tate´ *vt.* to drain of strength or energy —**de•bil•i•ta´tion** *n.*

de•bil´i•ty *n.* weakness; an infirmity

deb•o•naire´ *adj.* sophisticated, urbane; nonchalant, carefree

de•brief´ *vt.* to examine and instruct

dé•bris´ *n.* scattered remains; rubble

debt *n.* something owed; obligation

debt´or *n.* one who owes

de•bug´ *vt.* to correct errors or malfunctions

de•bunk´ *vt.* to expose; demystify

de•but´ *n.* a first public appearance; a beginning

deb´u•tante *n.* a young woman

dec´ade *n.* a group of ten; ten years

dec´a•dence *n.* deterioration or decline; a time of decline —**dec´a•dent** *adj.* —**dec´a•dent•ly** *adv.*

dec´a•gon *n.* a ten-sided form

dec•a•he´dron *n.* a ten-sided solid

de´cal *n.* a decorative transfer

de•cal´ci•fy *vt.* remove calcium —*vi.* to lose calcium

de•cant´ *vt.* to pour off a liquid; pour from one container to another —**de•can´ta´tion** *n.* —**de•cant´er** *n.*

de•cap´i•tate *vt.* to behead —**de•cap•i•ta´tion** *n.*

de•cath´lon *n.* an athletic competition comprising ten events

de•cay´ *n.* decomposition of organic matter; slow deterioration —*vi., vt.* decompose; deteriorate slowly

de•cease´ *vi.* to die —**de•ceased´** *adj.*

de•ceit´ *n.* a misrepresentation; a dishonest action; trickery

de•ceit´ful *adj.* marked by deception; fraudulent —**de•ceit´ful•ly** *adv.* —**de•ceit´ful•ness** *n.*

de•ceive´ *vt.* mislead by lying or trickery —*vi.* practice deceit

de•cel´er•ate *vi., vt.* reduce speed —**de•cel•er•a´tion** *n.*

de´cent *adj.* proper; respectable; conforming to public

standard; moderately good
—de**cen**•cy n.

de•cen'**tral**•ize vt. to disperse
—de•cen•tral•i•za'tion n.

de•cep'tion n. deceit; being
deceived; a misrepresentation

de•cep'tive adj. misleading;
designed to misrepresent —
de•cep'tive•ly adv. —de•
cep'tive•ness n.

de•cer'ti•fy vt. revoke

de•cide' vt. settle; bring to decision —vi. make a decision

de•cid'ed adj. certain, clearcut; without reservation; determined, resolute —de•cid'
ed•ly adv.

de•cid'u•ous adj. shed seasonally; temporary, ephemeral —de•cid'u•ous•ly adv.

dec'i•mal adj. of the number
10 —decimal system a
number system in base 10

dec'i•mate vt. to select and
kill one in ten; to destroy or
slaughter —dec•i•ma'tion n.

de•ci'pher vt. interpret the
obscure —de•ci'pher•a•ble
adj.

de•ci'sion n. a conclusion or
judgment

de•ci'sive adj. conclusive; resolving uncertainty; determined, positive; extremely
important

de•claim' vi., vt. recite dramatically; proclaim; to speak
out —vt. recite eloquently —
de•clam'a•to•ry adj.

de•clar'a•tive adj. effecting to
inform; making an assertion
—de•clar'a•tive•ly adv.

de•clare' vt. announce formally; state emphatically;
reveal or name —vi. make a
positive statement —dec'la•
ra'tion n. —de•clar'er n.

de•clen'sion n. a declining; a
slope; a deviation

dec•li•na'tion n. a slope or
descent; deviation; a courteous refusal

de•cline' n. a downward
trend; deterioration —vi. to
deteriorate; refuse politely;
slope downward —vt. refuse
to accept; cause to incline

de•cliv'i•ty n. a downward
sloping —de•cliv'i•tous adj.

de•code' vt. translate from
code

de•com•mis'sion vt. to take
out of service

de•com•pose' vt. break down
—vi. disintegrate or decay —
de•com'po•si'tion n.

de•com•press' vt. reduce
pressure; permit expansion

decompression chamber a
room with controlled air
pressure

decompression sickness a
painful, potentially fatal
condition caused by nitrogen
bubbles in the blood

de•con•tam'i•nate vt. to free
from harmful matter; to
make safe

de•cor' n. a style of decoration

dec'o•rate vt. to adorn; paint
and refurnish; plan and direct refurbishing; to honor
with a medal

dec'o•ra•tive adj. ornamental;
artistic —dec'o•ra•tive•ly
adv.

dec'o•rous adj. respectful;
demure —dec'o•rous•ly adv.

de•cor'ti•cate vt. to peel; remove an outer layer —
de•cor•ti•ca'tion n.

de•co'rum n. manners; propriety

de•cou•page' n, decorative
material mounted and

132

varnished —vt.

de·coy′ n. a thing used to mislead or lure —vi., vt. to lure, as into a trap

de·crease′ vi., vt. become gradually less or smaller — **de′crease** n. the process or lessening; the amount of reduction —**de·creas′ing·ly** adv.

de·cree′ n. an official proclamation —vt. to order —vi. issue a decree

de·crep′it adj. worn out by age or use —**de·crep′i·tude′** n.

de·cry′ vt. denounce; criticize or condemn —**de·cri′al** n.

ded′i·cate vt. to set apart, devote to a cause, etc.; open with ceremony; to pay homage —**ded·i·ca′tion** n.

ded′i·cat·ed adj. given over totally; for specific use

de·duce′ vt. conclude or infer by reasoning —**de·duc′i·ble** adj.

de·duct′ vt. to take away; subtract; conclude by reasoning; to deduce

de·duc′tion n. a subtraction; the process of reasoning; a determination —**de·duc′tive** adj.

deed n. an act; a notable achievement; document conveying interest in property —vt. to transfer by means of a legal document

deem vit., vt. to believe; to judge; to have as an opinion

de·em′pha·size vt. to reduce the importance of —**de·em′pha·sis** n.

deep adj. extending far; of a specific extent; penetrating; low in tone; abstract; earnest —**deep′ly** adv.

deep′en vi., vt. make deeper

deep′-fry vt. cook in hot grease

deep′-root·ed adj. having deep roots; firmly established

deep′-seat·ed adj. firmly established; difficult to overcome

deep space outer space

de·face′ vt. disfigure or mar; damage —**de·face′ment** n.

de fac′to Latin existing in fact

de·fame′ vt. slander or libel —**def·a·ma′tion** n. —**de·fam′a·to·ry** adj.

de·fault′ n. failure to fulfill an obligation; failure to appear —vi., vt. to fail in fulfilling

de·feat′ vt. overpower or conquer; to frustrate the efforts of another —n.

de·feat′ist n. one who expects or accepts defeat —adj. expecting misfortune

def′e·cate vi. eliminate waste from the body —vt. clear of impurities

de′fect, defect′ n. imperfection; deficiency —**de·fect′** vi. abandon a cause, etc.; join the opposition —**de·fec′tion** n. —**de·fec′tor** n.

de·fec′tive adj. imperfect or deficient —**de·fec′tive·ly** adv.

de·fence′ (Brit.) n. protection; means of protection; justification; in law, a defendant and solicitor or the arguments they present

de·fence′less (Brit.) adj. without protection; unable to defend; helpless

de·fend′ vt. to protect; justify one's actions; to contest — vi. make a defense —**de·fend′a·ble** adj.

133

de·fend´ant n. in law, one against whom an action is brought

de·fen·es·tra´tion n. the act of throwing out of a window

de·fense´ (US) n. protection; means of protection; justification; in law, a defendant and lawyer or the arguments they present

de·fense´less (US) adj. without protection; unable to defend; helpless —**de·fense´less·ly** adv.

de·fen´si·ble adj. able to be justified or defended —**de·fen´si·bly** adv.

de·fen´sive adj. resistant to criticism; recalcitrant; protective —n. prepared to resist —**de·fen´sive·ly** adv. —**de·fen´sive·ness** n.

de·fer´ vi., vt. to postpone; procrastinate; yield in deference to another —**defer´ra·ble** adj.

def´er·ence n. courteous regard

def´er·ent, def´er·en´tial adj. respectful; polite; obedient

de·fi´ance n. bold resistance; disposition to challenge —**de·fi´ant** adj.

de·fi´cience, de·fi´cien·cy n. a lack; something lacking

de·fi´cient adj. lacking; defective

def´i·cit n. a shortage

deficit financing borrowing to cover expenditures

deficit spending paying out in excess of income

de·file´ vt. corrupt or debase; pollute; profane —**de·file´ment** n.

de·fine´ vt. give precise value or meaning; describe, specify a limit —**de·fin´a·ble** adj.

def´i·nite adj. having exact limits; clear; positive —**def´i·nite·ly** adv.

def·i·ni´tion n. a statement of limits or meaning; clearly outlined

de·fin´i·tive adj. conclusive; precise; authoritative or accurate

de·flate´ vi., vt. collapse by release of gas; make smaller or less; to dishearten

de·flect´ vi., vt. turn aside —**de·flec´tion** n.

de·fo´li·ant n. chemical that causes a plant to shed—**de·fo·li·a´tion** n.

de·for´est vt. to clear of trees —**de·for·est·a´tion** n.

de·form´ vt. damage the appearance of; disfigure —vi. become disfigured —**de·for·ma´tion** n.

de·formed´ adj. misshapen or disfigured —**de·for´mi·ty** n.

de·fraud´ vt. take by deceit; swindle

de·fray´ vt. bear the expense of

de·frost´ vt. remove frost; to thaw

deft adj. skillful; dexterous -**deft´ly** adv. —**deft´ness** n.

de·funct´ adj. no longer existing; dead

de·fy´ vt. openly resist; baffle

de·gen´er·ate adj. morally depraved; deteriorated —n. one depraved or corrupted —vi. decline in quality

de·gen·er·a´tion n. worsening; progressive deterioration

de·grad´a·ble adj. that can be reduced chemically

de·grade´ vt. disgrace or debase; to reduce; erode —vi. to degenerate

134

de·grad·ed *adj.* reduced in rank, quality, etc.; corrupted or debased

de·grad·ing *adj.* debasing; humiliating —**de·grad·ing·ly** *adv.*

de·gree´ *n.* relative ranking; unit on a scale —**by degrees** little by little —**to a degree** somewhat

de·hu·man·ize *vt.* strip of human attributes; to make mechanical

de·hu·mid´i·fi·er *n.* a device that removes moisture from the air

de·hy´drate´ *vi.* to lose water —*vt.* to remove or deprive of water

de·ice´ *vt.*, *vi.* to remove ice; to prevent ice from forming

de´i·fy *vt.* to exalt, idealize; to worship —**de·i·fi·ca´tion** *n.*

de´ism *n.* belief in a supreme being not involved in the world

de´i·ty *n.* a god; a divinity

de·ject´ *vt.* to make unhappy; to depress —**de·jec´tion** *n.*

de·ject´ed *adj.* dispirited; depressed

delay´ *vt.* postpone; slow or detain —*vi.* to linger —*n.* that which causes lateness; a postponement

de´le *vt.* to take out: delete

de·lec·ta·ble *adj.* pleasing; delightful

de·lec·ta´tion *n.* delight; entertainment

del´e·gate´ *n.* one authorized to speak or act for others —*vt.* to authorize; send as a representative

de·lete´ *vt.* eliminate or erase

del·e·te´ri·ous *adj.* harmful; injurious

de·lib´er·ate *adj.* intentional; carefully planned; unhurried —*vi.*, *vt.* consider carefully

de·lib´er·a´tion *n.* careful consideration

de·lib´er·a·tive *adj.* contemplative

del´i·ca·cy *n.* beauty or refinement; frailty; requiring sensitivity: *a matter of some delicacy;* a special food

del´i·ca·te *adj.* fine or dainty; fragile; subtle; requiring or displaying tact

del·i·ca·tes´sen *n.* ready-to-eat foods; store selling these foods

de·li´cious *adj.* pleasing to the senses —**de·li·cious·ly** *adv.*

de´light *n.* a quality that pleases: charm —*vt.* give or take pleasure —*vt.* please or gratify —**de·light´ful** *adj.* —**de·light´ful·ly** *adv.*

de·lin´e·ate *vt.* depict with drawings or words —**de·lin·e·a´tion** *n.*

de·lin´quen·cy *n.* failure to perform as required; a fault or misdeed

de·lin´quent *adj.* contrary to duty or law; overdue, as an obligation —*n.* one acting contrary to duty or law

de·lir´i·ous *adj.* marked by delirium; extremely exerted

de·lir´i·um *n.* altered consciousness marked by anxiety, confusion, etc. — **de·lir´i·um tre´mens** delirium brought on by withdrawal or excessive ingestion of alcohol

de·liv´er *vt.* carry or give over to another; bring forth or produce a child; rescue —*vi.* fulfill a promise; to perform as promised

135

de·liv′er·ance n. a freeing; a pardon; redemption

de·liv′er·y n. liberation; conveyance or transference of goods; childbirth; one's speaking style

dell n. a small grove; a shady retreat

de·louse′ vt. to free of lice

del′ta n. symbol ($\triangle$) for the fourth letter of the Greek alphabet; thing shaped like a triangle; an alluvial deposit at the mouth of a river

del′toid adj. triangular —n. a triangular muscle

de·lude′ vt. to mislead or deceive

del′uge n. a great flood; heavy rainfall; a thing that overwhelms —vt. to flood; to overwhelm

de·lu′sion n. false or irrational belief —**de·lu′sion·al** adj.

de·luxe′ adj. luxurious; elegant

delve vi. search resolutely

de·mag′net·ize vt. to cancel or neutralize magnetic properties

dem′agogue n. a revolutionary; one who arouses by appeals to emotion or prejudice —**dem′a·gogu·er·y** n.

de·mand′ n. a bold request; a formal request; a claim; a need —vt. request boldly; claim as due; inquire formally; require —vi. make a demand

de·mand′ing adj. difficult, challenging; hard to please

de·mar·ca′tion n. a separation; a fixing of boundaries or limits

de·mean′ vt. to debase or humble

de·mean′or n. one's behavior or appearance

de·ment′ed adj. mentally ill

de·men′tia n. impairment of mental faculties; mental illness

dem′i·god n. one who is godlike

de·mise′ n. death; transfer of rights or authority —vt., vi. transfer or be transferred by will or abdication

dem′i·tasse n. a small cup; strong black coffee

dem′o n. a demonstration

de·mo′bi·lize vt. to disband; discharge from military service

de·moc′ra·cy n. the principle of equality, opportunity, etc. for all; control shared by the populace

dem′o·crat′ n. an advocate of government by the people

de·moc′ra·tize vt., vi. to make or become democratic

dem·o·graph′ics n. classification by age, sex, etc.

de·mog′ra·phy it. study of vital and social statistics in a population

de·mol′ish vt. tear down; destroy completely; severely damage

dem·o·li′tion n. the process of tearing down or destroying —**dem·o·li′tions** n. explosives

de′mon n. an evil being; one showing great energy or enthusiasm —**de·mon′ic** adj.

de·mo′ni·ac, de′mo·ni·a·cal adj. demon-possessed; fiendish; furious; frenzied

de′mon·ism n. belief in demons

de′mon·ol′a·try n. demon

worship

de·mon·ol´o·gy *n.* the study of demons and demonolatry

dem´on·strate´ *vt.* to prove; show in operation; make evident —*vi.* act in protest — **dem´on·stra·ble** *adj.*

de·mon´stra·tive *adj.* able to be verified; open and outgoing; openly affectionate

de·mor·al·ize´ *vt.* dishearten; cause confusion

de·mote´ *vt.* lessen in status or rank

de·mur´ *n.* a delay; an objection —*vi.* voice an objection; hesitate

de·mure´ *adj.* modest, reserved; affecting modesty

de·mur´rage *n.* compensation for delaying equipment

de·mys´ti·fy *vt.* to expose, explain

de·my·thol´o·gize *vi.* to explain away that considered mythological

den *n.* an animal's lair; a gathering place; a study or retreat

de·na´ture *vt.* change through chemical action

de·ni·a·ble *adj.* possible to dispute; that can be withheld or disowned

de·ni´al *n.* a refusal; a disavowal; unwillingness to acknowledge

de·ni´er *n.* one who denies

de·nier´ *n.* a measure of fineness

den´i·grate *vt.* cast aspersions

den´im *n.* a stout cloth

den´i·zen *n.* an inhabitant; one who frequents a particular place

de·nom·i·na´tion *n.* a designation; a unit of value; a religious group

de·nom·i·na´tion·al·ism *n.* a system of separation by classification

de·nom´i·na·tor *n.* one that names; an attribute in common; a fractional part

de·note´ *vt.* signify or indicate; serve as a symbol

de·nounce´ *vt.* openly condemn

dense *adj.* compact; thick; opaque; slow to grasp — **dense´ly** *adv.*

den´si·ty *n.* relative mass

dent *n.* an indentation; partial accomplishment —*vi.*, *vt.* to get or cause a dent

den´tal *adj.* of the teeth

den´tate *adj.* having teeth

den´ti·frice *n.* a product for cleaning the teeth

den´tist *n.* one who specializes in the care and treatment of the teeth —**den´tis·try** *n.*

den·ti´tion *n.* teething; the types and arrangement of the teeth

de´nu·date *adj.* naked; stripped of foliage —*vt.* to denude

de·nude´ *vt.* strip bare, as of foliage

de·nun´ci·ate *vt.* denounce

de·nun·ci·a´tion *n.* public condemnation —**de·nun´ci·a·tive** *adj*

de·ny´ *vt.* refuse to acknowledge

de·o´dor·ant *adj.* able to mask odors —*n.* a substance that masks or destroys odors —**de·o´dor·ize´** *vt.*

de·ox·y·ri´bo·nu·cle´ic ac´id DNA, that carries genetic code in cells

de·part´ *vi.*, *vt.* to leave

—**depart from** to deviate -
de·par´ture n.

de·part´ment n. an operating
division; a field of study; a
section in a periodical —
de·part·men´tal adj.

de·part·men´tal·ize vt. organize into separate operating units

department store a large retail establishment

de·par´ture n. a setting out;
devergence from a standard
course

de·pend´ vi. rely on; place
trust in; be contingent upon

de·pend´able adj. reliable;
trustworthy -**de·pen´d·a·bil´
i·ty** n.

de·pen´dence, de·pen´dance
n. reliance on another; faith
or trust; an addiction

de·pend´ent adj. relying on
another; contingent; subordinate; helpless —**de·pend´
ent, de·pen´dant** n.

de·per´son·al·ize vt. consider
objectively; cause loss of
distinctiveness —**de·per´
son·al·i·za´tion** n.

de·pict´ vt. to portray, to represent or describe —**de·pic´
tion** n.

dep´i·late vt. eliminate hair -
de·pil´a·to·ry adj., n.

de·plete´ vt. use completely;
lessen gradually —**de·ple´
tion** n.

de·plor´a·ble adj. tragic; distressing; unfortunate —**de·
plor´a·bly** adv.

de·plore´ vt. to condemn; to
regret

de·ploy´ vt. to position according to plan —**de·ploy´
ment** n.

de·pop·u·la´tion n. a sharp
reduction in inhabitants

deport´ vt. expel from a
country; to conduct oneself
in a particular way

de·por·ta´tion n. banishment

de·port´ment a. one's behavior

de·pos´it n. a thing placed for
safekeeping or security; a
thing left behind, as silt by a
flood —vt. to place —**de·
pos´i·to·ry** n.

dep·o·si´tion n. removal from
power; testimony taken outside court

de·pot´ n. a station; a store-
house

de·prave´ vt. to corrupt or
pervert —**de·praved´** adj. —
de·prav´i·ty n.

dep´re·cate vt. express disapproval; belittle —**dep·re·ca´
tion** n.

**dep´re·ca·tive, dep´re·ca·to·
ry** adj. tending to express
disapproval

de·pre´ci·ate´ vi. fall in value
—vt. to lessen in value; to
consider of little value —**de·
pre´ci·a·ble** adj.

de·press´ vt. lower one's
spirit; lessen in value; press
down —**de·press´ing** adj.

de·pres´sant n. an agent that
slows vital functions; a
sedative

de·pressed´ adj. pressed
down; despondent; reduced
in value, etc.

de·pres´sion n. despondency;
economic stagnation; indent

de·pres´sive adj. tending to
depress

de·prive´ vt. take from: dispossess; to keep from —**dep·
ri·va´tion** n.

de·prived´ adj. lacking necessities or opportunity; under-
privileged

dep′u•ty *n.* one acting for another; an aide or assistant; in some countries, a legislator —**dep•u•ta′tion** *n.* — **dep′u•tize** *vi., vt.*

de•rail′ *vi., vt.* cause to go off rails; cause to stop —**de•rail′ment** *n.*

de•range′ *vt.* to disorder or disturb; to make insane

de•range′ment *n.* mental illness

der′by *n.* a race; a type of felt hat

de•reg′u•late *vt.* free from government control —**de•reg•u•la′tion** *n.*

der′e•lict *adj.* abandoned; negligent or delinquent —*n.* a social outcast; a loiterer — **der•e•lic′tion** *n.*

de•ride′ *vt.* mock or ridicule

de•ri′sion *n.* ridicule; a display of scorn or contempt

de•ri′sive, de•ri′so•ry *adj.* marked by derision -**de•ri′sive•ly** *adv.*

der•i•va′tion *n.* something derived: a derivative; formation of a word

de•riv′a•tive *adj.* borrowed or learned —*n.* a thing produced from another source

de•rive′ *vt.* arrive at by reasoning; to trace to origin

der′ma *n.* the dermis —**der′mal** *adj.*

derma•ti′tis *n.* irritation of the skin

der•ma•tol′o•gy *n.* study of the skin, its diseases, and their treatment —**der•ma•tol′o•gist** *n.*

der′mis *n.* the layer of skin below the epidermis

de•rog′a•to•ry *adj.* disparaging; belittling

der′rick *n.* a machine for hoisting and moving heavy objects

der′rin•ger *n.* a small pistol

der′vish *n.* member of a Muslim sect

de•scend′ *vi., vt.* to progress downward, move from a higher level; derive from a source, as an ancestor

de•scend′ant, de•scend′ent *n.* one of particular lineage; that traced hack to art earlier form

de•scend′er *n.* the part of a typeset character below the baseline

de•scent′ *n.* a downward motion; an inclined surface; a lowering of status; a sudden onset

de•scribe′ *vt.* represent in speech or writing; draw or trace

de•scrip′tion *n.* an account that describes; a drawing or tracing

de•scrip′tive *adj.* serving to describe; illustrative —**de•scrip′tive•ly** *adv.*

de•scrip′tor *n.* identifying emblem

des′e•crate *vt.* violate that considered sacred; profane

de•sen′si•tize *vt.* benumb; make insensible by repeated exposure; protect from reaction to an antigen

des′ert *n.* a dry barren region

des•ert′ *vi., vt.* to abandon — **de•ser′tion** *n.*

de•serve′ *vi., vt.* be worthy of

de•served′ *adj.* honestly earned; justified or suitable

de•serv′ing *adj.* worthy of assistance, praise, etc.

des′ic•cate *vt.* dry thoroughly; preserve by drying —*vi.* to become dry

de·sign´ n. a detailed plan or schematic; an artistic rendering —vt to invent or devise; make a representation; have as a purpose

des´ig·nate vt. specify or appoint; to set aside for a specific purpose —**des·ig·na´tion** n.

designated driver one who abstains in order to chauffer those drinking

designated hitter in baseball, one who hits in place of the pitcher

de·sign´ed·ly adv. intentionally; deliberately

designer drug a synthetic drug

de·sign´ing adj. scheming, crafty, or treacherous — n. the art or business of making designs or patterns

de·sir´a·ble adj worth seeking or having; beneficial; pleasing or attractive —**de·sir·a·bil´i·ty** n.

de·sire´ n. a longing or craving; lust —vt. to want:; express a wish for —**de·sir´ous** adj.

de·sist´ vi. to cease; abstain from

desk n. a work station with drawers

desk´top adj. designed for use on a desk —n.

des´o·late adj. forsaken; dismal, dreary; forlorn —vt. lay waste; devastate —**des´o·la´tion** n.

de·spair´ n. loss of hope —vi. lose all hope —**de·spair´ing** adj.

des´per·ate adj. hopeless; dangerous; frantic —**des·per·a´tion** n.

des·pic´a·ble adj. detestable; deserving contempt; mean or vile

de·spise´ vt. regard with disdain; to look down on —**de·spis´al** n.

de·spite´ n. an insult; an act of spite —prep. notwithstanding

de·spond´ vi. lose hope; to become depressed or discouraged

de·spon´dent adj. suffering loss of hope; dejected —**de·spon´dence** n. —**de·spon´dent·ly** adv.

des´pot n. an absolute ruler; a tyrant —**des·pot´ic** adj.

des·sert´ n. final course of a meal

des´ti·na´tion n. the place to which someone or something is going

des´tine vt. determined for a special goal or purpose

des´ti·ny n. inevitable course

des´ti·tute´ adj. completely lacking; without means of survival

de·stroy´ vt. to ruin utterly; to make useless; to tear down or demolish

de·struc´ti·ble adj. capable of being destroyed; easily broken

de·struc´tion n. brought to ruin

de·struc´tive adj. producing destruction; tending to make ineffective —**de·struc´tive·ness** n.

des´ul·to·ry adj. lacking focus; random —**des´ul·to·ri·ness** n.

de·tach´ vt. disconnect; remove from attachment —**de·tach´a·ble** adj.

de·tached´ adj. aloof, impartial; separated

140

de•tach´ment n. separation; impartiality, indifference; a special unit

de´tail n. minute parts; a precise account; a detachment —vt. report precisely; dispatch for a purpose

de•tain´ vt. restrain or delay; hold in custody —**de•tain´ment** n.

de•tect´ vt. become aware of —**de•tect´a•ble, de•tect´i•ble** adj.

de•tec´tive n. one who investigates; one who painstakingly analyzes

de•tec´tor n. a device for discovering or disclosing

dé•tente´ n. a relaxing of tension

de•ten´tion n. custody; delay

de•ter´ vt. discourage by instilling doubt or fear

de•ter´gent adj. cleansing — n. a substance for cleansing

de•te´ri•o•rate vi., vt become worse —**de•te•ri•o•ra´tion** n.

de•ter´min•a•ble adj. able to be ascertained or established

de•ter´mi•nant n. that fixes or limits

de•ter´mi•nate adj. exactly fixed or limited; conclusive

de•ter´mi•na•tive adj. tending to influence —n. that determines

de•ter´mine vt. set bounds; render a decision; conclude after study and consideration —**de•ter´min•er** n.

de•ter´mined adj. resolved; steadfast

de•ter´min•ism n. belief that all is predetermined by other events

de•ter´rent adj. tending to cause restraint —n. a thing

that hinders; an obstacle — **de•ter´rence** n.

de•test´ vt. dislike intensely; despise; loathe —**de•tes•ta´tion** n.

de•test´a•ble adj. disgusting; abhorrent; despicable —**de•test•a•bil´i•ty** n. —**de•test´a•bly** adv.

de•throne vt. to remove from power —**de•throne•meat** n.

det´o•nate´ vi., vt. explode or cause to explode —**det•o•na´tion** n.

de•tox´i•fy vt. counteract poisonous properties; rid of effects of poison; end dependence on alcohol or narcotics —**de•tox´i•fi•ca´tion** n.

de•tract´ vt. take away or withdraw —vi. undergo removal of a valued quality or part —**de•trac´tor** n.

det´ri•ment n. damage or loss; a thing causing damage —**det´ri•ment´al** adj.

de•tri´tus n. particles or fragments of rock; disintegrated matter

de•val´u•ate, de•val´ue vt. reduce in value or significance

de•val´u•a´tion n. reduction in value

dev´as•tate vt. lay waste; overwhelm or stun —**dev•as•ta´tion** n.

de•vel´op vt. to realize potential or capability; expand or enlarge on; increase effectiveness —vi. to grow or evolve; become revealed

de•vel´oped adj. technologically advanced; seen as highly evolved; of cleared land used profitably

de•vel´op•er n. a builder or contractor; one who finances construction; chemical used in the processing of photographic film

de·vel´op·ing *adj.* in the process of building industry and economy

de·vel´op·ment *n.* a community of dwellings; an occurrence

de´vi·ant *adj.* contrasting with the usual or normal — *n.* one who does not conform to accepted standards

de´vi·ate *vi.* depart from a normal or standard course —**de´vi·a´tion** *n.*

de·vice´ *n.* anything contrived; an ornamental embellishment

dev´il *n.* an evil spirit; a wicked person; one who is mischievous —**poor devil** an unlucky person

dev´il·ment *n.* mischief

dev´il·ry, dev´il·try *n.* wickedness, sinfulness; mischief, impishness

devil's advocate one who explores the negative side of a proposition

de´vi·ous *adj.* deceptive; crafty; not direct, roundabout —**de´vi·ous·ly** *adv.* —**de´vi·ous·ness** *n.*

de·vise´ *n.* a giving of real property by will; property given; a will that bequeaths real property —*vi.*, *vt* to create or contrive; to bequeath real property

de·vis´er *n.* one who contrives

de·vi´sor *n.* one who bequeaths

de·vi´tal·ize *vt.* to weaken or enfeeble; to deprive of life

de·void´ *adj.* lacking entirely; empty

de·volve´ *vt.*, *vi.* to pass obligation to another

de·vote´ *vt.* to assign for a specific purpose; to give, as time or effort

de·vot´ed *adj.* dedicated; loving and faithful; thoughtful, solicitous

de·vo´tion *n.* affection or dedication; piety —**de·vo´tion·al** *adj.*

de·vour´ *vt.* eat or absorb completely

de·vout´ *adj.* religious; expressing devotion —**de·vout´ly** *adv.*

dew *n.* drops of moisture

dew point temperature at which moist air forms condensation

dew´y *adj.* moist; like dew; innocence —**dew´i·ness** *n.*

dew´y-eyed *adj.* innocent

dex·ter´i·ty *n.* skill —**dex´ter·ous, dex´trous** *adj.*

dex´trose *n.* sugar from starch

di·a·bol´ic, di·a·bol´i·cal *adj.* satanic; fiendish; wicked —**di·a·bol´i·cal·ly** *adv.* —**di·a·bol´i·cal·ness** *n.*

di·ab´o·lism *n.* demon worship; fiendish or wicked deeds

di·a·crit´ic *n.* pronunciation mark over or under a letter (ñ,ç,é,ü)

di·a·crit´i·cal *adj.* distinguishing; marking difference

di´a·dem *n.* a crown

di´ag·nose *vi.*, *vt* make a critical analysis —**di·ag·nos´a·ble** *adj.*

di´ag·no´sis *n.* a critical analysis —**di·ag·nos´tic** *adj.*

di´a·gram *n.* a sketch or drawing that clarifies; a chart or graph

di´al *n.* face of a clock; a rotating disk or knob; a gauge or indicator

dialling code (*Brit.*) telephone number prefix that identifies locality

di·a·lect *n.* language variations; speech characteristic of a class, trade, etc.

di·a·lec·tic *n.* examination of ideas through argumentation or deduction —**di·a·lec·ti·cal** *adj.*

di·a·logue *n.* conversation; an exchange of ideas; lines in a play; a conversational dissertation

di·al·y·sis *n.* a means for re moving impurities from the blood

di·am·e·ter *n.* distance across the center of a circle or sphere

di·a·met·ric, di·a·met·ri·cal *adj.* of a diameter; totally different or contrary —**di·a·met·ri·cal·ly** *adv.*

di·a·mond *n.* an extremely hard crystal of nearly pure carbon; a geometric form

di·aph·a·nous *adj.* extremely fine; transparent; thin and airy

di·a·phragm *n.* a membrane that serves to separate

di·a·ry *n.* a daily journal

di·a·tribe *n.* a harsh tirade; a denunciation

dice *n. pl., sing.* **die** small gaming cubes —*vt.* cut into small cubes

dic·ey *adj.* chancy; speculative

di·chot·o·my *n.* division into two; in biology, a forking

dick·er *vi.* barter; bargain

dic·tate *n.* a command; a guiding principle —*vi., vt.* to command; to speak for another to record

dic·ta·tor *n.* a ruler with unlimited power —**dic·ta·to·ri·al** *adj.*

dic·ta·tor·ship *n.* government by a dictator

dic·tion *n.* the choice of words and clarity of enunciation in speech

dic·tion·ar·y *n.* an alphabetical list of words or references

dic·tum *n., pl.* **dic·tums, dic·ta** a pronouncement

di·dac·tic, di·dac·ti·cal *adj.* instructive; inclined to sermonizing

die *vi.* to stop living; to stop running, as a motor —*n.* a metal stamp

die·-hard *adj.* stubborn —*n.* one firmly committed to a concept, etc.

di·et *n.* food and drink; special food —*vi.* limit intake of food —**di·e·tar·y, di·e·tet·ic** *adj.*

di·e·tet·ics *n.* study of diet

dif·fer *vi.* disagree; to he different

dif·fer·ence *n.* a distinctive characteristic; that differentiates one from another; a variance in quantity, quality, etc.; a disagreement

dif·fer·ent *adj.* unlike; changed; diverse —**dif·fer·ent·ly** *adv.*

dif·fer·en·tial *adj.* of a difference; able to cause varied results —*n.* a difference; a gear that alters output

dif·fer·en·ti·ate *vi.* become different —*vt.* make different; recognize a difference; display a difference

dif·fi·cult *adj.* requiring considerable effort —**dif·ficul·ty** *n.*

dif·fi·dence n. lack of confidence

dif·fi·dent adj. lacking confidence; shy; insecure — **dif·fi·dent·ly** adv.

dif·fuse´ adj. widely spread; of rambling or wordy speech — vi., vt. to disperse widely

dif·fus´er, dif·fus´or n. that diffuses, as frosted glass or a baffle

dif·fus´i·ble adj. suitable for effecting diffusion; able to be diffused

dif·fu´sion n. the spread of soft light or sound

dig vt. make a hole; uncover by careful study —n. a sarcastic remark —**dig in** get to work —**digs** living quarters

di·gest n. condensation of a literary work; a collection of works —**di·gest´** vt. to condense or summarize; convert food for absorption; to study and absorb

di·gest´ible adj. able to be digested

di·ges´tive adj. pertaining to absorption of food —n. anything that aids digestion

digestive system organs that ingest and process food, discarding waste

dig´gings pl. n. material unearthed; a place where digging takes place

dig´it n. a finger or toe; unit of a numbering system

dig´i·tal adj. discrete, having specific value; expressed in units

dig´ni·fied adj. displaying dignity; courtly or reserved

dig´ni·fy´ vt. to honor; make seem more worthy

dig´ni·tar´y n. one of high position

dig´ni·ty n. a presence that commands respect; poise; stateliness

di·gress´ vi. to stray from the subject —**di·gres´sion** n.

di·gres´sive adj. marked by rambling or departure from the subject

dike n. a river embankment

di·lap´i·date vi., vt. fall into disrepair or ruin —**di·lap·i·da´tion** n.

di·lap´i·dat·ed adj. broken down; fallen into disrepair

di·late´ vi., vt. to make or become larger; expand

di´lat·ed adj. expanded or distended

di·la´tion n. a widening or expansion; the process of dilating

di·la´tor n. that causes dilation, as a muscle or surgical instrument

dil´a·to·ry adj. intended or inclined to delay

di·lem´ma n. choice between equally unpleasant options; a serious predicament

dil·et·tan·te n. one who dabbles for personal amusement; a lover of the arts — **dil´et·tan·tish** adj.

dil´i·gent adj. industious; showing painstaking effort —**dil´i·gence** n.

dill n. a flavoring herb

dil´ly·dal·ly vi. waste time

di·lute´ adj. thinned or weakened —vt. make thinner or weaker

dim adj. faint, murky; ill defined; indistinct; not encouraging —vi., vt. to grow faint or indistinct

di·men´sion n. measure of a thing

di·min´ish vt., vi. to make or

become reduced —**di·min'·ish·a·ble** adj.

diminishing return less proportional increase as improvements or incentives are introduced

dim·i·nu'tion n. a lessening or reduction; something reduced

di·min·u'tive adj. very small; expressing small size —n. something small; a word form expeaaing small size

dim'mer n. a device for reducing the brightness of a lamp or light

dim'ple n. an indentation - vt. vi. to mark with or form dimples

din n. a loud clamor

dine vi. to eat

din'er n. one eating; (US) a small informal restaurant

di·nette' n. a small dining area; tables and chairs for a dining area

din'ghy a. a small boat

din'gy adj drab or dirty; grimy

dink'y adj. diminutive; small

din'ner n. main meal of the day; a social event featuring a large meal

dinner jacket a jacket worn on formal occasions; a tuxedo jacket

diph'thong n. a complex vowel sound

di·plo'ma n. document testifying to completion of a course of study

di·plo·ma·cy n. affairs between political entities; finesse and tact

dip'stick n. a rod for measuring liquid; a silly person

dire adj. serious; desperate; requiring immediate action

di·rect' adj. straight; of the shortest course; uninterrupted in line of descent; immediate;.absolute; sincere —vt. control or manage; point out or guide; to instruct; to aim —**di·rect·ly** adv. —**di·rect'ness** n.

di·rec'tion n. instruction; supervision; a command; the point faced —**di·rec'tion·al** adj.

di·rec'tive n. an official order —adj. serving to rule or govern

direct marketing sale of goods or services by mail or telephone

di·rec'tor n. one who supervises

di·rec·to·rate n. a board of directors; the office of a company director —**di·rec·to'ri·al** adj.

di·rec·to·ry n. an alphabetical reference; a directorate

dirge n. a mournful musical work

dir·i·gi·ble n. an airship

dirk n. a dagger

dirt adj. surfaced with earth —n. soil or earth; anything unclean; gossip or scandal; pornography

dirt-cheap extremely inexpensive

dirt'y adj. soiled; vulgar, lewd; contaminated —vi., vt. soil or stain —**dirty linen** embarrassing information —**dirty pool** unfair tactics

dis·a·ble vt. make unfit; incapacitate —**dis·a·bil'i·ty** n.

dis·a·bled adj. inoperative; incapacitated —n. one who is impaired

dis·a·buse' vt. to rid of a false notion; to clarify

dis´ad·van´tage n, a handicap; unfavorable circumstances —vt. hinder —**dis´ad·van´taged** adj.

dis·af·fect´ vt. cause estrangement, to alienate —**dis·af·fec´tion** n.

dis·a·gree´ vi. differ; quarrel; produce discomfort, as certain foods —**dis·a·gree´ment** n.

dis·a·gree´a·ble adj. unpleasant; quarrelsome

dis·al·low´ vt. refuse to permit; reject

dis·ap·pear´ vi. to pass from sight; become extinct

dis·ap·point´ vt. fail to satisfy; prevent fulfillment of expectation

dis·ap·point´ed adj. frustrated

dis·ap·point´ing adj. not meeting expectation

dis·ap·prove´ vi., vt. frown upon: to condemn —**dis·ap·prov´al** n.

dis·arm´ vt. take weapons from; to render powerless; to charm —vi. relinquish arms —**dis·arm´ing** adj. —**dis´arm´ing·ly** udv.

dis·ar´ma·ment n. reduction of military forces

dis·ar·ray´ n. state of confusion or disorder —vi. throw into confusion

dis·as·sem´ble vt. to tear down or dismantle

dis·as·so´ci·ate vt. to separate; withdraw from an alliance or relationship —**dis´as·so·ci·a´tion** n.

dis·as´ter n. great harm or distress —**dis·as´trous** adj.

dis·a·vow´ vt. to deny knowledge or responsibility —**dis·a·vow´al** adj.

dis·band´ vi. cease to function as a group —vt. to dissolve a group

dis·bar´ vt. withdraw a lawyer's right to practice —**dis·bar´ment** n.

dis·be·lieve´ vi., vt. refuse to believe; consider as false —**dis·be·lief´** n.

dis·burse´ vt. to pay out **dis·burse´ment** n.

dis·card´ n. that cast off —**dis·card´** vt. throw away; cast aside or reject

dis·cern´ vt. to perceive; differentiate —vi. recognize a difference —**dis·cern´i·ble** adj. —**dis·cern´ment** n.

dis·cern´ing adj. having good judgment; discriminating

dis·charge´ vt. unload; release from duty; fulfill an obligation; fire a weapon —**dis·charge´**, **dis´charge** n. the act of unloading, dismissing, etc.; that which is discharged

dis·ci´ple n. an active follower

dis´ci·pline n. branch of learning; formal training; self-control; acceptance of authority; punishment —vt. to train or control; to punish

dis·ci·pli·nar´i·an n. one who maintains or upholds strict discipline

dis´ci·pli·nar·y adj. of a branch of learning; punitive

dis·claim´ vt. to give up or deny a claim or connection

dis·claim´er n. denial of responsibility; relinquishing of a right

dis·close´ vt. reveal or make known —**dis·clo´sure** n.

dis·col´or vt. alter by fading or soiling —vi. become faded —**dis·col·or·a´tion** n

dis·com·bob·u·late *vt.* to embarrass, confuse

dis·com·fit *vt.* frustrate plans or aspirations; make un comfortable

dis·com·fort *rt.* physical or mental distress; uneasiness —*vt.* make uneasy —**dis·com·fort·a·ble** *adj.*

dis·com·mode *vt.* cause inconvenience —**dis·com·mo·di·ous** *adj.*

dis·con·cert *vt.* to confuse or embarrass

dis·con·cert·ed *adj.* characterized by confusion or embarrassment

dis·con·cert·ing *adj.* tending to cause confusion or embarrassment

dis·con·nect *vt.* to detach — **dis·con·nec·tion** *n.*

dis·con·nect·ed *adj.* separated; cut off; disjointed or incoherent

dis·con·so·late *adj.* dejected; inconsolable —**dis·con·so·late·ly** *adv.*

dis·con·tent *adj.* displeased —*n.* a lack of satisfaction — *vt.* to make displeased or dis satisfied

dis·con·tin·u·ance *n.* a temporary cessation; a suspension

dis·con·tin·ue *vi., vt.* to stop or end

dis·con·tin·u·ous *adj.* disordered; disconnected; irrational

dis·cord *n.* disagreement; harsh sounds —**dis·cor·dance** *n.* —**dis·cord·ant** *adj.*

dis·count *n.* a reduction or rebate —**dis·count** *vt.* sell at a reduction; reject as untrue or of little importance

dis·cour·age *vt.* advise

against; to dishearten — **dis·cour·age·ment** *n.*

dis·course *n.* conversation; lengthly treatment to writing or speech —**dis·course** *vi.* to converse; to write or speak at length

dis·cour·te·ous *adj.* impolite; rude —**dis·cour·te·ous·ly** *adv.*

dis·cour·te·sy *n.* bad manners

dis·cov·er *vt.* obtain knowledge; to detect or make known

dis·cov·er·y *n.* detection or disclosure; findings, a thing discovered

dis·cred·it *n.* damage to reputation —*vt.* cast doubt; damage a reputation — **dis·cred·it·a·ble** *adj.*

dis·creet *adj.* prudent; exercising caution —**dis·creet·ly** *adv.*

dis·crep·an·cy *n.* a variance or inconsistency

dis·crete *adj.* comprised of unconnected, distinct parts

dis·cre·tion *n.* quality of being discreet; freedom to make one's own decisions — **dis·cre·tion·ar·y** *adj.*

dis·crim·i·nate *vi., vt.* make distinction; differentiate — **dis·crim·i·na·tion** *n.*

dis·crim·i·nat·ing *adj.* discerning

dis·crim·i·na·to·ry *adj.* judgmental; discriminating

dis·cur·sive *adj.* rambling

dis·cuss *vt.* to talk or write about

dis·dain *n.* a show of contempt —*vt.* treat with contempt; deem unsuited

dis·dain·ful *adj.* showing contempt

dis•ease´ n. illness; an unsound or harmful condition —**dis•eased´** n.

dis•em•bark´ vi., vt. leave a conveyance —**dis•em•bar•ka´tion** n.

dis•em•bod´y vt. to separate from physical existence

dis•en•chant´ vt. free from delusion —**dis•en•chant´ment** n.

dis•en•cum´ber vt. relieve of burden

dis•en•fran´chise vt. deprive of right or privilege; deprive of right to vote

dis•en•tan´gle vt. unsnarl; extricate; free of confusion

dis•fa´vor n. disapproval —vt. look upon with disapproval

dis•fig´ure vt. to spoil the appearance of —**dis•fig´ure•ment** n.

dis•fran´chise vt. disenfranchise

dis•gorge´ vi., vt. discharge contents

dis•grace´ n. loss of honor; that brings dishonor —vt. bring dishonor upon; chastise publicly

dis•grun´tle vt. to make unhappy; to dissatisfy

dis•guise´ n. that used to conceal identity —vt. alter or conceal identity of; to misrepresent

dis•gust´ n. deep dislike; aversion —vt. to arouse dislike; to offend

dis•gust´ing adj. provoking disgust; nasty; distasteful, nauseating

dish n. a container for food; food prepared in a particular way —vt. to serve up

dis•ha•bille´ n. partial or incongruous dress

dis•har´mo•ny n. dissonance; discord

dis•heart´en vt. to lessen the courage, resolve, enthusiasm, etc. of

dis•heart´en•ing adj. causing loss of courage, enthusiasm, etc.

di•shev´eled, di•shev´elled adj. untidy; rumpled; disorderly —**di•shev´el** vt.

dis•hon´est adj. lacking honesty; deceitful; untrustworthy

dis•hon´or n. loss of respect, etc.; that causing lose of respect —vt. cause loss of honor; treat with disrespect; refuse to pay —**dis•hon´er•a•ble** adj.

dis´il•lu´sion vt. free from sentiment; to disappoint or disenchant —**dis•il•lu´sion•ment** n.

dis•in•clined´ adj. hesitant; reluctant

dis•in•fect´ vt. to sanitize; to sterilize

dis•in•fec´tant adj. serving to sanitize —n. substance used to sanitize

dis•in•fec´tive adj. disinfectant

dis•in•gen´u•ous adj. deceitful; insincere; crafty —**dis•in•gen´u•ous•ly** adv. —**dis•in•gen´u•ous•neas** n.

dis•in•her´it vt. deprive of a right or privilege —**dis•in•her´i•tance** n.

dis•in´te•grate vi., vt. to break into fragments —**dis•in•te•gra´tion** n.

dis•in•ter´ vt. to dig up from a grave —**dis•in•ter´ment** n.

dis•in´ter•est n. a lack of concern

dis´in´ter•est•ed adj. free of

bias; impartial; indifferent

dis•join´ vt. detach, separate
—vt. become separated

dis•joint´ vt. dismember; cut
or take apart; to separate

dis•joint´ed adj. disconnected; incoherent; rambling
—**dis•joint´ed•ly** adv.

dis•junc´tive adj. separating;
causing sharp divisions

disk n. a thin flat circular object

disk•ette´ n. a removable disk
for computer data storage

dis•like´ n. distaste or aversion —vt. look upon with
distaste

dis•lo´cate´ vt. to put out of
proper place or position

dislodge´ vt, to force from a
position

dis•loy´al adj. unfaithful —
dis•loy´al•ty n.

dis´mal adj. dreary, bleak —
dis´mal•ly adv.

dis•man´tle vt. take apart
systematically

dis•may´ n, loss of resolve —
vt. to cause loss of courage

dis•mem´ber vt. to cut up; to
mutilate

dis•miss´ vt. send away; release from employment; put
out of mind —**dis•mis´sal** n.
—**dis•miss´i•ble** adj.

dis•mis´sive adj. lack of concern

dis´o•be´di•ent adj. defiant;
insubordinate —**dis´o•be´di•ence** n.

dis´o•bey´ vi., vt. refuse to
obey

dis•or´der n. confusion or disarray; public disturbance;
illness —vt. to throw into
confusion or disarray

dis•or´der•ly adj. untidy;
lacking order; rowdy

dis•or´gan•ize vt. to cause
disorder

dis•o´ri•ent vt, confuse, bewilder

dis•own´ vt. refuse to acknowledge or accept; to
disinherit

dis•par´age vt. to discredit;
belittle —**dis•par´ag•ing** adj.

dis´pa•rate adj. dissimilar; diversified —**dis•par´ate•ly**
adv.

dis•par´i•ty n. difference

dis•pas´sion n. a lack of emotional involvment; freedom
from passion

dis•pas´sion•ate adj. free from
emotional involvement; detached

dis•patch´ n. a sending; a
message; promptness —vt.
send out; act quickly; kill

dis•pel´ vt. drive away; eliminate

dis•pen´sa•ble adj. not essential; that can be distributed

dis•pen´sa•ry n. a place for
obtaining medicines and
medical aid

dis•pen•sa´tion n. distribution; thing distributed; release or exemption

dis•pense´ vt. distribute; give
out; to administer; to absolve —**dispense with** do
without —**dis•pens´er** n.

dis•perse´ vt. scatter widely;
drive off; cause to dissipate,
as mist; separate light into
component colors —vi. be
scattered; disappear —**dis•per´sal, dis•per´sion** n.

dis•place´ vt. to move; take
the place of; remove from office —**dis•plac´a•ble** adj. —
dis•place´ment n.

dis•play´ n. a public showing
— vt, to show publicly

dis•please´ vi., vt. dissatisfy or annoy, to offend

dis•pos´a•ble adj. to be discarded after a single use

dis•pose´ vt. place in proper order; settle; adjust so as to be receptive

dis•po•si´tion n. one's temperament; a final settlement

dis•pos•sess´ vt. deprive of possession —**dis•pos•ses´sion** n.

dis´pro•por´tion n. lack of symmetry —vt. to make disproportionate

dis•pro•por´tion•ate adj. out of proportion; uneven

dis•prove´ vt. expose as false; refute

dis•pu´table adj. questionable; uncertain —**dis•put´a•bly** adv.

dis•pu´tant n. one who quarrels or disagrees —adj. involving dispute

dis´pu•ta´tion n. controversy; formal debate —**dis•pu•ta´tious** adj.

dis•pute´ n. a quarrel; disagreement —vi., vt. argue about; doubt the truth of

dis•qual´i•fy vt. to declare ineligible —**dis•qual•i•fi•ca´tion** n.

dis•qui´et n. anxiety —vt. to make anxious

dis•re•gard´ n. lack of respect —vt. to ignore or neglect

dis•re•pair´ re in need of repair

dis•rep´u•ta•ble adj. lacking respectability

dis•re•pute´ n. loss of reputation

dis•re•spect´ n. discourtesy; insolence —vt. treat discourteously —**dis´re•spect´ful** adj.

disr•obe´ vi., vt. to undress

dis•rupt´ vt. to intrude; upset an orderly process —**dis•rup´tion** n.

dis•rup´tive adj. rebellious; unruly; intruding —**dis•rup´tive•ness** n.

dis•sat´is•fac´to•ry adj. not acceptable

dis•sat´is•fy vt. fail to please —**dis•sat´is•fied** adj.

dis•sect´ vt. separate into parts; examine closely —**dis•sec´tion** n.

dis•sem´ble vt. conceal; deceive —vi. conceal one's true nature

dis•sem´i•nate vt. scatter; spread widely —**dis•sem´i•na´tion** n.

dis•sen´sion n. a disagreeing; difference of opinion

dis•sent´ n. a difference of opinion —vi. express disagreement —**dis•sent´er** n. —**dis•sent´ing** adj.

dis•sen´tious adj. opposing; disagreeing —**dis•sen´tious•ly** adv.

dis´ser•tate vi. speak at length

dis´ser•ta´tion n. lengthly discourse

dis•serve´ vt. harm; treat badly

dis•serv´ice n. a thoughtless deed

dis´si•dent adj. hostile; opposed; of those opposing —n. one who opposes —**dis´si•dence** n.

dis´sim´i•lar adj. different

dis•sim´i•lar´i•ty n. a difference; divergence or deviation

dis•sim´u•late vi., vt. conceal or disguise one's feelings —**dis•sim•u•la´tion** n. —**dis•sim´u•la•tive** adj.

dis·si·pate *vi.* waste in debauchery; vanish by dispersion —*vt.* to scatter or disperse; to use recklessly, waste —**dis·si·pa·tion** *n.*

dis·si·pat·ed *adj.* scattered; depleted; exhibiting effects of self-indulgence

dis·so·ci·ate *vi.*, *vt.* to separate; sever ties —**dis·so·ci·a·tion** *n.*

dis·so·ci·a·tive *adj.* tending to produce separation

dis·sol·u·ble *adj.* able to dissolve

dis·so·lute *adj.* lacking restraint; immoral —**dis·so·lute·ly** *adv.*

dis·so·lu·tion *n.* a dissolving, or termination, as of a business, etc.

dissolve *vi.*, *vt.* change into liquid; pass into solution; disintegrate or disappear; to end, as a marriage

dis·so·nance, dis·so·nan·cy *n.* disagreeable sound; lack of agreement —**dis·so·nant** *adj.*

dis·suad·a·ble *adj.* able to be persuaded against

dis·suade *vt.* to persuade from a course —**dis·sua·sion** *n.*

dis·sua·sive *adj.* intended to discourage or prevent

dis·tal *adj.* remote; far from origin or attachment

dis·tance *n.* time or space between; reserve, remoteness -*vt.* keep away; to act aloof

dis·tant *adj.* remote; far apart in time or space; reserved, aloof

dis·taste *n.* repugnance

dis·taste·ful *adj.* offensive; unpleasant —**dis·taste·ful·ly** *adv.*

dis·tem·per *n.* an affliction; an infectious disease of animals

dis·tend *vi.*, *vt.* to inflate; to stretch —**dis·ten·si·ble** *adj.*

dis·til´, dis·till´ *vt.* to extract or concentrate by distillation

dis·til·late *n.* result of distillation

dis·til·la·tion *n.* refinement by heating, then cooling and collecting condensation; that produced by distilling —**dis·til·er·y** *n.*

dis·tinct´ *adj.* undeniably different; definite, unmistakable; clearly perceptible —**dis·tinct´ly** *adv.*

dis·tinc´tion *n.* specific difference; distinguishing characteristic or quality; eminence or prestige

dis·tinc´tive *adj.* characteristic; having an uncommon quality

dis·tin´guish *vi.*, *vt.* set apart; recognize clearly; bring prestige to

dis·tin´guish·a·ble *adj.* able to discern; perceptible; unique or different

dis·tin´guished *adj.* celebrated, well-known; refined; extraordinary

dis·tort´ *vt.* bend out of shape; misrepresent; alter —**dis·tor´tion** *n.*

dis·tor´tive *adj.* causing distortion

dis·tract´ *vt.* divert attention; create confusion —**dis·tract´ing** *adj.*

dis·tract´ed *adj.* diverted; confused

dis·trac´tion *n.* that diverts one's attention; confusion or distress; a drawing away of one's attention

dis•traught´ *adj.* deeply troubled

dis•tress´ *n.* pain or anxiety; a condition requiring immediate help —*vt.* to inflict suffering

dis•tress´ful *adj.* causing worry or torment —**dis•tress´ful•ly** *adv.*

dis•trib´ute *vt.* disburse - **dis´tri•bu´tion** *n.*

dis•trib´u•tor *n.* serving to disseminate or classify

dis•trib´u•tor *n.* one authorized to market a product; a merchant; a device that dispenses

dis´trict *n.* an area specially defined

district attorney in the US, a prosecutor for the government

dis•trust´ *n.* lack of trust —*vt.* lack confidence in —**dis•trust´ful** *adj.*

dis•turb´ *vt.* upset serenity or order; to interrupt; make uneasy

dis•tur´bance *n.* a commotion; disorder; deviation from the usual

dis•turbed´ *adj.* distressed, troubled; mentally or emotionally unstable

dis•u•nite´ *vi., vt.* divide or separate

dis•use´ *n.* state of neglect —*vt.* take out of service; abandon or discard

ditch *n.* a trench or channel . —*vt.* get rid of; deliberately leave behind

di´the•ism *n.* belief in two supreme beings —**di•the•is´tic** *adj.*

dith´er *n.* nervous or excited state —*vi.* act nervous or excited; babble

dit´to *n.* same as previous; a repetition —*vt.* duplicate; make a copy; repeat —**ditto mark** a symbol (˝) to indicate a repeat of the above

dit´ty *n.* a simple song

ditty bag a small bag or pouch

di•u•ret´ic *adj.* tending to increase output of urine —*n.* a substance that increases output of urine

di•ur´nal *adj.* happening each day; in the daytime —**di•ur´nal•ly** *adv.*

di•van´ *n.* a davenport or sofa

dive *n.* a headlong leap; a sudden dropping; descent of an airplane —*vi., vt.* to plunge or drop

di•verge´ *vi.* move in different directions —**di•ver´gence** *n.*

di´vers *adj.* several

div´ers *n. pl.* those who dive

di•verse´ *adj.* dissimilar; assorted —**di•verse´ly** *adv.* —**di•verse´ness** *n.*

di•ver´si•fied *adj.* disparate; dissimilar; sundry —**di•ver´si•ty** *n.*

di•ver´si•fy´ *vt.* add variety; branch into new fields —**di•ver´si•fi•ca´tion** *n.*

di•ver´sion *n.* a turning aside; a distraction —**di•ver´sion•ar•y** *adj.*

di•vert´ *vt.* to turn aside; to distract

di•vert´ing *adj.* engaging; pleasing; entertaining

di•ver´tisse•ment *n.* amusement or distraction during an interlude

di•vest´ *vt.* get rid of; deprive of —**di•vest´i•ture, divest´ment** *n.*

di•vide´ *vt.* separate into parts or categories; distribute in portions; cause disagreement —*vi.* become separated; share

di•vid´ed *adj.* separated; in disagreement

divided highway (US) a road with separate lanes for opposing traffic

di•vid´er *n.* thing that serves to separate —**room divider** furniture or a screen that divides a room

div´i•dend *n.* a bonus; an unexpected benefit

divi•na´tion *n.* the art of prediction

di•vine´ *adj.* of the nature of a diety; godlike; pleasing —*vt.* predict

di•vin´er *n.* one who foretells; one who locates water underground

diving bell a device for exploring under water

diving board a springboard

divining rod a forked branch used to locate water underground

di•vin´i•ty *n.* a divine nature; the study of theology; a type of candy

di•vis´i•ble *adj.* easily separated; capable of being evenly divided

di•vi´sion *n.* a partition; a portioning; a rift or disagreement

di•vi´sive *adj.* provoking disagreement —**di•vi´sive•ness** *n.*

di•vorce´ *n.* legal dissolution of a marriage; any radical separation —*vt.* dissolve a marriage; separate entities from association or influence

di•vulge´ *vt.* to make known; reveal

di•vulse´ *vt.* to tear apart

diz´zy *adj.* light-headed; dazed; silly; flighty —**diz´zi•ness** *n.*

DNA *n.* deoxyribonucleic acid, that carries genetic code within cells

do *vi, vt,* perform; to cause; behave —**do in** to murder —**done in** tired; murdered —**do well** prosper

do´a•ble *adj.* able to be accomplished; profitable or expedient

do´cent *n,* a teacher or lecturer; (US) a tour guide —**do´cent•ship** *n.*

doc´ile *adj.* mild mannered; submissive —**do•cil´i•ty** *n.*

dock *n.* a pier or wharf —*vt.* bring a ship into dock; cut short deduct

dock´et *n.* a court calendar

doc´tor *n.* one licensed to practice medicine; highest degree awarded by college or university —*vt.* treat illness or injury; repair in makeshift fashion; to alter

doc´tor•ate *n. a* doctor's degree

doc´tri•naire´ *adj.* theoretical —*n.* one favoring theory over fact

doc´trine *n.* principals or policy —**doc´tri•nal** *adj.*

doc´u•ment *n.* a written record —*vt.* furnish supporting information —**doc•u•men•ta´tion** *n.*

doc•u•ment´ary *adj.* of documents or a report; based on documents —*n.* a factual presentation

dod´der *vt.* to totter, as from age —**dod´der•ing** *adj.*

dodge *vt.* sidestep; avoid or evade by trickery —*vi* move suddenly; employ trickery

—n. a deception or ruse —
dodg´er n.

do´er n. one who achieves

doff vt. to remove; to discard

dog n. an animal related to
the wolf

dog´-ear vt. to turn down a
corner a folded corner of a
page

dog´ged adj. persistent —**dog´
ged•ly** adv. —**dog´ged•ness**
n.

dog•ma n. a statement of doctrine

dog•mat´ic,   dog•mat´i•cal
adj. adhering strictly; dicta-
torial

doi´ly n. a table mat or run-
ner

dol´drums n. a depressed
state

dole n. a charitable gift —vt.
give charitably, portion out

dole´ful adj. mournful; full of
sadness —**dole´ful•ly** adv.

do´lor n. sorrow; anguish —
dol´or•ous adj. —**do´lo•
rous•ly** adv.

dolt n. one who is slow-witted

do•main´ n. sphere of influence or control; territory
controlled

do•mes´tic ndj. of a household, caring for home or
family; of a country; tamed
—n. a servant

do•mes´ti•cate´ or bring under control; adapt to a new
area

do•mes•tic´i•ty n. fondness
for home and family

dom´i•cile n. residence; a
home

dom´i•nate vt. control; have
preeminence —**dom´i•nance**
n. **dom´i•nant** adj.

dom•i•neer´ vi., vt. tyrannize,
bully

dom´i•neer´ing adj. assertive,
overbearing

do•min´ion n. sovereignty

do´nate vt. to contribute —
do•na´tion n.

done adj. completed

do´nor n. a contributor

doom n. inevitable ruin; condemnation —vt. destine for
ruination; to condemn

dooms´day n. final judgment

door n. an entryway

dope n. a drug; information

dor´mant adj. temporarily inactive —**dor´man•cy** n.

dor´mi•to´ry n. living quarters
for students; room with
sleeping accommodations for
many people

dor´y n. a small rowboat

dose n. amount to be taken at
one time —vt. give in measured amounts —**dos´age** n.

dos´si•er n. information relating to a particular matter
or person

dot´age n. childish behavior
in old age: senility; extravagant affection

do´tard n. a senile old person

dote vi. be excessively attentive —**dot´ing•ly** adv.

dou´ble adj. twofold, dupli-
cated, paired; made for two
—n. twice as much; look-
alike —vt. make twice as
much; to fold —vi. increase
twofold; reverse course;
serve in extra capacity —
dou´bly adv.

dou´ble-deal´ing adj. treacherous

dou´ble-deck´er n. a thing
with two levels or layers

dou´ble-en•ten´dre n. word or
phrase having two meanings

double helix coiled structure
of DNA

double standard unevenly applied

dou´blet n. a pair; a short, close-fitting outer garment

double take a delayed reaction

doubt n. uncertainty; lack of trust; skepticism —vi., vt. be uncertain; skeptical — **doubt´ful** adj.

doubt´less adj. without question

dough´ty adj. valiant

dour adj. dreary; gloomy

douse vt. immerse; wet thoroughly

dove´tail´ n. a type of joint —vi., vt. to connect; fit closely

dow´a•ger n. a dignified elderly lady

dow´dy adj. shabby

dow´el n. a round pin used to join

dow´er n. an endowment —vt. to furnish with an endowment

down adv. from higher to lower; from an earlier time; to a diminished volume; to greater intensity —adj. toward a lower position; in a lower place; dejected —vt. subdue; swallow —n. a descent; a reversal of fortune

down-and-out´ destitute

down´cast adj. dejected; despondent

down´fall n. a failure; disgrace

down´grade vt. to reduce or lower

down´heart•ed adj. dejected, discouraged —**down´heart•ed•ly** adv.

down´pour n. a heavy rain

down´right adj. absolute; straightforward —adv. utterly

down´trod•den idj oppressed

down´turn n. an economic decline

down´ward adj, adtr toward a lower point —**down´wards** adv.

dow´ry n. property brought to a marriage by the bride

doze n. brief sleep —vi. sleep briefly

doz´en n. a set of twelve

drab adj. dull; colorless

draft (US) adj. drawn from a keg —n. a preliminary work; air current; an order directing payment; selection for some purpose; depth of a vessel below water —vt. make a layout; sketch or write; select for service

drag n. act of pulling; a device normally pulled or that checks motion; an impedence; slow laborious movement; a tiresome thing; influence —vi. be pulled; lag behind; move slowly —vt. pull; draw slowly or with difficulty —**main drag** a main road

drag´on n. a legendary beast

dra•goon´ n. a cavalryman

drain n. a duct for waste water, etc.; that which draws off — vi., vt. draw off; depletion of energy, resources, etc. —**drain´age** n.

drake n. a male duck

dram n. a unit of weight; a small portion

dra´ma n. a serious play or event; plays collectively — **dra•mat´ic** adj. —**dra•mat´i•ca•ly** udv.

dra•ma•tis per•so•nae n. a cast of characters

dra•mat´ics n. the art of staging drama; histrionics

dram´a•tize´ *vt.* adapt for a play; present in an exaggerated fashion —**dram•a•ti•za´tion** *n.*

drape *n.* a hanging cloth; the way cloth hangs —*vt.* cover with cloth; arrange cloth; hang loosely

dras´tic *adj.* extreme; strong and rapid —**dras´ti•cal•ly** *adv.*

draught (*Brit.*) *adj.* drawn from a keg —*n.* a preliminary work; air current; order directing payment; selection for purpose; depth of a vessel below water —*vt.* make a layout; sketch or write; select

draughts *n.* (*Brit.*) a board game similar to checkers

draw *n.* that attracts or entices; a tie —*vi., vt.* pull or drag; suck; entice; compose or portray; to pull out — **draw the line** to set a limit

draw´back´ *n.* a disadvantage

draw´er *n.* one who draws; a sliding container in furniture

drawl *n.* a manner of speaking —*vi., vt.* speak slowly

dray *n.* a low, heavy cart

dray´age *n.* a fee for hauling

dread *n.* fearful anticipation —*vt.* anticipate with fear or reluctance

dread´ful *adj.* inspiring dread; unpleasant. distasteful

dread´nought *n.* a battleship

dream *n.* images during sleep; a vision; something pleasant —*vi.* experience in a dream, deem practical —*vt.* envision; waste time

dream´y *adj.* pleasant; soothing —**dream´i•ly** *adv.*

drear´y *adj.* bleak, dismal;

dull —**drear´i•ly** *adv.* — **drear´i•nest** *n.*

dredge *n.* machine for clearing waterways —*vt., vi.* dig

dregs *pl. n,* residue; waste

drench *vt.* saturate; wet thoroughly

dress *vt.* clothe; trim or adorn —*vi.* don clothing —*n.* apparel —**dress up** improve appearance; don one's best clothing —**dress´mak•er** *n.*

dress´er *n.* a decorator; one who dresses well; (*US*) chest of drawers

dressing gown (*Brit.*) a loose, casual garment

drib´ble *n.* a small amount — *vi., vt.* trickle; flow a little at a time

drift *n.* something carried by wind or water; a gradual change, a trend —*vi.* carried by wind or water; wander aimlessly; to stray

drift´er *n.* a homeless person

drill *n.* practice exercises; a boring tool —*vt.* to bore a hole; to train

drink *n.* a beverage —*vi., vt.* ingest a liquid —**drink´a•ble** *adj.*

drip *n.* a drop of liquid; the sound of a falling drop —*vi., vt.* fall in drops

drive *n.* operating a motor vehicle; an auto trip; path for an auto; a sharp blow to a ball; an organized effort; enthusiasm —*vi., vt.* operate or propel; hit a ball; press toward a goal

driv´el *n.* foolish talk —*vi., vt.* utter foolishly

drive´way *n.* a private access road

driz´zle *n.* light rain —*vi., vt.* fall in small drops

droll *adj.* quaintly humorous

drone *n.* a loafer; a dull humming sound —*vi.* to speak monotonously

droop *vi.* hang down; become dejected —**droop´y** *adj.*

drop *n.* a small amount; a sharp decline; distance between two levels; a location for depositing; material deposited —*vi., vt.* to fall or decline; to deposit

drop´let *n.* a small drop

drop´out´ *n.* one who abandons an undertaking

dross *n.* waste matter

drought *n.* a long period of dry weather; any prolonged shortage

drove *n.* a large number moving together —**dro´ver** *n.*

drown *vi.* to die in liquid —*vt.* to kill in liquid; to overwhelm

drowse *vt., vi.* become sleepy

drow´sy *adj.* sleepy; sluggish

drub *vt.* beat with a stick; to vanquish —*n.* a heavy blow

drub´bing *n.* a one-sided defeat

drudge *n.* a menial worker — *vi.* to labor at a menial or dull task

drudg´er•y *n.* tiresome work

drug *n.* substance that alters a body function —*vt.* to medicate; add a narcotic to food or drink

dru´id *n.* a priest in ancient Gaul

drum *n.* a percussion instrument; a cylindrical receptacle; repetition —*vt.* beat constantly —**drum out** expel —**drum up** summon or seek by persistence

drunk *adj.* affected by drink to the point of impairment;

overcome by emotion —*n.* one legally or noticeable overcome by drink

dry *adj.* lacking moisture; of a non-liquid; plain, as of food or wine; boring; unproductive —*vi., vt.* become or make dry —**dry´ness** *n.*

dry´ad *n.* a mythical wood nymph

dry cell *n.* a sealed battery

dry´dock *n.* a mooring for the repair of ships —*vi., vt.* to go into drydock

dry goods textile, fabrics

dry rot *n.* a fungal disease

dry run *n.* a rehearsal

dual *adj.* comprised of two parts

dual carriageway (*Brit.*) a road with separate lanes for opposing traffic

dub *vt.* bestow knighthood; confer with a title; to add music, subtitles, etc. to a film or recording

du•bi´e•ty *n.* doubt; uncertainty

du´bi•ous *adj.* questionable; suspect; causing doubt or uncertainty

du´bi•ta•ble *adj.* uncertain

du´cal *adj.* of a duke or duchy

duch´ess *n.* wife or widow of a duke

duch´y *n.* realm of a duke

duck *n.* a web-footed water bird —*vi., vt.* plunge into water; to evade

duck´ling *n.* a small or baby duck

duct *n.* a tubular channel

duc´tile *adj.* able to be hammered thin; easily led — **duc´til´i•ty** *n.*

dude *n.* a dandy

dud´geon *n.* sullen displeasure

due *adj.* scheduled or expected; fitting or deserved — *n.* anything owed or deserved

du´el *n.* formal combat between two persons —*vi.*, *vt.* fight a duel

du•et´ *n.* a musical work for two

dug´out *n.* a canoe; an underground shelter

duke *n.* an English peer

duke´dom *n.* a duchy

dul´cet *adj.* pleasing to the ear; soothing —**dul´cet•ly** *adv.*

dul´ci•mer *n.* a stringed instrument

dull *adj.* mentally or physically slow; lacking spirit; boring; blunt; lacking brightness —*vt.*, *vi.* make or become dull —**dull´ish** *adj.*

dul´lard *n.* a dull person

duly *adv.* in a proper manner

dumb *adj.* unable to speak; lacking intelligence

dumb´found, dum´found *vt.* astonish; make speechless from shock

dumb´struck *adj.* speechless

dum´my *n.* a stupid or foolish person; a representation; a silent player, as in bridge — *adj.* fake or counterfeit; represenlational

dump *vt.*, *vi.* empty or unload; get rid of —*n.* a place for refuse; a distribution point

dump´ling *n.* a filled pastry; dough cooked in soup or stew

dump´ster *n.* (US) a trash container

dump´y *adj.* short and thick

dun *vt.*,*vi.* press for payment

dunce *n.* an ignorant person

dune *n.* a hill or ridge of sand

dung *n.* animal excrement

dun•ga•ree´ *n.* a sturdy cotton cloth —**dun•ga•rees´** work clothes

dun´geon *n.* an underground cell

dunk *vi.*, *vt. to* dip *into* liquid

du•o•de´num *n.* the part of the small intestine nearest the stomach

dupe *n.* one easily deceived — *vt.* to deceive

du´plex *adj.* double —*n.* (US) two connected housing units

du´pli•cate *adj.* copied —*n.* a copy —*vt.* make a copy; repeat

du•plic´i•ty *n.* deception —**du•plic´i•tous** *adj.* —**du•plic´i•tous•ly** *adv.*

du´ra•ble *adj.* able to withstand heavy use —**du´ra•bil´i•ty** *n.*

durable goods products having a relatively long life

du•ra´tion *n.* an interval of time

du•ress´ *n.* threat or coercion

dur´ing *prep.* throughout; in the course of

dusk *n.* early evening darkness

dust *n.* powder —*vt.* remove dust; sprinkle lightly — **dust´y** *adj.*

dust´er *n.* a protective garment

du´te•ous *ndj* obedient; attentive to duty — **du´te•ous•ly** *adv.*

du´ti•ful *adj.* having a sense of duty; obedient —**du´ti•ful•ly** *adv.*

duty *n.* that required; an assigned task; a tax on imported goods

dwarf *n.* a thing notably smaller than most —*vt.* curb the growth of

dwell *vi.* reside; linger —
dwell´er *n.*

dwin´dle *vi.* lessen gradually

dye *n.* coloring matter —*vt.,
vi.* to stain with liquid coloring

dy•nam´ic *adj.* relating to
force; marked by change;
forceful, intense —**dy•nam´
i•cal•ly** *adv.*

dy•nam´ics, *n.* the study of
force; the forces that make
up a system

dy´na•mite *n.* an explosive —
vt. destroy with an explosive

dy´na•mo *n.* a mechine for
converting mechanical en-
ergy to electrical energy

dy´nas´ty *n.* a succession of
rulers

dyne *n.* a unit of force

dys´en•ter•y *n.* inflammation
of the large intestine

dys•func´tion *n.* impaired
function —**dys•func´tion•al**
adj.

dys•lex´i•a *n.* a visual impairment —**dys•lex´ic** *adj.*

dys´pep´sia *n.* distressed digestion —**dys´pep´tic** *adj.*

dys•pha´gia *n.* difficulty in
swallowing —**dys•phag´ic**
adj.

dys•pha´sia *n.* difficulty with
speech —**dys•pha´sic** *adj.*

dys´tro•phy *n.* a disorder
caused by faulty nutrition

e, E fifth letter of the English
alphabet

each *adj.* one of two or more
—*adv.*

ea´ger *adj.* impatient or anxious

eagle-eyed *adj.* having keen
sight

ear *n.* organ of hearing; heed

ear´ful *n.* gossip

ear´ly *adj.* near the beginning;
before the usual or expected
time

ear´mark *vt.* mark for identification; set aside —*n.* an
owner's mark

earn *vt.* receive as payment;
deserve for effort; to yield a
profit

earnings *pl. n.* wages; profit

ear´nest *adj.* serious; intense;
important —**earnest money**
payment to seal a bargain

ear´shot *n.* hearing distance

earth *n.* dry land; a place of
being as contrasted to the
spirit world

earth´en *n.* made of earth or
baked clay —**earth´en•ware**
n.

earth´quake´ *n.* a surface
tremor

earth´work *n.* a fortification

earth´y *adj.* crude, unrefined,
natural —**earth´i•ness** *n.*

ease *n.* comfort; rest; freedom
from difficulty —*vi., vt.* to
lessen; move slowly and
carefully —**ease´ful** *adj.*

ea´sel *n. a* stand for displaying

ease´ment *n.* relief; that providing relief; a right to use of
properly

east *n.* the direction from
which the sun rises —**the
East** an eastern region; Asia
—**east´er•ly** *adj., adv.*

eas´y *adj.* without difficulty;
unhurried, relaxing —
eas´i•ly *adv.*

eas´y•go•in *adj.* relaxed; unhurried

eat *vi., vt.* take in food; consume or destroy; annoy —
eat´a•ble *adj.*

eat´er•y *n.* a restaurant

eaves *pl. n.* projecting edge of a roof

eaves´drop *vi.* to listen secretly

ebb *n.* a decline; receding tide (also **ebb tide**) —*vi.* decline; recede

eb·on·y *n.* hard wood, usually black —*adj.* made from ebony; black

e·bul´lient *adj.* exuberant; enthusiastic **e·bul´lience, e·bul´lien·cy** *n.*

ec·cen´tric *adj.* off center; having different centers; unconventional —*n.* device for transferring motion; an odd or unconventional person

ec·cle·si·as´tic *n.* a cleric — **ec·cle·si´as·tic, ec·cle·si·as´ti·cal** *adj.* pertaining to the church

ec·cle·si·ol´o·gy *n.* study of church function or ornamentation

ec·dys´i·ast *n.* a striptease

ech´e·lon *n.* a military formation; a level of responsibility or function

e·chid´na *n.* a spiny anteater

echo *n.* reflected sound —*vi.* to resound; be repeated —*vt.* to repeat

ech·o·lo·cate *vt.* to position by sound waves —**ech·o·lo·ca´tion** *n.*

e·clair´, e·clair´ *n.* a filled pastry

e·clat´ *n.* a dazzling display; celebrity or renown

ec·lec´tic *adj.* from varied sources —*n.* one using various sources

e·clipse´ *n.* the obscuring of a celestial body; a dimming or diminishing —*vt.* to diminish; overshadow

e·clip´tic *n.* the plane that intersects the sun and the earth's orbit

e·col´o·gy *n.* study of a changing environment — **ec·o·log´i·cal** *adj.*

e·co·nom´ic *adj.* of the production and management of wealth

e·co·nom´i·cal *adj.* done without waste; economic; of economics

e·co·nom´ics *n.* study of the production and management of wealth

e·con´o·my *n.* management of finances; care in use of resources; a system for managing resources

e·con´o·mize *vi.* to use carefully

ec´o·sys·tem *n.* a community of organisms and their environment

ec´ru *adj.* light brown.

ec´sta·sy *n.* emotional rapture or delight —**ec·stat´ic** *adj.*

ec·u·men´ic, ec·u·men´i·cal *adj.* general or universal; promoting unity —**ec´u·me·nism** *n.*

ec·ze·ma *n.* a skin inflammation

e·da´cious *adj.* voracious

ed´dy *n.* a circling current — *vi., vt.* to move or cause to move in circles

e·de´ma *n.* morbid accumulation of fluid

e·den´tate *adj.* toothless

edge *n.* a border or margin; cutting part; a dividing line —*vt.* to border; sharpen; advance gradually

edg´y *adj.* irritable; nervous —**edg´i·ness** *n.*

ed´i·ble *adj.* fit to be eaten

e´dict *n.* formal decree; a strict order

ed·i·fice *n.* an imposing building

ed·i·fy *vt.* instruct, enlighten

ed·it *vt.* prepare for publication; to correct or alter - **ed·i·tor** *n.*

e·di·tion *n.* a published work; the number of copies issued

ed·i·to·ri·al *adj.* of an editor —*n.* an article expressing opinion

ed·u·cate *vt.* teach or train; inform

ed·u·cat·ed *adj.* well-schooled, cultivated in speech, manner, etc.

ed·u·ca·tion *n.* training the mind; knowledge; the art of teaching

ed·u·cat·ive *adj.* instructive

e·duce´ *vt.* to draw out; formulate

ee·rie, ee·ry *adj.* weird; awesome; strange —**ee´ri·ness** *n.*

ef·face´ *vt.* obliterate; make oneself insignificant —**ef·face´ment** *n.*

ef·fect´ *n.* something brought about; power to influence — *vt.* produce or cause —**ef·fec´tive** *adj.*

ef·fec·tu·al *adj.* possessing power; in force —**ef·fec´tu·al·ly** *adv.*

ef·fec·tu·ate *vt.* bring about

ef·fem·i·nate *adj.* having female traits; marked by weakness and overrefinement —**ef·fem´i·na·cy** *n.*

ef·fer·ves´cent *adj.* emitting tiny bubbles; lively, vivacious —**ef·fer·vesce´** *vi.* — **ef·fer·ves´cence** *n.*

ef·fete´ *adj.* unproductive self-indulgent —**ef·fete´ness** *n.*

ef·fi·ca´cious *adj.* producing

desired effect —**ef·fi·ca·cy** *n.*

ef·fi´cient *adj.* produced with minimum effort, waste, etc.

ef´fi·gy *n.* a representative figure

ef·flo·resce´ *vi.* bear flowers

ef·flu·ence *n.* that flowing out

ef·flu´vi·um *n.* an emanation; noxious vapor —**ef·flu´vi·ous** *adj.*

ef·fort *n.* energy required to accomplish a task; an attempt

ef·fort·less *adj.* requiring little effort

ef·fron´ter·y *n.* boldness; insolence

ef·ful´gence *n.* a shining forth; radiance —**ef·ful´gent** *adj.*

ef·fuse´ *vt., vi.* pour forth

ef·fu´sive *adj.* overly demonstrative; gushing —**ef·fu´sive·ly** *adv.*

e·gal·i·tar·i·an *adj.* of political and social equality

egg *n.* a reproductive body; a female gamete —**lay an egg** fail —**egg on** to incite

egg´head´ *n.* an intellectual

e´go *n.* the conscious self

e·go·cen´tric *adj.* self-centered

e´go·ism *n.* excessive concern with one's self; conceit; belief in self-interest as a primary goal —**e´go·ist** *n.* — **e·go·is´tic** *adj.*

e·go·ma´ni·a *n.* excessive concentration on one's self

e´go·tist *n.* one with an overblown sense of self-importance

e·gre´gious *adj.* exceptionally bad

e´gress *n.* a going out; an exit

ei´der *n.* a large sea duck

ei´ther *adj.* one of two

e•jac´u•late vt. utter or eject abruptly —**e•jac•u•la´tion** n.

e•ject´ vt. cast out —**e•jec´tion** n.

eke ut. to supplement; produce with difficulty

e•lab´o•rate adj. intricate —vi., vt. to work out m great detail —**e•lab´o•rate•ly** adv.

é•lan´ n. dash; vivacity

e•lapse´ vi. to pass by

e•las´tic adj. capable of quick recovery; easily adapting —n. a stretchable fabric —**e•las•tic´i•ty** n.

e•late´ vt. raise the spirits of —**e•lat´ed** adj.

e•la´tion n. exultation

el´bow n. joint at the bend of the arm; any angular joint or fitting

el´der adj. older, superior in rank —n. an older person

el´der•ly adj. somewhat old

el´dest adj. first-born

e•lect´ adj. chosen; singled out, exclusive —n. one chosen or singled out —vt. to choose or vote for —**the elect** a favored group

e•lect´a•ble adj. able or likely to be elected

e•lec´tion n. the process of selecting

e•lec•tion•eer´ vi. canvass for votes

e•lec´tive adj. chosen by votes; open to choice; optional

e•lec´tor n. a voter; a member or the electoral college —**e•lec´tor•al** adj.

electoral college people chosen to formally elect the president and vice president of the U.S.

e•lec´tor•ate n. a body of voters

e•lec´tric, e•lec´tri•cal adj. of or operated by electricity; emotionally charged —**e•lec´tri•cal•ly** adv.

e•lec•tric´i•ty n. a common source of energy; emotional excitement

e•lec´tri•fy n. to equip for operation by electricity; to startle or thrill

e•lec´tro•car´di•o•gram n. a graph showing heart activity

e•lec´tro•car´di•o•graph´ n. instrument for recording heart activity

e•lec´trode n. a conducting element fur an electric charge

e•lec•tro•dy•nam´ics n. interaction of electicity and magnetism

e•lec•tro•en•ceph´a•lo•gram n.a record of the brain's activity

e•lec•tro•mag´net n. magnet produced by electricity

e•lec´tron n. a negatively charged atomic particle

e•lec•tron´ics n. the study of carriers of electric charge

el•ee•mos´y•nar•y adj. charity; nonprofit

el´e•gance n. a sense of propriety, grace, or beauty; tasteful luxury —**el´e•gant** adj. —**el´e•gant•ly** adv.

el´e•gy n. a classical poem —**el•e•gi´ac** adj. —**el´e•gize** vt., vi.

el´e•ment n. a basic component; one's natural environment —**el´e•men´tal, el´e•men´ta•ry** adj.

el´e•phant n. is huge mammal with a flexible trunk and tusks

el´e•vate vt. to raise or lift; improve one's moral or

intellectual awareness; improve the spirits of

elf n. a mischievous sprite — **elf´in, elf´ish** adj.

e•lic´it vt. to draw out; to bring out

e•lide´ vt. omit; ignore

el´i•gi•ble adj. qualified to participate

e•lim´i•nate vt. remove, reject

e•lite´ n. the aristocracy; a small powerful group — **e•lit´ist** n.

e•lix´ir n. a cure-all

elk n. a large deer with broad antlers

el•lipse´ n. an oval geometric form — **el•lip´tic, el•lip´ti•cal** adj.

el•lip´sis n., pl **el•lip´ses** the omission of a word or phrase; marks that indicate omission as ... or ***

elo•cu´tion n. the art of public speaking — **el•o•cu´tion•ar•y** adj.

e•lon´gate vt., vi. to make or grow longer — **e•lon´gate, e•lon´ga•ted** adj. made longer, slender

e•lope´ vi. run away to marry

el´o•quence n. expressive speech of writing — **el´o•quent** adj.

else adj. different or other, more

e•lu´ci•date vt. clarify; explain — **e•lu•ci•da´tion** n.

e•lude´ of evade or escape; slip from memory — **e•lu´sive, e•lu´so•ry** adj.

e•ma´ci•ate vt. make abnormally thin — **e•ma´ci•at•ed** adj.

em´a•nate´ vt. come forth

e•man´ci•pate´ vt. release from bondage — **e•man´ci•pa´tion** n.

e•mas´cu•late vt. to deprive of force — **e•mas´cu•la´tion** n.

em•balm´ vt. preserve a dead body; protect from change

em•bank´ment n. a protective mound — **em•bank´** vt.

em•bar´go n. restriction of trade — vt. place restriction on

em•bark´ vi., vt. go aboard — **em•bar•ka´tion** n. — **em•bark´ment** n.

em•bar´rass vt. make ill at ease; involve in financial difficulties — **em•bar´rass•ment** n.

em•bas•sy n. the post, trappings. staff, etc. of an ambassador

em•bat´tle vt. to equip for battle; to fortify — **em•bat´tied** adj.

em•bed´ vt. to set firmly

em•bel´lish vt. add detail or adornment; add particulars to an account — **em•bel´lish•ment** n.

em´ber n. a live coal — **em´bers** n. a dying fire

em•bez´zle vt. take illegally — **em•bez´zle•ment** n.

em•bit´ter vt. give rise to unhappiness

em•bla´zon vt. to adorn or decorate

em´blem n. a symbol; a representation — **em´blem•at´ic** adj.

em•bod´y vt. collect into a whole; include or incorporate

em•bold´en vt. give courage to

em´bo•lism n. stoppage in a blood vessel

em´bo•lus n. an obstruction

em•bos´om vt, to take in; shelter

em•boss vt, to adorn with a

raised design

em·brace´ n. a hug; acceptance —vi. join in a hug —vt. to hug; accept; to include — **em·brace´a·ble** adj.

em·broi´der·y n. ornamental needlework —**em·broi´der** vt.

em·broil´ vt. draw into a conflict

em´bry·o n. the early stage of an organism —**em´bry·on´ic** adj.

em·bry·ol´o·gy n. the study of embryos —**em·bry·ol´o·gist** n.

e·mend´, e´men·date vt. to correct

em´er·ald n. a green precious stone

e·merge´ vi. come forth; come into view; form or evolve — **e·mer´gence** n. —**e·mer´gent** adj.

e·mer´gen·cy n. a situation requiring immediate action

e·mer´i·tus adj. retired, but retained in a honorary position

em´er·y n. a very hard mineral

e·met´ic n. medicine used to induce vomiting —adj. causing vomiting

em´i·grate vi. leave a country to settle in another — **é·mi·gre´** n.

em´i·nent adj. renowned, exalted; above others —**em´i·nence** n.

eminent domain the right to take private property for public use

em´is·sar´y n. one sent on a mission

e·mis´sion n. something omitted

e·mit´ vt. give out; discharge

e·mol´u·ment n. compensation for office or employment

e·mote´ vi. to act melodramatically

e·mo´tion n. strong feeling; mental agitation —**e·mo´tion·al** adj.

e·mo´tion·a·lize vt. make emotional

e·mo´tive adj. arousing emotion

em´pa·thy n. identification with the emotions, thoughts, etc. of another

em´per·or n. ruler of an empire

em´pha·sis n. forcefulness; special importance —**em´pha·size´** vt.

em·phat´ic adj. forceful; definite —**em·phat´i·cal·ly** adv.

em·phy·se´ma n. a lung condition marked by shortness of breath

em´pire n. a vast organization

em·pir´ic, em·pir´i·cist n. a seeker of knowledge through experience —adj. empirical

em·pir´i·cal adj. based on experience —**em·pir´i·cal·ly** adv.

em·ploy´ vt. engage the services of; to use —**em·ploy´ment** n.

em·ploy´a·ble adj. capable of being put to use —**em·ploy´a·bil´i·ty** n.

em·po´ri·um n. a marketplace

em·pow´er vt. to enable or permit

emp´ty adj. having nothing within; insincere; frivolous —vt., vi. make or become empty; transfer contents — **emp´ti·ness** n.

e·mu´ n. a flightless bird of Australia

em´u·late *vt.* imitate; to strive to equal —**em´u·la´tion** *n.*

e·mul´sion *n.* particles suspended in liquid —**e·mul´sive** *adj.*

e·mul´si·fy *vt.* mix or whip —**e·mul·si·fi·ca´tion** *n.*

en·a´ble *vt.* make possible

en·act´ *vt.* make into law

en·am´el *n.* a glossy coating —*vt.* to surface with a protective coating

en·am´or *vt.* to inspire love

en·cap´su·late *vt.* summarize

en·ceph·a·li´tis *n.* an inflammation of the brain —**en·ceph·a·lit´ic** *adj.*

en·ceph´a·lon *n.* the brain

en·chant *vt.*, delight or charm —**en·chant´ing** *adj.* —**en·chant´ment** *n.*

en·ci´pher *vt.* to translate into code

en·cir´cle *vt.* to surround

en´clave *n.* a distinct area enclosed within a larger one

en·close´ *vt.* to surround or contain

en·co´mi·um *n.* a eulogy

en·com´pass *vt.* include; encircle or surround —**en·com´pass·ment** *n.*

en´core *n.* a repeat performance

en·coun´ter *n.* a meeting —*vi.*, *vt.* to meet unexpectedly or in conflict

en·cour´age *vt.* support; inspire —**en·cour´age·ment** *n.*

en·croach´ *vi.* to intrude —**en·croach´ment** *n.*

en·crust´ *vt.* cover with a hard coating; to decorate with jewels —**en·crus·ta´tion** *n.*

en·cum´ber *vi.* to weigh down —**en·cum´brance** *n.*

en·cy·clo·pae´di·a, en·cy´clo·pe´di·a *n.* an authoritative reference

end *n.* a terminal point

en·dan´ger *vt.* imperil —**en·dan´ger·ment** *n.*

en·dear´ *vt.* make beloved —**en·dear´ing** *adj.*

en·dear´ment *n.* an expression of affection

en·deav´or *n.* sincere effort; an undertaking —*vi.*, *vt.* make an effort

en·dem´ic *adj.* peculiar to a particular area or people

end´less *adj.* boundless; without end; forming a closed loop —**end´less·ly** *adv.* —**end´less·ness** *n.*

en·dorse´ *vt.* approve or support —**en·dorse´ment** *n.*

en·dow´ *vt.* provide income; equip —**en·dow´ment** *n.*

en·dure´ *vi.*, *vt.* continue; bear up —**en·dur´a·ble** *adj.* **en·dur´ance** *n.*

en´e·my *n.* one hostile to another

en·er·get´ic *adj.* displaying energy

en´er·gize *vt.* bring to action

en´er·gy *n.* power to act; power from natural sources —*adj.* pertaining or relating to power

en·er´vate *vt.* deprive of energy; weaken —**en·er·va´tion** *n.*

en·fee´ble *vt.* weaken; render helpless —**en·fee´ble·ment** *n.*

en·fold´ *vt.* embrace; to wrap

en·force´ *vt.* compel obedience —**en·force´a·ble** *adj.* —**en·forc´er** *n.*

en·fran´chise *vt.* endow with rights; free from bondage

en·gage´ *vi.*, *vt.* hire; promise to marry; to occupy oneself with

en·gag'ing *adj.* charming

en·gen'der *vt.* bring about; produce

en·gine *n.* a machine that converts energy into force

en'gi·neer' *n.* one who plans and manages —*vt.* to contrive; to plan and supervise

en'gi·neer'ing *n.* application of science to practical problems

en·grave' *vt.* to carve or etch into a surface

en·gross' *vt.* absorb entirely

en·gulf' *vt.* swallow up; overwhelm

en·hance *vt.* embellish so as to improve **—en·hance' ment** *n.*

e·nig'ma *n.* something ambiguous or perplexing **—en' ig·mat'ic** *adj.*

en·join' *vt.* forbid or prohibit

en·joy *vt.* pleasure in; have use of **—en·joy'a·ble** *adj.*

en·kin'dle *vt.* set on fire; to excite

en·large' *vt., vi.* make or become larger **—en·large' ment** *n.*

en·light'en *vt.* inform; impart knowledge **-en'light'en· ment** *n.*

en·liv'en *vt.* to stimulate

en·mesh' *vt.* to entangle

en'mi·ty *n.* hostility

en·no'ble *vt.* confer nobility; honor or venerate

en'nui *n.* listlessness or indifference

e·nor'mous *adj.* of great size **—e·nor'mi·ty** *n.*

e·nough' *adj.* adequate; sufficient **—***adv.* sufficiently **—***n.* an adequate supply **—***interj.*

en·rage' *vt.* make angry; infuriate

en·rap'ture *vt.* delight

en·rich' *vt.* to increase the wealth or quality of **—en· rich'ment** *n.*

en·rol, enr·oll' *vt.* register; place on record; enlist

en·sconce' *vt.* settle snuggly

en·sem'ble *n.* a suitable or pleasing combination; group of performers

en·shrine' *vt.* to hold sacred

en·shroud' *vt.* to cover or conceal

en·sign *n.* a flag, banner, or symbol; a naval officer

en·si'lage *n.* stored fodder

en·slave' *vt.* place in bondage; dominate

en·snare' *vt.* to trap

en·sue' *vi.* result; follow after

en·sure' *vt.* to make safe or secure; make certain; guarantee

en·tail' *vt.* impose as a consequence

en·tan'gle *vt.* complicate; involve In difficulties **—en· tan'gle·ment** *n.*

en·tente' *n.* an understanding between nations

en'ter *vt.* gain admission; become a member; to begin; to record

en'ter·pris'ing *adj.* displaying initiative **—en'ter'prise'** *n.*

en·ter·tain' *vt.* amuse; offer hospitality; consider **—en· ter·tan'ing** *adj.* **—en·ter· tain'ment** *n.*

en·thral', en·thrall' *vt.* to charm or fascinate

en·thu'si·asm *n.* great excitement or interest **—en' thu·si·as'tic** *adj.*

en·tice' *vt.* attract with promises **—en·tice'ment** *n.* **—en·tic'ing** *adj.*

en·tire' *adj.* complete; undivided

en·ti·tle vt. give right to; authorize

en·ti·ty vt. any being; anything that exists

en·tomb´ vt. place for burial

en·to·mol´o·gy n. study of insects —**en·to·mo·log´i·cal** adj.

en·tou·rage´ n. companions; attendants

en´trance[1] n. act or means of entering —**en´trance·way** n.

en·trance[2] vt. fill with delight or enchantment —**en·tranc´ing** adj.

en´trant n. one taking part

en·trap´ vt. catch or ensnare; trick or lure into danger or difficulty; lay a trap for — **en·trap´ment** n.

en·treat´ vt., vi. to plead or implore

en·trench´ vt. fortify; establish firmly —**en·trench´ment** n.

en·tre·pre·neur´ n. one starting a business venture —**en·tre·pre·neur´i·al** adj.

en·trust´ vt. give for safekeeping

en´try n. means of access; act of entering; item entered; an entrant

en·twine´ vt., vi. to twist together

e·nu´mer·ate vt. name one by one; to count —**e·nu·mer·a´tion** n.

e·nun´ci·ate vt. pronounce distinctly; state precisely; to proclaim

en·vel´op vt. surround completely

en´ve·lope´ n. that which envelops; a wrapper for letters, etc.

en´vi·a·ble adj. provoking envy or admiration

en´vi·ous adj. experiencing or expressing envy —**en´vi·ous·ly** adv.

en·vi´ron·ment n. conditions affecting growth and development of an organism; one's surroundings

en·vi·ron·men´tal·ist n. advocate for environmental preservation

en·vi´rons pl. n. surrounding area; the environment

en·vis´age vt. visualize; form an image of

en·vi´sion vt. imagine; foresee

en´voy´ n. a diplomatic agent

en´vy n. resentment aroused by jealousy —vt. regard jealously

e´on n. an incalculable time

ep´au·let´ n. a shoulder ornament

e·phem´eral adj. short-lived; transitory —**e·phem´er·al·ly** adv.

ep´ic n. a work having a heroic theme —adj. grand; heroic

ep´i·cen·ter n. point above an earthquake source; a central point

ep´i·cure n. a discriminating person —**ep·i·cu·re·an** adj., n.

ep·i·dem´ic n. a widespread condition —**ep·i·dem´ic** adj. affecting many at once

ep·i·de·mi·ol´o·gy n. study of epidemics

ep·i·de·mi·ol´o·gist n.

ep´i·der´mis n. outer layer of skin

ep´i·gram´ n. a thought-provoking saying

ep´i·lep·sy n. a nervous disorder

ep´i·logue n. a concluding section

e·pis·co·pa·cy *n.* church government by bishops —**e·pis´co·pal** *adj.*

e·pis´co·pate *n.* office of a bishop

ep´i·sode´ *n.* one in a series of events; a notable incident

e·pis·te·mol´o·gy *n.* study of human knowledge —**e·pis·te·mol´o·gist** *n.*

e·pis´tle *n.* a letter of instruction

ep´i·taph´ *n.* inscription on a tomb

ep´i·thet´ *n.* a word or phrase that characterizes a person or thing

e·pit´o·me *n.* a typical example; a brief summary

e·pit´o·mize *vt.* abridge; be typical of

ep´och *n.* period marked by extraordinary events —**ep´och·al** *adj.*

eq´ua·ble *adj.* of uniform condition; not easily disturbed

e´qual *adj.* of the same value; fair and impartial; balanced —*vt.* be equivalent —*n.* that which closely matches another —**e´qual·ly** *adv.*

e·qual´i·ty *n.* condition of being equal —**e´qual·ize** *vt.*

e´qua·nim´i·ty *n.* calmness; composure

e·quate´ *vt.* make equal; to compare

e·qua´tion *n.* a complex array; a statement expressing equality

e·qua´tor *n.* a circle around the earth equidistant from the poles

e·ques´tri·an *adj.* of horses or horsemanship

e´qui·lat´er·al *adj.* having all sides equal —**e´qui·lat´er·al·ly** *adv.*

e´qui´li·brate *vi., vt.* balance; to be or bring to a state of equilibrium

e·qui·lib´ri·um *n.* a condition in which all are equal or balanced

e´quine *adj.* of horses —*n.* a horse

e´qui·nox *n.* time when day and night are of equal length

e·quip´ *vt.* to prepare, as by outfitting or training —**e·quip´ment** *n.*

eq´ui·ta·ble *adj.* fair; impartial —**eq´ui·ta·bly** *adv.*

eq´ui·ty *n.* fairness; impartiality; net assets

e·quiv´a·lent *adj.* equal or corresponding —*n.* that corresponds —**e·quiv´a·lence** *adj.*

e·quiv´o·cate´ *vi.* speak with intent to deceive —**e·quiv´o·ca´tion** *n.*

e´ra *n.* a period encompassing important dates, events, etc.

e·rad´i·cate´ *vt.* to destroy utterly —**e·ra·di·ca´tion** *n.*

e·rase´ *vt.* wipe out; remove

e·rect´ *adj.* upright; vertical; standing —*vt.* construct; set in an upright position —**e·rec´tion** *n.*

e·rec´tile *adj.* able to become erect or raised to an upright position

erg *n.* a unit of work or energy

er·go·nom´ics *n.* design of equipment or workplace to minimize operator fatigue —**er·go·nom´ic** *adj.*

e·rode´ *vt., vi.* wear or become worn away —**e·ro´sion** *n.*

e·rog´e·nous *adj.* exciting sexually

e·rot´ic *adj.* arousing sexually

e·rot´i·ca *n.* erotic materials

err *vi.* make a mistake; to sin

168

er´rand n. short trip; tend to a task

er´rant adj. wandering; straying from a proper course

er·rat´ic adj. deviating from the expected; lacking consistency

er·ro´ne·ous adj. inaccurate, incorrect —**er·ro´ne·ous·ly** adv.

er´ror n. wrongly done; inaccuracy

er´satz adj. being substitute

erst´while adj. former

er´u·dite adj. scholarly; learned

e·rupt´ vi., vt. burst forth — **e·rup´tion** n. —**e·rup´tive** adj.

es·ca·late´ vi., vt. increase; to ascend or carry up

es·ca·la´tor n. a moving staircase

es·ca·pade´ n. prank

es·cape´ n. breaking free; means to break free —vi., vt. to elude, avoid, or break free

es·ca´pism n. a turning from unpleasant reality

es·carp´ment n. a steep slope

es·cha·tol´o·gy n. theological study of the destiny of man

es·cheat´ n. reversion of property in the absence of heirs vi., vt. to revert or cause to revert to the state

es·chew´ vt. to shun or refrain from

es´cort n. one accompanying —**es·cort´** vt. to accompany

es´crow n. thing of value held until certain conditions are satisfied

es·cutch´eon n. a heraldic shield

e·soph´a·gua n. the tube that connects the mouth to the stomach

es·o·ter´ic adj. understood by a limited group; confidential

es·pe´cial adj. exceptional

es´pi·o·nage n. spying

es·pla·nade´ n. a level public space

es·pouse´ vt. to give or take in marriage; to take up as a cause

es·pres´so n. coffee from darkly roasted and finely ground beans

es·py´ vt. to catch sight of

es·quire´ n. a title of courtesy; a candidate for knighthood

es´say n. a brief written work; a testing —vt. to test ore

es´sence n. basic nature or quality

es·sen´tial adj. fundamental; necessary —n. something required

es·tab´lish vt. to create or install; to authenticate —**es·tab´lish·ment** n.

es·tate´ n. one's entire wealth; landed property

es·teem´ n. respect; reverence —vt. to value; to regard as

es´ti·ma·ble adj. deserving of esteem

es´ti·mate vt. approximate; form an opinion —n. appraisal or evaluation; an opinion —**es´ti·ma´tion** n.

es·top´ vt. to prevent

es·trange´ vt. alienate

es´tu·a´ry n. mouth of a river

etch vi., vt. engrave with acid; make a clear impression — **etch´ing** n.

e·ter´nal adj. without end; perpetual —**e·ter´nal·ly** adv. —**e·ter´ni·ty** n.

e·the´re·al adj. light, airy

eth´ic n. a set of principals

eth´i·cal adj. morally right

eth´ics n. accepted morality

eth·nic *adj.* of customs, food, etc. of a group or culture

eth·nol´o·gy *n.* the study of cultures

e·ti·ol´o·gy *n.* the study of origins

et´i·quette´ *n.* the rules for socially acceptable behavior

e´tude *n.* a musical exercise

et´ymol´o·gy *n.* the origin and development of words

eu·gen´ics *n.* improvements to the human race by selective breeding

eu·lo·gy *n.* a tribute —**eu´lo·gize** *vt.*

eu·phe·mism *n.* a substitute word or phrase —**eu´phe·mis´tic** *adj.*

eu·phon´ic, eu·pho´ni·ous *adj.* pleasant or agreeable sounding

eu·pho´ni·um *n.* a brass instrument

eu´pho·ny *n.* a pleasant sounding word combination

eu·pho´ri·a *n.* a feeling of well-being

eu·ryth´mics *pl. n.* musical interpretation through rhythmic body movements —**eu·ryth´mic** *adj.*

eu·tha·na´sia *n.* ending the life of a suffering person —**eu·tha·nize** *vt.*

e·vac´u·ate´ *vt.* to depart from; to withdraw —**e·vac´u·a´tion** *n.*

e·vade´ *vi., vt.* avoid by deceit

e·val´u·ate *vt.* determine the worth of; appraise —**e·val´u·a´tion** *n.*

ev´a·nesce´ *vt.* to vanish slowly

e´van·gel´ic, e´van·gel´i·cal *adj.* adhering closely to Christian scripture; marked by enthusiasm or ardor

e·van·gel·is´tic *adj.* of a crusading nature

e·van´gel·ize *vi., vt.* to preach

e·vap´o·rate *vi., vt.* to convert liquid into vapor —**e·vap·o·ra´tion** *n.*

e·va´sive *adj.* deliberately vague; intended to avoid —**e·va´sion** *n.*

eve *n.* night before an event

e´ven *adj.* smooth; level; unchanging, constant; calm, tranquil; balanced —*vt., vi.* to make or become smooth, level, etc. —*adv.*

eve´ning *n.* close of the day

e·vent´ *n.* an important occasion; an incident; one of a series

e·vent´ful *adj.* momentous —**e·vent´ful·ly** *adv.* —**e·vent´ful·ness** *n.*

e·ven·tu·al *adj.* future, impending —**e·ven·tu·al´i·ty** *n.*

ev´er *adv.* at any time; in any way; always

e·vert´ *vt.* turn inside out

eve´ry *adj.* all, taken singly

e·vict´ *vt.* to turn out; to dispossess

ev´i·dence *n.* that serves to make clear or prove —*vt.* make plain; attest —**ev·i·den´ti·ar·y** *adj.*

evi´dent *adj.* clear; obvious

e´vil *adj.* wicked, depraved; harmful —*n.* sinfulness; that which harms

e·vince´ *vt.* to demonstrate clearly

e·vis´cer·ate *vt.* disembowel

e·voke´ *vt.* to call forth or summon

evo·lu´tion *n.* process of evolving; gradual development or growth

evo·lu´tion·ism *n.* gradual biological change; a belief in biological evolution —**ev•o•lu′tion•ist** n.

e•volve′ vi., vt. develop gradually

ew′er n. a large pitcher

ex•ac′er•bate vt. make more intense

ex•act′ adj. very accurate; precise —vt. obtain by force or authority

ex•ac′tion n. extortion

ex•ag′ger•ate vi., vt. to overstate

ex•alt′ vt. to glorify or praise

ex•am′i•ne vt. inspect or test

ex•am′ple n. that which typifies

ex•as′per•ate vt. to annoy or irritate

ex′ca•vate vt. make a hole; uncover by digging —**ex′ca•va′tion** n.

ex•ceed′ vt. to go beyond

ex•ceed′ing adj. surpassing

ex•cel′ vi., vt. to be better or superior; to surpass

ex′cel•lent adj. outstanding; of exceptional quality —**ex′cel•lence** n.

ex•cel′si•or n. packing material

ex•cept′ vt. to exclude —vi. to object —prep. with the exception of

ex•cep′tion n. that different or excluded; an objection

ex′cerpt n. an extract —**ex•cerpt′** vt. remove or extract; to quote

ex•cess′ n. amount greater than needed; amount greater than another; overindulgence —**ex•cess′** adj. surplus —**ex•ces′sive** adj.

ex•change′ vt. to trade; reciprocate; replace —vi. make a trade —n. trading or reciprocating; a substitution; a place for trading

ex′cise n. an indirect tax or fee —**ex•cise′** vt. remove —**ex•ci′sion** n.

ex•cit′a•ble adj. high-strung; emotional; easily excited

ex•cite′ vt. stir the emotions, provoke —**ex•cit′ed** adj.

ex•cite′ment n. a state of high emotion; something that thrills

ex•cit′ing adj. exhilarating; intensely emotional

ex•claim′ vi., vt. cry out suddenly —**ex•clam′a•to•ry** adj.

ex•clude′ vt. put out; leave out, except —**ex•clu′sion** n.

ex•clu′sive adj. limited; regarded as incompatible; restricted

ex•com•mu′ni•cate vt. to expel —adj. expelled or excluded

ex•co′ri•ate vt. to abrade the skin; to denounce

ex′cre•ment n. refuse matter; feces

ex•cre′ta n. the body's waste matter —**ex•cre′tion** n.

ex•cru′ci•at•ing adj. causing severe mental or physical pain; intense

ex′cul•pate vt. prove innocent

ex•cur′sion n. a short journey; a group tour

ex•cuse′ vt. to overlook; free from blame; offer a reason or apology; free from obligation —n. justification for offense; that relieving obligation —**ex•cus′a•ble** adj.

ex′e•cra•ble adj. appallingly bad

ex′e•crate vt. to denounce; to loathe

ex′e•cute vt. to perform; put into effect; put to death

ex·ec´u·tive n. an official exercising control —adj. administrative; having ability to direct or control

ex·em´plar n. typical example

ex·em´pla·ry adj. worthy of imitation; commendable

ex·em´pli·fy vt. to show by example

ex·empt´ adj. freed from obligation —vt. free from a duty or obligation

ex·er·cise n. activity to improve strength or endurance; practice to develop a skill; a ceremony —vt. to train; to make use of

ex·ert´ vt. to put forth; bring to bear

ex·fo´li·ate vt., vi. to peel off; come off in flakes, layers, etc.

ex·hale´ vi. to breathe out

ex·haust´ vt. use up; drain of resources, energy; etc.

ex·haust´ed adj. used up; consumed; extremely tired

ex·haust´ing adj. tiring

ex·haus´tion n. extreme fatigue

ex·haus´tive adj. extensive; complete —**ex·haus´tive·ly** adv.

ex·hib´it vt. display; present for inspection —vi. place on display —n. a display; something displayed

ex·hi·bi´tion·ist n. one who seeks attention; one driven to indecent exposure —**ex·hi·bi´tion·ism** n.

ex·hil´a·rate vt. to cheer; stimulate or enliven —**ex·hil´a·rat·ing** adj.

ex·hil·a·ra´tion n. elation; excitement

ex·hort´ vt. advise strongly; entreat

ex·hume´ vt. to disinter; to disclose

ex·i´gen·cy n. an emergency; a pressing need —**ex´i·gent** adj.

ex·ig´u·ous adj. meager, sparse

ex´ile n. expulsion, banishment; one banished —vt. to expel or banish

ex·ist´ vi. have reality; be present; to continue to be —**ex·ist´ence** n.

ex·is·ten´tial·ism n. philosophy that stresses free will and personal responsibility —**ex·is·ten´tial·ist** n.

ex´it n. a going out; a way out

ex´o·dus n. a departure or leaving

ex·og´a·my n. marrying outside one's social unit

ex·on´er·ate vt. clear of an accusation; prove blameless

ex·or´bi·tant adj. excessive

ex·or·cise´, ex´or·cize´ vt. to drive out an evil spirit; free from evil influence —**ex´or·cism** n.

ex·ot´ic adj. foreign; strange or unusual; alluring

ex·pand´ vi., vt. to make or become greater; spread or extend

ex·panse´ n. unbroken space; wide extent —**ex·pan´sion** n.

ex·pan´sive adj. extensive; amiable or outgoing —**ex·pan´sive·ly** adv.

ex·pa´ti·ate vi. to speak at length and in great detail; to elaborate

ex·pect´ vt. to anticipate as likely or deserving —**ex·pect´ant** adj.

ex·pec·ta´tion n. something expected; hope for good

ex·pec´to·rant *n.* medication to help clear mucus from the lungs

ex·pec´to·rate *vi., vt.* to spit

ex·pe´di·ent *adj.* appropriate; convenient; useful —*n.* thing suited to a pressing need

ex´pe·dite *vt.* hasten; to speed the progress of

ex·pe·di´tion *n.* a voyage; those who journey and their equipment

ex·pe·di´tious *adj.* rapid, speedy

ex·pel´ *vt.* to drive out by force; to eject by authority

ex·pend´ *vt.* spend or use up

ex·pend´i·ture *n.* an expense; a disbursement

ex·pense´ *n.* an outlay; a cost

ex·pen´sive *adj.* costly

ex·pe´ri·ence *n.* that learned from observation or involvement —*vt.* live through

ex·per´i·ment *n.* a test to learn or verify —*vi.* to try or test

ex·per·i·men´tal *adj.* in development —**ex·per´i·men´tal·ly** *adv.*

ex·per·i·men·ta´tion *n.* the process of testing and recording results

ex·pert´ *adj.* having great skill or knowledge —*n.* one knowledgeable or skilled —**ex´pert·ly** *adv.*

ex·per·tise´ *n.* the skill, knowledge, etc. of an expert

ex´pi·ate´ *vt.* make amends; to atone

ex·pire´ *vi.* to die; to come to an end

ex·plain´ *vi., vt.* make clear or understandable —**ex·pla·na´tion** *n.*

ex´ple·tive *n.* an exclamation

ex·pli·ca·ble *adj.* explainable

ex´pli·cate *vt.* to explain

ex·plic´it *adj.* distinct; clearly stated or established —**ex·plic´it·ly** *adv.*

ex·plode´ *vi., vt.* to blow up; to burst

ex·ploit, ex·ploit´ *n.* a remarkable or daring feat —**ex·ploit´** *vt.* use to one's advantage; take unfair advantage of —**ex·ploit´a·ble** *adj.* —**ex·ploi·ta´tion** *n.*

ex·plore´ *vi., vt.* investigate or examine exhaustively

ex·plor´a·ble *adj.* able to be explored

ex·plo´sion *n.* a blowing up; a sudden outburst; a sudden increase

ex·plo´sive *adj.* pertaining to explosion; liable to cause violence or an outburst —*n.* a substance that can explode —**ex·plo´sive·ly** *adv.*

ex·po´nent *n.* one who promotes; a mathematic symbol

ex´port *n.* goods sent out of a country —**ex·port´** *vt.* to send out

ex·po·sé´ *n.* a description or airing

ex·pose´ *vt.* leave unprotected

ex·po·si´tion *n.* a public exhibition; detailed explanation

ex·po´sure *n.* a revealing; the condition of being open to the elements

ex·pos´tu·late´ *vi.* to argue against

ex·press´ *vt.* convey in words; represent by symbols; to press or force out —*adj.* deliberate, definite; of a high speed or non-stop train —*adv.* by fast delivery —*n.* a system for transporting rapidly

ex·pres´sion *n.* a means of

conveying; something conveyed; a saying

ex·pres´sive *adj.* demonstrative; meaningful —**ex·pres´sive·ly** *adv.*

ex·pul´sion *n.* bring forced out or expelled —**ex·pul´sive** *adj.*

ex·punge´ *vt.* erase or delete

ex´qui·site *adj.* beautiful; delicately crafted —**ex·quis´ite·ly** *adv.*

ex´tant *adj.* still existing

ex·tem´po·ra´ne·ous, extem´po·rar´y *adj.* improvised; speaking without notes

ex·tend´ *vi., vt.* enlarge; stretch out

ex·ten´sive *adj.* great in amount, extent, etc. —**ex·ten´sive·ly** *adv.*

ex·tent´ *n.* scope or range of a thing

ex·ten´u·ate *vt.* lessen seriousness by offering excuse

ex·te´ri·or *adj.* outermost; of the outside —*n.* the outside; an outer surface

ex·ter´mimate *vt.* destroy; eradicate completely —**ex·ter·mi·na´tion** *n.*

ex·ter´nal *adj.* on or of the outside

ex·tinct´ *adj.* no longer in existence

ex·tin´guish *vt.* to quench; destroy

ex´tir·pate *vt.* uproot, destroy completely, exterminate

ex·tol´, ex·toll´ *vt.* to praise; exalt

ex·tort´ *vt.* to obtain by violence or threats —**ex·tor´tion** *n.*

ex´tra *adj.* more than required; additional —*n.* something special or additional —*adv.* unusually

ex´tract *n.* a distillation; a quote —**ex·tract´** *vt.* to draw out; to quote

ex·tra·cur·ric´u·lar *adj.* outside the regular course of studies or work

ex´tra·dite *vt.* give over an accused person to another jurisdiction

ex·tra´ne·ous *adj.* not belonging; unrelated —**ex·tra´ne·ous·ly** *adv.*

ex·tra·or´di·nar·y *adj.* unusual; out of the ordinary; exceptional

ex·trap´o·late *vt.* to project a value from available data

ex·tra·sen´so·ry *adj.* outside the range of normal senses

ex·trav´a·gance *n.* excess spending; immoderation —**ex·trav´a·gant** *adj.* —**ex·trav´a·gant·ly** *adv.*

ex´tra·vert, ex´tro·vert *n.* one active and aggresive

ex·treme´ *adj.* most remote; utmost; to the greatest degree —*n.* a limit; a thing as far from another as possible —**ex·treme´ly** *adv.*

ex´tri·cate *vt.* release from difficulty; disentangle —**ex´tri·ca·ble** *adj.*

ex·u´ber·ant *adj.* spirited; enthusiastic —**ex·u´ber·ance** *n.*

ex·ult´ *vi.* to rejoice, celebrate

ex·ur´ban·ite *n.* one who lives in the suburbs of a city

f, F sixth letter of the alphabet

fa´ble *n.* story that teaches a lesson

fab´ric *n.* cloth; structure of a thing

fab´ri·cate´ *vt.* to manufacture or assemble; to invent a story; to lie

fab·u·lous adj. imaginary; fictitious; incredible, astonishing

fac´et n. the small plane surface of a gem; any aspect of a thing

fa·ce´tious adj. amusing; whimsical

fac´ile adj. easily accomplished

fa·cil´i·tate´ vt. to make convenient or easier

fa·cil´i·ty n. absence of difficulty; skill; building or equipment

fac·sim´i·le n. a reproduction

fact n. the truth; reliable information; anything that happens

fac´tion n. an opposition group within an organization

fac´tious adj. tending to cause dissension —**fac´tious·ly** adv.

fac·ti´tious adj. forced or artificial; not genuine

fac´tor n. one who acts as agent for another; any cause or condition

fac´to·ry n. a building for the manufacture or assembling of goods

fac´ul·ty n. ability to act; mental or physical ability; a body of teachers

fade vi. to lose color or distinction; to diminish in some way

fail vi., vt. fall short of need; cease to function properly; be unsuccessful

faint adj. lacking strength; indistinct —vi. to swoon —**faint´ly** adv.

faith n. unflagging trust; belief without proof; belief in a supreme being: a religion; fidelity

fal´con n. a bird of prey

fall vi. descend; decline; collapse —n. the act of falling; (US) autumn

fal´la·cy n. illogical reasoning —**fal·la´cious** adj.

fal´li·ble adj. questionable; liable to err —**fal·li·bil´i·ty** n.

false adj. deceitful; unfaithful; artificial —**false´ly** adv.

fal´si·fy vt. to misrepresent; alter with fraudulent intent

fa·mil´iar adj. intimate, informal; common; presumptuous

fam´i·ly n. members of a household; close relatives; a social unit; a related group of plants or animals

fam´ine n. a critical shortage of food

fam´ish vt. be hungry; to starve or cause to starve

fa´mous adj. very well known; renowned —**fa´mous·ly** adv.

fa·nat´ic, fa·nat´i·cal adj. overly enthusiastic —n. one unreasonably zealous —**fa·nat´i·cism** n.

fan´cy adj. elaborate; intricate —n. a whim; a delusion —vt. to imagine; to be fond of —**fan´ci·ful** adj.

fang n. a long, pointed tooth

fan·tas´tic adj. imaginary; strange, odd; fanciful

farce n. a broad comedy or satire; empty actions or ceremony

fare n. price for transport; a passenger; food —vi. prosper; to turn out.

far´ther adj. more distant —adv. more remote in time or place

fas´ci·nate vt. to charm, bewitch; to captivate —**fas·ci·na´tion** n.

fash′ion n. a popular style of dress —vt. to make or adapt —**fash′ion•a•ble** adj. —**fash′ion•a•bly** adv.

fas′ten vi. to become attached —vt. to attach or secure— **fas′ten•er** n.

fas•tid′i•ous adj. particular; difficult to satisfy; oversensitive

fa′tal adj. deadly; decisive; fateful —**fa′tal•ist** n. — **fa•tal•is′tic** adj.

fate n. inescapable future; destiny —vt. to predestine — **fat′ed** adj.

fath′om n. a measure for depth, equal to 6 feet —vt. to comprehend

fa•tigue′ n. weariness, exhaustion —vi., vt. to make or grow exhausted

fat′u•ous adj. silly, foolish; dim-witted —**fat′u•ous•ly** adv.

fau′cet (US) n. a device for regulating flow of a liquid

fault n. a flaw; a mistake; a liability —**fault′i•ness** n. — **fault′y** adj.

faux pas′ n. a socially unacceptable error; a tactless deed

fa′vour (Brit.), **fa′vor** (US) n. approval; a generous act; preferential treatment; a small gift —vt. to approve; to assist —**fa′vour•a•ble, fa′vor•a•ble** adj. —**fa′vour•a•ble•ness, fa′vor•a•ble•ness** n. —**fa′vour•a•bly, fa′vor•a•bly** adv.

fa′vour•ite (Brit.), **fa′vor•ite** (US) n. thing regarded fondly; one granted privileges; one most likely to win —adj. especially liked; preferred

fawn vi. to dote on; to curry favor

faze vt. to disturb; confuse

fear n. anxiety or dread; uneasiness or concern —vi. be afraid —vt. dread; regard with awe —**fear′ful** adj. — **fear′ful•ly** adv.

fea′si•ble adj. within reason; possible —**fea•si•bil′i•ty** n.

feast n. a festivity; a banquet —vi. to dine extravagantly — vt. entertain

feat n. an extraordinary deed

fea′ture n. a property or characteristic; a prominent written article

fe′ces n. pl. waste matter expelled by the body; excrement

fed′er•al adj. of a coalition of states

fed′er•ate vi., vt. unite under common authority —**fed•er•a′tion** n.

fee n. a charge

fee′ble adj. weak, infirm

feed vi. to eat; flow steadily— vt. furnish with food; to supply with material —n. food for animals

feel n. sense of touch; emotional or intuitive perception —vi., vt. to sense by touch; to base on emotion or intuition —**feel′ing** adj.

feign vi., vt. to pretend

feint n. a deceptive move -. vi., vt. make a deceptive move

feis′ty adj. lively or flamboyant; spirited —**feis′ti•ness** n.

fe•lic′i•tate vt. to congratulate; wish well; make happy

fe•lic′i•ty n. happiness; lightheartedness; a pleasing quality

fe`line *adj.* of or like a cat —*n.* a cat

fel`low *n.* an associate or colleague; a scholar

fel`on *n.* one guilty of serious crime

fel•o•ny *n.* serious crime — **fe•lo`nious** *adj.* —**fe•lo`ni•ous•ly** *adv.*

fe`male *adj.* of the sex that bears offspring; of a mechanical part —*n.* a female animal or plant

fem`i•nine** *adj.* having the qualities of a female —**fem`i•nin`i•ty *n.*

fem`i•nist *n.* one who advocates equal rights for women

fence *n.* a barrier that divides or protects; a dealer in stolen goods —*vi.* be evasive; deal in stolen goods —*vt.* to restrict by a barrier; sell to a dealer in stolen goods

fenc`ing *n.* the art of combat with a foil, saber, etc.

fend *vi.* to provide for oneself —*vt.* to ward off; to defend

fend`er (*US*) *n.* a guard that protects from damage by contact

fer•ment` *n.* substance that causes fermentation; state of agitation —*vt., vi.* cause or undergo fermentation; to agitate or be agitated

fer•men•ta`tion *n.* chemical conversion by a ferment; agitation

fe•ro`cious** *adj.* savage; unmerciful; ravenous —**fe•ro`cious•ly *adv.*

fer`ry *vt.* convey freight or passengers —*n.* vehicle for conveyance

fer`tile** *adj.* productive; teeming; rich in resources —**fer•til`i•ty *n.*

fer`vid *adj.* impassioned; zealous

fer`vour** (*Brit.*), **fer`vor (*US*) *n.* ardor; zeal; enthusiasm

fes`ter *vi., vt.* form pus; to rankle

fes`ti•val *n.* a celebration

fes`tive *adj.* joyous, lighthearted

fes•tiv`i•ty *n.* festival or celebration

fes•toon` *n.* a hanging garland; a decorative molding —*vt.* to decorate with garlands

fete, fête *n.* al festival —*vt.* to honor with a festival or celebration

fe`tish *n.* object having magical powers; an object of devotion

fet`id *adj.* having an offensive smell; stinking

fe•tol`o•gy *n.* the discipline dealing with the study and care of a fetus

fet`ter *n.* a shackle for the feet; a restraint —*vt.* to constrain; restrain

fe`tus *n.* an unborn young

feud *n.* a bitter, long-lasting quarrel —*vi.* sustain a quarrel

fe`ver *n.* a condition characterized by increased body temperature; a state of exceptional excitement

fi•an•cé` *n.* a man engaged to marry

fi•an•cée` *n.* a woman engaged to marry

fi•as`co *n.* a complete and utter failure; a debacle

fi`at *n.* a legal order; a decree

fi`ber** (*US*), **fi`bre (*Brit.*) *n.* a threadlike structure —**fi`brous** *adj.*

fick`le *adj.* flighty or unstable

fic´tion *n.* an imaginary story; a narrative portraying imaginary characters and events

fic·ti´tious *adj.* pretended; made up, imaginary — **fic·ti´tious·ly** *adv.*

fi·del´i·ty *n.* loyalty; devotion to duty; accuracy

fi·du´ci·ar´y *adj.* of one who holds In trust for another; of that held in trust — *n.* one who holds in trust

field *n.* open land; a plot of ground for crops or pasture; any unbroken expanse; an area of endeavor

fiend *n.* an evil spirit, a demon; one exceptionally cruel; one addicted

fierce *adj.* savagely cruel; violent; passionate or intense

fi´er·y *adj.* containing or like fire; impetuous or emotional

fight *vi., vt.* take part in con flict — *n.* conflict or struggle; boldness; readiness to struggle — **fight´er** *n.*

fig´ur·a·tive *adj.* symbolic; not taken literally — **fig´u·ra·tive·ly** *adv.*

fig´ure *n.* a form or likeness; a diagram; a character repre senting a value — *vi., vt.* calculate; consider

fil´a·ment *n.* threadlike component

file *n.* a storage cabinet, folder. etc.; a collection of data; a line of people or things; a tool for smoothing — *vi.* march in line; formally petition to a court — *vt.* place and store documents, data, etc.; place on record; to smooth or scrape

fil´i·al *adj.* due of a son or daughter

fil´i·gree´ *n.* ornamental work

fill *n.* a thing used to take space or make full; built up land; a satisfactory amount — *vt.* bring to a desired level; make full; occupy; furnish that needed; satisfy hunger

fil´ly *n.* a young mare

film *n.* a thin layer or coating; sensitized material in photography; a motion picture — *vi., vt.* to coat; make a motion picture

fil´ter *n.* a porous substance for separating materials — *vi., vt.* pass through a filter

filth *n.* dirt; grime; contamination; lewd material; an obscenity

filth´y *adj.* dirty; obscene

fil´trate *vt.* strain or separate — *n.* a filtered substance — **fil·tra´tion** *n.*

fi´nal *adj.* at the end; conclusive — *n.* last of a series

fi·nance´, fi·nance´ *n.* money management — *vt.* furnish money or credit — **fi·nan´cial** *adj.*

finances the resources of a person, company, etc.

fin·an·cier´ *n.* one specializing in financial operations

find *n.* an amazing discovery — *vt.* to discover or perceive; to experience

fine *adj.* of exceptional quality; small, thin, or keen — *n.* payment as a penalty — *vt.* impose a fine

fin´ger *n.* a digit; thing resembling a finger — *vt.* to touch; point out

fin´ish *n.* an end; a completion; surface of an object; fineness of manner — *vt.* bring to an end; use up; apply a final coat

fi´nite *adj.* of a defined limit

fir *n.* a cone-bearing ever-green tree

fire *n.* combustion; strong feeling, ardor; a discharge of firearms —*vt., vi.* set afire; bake in a kiln; excite, inspire; discharge a firearm; dismiss an employee

fire'proof *adj.* not easily burned —*vt.* make less combustible

firm *adj.* solid or dense; not yielding to pressure; secure, immovable; settled, as a contract; determined —*n.* a business

fir'ma•ment *n.* the heavens

first *adj.* before all others —*n* one above all; the beginning —*adv.*

first aid emergency treatment

first'-class', first'-rate' *adj.* of the best quality —*adv.*

fis'cal *adj.* of taxation or public finances; of financial policy

fish *n.* an aquatic animal — *vi., vt.* try to catch fish —*adj.* pertaining to or made from fish

fis'sion *n.* a splitting —**nuclear fission** splitting of atoms to release energy — **fis'sion•a•ble** *adj.*

fis'sure *n.* a long, narrow crack

fit *adj.* able, competent; appropriate, suitable; trim, healthy —*n* being appropriate; a seizure —*vi.* to be suited —*vt.* be appropriate; alter to make suitable; insert in position

fit'ting *adj.* appropriate; suitable —*n.* process of testing or altering; a connector — **fit'ting•ly** *adv.*

fix *n.* an awkward situation

—*vt.* to fasten firmly; establish with certainty; repair

fix•a'tion *n.* a preoccupation; obsession —**fix'ate** *vi., vt.*

fix'ture *n.* a thing firmly fastened; that which seems permanent

flab'by *adj.* soft, weak; lacking good physical form — **flab'bi•ness** *n.*

flac'cid *adj.* weak, feeble, soft

flag *n.* a cloth banner —*vi.* to grow weak; tire —*vt.* signal by waving

flab'el•late *vt.* to whip

fla'grant *adj.* outragious; openly disgraceful —**fla'gran•cy** *n.*

flake *n.* a small, thin piece; one flightly or fickle —*vi., vt.* to form or chip off into flakes —**flak'y** *adj.*

flame *n.* light from a fire —*vi.* burn brightly; become excited; show the flush of excitement —**flam'ing** *adj.*

flange *n.* a projecting edge

flank *n.* side —*vt.* to be at the side of

flap *n.* a flat, broad piece; a slapping sound; a state of excitement —*vi., vt.* move back and forth; to flutter

flare *n.* a bright light; a sudden burst —*vi.* emit a sudden burst of light; spread out at one end

flash *adj.* happening suddenly —*n.* a brief gleam; that comes and goes quickly; ostentation —*vi.* emit a sudden light; pass swiftly —*vt.* display briefly —**flash'i•ness** *n.*

flash'back *n.* a memory or reminiscence; an interruption to portray an earlier event

flask *n.* a small bottle

flat¹ *adj.* even; with no variation; lying prone; bland; lacking finances —*n.* a level surface; a musical note — *adv.* —**flat´ten** *vi., vt.*

flat² *n.* (Brit.) living quarters

flat´ter *vt.* compliment excessively or disingenuously — **flat´ter•y** *n.*

flaunt *vi., vt.* make an ostentatious or impudent display

fla´vor (US) *n.* taste; a thing added to alter taste; a distinctive quality —*vt.* impart flavor to —**fla´vor•er** *n.*

fla´vor•ful (US) *adj.* full of flavor; delectable

fla´vor•ing (US) *n.* a substance, such as an extract, that imparts flavor

fla´vor•less (US) *adj.* lacking flavor; flat or insipid

fla´vour (Brit.) *n.* taste; thing added to alter taste; distinctive quality —*vt.* impart flavor to —**fla´vour•er** *n.*

fla´vour•ful (Brit.) *adj.* full of flavor; delectable

fla´vour•ing (Brit.) *n.* a substance that imparts flavor

fla´vour•less (Brit.) *adj.* lacking flavor; flat or insipid

flaw *n.* a defect —*vt., vi.* to make or become defective

flay *vt.* to strip the skin from, as by whipping; to criticize harshly

fleck *n.* a small particle —*vt.* to cover with specks

flee *vi., vt.* to run away or escape

fleece *n.* a coat of wool —*vt.* to clip the wool from a sheep; to defraud

fleet *adj.* swift; temporary — *vi.* proceed swiftly —**fleet´ness** *n.*

fleet *n.* the ships, planes, etc.,

operating under a single authority

fleet´ing *adj.* passing quickly; transitory —**fleet´ing•ly** *adv.*

flesh *n.* meat of an animal; edible portion of fruits and vegetables; the human body; human desires

flesh´ly *adj.* pertaining to the body; sensual; plump — **flesh´li•ness** *n.*

flex´i•ble *adj.* able to bend; amenable to change —**flex´i•bil•i•ty** *n.*

flex´time *n.* varied working hours

flight *n.* travel by air; fleeing; running away; a set of steps

flight´y *adj.* frivolous; whimsical

flim´sy *adj.* easily damaged; fragile; poorly fashioned — **flim´si•ness** *n.*

flinch *vi.* to wince or shrink back

fling *vt.* throw forcefully or violently; act spontaneously —*n.* a violent throw; a time of wild abandon

flint *n.* a very hard stone

flint´y *adj.* like flint; unyielding

flip´pant *adj.* frivolous; lacking reverence; impertinent

flirt *n.* a trifler; a coquette — *vi.* trifle with affection; consider briefly —**flir´ta´tion** *n.* —**flir•ta´tious** *adj.*

float *n.* that resting on the surface; a decorated platform —*vi.* rest on the surface; drift on the air

flock *n.* a group or congregation —*vi.* assemble in a group

flog *vt.* beat with a whip

flood *n.* covering of dry land

with water; a deluge or glut —*vt.* to overflow, inundate, or glut

floor *n.* surface of a room; a bottom surface; level of a building; recognition to speak —*vt.* to build or refinish a surface; defeat or astound

flo´ra *n.* the plants of a region

flo´ral *adj.* of or like flowers

flor´id *adj.* gaudy, ornate; of a rosy complexion —**flor´id•ness** *n.*

flor´ist *n.* one who sells flowers

flo•til´la *n.* a fleet of boats

floun´der *n.* a flatfish —*vi.* have difficulty; struggle

flour *n.* a fine meal —*vt.* to make into flour; to sprinkle with flour

flour´ish *n.* anything showy; a sweeping motion; an elaborate fanfare —*vi.* prosper — *vt.* decorate ornately; wave with a sweep of the arm

flout *vi. vt.* to mock; to regard contemptuously —*n.* a mocking insult

flow *n.* emanation; rate of discharge; course of a river, etc.; a continuous stream — *vi.* move in a stream; progress smoothly

flow´er *n.* a bloom; a plant cultivated for blossoms; the best part —*vi.* to bloom; attain the best level

fluc´tu•ate *vi.* vary continuously; to waver —*vt.* cause to waver

flue *n.* an exhaust for smoke, etc

flu´ent *adj.* smooth flowing; able to speak or write well— **flu´en•cy** *n.*

flu´id *adj.* flowing; graceful in movement; readily changed —*n.* a substance that flows

fluke *n.* that happening by chance

flunk *vi., vt.* to fail in school

flunk´y *n,* a servant; one engaged for menial tasks

flush *adj.* well supplied; even —*n.* a rapid flow; a warm glow; sudden exhilaration — *vi., vt.* flow rapidly; clean with flowing liquid; to blush

flus´ter *vi., vt.* to make or become nervous or confused

flut´ter *n.* rapid waving or fluctuation; a commotion — *vi., vt.* wave or fluctuate rapidly; move restlessly

flux *n.* a flowing; constant change

fly *n.* a flap over an opening; an insect —*vi., vt.* to travel by air; to operate an aircraft; to flee

fo´cus *n.* a point of convergence or concentration —*vi., vt.* to adjust to produce a clear image —**fo´cal** *adj.*

foe *n.* an adversary, enemy

fog *n.* a dense mist —*vt.* to obscure —**fog´gi•ness** *n.* — **fog´gy** *adj.*

foi´ble *n.* a minor weakness

foil *n.* a thin sheet of metal; a fencing sword —*vt.* to frustrate

foist *vt.* to pass off by trickery

fold *n.* a doubling; a pen for sheep —*vt.* close a business —*vt.* to double; to envelop

fo´li•age *n,* plant leaves

folk *adj.* of the common people —*n.* people generally; a tribe, family, nation, etc. — **folks•y** *adj.*

folk´lore´ *n.* traditions of a culture

fol´low *vi., vt.* come next;

conform; happen as a result; trail or pursue —**follow through** to complete

fol•low•ing adj. ensuing —n. supporters; a calling

fol´ly n. foolishness; a frivolous act or undertaking

fo•ment´ vt. advocate; incite

fond adj. cherished; doting or indulgent —**fond´ly** adv. — **fond´ness** n.

fon´dle vt. caress or stroke

font n. size and style of type; a water basin or fountain; a place of origin

food n. a substance that nourishes; something that stimulates

fool n. one lacking sense; a silly person —vi. act silly — vt. mislead or cheat — **fool´ish** adj.

fop to one overly devoted to personal appearance

for´age n. food for animals, fodder —vi., vt. search for food or supplies

for´ay n. a raid or venture — vt. raid

for•bear´ vt. abstain; to restrain oneself —**for•bear´ ance** n.

for•bid´ vt. prohibit; order against; to prevent —**for• bid´den** adj.

for•bid´ding adj. frightening; unpleasant —**for•bid´ding•ly** adv.

force n. potency; might; power to compel; an organized group —vt; to overpower; to compel by might

fore´bear n. an ancestor

fore•bode´ vi., vt. predict; anticipate

fore´cast n. a prediction —vi., vt. to anticipate

fore•close´ vi., vt. take away

the right to property —**fore• clo´sure** n.

fore´fa•ther n. an ancestor

for´eign adj. from another country; unfamiliar; exotic.

fore´man n. one in charge of a group

fo•ren´sic adj. pertaining to legal or formal argumentation

fore´run´ner n. one coming before; an ancestor; a sign or omen

fore•see´ vt. to predict; foretell

fore´sight´ n. ability to anticipate

for´est n. extensive growth of trees

fore•tell´ vi., vt. predict

for•ev´er adv. for all time

for´feit n. that lost by neglect, etc. —vt. to give up —**for´ fei•ture** n.

fore•warn´ vt. to warn beforehand

forge n. a furnace for heating metal —vi., vt. to form laboriously, as metal; to falsify in order to deceive

for´ger•y n. an illegal making or altering; an imitation or fake

for•get´ vi., vt. to lose from memory; to overlook or neglect

for•get´ful adj. losing ability to remember; careless or neglectful

for•give´ vt. to pardon; overlook

fork n. a device with prongs; a dividing —vi., vt. split into branches

for•lorn´ adj. abandoned; wretched; without hope

form n. configuration; a mold; type; convention; method — vi., vt. mold or shape;

formal   fraudulent

for·mal *adj.* according to custom; correct or suitable; precise; stodgy

for·mal´ity *n.* careful adherence to custom; an official act

for·ma´tion *n.* a thing formed; arrangement or configuration

for´mer *adj.* coming before; preceding; the first of two

for´mi·da·ble *adj.* awesome; threatening; overwhelming

for´mu·la *n.* a representation using symbols; a precise specification

for´mu·late *vt.* to conceive or develop; express as a formula

for·ni·ca´tion *n.* sexual intercourse between unmarried persons

for·sake´ *vt.* forgo; leave or abandon

forte *n.* one's special ability

for´ti·fy *vt.* make stronger

for´ti·tude *n.* strength of character; determination

fort´night *n.* two weeks time

for·tu·i´tous *adj.* occurring by chance; fortunate —**for·tu´i·ty** *n.*

for´tu·nate *adj.* lucky; auspicious

for´tune *n.* luck; fate; riches

fo´rum *n.* a gathering for discussion

fos´sil *n.* preserved remains

fos´ter *vt.* to promote; to nurture

foul *adj.* offensive; profane; underhanded; entangled; unpleasant —*vi., vt.* to soil; to entangle

found *adj.* discovered —*vt.* to bring into being; to cast metal

foun·da´tion *n.* a fundamental principle; a charitable endowment

foun´dry *n.* the process of casting metal; a place where metal is cast

foun´tain *n.* a natural or artificial spring; a reservoir

fox´y *adj.* crafty, cunning; attractive, seductive —**fox´i·ness** *n.*

fra´cas *n.* a brawl

fraction *n.* is small part; value expressed as parts of a whole

frac´tious *adj.* unruly; difficult to manage; irritable or testy

fracture *n.* a crack or break —*vi.* to crack or break

frag´ile *adj.* easily damaged; delicate

frag´ment *n.* a part or piece

fra´grance *n.* a pleasant odor

frail *adj.* easily damaged; delicate; feeble or weak —**frail´ty** *n.*

frame *n.* skeletal structure; general form; field of view —*vt.* shape or form; provide a border

frame of reference a point or aspect from which something is viewed

fran´chise´ *n.* a right or privilege

fran´gi·ble *adj.* fragile; brittle

frank *adj.* open and honest

frantic *adj.* distraught; highly emotional —**fran´ti·cal·ly** *adv.*

fra·ter´nal *adj.* brotherly

fraternize *vi.* have friendly relations with —**frat·er·ni·za´tion** *n.*

fraud *n.* deception; swindler; faker

fraud´u·lent *adj.* deceitful;

marked by fraud —**fraud´u·lence** n.

fray n. a brawl —vi., vt. become worn

freak adj. abnormal; bizarre —n. an abnormality — **freak´ish** adj.

free adj. not busy; independent; unrestrained; without obligation; without cost —vt. release or make available — **free´ly** adv.

fren´zy n. a sudden burst of agitation or activity —**fren´zied** adj.

fre´quent adj. happening often —**fre·quent´** vt. to stop by often

fres´co n. a painting on wet plaster

fresh adj. newly made; natural; uninitiated; impertinent, impudent

fret vi., vt. be irritated or annoyed —**fret´ful** adj. —**fret´ful·ly** adv.

fri´a·ble adj. easily crumbled

fric´tion n. a rubbing or abrasion; discord caused by differences

friend n. an ally or supporter

fright n. sudden alarm or terror; a startling sight

fright´en vt. to cause alarm or terror

frill n. gathered edging; an unnecessary adjunct — **frill´y** adj.

fringe adj. at the edge; minor or peripheral —n. edging; an outer edge —vt. decorate with a fringe

fringe benefit indirect compensation

frisky adj. energetic; playful

frit´ter n. deep-fried food coated with batter —vt. waste bit by bit

friv´o·lous adj. trivial; not serious or sensible —**frivol´i·ty** n.

frol´ic n. merriment, play —vi. play

front n. the forward part; appearance or demeanor; an area of activity —**fron´tal** adj.

fron·tier´ n. the border of a country; an unexplored area

frost n. ice crystals; coldness —vt. to coat with frosting — **frost´i·ness** n.

froth n. foam; something trivial —vi., vt. to foam

frown n. a stern look —vi., vt. scowl; show disapproval

frugal adj. thrifty; inexpensive

fruit n. the edible portion of a plant; a consequence — **fruit´ful** adj.

fru·i´tion n. the yielding of results; fulfillment

frus´trate vt. to nullify the efforts of another —**frus·tra´tion** n.

fu´el n. anything consumed to produce energy

fu·gi·tive n. one who flees; something elusive

ful´crum n. support for a lever

ful·fill´ vt. to perform or accomplish

full adj. containing all possible; of the highest degree; puffed out

ful´mi·nate´ n. an explosive salt —vi., vt. to denounce loudly; explode

ful´some adj. obsequious or fawning; abundant

fum´ble vi.,vt. to grope awkwardly; blunder

fume n. a vapor —vi. give off vapor; show anger

fu´mi·gate´ vt. disinfect

func´tion *n.* normal use, an event —*vi.* to perform as designed

fund *n.* an institution that manages designated assets —*vt.* to finance

fun´da•men´tal *adj.* essential; basic —*n.* a principle; an essential part

fu´ner•al *n.* ceremony concerned with burial of the dead

fu•ne´re•al *adj.* solemn

fur´bish *vt.* restore; to polish

fu´ri•ous *adj.* enraged; frenzied

fur´nace (*US*) *n.* an appliance for producing heat

fur´nish *vt.* supply; to provide

fur´nish•ings *pl. n.* household goods; clothing and accessories

fur´ni•ture *n.* equipment that makes a room fit for habitation or work

fu´ror *n.* a state of excitement

fur´row *n.* a rut; a deep wrinkle —*vt., vt.* make a rut or wrinkle

fur´ther *adj.* additional; more distant —*adv.* farther; to a greater extent; moreover —*vt.*— to aid or promote —**fur´ther•more** *adv.*

fur´tive *adj.* stealthy, sneaky

fu´ry *n.* violent anger; violence

fuse *n.* device for setting off an explosive; device that prevents overloading an electrical circuit —*vi., vt.* to unite or blend

fu´sion *n.* a melting or joining by heat; a nuclear reaction

fuss *n.* a quarrel; a commotion; needless concern —*vi.* complain; bother over trifles —*vt.* worry needlessly

fu´tile *adj* hopeless; trivial

fu´ture *adj.* to come; expected —*n.* a time or event to come; outlook

fuzz´y *adj.* indistinct

g, G seventh letter of the alphabet; slang term for 1000 dollars

gab *n.* idle talk —*vi.* to gossip

gabble *n.* meaningless chatter —*vi., vt.* to jabber or chatter

gadg´et *n.* any implement; a device of limited utility

gag *n.* a joke; a thing placed over the mouth; restriction of free speech —*vi.* choke or retch —*vt.* to silence

gai´e•ty *n.* mirth; festivity; gaudiness

gain *n.* an increase; an advantage —*vi., vt.* to acquire; to reach

gala *adj.* joyful —*n.* a celebration

gal´ax•y *n.* a star system; a gathering of distinctive persons or things

gale *n.* a strong wind

gall *n.* bile; impertinence

gal´lant *adj.* chivalrous; dashing —**gal•lant´** *n.* a lover; one who is chivalrous —**gal´lant•ly** *adv.*

gal´lon *n.* a liquid measure equal to four quarts

gam´bit *n.* a strategy designed to gain an advantage

gam´ble *n.* a risk —*vi., vt.* take a risk

gam´bol *vi.* jump about; frolic

gan´der *n.* a male goose —**take a gander** look

gang *n.* a group

gang´ster *n.* a criminal

gaol (*Brit.*), **jail** (*US*) *n.* a place of confinement —*vt.* to confine —**gaol´er** (*Brit.*), **jail´er** (*US*) *n.*

gape *n.* a large opening; an open-mouthed stare —*vi.* yawn; stare in amazement; to open wide

ga·rage´ *n.* a building for storing or repairing an automobile

garb *n.* clothing —*vt.* to clothe

gar´ble *vt.* confuse or distort

gar´bage (US) *n.* waste, trash

gar´den *n.* a plot of cultivated land —*vi.*, *vt.* to cultivate a plot of land

gar´gle *n.* a solution for medicating or cleansing the throat —*vi.*, *vt.* to cleanse or medicate the throat

gar´ish *adj.* overly ornate, gaudy

gar´ment *n.* an article of clothing

gar´ner *n.* collect and store; acquire

gar´nish *n.* a decoration —*vt.* to decorate

gar´ret *n.* an attic room

gar´ru·lous *adj.* chattering; wordy

gas *n.* vapor; a mixture used for anesthesia, fuel, etc.; something enjoyable; (US) gasoline

gash *n.* a deep cut —*vt.* make a cut

gasket *n.* a washer, a seal

gas·o·line´ *n.* a liquid fuel

gasp *n.* a catching of the breath —*vi.* inhale sharply or with difficulty

gas´tric *adj.* relating to the stomach

gath´er *vi.*, *vt.* convene or assemble; accumulate; draw together; to infer or conclude

gaud´y *adj.* garish; vulgar

gauge *n.* a standard measure; a measuring device —*vt.* to measure or estimate

gaunt *adj.* thin and bony; drawn; dreary, barren

gay *adj.* lively, merry; bright.

gaze *n.* a steady look —*vi.* to look intently; to stare

gaz´et·teer´ *n.* a geographical dictionary or index

gear *n.* personal property; equipment, a device that transmits energy

gem *n.* a precious stone; anything prized for its value

gene *n.* unit that transmits hereditary characteristics

gen´e·al´o·gy *n.* a record of one's lineage, the study of lineage

gen´er·al *adj.* extensive and diversified; non-exclusive; imprecise

gen´er·ate´ *vt.* to originate or bring into being; produce

gen´er·a´tion *n.* the process of producing; a stage of development

ge·ner´ic *adj.* of a class or group

gen´er·ous *adj.* gracious, unselfish; ample —**gen·er·os´i·ty** *n.*

gen´e·sis *n.* origin

ge·net´ic, ge·net´i·cal *adj.* of origin or ancestry **ge·net´i·cal·ly** *adv.*

ge·net´ics *n.* the study of ancestry

gen´ial *adj.* pleasant; amiable

gen´ius *n.* exceptional natural ability or mental capacity

gen´o·cide´ *n.* the systematic extermination of a people

gen´tle *adj.* kindly; temperate; courtly; tame

gen´u·ine *adj.* authentic; sincere and honest

ge·og´ra·phy *n.* study of the earth and its inhabitants; physical nature of an area

ge•ol´o•gy *n.* the study of the earth's structure and development

germ *n.* basic form; a microorganism; a basic concept

ger´mi•nate *vi., vt.* sprout; to begin growth —**ger•mi•na´tion** *n.*

ges•tic´u•late´ *vi., vt.* gesture

ges´ture *n.* a move that emphasizes; something done for effect

get *vt.* to acquire; to understand

ghast´ly *adj.* shocking; terrifying; ghostlike; offensive

ghet´to *n.* an isolated community

ghost *n.* a disembodied spirit; a faint suggestion

gi´ant *adj.* of great size —*n.* anything of exceptional size

gibe *n.* a taunting remark —*vi., vt.* to taunt or ridicule

gift *n.* something freely given; a natural ability

gi•gan´tic *adj.* enormous

gig´gle *n.* a silly nervous laugh —*vi.* to laugh nervously

gild *vt.* to coat with gold; make attractive; to make seem attractive

gilt *adj.* gilded —*n.* gildingç

gim´mick *n.* a thing designed to deceive; a device to gain attention

gird *vt.* encircle with a belt or band

gird´er *n.* a large supporting beam

gist *n.* the primary concept

give *vi.,vt.* to contribute; impart; to yield to pressure

glad *adj.* happy; pleased —**glad´den** *vt.* —**glad´ly** *adv.*

glade *n.* open space in a woods

glance *n.* a brief look; a deflecting —*vi.* to fly off at an angle; look briefly

glare *n.* intense light; a fixed stare —*vi.* shine intensely; stare

glaze *n.* a glassy finish —*vt.* give a glassy finish; fit with glass

gleam *n.* a flash of light; a faint display —*vi.* to appear briefly

glean *vt.* collect grain left by reapers; obtain piecemeal —**glean´ings** *n.*

glee *n.* gaiety, merriment

glib *adj.* fluency —**glib´ly** *adv.*

glide *n.* a smooth,. flowing movement —*vi.* move smoothly

glim´mer *n.* a faint light; a trace —*vi.* to appear faintly

glimpse *n.* a quick view —*vi.* to glance —*vt.* view briefly

glis´ten *vi.* to sparkle or shine

glit´ter *n.* sparkling light; bits of decorative material —*vi.* sparkle; be brilliant —**gilt´ter´y** *adj.*

gloat *vi.* to view with malicious pleasure

glob´al *adj.* world-wide; comprehensive

globe *n.* a sphere; the earth

glob´ule *n.* a tiny globe, a drop

gloom *n.* dimness or darkness; despondency —**gloom´y** *adj.*

glo´ri•ous *adj.* splendid, pleasant; famed —**glo´ri•ous•ly** *adv.*

glo´ry *n.* splendor; fame; a state of well-being —*vi.* be proud of; rejoice in —**glo´ri•fy** *vt* —**glo´ri•ous** *adj.*

gloss *n.* shine or luster; a superficial image —*vt.* make

shiny; pass over or cover up
—**gloss´i•ness** *n.*

glos´sa•ry *n.* list of definitions

glow *n.* soft light; a feeling of warmth give off light; be flushed

glow´er *n.* a scowl —*vi.* to scowl

glue *n.* an adhesive —*vt.* to affix

glum *adj.* sullen, dejected

glut *n.* an oversupply —*vt.* to oversupply; to overburden

glut´ton *n.* an overeater

gnaw *vi., vt.* wear away with the teeth; to worry

goad *vt.* to prod or urge; provoke

goal *n.* an objective

gob´ble•dy•gook *n.* wordy, ambiguous language

gob´let *n.* a stemmed drinking glass

gob´lin *n.* a mischievous elf

gone *adj.* departed; used up

gon´er *n.* one beyond help

gore *n.* blood from a wound —*vt.* wound with a horn

gorge *n.* a ravine —*vi., vt.* to devour

gor´geous *adj.* exceptionally beautiful; delightful

gos´sip *n.* idle chatter; one who gossips —*vi.* engage in idle chatter

gouge *n.* a type of chisel; an overcharging —*vt.* to cut into; to cheat

gour•mand´ *n.* one fond of good food

gour•met´ *n.* a good judg of fine food and drink

gov´ern *vt.* to control or influence; to regulate or restrath

gov´ern•ment *n.* a system of administration and its agencies

gown *n.* a long flowing garment

grab *vt.* seize roughly; take by deceit; attract one's attention; to impress

grace *n.* a pleasing quality; good will; a temporary extension; a blessing —*vt.* adorn; dignify

grace´ful *adj.* having elegance

gra´cious *adj.* courteous and affable; compassionate; comfortable or luxurious —**gra´cious•ly** *adv.*

gra•da´tion *n.* a gradual progression

grade *n.* a level in a progression; a rating; degree of slope —*vt.* to rate or classify; change the slope of

gradient *adj.* sloping —*n.* a slope

grad´u•al *adj.* progressing in slow or regular steps —**grad´u•al•ly** *adv.*

grad´u•ate *n.* one completing a course of study; a container for measuring —*vi.* complete a course of study —*vt.* award a diploma; mark a container for measuring

graf•fi´to *n., pl.* **graf•fi´ti** a crudely-drawn inscription

graft *n.* joining of tissue; tissue so joined; profit by extortion —*vi., vt.* to join tissue; obtain by extortion

gram´mar *n.* the structure of a language; rules for use of a language

grand *adj.* high in rank; imposing; luxurious; noble —**grandeur** *n.*

grad´dil•o•quent *adj.* spoken pretentiously

gran´di•ose *adj.* pompous

grant *n.* something given —*vt.* to give

gran´ular *adj.* grainy

granule *n.* a small particle

graphic, graphical *adj.* explicit; described clearly; regarding anything written or pictorial

grap´ple *vi.* to struggle —*vt.* to seize

grasp *n.* a firm hold; comprehension —*vt. to* take hold; comprehend

grasp´ing *adj.* greedy

grate *n. a* framework *of* metal bars —*vt., vi.* make a harsh sound; irritate; to shred

grate´ful *adj.* appreciative

grat´i•fy´ *vt.* to afford pleasure; to indulge —**grat´i•fi•ca´tion** *n.*

grat´i•tude *n.* appreciation

gra•tu´i•tous *adj. given* freely; without cause —**gra•tu´i•tous•ly** *adv.*

gra•tu´i•ty *n.* gift for services

grave *adj.* serious; somber — *n.* a place for burial

grav´el *n.* crushed rock

grav´i•tate´ *vi.* to be inclined or attracted towards —**grav•i•ta´tion** *n.*

grav´i•ty *n.* seriousness; the attraction between celestial bodies

graze *vi., vt.* to feed on; touch lightly

grease *n.* melted animal fat; a lubricant —*vt.* to lubricate

great *adj.* large; extensive; important; skillful

greed *n.* excessive desire

greet *vt,* to welcome; to acknowledge

gre•gar´i•ous *adj.* sociable; tending to join or associate in groups

grid *n.* a network of horizontal and vertical parallel lines, bars, etc.

grid´dle *n.* a flat iron pan

grief *n.* sadness, sorrow; a difficulty

griev´ance *n.* a wrong; a complaint

grieve *vt., vi.* to express grief

grim *adj.* stern; forbidding

grime *n.* dirt; filth —**grim´y** *adj.*

grin *n.* a broad smile —*vi.* to smile

grind *vt.* to crush; shape by rubbing

grip *n. a* hold; a device for grasping; a small suitcase — *vi., vt.* to hold

gripe *vi. a* complaint —*vi.* complain

gris´ly *adj.* horrible, ghastly

grit *n.* small, hard particles; determination or pluck —*vt.* to clench or grind the teeth —**grit´ty** *adj.*

groan *n.* a sound of distress; a moan —*vi.* make *a* low moaning sound

grog´gy *adj.* sluggish or dazed

grom´met *n.* reinforcement for a hole *in* cloth or other light material

groom *n.* a bridegroom; one who tends horses —*vt.* to make attractive; train for a purpose

groove *n.* a channel; *a* settled pattern —*vt.* cut a channel

grope *vi.* to feel around or search uncertainly —*vt.* to fondle

gross *adj.* coarse, unrefined; offensive; flagrant; total —*n.* a total; twelve dozen —*vi., vt.* earn in total

gro•tesque´ *adj.* bizarre; distorted; *hideous* —**gro•tesque´ly** *adv.*

grot´to *n.* a cavern

grouch *n.* one prone to

complain; a discontented person — *vi.* to grumble or complain; to sulk

ground *n.* a surface; soil; an area set aside for a special use; a basis or foundation — *vt* place on the surface; provide a basis

grounds *pl. n.* land around an estate

ground´less *adj.* without cause

group *n.* a number of persons or things —*vi., vt.* arrange together

group´ie *n.* an avid fan

grouse *n.* a game bird —*vi.* complain

grove *n.* a stand of trees

grov´el *vi.* to cower; to fawn over; to humble oneself

grow *vi.* come to be; to increase —*vt.* cultivate — **growth** *n.*

grown *adj.* mature; cultivated

grub´by *adj.* filthy; wretched

grudge *n.* ongoing resentment

gru´el•ing *adj.* extremely demanding; exhausting

grue´some *adj.* frightful; hideous; grotesque

gruff *adj.* brusque; surly

grum´ble *vi.* complain; rumble

grump´y *adj.* grouchy

grun´gy *adj.* filthy; shabby

guar´an•tee´ *n.* assurance; surety —*vt.* assure —**guar´an•tor** *n.*

guard *n.* protection —*vt.* keep watch; to protect

guard´ed *adj.* protected; cautious

gu´ber•na•to´ri•al *adj.* relating to the office of governor

guess *n.* an estimate —*vi., vt.* to estimate; presume

guest *n.* a visitor; a visiting artist

guide *vt.* lead, direct —**guid´ance** *n.*

guild *n.* an association

guile *n.* craftiness, cunnin

guilt *n.* liability —**guilt´y** *adj.*

guise *n.* appearance; pretense

gulch *n.* a ravine

gulf *n.* a large inlet; a wide expanse

gul´li•ble *adj.* easily deceived —**gul•li•bil´i•ty** *n.* —**gul´li•bly** *adv.*

gul´ly *n.* a small ravine

gump´tion *n.* initiative; nerve

gu´ru *n.* a spiritual advisor

gush *n.* a strong flow —*vi.* to surge; to be overly enthused — **gush´y** *adj.*

gust *n.* sudden burst or rush

gus´ta•to´ry *adj.* pertaining to the sense of taste

gus´to *n.* enthusiasm, ardor

gut´tur•al *adj.* harsh or throaty

guz´zle *vi., vt.* drink greedily

gyp *n.* a swindle or swindler —*vi., vt.* to swindle or cheat

gy´rate´ *vi.* revolve in a circle

h, H eighth letter of the alphabet

hab´er•dash•er *n.* (Brit.) seller of sewing needs; one who sells men's clothing —**hab´er•dash•er•y** *n.*

hab´it *n.* customary behavior; addiction; a manner of dress

hab´i•tat *n.* native environment

hab•i•ta´tion *n.* a dwelling

habit´u•é *n.* a habitual visitor

hack´neyed *adj.* commonplace; trite

hag *n.* an ugly old woman; a witch

hag´gard *adj.* drawn or gaunt

hag´gle *vi.* bargain

hail *n.* frozen rain; a greeting;

a barrage —*vt.* fall as frozen
rain —*vt.* greet with cheers;
call out

hair grip (*Brit.*) a metal hair
pin

hair slide (*Brit.*) a small appliance for keeping hair in
place

hal´cy•on *adj.* tranquil

hale *adj.* healthy

half *adj.* partial —*adv.* partly
—*n* one of two equal parts

half´heart´ed *adj.* lacking
enthusiasm —**half´heart´ed•
ly** *adv.*

hal´i•to´sis *n.* stale breath

hall *n.* a large room; a passageway

hall´mark *n.* a mark of quality; a distinctive feature

hal´low *vt.* to make or regard
as holy

hal•lu´ci•nate *vi., vt.* see that
which is not real; fantasize
—**hal•lu´ci•na´to•ry** *adj.*

hal•lu´ci•no•gen *n.* a substance that causes one to
hallucinate

halt *n.* a stop —*vi.* stop;
hesitate or be uncertain —
vt. cause to stop

halve *at.* divide; to reduce by
half

ham´let *n.* a small village

ham´per *n.* a large basket —
vt. prevent from moving
freely

hand *n.* part of the body at
the end of the arm —*vt.* provide

hand´book *n.* a manual

hand´ful *n.* a small amount;
that difficult to manage

hand´i•cap´ *n.* a hindrance —
vt. to hinder

hand´i•work´ *n.* that done by
one's own efforts

han´dle *n.* part designed for

gripping —*vt.* to touch, hold,
etc.; manage or deal with; to
trade in

hand´out *n.* a gift; a promotional flyer

hand´pick´ *vt.* choose with
care

hand´some *adj.* attractive;
impressive

hand-to-mouth *adj.* barely
subsisting

hand´y *adj.* easily accessible;
useful; skillful —**hand´i•ly**
adv.

hang *vi., vt.*   suspend

hang´ing *adj.* suspended —*n.*
a decorative device

hang-up *n.* a difficulty or in-
hibition

hap´haz´ard *adj.* random —
adv. by chance

hap´less *adj.* unlucky

hap´pen *vi.* occur

hap´pen•ing *n.* an important
event

hap´py *adj.* fortunate, pleased

ha•rangue´ *n.* a bombastic
lecture —*vi., vt.* to lecture
harshly

har´ass *vt.* to pester or worry

har´hin•ger *n.* precursor —*vt.*
herald

har´bor *n.* a refuge —*vt.* to
provide shelter; to entertain
or cling to

hard *adj.* inflexible; intense;
unyielding; difficult —*adv.*
with difficulty; diligently;
with force

hard-bitten *adj.* tough

hard´en *vi, vt.* make tougher

hard´head´ed *adj.* practical;
obstinate

hard´ly *adv.* barely; probably
not

hard´-nosed´ *adj.* stubborn;
practical

hard´ship *n.* difficulty

har´dy adj. strong; resolute

harm n. damage —vt. cause damage

harm´less adj. unlikely to cause damage or distress

har´mo•ny n. agreement; a pleasing combination — **har´mo´ni•ous** adj.

har´row•ing adj. distressing

har´ry vt. to raid or harass

harsh adj. disagreeably coarse or rough; stern — **harsh´ly** adv.

har´vest n. a season's crop; gathering a crop; time for gathering; outcome of an action —vi., vt to get as the result of effort

has´-been n. one no longer famous, productive, etc.

has´sle n. a quarrel; difficulty —vi. to quarrel —vt. to annoy

haste n. quickness; fast action

has´ten vi. be quick; accelerate

hast´y adj. overly quick; done in a hurry; impetuous — **hast´i•ly** adv.

hate n. intense dislike —vi., vt. dislike intensely —**ha´ teed** n.

haugh´ty adj. proud, arrogant; contemptuous of others

haul n. pulling or carrying; that carried; distance traveled —vi., vt. to pull or carry

haunt n. place often visited — vt. visit often; pervade

have vt. possess; gain; control

ha´ven n. a shelter; a refuge

hav´oc n. chaos; destruction

haz´ard n. uncertainty, danger —vt. endanger; venture

haze n. light mist; vagueness —**haz´i•ness** n. —**haz´y** adj.

head n. part of the body with organs for sight, smell, taste, hearing, and feeding; intellect; foremost part; a leader —vt. to lead or direct

head´ing n. forming a head; direction of motion

head´long adj. uncontrollable; reckless —adv. recklessly

head´-on´ adj. direct —adv. directly

heal vi., vt. become or make healthy

health n. soundness of body or mind

heap n. an accumulation; a mound; large amount —vt. to amass; give in large amounts

hear vi., vt. sense sound; be informed; heed; consider formally

hear´say n. rumor

heart n. body organ that pumps blood; essence or core

heart´en vt. encourage

heart´felt adj. sincere

heart´less adj. insensitive

heart´rend•ing adj. distressing

heart´y adj. enthusiastic; robust; unreserved —**heart´i• ness** n.

heat n. warmth; warming — vi., vt. become hot; become aroused

heat´ed adj. intense

heav´y adj. weighty; overweight; serious or intense; greater than normal —**heav´ i•ness** n,

heav´y-hand´ed adj. tactless

heav´y-heart´ed adj. sad

heckle vt. to taunt —**heck´ ler** n.

hec´tic adj. frenzied

hedge n. a boundary of

bushes —*vi.* be evasive; make compensating investments to lessen risk —*vt.* set a border of bushes; to surround with restrictions; lessen a risk

heed *n.* close attention —*vi., vt.* to pay attention

heft´y *adj.* large; weighty

height *n.* an extreme; an elevation; distance from bottom to top

height´en *vi., vt.* to become or make higher or more intense

hein´ous *adj.* atrocious

help *n.* aid; a remedy; employees —*vi., vt.* assist; remedy or improve —**help´ful** *adj.* —**help´ful•ly** *adv.*

help´less *adj.* powerless; incapable of aiding —**help´less•ly** *adv.*

hence *adv.* from now; therefore

hence´forth´ *adv.* from now on

her´ald *n.* a harbinger —*vt.* to foretell or publicize

her´biv•ore *n.* an animal that feeds on plants —**her•biv´o•rous** *adj.*

herd *n.* a large group —*vi., vt.* gather or move; tend a group of animals

he•red´i•tar•y *adj.* inherited

he•red´i•ty *n.* inherited

her´e•sy *n.* rejection of an accepted or established concept or belief

her´e•tic *n.* one whu rejects an established belief —**he•ret´i•cal** *adj.*

her´it•age *n.* that inherited; culture, tradition, etc. that is handed down

her´mit *n* a recluse

he´ro *n.* one noted for courage, greatness, etc.; central

figure in a story —**he•ro´ic, he•ro´i•cal** *adj.*

hes´i•tant *adj.* uncertain, doubtful

hes´i•tate´ *vi.* to pause or waver; be uncertain —**hes´i•ta´tion** *n.*

hes´si•an *n.* (*Brit.*) a coarse cloth

hew *vt.* to chop or hack

hex (*US*) *n.* a spell —*vt.* cast a spell

hi•a´tus *n.* a break in continuity; an interruption

hic´cup, hic´cough *n.* an involuntary closing of the respiratory tract

hid´den *adj.* concealed; secret

hide *vi., vt.* to conceal

hide´bound *adj.* opinionated

hid´e•ous *adj.* repulsive; terrifying

high *adj.* elevated; prominent; greater than normal —**high and mighty** haughty; snobbish

high´er-up *n.* one superior

high´hand•ed *adj.* haughty

high´-spir•it•ed *adj.* lively

high´-strung *adj.* nervous

high´way (*US*) *n.* a main road

hi´jack *vt.* take by force

hike *n.* a long walk; a rise in prices —*vi.* to walk —*vt.* to raise; pull up

hi•lar´i•ous *adj.* very funny

hill *n.* high ground; a pile or mound

hill´ock *n.* a small hill

hin´der *vi., vt.* to delay or ob struct

hin´drance *n.* an obstacle

hinge *n.* a flexible joint —*vi. vt.* make contingent on something else

hint *n.* a slight indication — *vi., vt.* to intimate

hire *vt.* to employ for payment

hir´sute *adj.* hairy

his•tor´ic, his•tor´i•cal *adj.* relating to the past; notable

his´to•ry *n.* an account of the past

hit *n.* a blow; a success —*vi., vt.* to strike; to discover

hoard *n.* a hidden supply —*vt.* obtain and store in reserve

hoarse *adj.* harsh sounding

hoar´y *adj.* grayish-white; old

hoax *n.* a deception

hob´by *n.* a favored pastime

hob´nob *vt.* to socialize

ho´bo (*US*) *n.* a vagrant

hod *n.* a V - shaped trough for hauling bricks or mortar; a coal scuttle

hoist *n.* act of lifting, device for raising loads —*vt.* to lift or pull up

ho´kum *n.* nonsense

hold *n.* act of grasping; an in--luence or controlling force —*vi., vt.* to grasp; to sustain; contain

hole *n.* an opening; a hollow; a crude or squalid shelter

hol´i•day´ *adj.* festive —*n.* a day of rest, commemoration, etc.

hol´ler *n* a yell —*vi.,vt.* to call out

hol´low *adj.* empty inside; sunken or indented —*n.* a recess —*vi., vt.* become or make hollow

hol´o•caust´ *n.* great destruction

hom´age *n.* a profession of fealty or loyalty; worship

home *n.* where one lives, one's native state, country, or land —*adj.* relating to residence or origin —*adv.* at or in the direction of home

home´ly *adj.* plain; unpretentious

home´stead´ *n.* buildings and land that constitute a home

home´y *adj.* simple; comfortable

hom´i•cide *n.* killing; one who kills another —**hom´i•ci´dal** *adj.*

hom•i•let´ics *n.* art of sermonizing

hom´i•ly *n.* a sermon or lecture

hom´i•ny *n.* hulled and dried corn

ho•mog´e•ne•ous *adj.* of a similar kind or type; uniform throughout

ho•mog´e•nize *vt.* make homogeneous; to disperse evenly throughout

ho•mol´o•gous *adj.* corresponding or similar in many aspects

hom´o•nym *n.* word that sounds like another but differs in meaning

Ho´mo sa´pi•ens *n.* the human race

ho´mo•sex´u•al *n.* one attracted to persons of the same sex

hone *vt* to sharpen —*n* a stone for sharpening

hon´est *adj.* free of deceit, marked by integrity; respectable; trustworthy; fair —**hon´es•ty** *n.*

hon´ey *n.* a thick, sweet liquid —*vt.* to sweeten with honey

hon´ey•comb *n.* a network of cells —*vt.* to permeate with small holes

hon´ey•moon *n* a wedding trip; a brief period of accord

honk *n* the call of a wild goose, any similar sound — *vi., vt.*

hon´or *n.* great respect; special recognition; reputation;

exalted rank —*vt.* esteem or respect; afford special recognition; to recognize as a due debt —**hon′or•a•ble** *adj.*

hon•o•rar′i•um *n.* fee paid a speaker

hon′or•ar′y *adj.* conferred without duties or pay

hon•or•if′ic *adj.* that which shows respect —*n.* an honorary title

hon′our (*Brit.*) *n.* great respect; special recognition, reputation, an exalted rank —*vt.* esteem or respect; afford special recognition, recognize as a due debt

hood *n.* a covering; a hoodlum —*vt.* cover with a hood

hood′lum *n.* a rowdy; a gangster

hood′wink *vt.* to deceive

hoof *n.* a horny covering of the feet of certain mammals —*vt., vt.* walk or dance

hoof′er *n.* one who dances

hook *n.* a connector, a fish hook; a means to attract or snare —*to* catch, connect, or suspend; steal

hoo′li•gan *n.* a hoodlum

hoop *n.* a band of metal of wood, anything similar —*vt* secure with a band

hoot′e•nan′y *n* an Informal gathering of folk musicians

hop *vi.* jump on one fool, move quickly —*n* a short distance; a quick trip

hope *vi.* to desire or anticipate —*n.* confident expectation

hop′per *n.* a container emptied through the bottom; one that hops

horde *n.* a great crowd; a throng

ho•ri′zon *n.* convergence of earth and sky; extent of one's interest

hor′i•zon′tal *adj.* level with or parallel to the horizon

hor′mone *n.* a substance produced in the body to regulate activity

horn *n.* a projection from the head of an animal; coating of an animal horn; something the shape of a horn; a wind instrument

hor′net *n.* a type of wasp

ho•rol′o•gy *n.* the study of time, the art of creating timepieces

hor′o•scope *n* aspect of the heavens kept to foretell the future

hor•ren′dous *adj.* dreadful

hor′ri•ble *adj.* inspiring horror; dreadful

hor′rid *adj.* hideous; shocking

hor′ri•fy′ *vt.* overwhelm with terror

hor′ror *n.* great revulsion or fear

hors d′oeu•vre *pl. n.* appetizers

horse *n.* a hoofed mammal; a carpenter's frame, cavalry —*adj. of* a horse —*vt.* to provide with a horse

horse′play *n.* rough boisterous play

horse′pow•er *n.* a unit of power

hor′ta•to•ry *adj.* expressing encouragement

hor′ti•cul′ture *n.* the science of cultivating plants

hose *n.* socks or stockings; a flexible pipe —*vt.* wet with a hose; deceive

ho′sier•y *n.* socks and stockings

hos′ pice *n.* a lodging or shelter

hos′pi•ta•ble *adj.* cordial,

helpful, or generous; suitable for habitation

hos·pi·tal *n.* location for care of the sick and injured

host *n.* one who receives guests; a master of ceremonies; a throng; an organism on which another lives

hos´tage *n.* one held as security

hos´tel *n.* lodging for hikers

host´ess *n.* a female host; a greeter at a restaurant or club

hos´tile *adj.* feeling ill will; threatening; antagonistic; detrimental to health or well-being —*n.* an enemy

hot *adj.* of high temperature; burning to taste or touch; marked by passion; angry — *adv.* in a hot manner — **hot´ly** *adv.*

hot´-blood´ed *adj.* passionate

hot´dog´ *n.* a frankfurter served on a long roll; a daredevil or showoff

ho·tel´ *n.* an establishment offering lodging and meals

hot´house *n.* a greenhouse with controlled heat and humidity

hot´line *n.* a direct channel of communication

hot´-rod´ *n.* a car modified to increase acceleration or speed

hound *n.* a dog used in hunting; one diligent in pursuit —*vt.* to badger

hour *n.* sixty minutes; set time for an activity; a significant time —**hour´ly** *adv.*

house *n.* a dwelling or shelter; family or lineage; a business establishment; branch of the legislature —*vt.* provide living space; to shelter

house´hold *n.* all sharing a dwelling —*adj.* pertaining to- or used in a dwelling; commonplace

hov´el *n.* a wretched dwelling

hov´er *vi.* to remain over, in, or near

how *adv.* in what manner; by what means; to what extent

how·ev´er *adv.* by whatever means

howl *n.* a plaintive wail;; something funny —*vi., vt.* utter a wail

hoy´den *n.* boisterous woman

hub *n.* center of a wheel; a center of interest or activity

hub´bub´ *n.* uproar, bustle

hub´cap´ *n.* covering for a hubs

huck´ster *n.* a pitchman; one. who promotes with overblown claims

hud´dle *vi., vt.* to crowd together; to crouch —*n.* a dense crowd; a quick, informal meeting

hue *n.* a gradation of color; a tint

huff *vi.* be indignant or offended —*n.* a feeling of anger or annoyance

huff´y *adj.* easily offended

hug *vt.* embrace; keep close to; hold fast —*n.* an embrace.

huge *adj.* exceedingly large; of great extent

hulk *n.* an old unwieldy or unseaworthy ship; an abon doned hull; anything bulky or unwieldy

hull *n.* a husk: the outer covering of a seed or fruit; the body of a ship —*vt.* remove the husk from

hum *vi., vt.* make a low droning sound; sing without words —*n.* a low, dronint sound

196

hu´man *adj.* having form or characterstics of a human being; of human attributes —*n.* a human being —**hu´man•ly** *adv.*

hu•mane´ *adj.* marked by compassion; pertaining to human values

hu•man´i•tar´i•an *n.* one concerned with the welfare of others

hu•man´i•ty *n.* the human race; the quality of being human or humane

hu´man•ize *vt., vi.* to make or become human or humane

hum´ble *adj.* meek; submissive; unpretentious —*vt.* to humiliate; to abase

hu´mid *adj.* moist or damp

hu•mid´i•fi•er *n.* a device for adding moisture to the air

hu•mid´i•ty *n.* dampness; a measure of moisture in the air

hu•mi•dor *n.* a tobacco container

hu•mil´i•ate´ *vt.* embarrass or shame —**hu•mil´i•a´tion** *n.*

hu•mil´i•ty *n.* humbleness; modesty

hum´ming•bird´ *n.* a tiny bird noted for the ability to hover and dart

hu´mor (*US*) *n.* an amusing quality; that intended to incite laughter; one's disposition —*vt.* to indulge

hu´mor•ist *n.* one who specializes in relating amusing stories

hu´mor•ous *adj.* expressing humor; amusing **hu´mor•ous•ly** *adv.*

hu´mour (*Brit.*) *n.* an amusing quality; that intended to incite laughter; one's disposition —*vt.* indulge

hu´mus *n.* organic matter in soil

hun´ger *n.* desire or craving —*vi.* a strong desire —**hun´gry** *adj.*

hunk *n.* a large piece

hunt *vi., vt.* seek or search —*n.* the seeking of wild game; a hunting expedition; a diligent search

hur´dle *n.* a barrier or obstacle —*vt., vi.* surmount an obstacle

hurl *vt.* throw violently; utter vehemently; to vomit

hur´ri•cane *n.* a violent storm

hur´ry *vi., vt.* move with haste —*n.* haste

hurt *vt.* to injure; impair or lessen —*n.* something that causes suffering —**hurt´ful** *adj.*—**hurt´ful•ly** *adv.*

hur´tle *vt., vi.* throw; move violently

hus´band *n.* a married man —*vt.* to conserve or use economically

hus´band•ry *n.* study of agriculture or livestock breeding; careful management

husk *n.* outer covering of seeds, fruits, or vegetables —*vt.* remove the covering from

husk´y *adj.* of a voice with a hoarse or rough quality; sturdily built

hus´sy *n.* a saucy female

hus´tle *vi., vt.* move energetically; convince by questionable means

hut *n.* a crude dwelling

hy´brid *n.* a combination of dissimilar species or elements —*adj.* pertaining to a hybrid

hy´dra *n.* a freshwater polyp; persistent evil

hy´drant n. outlet from a water main

hy´drate n. a compound of water and other molecules or atoms —vt.

hy·drau´lic adj. operated by fluid

hy·drau´lics n. science of the dynamics of fluid in motion

hy´dro·e·lec´tric adj. of electricity generated by water power

hy´dro·foil n. structure that holds a boat out of water when in motion; a boat equipped with hydrofoils

hy´dro·gen n. a flammable gas, lightest of all the elements

hydrogen bomb a powerful explosive device

hy·drom´e·ter n. a device to measure the specific gravity of a liquid

hy´dro·plane n. a seaplane; a boat that skims the surface of water; a hydrofoil —vt. skim atop water

hy´dro·pon´ics n. the cultivation of plants without soil

hy·e´na n. a scavenging carnivorous mammal of Africa and Asia

hy´giene n. practice that serves to promote health

hymn n. a song of praise

hym´nal n. a book of hymns

hy·per·bo´la n. a geometric curve

hy·per´bo·le n. a figure of speech using exaggeration for emphasis

hy·per·bol´ic adj. shaped like a hyperbola; containing hyperbole

hy·per·crit´i·cal adj. exacting

hy·per·sen´si·tive adj. excessively tense or delicate

hy·per·son´ic adj. capable of moving at several times the speed of sound

hy´per·ten´sion n. high blood pressure

hy´per·thy´roid·ism n. a disorder caused by an overly active thyroid

hy´phen n. a punctuation mark (-)

hyp·no´sis n. a sleep-like state

hyp·not´ic adj. of hypnosis; spellbinding

hyp´no·tism n. the act of inducing hypnosis —**hyp´no·tize´** vt.

hy·po·chon´dri·a n. excessive anxiety about one's health

hy·poc´ri·sy n. pretending to a belief —**hyp´o·crite** n.

hy´po·der´mic adj. of tissue or injection beneath the skin —n. an injection, needle, or syringe

hy´po·ten´sion n. low blood pressure

hy·pot´e·nuse´ n. side opposite the right angle of a right triangle

hy·poth´e·sis n., pl. **hy´poth´e·ses** a theory put forth for testing

hys·ter·ec´to·my n. surgical excision of the uterus

hys·te·ri·a n. uncontrollable emotion; neurosis marked by physical ailment without apparent cause

hys·ter´ic, hys·ter´i·cal adj. characterized by hysteria

hys·ter´ics n. an attack of hysteria

i, I ninth letter of the alphabet; Roman symbol for one

ice n. frozen water; a dessert of shaved ice and flavoring

—*vt.* to cool with ice; decorate a cake

ice´berg´ *n.* a mound of floating ice

ice´box´ *n.* a refrigerator; an insulated cabinet used to cool food

ice´cap´ *n.* ice covering a tract of land

ice sheet *n.* a continental glacier

ich•thy•ol´o•gy *n.* the study of fishes

i´ci•cle *n.* a hanging taper of ice

i´ci•ly *adv.* in a cold or haughty manner

ic´ing *n.* mixture to decorate a cake

icon *n.* an image; a sacred picture; one revered; an image on a computer that represents a command

i´con´o•clast *n.* a destroyer of sacred images or traditional institutions

i´cy *adj.* covered with ice; cold or slippery; cold and unfriendly

id *n.* the subconscious concerned with primitive impulses

i•de´a *n.* a mental image; a scheme; concept or opinion

i•de´al *adj.* perfect or excellent; typical; existing in theory —*n.* a model for perfection —**i•de´al•ly** *adv.*

i•de´al•ism *n.* seeking the best in everything; belief that all is good

i•de´al•ist *n.* a visionary; one inspired by that which is ideal

i•de´al•ize *vt.* to envision as ideal

i•den´ti•cal *adj.* alike in every way

i•den´ti•fi•ca´tion *n.* recognition or classification; credentials

i•den´ti•fy *vt.* establish identity —*vi.* establish unity with certain others

i•den´ti•ty *n.* that by which a person or thing is recognized or defined

id•e•ol´o•gy *n.* set of beliefs or doctrines —**i•de•ol´o•gist** *n.*

id´i•o•cy *n.* folly; mental retardation

id´i•om *n.* usage peculiar to a language or region

id•i•o•syn´cra•sy *n.* a characteristic peculiar to a person or group

id´i•ot *n.* one foolish or stupid

id•i•ot´ic *adj.* foolish or stupid

idle *adj.* not busy or in use —*vt.* waste time —**i´dly** *adv.*

i´dol *n.* an image; an object of worship; one revered or adored

i´dol•a•try *n.* the worship of idols; excessive devotion —**i•dol´a•ter** *n.*

i´dol•ize´ *vt.* subject to devotion

i´dyl, i´dyll *n.* a short work describing the pastoral or romantic

if *conj.* on condition that; whether or not —*n.* a supposition or condition

ig´ne•ous *adj.* pertaining to fire; formed by fire

ig•nite´ *vt.* to set afire; to arouse passion —*vi.* to burn

ig•ni´tion *n.* setting or being set on fire; a system for igniting the fuel in an internal-combustion engine

ig•no´ble *adj.* base; vulgar; of low birth

ig´no•min´y *n.* disgrace; shame

ig·no·ra·mus *n.* an ignorant person

ig·norance *n.* lack of experience or knowledge; being uninformed

ig·no·rant *adj.* lacking knowledge; uninformed

ig·nore *vt.* to disregard

ilk *n.* type or kind

ill *adj.* sick; harmful; hostile —*n.* harmful; a cause of suffering

ill-ad·vised *adj.* unwise; evidencing a lack of careful thought

ill·-bred *adj.* crude; impolite

il·le·gal *adj.* prohibited by law —*n.* one who enters the country illegally —**il·le·gal·i·ty** *n.*

il·leg·i·ble *adj.* impossible to decipher; unreadable

il·le·git·i·mate *adj.* contrary to law; illegal; born out of wedlock

ill·-fat·ed *adj.* likely to end badly

ill·-got·ten *adj.* obtained dishonestly

il·lib·er·al *adj.* selfish; bigoted; vulgar; ill-bred

il·lic·it *adj.* unlawful; prohibited

il·lit·er·a·cy *n.* the state of being unable to read or write

il·lit·er·ate *adj.* lacking education; lacking comprehension —*n.* one unable to read and write

ill·ness *n.* sickness or disease

il·log·i·cal *adj.* contrary to reason; unreasonable or unreasoning

ill·-tem·pered *adj.* querulous; irritable—**ill·-tem·pered·ly** *adv.*

il·lum·i·nate, il·lu·mine *vi., vt.* light or make brighter; to clarify; to decorate a printed page

il·lu·mi·na·tion *n.* lighting; clarification or instruction

il·lu·sion *n.* an erroneous or deceptive impression

il·lu·so·ry *adj.* based on illusion; deceptive; not real

il·lus·trate *vt.* to clarify or explain; decorate with pictures

il·lus·tra·tion *n.* an example or explanation; a picture

il·lus·tra·tive *adj.* serving to illustrate or explain; symbolic

il·lus·tri·ous *adj.* distinguished; eminent

ill will malevolence; hostility

im·age *n.* a likeness; a thing closely resembling another; a concept

im·a·ge·ry *n.* a mental image; imaginative language

im·ag·i·na·ble *adj.* that can be imagined; conceivable; plausible

im·ag·i·na·ry *adj.* fanciful; theoretical; nonexistent

im·ag·i·na·tion *n.* creativity; the formation of mental images

im·ag·i·na·tive *adj.* inventive; creative —**im·ag·i·na·tive·ly** *adv.*

im·ag·ine *vi., vt.* picture in the mind

im·bal·ance *n.* a state of unevenness

im·be·cil·ic *adj.* silly; foolish

im·be·cile *n.* a foolish person; one lacking intellect—**im·be·cil·i·ty** *n.*

im·bibe *vt.* to drink

im·bro·glio *n.* an entanglement; confusion

im·bue *vt.* to permeate

im·i·tate *vt.* to copy in appearance or style; to mimic

im•i•ta´tion n. a copy or likeness; a substitute of lesser quality

im•i´ta•tive adj. involving imitation; not original or genuine; deceptive

im•mac´u•late adj. absolutely pure or clean; without blemish

im•ma•nent adj. existing within; deep-seated —**im´ma•nence** n.

im•ma•te´ri•al adj. lacking importance or substance; insignificant

im•ma•ture´ adj. not ripe; not fully grown; childish; wanting of adult qualities

im•meas´ur•a•ble adj. boundless; incapable of being measured

im•me´di•ate adj. at this instant; near the present time; near at hand —**im•me´di•a•cy** n.

im•me•mo´ri•al adj. before memory or recorded history

im•mense´ adj. extremely large

im•merse´ vt. to submerge; become deeply involved; baptize by submersing completely in water

im´mi•grant n. one newly-arrived in a country with intent to settle

im´mi•grate vi. enter a country with intent to settle

im•mi•gra´tion n. settlement in a new land

im´mi•nent adj. impending; about to occur

im•mo•bil´i•ty n. the state of being motionless or unable to move

im•mod´er•ate adj. excessive

im•mod´est adj. bold; egotistical; lacking modesty

im´mo•late vt. to sacrifice

im•mor´al adj. lacking virtue; counter to accepted morality

im•mo•ral´i•ty n. a lack of virtue; an immoral act

im•mor´tal adj. that cannot die; everlasting; enduring — n. a god; a person worth remembering

im•mor•tal´ity n. the condition of living or being remembered forever

im•mov´able adj. fixed in place; unable to be moved

im•mune´ adj. not affected; exempt

im•mu´ni•ty n. exemption from restriction; protection from disease

im´mu•nize vt. protect from disease

im•mu•nol´o•gy n. the science dealing with the immune system

im•mure´ vt. to confine within a wall; to protect or imprison

im•mu´ta•ble adj. not subject to change

imp n. a small demon; a mischievous child

im´pact n. a collision; force of collision; an effect —**im•pact´** vt. to strike with force; to pack firmly; to have effect on —**im•pact´ed** adj.

im•pair´ vt. cause to diminish, as in quantity or value

im•pale´ vt. to thrust a sharp stake through the body; render helpless

im•pal´pa•ble adj. not perceived by touch; not easily grasped

im•pan´el vt. prepare a list for duty

im•part´ vt. to give or confer; convey knowledge

im•par´tial adj. not biased;

without prejudice —**im·par´tial·ly** adv.

im·par·ti·al·i·ty n. objectivity; not partial or biased

im·pass´a·ble adj. unable to be travelled over or through

im´passe n. lacking room for compromise; a stalemate

im·pas´si·ble adj. apathetic; not easily aroused

im·pas´sioned adj. ardent; designed to arouse passion

im·pas´sive adj. insensible to pain; showing no emotion

impa´tience n. restlessness; intolerance

im·pa´tient adj. unable to wait; restless; anxious; intolerant

im·peach´ vt. charge with misconduct in office; attempt to discredit

im·pec´ca·ble adj. nattily attired; without flaw or imperfection

im·pe·cu´ni·ous adj. lacking means; penniless

im·pede´ vt. to slow the progress of; to obstruct

im·ped´i·ment n. an obstruction; that which prevents clear articulation; in law, an obstacle that bars the making of a legal contract

im·pel´ vt. to drive or urge forward; to spur to action

im·pend´ vi. about to happen; to approach and threaten

im·pen´e·tra·ble adj. unable to be penetrated; incomprehensible

im·pen´i·tent adj. without regret or remorse **im·pen´i·tence** n.

im·per´a·tive adj. pressing; obligatory —n. an order or obligation

im·per·cep´ti·ble adj. that

cannot be perceived —**im·per·cep´ti·bly** adv.

im·per´fect adj. deficient; flawed

im·per·fec´tion n. a flaw

im·pe´ri·al adj. of a ruler or empire; majestic; of great size

im·pe´ri·al·ism n. extending an empire by acquiring territory or establishing dominance

im·per´il vt. to endanger

im·pe´ri·ous adj. arrogant; overhearing —**im·pe´ri·ous·ly** adv.

im·per´ma·nent adj. not lasting; transient —**im·per´ma·nence** n.

im·per´me·a·ble adj. not subject to penetration by moisture

im·per´son·al adj. cold or indifferent

im·per´son·ate´ vt. to pretend to he another; to mimic for the purpose of entertaining

im·per´ti·nent adj. disrespectful or insolent —**im·per´ti·nence** n.

im·per·turb´a·ble adj. calm; not disposed to becoming agitated

im·per´vi·ous adj. impenetrable; not influenced by emotion

im·pet´u·ous adj. marked by sudden impulse or passion; spontaneous

im´pe·tus n. a stimulus; action caused by a stimulus; momentum

im·pinge´ vi., vt. to touch or encroach upon

im´pi·ous adj. lacking piety; blasphemous —**im´pi·ous·ly** adv.

im·pla´ca·ble adj unable to

im•plant' *vt.* to establish or instill; to plant surgically — *n.* a thing inserted by surgery

im•plau•si•ble *adj.* not believable

im'ple•ment *n.* a tool or device — *vt.* to use or put into force

im•pli•cate *vt.* to incriminate; imply; to entangle or involve

im•pli•ca'tion *n.* something implied

im•plic'it *adj.* understood or implied; absolute — **im•plic'it•ly** *adv.*

im•plode' *vt., vi.* to burst inward

im•plore' *vt.* to beg or plead

im•ply' *vt.* to infer; signify indirectly

im•po•lite' *adj.* rude; discourteous

im•pol'i•tic *adj.* imprudent; unwise

im•pod'der•a•ble *adj.* impossible to evaluate — **im•pon•der•a•bil'i•ty** *n.*

im•port' *vt.* bring from another country; to transfer computer data — *vi.* to be of significance — **im'port** *n.* a thing brought in, meaning or significance — **im'por•ta'tion** *n.*

im•port'ed *adj.* foreign; brought from elsewhere

im•por'tance *n.* significance; personal distinction or standing

im•por'tant *adj.* significant

im•por'tu•nate *adj.* persistently pleading; urgently requesting

im'por•tune' *vi., vt.* to plead

im•pose' *vt.* apply with authority, force on others;

lay out a publication for printing — *vi.* to take advantage of

im•pos'ing *adj.* impressive by virtue of size or power

im'po•si'tion *n.* something burdensome or forced upon; advantage taken; layout of a publication

im•pos•si•bil'i•ty *n.* that on attainable or likely to end in failure

im•pos'si•ble *adj.* unattainable; not believable of existing; difficult to cope with — **im•pos•si•bil'i•ty** *n.*

im•pos'tor *n.* one who assumes a false identity

im•pos'ture *n.* deception using an assumed identity

im'po•tence *n.* weakness; inability to have sexual intercourse

im'po•tent *adj.* lacking strength or power; ineffective; unable to have sexual intercourse

im•pound' *vt.* legally seize and hold

im•pov'er•ish *vt.* deprive of wealth

im•pov'er•ished *n.* devoid of wealth or resources; poverty stricken

im•prac'ti•cal *adj.* not effective, prudent, or economical, unable to function in an efficient manner

im'pre•cate' *vt.* to call evil down upon; to curse — **im'pre•ca'tion** *n.*

im•preg'na•ble *adj.* impossible to take by assault; impossible to contest or challenge

im•preg'nate' *vt.* to saturate; make pregnant

im•pre•sa'ri•o *n.* an organizer

or manager of musical entertainment

im·press´ *vt.* find favor; attract notice; plant in the mind; to mark by pressure; to force into service

im·pres´sion *n.* an image in the mind; a vague notion; a mark made by pressure; a printed image; all of the copies of a publication printed at one time

im·pres´sion·a·ble *adj.* receptive to outside influence

im·pres´sion·ism *n.* a school of art that focuses on a quick concept

im·pres´sive *adj.* stirring; tending to impress

im·pri·ma´tur *n.* approval; sanction

im´print *n.* a distinguishing mark —**im·print´** *vt.* to produce a mark on

im·pris´on *vt.* to confine

im·prob´a·ble *adj.* unlikely or doubtful —**im·prob·a·bil´i·ty** *n.*

im·promp´tu *adj.* spontaneous; unrehearsed —*adv.* extemporaneously

im·prop´er *adj.* unsuitable or inappropriate; not in compliance with common decency

im·prove´ *vt., vi.* make more useful

im·prove·ment´ *n.* an enhancement or addition; an enhanced condition

im·prov´i·dent *adj.* without due caution; rash

im´pro·vise´ *vt.* to perform without advance preparation; create from materials at hand

im·pru´dent *adj.* unwise

im´pu·dent *adj.* marked by audacity; impertinent; bold

im·pugn´ *vt.* challenge as false

im´pulse´ *n.* a surge; a sudden urge that leads to action; a stimulus

im·pul´sive *adj.* acting on a whim; characterized by rash action

im·pun´i·ty *n.* immunity or deliverance from punishment or loss

im·pure´ *adj.* contaminated; adulterated; lewd or obscene

im´pu·ta´tion *n.* an insinuation

im·pute´ *vt.* assign a quality

in·a·bil´i·ty *n.* lack of capability

in·ac·ces´si·ble *adj.* not approachable; remote; unattainable

in·ac´cu·ra·cy *n.* an error

in·ac´cu·rate *adj.* incorrect; not exact; misleading

in·ac´tion *n.* immobility or idleness

in·ac´tive *adj.* immobile or idle; not currently in use; retired from service —**in´ac·tiv´i·ty** *n.*

in·ad´e·qua·cy *n.* a weakness; ineptitude

in·ad´e·quate *adj.* not sufficient

in·ad·mis´si·ble *adj.* not allowed

in´ad·vert´ent *adj.* careless or thoughtless; not intentional

in·al´ien·a·ble *adj.* not allowing of change or transfer

in·am·o·ra´ta *n.* a woman one loves

in·ane´ *adj.* pointless; lacking substance; empty of meaning

in·an´i·mate *adj.* lacking spirit or energy

204

in·ap·pro′pri·ate *adj.* unsuitable

in·apt′ *adj.* inept; inappropriate

in·ar·tic′u·late *adj.* unable to express in words; unable to speak distinctly; incomprehensible

in·at·ten′tive *adj.* indifferent, preoccupied —**in·at·ten′tive·ly** *adv.*

in·au′gu·rate′ *vt.* bring into use with ceremony; cause to begin

in·au·gu·ra′tion *n.* a ceremony of installation or induction

in·aus·pi′cious *adj.* unfavorable

in′born′ *adj.* present at birth; innate

in′bred′ *adj.* inborn

in·cal′cu·la·ble *adj.* that cannot be calculated; unpredictable

in·can·des′cent *adj.* glowing from being heated; shining brilliantly

in·can·ta′tion *n.* a chant to invoke magic; a ritual supplication

in·ca′pa·ble *adj.* lacking qualification or competence

in·ca·pac′i·tate′ *vt.* deprive of potential; to invalidate or disqualify

in·ca·pac′i·ty *n.* a lack of ability; something that disqualifies

in·car′cer·ate′ *vt.* to imprison; to confine —**in·car′·cer·a′tion** *n.*

in·car′nate *adj.* manifest in human form; personified —*vt.* to manifest or personify —**in′car·na′tion** *n.*

in·cen·di·ar′y *adj.* causing fire; inclined to inflame emotions —*n.* that causing fire; one who sets fire; one who incites rebellion

in′cense *n.* substance that creates a pleasing aroma —**in·cense′** *vt.* excite to anger

in·cen′tive *n.* something that encourages or inspires; the prospect of penalty or reward

in·cep′tion *n.* a beginning

in·ces′sant *adj.* continuous; without interruption —**in·ces′sant·ly** *adv.*

in′cest *n.* sexual intercourse between closely related persons

in′ci·dence *n.* the act of occurring; rate of occurrence

in′ci·dent *n.* a single event; a relatively minor occurrence

in·ci·den′tal *adj.* accidental, unplanned —*n.* a minor expense

in·cin′er·ate′ *vi., vt.* to burn entirely

in·cip′i·ent *adj.* starting to come into being —**in·cip′i·ence** *n.*

in·cise′ *vt.* cut into; engrave

in·ci′sion *n.* a cut; a surgical scar

in·ci′sive *adj.* keen or sharp

in·ci′sor *n.* a front cutting tooth

in·cite′ *vt.* provoke to action; to instigate

in·clem′ent *adj.* stormy; cruel or merciless

in·cli·na′tion *n.* a disposition or preference; an inclined surface

in·cline′ *vi.* slope or lean; tend toward; show a preference; deviate —*n.* a slope

in·clined′ *adj.* sloping or leaning; tending toward as a preference

in•clude´ *vt.* to take in, embrace, or contain as a part —**in•clu´sion** *n.*

in•clu´sive *adj.* incorporating most or all; including all in the range specified —**in•clu´sive•ness** *n.*

in•cog•ni´to *adj., adv.* with identity hidden or obscured

in•co•her´ence *n.* lack of order; the inability to communicate clearly

in•co•her´ent *adj.* lacking order or agreement; disjointed; unable to communicate in a distinct or organized manner; inarticulate

in´come *n.* a thing received in exchange for labor; earnings

in´com•ing *adj.* coming in; about to come in

in•com•men•su•ra•ble *adj.* not to be measured or compared

in•com•men´su•rate *adj.* disproportionate; inadequate

in•com•mo´dious *adj.* inconvenient or uncomfortable

in•com•pa•ra•ble *adj.* exceptional; beyond compare

in•com•pat•i•bil´i•ty *n.* the inability to exist harmoniously

in•com•pat´i•ble *adj.* unsuited; contradictory; mutually exclusive; irreconcilable; mutually repelling; in•congruous

in•com´pe•tence *n.* a lack of ability

in•com´pe•tent *adj.* inadequate or unsuited; not mentally qualified —*n.* one unable to function in certain circumstances

in•com•plete´ *adj.* not finished; missing a part; failure to complete requirements of

a course of study

in•com•pre•hen´si•ble *adj.* difficult to understand or accept

in•con•ceiv´a•ble *adj.* impossible to grasp or accept; highly improbable

in•con•gru´i•ty *n.* inconsistency; something inconsistent

in•con´gru•ous *adj.* inappropriate or incompatible; inconsistent

in•con•se•quen´tial *adj.* of little importance

in•con•sid´er•a•ble *adj.* trivial

in•con•sid´er•ate *adj.* thoughtless of others; insensitive; lacking consideration —**in•con•sid´er•ate•ly** *adv.*

in•con•sist´en•cy *n.* a discrepancy

in•con•sis´tent *adj.* lacking agreement; not logical; erratic; unpredictable —**in•con•sis´tent•ly** *adv.*

in•con•spic´u•ous *adj.* not easily seen; hardly noticeable

in•con´stant *adj.* fickle —**in•con´stan•cy** *n.* —**in•con´stant•ly** *adv.*

in•con•test´a•ble *adj.* unquestionable —**in•con•test´a•bly** *adv.*

in•con´ti•nent *adj.* lacking self-control —**in•con´ti•nence** *n.*

in•con•tro•vert´i•ble *adj.* not subject to question; unable to deny or disprove —**in•con•tro•vert´i•bly** *adv.*

in•con•ven´ience *n.* that not convenient; a source of bother —*vt.* to cause difficulty or annoyance

in•con•ven´ient *adj.* unsuited to comfort or needs; difficult to use; poorly timed

in•cor´po•rate vi., vt. become united or combined; (US) form a legal corporation

in•cor•po•ra´tion n. a thing added; (US) legally incorporating

in•cor•po´re•al adj. lacking physical form; spiritual

in•cor•rect´ adj. inaccurate; unsuitable or improper

in•cor´ri•gi•ble adj. incapable of reform; difficult to control or restrain —n. one who cannot be changed or reformed

in•crease´ vt., vi. become more or larger —in´crease n, the amount or rate of augmentation

in•cred´i•ble adj. so unlikely as to cause disbelief; amazing; startling

in•cred´u•lous adj. not inclined to believe; showing disbelief

in´cre•ment n. steady growth; an addition; a slight increase; one of a series —

in•cre•men´tal adj.

in•crim´i•nate vt. accuse of involvement; implicate by inference

in´cu•bate vt. provide environment suitable for growth and development; to hatch —vi. develop and hatch —in•cu•ba´tion n.

incu´ba•tor n. a controlled environment, as for life support

in•cu´bus n. a nightmare; a male demon

in•cul´cate vt. teach by repeated instruction —in´cul•ca´tion n.

in•cul´pate vt. incriminate —in´cul•pa´tion n.

in•cum´bent adj. obligatory; resting on something else; in office —n. one who holds an office

in•cur´ vt. become liable for

in•cur´able adj. incapable of being remedied —in•cur´a•bly adv.

in•cur´sion n. entering into another's territory; an invasion

in•debt´ed adj. obligated

in•dec´ent adj. contrary to good taste —in•dec´ent•ly adv.

in•de´cen•cy n. immodesty, lewdness

in•de•ci´sion n. inability to decide

in•de•ci´sive adj. prone to doubt; inconclusive

in•de•fat´i•ga•ble adj. tireless

in•de•fen´si•ble adj. unable to be defended —in•de•fen•si•bil´i•ty n.

in•def´i•nite adj. lacking precise limits; uncertain; vague

in•del´i•ble adj. impossible to remove; unable to forget

in•dem´ni•fy vt. compensate

in•dem´ni•ty n. protection or compensation from loss or injury

in•den´ture n. a contract; a legal binding of servant to master

in•de•pend´ence n. autonomy; freedom

in•de•pend´ent adj. free from control; self-supporting

in-depth´ adj. detailed

in•de•struct´i•ble adj. permanent; unable to be destroyed

in•de•ter´mi•nate adj. not precisely fixed; indefinite

in´dex n., pl. in´dex•es, in´di•ces a list of contents; any list or directory, an indicator that characterizes data —*vt.* provide an index; to list, catalog, or otherwise arrange

in·di·cate *vt.* point out or signify; to comment briefly

in·di·ca·tion *n.* a hint or suggestion; something suggested as practical for treatment of an illness

in·dic·a·tive *adj.* serving to designate; characteristic

in·di·ca·tor *n.* that which serves to measure or quantify a value; *(Brit.)* a turn signal on a car

in·dict´ *vt.* charge with wrongdoing

in·dict´ment *n.* a formal accusation

in·dif·fer·ence *n.* unconcern or detachment; coldness, aloofness

in·dif·fer·ent *adj.* not involved; neutral or unconcerned; of little consequence or quality

in·dig·e·nous *adj.* native; natural; inherent —**in·dig´e·nous·ly** *adv.*

in·di·gence *n.* poverty

in´di·gent *adj.* impoverished —*n.* one poor or needy

in·di·gest´i·ble *adj.* impossible or difficult to digest

in·di·ges´tion *n.* discomfort caused by difficulty in digesting

in·dig´nant *adj.* angry over a wrong or injustice —**in·dig´nant·ly** *adv.*

in·dig·na´tion *n.* righteous anger

in·dig´ni·ty *n.* an affront; humiliation

in´di·go *n.* a blue dye

in·di·rect´ *adj.* roundabout; devious

in·dis·creet´ *adj.* tactless;

imprudent; thoughtless

in·dis·crete´ *adj.* undivided; tightly bound; that can not be divided

in·dis·cre´tion *n.* tactlessness

in·dis·crim´i·nate *adj.* random; without order

in·dis·pen·sa·ble *adj.* essential; definitely needed

in·dis·posed´ *adj.* reluctant or unwilling to honor; ill or ailing

in·dis·put´a·ble *adj.* not to be denied; incontestable

in·dis·sol·u´ble *adj.* that cannot be destroyed; perpetually binding

in·dis·tinct´ *adj.* not clear; dim or faded; not easily understood

in·di·vid´u·al *adj.* of one only; by or for one; distinctive —*n.* a thing considered apart from its group; one marked by a special quality

in·di·vid·u·al´i·ty *n.* qualities that make one distinctive; uniqueness

in·doc´tri·nate *vt.* instruct in a doctrine or ideology; acquaint with new rules or policies

in·doc·tri·na´tion *n.* instruction or training

in´do·lent *adj.* habitually lazy; idle —**in´do·leace** *n.*

in·dom´i·ta·ble *adj.* unable to be subdued; unconquerable

in·du·bi´ta·ble *adj.* undeniable; too obvious to be doubted

in·duce´ *vt.* to persuade to action; to cause or bring about

in·duce´ment *n.* an incentive; something that persuades

in·duct´ *vt.* formally place in office; acquaint with or instruct in

in•duc´tion *n.* entrance into office; reasoning that draws broad conclusions from specific facts

in•duc´tive *adj.* relating to logical induction —**in•duc´tive•ly** *adv.*

in•dulge´ *vt.* yield to desires — at to gratify one's desires; take part in

in•dul´gence *n.* an act of gratification; intemperance

in•dus´tri•al *adj.* of or relating to manufacturing and trade

in•dus´tri•al•ize *vt.* convert to economy based on industry; make into an industry

in•dus´tri•ous *adj.* dedicated to a task —**in•dus´tri•ous•ly** *adv.*

in•dus´try *n.* manufacture and trade in commercial goods; active dedication to a task

in•e´bri•ate *vt.* intoxicate; exhilarate —**in•e´bri•ate, in•e´bri•a•ted** *adj.* intoxicated; drunken

in•ef´fa•ble *adj.* indescribable; taboo to utter —**in•ef´fa•bly** *adv.*

in•ef•fec´tive *adj.* not as intended effect; inadequate

in•ef•fec´tu•al *adj.* fruitless

in•ef•fi´cient *adj.* wasteful; incompetent —**in•ef•fi´cien•cy** *n.*

in•el´i•gi•ble *adj.* precluded by restrictions or lack of ability

in•ept´ *adj.* lacking ability; incompetent; clumsy —**in•ept´i•tude** *n.*

in•equal´i•ty *n.* a difference or disparity

in•eq´ui•ta•ble *adj.* unfair —**in•eq´ui•ta•bly** *adv.*

in•eq´ui•ty *n.* an injustice

in•ert´ *adj.* motionless; inactive; unable to move; lethargic

in•er´tia *n.* resistance to change; reluctance to move or act

in•ev´i•ta•ble *adj.* impossible to prevent; unavoidable; inescapable

in•ex´o•ra•ble *adj.* unyielding; implacable; not to be persuaded

in•ex•pe´ri•ence *n.* a lack of skill

in•ex•pe´ri•enced *adj.* lacking skill or knowledge

in•ex´pert *adj.* unskilled

in•ex´pi•a•ble *adj.* that may not be atoned for

in•ex´pli•ca•ble *adj.* impossible to explain or understand

in•ex•press´i•ble *adj.* that cannot be described —**in•ex•press´i•bly** *adv.*

in•ex´tri•ca•ble *adj.* that cannot be disentangled; impossible to resolve

in•fal´li•ble *adj.* incapable of failure or error —**in•fal´li•bil´i•ty** *n.*

in´fa•mous *adj.* having a bad reputation; deserving of low regard

in´fa•my *n.* disgrace

in´fan•cy *n.* childhood; the early stages of development

in´fant *n.* a young child; a minor —*adj.* of a young or early state

in´fan•tile *adj.* relating to infancy; childlike

in´fan•try *n.* soldiers trained to fight on foot

in•fat´u•ate *vt.* provoke unreasoning affection; incite foolish behavior

in•fect´ *vt.* contaminate or corrupt

in·fec´tion n. invasion of the body by disease; an infectious disease

in·fec´tious adj. caused by infection; tending to spread

in·fer´ vt. presume from available evidence; insinuate or hint

in·fer·ence n. reaching a conclusion from information available

in·fe´ri·or adj. of a lesser quality or value; subordinate —n. one who is lower in rank or station

in·fe·ri·or´i·ty n. a state of low rank

in·fer´nal adj. fiendish

in·fer´no n. place of fiery heat

in·fest´ vt. to inhabit in overwhelming numbers

in·fi·del´i·ty n. sexual unfaithfulness; a lack of loyalty

in·fight·ing n. struggle or dissension between rivals in an organization

in·fil´trate vt. secretly enter; to permeate by a liquid

in·fi´nite adj. without limit

in·fin·i·tes´i·mal adj. minuscule; immeasureably small

in·fin´i·ty n. a limitless expanse, time, or quantity

in·firm´ adj. feeble or weak from old age or disease; irresolute

in·fir´ma·ry n. a small clinic or dispensary

in·fir´mi·ty n. ailment or weakness

in·flame´ vi., vt. become excited or aroused; to redden and swell; set on fire

in·flam´ma·ble adj. combustible; easily excited

in´flam·ma´tion n. redness or swelling from irritation or infection

in·flam´ma·to·ry adj. intended to arouse passion, violence, etc.; causing inflammation

in·flate´ vt. fill with air; to enlarge or expand —vi. to become enlarged or swelled —in·fla´tion n.

in·flect´ vt. modify in tone or pitch

in·flex´i·bil´i·ty n. unwillingness or inability to change

in·flex´i·ble adj. not easily bent or changed; inelastic; rigid

in·flict´ vt. to impose punishment or hardship

in´flu·ence n. power that effects; an effect shaped by control or persuasion —vt. effect by persuasion

in·flu·en´tial adj. having the power to influence

in·flu·en´za n. a contagious viral disease

in´flux n. a flowing in

in·form´ vi., vt. make known; provide information; reveal

in·for´mal adj. casual; unofficial

in·for·mal´ity n. casualness; the absence of ceremony or formality

in·form´ant n. one who testifies

in·for·ma´tion n. a body of knowledge or data

in·for´ma·tive adj. providing information; revealing

in·frac´tion n. a violation of rules

in·fran·gi·ble adj. incapable of being smashed

in·fra·red´ adj. pertaining to radiation between red and microwave

in´fra·struc·ture n. elements of a structure, system, etc.

in•fre´quent *adj.* at large intervals of time or space — **in•fre´quen•cy** *n.*

in•fringe´ *vi., vt.* to intrude upon; to transgress — **in•fringe´ment** *n.*

in•fu´ri•ate *vt.* to enrage

in•fuse´ *vt.* introduce into; to inspire; to steep in order to extract

in•gen´ious *adj.* resourceful, clever

in•ge•nu´ity *n.* resourcefulness

in•gen´u•ous *adj.* innocent; lacking sophistication; straightforward

in•gest´ *vt.* take into the body; to eat

in•glo´ri•ous *adj.* marked by failure or disgrace — **in•glo´ri•ous•ly** *adv.*

in´got *n.* a lump of cast metal

in•grain´ *vt.* to fix in the mind

in´grate *n.* one who is ungrateful

in•gra´ti•ate *vt.* to curry favor

in•gre´di•ent *n.* part of a mixture

in•hab´it *vt.* to occupy or reside in; to fill — **in•hab´it•ant** *n.*

in•hal´ant *n.* medicine inhaled as a vapor — **in´ha•la•tor** *n.*

in•hale´ *vt.* draw into the lungs; take in quickly — *vi.* to breathe in

in•her´ent *adj.* inherited; intrinsic

in•her´it *vt.* to receive, acquire, or take over from another

in•hib´it *vt.* to hold back or restrain

in•hi•bi´tion *n.* a restraint; something that inhibits

in•hos•pi´ta•ble *adj.* unfriendly; barren: offering little to promote life or growth

in•hu´man, in•hu•mane´ *adj.* lacking human qualities

in•im´i•cal *adj.* unfriendly

in•im´i•ta•ble *adj.* that cannot be imitated

in•iq´ui•ty *n.* wickedness; evil; a wicked or evil act

in•i´tial *adj.* first instance; beginning —*n.* first letter of a proper name —*vt.* to sign with initials

in•i´ti•ate *vt.* introduce; to start; induct into a club —*n.* one newly allowed membership; an inductee

in•i•ti•a´tion *n.* a ceremony for induction; bringing into being

i•ni´ti•a•tive *n.* motivation that drives one to begin; a first move; the power to originate

in•ject´ *vt.* to insert or introduce into

in•ju•di´cious *adj.* unwise; lacking judgement —**in•ju•di´cious•ly** *adv.*

in•junc´tion *n.* a command or directive; a legal order that prohibits

in´jure *n.* cause harm to, to wound

in•jur´i•ous *adj.* harmful

in´ju•ry *n.* damage or harm; a basis for legal redress

in•jus´tice *n.* an instance of wrongdoing; a violation of rights

ink *n.* colored liquid used for writing or printing —*vt.* to mark with ink

ink´ling *n.* a hint, suggestion, or notion

in´lay *n.* to set decorative material into —*n.* —**in´laid** *adj.*

in´let n. a coastal recess; an access from the sea to inland waters

in´mate n. one confined

in´most adj. furthest from the exterior; secret or intimate

inn n. lodging for travelers; a tavern or restaurant

in•nate´ adj. inborn

in´ner adj. further inside; private or secret

in´ner•most adj. most intimate

inn´keep•er n. one who operates a public hostelry

in´no•cence n. freedom from guilt; a lack of cunning or guile

in´no•cent adj. uncorrupted; blameless; unsophisticated; harmless —n. an unsophisticated person

in•noc´u•ous adj. inoffensive; unlikely to stimulate; having no harmful qualities

in´no•vate vi., vt. to introduce or change

in•no•vi´tion n. something new; introduction of something new

in•nu•en´do n. an insinuation

in•nu´mer•a•ble adj. incalculable; too many to count

in•oc´u•late´ vt. to immunize by vaccination —**in•oc´u•la•tion** n.

in•of•fen´sive adj. harmless; without fault

in•op´er•a•ble adj. unable to function; inappropriate for surgery

in•op´er•a•tive adj. not working; no longer in force

in•op•por•tune´ adj. ill-timed

in•or´di•nate adj. excessive; exceeding reasonable bounds

in´put n. that directed into; data entered in a computer

in´quest n. investigation or inquiry

in•qui´e•tude n. a state of unrest

in•quire´ vt. to investigate or ask about

in•quir•y n. investigation; a question

in•qui•si´tion n. an investigation

in•quis´i•tive adj. overly curious; eager to learn

in•quis´i•tor n. an examiner

in´road n. encroachment or invasion

in•sane´ adj. psychotic; marked by immoderate or foolish action

in•san´i•ty n. mental disorder; an extremely foolish action

in•sa´ti•a•ble, in•sa´ti•ate adj. unable to be satisfied

in•scribe´ vt. write or carve; engrave; dedicate a book, treatise, etc.

in•scrip´tion n. words written or engraved; a dedication

in•scru´ta•ble adj. incomprehensible

in´sect n. a small animal with segmented body and six legs

in•sec´ti•cide n. a chemical used to kill insects

in•se•cure´ adj. uncertain; lacking stability —**in•se•cur´i•ty** n.

in•sem´i•nate vt. impregnate

in•sen´sate adj. inanimate: lacking reason; incapable of sensation; hard-hearted

in•sen´si•ble adj. unconscious; indifferent

in•sen´si•tive adj. incapable of feeling; numb; unconcerned with others —**in•sen•si•tiv´i•ty** n.

in•sen´ti•ent adj. inanimate:

totally lacking in life or consciousness

in•sep´a•ra•ble *adj.* indivisible; closely associated

in•sert´ *vt.* to place into or among —**in´sert** *n.* an enclosure in a publication

in•ser´tion *n.* something added; the act of adding or inserting

in•side´ *adj.* inner; select or confidential —*adv.* into —*n.* an interior surface or part —**in•sid´er** *n.*

in•sid´i•ous *adj.* harmful and subtly conveyed or accumulated

in´sight *n.* the ability to recognize the true nature of a situation

in•sig´ni•a *n.* a badge or emblem

in•sig•nif´i•cance *n.* unimportance

in•sig•nif´i•cant *adj.* unimportant; having little force or value; of small size or quantity

in•sin•cere´ *adj.* pretentious; deceitful or hypocritical

in•sin•cer´i•ty *n.* deceit; hypocrasy

in•sin´u•ate *vt.* to convey a notion or opinion in a subtle manner

in•sin•u•a´tion *n.* a subtle hint

in•sip´id *adj.* uninteresting; dull; lacking flavor —**in•sip´id•ly** *adv.*

in•sist´ *vi.* be firm or persistent —*vt.* demand firmly or persistently

in´so•lent *adj.* rude or disrespectful; insulting —**in´so•lence** *n.*

in•sol´u•ble *adj.* not to be dissolved; insolvable

in•solv´a•ble *adj.* impossible to solve or explain

in•sol´vent *adj.* unable to pay debts —*n.* one who is bankrupt

in•som´ni•a *n.* inability to sleep

in•spect´ *vt.* to examine carefully or critically

in•spec´tion *n.* examination

in•spec´tor *n.* one who examines; a police officer

in•spi•ra´tion *n.* stimulation to creativity; a sudden creative idea

in•spire´ *vt.* to invigorate or encourage

in•spir´it *vt.* to exhilarate; instill with courage

in•stall´ *vt.* to set up or build into; admit into office

in•stal•la´tion *n.* the placement of fixtures or equipment; something installed

in•stall´ment *n.* one of a series

in´stance *n.* an occurrence; an example or illustration

in´stant *adj.* immediate; designed for quick preparation —*n.* a point in time —**in•stan•ta´ne•ous** *adj.*

in´stant•ly *adv.* immediately

in•stead´ *adv.* alternatively

in´sti•gate *vt.* initiate, incite, or urge —**in•sti•ga´tion** *n.*

in•still´ *vt.* to implant or infuse; to teach or indoctrinate

in´stinct *n.* inborn or natural behavior

in•stinc´tive *adj.* intuitive; natural

in´sti•tute *n.* established organization; buildings and land of an organization —*vt.* enact or establish

in•sti•tu´tion *n.* a founding or establishing; custom or tradition; an organization or its buildings and land —**in·sti·tu´tion·al** adj.

in·struct´ vt. educate or edify; order or direct —vi. to discharge the duties of an instructor

in·struc´tion n. guidance; imparting of knowledge; a direct order

in·struc´tor n. a teacher; one who passes on knowledge

in´stru·ment n. an implement or tool; a device for producing musical sounds; a legal contract

in·stru·men´tal adj. serving as agency for; responsible; of music without words

in·stru·men·tal´i·ty n. agency

in·sub·or´di·nate adj. rebellious; hesitant or unwilling to obey

in·sub·or·di·na´tion n. rebellion against authority

in·suf´fer·a·ble adj. intolerable; difficult to endure

in·suf·fi´cient adj. not enough; lacking —**in·suf·fi´cient·ly** adv.

in´su·lar adj. detached; isolated

in´su·late vt. separate or protect with a barrier

in·su·la´tion n. protective covering; protection from external influence

in·sult´ vi., vt. to offend; treat offensively —**in´sult** n. an offensive act or utterance

in·su´per·a·ble adj. impossible to be overcome —**in·su´per·a·bly** adv.

in·sup·port´a·ble adj. intolerable; that cannot be justified

in·sur´ance n. protection from loss

insure´ vt. make certain;

protect against loss —**in·sured´** adj.

in·sur´gent n. one rebeling against authority —adj. rebellious

in·sur·mount´a·ble adj. that cannot be overcome

in·sur·rec´tion n. open rebellion

in·sus·cep´ti·ble adj. not vulnerable

in·tact´ adj. complete; not damaged or diminished in any way

in·tan´gi·ble adj. indefinable by the senses

in´te·ger n. a whole number

in´te·grat adj. necessary; essential

in´te·grate vt. bring together; unify

in·te·gra´tion n. a unifying or blending

in·teg´ri·ty n. compliance to a standard; being whole or sound

in·tel·lect n. the capacity for reason or understanding

in·tel·lec´tu·al adj. appealing to the intellect; intelligent — n. one given to intellectual pursuits

in·tel´li·gence n. capacity for knowledge; information or news

in·tel´li·gent adj. having knowledge; able to acquire knowledge

in·tel·li·gent´si·a n. intellectual elite

in·tel´li·gi·ble adj. understandable

in·tem´per·ance n. excessive indulgence

in·tend´ vt. to have in mind

in·tend´ed adj. intentional

in·tense´ adj. extreme in force or magnitude; emotional

in•ten´si•fy *vi.*, *vt.* grow stronger

in•ten´sive *adj.* marked by vigor or concentration

in•tent´ *adj.* firmly fixed in the mind —*n.* something intended

in•ten´tion *n.* aim; purpose

in•ten´tion•al *adj.* deliberate; planned —**in•ten´tioa•al•ly** *adv.*

in•ter´ *vt.* to bury or entomb

in•ter•act´ *vi.* relate or act mutually

inter•cede´ *vt.* to plead on behalf of another

inter•cept´ *vt.* interrupt the progress of —**in•ter•cep´tion** *n.*

in•ter•ces´sion *n.* a plea for another; mediation

in•ter•change *vi.*, *vt.* to change successively —**in´ter•change** *n.* a system of highway access ramps

in´ter•course *n.* communication between persons; sexual relations

inter•de•pen´dence, in•ter•de•pend´en•cy *n.* mutually dependent

in•ter•dict´ *vt.* prohibit by law or order of the church

in•ter•dic´tion *n.* a legal prohibition; censure by the church

in´ter•est *n.* curiosity; the right to a share; fee for the loan of money —*vt.* hold one's attention

in´ter•est•ed *adj.* connected or affected in some way

in´ter•est•ing *adj.* inviting attention

in•ter•fere´ *vt.* to invene

in•ter•fer´ence *n.* an obstruction; an act of interrupting or obstructing

in•ter•´ga•lac´tic *adj.* existing between galaxies

is´ter•im *n.* a time between events —*adj.* effective for a time

in•te´ri•or *adj.* inside; away from the coast —*n.* the internal part; the internal af-fairs of a political entity

in•ter•ject´ *vt.* insert between other components —**in•ter•jec´tion** *n.*

in•ter•lace´ *vt.* to weave or entwine

in´ter•leaf *n.* a blank sheet between pages to a book

in´ter•lock *vt.*, *vi.* join together; link

in´ter•lop•er *n.* one who meddles

in´ter•lude *n.* a lull; intervening time

in•ter•me´di•ar•y *n.* an agent or mediator

in•ter•me´di•ate *adj.* occurring between

in•ter´ment *n.* burial

in•ter´mina•ble *adj.* without terminus; endless; tiresome

in•ter•min´gle *vt.*, *vi.* combine or become mingled together

in•ter•mis´sion (*US*) *n.* a pause between events, as the acts of a play

in•ter•mit´tent *adj.* not continuous

in•ter•mix´ *vt.*, *vi.* to mix together

in´tern *n.* an apprentice —**in•tenr´** *vt.* to confine —*vi.* to serve as apprentice

in•ter´nal *adj.* of the area within borders —**in•ter´nal•ly** *adv.*

inter•na´tion•al *adj.* worldwide; between nations

in•ter•nec´ine *adj.* of an internal struggle; mutually

destructive

in•tern′ment n. confinement

in•teir′nist n. a physician

in•ter•per′son•al adj. between persons

in′ter•play n. interaction

in•ter′po•late vt. to derive data from that which precedes and follows it

in•ter•pose′ vt. to inject into or between elements

in•ter′pret vt. to translate, explain, or illuminate

in•ter•pre•ta′tion n. an explanation; a presentation marked by a particular style or point of view

in•ter′pret•er n. one who translates or explains

in•ter•re•late′ vt.,vi. to come into interdependent association

in•ter′ro•gate vt. cross-examine

in•ter•ro•ga′tion n. a formal questioning

in•ter•rupt′ vt. break in or interfere

in•ter•rup′tion n. delay or intrusion

in•ter•sect′ vt., vi. to cross or abut; form an intersection

in•ter•sec′tion n. a point where lines, streets, etc. abut or cross

in•ter•sperse′ vt. place at regular intervals

in′ter•twine vt., vi. to unite by interlacing

in′ter•val n. space or time between

in•ter•vene′ vi. to come between; to interfere

in•ter•ven′tion n. interference in the affairs of another

interview n. meeting to elicit or exchange information

in•tes′tine n. the passage

between stomach and anus that plays a major role in digestion

in′ti•ma•cy n. closeness

in′ti•mate adj. marked by innermost thoughts, feelings, etc.; closely associated; of informality and privacy —n. a close associate —vt. hint

in•ti•ma′tion n. information communicated subtly and indirectly; a hint

in•tim′i•date vt. to frighten; to pressure by threatening

in•tol′er•a•ble adj. unbearable; grossly offensive

in•tol′er•ant adj. bigoted or prejudiced; unwilling to accept: intolerant of evil

in•to•na′tion n. voice modulation

in•tone′ vt., vi. to recite or chant in a monotone

in•tox′i•cant n. agent of intoxication

in•tox′ i•cate vt. to inebriate or befuddle by strong drink; to stimulate, as by good news, beauty, etc.

in•tox•i•ca′tion n. drunkenness; stimulation

in•trac′ta•ble adj. obstinate or undisciplined; difficult to control

in•tran′si•gence n. refusal to compromise; obstinacy; stubborness

in•tran′si•gent adj. intolerant and inflexible; obstinate

in•tra•ve′nous adj. injected into or situated within a vein

in•trep′id adj. fearless — **in•trep′id•ly** adv.

in′tri•ca•cy n. something extremely complex

in′tri•cate adj. complex or involved

in•trigue′ n. a secret scheme

—*vi.* to plot secretly —*vt.* arouse interest

in•trin´sic *adj.* of an inborn quality

in•tro•duce´ *vt.* present for consideration; acquaint one with another

in•tro•duc´tion *n.* presentation of a person, idea, etc.; a time or ceremony of presentation

in•tro•duc´to•ry *adj.* of presentation of something new

in•tro•spec´tion *n.* contemplation and self-examination

in´tro•vert *n.* one whose interests are directed inward

in•trude´ *vi., vt.* to intervene where one is not wanted

in•trud´er *n.* one who meddles or enters improperly

in•tru´sion *n.* an interruption; meddling —**in•tru´sive** *adj.*

in•tu•i´tion *n.* an instinctive feeling

in•tu´i•tive *adj.* instinctive; perceived or determined without reason —**in•tu´i•tive•ness** *n.*

in´un•date *vt.* to overwhelm

in•un•da´tion *n.* a flooding or overflowing

in•ure´ *vt.* to acclimate or accustom to something unpleasant

in•vade´ *vt.* to attack; to enter and remain —**in•vad´er** *n.*

in•val´id *adj.* not legal; not legally binding; faulty —

in•va•lid *n.* one who is disabled by illness or injury

in•val´i•date *vt.* to revoke or nullify

in•val´u•a•ble *adj.* priceless

in•var´i•a•ble *adj.* unchanging

in•va´sion *n.* an attack; infestation

in•va´sive *adj.* tending to

invade or intrude

in•vec´tive *adj.* marked by abusive language —*n.* abusive language; denunciation

in•veigh´ *vt.* to protest vigorously

in•vei´gle *vt.* to entice or trick by coaxing or flattery

in•vent´ *vt.* create something new; to misrepresent, as by way of excuse

in•ven´tion *n.* something newly created

in•ven´tive *adj.* clever; creative; resourceful —**in•ven´tive•ly** *adv.*

in´ven•to•ry *n.* goods in stock; an accounting —*vt.* to count and record goods on hand

in•verse´ *adj.* reversed

in•vert´ *vt.* to reverse position

in•ver´te•brate *adj.* lacking a backbone —*n.* an animal that has no backbone

in•vest´ *vt.* buy in anticipation of profit; to charge with authority; to formally install in office

in•ves´ti•gate *vi., vt.* to make careful inquiry

in•ves•ti•ga´tion *n.* detailed inquiry

in•vest´ment *n.* the placing of resources in the hope of profit

in•vet´er•ate *adj.* well-established; persisting

in•vid´i•ous *adj.* expressing ill-will; malicious —**in•vid´i•ous•ly** *adv.*

in•vig´o•rate *vt.* enliven; energize —**in•vig•o•ra´tion** *n.*

in•vig´o•rat•ing *adj.* tending to energize; refreshing or stimulating

in•vin´ci•ble *adj.* unconquerable —**in•vin•ci•bil´i•ty** *n.*

in•vi´o•la•ble *adj.* that cannot

be profaned; invincible

in•vi´o•late *adj.* not violated; pure

in•vis´ible *adj.* unseen; not open to view **—in•vis´i•bly** *adv.*

in•vi•ta´tion *n.* a formal request; an allurement or temptation

in•vi•ta´tion•al *n.* an event limited to those invited — *adj.* restricted to invited participants

in•vite´ *vt.* formally request; tempt

in•vit´ing *adj.* attractive, en tieing

in•vo•ca´tion *n.* an appeal; a prayer

in´voice *n.* a statement of charges *—vt.* to tender a bill

in•voke´ *vt.* to call up, as a spirit; to beseech or appeal earnestly

in•vol´un•ta•ry *adj.* unintentional; instinctive

in•vo•lu´tion *n.* involvement; complexity

in•volve´ *vt.* include or connect to, implicate or incriminate; become engrossed in; complicate

in•volved´ *adj.* complicated; engrossed; emotionally committed

in•volve´ment *n.* participation; entanglement

in•vul´ner•a•ble *adj.* invincible; impossible to harm or damage

in´ward *adj.* related to the inside *—adv.* toward the inside

i•o´ta *n.* a small amount

i•ras´ci•ble *adj.* irritable; quick to anger; marked by anger

i´rate, i•rate´ *adj.* incensed; marked by anger

ire *n.* anger

irk *vt.* vex or annoy

irk´some *adj.* annoying; dis--urbing

i´ron *n.* a metallic element; something made from iron; a symbol of strength *—vt., vi.* smooth clothing *—adj.* made of or containing iron; strong and unyielding

i•ron´ic, i•ron´ical *adj.* paradoxical; mocking **—iron´i•cal•ly** *adv.*

i´ro•ny *n.* a paradox; a literary syle that mocks or satirizes convention

ir•ra´di•ate *vt.* to clarify or illuminate; to expose to radiation

ir•rad´i•ca•ble *adj.* impossible to destroy

ir•ra´tion•al *adj.* not subject to reason; illogical; silly

ir•rec•on•cil´a•ble *adj.* that cannot be justified

ir•re•deem´a•ble *adj.* that cannot be redeemed; impossible to recover or reform

ir•re•fut´a•ble *adj.* indisputable; not subject to argument or dispute

ir•reg´u•lar *adj.* contrary to the normal or conventional, not symmetrical or uniform

ir•reg•u•lar´i•ty *n.* an abnormality or oddity

ir•rel´e•vance, ir•rel´e•van•cy *n.* the quality of being trivial or not pertinent

ir•rel´e•vant *adj.* not pertinent

ir•re•li´gious *adj.* not religious; hostile to religion

ir•re•mis´si•ble *adj.* incurable; unpardonable

ir•rep´a•ra•ble *adj.* hopeless; impossible to mend or coo rect

ir·re·place´a·ble *adj.* priceless; that cannot be replaced

ir·re·press´i·ble *adj.* that cannot be controlled; overly enthusiastic

ir·re·proach´a·ble *adj.* blameless

ir·re·sist´i·ble *adj.* overwhelming; compelling —**ir·re·sist´i·bly** *adv.*

ir·res´o·lute *adj.* lacking in purpose or resolution; wavering —**ir·res´o·lute·ly** *adv.* —**ir·res·o·lu´tion** *n.*

ir·re·spec´tive *adj.* regardless

ir·re·spon´si·ble *adj.* lacking a sense of duty; thoughtless; unpredictable

ir·rev´er·ence *n.* a lack of respect

ir·rev´er·ent *adj.* disrespectful of that considered proper

ir·rev´o·ca·ble *adj.* that cannot be retracted or changed

ir´ri·gate *vt.* furnish water for growing plants; to cleanse with liquid

ir·ri·ga´tion *n.* a system or process of providing water for plants or liquid for cleansing

ir´ri·table *adj.* ill-tempered, easily provoked or offended

ir´ri·tant *n.* something that annoys

ir´ri·tate *vt.* provoke to anger; chafe or abrade —**ir´ri·tat·ing·ly** *adv.*

ir´ri·tat·ed *adj.* troubled of disturbed

ir·ri·ta´tion *n.* something that troubles or vexes; an irritant

is´land *n.* land surrounded by water, an isolated structure or area

i´so·late *vt.* set apart

i·so·la´tion *n.* separation; seclusion

i·so·la´tion·ist *n.* one opposed to involvement in the affairs of others

is´sue *n.* a flowing out, something published or distributed; an edition —*vi., vt.* to flow out; orginate from a source; to distribute

itch *n.* a skin irritation; a desire —*vi.* sense an irritation or desire

i´tem *n.* a single element that is part of a whole

i´tem·ize *vt., vt.* to enumerate,one by one—**i´tem·i·za´tion**

it´er·ance, it·er·a´tion *n.* repetition

it´er·ate *vt.* to repeat

i·tin´er·ant *adj.* roving —*n.* a wanderer —**i·ti´ner·ant·ly** *adv*

i·tin´er·ar·y *n.* a travel plan

i´vied *adj.* coated with ivy

i´vy *n.* a climbing or trailing plant

j, J tenth letter of the alphabet

jab *n.* a quick poke or punch —*vi., vt.* to poke or punch sharply

jab´ber *vi., vt.* speak rapidly of nonsensically —*n.* senseless talk

ja·bot´ *n.* ornamental ruffles

jack *n.* a device for raising heavy objects; a type of food fish; (*US*) a plug for electronic devices —*vt.* raise with a jack; to raise prices

jack´al *n.* a wild dog

jack´ass *n.* the male ass; a stupid person

jack´boot *n.* a heavy boot reaching above the knee

jack´daw *n.* a small black bird related to the crow

jack´et n. a short coat; an outer covering or container —vt. to cover —**jack´et•ed** adj.

jack´knife n. a pocket knife

jack´pot n. a prize or pool of money; winnings; a bonanza or reward

jack´rab•bit n. a large American hare

jade vt., vi. wear out by overindulgence —n. a shrewish woman; a gemstone, usually pale green

jad´ed adj. world-weary; pretentiously indifferent

jag´ged adj. characterized by an irregular edge —**jag´ged•ness** n.

jag´uar n. a large spotted cat

jail (US), **gaol** (Brit.) n. a place of confinement —vt. confine in a jail

jail´er (US), **gaol´er** (Brit.) n. one charged with the upkeep of a jail

ja•la•pe´ño n. a pungent tropical pepper having red or green fruit

ja•lop´y n. an old, broken-down car

jal´ou•sie n. a door or window covering with adjustable slats

jam n. a preserve of sugar and fruit; a crush of people; a difficult situation —vt., vi. cram in a tight space

jamb n. side of a door or window

jam•ba•lay´a n. a spicy Creole dish

jam•bo•ree´ n. a large gathering; a festive celebration

jam session an unrehearsed gathering or meeting

jan´gle n. discordant metallic sound —vi., vt.

jan´i•tor (US) n. one charged with the maintenance of a building

ja•pan´ n. a hard glossy coating; an item coated in the Japanese manner —vt. coat with japan

jape n. a jest or prank —vi. to joke or jest —**jap´er** n. — **jap´ery** n.

jar n. a small jar container; a jolt or bump —vi., vt. to shake or cause to shake; to irritate or shock

jar´di•niere´ n. an ornamental pot or stand for flowers

jar´gon n. a patois or dialect; the terms of a profession or trade

jas´mine n. a species of flowering shrubs used in trio grances and tea; a fragrance or tea of jasmine

jas´per n. a type of yellow, red, or brown quartz

jaun´dice n. abnormal yellowing of the skin, eyeballs, etc.; hostility —vt. to affect with jaundice; influenced by envy or distrust

jaunt n. an excursion; a short pleasure trip —vi. to make a short trip

jaun´ty adj. in a free and easy manner; buoyant; self-confident

jav´e•lin n. a short light spear

jaw n. bony structures that frame the mouth; anything that grips like a jaw —vi., vt. to talk or scold

jaw´bone n. a bone of the jaw —vt., vi. to urge or argue vigorously

jazz n. an American musical form —adj. pertaining to jazz

jeal´ous adj. envious; fearful of competition; protective

jeal´ou·sy n. possessive envy

jeer n. an abusive or mocking remark —vi., vt. to mock or ridicule

je·june´ adj. dull or lifeless; childlike

jell vi.,vt. become firm; take shape

jel´ly n. a gelatinous food

jeop´ar·dize vt. to expose to danger

jeop´ar·dy n. risk of loss; danger

jerk n. a sudden action; a silly or foolish person —vt., vi. make a lurching or quivering move

jer´kin n. a short jacket

jerk´y adj. marked by short, abrupt movement

jer´ky n. cured meat

jer·o·bo´am n. a 3 liter wine bottle

jer´ry-built adj. shoddily constructed; improvised

jer´sey n. knitted fabric; a pullover shirt or sweater

jest n. a joke or prank —vi. to tease or mock; speak in fun

jest´er n. a professional comedian; one given to light banter

jet n. a flow of fluid at high pressure; a vehicle creating such a flow; a vehicle propelled by this flow; a dense, black color —vi. to travel in a jet-propelled aircraft

jet engine n. an engine that develops thrust. from exhaust

jet´sam n. material jettisoned by a ship in distress

jet´ti·son vt. to throw overboard, as from a ship; to discard

jet´ty n. a structure protecting a harbor or shoreline

jew´el n. a precious stone; an ornament set with precious stones; something highly prized

jew·el·ler·y (Brit.) **jew´el·ry** (US) n. ornaments made of precious metals and set with precious stones

jif´fy n. a brief span of time

jig n. a lively dance; a device for holding or guiding —vi. dance a jig

jig´ger n. a 1½ ounce measure

jig´gle vi. to bounce lightly up and down or from side to side

ji·had´ n. a holy war or pious quest

jilt vi. to reject suddenly

jim´my n. a short crowbar —vt. to force with a crowbar

jin´gle n. a short rhyme or song; a light metallic sound —vi., vt. to make a metallic sound

jin´go n. one who aggressively supports his or her nation

jin´go·ism n. extreme nationalism

jinx n. a hex or spell; thing bringing bad luck —vt. to bring bad luck

jit´ney n. a small passenger vehicle; a delapidated vehicle

jive n. the jargon of jazz; nonsensical talk —vt., vi talk nonsensically

job n. work for pay; the work one does; a task or duty; something worked on or at

job´ber n. one who buys in large quantities and sells to retailers

job´less adj. out of work

jock´ey n. a professional rider; one associated with a

particular vehicle, profession, etc. —*vi.*, *vt.* to ride a horse; to manuever

jo•cose´ *adj.* given to humor —**jo•cose´ly** *adv.*

joc´u•lar *adj.* given to joking

joc´und *adj.* lighthearted —**jo•cun´di•ty** *n.* —**joc´und•ly** *adv.*

jodh´purs *n.* riding pants

jog *n.* a slow, steady trot; a slight jostling or nudge —*vi.*, *vt.* move at a slow run; to jostle or nudge

jog´gle *vt.*, *vi.* to shake lightly

join *vt.*, *vi.* to bring together; connect

join´er *n.* a carpenter; a tool designed to fashion joints

joint *n.* a place where pieces come together; a seedy establishment; a marijuana cigarette —*adj.* shared

joist *n.* a horizontal beam

joke *n.* an amusing story or act — *vi.* speak or act in fun

jok´er *n.* a jester or prankster

jol´lity *n.* merriment

jol´ly *adj.* cheerful; exhibiting good humor —**jol´li•ly** *adv.*

jolt *n.* a jarring bump; a shock or surprise —*vt.* to jar with a sharp blow; to shock

josh *vi.* to joke; to tease playfully

jos´tle *vt.* to push or bump while passing

jot *n.* a small amount —*vt.* to write hastily

jot´ted *adj.* written hastily

jot´ting *n.* a short note

jounce *n.* a jolting movement —*vt.* to move with a jolt

jour´nal *n.* an account of fi nances or activities; a news paper or periodical —**jour´nal•ize** *vt.*

jour´nal•ism *n.* the writing

and editing of news items

jour´nal•ist *n.* one who writes for a newspaper or periodical

jour´ney *n.* the act of traveling; distance traveled —*vi.*, *vt.* to travel

jour´ney•man *n.* one who has completed an apprenticeship

joust *n.* medieval combat; a competition; a confrontation —*vi.* to compete; engage in a battle of words or wits

jo´vi•al *adj.* extremely cordial and sociable —**jo´vi•al•ly** *adv.*

jowl *n.* the flesh of the cheek or jaw

jowl´y *adj.* having loose hapging flesh about the cheeks and jaws

joy *n.* intense happiness or pleasure; the cause of such pleasure

joy´ful *adj.* expressing or feeling joy

joy´less *adj.* lacking joy; sad

joy´ous *adj.* causing or expressing joy —**joy´ous•ly** *adv.*

joy´stick *n.* a cursor control

ju´bi•lant *adj.* extremely happy; rapturous —**ju´bi•lance** *n.*

ju´bi•late *vi.* to rejoice

ju•bi•la´tion *n.* rapture; a manifestation of joy

ju´bi•lee *n.* a celebration; an occasion for rejoicing

judge *n.* an officer of the court; one appointed to arbitrate or decide after argument; to form an opinion based on careful study

judg•mat´ic, judg•mat´i•cal *adj.* judicious —**judg•mat´i•cal•ly** *adv.*

judge´hip n. the office and authority of a judge

judge´ment, judg´ment n. ability to discern; opinion based on observation and consideration

judg•men´tal adj. tending to judge; relating to judgment

ju•di´cial adj. relating to a court —of law; pronouncing judgment

ju•di´ciar•y n. the court system; those who administer justice

ju•di´cious adj. marked by prudence; careful; discreet; sensible

ju´do n. a form of combat

jug n. a large, rounded container with a small mouth and a handle

jug´ger•naut n. overwhelming force

jug´gle vt. keep in the air by alternately tossing and catching; to have difficulty moving between activities; alter so as to deceive

jug´u•lar adj. about the neck or throat

juice n. liquid derived from plant or animal tissue

juic´y adj. full of juice; mouth-watering; having special meaning

juke´box n. a coin-operated phonograph

ju•li•enne´ n. a broth containing strips of vegetable — adj. cut into long, thin strips

jum´ble n. a confusing mixture —vt., vi. to mix in a haphazard fashion

jum´bo adj. large in size

jump n. a leap; span of a leap —vi., vt. to move or change suddenly

jump´er n. one who jumps; a shunt for an electrical circuit; (Bnt.) a sweater; (US) a sleeveless dress

jump´i•ness n. nervousness

jump´suit n. a one-piece garment

jump´y adj. nervous

junc´tion n. place where two things meet —junc´tion•al adj.

junc´ture n. a junction; place where two things are joined

jun´gle n. tangled undergrowth; a jumbled or confusing accumulation; intense rivalry

jun´ior adj. younger; lower in rank —n. younger of two; one lower in rank; a third year student

junk n. objects. cast off; something of poor quality — vt. discard —adj. worthless

junk bond a high yield corporate bond entailing high risk

junk´er n. an old, beat-up car

junk´et n. an outing; a trip at public expense —jun´ke•teer´n.

junk food snack food

jun´ta n. a group of rulers

ju´ral adj. relating to the law

ju´rat n. certification on an affidavit

ju•rid´ic, ju•rid´i•cal adj. relating to administration of the law

juris•dic´tion n. the range or extent of one's authority

juris•dic´tion•al adj. relating to the limits of one's rights or authority

juris•pru´dence n. the science of law —ju•ris•pru´dent adj., n.

ju´rist n. one experienced in the law

ju•ris´tic adj. relating to a

jurist or matters of the law

ju´ror n. one serving on a jury

ju´ry n. a group sworn to hear an issue and to pass judgment

ju´ry-rig vt. rig for emergency use; improvise

just adj. fair and fitting; conforming to what is right; im partial —adv. precisely; barely —**just´ly** adv.

jus´tice n. adhering to what is right or just

jus·ti·fi·a·ble adj. proved correct; warranted —**jus´ti·fi·a·bly** adv.

jus·ti·fi·ca´tion n. defense; explanation

jus´ti·fy vt. prove correct; absolve of blame

jut vi., vt. to extend outward

ju´ve·nile adj. young; relating to the young; marked by immature behavior

jux´ta·pose vt. place side by side for comparison —**jux·ta·po·si´tion** n.

k, K eleventh letter of the alphabet

ka·lei´do·scope n. an optical device that produces changing colored patterns; somethin constantly changing —**ka·lei·do·scop´ic** adj.

kan´ga·roo´ n. an Australian marsupial

kan´ji n. Japanese picture writing

ka´pok n. a cottonlike fiber

ka·put´ adj. not working; used up or gone bad

ka·ra´te n. a system of self-defense

kar´ma n. one's destiny

katz´en·jam·mer n. a hangover; a bewildered state

kay´ak n. an enclosed canoe propelled with a double—ended paddle

ka·zoo´ n. an instrument with a vibrating membrane that produces a humming sound

ke·bob´ n. bits of food broiled on a skewer; a shish kebob

kedge n. a light anchor

keel n. the lowest point along the length of a vessel —vi. to roll over

keen adj. sharp; intelligent and perceptive; sensitive; eager for

keep vt. retain; tend or care for; continue without change; restrain or prevent —vi. continue; remain unchanged —n. care or support; a stronghold, as in a castle

keep´er n. an overseer

keep´sake n. a memento

ke·fir´ n. a drink made from fermented row's milk

keg n. a small barrel; a 100 pound measure for nails

keg´ler n. one who bowls

kelp n. a type of seaweed

kempt adj. neat; orderly

ken´nel n. an animal shelter; the boarding or. breeding of dogs

ker´a·tin n. a tough protein that forms nails, horns, etc.

ker´chief n. large handkerchief; a bandanna

kerf n. a cut made by an axe or saw

ker´nel n. a grain or seed; the most significant or central part

ker·o·sene (US) n. a fuel distilled from petroleum

ketch n. a two-masted vessel

ket´tle n. a metal pot, often with a handle and a lid; a teakettle

key *n.* a notched device for unlocking, winding, etc.; a critical element; pitch of a musical tone

key´board *n.* a set of keys as on a typewriter, piano, etc.

key´board•ist *n.* one who plays a piano, synthesizer, etc.

keycard *n.* a rigid card that unlocks with a coded electronic strip

key club a private club

keynote address an opening speech

key´pad *n.* device for inputting data

key´stone *n.* the topmost stone in an arch; a fundamental element

khak´i *n.* a tannish brown color; a cloth of this color

kib´itz *vi.* chat informally; intrude; offer unwanted advice

kick *n.* a blow with the foot; a thrust of the foot; vigor or stimulation —*vi., vt.* to strike out with the foot

kick´back *n.* payback: a bribe; a violent reaction; a backlash

kick´er *n.* one who kicks; an important contingency

kick´off *n.* a traditional beginning

kid *n.* young of certain animals; the meat or hide of a young goat; a young person —*vi., vt.* to engage in good-natured banter —**kid´der** *n.*

kid´nap *vt.* to abduct or hold illegally

kid´ney *n.* one of a pair of organs that filter body fluids

kid´skin *n.* leather from the skin of a young goat

kill *vt.* put to death; to destroy, extinguish, or end; to overwhelm —*n.* an act of killing; that killed

kill´joy *n.* one who undermines the pleasure of other

kiln *n.* an oven for baking or drying

kil´o•byte *n.* a computer unit equal to 1,024 bytes

kil´o•cal•o•rie *n.* a unit of po-tential energy in food; a nu-tritionist's calorie, a large calorie

kil´o•cy•cle *n.* one thousand cycles

ki•lom´e•ter *n.* one thousand meters

ki•mo´no *n.* a robe-like outer garment indigenous to Japan

kin *adj.* of the same ancestry —*n.* those to whom one is related

kind *adj.* benevolent, compassionate, and humane —*n.* a class unified by common traits; something similar

kin´der•gar•ten *n.* school for young children

kind´heart•ed *adj.* having a kind and sympathetic nature

kin´dle *vt., vi.* to set on fire; to stimulate emotion —**kin´dling** *n.*

kind´ly *adj.* of a kind disposition — *adv.* pleasantly or politely

kind´ness *n.* being kind; acting in a kind manner; a courtesy; an act of charity

kin´dred *adj.* of common origins or nature

ki•net´ic *adj.* producing motion

kinetic energy t he energy of a body attributable to its motion

ki·net´ics n. the study of the dynamics of material bodies

king n. a male sovereign; one superior in a field —adj. preeminent

king´dom n. domain of a king; a broad domain: *the animal kingdom*

king´ly adj. regal; in the manner of a king —adv. —**king´li·ness** n.

king´pin n. a leader; the most important person

kink n. a tight curl; a cramp; a quirk or impediment

kink´y adj. tightly curled; strange or quirky —**kink´i·ness** n.

kin´ship n. relationship by blood

ki´osk n. a small, free-standing structure, such as a gazebo

kip´per n. a fish cured by salting and smoking —vt. to cure

kir n. dry white wine flavored with creme de cassis

kirk n. a Scottish church

kirsch n. a clear cherry brandy

kiss n. a touching of the lips; alight, fleeting touch —vi., vt. touch with the lips; touch lightly

kit n. a collection of articles or the container for such a collection

kitch´en n. an area for food preparation; a staff or implements for preparing food

kitch·en·ette´ n. a small kitchen

kitch´en·ware n. implements used in the preparation of food

kite n. a hawk; a paper-covered frame flown in the wind; a counterfeit negotiable instrument —vt., vi. obtain money by counterfeiting

kit´ty n. money pooled for a purpose

klep·to·ma´ni·ac n. one with an obsessive urge to steal

klutz n. one clumsy or lacking in social grace —**klutz´y** adj.

knack n. a special talent or skill

knap´sack n. a sturdy bag with shoulder straps

knave n. one of humble birth; a rascal or rogue —**knav´ish** adj.

knav´er·y n. deceitful or underhanded transactions

knead vt. to fold and press with the hands; to massage

knee n. a joint of the leg; part. of a garment that covers the knee —vt. to strike with the knee

knee´-jerk adj. involuntary, as a reaction; unthinking acceptance

kneel vi. rest on one or both knees

knell n. slow, solemn tolling of a hell

knick´er·bock·ers (US) n. full trousers that are cut off and tied just below the knee

knick´knack n. a small curio or ornamental piece

knife n. a tool consisting of a thin blade attached to a handle

knight n. a medieval mounted soldier; one who champions a cause

knight-er·rant n. a knight seeking adventure; an adventure-seeker

knight´hood n. a rank conferred by a sovereign for outstanding service

knish *n.* a savory filled pastry that is baked of fried

knit *vt., vi.* intertwine strands of yarn; to join tightly; to draw together in wrinkles

knit´ting, knit´wear *n.* garments made by knitting

knob *n.* a stubby projection; a rounded handle —**knobbed** *adj.*

knob´by *adj.* have the appearance of a knob, as *knobby* knees

knock *vi., vt.* strike solidly; to collide; to criticize —*n.* a sharp blow

knock´off *adj.* a cheap imitation

knoll *n.* a low, rounded hill; a hillock

knot *n.* fastener or decoration made by tying; a tight group of people; a tight feeling; joint of a tree; one nautical mile; a speed of one nautical mile per hour —*vt., vi.* form unto a knot; become entangled

knot´ty *adj.* snarled; having many knots; difficult to resolve

know *vt., vi.* to possess information and understanding; comprehend

know´-how *n.* expertise

know´ing *adj.* knowledgeable; shrewd; secretly aware; deliberate or intentional —**know´ing•ly** *adv.*

knowl´edge *n.* awareness or information from study or experience

knowl´edge•a•ble *adj.* possessing learning or experience

knuck´le *n.* bulge *of* bones in a joint

knurl *n.* a protuberance; small ridges that aid in gripping

ko•a´la *n.* an Australian arborial marsupial

ko´an *n.* a Zen riddle in the form of a paradox

kook *n.* an unconventional person —**kook´y** *adj.*

ko´sher *adj.* conforming to Jewish dietary laws; valid or legitimate

ko´to *n.* a Japanese stringed instrument

kraut *n.* sauerkraut

kris *n.* a Malaysian dagger

kryp´ton *n.* an inert gas

ku´chen *n.* yeast dough coffee cake

ku´dos *n.* aclaim for achievement

kum´mel *n.* caraway seed liqueur

kum´quat *n.* a small, orange-like fruit

kung fu *n.* Chinese martial art similar to karate

l, L twelfth letter of the alphabet

lab *n.* laboratory

la´bel *n.* a tag or stamp; a distinguishing appellation —*vt* attach or ascribe with a label

la´bor (*US*) *n.* physical effort; workers collectively; the exertion of childbirth —*vi.* expend energy; toil conscientiously; move with difficulty; experience childbirth

lab•o•ra•to•ry *n.* a place of research or learning

la´bored (*US*) *adj.* accomplished with great effort

la´bor-inten•sive *adj.* reduffing an excessive amount of physical labor

la•bo´ri•ous *adj.* difficult or

exhausting —**la•bo´ri•ous•ly** adv.

la´bour (*Brit.*) *n.* physical effort; workers collectively; the exertion of childbirth —*vi.* expend energy; toil conscientiously; move with difficulty; experience childbirth

la´boured (*Brit.*) *adj.* accomplished with great effort

lab´y•rinth *n.* a maze; something intricate —**lab•yrin´thi•an** *adj.*

lace *n.* a cord used to fasten; a delicate fabric —*vt.* place by threading or intertwining; spread throughout —**lace into** to assail verbally

lac´er•ate *vt.* to cut or tear, as flesh —*adj.* torn

lac•er•a´tion *n.* a jagged wound

lach´ry•mose *adj.* tearful; causing tears —**lach´ry•mal** *adj.*

lack *n.* a deficiency in substance or quality —*vi.*, *vt.* have little; need

lack•a•dai´si•cal *adj.* languid; lacking spirit

lack´ey *n.* a menial; a fawning attendant

lack´lus•ter *adj.* wanting in vitality

la•con´ic, la•con´i•cal *adj.* not wordy; disinclined to converse

lac´quer *n.* a clear, protective coating —*vt.* coat with lacquer

la•crosse´ *n.* a type of field hockey

lac´tate *vi.* produce milk

lac•ta´tion *n.* production of milk in mammary glands; period of such production —**lac•ta´tion•al** *adj.*

lac´te•al *adj.* relating to milk

lac´tic *adj.* relating to or derived from milk

lac´y *adj.* resembling lace; flimsy —**lac´i•ness** *n.*

lad *n.* a young man

lad´der *n.* parallel sides joined by rungs for climbing; an analogous means of ascent or descent

lade *vt.* load with cargo; dip or ladle

lad´en *adj.* weighed down; oppressed

la´dle *n.* a deep-bowled serving spoon —*vt.* to serve or apportion

la´dy *n.* a well-mannered woman; the female head of a household

la´dy•like *adj.* having the manners or bearing of a lady

lag *vt.* to fall behind; falter

la´ger *n.* a type of beer

lag´gard *n.* one who falls behind; a straggler —*adj.* slow

la•goon´ *n.* a shallow body of water

la´ic, la´i•cal *adj.* secular —*n.* a layperson

laid´-back´ *adj.* serene or casual

lair *n.* an animal's den; one's habitat or domain

lais´sez-faire´ *n.* a policy of noninterference

la´i•ty *n.* those not of the clergy

lake *n.* a large inland body of water

lam•baste´ *vt.* to rebuke sharply; to reprimand

lame *adj.* disabled; halting; weak or ineffective —*vt.* to disable

la•mé´ *n.* a fabric of metallic thread

la•ment´ *n.* an expression of sorrow —*vi.*, *vt.* express

grief, sorrow, or remorse —
lamentable adj.
lam•en•ta´tion n. a lament
lam´i•nate n. a thin covering
material —vt. to cover with a
thin material; to form from
thin layers
lam´i•nat•ed adj. coated with
or formed from thin layers
lam•i•na´tion n. a coating or
joining; material formed from
such process
lamp n. a device that provides
light or heat
lamp´black n. fine carbon
used as a pigment
lam•poon´ n. a satirical work
that ridicules —vt. to satirize
la•nai´ n. a roofed porch or
patio
lance n. a long shaft with a
pointed end —vt. to pierce
with a pointed weapon or instrument —**lanc´er** n.
lan´cet n. a surgical knife
land n. real estate; a nation or
country —vi., vt. to come to
a place
land bridge dry ground that
joins two land masses
land´ed adj. possessing property
land´fill n. land created by
depositing waste between
layers of soil
land grant property deeded by
a government
land´hold•er n. a property
owner
land´ing n. termination of a
voyage; a place for transferring cargo; the termination
of a staircase
land´locked adj. without access to the sea
land´mark n. a boundary
marker; a prominent feature; a building or area

preserved for posterity
landscape n. a scenic view —
vt., vi. beautify by contouring, planting, etc.; beautify
land as a vocation
lane n. a narrow byway; a defined channel
lan´guage n. a system of
sounds, symbols, gestures,
etc. for communicating
lan´guid adj. lacking vitality or
force; sluggish —**lan´
guid•ness** n.
lan´guish vi. be or become
weak or neglected
lan´guor n. lack of energy; a
lethargic condition —**lan´
guor•ous** adj.
lank adj. lean and gaunt
lank´y adj. tall and thin;
awkward
lan´tern n. a lamp with a
protective case
lan´yard n. a short rope; a
decorative cord
lap n. the surface formed when
one is seated; amount by
which one piece lies over
another; act or sound of
taking in liquid with the
tongue —vi., vt. to lie over;
overlap; take in or make
sounds of taking in with the
tongue
la•pel´ n. an extended collar
that folds back against a
garment
lap´i•dar•y n. one who finishes or deals in gems
lapse n. a temporary fault or
break; a deterioration; termination of a right —vi. deteriorate or deviate from accepted course; lose a right
lap´top n. a portable computer
lar´ce•nous adj. given to larceny

lar·ce•ny *n.* unlawful taking of property

lard *n.* rendered fat —*vt.* to prepare meat by injecting with strips of fat

lar´der *n.* a store of food; a pantry

large *adj.* of greater than average size or scope; extensive; important; significant —**large´ly** *adv.*

lar•gess´ *n.* generosity: generous gift

lark *n.* a songbird; a spontaneous escapade —**lark´er** *n.*

las·civ•i•ous *adj.* lewd; arousing sexual desire

lash *n.* a whip; a sudden blow; a stinging attack of words; an eyelash —*vi., vt.* strike suddenly; attack with words

las·si•tude *n.* lethargy; a feeling of apathy or fatigue

las´so *n.* a noose used mainly to control livestock —*vt.* to catch with a noose

last *n.* the end or one at the end —*adj., adv.* final; the only one left; most recent but one —*vi., vt.* to continue; endure or persist

last´ing *adj.* permanent; enduring

last name (*US*) a surname; a family name

last word final say; latest or most modern

latch *n.* a catch or lock as for a door *vt.* close or lock

latchkey child a child of working parents left at home unsupervised

late *adj.* after the usual or expected time; well on in time; recent; former or deceased —*adv.* after the usual or expected time; recently

late´ly *adv.* recently

lat´en *vi., vt.* to become late latent *adj.* potential; undeveloped

lat´er•al *adj.* to the side; sideways

lat´est *n.* newest; most recent

lath *n.* a thin wood strip

lathe *n.* a machine for cutting and shaping wood or metal

lath´er *n.* foam —*vt., vi.* to coat with lather

lat´i•tude *n.* an angular distance from the equator or a celestial body; a range in which to function

la•trine´ *n.* a communal toilet

lat´ter *adj.* the second of two; nearer the end

lat´tice *n.* a panel of crisscrossed slats

laud *vt.* to praise —**laud•a•bil´i•ty** *n.*

laud´a•ble *adj.* worthy of praise —**laud´a•bly** *adv.*

lau´da•to•ry *adj.* bestowing praise

laugh *vi.* express amusement by an impromptu, inarticulate sound; to mock with such sounds

laugh´a•ble *adj.* disdainful

laugh´ing *adj.* expressing amusement

laugh´ter *n.* the sound of merriment or derision

launch *vt.* set in motion — *vi.* begin

launch pad a platform and scaffold for launching a spacecraft

laun´der *vt.* to wash; to conceal or obscure the origin of

laun´dry *n.* clothes to be washed; *a place* for washing. clothes

lau´re•ate *adj.* decked with laurel; distinguished —*n.* one deserving of special honor for achievement

la´va *n.* molten rock from a volcano; cooled and hardened volcanic rock

lav´atory *n.* a public bathroom; a washbasin; a toilet

lave *vt.* to bathe

lav´ish *adj.* extravagant; profuse —*vt.* to furnish in abundance

law *n.* a code or system of conduct

law´-a•bid´ing *adj.* faithful to law

law´ful *adj.* sanctioned by law —**law´ful•ly** *adv.*

law´less *adj.* not founded in law; without sanction; disregarding legal constraints

law´mak•er *n.* a legislator

lawn *n.* a tended tract of grass

law´suit *n.* a court action

law´yer *n.* one who gives counsel and support in legal matters

lax *adj.* slack, indifferent; not exacting or demanding —**lax´i•ty** *n.*

lay *vt.* place or arrange —*adj.* of the laity; not of a particular profession

lay´a•bout *n.* a loafer

lay´er *n.* a single thickness; a hen kept for egg production — *vi*, *vt.* to form in layers

lay´off *n.* suspension for lack of work; period of inactivity

laze *vi.*, *vt.* to loaf

la´zy *adj.* inclined to inactivity; inviting idleness —**la´zi • ness** *n.*

lea *n.* a meadow

lead *vt.*, *vi.* guide or direct; go first —*n.* first position; amount by which one is ahead; a clue or suggestion

lead´en *adj.* heavy; dull or listless

lead´er *n.* a guide; one in command; a person of influence or importance; that which precedes or joins

lead´er (*Brit.*) *n.* a written work expressing editorial opinion

lead´er•ship *n.* guidance; capacity to guide or command

lead´-in *n.* an introduction

lead´ing *adj.* most prominent; at the front; designed to elicit a response; directing or guiding

leaf *n.* an appendage issuing from the stem of a plant; a thin sheet of material; a page of a book —*vi.*, *vt.* to browse through

leaf´let *n.* a pamphlet or flier

leaf´y *adj.* having leaves; producing leaves

league *n.* an association —*vi.*, *vt.* to come or bring together in association

leak *n.* an opening that allows escape; substance that has escaped —*vi.*, *vt.* allow escape; disclose through unauthorized channels

leak´y *adj.* inclined to leak

lean *adj.* having little fat; thin or spare; without excess or waste —*vi.*, *vt.* to incline

lean´ing *n.* a tendency or preference

lean´-to *n.* a makeshift shelter; a structure with a roof that slopes

leap *vi.*, *vt.* to jump or act abruptly

learn *vi.*, *vt.* to acquire knowledge or understanding; to memorize —**learn´er** *n.*

learn´ed *adj.* scholarly

learn´ing *n.* knowledge or understanding acquired by study

learning curve time needed to acquire a skill

lease n. a contract for the use of property —vt. to grant use by contract —**leas´a·ble** adj.

lease´hold n. property controlled by a lease

leash n. a restraint —vt. to restrain

least adj. lowest in rank, importance, or magnitude —adv.

leath´er n. dressed hide of an animal

leath´er·work n. things made from leather; decorative work on leather

leath´er·y adj. having the texture or consistency of leather; tough

leave n. consent; a departure —vt. to depart; to abandon or overlook

leav´en, leav´en·ing n. a substance that causes fermentation

leav´ings n. remains or residue

lech´er·y n. preoccupation with sex; lust —**lech´er·ous** adj.

lec´tern n. a speaker's stand

lec´ture n. an address intended to enlighten; a reprimand —vi., vt. to expound; deliver a talk; admonish

lec´tur·er (Brit.) n. an educator; instructor at a college or university

ledge n. horizontal projection

ledg´er n. a book for recording financial transactions

leech n. a worm that feeds on blood; a parasite —vi., vt. to draw off resources

leer n. a sly look of lust —vi. to view with lust or maliciousness

leer´y adj. wary; distrustful

lee´way n. a margin; latitude

left´ist n. a radical —adj. liberal or radical

leg n. a limb that supports or propels; part of clothing covering the leg; a segment, as of a journey or a contest

leg´a·cy n. something passed on from an ancestor or predecessor

le´gal adj. based on, established by, or in conformity with the law

le·gal·ese´ n. jargon of the legal profession

le·gal·ism n. overly strict interpretation of the law

le´gal·ize vt. make legal; sanction by law —**le·gal·i·za´tion** n.

legal pad a writing tablet of ruled sheets, 8½ x 14 inches

legal tender currency that must be accepted for the payment of debts

leg´end n. a heroic fable; a famed person or deed; an inscription

leg´end·ary adj. of the nature of a legend; celebrated

leg´er·de·main n. sleight of hand; trickery

leg´i·ble adj. clear; able to be read

le´gion n. large number; a multitude

leg´is·late vi., vt. to write or enact laws —**leg´is·la·tor** n.

leg·is·la´tion n. a law or set of laws

leg´is·la·tive adj. of a governing body; of the making of law

leg´is·la·ture n. a governing body charged with the making of laws

le·git´i·mate adj. complying

with the law or standards; reasonable or logical — **le•git′i•ma•cy** n.

leg′ume n. a pod that splits to reveal edible seeds — **le•gu′mi•nous** adj.

lei n. a crown or wreath of flowers

lei′sure n. free time

lei′sure•ly adj. marked by an unhurried pace—adv. in an unhurried way

lemon law law requiring repair or replacement of a defective product

lend vt. permit temporary use of; offer or impart

length n. measure of distance or duration —**go to great length** make significant effort; do all that is necessary

length′en vi., vt. make longer

length′y adj. somewhat long; longer than seems necessary

le′ni•ent adj. indulgent; not strict —**le′ni•ence, le′ni•en•cy** n.

lens n. transparent material shaped to bend light rays

le•o•tard n. a close-fitting garment

lep′er n. one afflicted with leprosy; one shunned —**lep′rous** adj.

lep•re•chaun n. a fairy cobbler of Irish folklore

lep′ro•sy n. a tropical disease that can cause paralysis, numbness, and deformity

les′bi•an n. a homosexual woman

le′sion n. a wound or abrasion

less, less′er adj. smaller or not as important

lessee′ n. one who leases

lessen vt., vt. make or become less

les′son n. something learned; a part of a course of instruction

les′sor n. one who leases to another

let vt., vi. permit or allow; rent or lease

let′down n. disappointment

le′thal adj. harmful; able to cause death

le•thar′gic, le•thar′gi•cal adj. sluggish; listless; apathetic

leth′ar•gy n. dullness; apathy

let′ter n. a written symbol; written communication

let′tered adj. learned; inscribed with letters

let′up n. a pause or lull

leu•ke′mi•a n. a disease of the blood

lev′ee n. an embankment to hold back water

lev′el n. relative ranking; a flat surface; device for determining deviation from the horizontal —adj. having the same ranking; horizontal — vt. make horizontal or flat; measure deviation from the horizontal —**on the level** honest; fair

lev′el•head′ed adj. having common sense

lev′er n. a simple machine composed of a rigid rod pivoting on a fulcrum; a protruding handle

lev′er•age n. an advantage, as provided by a lever; political or financial power

leveraged buyout use of a company's own assets to finance its acquisition

le•vi′a•than n. a monster; an exceptionally large specimen

lev′i•tate vi., vt. float in the air with no visible means of support —**lev•i•ta′tion** n.

lev′i•ty *n.* frivolity; flippancy

lev′y *vt.* assess and collect, as taxes —*n.* monies collected

lewd *adj.* obscene; depraved

lex•i•cog′ra•phy *n.* the work of compiling a dictionary

lex′i•con *n.* a dictionary; a collection of terms peculiar to a discipline

li•a•bil′i•ty *n.* a debt or obligation

li′a•ble *adj.* legally responsible; at risk; extremely likely

li′ai•son *n.* a connection or link; one who serves as a link; a clandestine affair

li′ar *n.* one who deceives by lying

li•ba′tion *n.* a beverage

li′bel *n.* a malicious falsehood that defames —*vt.* —**li′bel•ous, li′bel•lous** *adj.* —**li′bel•ous•ly, li′bel•lous•ly** *adv.*

lib′er•al *adj.* open to new ideas and concepts; not strict; lavish in gift-giving

lib′er•al•ize *vi., vt.* become or make more liberal

lib′er•ate *vt.* set free, as from bondage or onerous convention

lib•era′tion *n.* the act of treeing or being set free

lib•ertar′i•an *n.* a believer in freedom from government intervention

lib′er•tine *n.* one lacking moral restraint; a reprobate

lib′arty *n.* freedom from restraint or restriction; rights granted

li•bid′i•nous *adj.* displaying lust; salacious —**li•bid′i•nous•ly** *adv.*

li•bi′do *n.* energy associated with biological impulses; sexual appetite

li′brar•y *n.* a collection of printed matter, recordings, etc.; the place where a collection is kept

li•bret′to *n.* words set to music

li′cence (*Brit.*) *n.* legal authorization; lack of restraint or adherence to common practice

li′cense (*US*) *n.* legal authorization; lack of restraint or adherence to common practice —*vt.* grant authorization; formally permit

li•cen′tious *adj.* lacking restraint or regard for accepted morality

lic′it *adj.* legal

lick *n.* a stroking or touching with the tongue; a small amount; a blow —*vt.* stroke with the tongue; overcome; to punish by striking

lick′ing *n.* a spanking; a hard loss

lid *n.* cover for a container

lie *n.* something meant to deceive; the manner in which a thing is positioned —*vi.* pass on false information or create a false impression; recline; be in a certain place

lien *n.* the right to property as security for a debt

lieu•ten′ant *n.* an officer in a military or quasi-military organization; a deputy or assistant

life *n.* the condition of a functioning creature; the time between birth and death; a group of living things; a segment of one's existence

life′-and-death′ *adj.* critical

life cycle the stages of development of a living creature

life′less *adj.* dead; inanimate; lacking spirit

life´like *adj.* precisely imitating life

life style a mode of living

lift *vi.* rise; disperse —*vt.* raise; give a ride to; steal — *n.* an Instance of rising; a ride offered; a rise in condition or attitude

lift (*Brit.*) *n.* a conveyance heiween floors of a building; an elevator

lig´a•ment *n.* connective tissue of the body

lig´a•ture *n.* a cord, bandage, etc. that hinds; a symbol created from two or more characters, such as æ

light *n.* illumination, or its source; clarification; source of fire —*vi.*, *vt.* give off illumination; start to burn; dismount from a vehicle — *adj.* illuminated; of color that is less dark; relatively little in weight, quantity, force, etc.; insubstantial

light´en *vi.*, *vt.* make brighter; make less heavy or oppressive

light´-fin•gered *adj.* inclined to steal; adept at petty theft

light´heart•ed *adj.* free of care

light´ing *n.* style or fixtures for artificial illumination; light provided

light´ly *adv.* with little exertion; delicately; in a free and easy way

light´ning *n.* a natural electric discharge —*adj.* quick or abrupt

light show a display of laser light

light´weight *n.* a weight class in sports; one lacking in knowledge, ability, etc. — *adj.* relatively light in substance or weight

light´-year *n.* distance traveled by light in one year

like *vt.* enjoy or he inclined toward show preference for —*n.* a preference —*adj.* similar —*prep.* in the same or a similar manner — **lik´a•ble, like´a•ble** *adj.*

like´li•hood *n.* probability

likely *adj.* possible; believable

like´-mind´ed *adj.* in agreement

lik´en *vt.* to compare

like´ness *n.* a representation

like´wise *adj.* also

liki´ng *n.* fondness; preference

lilt *n.* a light, cheerful style; a jaunty walk —*vi.*, *vt.* to speak or sing in a light, cheerful style

limb *n.* an appendage

lim´ber *adj.* flexible; supple

limber up to flex; make flexible

lime´light *n.* a center of attention

lim´er•ick *n.* a light verse of five lines

lim´it *n.* a boundary; restriction or condition; an amount not to be exceeded — *vt.* confine within a boundary; firmly establish

lim•i•ta´tion *n.* a restriction; a deficiency

lim´it•ed *adj.* restricted or deficient; cramped or confined —*n.* a train making only express stops

limited edition a work produced in specified numbers

lim´it•ing *adj.* serving to limit

lim´it•less *adj.* unbounded; without limit; infinite

lim´o, lim´ou•sine *n.* a large, elegant automobile

limp n. a hesitant or hobbling gait —vi. move haltingly; hobble —adj. lacking rigidity; lacking strength or vigor

lim´pid adj. of a clear, serene liquid; logical and lucid

line n. a real or imaginary striper *firing line*; things in a row or series; a sequence; a connection: *phone line*; a transportation system; field of competence or employment; a row of words or symbols; a brief note; a concept or notion —vt. cover the interior of

lin·e·age n. ancestry

lin´e·al adj. directly descended; relating to lineage

lin´e·ar adj. in a line; one-dimensional —**lin´e·ar·ly** adv.

lin´en n. cloth made from flax thread —adj. made of or resembling linen

linen closet a storage area for bedding, tablecloths, etc.

lin´er n. material covering the inside; a large passenger ship or airplane

lines´man n. a sports official who judges from the sideline

line´up n. persons assembled for identification; a group of people identified with a common purpose

lin´ger vi. remain longer than anticipated; be slow to act

lin·ge·rie´ n. women's underclothing

lin´guist n. one who studies language —**lin·guis´tic** adj.

lin·guis´tics n. the study of human speech

lin´i·ment n. a liquid applied to relieve pain or tension

lin´ing n. backing material

link n. one of a series; a connector —vi., vt. to connect

linked adj. connected

li·no´le·um n. a floor covering

lint n. bits of shed fiber; downy fibers from linen, used as dressing

lin´tel n. the brace at the top of a window or door frame

li´on n. a large carniverous feline; a distinguished person

li´on·heart·ed adj. extremely brave

li´on·ize vt. treat as a celebrity

lip n. fleshy structure surrounding the mouth; impertinent speech

lip service insincere agreement

liq´ue·fy vi., vt. to make liquid

li·queur´ n. a sweet beverage, often flavored with fruit, herbs, or spices

liq´uid adj. capable of flowing; of assets readily convertible

liq´ui·date vt. discharge an obligation; convert into cash; destroy —vi. close out a business by disposing of assets —**liq´ui·da·tor** n.

li´quor (US) n. a distilled beverage; liquid obtained from cooking

lisle n. a fine cotton fabric

lisp n. a speech defect —vi., vt. to speak with a lisp

list n. a catalog of items, as for shopping, etc.; a tilting —vi., vt. itemize; cause to tilt

lis´ten n. be attentive; heed

lis´ten·a·ble adj. pleasing to the ear

list´less´ adj. lacking vitality or spirit; apathetic, indifferent

list price recommended selling price

lit´a·ny n. responsive prayer; something often repeated

li´ter (*US*) *n.* a unit of volume

lit´er•a•cy *n.* education, as the ability to read and write

lit´er•al *adj.* precise interpretation; verbatim

lit´er•al•ly *adv.* precisely; word for word

lit´er•ar•y *adj.* relating to or fond of literature

lit´er•ate *adj.* educated; well-informed —**lit´er•ate•ness** *n.*

lit•e•ra´ti *n. pl.* cultivated or well-educated persons

lit´era•ture *n.* printed matter; a collection of writings

lithe, lithe´some *adj.* supple or graceful

lith´o•graph *n.* a print made by lithography —*vt.* — **lith´o•graph´ic** *adj.*

li•thog´ra•phy *n.* a process for printing fine reproductions

lit´i•gant *n.* one involved in a lawsuit —*adj.* engaged in a lawsuit

lit´i•gate *vi., vt.* take part in legal action —**lit•i•ga´tion** *n.*

lit•i´gious *adj.* tending to be involved in legal action

litmus test a chemical test to determine acidity; use of a single determinant to test

li´tre (*Brit.*) *n.* a unit of volume equal to approximately 33.8 US ounces

lit´ter *n.* discarded trash; young from a single birth; material lining a cage; a framework for transporting —*vi., vt.* scatter trash

lit´tle *n.* a small amount — *adj.* modest in size or amount; unimportant —*adv.* slightly; not at all

lit´ur•gy *n.* a set form for worship or ritual —**li•tur´gi•cal** *adj.*

liv´a•ble, live´a•ble *adj.* fit for habitation; acceptable or tolerable

live *vi.* possess life; exist — *adj.* having life; useable, having potential: *live wire*; physically present

live´li•hood *n.* means of support

live´ly *adj.* marked by energy and spirit; active —*adv.*

liv´en *vi., vt. to* become lively

liv´er•ied *adj.* uniformed

liv´er•y *n.* a uniform; care and boarding of horses; a service that rents vehicles

live´stock *n.* domestic animals

live wire *n.* wire attached to a power source; a dynamic person

liv´id *adj.* extremely angry

liv´ing *adj.* having life; pertaining to existence —*n.* being alive; a means to support life

living wage earnings sufficient to provide necessities

living will *n.* a stipulation for treatment if the maker is alive but unable to respond

load *n.* that which is carried, supported, etc.; burden of work or responsibility —*vi., vt.* put or place

load´ed *adj.* carrying a full load; of a troublesome or hidden meaning

loaf *n.* an oblong mass

loa´fer *n.* one frequently inactive or unemployed —**loaf** *vi.*

loan *n.* something given or received for temporary use

loan shark one who lends money at high interest

loath *adj.* hesitant or reluctant

loathe *vt.* despise

loath´ing *n.* aversion

loath´some *adj.* arousing intense dislike

lob´by (*US*) *n.* an entryway; persons attempting to influence —*vi.*, *vt.* attempt to influence legislators —**lobby·ist** *n.*

lo´cal *adj.* of a relatively small area or political subdivision; not widespread —*n.* a regional chapter; a train that stops at every station

lo·cale´ *n.* a site or setting

lo·cal´i·ty *n.* a specific place

lo·cal·ize *vt.* restrict to a particular area

lo·cate *vi.* situate—*vt.* learn the position of; assign to a place

lo·ca´tion *n.* a place or position; a place designated

lock *n.* device for securing; closed section of a channel for raising or lowering water level; a bit of hair —*vi.*, *vt.* make secure; immobilize; link together

lock´er *n.* a storage compartment

locket *n.* a small hinged case

lock´out *n.* closing *of* a workplace to striking employees

lo·co·mo´tion *n.* the act of moving

lo·co·mo´tive *adj.* able to move —*n.* a self-propelled engine

lode *n.* a mineral deposit; an abundant source

lodge *n.* a rustic dwelling; a meeting hall —*vi.*, *vt.* to provide temporary living space; to place or plant

lodg´ing *n.* place to live — **lodg´er** *n.*

loft *n.* an open area directly under a building's roof; a gallery or alcove

loft´y *adj.* tall or towering; arrogant or haughty

log *n.* a cut tree; a record, as of performance —*vt.* set down in writing; accumulate, as time or distance

log´book *n.* book for recording official data

loge *n.* front rows of the mezzanine or box in a theater

log´ic *n.* fundamentals of reasoning; sound reasoning; comparable functions in a computer program

log´i·cal *adj.* capable of analytical thought; reasonable

lo·gis´tics *n.* planning and managing of an operation

lo´go, log´o·type *n.* symbol or trademark of a business

lo´gy *adj.* lethargic; muddled

loi´ter *vi.* loll or linger about; waste time

loll *vi.* to move or lie about

lone *adj.* without anyone or anything else; lacking companionship

lone´ly *adj.* saddened by being alone; deserted —**lone´li·ness** *n.*

lon´er *n.* one who works alone or shuns company *of* others

lone´some *adj.* lonely

long *vi.* have a craving or desire —*adj.* relatively lengthy; of specific length or duration

lon·gev´i·ty *n.* long life or duration

long´hair *n.* one with refined taste in art —**long´hair, long´haired** *adj.*

long´hand *n.* cursive writing

long´ing *n.* craving or desire

lon´gi·tude *n.* angular distance from the prime meridian or a celestial body

lon·gi·tu´di·nal *adj.* of longitude; running lengthwise

long´shore•man *n.* a dock worker

long shot a venture with little prospect of success.

long´-suf´fe•ring *adj.* uncomplaining; patiently enduring

long´-wind•ed *adj.* wordy or tiresome

loo´fa, loo´fah *n.* dried spongelike part of a tropical fruit, used for cleansing the skin

look *n.* a gaze, stare, glance, etc.; appearance or fashion —*vi., vt.* use sight; occupy one's attention; seek out or search; appear to be

loom *vi.* hover over; menace

loop *n.* a circular pattern; a circle —*vi., vt.* form or fasten into a circle; move in a circular pattern

loop´hole *n.* an oversight that provides escape

loose *adj.* not attached or confined; poorly attached or fitted; lacking discipline; vague —*vi., vt.* become or makeless restrained; release

loose end unresolved detail

loos´en *vi., vt.* make loose or looser

loot *n.* stolen goods —*vi., vt.* to plunder —**loo´ter** *n.*

lop *vt.* cut off or eliminate

lope *n.* a leisurely gait —*vi.*

lop´sid•ed *adj.* tipped to one side

lo•qua´cious *adj.* talkative — **lo•quac´i•ty** *n.*

lord *n.* one of high rank; a god —*vi.* to domineer

lord´ly *adj.* majestic or noble; pretentious; domineering

lore *n.* collected traditions or wisdom; knowledge

lor•gnette´ *n.* corrective lenses on a short handle

lose *vt.* be deprived of, unable to keep; rid oneself of —*vi.* endure loss —**los´er** *n.*

loss *n.* deprivation; something taken, misplaced, etc.

lost *adj.* no longer in one's possession or inevidence

lot *n.* a group of associated things; a large amount; a token selected at random; one's fate; a plot of land

lo´tion *n.* a liquid applied as medication or cosmetic

lot´ter•y *n.* a selection made by lot

loud *adj.* of high amplification; bright in color; glaringly bad design

loud´mouth *n.* one who speaks loudly or thoughtlessly

lounge *n.* a waiting room; a tavern or cafe; a type of couch —*vi., vt.* recline; pass time leisurely

louse *n.* a parasitic insect; disreputable person

lous´y *adj.* infested; of poor quality; unpleasant

lout *n.* one regarded as ill-mannered or tiresome — **lout´ish** *adj.*

lou´ver *n.* angled slats that provide ventilation

lov´a•ble, love´a•ble *adj.* having qualities that invite affection

love *n.* strong attraction; an object of affection or desire; sexual intercourse —*vt.* have affection or desire for; engage in sexual intercourse

love affair an intimate relationship; a strong attraction

love feast a symbolic meal to promote friendship

love´-in *n.* a gathering intended to promote love and understanding

love´lorn adj. deprived of love or a lover

love´ly adj. beautiful and charming; attractive or appealing —adv.

lov´er n. one devoted to a person, activity, etc.; a sexual partner

love´sick adj. distracted by love

lov´ing adj. affectionate

loving cup decorative urn; an award

low adj. less than usual or acceptable in height, quality, etc. —adv.

low´born adj. of humble birth

low´boy n. a chest of drawers

low´bred adj. unrefined

low´brow n. one of unrefined tastes —adj. suited to the unrefined

low comedy burlesque or slapstick comedy

low´down n. gossip; the latest information

low´-down adj. base; contemptible

low´er adj. less in pnce, position, etc. —n. a menacing look —vi., vt. to become less; to look menacing

low-key´ adj. restrained; subdued

low´life n. a disreputable person

low´ly adj. unpretentious; humble —adv.

low´-pres•sure adj. relaxed; easygoing

low´-pro´file adj. acting so as to avoid undue attention

low-tech adj. of that which does not employ or require modern technology

lox n. smoked salmon

loy´al adj. marked by allegiance; faithful —**loy´al•ty** n.

loz´enge n. a medicated candy

lu´au n. a traditional Hawaiian feast

lu´bri•cate vt. apply a substance to reduce friction —**lu´bricant** n.

lu´cent adj. clear or transparent; luminous —**lu´cency** n.

lu´cid adj. clear; easily understood; sane or rational —**lu•cid´i•ty** n.

luck n. chance events

luck´i•ly adv. by good fortune

luc´ky adj. having or bringing good fortune

lu´cra•tive adj. profitable

lu´cre n. money

lu´di•crous adj. incongruous; laughable

lug n. id. pull or carry with difficulty

luge n. a racing sled

lug´gage n. travelling bags; effects carried by a traveler

luke´warm adj. slightly warm; lacking enthusiasm

lull n. relative quiet or calm —vt. to calm or quiet, as fears

lull´a•by n. song that soothes

lumber n. (Brit.) unwanted items; (US) wood used in construction —vi. to move clumsily; to plod

lu´mi•nar•y n. a distinguished person; a model for others

lu•mi•nes´cence n. light accompanied by little heat

lu´mi•nous adj. emitting light; easily understood

lump n. a bulge or swelling; a clump; a total amount —adj. complete: lump sum —vt. consider as a whole —**lump´y** adj.

lu´na•cy n. madness; foolishness or silliness

lu´nar adj. involving the moon

lunar month time of a moon's orbit

lunch, lunch´eon n. midday meal eat a midday meal

lunge n. sudden thrust —vi. vt. thrust forward suddenly

lurch n. a jerking movement; an unsteady gait —vi. move jerkily; walk unsteadily

lure n. an enticement —vt. attract or entice, especially with inducement

lu´rid adj. gruesome or ghastly; pale or sallow

lurk vi. prowl stealthily; lie in wait

lus´cious adj. sweet and juicy; beautiful or sensuous

lush adj. marked by abundance; luxurious

lust n. intense craving —vi. have an intense desire

lus´ter (US), **lus´tre** (Brit.) n. radiance; brilliance; gloss on pottery achieved by glazing —vt. apply a glaze —vi. become glossy —**lus´trous** adj.

lust´y adj. robust; boisterous

lux·u´ri·ant adj. marked by abundant growth; lavish

lux·u´ri·ate vi. revel in luxury

lux·u´ri·ous adj. marked by extravagance or indulgence

lux´u·ry n. that contributing to comfort and enjoyment

lyr´ic adj. of musical verse

lyr´i·cal adj. melodious

lyr´i·cist, lyr´ist n. one who writes song lyrics

m, M thirteenth letter of the alphabet; 1000 in Roman characters

ma·ca´bre adj. gruesome; horrible

mac´er·ate vi., ut. make soft by soaking

mach´i·nate vt. to plot

ma·chine´ n. a device to modify and transfer energy; any contrivance that aids; one who performs in a predictable manner —adj. of or like a mechanical device —vi., vt. to fashion by mechanical device —**ma·chin´er·y** n.

ma·chis´mo n. an inflated notion of masculinity

ma´cho adj. marked by show of masculinity —n. one overly impressed with masculinity or virility

mac·ro·bi·ot´ics n. promotion of health and well-being by regulation of diet

mac´ro·cosm n. the universe; a. multifaceted aggregate

mac´ro·scop´ic adj. that can be seen with the naked eye

mad adj. angry; insane; lacking judgment

mad´am n. a polite form for addressing a woman

mad´cap adj. wild and reckless; uninhibited

mad´den vt., vt. make angry

mad´den·ing adj. tending to cause anger

made adj. fashioned or produced

made´-to-or´der adj. fashioned according to instructions; well-suited

made´-up´ adj. fictitious; complete

mad´ly adv. in a foolish or frenzied manner

mad´ness n. insanity; excessive enthusiasm

mad´ri·gal n. a vocal composition for several voices

mael´strom n. a large whirlpool; a turbulent situation

mae´stro n. a master

mag´a·zine´ n. a printed periodical; storage compartment

mag´got n. an insect larva; a grub

mag´ic n. supernatural power; sorcery; sleight of hand, misdirection, illusion, etc.; a mystifying quality —adj. relating to the supernatural; mystical —**mag´i•cal** adj.

mag´is•trate n. a local official such as justice of the peace

magis´tra•cy n. office or jurisdiction of a magistrate

mag´ma n. molten rock that forms part of Earth's core

mag•na•nim´i•ty n. generosity

mag•nan´i•mous adj. generous; inclined to forgive

mag´nate n. a prominent industrialist

mag´net n. anything that attracts

magnet´ic adj. having power to attract

mag´net´ism n. energy of a magnet; power to attract

mag´net•ize vt. to make magnetic; to fascinate or attract

mag•ni•fi•ca´tion n. enlargement of an image

mag•nif´icence n. grandeur

mag•nifi´cent adj. majestic or noble; exceptionally good

mag´ni•fy vt. make or appear larger

mag´ni•tude n. size or extent; importance

magnum opus a masterpiece

maid´en n. an unmarried woman —adj. unmarried; original or beginning

mail (US) n. material delivered by the postal system —vi., vt. send by post

mail order buying or selling by mail

maim vt. mutilate or disable

main adj. most significant — n. the dominant part; a large

pipe or conduit; open sea

main´frame n. a large computer serving many users

main´land n. large body of land; a continent

main´ly adv. largely; predominantly

main´stream n. dominant or accepted views —adj. conventional or traditional

main•tain´ vt. uphold; preserve in a desired state

main´te•nance a. care required to preserve

maî´tre d'hô•tel´ n. a head-waiter

ma•jes´tic adj. stately or dignified; magnificent

maj´es•ty n. grandeur and nobility of a sovereign; elegance or splendor

ma´jor n. a military rank — adj. among the most important; of exceptional scope, size, etc.

major-do´mo n. chief steward of a household; a butler

ma•jor´i•ty n. more than half; group that controls the most votes; legally of age

make vt., vt. assemble or fashion; create or produce; to cause

make´-be•lieve n. a flight of. fancy —adj faniful

make´-do, make´shift n. a convenient substitute —adj. temporary; provisional

make´up n. manner of arrangement; cosmetics; compensation for missing or um satisfactory work

mal´ad•just´ed adj. poorly fitted to the stresses of life

mal´a•droit´ adj. inept; unskilled

mal´a•dy n. an ailment or affliction

mal•aise′ *n.* a feeling of uneasiness or despondency

mal′a•prop•ism *n.* substitution of a word for one that sounds similar

ma•lar′ia *n.* infectious disease marked by chills and fever

mal′con•tent *n.* one habitually disgruntled; an agitator —*adj.* disgruntled

male *adj.* of the sex that fertilizes eggs of the female; masculine; of a coupling device —*n.*

mal•e•dic′tion *n.* a curse

mal′e•fac•tor *n.* a criminal

ma•lef′i•cent *adj.* harmful orhurtful; wicked

ma•lev′o•lence *n.* malicious or spiteful behavior

ma•lev′o•lent *adj.* malicious, spiteful; giving rise to evil

mal•fea′sance *n.* impropriety by a public official

mal′for•ma′tion *n.* deformity

mal•func′tion *n.* a breakdown —*vi.* perform poorly

mal′ice *n.* a desire to harm; spite —**ma•li′cions** *adj.*

malign′ *vt.* speak ill of; slander

ma•lig′nant *adj.* extremely harmful; malevolent

ma•lin′ger *vi.* avoid duty by feigning illness

mall (US) *n.* a shaded walk; an enclosed shopping complex; a park-like public area

mal′le•a•ble *adj.* flexible or adaptable; able to be molded

mal′let *n.* a type of hammer

mal•nour′ished *adj.* lacking proper food

mal•o′dor•ous *adj.* foul smelling

mal•prac′tice *n.* improper treatment or conduct by a professional

malt *n.* grain that has germinated and dried; a beverage brewed or flavored with malt

mal′treat′ *n.* to abuse

mam′mal *n.* any of a class of warm-blooded vertebrates that suckle their young —

mam•mal′i•an *adj.*

mam•mal′o•gy *n.* the study of mammals

mam′mon *n.* wealth deemed to exert a harmful influence

mam′moth *n.* a large extinct elephant; anything very large —*adj.* huge; enormous

man *n.* an adult male human; humans generally; a male underling —*vt.* to assign or take a position; hire a staff

man•a′cle *n.* a restraint —*vt.* to constrain

man•age *vi., vt.* direct or control; administer; bring about; have control of — **man′a•ge′ri•al** *adj.*

man′age•a•ble *adj.* compliant; submissive

man′age•ment *n.* those who guide or direct a business

man′date *n.* a declaration; an assignment; a charge —*vt.* assign or require

man′da•to•ry *adj.* required; compulsory

mane *n.* long hair growing about the neck

ma•neu′ver (US) *n.* a change in speed, direction, etc.; a move or series of moves — *vi., vt.* change course; influence people or events

mange *n.* a skin disease of animals

man′ger *n.* a feeding trough

man′gle *vt.* disfigure; ruin through ineptness

man′han•dle *vt.* treat roughly

ma′nia *n.* an obsession;

243

irrational behavior

ma´ni•ac n. an insane person; one who acts in an irrational or capricious manner

man´i•cure n. cosmetic care of fingernails —vt. care for fingernails; crop closely and evenly

man´i•fest adj. evident; obvious —n. list of cargo, passengers, etc. —vt. become evident

man•i•fes•ta´tion n. evidence or proof; embodiment of a spirit

ma•nip´u•late vt. control or shape; persuade deviously —ma•nip•u•la´tion n.

man´kind´ n. humanity; the human race

man´ly adj. masculine

man´-made´ adj. manufactured; artificial

man´ne•quin n. a model used to display clothing

man´ner n. a style or mode

man´ner•ism n. a distinctive trait; an affectation; an artistic style

man´ner•ly adj. having excellent manners —adv. politely

ma•noeu´vre (Brit.) n. a change in speed, direction, etc.; a move or series of moves —vi., vt. change course; influence

man´or n. a landed estate; main house on an estate —ma•no´ri•al adj.

man´sard n. roof with a double pitch

manse n. a clergyman's house

man´sion n. a large house

man´slaugh•ter n. **murder by** accident

man•teau´ n. a cloak

man´tel, man´tel•piece n. shelf over a fireplace

mantle n. a cloak; thing that covers or conceals —vt., vi. cover or conceal

man´tra n. a chant that aids in meditation

man´u•al adj. of the hands —a. reference or instruction book

manual training training in practical arts

man•u•fac´ture vi., vt. fashion, fabricate, or assemble; create a false report —n. production of goods

man•u•mit´ vt. to liberate

ma•nure´ n. dung or decaying matter —vt. to fertilize

man´u•script n. text lettered by hand; unpublished text

man•y n., pron. a large number —adj. numerous

man´y•fold adv. a large number

map n. depiction of an area —vt. to survey and depict graphically; set out in detail

mar vt. damage or deface

mar´a•thon n. competition requiring endurance

ma•raud´ vi., vt. attack and plunder

mar´ble n. a multicolored stone —**mar´ble, mar´ble•ize** vt. streak with color —**marbled** adj.

marble cake a cake streaked with colored batters

mar´bling n. streaking resembling marble

march n. orderly forward movement; a gathering to protest or champion a cause —vi., vt. move forward in an orderly, methodical manner

mar´ga•rine n. a butter substitute

mar´gin n. a limit; an allowance for variation

mar´gi•nal *adj.* barely acceptable

ma•ri´na *n.* a docking area

mar´i•nade´ *n.* seasoned liquid

mar´i•nate *vi., vt.* to soak in a marinade —**mar´i•ni´tion** *n.*

marine´ *adj.* relating to the sea or seamen

mar´i•o•nette´ *n.* a puppet

mar´i•tal *adj.* relating to marriage

mar´i•time *adj.* at or near the sea; of the sea or seamen

mark *n.* a random impression; a representative symbol; a rating; an objective —*vt.* imprint; scratch or blotch; identify by symbol; label; notice —**make one´s mark** be successful or notable —**mark time** wait for a propitious time —**wide of the mark** a failure

marked *adj.* noticeable; prominent

mark´er *n.* thing that identifies; writing implement

market *n.* the business of buying and selling; a place where goods are traded; trade in a commodity —*vi., vt.* to buy or sell

mar´ket•pace *n.* site where goods are traded; a distinct domain: *literary market place*

market research accumulation and analysis of consumer-related data

mark´ing *n.* a characteristic feature or pattern

mar´ma•lade *n.* thick fruit preserve

mar´riage *n.* legal union of two people; joining of two elements

mar´riage•a•ble *adj.* suited or able to be married

mar´ry *vt.* join; combine or closely unite —*vi.* take as a life partner —**mar´ried** *adj.*

marsh *n.* land that is wet and muddy —**marsh´and** *n.*

mars´hal *n.* an officer of the law —*vt.* gather or arrange: marshal forces

marsh´mal•low *n.* a soft, spongy confection

marsh•y *adj.* wet and muddy

mar•su´pi•al *n.* mammal that bears its young in an external pouch

mart *n.* a market

mar´tial *adj.* referring to war or warriors —**mar´tial•ist** *n.*

mar´ti•net´ *n.* a strict disciplinarian

mar´tyr *n.* one who suffers for a belief; one who suffers without complaint; one who exaggerates discomfort for sympathy —*vt.* persecute for devotion to a belief or cause —**mar´tyr•dom** *n.*

mar´vel *n.* a thing of awe or wonder —*vi., vt.* wonder at; be amazed

mar´vel•ous *adj.* **wonderous;** impressive

mas´cot *n.* a symbol believed to bring good fortune

mas´cu•line *n.* characteristic of a male; attributes associated with a male —**mas•cu•lin´i•ty** *n.*

mash *n.* a pulpy mass —*vt.* reduce to a pulpy mass

mask *n.* concealment or protection for the face; a representational wall ornament —*vi., vt.* to conceal or cover

mas´och•ist *n.* one who derives pleasure from abuse

ma´son *n.* one who works with stone

masquerade´ *n.* a costume

party; a deception —*vi.* assume a disguise

mass *n.* a clump; physical bulk; undetermined amount —*vi.*, *vt.* assemble into a mass —*adj.* large in number or scale

mas'sa•cre *n.* indiscriminate slaughter —*vt.* to slaughter

mas•sage' *n.* a rubdown —*vt.* relax muscles by rubbing or kneading; manipulate data

mas•seur', **mas•seuse'** *n.* one trained in the art of massage

mas'sive *adj.* large or bulky; imposing; cumbersome

mass'-produce' *vt.* manufacture in large quantities

mass transit local transportation systems that regularly carry large numbers

mas'ter *adj.* primary or controlling; proficient or knowledgeable —*n.* one who owns or controls; a teacher; one proficient in a craft; one who possesses exception knowledge or ability —*vt.* control; acquire knowledge or ability

mas'ter•ful *adj.* domineering; exhibiting skill

mas'ter•mind *n.* one . with ability to conceive or direct a complex operation —*vt.* to plan and direct

master of ceremonies one who presides over a formal gathering

mas'ter•piece *n.* outstanding work

mas'ter•stroke *n.* a notable action or achievement

mast'head *n.* name of a publication as it appears on a cover or leading page; the listing in a publication of its ownership, staff, etc.

mas'ti•cate *vi.*, *vt.* chew food;

reduce to a pulp

mas'to•don *n.* an extinct elephant-like animal

mas•tur•ba'tion *n.* sexual stimulation without intercourse

mat *n.* material for a bed, covering, protection, etc.; border for a picture —*vi.*, *vt.* to press or tangle

mat'a•dor *n.* a bullfighter

match *n.* a small strip used to produce fire; a thing nearly like another; thing compatible or harmonious; a sporting contest —*vt.* give or get something identical, comparable, or compatible

match'less *adj.* without equal

match'mak•er *n.* one who arranges marriages

mate *n.* one of a pair; a close friend or ally —*vi.*, *vt.* to pair

ma•te'ri•al *adj.* relevent; tangible —*n.* unprocessed matter, information, etc.

ma•te'ri•al•ism *n.* excessive concern for possessions

mate'ri•al•ize *vi.* appear suddenly —*vt.* come forth

ma•ter'nal *adj.* of a mother or motherhood

mater'ni•ty *n.* emotions associated with motherhood —*adj.* relating to pregnancy or childbirth

math, **math•e•mat•ics** *n.* the science of numbers

math•e•mat'i•cal *adj.* pertaining to numbers

mat•i•nee' *n.* afternoon performance

ma'tri•arch *n.* woman who heads a family; a respected woman

ma'tri•ar•chy *n.* society that traces its lineage through women

ma·tric′u·late *vt.*, *vi.* be permitted into a course of study

ma·tri·lin′e·age *n.* maternal lineage

mat′rimo·ny *n.* union of two persons; being married

ma′trix *n.* a mold or pattern

ma′tron *n.* a mature woman; a female supervisor

matte *n.* a soft or dull finish —*adj.* having a dull finish

mat′ter *n.* substance; something of interest —*vi.* be important

mat′ter-of-fact′ *adj.* objective; unimaginative

mat′ting *n.* a rough fabric, as for floor covering

mat′tress *n.* pad for sleeping

mat′u·rate *vi.* mature or ripen

mature′ *adj.* fully developed; ripe —*vi.*, *vt.* ripen; become due —**ma·tur′i·ty** *n.*

maud′lin *adj.* tearful; nauseatingly sentimental

maul *n.* a heavy hammer —*vt.* beat or batter; mangle

mau·so·le′um *n.* a tomb; a tomb-like room or building

maven *n.* an expert

mav′er·ick *adj.* independent; radical —*n.* a nonconformist; one acting independently

mawk′ish *adj.* overly sentimental

max′im *n.* an adage or motto

max′i·mize *vt.* increase or emphasize to the utmost

max′i·mum *adj.* of the largest possible —*n.* largest amount or extent

may′be *adze.* possibly —*n.* a possibility

may′hem *n.* deliberate injury; reckless damage or destruction; a state of turmoil

may′o, may′on·aise *n.* a thick, rich sauce or dressing

may′or *n.* a municipal administrator

maze *n.* a complex pattern of paths; a network of complicated or confusing elements

mead′ow *n.* an expanse of pasture or grassland

mea′ger (*US*), **mea′gre** (*Brit.*) *adj.* scant; lacking

meal *n.* edible grain; food eaten at a sitting

mean *adj.* cruel or malicious; low in quality or amount; selfish or miserly —*n.* midway between extremes —*vt.* indicate or intend

mean′der *vi.* wander aimlessly —*n.* a winding course

mean′ing *adj.* having purpose —*n.* significance or purpose; that understood

mean′ing·less *adj.* without purpose; insignificant

mean′ly *adv.* in a shabby way

mean′nest *n.* cruelty or malice; a lack; selfishness

mean′-spir′it·ed *adj.* characterized by pettiness

mea′sur·a·ble *adj.* that can be quantified; finite; significant

mea·sure *n.* a standard unit of size, weight, etc.; a device calibrated to a standard; an unspecified amount; an unspecified action —*vi.*, *vt.* express or gauge in terms of a standard unit —**beyond measure** Incalculable —**in some measure** In an unspecified extent—**measure up** fulfill expectations

measured *adj.* steady and deliberate

mea′sure·ment *n.* determination of size, capacity, etc.

meat *n.* edible flesh; a main idea

meat′y *adj.* containing meat;

important or significant

me•chan´ic *n.* one who repairs machines

me•chan´i•cal *adj.* relating to mechanical action; perfunctorily

mechanical advantage ratio of output to input energy

me•chan´ics *n.* the study of force; study of machinery

mech•a´nism *n.* the parts, action, or operation of a mechanical device

mech´a•nize *vt.* to equip with machines; automate

med´al *n. an* ornament recognizing a person, event, etc.

me•dal´lion *n.* medal or emblem that serves as ornament, identification, etc.; food cut or formed in circles

med´dle *vi.* interfere in the affairs of another

med´dle•some *adj.* tending to interfere

med´e•vac *n.* medical evacuation; transporting of injured by air to a medical facility

media *n.* mass communication collectively, as newpapers, television, etc.

me´di•al *adj.* median

me´di•an *adj.* relating to the middle —*n.* a middle part

me´di•ate *vt.* resolve a dispute —*vi.* act as an agent of reconciliation —**me•di•a´tion** *n.*

med´i•cal *adj.* of the science of healing

me•dic´a•ment *n.* a medicine

med´i•cate *vt.* treat with medicine —**med•i•ca´tion** *n.*

med´i•cine *n.* science of healing; something to treat illness —**me•dic´i•nal** *adj.*

me•di•e´val *adj.* of the Middle Ages; antiquated; barbaric

me•di•e´val•ism *n.* study of

life in the Middle Ages

me´di•o•cre *adj.* unexceptional; barely acceptable; inferior

med´i•tate *vi., vt.* deliberate or consider; spend time in quiet contemplation —**med•i•ta´tion** *n.*

med´i•ta•tive *adj.* thoughtful or reflective; marked by quiet contemplation

me´di•um *adj.* between extremes —*n.* a thing midway between; means by which something is attained

medium of exchange accepted currency

med´ley *n.* an assortment; a conglomeration

meek *adj.* subdued or sub-. missive; humble

meet *vt.* come upon or confront; make acquaintance of; gather; satisfy —*vi.* come together; assemble; be introduced —*n.* a gathering

meet´ing *n.* encounter or confrontation; a gathering; an intersecting

meg´a•herz *n.* one million cycles per second

meg´a•lith *n.* a large stone monument

meg•a•lo•mi´ni•a *n.* obsession with wealth or power

meg•a•lop´o•lis *n.* an area of closely joined cities

meg´a•phone *n.* a device that amplifies

mel´an•cho´lia *n.* mental disorder marked by depression

mel´an•choly *adj.* sadly quiet and contemplative —*n.* a condition marked by gloom and quiet attitude

melange´ *n.* a collection or jumble

mel•a•no´ma *n.* dark growth

on the skin, often malignant

meld *n.* a blending together — *vi., vt.* to become mingled

me´lee *n.* a violent clash

mel´io•rate *vi., vt.* to improve

mel´low *adj.* soft and rich, as of sound; pleasant and unhurried —*vi., vt.*

me•lod´ic *adj.* tuneful

me•lo´di•ous *adj.* pleasing to the ear; harmonious

mel´o•dra•ma *n.* theatre marked by overdrawn characterizations and exaggerated emotion

mel´o•dy *n.* a musical strain; theme of a musical composition

melt *vt., vt.* transform from solid to liquid; to soften, dissolve, or disappear

mem´ber *n.* one who belongs; part of an organism; a distinct part

mem´ber•ship *n.* affiliation; collectively, those affiliated

mem´brane *n.* thin tissue that serves as cover or lining

me•men´to *n.* a keepsake

mem´o, mem•o•ran´dum *n.* a written communication

mem´oir *n.* an autobiography

mem•o•ra•bil•ia *pl. n.* souvenirs or mementos

mem´o•ra•ble *adj.* worth remembering; unusual

memo´ri•al *adj.* commemorative —*n.* a monument or ceremony

memo´ri•el•ize *vt.* to commemorate

mem´o•rize *vt.* to commit to memory

mem´o•ry *n.* ability to remember and recall; thing remembered

men´ace *n.* a threat —*vt.* to threaten

me•nag´er•ie *n.* an assortment of animals; a place where animals are confined; a collection

mend *vi., vt.* make better; to correct, repair, or heal

men•da´cious *adj.* lying or deceitful —**men•dac´i•ty** *n.*

men´di•cant *adj.* of a beggar; depending on alms —*n.* a beggar —**men•dic´i•ty** *n.*

me´ni•al *adj.* servile or humble; befitting a servant —*n.* a servant

men´tal *adj.* relating to the mind —**men´tat•ly** *adv.*

men´tal•ism *n.* concept of mental phenomena beyond explanation; parapsychological incident, as telepathy

men•tal´i•ty *n.* intellectual capacity; manner of thinking

men´tion *n.* casual reference; a tribute —*vt.* refer to

men´tor *n.* advisor or teacher

menu *n.* a list of food items; any list of options

mer•can´tile *adj.* relating to marketing; commercial

mer´ce•nary *n.* one in the pay of a foreign government; one motivated by personal gain —*adj.* desire for gain

mer´chan•dise *n.* goods bought and sold —*vi., vt.* to sell; promote the sale of

mer´chant *adj.* pertaining to trade —*n.* one who sells for profit

mer´ci•ful *adj.* showing mercy

mer´ci•less *adj.* showing no mercy; lacking compassion

mer•cu´ri•al *adj.* volatile; fluctuating; prone to abrupt change

mer´cy *n.* compassion; an act of forgiveness or compassion

mere adj. insignificant; inconsequential —**mere´ly** adv.

mere·tri´cious adj. gaudy; insincere

merge vt., vi. combine

merg´er n. a combining

me·ringue´ n. stiffened egg whites baked as a topping

mer´it n. a worthwhile quality —vt. he worthy of, deserve

mer·i·toc´ra·cy n. hierarchy based on ability

mer·i·to´ri·ous adj. praiseworthy, commendable

mer´ri·ment n. lively fun; gaiety

mer´ry adj. joyous; happy; marked by mirth

mesa n. a broad plateau

mesh n. a loose, open fabrication of thread, wire, etc.— vi., vt. fit together

mes´mer·ize vt. fascinate; hypnotize

mess n. disordered clutter; a jumble; a large quantity — vi., vt. clutter; make untidy

mes´sage n. a communication; an underlying lesson or guidance

mess´y adj. disorderly; un pleasant

met·a·bolic adj. relating to metabolism

me·tab´olism n. process of converting food, synthesizlug needed substances, manufacturing tissue, etc.

met´al n. elements that are usually shiny, good conductors, and ductile — **me·tal´lic** adj.

metal·lur´gy n. the extraction or combining of metals

met·a·mor´pho·sis n. translormation, esp. one that seems miraculous

met´a·phor n. a figure of speech using one thing to designate another

met´a·phys´ics n. branch of philosophy dealing with the nature of reality

mete vt. measure and distribute

me´te·or n. bright streak in the sky as a meteoroid enters the earth's atmosphere

meteor´ic adj. of atmospheric phenomenon; swift

me´te·orite n. object from space fallen Into the earth's atmosphere

mete´or·oid n. matter moving through space

me·te·o·rol´o·gy n. the study of atmospheric phenomenon

me´ter n. (Brit. & US) a measuring device; (US) a rhythmic pattern, as in poetry; unit of length in the metric system —vt. to measure

meth´od n. systematic procedure; orderliness

me·thod´i·cal adj. in a systematic or orderly fashion

meth·od·ol´o·gy n. systematic procedures for study or investigation

me·tic´u·lous adj. precise, attentwe to detail

me´tre (Brit.) n. a rhythmic pattern, as in poetry; unit of length in the metric system —vt. measure with a meter; give in measured amounts

metric system n. a decimal system of weight and measure

me·trop´o·lis n. a major urban area —**metro·pol´i·tan** adj.

met´tle n. courage; strength of character

mez·sa·nine´ n. a balcony; a landing between floors

mi·as·ma *n.* foul air; corrupting influence

mi'crobe *n.* a microorganis

mi·cro·bi·ol·o·gy *n.* study of microorganisms —**micro·bi·ol'o·gist** *n.*

mi'cro·cosm *n.* small representation of a larger system

mi·cro·or'ga·nism *n.* a microscopic creature

mi'cro·scope *n.* device for viewing that which cannot be seen with the naked eye

mi'cro·wave *n.* electromagnetic energy wave; microwave oven —*vt.* to cook in a microwave oven

mid'dle *adj.* positioned midway between —*n.* a center or midpoint

mid'dle·man *n.* a go-between

mid'land *n.* central part of a country

mid'riff *n.* the part of the body between the chest and the abdomen

midst *n.* positioned in or among; located at or near the midpoint

mid'way *n.* carnival sideshows, games, etc.; halfway

mid'wife *n.* one trained to assist in childbirth

mien *n.* appearance or demeanor

miff *vi., vt.* be offended or annoyed

might *n.* strength or power

might'y *adj.* strong or powerful; imposing; impressive

mi'graine *n.* a severe headache

mi'grant *adj.* migratory —*n.* one who moves regularly

mi'grate *vi.* move regularly from one place to another

mi·gra'tion *n.* a moving together

mi'gra·to·ry *adj.* tending to move with the seasons

mild *adj.* gentle or moderate

mil'dew *n.* a type of fungus; a coating caused by fungus

mile *n.* a measure of distance

mile'age *n.* distance traveled; an amount paid or allowed for travel

mile'post, mile'stone *n.* a distance marker beside a road; a mark of progress

mi·lieu' *n.* environment; surroundings

mil'i·tant *adj.* belligerent or aggressive —**mil'i·tance** *n.*

mil'i·ta·rism *n.* emphasis on military preparedness; belief in military spirit or values —**mil'i·ta·ristic** *adj.*

mil'i·tar·y *adj.* of the armed forces or war

mi·li'tia *n.* a citizen army

milk *n.* fluid from mammals to feed their young; similar fluid from a plant —*vt.* to extract milk from; take advantage of —**milk'y** *adj.*

mill *n.* place for grinding grain; a factory; device that transforms by grinding, shaping, etc.; thing that functions methodically —*vt.* transform by a machine —*vi.* move about in a disorderly fashion

mil'li·ner *n.* one who makes or sells women's hats

mi'lion·aire' *n.* a wealthy person

mill'stone re a stone used in milling grain; a burden

milque'toast *n.* timid person

mime *n.* silent performer; a pantomime —*vi., vt.* communicate with gestures

mim'ic *n.* one who portrays another —*vt.* imitate closely

min´a•ret´ n. tower on a mosque

mince vi. walk or speak in an affected manner —vt. chop; lessen or cushion to be polite: *mince words*

mince´meat n. a thick, spicy concoction of fruit and meat

mind n. awareness of being; intellect; ability to think —vi., vt. behave; give heed to; be concerned

mind´ful adj. careful, attentive

mind´less adj. without reason or purpose, lacking care or caution; indifferent

minds•et, mind´-set n. a fixed attitude or response; a predilection

mind´s eye imagination

mine n. a hole or tunnel; a source; an explosive device —vi., vt. dig a tunnel; extract minerals; set an explosive

mine´field n. area seeded with explosive devices; something potentially dangerous or unpleasant

min´er•al n. naturally occurring inorganic matter —adj. of inorganic matter

min•er•al•o•gy n. the study of minerals

mingle vi., vt. to combine or mix together

min´i•a•ture adj. small for its type —n. something small; a copy or model

min´i•a tur•ize vt. make smaller; make a model

min´i•bus n. a small bus; a public conveyance

min´i•mal adj. the smallest possible; barely adequate

min´i•mal•ism n. an art form characterized by simplicity of form, color, etc.

min´i•mize vt. to downplay

min´i•mum n. the least possible or allowable —adj.

min´ ion n. a subordinate; a toady

min´i•se•ries n. a program aired in several episodes

min´is•ter n. a clergyman; a government official —vi. care for others —**min´is•te´ri•al** adj.

min•is•tra´tion n. the act of caring for another

min´is•try n. office and duties of a minister; department of government; care of others

min´now n. a small fish

mi´nor adj. of less significance—n.lessbycomparison; one not of legal age

mi•nor´i•ty n. a smaller group; time before legal age

min´strel n. wandering singer and poet

mint adj. new in appearance —n. place where coins are struck; plentiful amount —vt. make or strike coins

min´us•cule adj. tiny

min´ute n. a short time; part of an hour —**mi•nute´** adj. very small; detailed or exacting

mi•nu´ti•a n., pl. **mi•nu´ti•ae** a small insignificant detail

minx n. a flirtatious or defiant woman —**minx´ish** adj.

mir´a•cle n. an unexplainable event; a supernatural occurrence

mi•rac´u•lous adj. of the nature of a miracle

mi•rage´ n. an illusion; something flimsy or fanciful

mire n. wet, muddy ground; a swamp; a difficult situation —vi., vt. become stuck

mirror n. a surface that

reflects; something thought of as representing an image

mirror image a reverse

mirth n. lighthearted merriment —**mirth′ful** adj.

mirth′less adj. lacking gaiety; somber —**mirth′less•ly** adv.

mis•ad•ven′ture n. misfortune

mis′an•thrope n. one who dislikes or distrusts people; a recluse

mis•an′thro•py n. hatred or distrust of people

mis•ap•pre•hend′ vt. misunderstand

mis•ap•pro′pri•ate vt. take or use improperly or illegally

mis•be•have′ vt. conduct oneself badly or improperly behave badly

mis•cai′riage n. premature birth of a nonviable fetus; a spontaneous abortion; a failure or malfunction

mis•cel•la′ne•a pl. n. a collection of written works

mis•cel•la′ne•ous adj. comprising a variety

mis•chance′ n. misfortune

mis′chief n. a deliberate act causing damage or distress

mis′chie•vous adj. inclined to he playful or bothersome

mis•con•cep′tion n. a misunderstanding

mis′con•strue′ vt. misinterpret

mis′cre•ant n. a villain; a criminal—adj. villainous

mis′deed′ n. a violation

mis•de•mean′or n. a minor crime

mis•di•rect′ vt. improperly instruct; draw attention away from —**mis•di•rec′tion** n.

mi′ser n. one who hoards

mis•er•a•ble adj. wretched; unpleasant

mi′ser•ly adj. stingy

mis′er•y n. suffering, distress; thing that causes suffering

mis′fit′ n. a nonconformist; a maladjusted person

mis•for′tune n. had luck; adversity

mis•giv′ing n. doubt or uncertainty

mis•guid′ed adj. improperly directed; based on bad information —**mis•guide′** vt.

mis•guid′ance n.

mis•han′dle vt. mismanage; treat roughly or clumsily

mis′hap n. an accident

mis•in•form′ vt. advise inadequately or inaccurately; mislead

mis•in•ter′pret vt. misunderstand; explain incorrectly

mi•sjudge′ vt. form a wrong or unfair opinion

mis•lay′ vt. place and forget

mis•lead′ vt. direct wrongly or improperly; lead astray

mis•lead′ing adj. deceptive

mis•no′mer n. an inappropriate name or designation

mis•og′a•mist n. one who hates marriage

mis•og′y•nist n. one who hates women

mis•pri′sion n. concealment of crime

mis•rep•re•sen•ta′tion n. a false or misleading depiction

miss n. a failing; form of address for an unmarried woman —vi., vt. fail to make contact; to exclude or allow to pass; endure loss of

mis′sal n. a prayer book

mis′sile n. a projectile

miss′ing adj. absent or lacking; gone

mis′sion n. an organization

established for a purpose; function or task of a group

mis´sive n. a letter or memo

mis•step´ n. a slip or stumbling; a mistake or blunder

mist n. droplets forming a haze; thing that obscures — vt., vi make dim; rain in fine droplets —**mist´y** adj.

mis•take´ n. error; misunderstanding —vi. make a mistake —vt. misinterpret; to wrongly identify

mis•tak´en adj. misinformed or misguided; wrong

mis´ter n. form of address for a man

mis•treat´ vt. handle roughly or clumsily

mis´tress n. a woman in authority, who owns or controls; a teacher; one of exception knowledge or ability; a companion supported by a man not her husband

mis•tri´al n. a trial without verdict or declared invalid

mis•trust´ n. uncertainty, doubt, or suspicion —vi., vt. doubt or suspect

mist´y-eyed adj. sentimental; tearful

mi´ter n. ornamental headdress worn by a bishop; one of the bevels of a miter joint —vt. raise to the rank of bishop; join with a miter

miter joint a coupling of two angled pieces, as at a corner

mit´igate vi., vt. to become or make less intense or severe

mitt n. a glove

mit´ten n. a mitt with a pocket for the thumb

mix n. a combination of ingredients —vi., vt. to become combined; to blend in; confuse —**mix´a•ble** adj.

mixed adj. combined; consisting of differing elements

mixed´-up´ adj. confused or befuddled

mix´er n. a device that combines or blends; non-alcoholic beverage in a cocktail; a type of gathering; one who meets easily with others

mix´ture n. a mix; that which results from combining

mix´-up n. a state of turmoil or confusion

mne•mon´ics n. a technique used as a memory aid

moan n. a low, doleful sound

moat n. a protective ditch

mob n. a large crowd; a group of criminals —vt. crowd; overwhelm

mo´bile adj. movable; easily moved —n. hanging art made of freely moving pieces

mo•bil´i•ty n. movement; the ability to move easily

mo´bi•lize vt. make moveable; organize and deploy

mob´ster n. a criminal

moc´ca•sin n. footwear

mo´cha n. rich coffee; flavoring of coffee and chocolate

mock adj. imitation; false — vi., vt. to ridicule or imitate derisively —**mock´ery** n.

mock´-up n. a scale model; layout for a printed page

mode n. a particular manner or fashion —**mod´al** adj.

mod´el n. a copy or prototype; one who poses; displays clothing, etc.; an ideal —vi., vt. make a model; pose; display by wearing

mod´erate adj. not extreme or excessive —n. one not inclined to extreme views —vi., vt. make less extreme; to preside

mod´era•tor n. one who mediates or officiates

mod´ern adj. of recent time or development

mod´ern•ize vi., vt. make contemporary

mod´est adj. unpretentious; diffident; conforming to convention; not extreme —**mod´es•ty** n.

mod´i•cum n. a small amount

mod•i•fi•ca´tion n. change or alteration —**mod´i•fy** vt.

mod´ish adj. smart or trendy; in the current style

mod´ule n. a separate component, as part of a sound or computer system — **mod´u•lar** adj.

mo´dus ope•ran´di n. a manner of operating

mo´gul n. one rich or powerful

moi´e•ty n. a half; a portion

moist adj. slightly wet; damp

moist´en vi., vt. to become or make slightly wet

mois´ture n. slight wetness

mois´tur•ize vt. make wet

mo´lar n. a large tooth

mo•las´ses n. a thick, sweet syrup

mold[1] (US) n. a form for casting —vi. shaped in a form —vt. form or shape

mold[2] (US) n. a fungal growth

mold´er (US) vi. gradually decay

mold´ing n. decorative trim, as around a door or window

mold´y (US) adj. spoiled by a fungal growth; having a musty odor

mol´e•cule n. the smallest particle with distinct chemical and physical properties

mo•lest´ vi. disturb or annoy; accost improperly

mol´li•fy vt. soothe or pacify

mol´lusk n. marine invertebrate with soft body and protective shell

molt (US) vi., vt. to shed

mol´ten adj. extremely hot and melted or liquified

mo´ment n. a brief interval; importance

mo´men•tary adj. existing briefly

mo•men´tous adj. of great importance

mo•men´tum n. force of a body in motion; energy generated by ideas or events

mon´arch n. an absolute ruler

mon´aster•y n. religious community

mon´e•lary adj. regarding money or finance

mon´ey n. legal tender; currency, etc. issued by a government; an expression of wealth

mon´eyed adj. wealthy

mon´ger n. a tradesman; a promoter or advocate

mon´grel adj. of mixed breed —n. an interbred plant or animal

mon´i•tor n. device that controls or oversees; an adviser or assistant; an overseer — vt. oversee or regulate

mon´i•to•ry adj. admonishing; cautionary

monk n. member of a religious order

monk´ish adj. characteristic of a monk or a monastic life; austere or disciplined

mo•nog´a•my n. having one mate at a time; taking one spouse or mate for a lifetime

mon´o•gram n. letters designed as a distinguishing emblem —vt. adorn with a monogram

mon´o•graph n. a scholarly dissertation

mon´o•lith n. a large stone column or monument

mon´o•log, mon´o•logue n. discourse by one person

mon•o•pho´bi•a n. fear of being alone

mo•nop´o•lize vt. dominate; to solely control

mo•nop´o•ly n. absolute control of a market

mon´o•rail n. a train suspended from a single rail

mon´o•syl•lab´ic adj. of one syllable

mon´o•the•ism n. belief in a single god

mon´o•tone —n. single tone; listless or boring delivery

mo•not´o•nous adj. tedious or tiresome

mon´ster n. a frightening creature; one abnormally cruel; a deformed organism

mon´strous adj. frightening; abnormally cruel; deformed; huge

mon•tage´ n. art made up of a number of elements

month n. time of one cycle of the moon

month´ly adj. occurring every month —n. a periodical that is published every month

mon•u•ment n. a memorial; an anchored structure: a boundry marker

mon•u•men´tal adj. impressive to size or significance

mooch vi., vt. freeload or get by begging —**mooch´er** n.

mood n. state of mind or attitude

mood´y adj. sullen; susceptible to depression; temperamental

moon n. a satellite —vi. to languish about —vt. bare the buttocks playfully

moon´light n. light reflected from the moon —vi. work a second job

moon´shine n. illegal whiskey

moon´struck adj. beguiled by romantic notions

moor vi., vt. secure or anchor

moor´age, moor´ing n. place for securing a vessel; charge for use

moot adj. that can be dis-puted; of no significance

mop n. soft material used for cleaning; a soft clump or mass —vi., vt. wash by rub king; make clean

mope vi. act dejected; sulk

moppet n. a child

moraine´ n. debris deposited by a glacier

mor´al adj. conforming to what is right or just —n. a truth or principle; a lesson

morale´ n. attitude, enthusiasm, resolve, or confidence

mor´al•ist n. one overly concerned with morals; one inclined to impose values on others

mo•ral´i•ty n. a sense of what is right or lust

mor´al•ize vi., vt. pronounce judgement or lecture

mo•rass´ n. a wetland; a marsh or bog; something that impedes

mor•a•to´ri•um n. a suspension or delay

mor´bid adj. diseased; gruesome; abnormally preoccupied by the gruesome

mor´dant adj. sharp or incisive; caustic

more adj. greater in number or degree; enhanced or extended —n. an additional amount —*adv.*

mo´res *n.* accepted standards, as in customs, morals, etc.

morgue *n.* a place where dead await burial; a library or reference file

mor·i·bund *adj.* nearing death; outdated

morn´ing *n.* that part of the day from midnight to noon or from sunrise to noon

mo·rose´ *adj.* surly or gloomy

mor·phol´o·gy *n.* scientific study of form and structure

mor´sel *n.* a bit of food; a small amount

mor´tal *adj.* of the physical person; susceptible to death; deadly —*n.* a human being

mor´tar *n.* bonding material; type of cannon; a container in which material is ground with a pestle

mart´gage *n.* pledge of property as security to pledge property

mor·ti´cian *n.* one who prepares dead for burial

mor·ti·fi·oa´tion *n.* humiliation or shame; discipline or pennance

mor´ti·fy *vi.* undergo self-denial to humiliate or shame; discipline oneself by self-denial

mor´tise *n.* a slot designed for a tenon to form a joint

mor´tu·ary *n.* a place where bodies are kept for burial

mo·sa´ic *n.* a design of joined colored pieces, such as tiles

mosque *n.* Muslim house of worship

most *adj.* of the greatest number or amount —*n.* the larger part; the greatest amount —*adv.* to the greatest degree, extent, etc.

mot *n.* a witty remark

mote *n.* a speck

mo·tel´ *n.* lodging for travelers

moth´er *adj.* being derived from —*n.* a female parent; one who gives birth —*vt.* to give birth; to rear

moth´er·ly *adj.* nurturing; having qualities of a mother

mo·tif *n.* a recurring theme

mo´tile *adj.* able to move

mo·tion *n.* a movement; act of moving; a proposal put before a group —*vi., vt.* gesture or guide

mo´ti·vate *vt.* rouse to action

mo·tiva´tion *n.* an inducement —**mo·ti·va´tion·al** *adj.*

mo·tive *n.* that which induces

mot´ley *adj.* varied; marked by variety or incongruity; multicolored —*n.* an incongruous mixture

mo´tor *adj.* of motion —*n.* device that produces mechanical energy —*vi., vt.* travel by motor vehicle

mot´tled *add.* spotted

mould[1] (*Brit.*) *n.* a form for casting —*vi.* shaped in a form —*vi.* to form or shape

mould[2] (*Brit.*) *n.* a fungal growth

mould´er (*Brit.*) *vi.* gradually decay

mould´y (*Brit.*) *adj.* spoiled by fungal growth; having a musty odor

moult (*Brit.*) *vi., vt.* to shed

mound *n.* a pile or heap; a knoll or small hill —*vt.* make into a heap

mount *n.* a riding horse; a device that holds —*vi., vt.* to ascend; get onto; fix in place; increase, as cost

mount, mountain *n.* elevated land of substantial

257

height and mass; a large amount —**moun´tain•ous** *adj.*

moun´te•bank *n.* a charlatan; a fast-talking salesman

mourn *vi., vt.* express grief or sorrow —**mourn´ful** *adj.*

mourn´ing *n.* a grieving for the dead; signs or symbols of grieving

mouse *n.* small rodent; timid person; a computer device

mousse *n.* food bound by whipped cream and gelatin, served cold, a preparation used to style the hair

mous´tache *n.* hair on the upper lip

mouth *n.* a body opening for feeding; opening of a river or cave —*vi., vt.* to speak; form words without sound

mouth´y *adj.* given to excessive or offensive speech; talkative

move *vi., vt.* advance from one place to another; alter posinon; act or be active; be emotionally aroused; propose, as in formal meeting

move´ment *n.* a steady or gradual change

mov´ing *adj.* in motion; of the transfer of goods; arousing emotional response

much *adj.* considerable in quantity or extent —*n.* con sidcrable amount *adv.* to a great degree; approximately

muck *n.* a wet sticky mixture; filth; something offensive —*vt.* soil, botch —**muck´y** *adj.*

mud *n.* mix of soil and water; plaster or mortar

mud´dle *n.* confusion or dis order; a predicament —*vt.* to confuse; mismanage

mud´dy *adj.* stained; murky

or hazy

muf´fle *vt.* suppress or deaden; maintain secrecy

muf´fler *n.* heavy scarf; (US) device for deadening sound of an engine

mug *n.* a heavy cup; one's face or expression; a gangster —*vi.* contort the face for effect —*vt.* assault

mulch *n.* ground cover around plants—*vt.*

mul´ish *adj.* obstinate

mull *vi., vt.* ponder

mul´ti•far´i•ous *adj* having great sanely; diverse

mul´ti•ple *adj.* relating to several

mul´ti•pli•ca´tion *n.* increasing a number by adding to itself; organic reproductmn —**mul´ti•ply** *vt., vt.*

mul´ti•plic´i•ty *n.* a large or varied collection

mul´ti•tude *n.* a large number; the general public

mum´ble *n.* indistinct articulation ot. speak indistinctly —**mum´bler** *n.*

mum•mi•fi•ca´tion *n.* preparation for burial in the manner of ancient Egyptians; natural drying and preservation— **mum´mi•fy** *vi., vt.*

mun•dane´ *adj.* common or ordinary; not exceptional

mu•nic´i•pal *adj* relating to a local government

mu•nic•i•pali•ty *n.* a local governmental unit

mu•nif´i•cent *adt* generous

mural rr art applied directly to a wall or ceiling

mur´der *n.* unlawful killing; something arduous or unpleasant —*vt.* kill or destroy; corrupt —**mur´der•ous** *adj.*

murk´y *adj.* dark or hazy

mur´mur n. a low-pitched, indistinct sound —vi., vt. complain or utter in a low tone

mus´cle n. fibrous tissue that serves to achieve movement; strength or force crowd or intrude

mus´cu•lar adj. relating to muscles; inferring power

muse n. a spiritual or intellectual guide to ponder or meditate

mu•se´um n. a place for pres emotion of art or history

mush n. porridge, a pasty mass, exaggerated affection

mush´room n. a type of fungus; the shape of a mushroom — vi. grow rapidly — adj. relating to or like a mushroom

mu´sic n. sound that is pleasant to the ear; a musical score —mu´si•cal adj.

mu•si´cian n. one who composes or performs music

mu•si•col´o•gy n. the study of music

mus´lin n. a coarse fabric

mus´sel n a type of marine or freshwater mollusk

must n. something required — aux verb a requirement; a command: you must do this; a likelihood: they must know; a certainty: this must end; intentiun: I must go

mus´ter n. a gathering —vi. assemble —vt. call together; summon or marshal

must´y adj. stale, as of a smell; old or out of date

mu´ta•ble adj. changeable

mu•ta´tion n. a modification; process of changing; thing created by change —mu´tant n.

mute adj. unable or unwilling to speak —n. one who can not speak

mut´ed adj. subdued

mu´ti•late vt. maim or cripple; disfigure

mu´tiny n. open rebellion; revolt —mu´ti•nous adj.

mu´tu•al adj. reciprocal or common

muz´zle n. snout of an animal; device to cover a snout, that prevents free speech — vt. restrain, prevent from speaking

my•o´pia n. nearsightedness

myr´i•ad adj. innumerable — n. a large number

mys´ter•y n. that not easily understood; a work of fiction — mys•te´ri•ous adj.

mys´tic, mys´ti•cal adj. of mysticism; mystenous; incomprehensible —mys´ti•cism n.

mys´ti•fy vt. puzzle or perplex

mys•tique´ n. a mysterious quality

myth n. a legend or folk tale, something untrue —myth´ic, myth´i•cal adj

my•thol´o•gy n. a collector of myths; the study of myth —myth•olog´i•cal adj.

n, N fourteenth letter of the alphabet, symbol for an rn exact number

nab vt. snatch or seize; arrest

na´dir n. the lowest point

na•ive´ adj. unsophisticated, guileless; gullible

na•ive•te´ n. inexperience, ingenuousness

na´ked adj uncovered or un protected —na´ked•ness n.

name n. word by which a thing is known; designation

or title; a disparaging epithet —*vt.* give a designation; appoint or assign, as to a rank

nap *n.* brief sleep; soft raised surface as on a carpet —*vi.* sleep briefly

nape *n.* back of the neck

na·per·y *pl. n.* household linens

nar·cis·sism *n.* excessive devotion to one's self —**nar·cirais´tic** *adj.*

nar´rate *vti., vt.* recite, describe; give an account; provide commentary

nar·ra´tion *n.* a recounting of events; that which is related

nar´ra·tive *n.* a vocal account —*adj.* marked by narration

nar´row *adj.* small in width; confined or limited; extremely close —*vt., vt.* make confined or restricted

nas´cent *adj.* beginning; emerging

nas´ty *adj.* offensive; unpleasant

na´tal *adj.* of birth

na´tion *n.* people bound by common government, heritage, etc.

na´tive *adj.* associated with a particular place; connected by birth; natural or inherited —*n.* one connected by birth

na·tiv´i·ty *n.* birth

nat·u´ral *adj.* occurring in nature; usual, typical, or characteristic; simple and unrehearsed —*n.* one well-suited —**nat´u·ral·ness** *n.*

nat·u·ral·ist *n.* one who studies natural history; one in harmony with nature

nat·u·ral·i·za´tion *n.* the process of becoming accepted or acclimated

natural law principles that derive from nature

na´ture *n.* realm of the living; processes and power that control the living; a personal quality

nau´sea *n.* illness marked by a queasy stomach; revulsion —**nau´se·ate** *vi., vt.* —**nau´seous** *adj.*

nau´ti·cal *adj.* of ships or shipping

nave *n.* the central aisle of a church

na´vel *n.* process on a mammal left by an umbilical cord

nav´i·gate *vi., vt.* plot or direct a course; travel by ship —**nav·i·ga´tion** *n.* —**nav´i·ga·tor** *n.*

near *adj., adv.* approaching or close to; almost —*vi., vt.* come or draw near —**near´ly** *adv.* —**near´ness** *n.*

neat *adj.* orderly or tidy; clever or adroit; undiluted

neat´en *vt.* put in order; make tidy

neb´u·lous *adj.* hazy or indistinct; vague or confused

nec´es·sary *adj.* essential; required

ne·cei´si·tate *vt.* require; make compulsory

ne·ces´ar·ty *n.* something essential or required

neck *n.* a narrow body part that joins; a narrow section —*vi., vt.* to kiss and caress

neck´wear *n.* clothing or jewelry worn about the neck

nec·ro·man·cy *n.* communication with the dead; black magic

nec·ro·phil´i·a *n.* obsession with death and dead bodies

nec·ro·pho´bi·a *n.* abnormal fear of death

necrop´o•lis *n.* place of burial, esp. near an ancient city

need *n.* a lack; a thing required or desired; a necessity; state of poverty —*vt.* have want of; require —*vi.* be in want; be obliged or compelled —**need´ful** *adj.*

needless *adj.* unnecessary; useless

need´y *adj.* poor; overly dependent on others

ne•far´i•ous *adj.* extremely wicked

ne•gate´ *vt.* nullify or retract

neg´a•tive *adj.* expressing opposition or denial; lacking any affirmative quality — **neg•a•tiv´i•ty** *n.*

neg•lect *n.* indifference or carelessness —*vt.* disregard; be indifferent; be careless or irresponsible —**ne•glect´ful, neg´li•gent** *adj.*

neg´li•gi•ble *adj.* insignificant; inconsequential

ne•go´ti•ate *vi.* confer in attempt to reach agreement — *vt.* compromise or agree; transfer ownership —**ne•go´ti•a•ble** *adj.*

neigh´bor (*US*), **neigh´bour** (*Brit.*) *n.* one who lives near; that near or adjacent — *vi., vt.* live or be situated near —*adj.* near to; adjacent — **neigh´bor•ly, neigh´bour•ly** *adj.*

nei´ther *adj.* not either; not one or the other

nem´e•sis *n.* an enemy; one seeking retribution or revenge; something harmful

neo•clas´sic, ne´o•clas•si•cal *adj.* of the revival of earlier forms in music or literature

ne´o•phyte *n.* a novice; a recent convert

nep´o•tism *n.* favoritism to a relation

nerd *n.* one engrossed in scholarly pursuits —**nerd´y** *adj.*

nerve *n.* fiber that transmits signals throughout the body; courage; impudence

ner´vous *adj.* of the nerves; high-strung or excitable; agitated, apprehensive

ne´science *n.* ignorance; lack of knowledge or awareness

nest *n.* a cozy shelter; a refuge; objects that fit together —*vi., vt.* fit together snugly

nes´tle *vi., vt.* to lie or place snugly or comfortably

net *adj.* remaining after deductions —*n.* amount remaining; mesh —*vt.* produce profit; to catch

net´tle•some *adj.* irritating

network *n.* a system or structure with interconnecting bonds

neu´ral *adj.* regarding the nerves or nervous system

neu•ri´tis *n.* inflammation of a nerve —**neu•rit´ic** *adj.*

neu•rol´o•gy *n.* study of the nervous system

neuron *n.* a nerve cell

neu•ro´sis *n.* a mental or emotional disorder

neu´tral *adj.* not supporting either side; unbiased or disinterested; drab or colorless —**neu´tral•ize** *vt.*

nev´er *adv.* not ever

new *adj.* recently formed or discovered; previously unused; different; inexperienced —**new´ ly** *adv.*

next *adj.* following immediately in sequence —*n.* that which comes immediately after —*adv.*

nib´ble n. a small bite — vi., vt. take or eat in small bites —**nib´bler** n.

nice adj. pleasing; courteous, considerate; delicate, subtle

ni´ce·ty n. a precise, subtle, or refined quality

niche n. a recess or alcove; a special area of interest

nig´gard·ly adj. closefisted; reluctant to give or spend

nig´gle vi. to nag or complain over trifles —**nig´gling** adj.

nigh adj., adv. near; nearly

night n. period between sunset and sunrise; evening before midnight

night´ly adj. every night; during the night —adv. by night; every night

ni´hi·lism n. philosophy that denies all existence; rejection of religion and morality

nim´ble adj. quick and agile; sharp witted —**nim´bly** adv.

nim´bus n. a halo or disk of light

nip n. a sip; a small bite or particle; a sharp or stinging quality sip; bite or pinch off; sting —**nip´py** adj.

nir·va´na n. an ideal state

nit´pick vi. quarrel over trifles

no´ble adj. pertaining to or having qualities attributable to nobility —**no·bil´l·ty** n.

no´cent adj. harmful

noc·tur´nal adj. occurring in the night

noc´turne n. a night scene; a gentle, dreamy musical corn position

noc´u·ous adj. harmful or detrimental

nod n. assent or agreement — vi., vt. move the head in assent or acknowledgement; to briefly drift off to sleep

nod´ule n. a small lump

noise n. a loud or unpleasant sound; complaint; interference; unwanted or meaningless data —vt. spread gossip —**nois´y** adj.

noi´some adj. disgusting, esp. of an odor; dangerous or deadly, as fumes

nomad n. a wanderer; one lacking a permanent home —**no·mad´ic** adj.

no´men·cla·ture n. a name or designation; a system of names

nom´i·nal adj. of a name or designation; of a token amount; existing in name only —**nomi·nal·ly** adv.

nom´i·nate vt. name as a candidate; appoint to office

non·age n. legally underage

non´cha·lant´ adj. seemingly casual or indifferent

non·com·mit´tal adj. guarded about feelings or opinions

non´de·script adj. lacking distinctive characteristics

none adv. not at all —pron. no one

non·en´ti·ty n. thing of no importance

non·fei´sane n. failure to discharge an obligation

non´pa·reil´ adj. without equal

non·par´ti·san adj. neutral; unaligned with a group or cause —n.

non´plus´ vt. bewilder; put at a loss for words

non´sense n. lacking meaning; of no value; foolishness —**non·sen´si·cal** adj.

noon n. midday; time when the sun is at or near its highest point

nor´mal adj. typical, usual, or

standard; sane

north *n.* to the left of sunrise, perpendicular to the path of the sun

nose *n.* the organ for detecting odors; sense of smell; aroma, as of wine; ability to find as if by smell; the front

nos•tal´gia *n.* sentimental lunging for the past

nos´tril *n.* opening of the nose

nostrum *n.* an untested medicine or remedy

not *adv.* in no way

no´ta•ble *adj.* distinctive or remarkable; deserving notice

no´ta•ry, no´ta•ry pub´lic *n.* one certified for certain legal duties —**no´ta•rize** *vt.*

no•ta´tion *n.* a note or comment; a system of symbols

note *n.* a short, informal letter; an annotation, reminder, etc.; currency or convertible to currency —*vt.* make a written record of; take notice of

not´ed *adj.* distinguished; famous

note´wor•thy *adj.* deserving notice

noth´ing *adj.* meaningless — *n.* thing of no value —*pron.* not anything

no´tice *n.* announcement or warning; observation or attention —*vt.* observe; become aware of

no´ti•fy *vt.* serve notice; to inform or make known

no´tion *n.* idea or opinion; theory; disposition toward

no•to•ri´e•ty *n,* fame; reputation

no•to´ri•ous *adj.* infamous; well-known

not•with•stand´ing *prep.* in spite of —*adv.*

noun *n.* a word that names a person, place, thing, etc.

nour´ish *vt.* promote development of; provide with food or other necessities

nou•velle´ cui•sine´ a style of cooking that stresses fresh ingredients and light sauces

nov´el *adj.* new and unusual —*n.* a book-length, fictional story —**novelist** *n.*

nov´el•ette´ *n.* a short novel

nov´el•ty *n.* being original or fresh; something unique; a fad; a trinket

nov´ice *n.* one new to a trade or activity; an apprentice

now *adj.* at this time —*adv.* immediately; promptly

nox´ious *adj.* harmful

noz´zle *n.* a spout or outlet for controlling flow

nu´ance *n.* subtlety; slight variation

nu´bile *adj.* of marriageable age; sexually mature

nu´cle•ar *adj.* of a nucleus; atomic

nuclear reactor a device for harnessing nuclear energy

nu´cle•us *n.* center or essence

nude *adj.* unclothed or uncovered —*n.* a naked body —**nu´dity** *n.*

nudge *n.* a light push —*vt.* touch or push gently

nui´sance *n.* bother or annoyance; interference with rights of others

null *adj.* nonexistent or insignificant; invalid —**nul´li•fy** *vt.*

numb *adj* lacking feeling — *vt., vi.* make numb

num´ber *n.* an integer; one in a progression; numerals that represent something—*telephone number*—*vt.* assign a position; to count or total

nu´mer•al n. a symbol representing a number —**nu´mer´ic, nu•mer´i•cal** adj.

nu•mer•ol´o•gy n. belief in secret meaning associated with numbers

nu´mer•ous adj. many; a large number

nu•mis•mat´ics n. the study or collection of coinage

nup´tial adj. of marriage or a marriage ceremony

nurse n. one who ministers to the sick; one in charge of young children —vt. tend or care for another; sustain or conserve —**nurs´er** n.

nurs´ing n. the profession of a nurse; the care of a nurse

nur´ture vt. care for; aid to grow and improve

nut n. a seed within a hard shell; an eccentric; a fanatic

nu´tri•ent adj. nourishing —n. a source of nourishment

nu´tri•ment n. food; anything that promotes growth and development

nu•tri´tion n. study of nourishment; process by which food is used in the body

nu•tri´tious adj. nourishing

nuz´zle vi., vt. nestle; push gently with the nose

o, O fifteenth letter of the alphabet

oaf n. one slow-witted or clumsy

oa´sis n., pl. **oa´ses** a haven of greenery in a wasteland; a place of refuge

oath n. solemn promise; an irreverent or blasphemous utterance

ob´du•rate n. hardhearted; stubborn

o•be´di•ent adj. deferential to authority; submissive

o•bese´ adj. overweight

o•bey´ vi., vt. accept or comply

ob•fus´cate vt. make confused

obit´uary n. published account of a death

ob´ject n. thing perceived by the senses; goal or objective; a recipient —**object´** vi., vt. oppose or dissent

ob•jec´tion n. opposition; a reason for opposing

ob•jec´tion•a•ble adj. offensive

ob•jec´tive adj. fair and unbiased —n. a tangible goal

ob´li•gate adj. essential —vt. bind or compel by indebtedness, etc. —**ob•li•ga´tion** n.

o•blig´a•to•ry adj. required; morally or legally binding

o•blige´ vt. require; accommodate or assist

o•blique´ adj. inclined or slanting; angled; indirect: *oblique reference*

ob•lit´er•ate vt. remove completely —**ob•lit•er•a´tion** n.

ob•liv´i•on n. obscurity; nonexistence

ob•liv´i•ous adj. preoccupied; lacking awareness

ob´long adj. elongated

ob•nox´ious adj. offensive or objectionable; impolite

ob•scene´ adj. contrary to accepted morality or propriety —**ob•scen´i•ty** n.

ob•scure´ adj. not clearly perceived; indistinct —vt. conceal or make indistinct

ob•scurity n. being unknown or indistinct

ob•se´qui•ous adj. groveling or subservient; fawning

ob•serv´a•ble adj. noticeable; perceived by eye

ob•serv´ance n. traditional rite or celebration; an act of compliance —**ob•serv´ant** adj. —**ob•ser•va´tion** n.

ob•serve´ vt. notice; watch carefully; celebrate a tradtion; abide by custom or law; mention —vi. make a casual remark; take notice

ob•ses´sion n. unnatural or irrational fascination

ob•ses´sive adj. compulsive

ob•so•lete´ adj. no Longer useful or in use; out-of-date —**ob•so•les´cence** n.

ob´sta•cle n. a hindrance; a barrier or obstruction

ob•stet´rics n. care during and directly following pregnancy —**ob•ste•tri´cian** n.

ob´sti•nate adj stubborn; defying control or treatment

ob•strep´er•ous adj. unruly; defiant

ob•struct´ vt. interfere or hin der; block view of —**ob•struc´tive** adj. —**ob•struc´tion** n.

ob•tain´ vt. gain possession of

ob•tru´sive adj. interfering; overly conspicuous —**ob•tru´sive•ness** n.

ob•tuse´ adj. dull or ignorant; lacking understanding

ob´vi•ate vt. make unnecessary

ob´vi•ous adj. clearly seen or understood

oc•ca´sion n. an event or opportunity —vt. to cause

oc•ca´sion•al adj. occurring Infrequently

oc•cult´ adj. obscured or hidden; mysterious; relating to the supernatural —**oc•cult´ism** n.

oc•cu•pan•cy n. possession of an office, home, etc.

oc´cu•pant n. one who fills a position or inhabits a place

oc•cu•pa´tion n. activity, esp. for livlihood; occupancy

oc´cu•py vt. fill time or space; hold one's attention; control after conquest

oc•cur´ vi. happen; present itself, as an idea —**oc•cur´rence** n.

o´cean n. large body of salt water; large amount —**o•ce•an´ic** adj.

o•cean•og´ra•pby n. study of the ocean and its phenomena —**o•cea•nog´ra•pher** n.

oc´ta•gon n. an eight-sided polygon —**oc•tag´o•nal** adj.

oc•tet´ n. a group of eight

oc´u•lar adj. of eyes or sight

oc´u•list n. a physician who treats the eyes, an optomotrist or opthalmologist

odd adj. strange or different; unusual or unexpected; an uneven amount

odds n. pl. probability

ode n. lyric poem —**od´ic** adj.

o´di•ous adj. offensive; engendering aversion

o´di•um n. hatred or aversion

o•dom´e•ter n. a device for measuring distance traveled

o´dor (US) n. something perceived by smell; an aroma

o•dor•if´er•ous adj. having an aroma

o´dor•ous adj. having a distinctive aroma

o´dour (Brit.) n. thing perceived by smell; an aroma

off adj., adv., prep. away from; at a distance; removed

of´fal n. waste

of•fence´ (Brit.) n. a violation; that arousing disapproval

of•fend´ vi., vt. arouse disapproval —**of•fend´er** n.

offense´ (US) n. a violation; that arousing disapproval

of·fen´sive adj. disagreeable; vulgar or insulting

of´fer n. something for consideration —vt. present or submit

of´fer·ing n. a gift

of´fi·cer n. one in authority

of·fi´cial adj. relating to an office or position; authorized —n. one in authority

of·fi´ci·ate vt. preside; perform the duties of office

of·fi´cious adj. overly eager

of´ten adv. frequently

o´gle vi. , vt. stare rudely

o´gre n. a mythical monster

oint´ment n. a salve

old adj. aged or elderly; of a specific age; showing signs of age or wear; seasoned or matured

o·le·o·mar´ga·rine n. margarine, a substitute for butter

ol·fac´to·ry adj. of the sense of smell

ol·i´gar·chy n. government controlled by a small group

ol·i·gop´o·ly n. market dominated by few suppliers

ol·i·gop´so·ny n. market dominated by lew buyers

o·li·o n. a stew, mixture or collection

om·buds´man n. an investigator and mediator

o´men n. a sign or indication

om´i·nous adj. threatening; inauspicious

o·mis´sion n. something omitted; failure to perform

omit´ vt. leave out

om´ni·bus adj. including many —n. a large passenger vehicle: a bus

om·nip´o·tent adj. having unlimited power

om·nis´cient adj. having unlimited knowledge

om·niv´o·rous adj. subsisting on either plants or animals —om´ni·vore n.

on´er·ous adj. difficult or troublesome

o´nus n. responsibility; burden

ooze n. that leaks out; slimy mud —vi., vt. flow or leak out slowly; give off

o·paque´ adj. not transparent; mtpervious to light; ambiguous, obscure —o·pac´i·ty n.

o´pen adj. accessible; unobstructed; unrestricted; available; candid and straightforward; lacking prejudice— vi., vt. become accessible; to begin —o´pen·ing n.

op´er·a n. a musical drama

op´er·ate vi. function; perform surgery —vt. control or cause to function; manage a business —op´er·a·ble adj. —op´er·a·tor n.

op·er·a´tion n. a condition of functioning; a procedure or method; surgery

op´er·a·tive adj. functioning

op·er·et´ta n. a light opera

oph·thal·mol´o·gy n. study of the eye, its diseases, and treatment —oph·thal·mol´o·gist n.

o´pi·ate n. a sedative; anything that dulls the senses

o·pin´ion n. belief or judgment

o·pin´ion·at·ed adj. having strong beliefs

o´pi·um n. a narcotic derived from the opium poppy

op·po´nent adj. acting in opposition —n. one opposing

op´por·tune´ adj. timely or suitable

op•por•tun´ist *n.* one who takes advantage

op•por•tu´ni•ty *n.* an advantageous occasion or time

op•pos´a•ble *adj.* able to be reversed; that can be confronted or countered

op•pose´ *vt.* act in conflict; place across from —**op´po•site** *adj.*

op•po•si´tion *n.* conflict; those disagreeing

op•press´ *vt.* suppress by maltreatment or abuse; overburden —**op•pres´sor** *n.* —**op•pres´sive** *adj.*

op•pro´bri•ous *adj.* contemptuous, reproachful; shameful —**op•pro´bri•um** *n.*

op´ti•cal *adj.* relating to vision

op´tics *pl. n.* the branch of science dealing with vision and light —**op•ti´cian** *n.*

op´ti•mal *adj.* most favorable

op´ti•mism *n.* expectation of a favorable outcome

op´ti•mize *vt.* maximize effectiveness

op´ti•mum *adj.* favorable

op´tion *n.* a choice; a right to choose —**op´tion•al** *adj.*

op•tom´e•try *n.* examination, diagnosis, and treatment for problems of the eyes —**op•tom´e•trist** *n.*

op´u•lent *adj.* marked by wealth or abundance

o´pus *n.* a creative literary or musical composition

o´ra•cle *n.* a prophet; a visionary; one having great wisdom —**o•rac´u•lar** *adj.*

o´ral *adj.* spoken; relating to speech or the mouth

o•rate´ *vt.* speak formally

ora•tor´i•cal *adj.* pertaining to an orator or oratory

or´a•to•ry *n.* public speaking

orb *n.* a sphere

or´bit *n.* the path of one body around another; a sphere of influence —*vi.* travel an orbit —*vt.* place in orbit

or•dain´ *vt.* charge with holy orders; decree or dictate

or•deal´ *n.* a trying experience

or´der *n.* logical arrangement; a command; a group or organization —*vt.* arrange; instruct or direct

or´der•ly *adj.* neat; systematic; peaceful and law-abiding —*n.* an attendant

or´di•nance *n.* a local law

or´di•nary *adj.* common; unexceptional

ore *n.* mineral rock

or´gan *n.* a musical instrument; a body part; a publication

or•gan´ic *adj.* of or relating to living tissue

or´ga•nism *re* a hie form

or•ga•ni•za´tion *n.* a bringing together, persons united for a common purpose

or´ga•nize *vt.* make orderly or functional; bring together —**or´ga•nized** *adj.*

or´gasm *n.* sexual climax

or´gy *n.* revelry; uncontrolled indulgence

o´ri•ent *vt.* position to points of the compass; familiarize

or´i•fice *n.* an opening

or´i•gin *n.* beginning; a source

o•rig´i•nal *adj.* first or new, different or imaginative —*n.* that from which others derive, a prototype —**o•rig•i•nal´i•ty** *n.* —**o•rig´i•nal•ly** *adv.* —**o•rig´i•nate** *vi., vt.*

or´na•ment *n.* decoration or embellishment —*vt.*

or´na•men´tal *adj.* decorative

or•nate´ *adj.* elaborately

styled or decorated

or•ni•thol′o•gy n. the study of birds

or′phic adj. mystical

ort n. a scrap, esp. of food

or•tho•don′tia, or•tho•don′tics n. prevention and correction of dental irregularities —**or•tho•don′tist** n.

or′tho•dox adj. adhering to traditional or established ways —**or′tho•dox•y** n.

or•tho•pe′dics n. medical treatment for ailments of the skeletal system

os•cil′late vi. move back and forth; to vibrate

os′cu•late vi. come together — vt. to kiss —**os•cu•la′tion** n.

os•mo′sis n. passage of fluids through a membrane; gradual process of absorbing or learning —**os•mot′ic** adj.

os•si•fi•ca′tion n. process of forming bone or hardening

os•ten′si•ble adj. appearing as; professed or pretended

os•ten•ta′tion n. pretentious display

os′tra•cize vt. isolate; banish

oth′er adj. distinct from

o′ti•ose adj. idle, indolent

oust vt. eject; force out

out adj., adv. exterior; away or apart from; distinct from the usual or accepted

out′er adj. external or exterior

out′fit vt. furnish with clothing or equipment

out′growth n. a result

out′lay n. an expenditure

out′rage n. an offensive act; anger —vt. make violently angry —**out•ra′geous** adj.

out•side′ adj. of an outer limit —n. an outer surface or limit

out′spo′ken adj. candid

out•wit′ vt. trick or deceive

o′val adj. elliptical; egg-shaped —n.

o•va′tion n. spirited applause

o′ver adj. extreme; extra — adv. above; across; as far as; completed or done —prep.

o′ver•age n. an excess

o′ver•alls n. (Brit.) a one-piece garment worn over street clothes; (US) loose trousers with a bib front

o′ver•bear′ing adj. domineering or arrogant

o′ver•flow n. excess; a device that allows excess to escape —vi., vt. spill over; abound

o′ver•joyed adj. delighted

o′ver•look n. a vantage point —**o′ver•look′** vt. watch over, supervise; disregard or omit

o′ver•pow′er vt. to overwhelm

o′ver•shad′ow vt. dominate

o′ver•sight n. supervision; an unintentional error

o•vert′ adj. open and public; sanctioned —**o•vert′ly** adv.

o′ver•ture n. musical introduction; an approach signaling readiness to negotiate

o′vine adj. pertaining to sheep; sheeplike

o′void adj. shaped like an egg

owe vi.,vt. be indebted

ow′ing adj. unpaid

own adj. of one's possession —vt. possess or control — vi., vt. admit or acknowledge

ox•i•da′tion n. a combining with oxygen —**ox′i•dize** vt.

ox′y•gen n. a nonmetallic element necessary for plant and animal respiration

ox•y•mo′ron n. a contradictory phrase: *sweet sadness*

p, P sixteenth letter of the alphabet

pace n. manner of walking;

speed of a walk, action, event, etc.; a stride —*vt.*, *vi.* walk; measure by paces

pa•cif´ic *adj.* peaceful, tranquil —**pac´i•fi•ca´tion** *n.*

pac´i•fy *vt.* ease anger or conflict —**pac´i•fist** *n.*

pack *n.* a small package; set of items; a bag with straps; a group functioning as a unit —*vt.*, *vi.* place in a container; compress

pack´age *n.* a container; a group of elements taken together —*vt.* offer as a unit

pact *n.* agreement; contract

pad *n.* a cushion; joined sheets of paper —*vt.* cushion; increase deceitfully

pa´gan *adj.* without religion —*n.* a nonreligious person

page *n.* one side of a sheet of paper —*vt.* to summon

pag´eant *n.* an elaborate procession or celebration

pa•go´da *n.* an ornate multistoried Buddhist shrine

pail *n.* a cylindrical container with a handle

pain *n.* a disagreeable sensation; suffering —*vi.*, *vt.* cause pain

pains´tak•ing *adj.* requiring great care, careful

pair *n.* two persons or things —*vi.*, *vt.* tiring two together

pal *n.* a friend

pal´ace *n.* a grand and sumptuous residence

pal´at•a•ble *adj.* edible; acceptable —**pal´ate** *n.*

pa´lette *n.* a flat for mixing colors; an artist's colors

pal´in•drome *n.* a word or phrase that reads backward or forward

pal•i•sade´ *n.* a steep cliff

pall *n.* gloom; dark cover

pal´li•ate *vt.* relieve or ease

pal´li•a•tive *adj.* serving to relieve

pal´lid *adj.* pale; ashen

pal´pa•ble *adj.* obvious; tangible

pal´pi•tate *vi.* tremble or quiver; pulsate

pal´try *adj.* trivial; insignificant; of little worth

pam´per *vt.* cater to; indulge

pan *n.* a container, as for cooking; harsh critcism —*vi.*, *vt.* separate by rinsing; criticize

pan•a•ce´a *adj.* a cure-all

pan•dem´ic *adj.* general; universal

pan•de•mo´ni•um *n.* noisy confusion

pan´der *vt.* procure for sexual affairs —*n.* procurer or pimp

pane *n.* a panel of glass; a flat piece or surface

pan´el *n.* a flat or decorative section; a group formed to judge, discuss, etc. —*vt.* provide with panels

pang *n.* a sudden sharp pain

pan•han•dle (US) *vi.* to beg

pan´ic *n.* sudden fear; general hysteria —*vi.*, *vt.* —**pan´icked, pan´ick•ing, pan´ic-strick•en,** *adj.*

pan´o•ply *n.* an extensive or impressive display

pan•o•ram´a *n.* extensive view

pant *vi.* take short rapid breaths

pan´to•mime *n.* communication by gestures —*vt.*, *vi.* perform without speech

pan´try *n.* an area where foods are stored or prepared

par *adj.* normal —*n.* an established standard; face value

par´a•ble *n.* story with a moral

pa•rade´ *n.* a procession

par´a•digm n. an example or modal

par´a•dise n. a perfect place of peace and beauty

par´a•dox n. a seeming contradiction; an enigma

par•al•lax n. optical displacement from change in position —**par•al•lac´tic** adj.

par´al•lel adj. of equal distance at all points; being or moving in concert —n. a resemblance —vt.

par´a•lyse (Brit.) vt. render unable to move or function

pa•ral´y•sis n. loss of ability to move or function

par´a•lyze (US) vt. render unable to move or function

par•a•med´ic n. one providing emergency treatment or assisting a doctor

par•ram´e•ter n. a houndry

par´a•mount adj. of primary importance; dominant

par´amour n. a lover

par•a•noi´a n. irrational fear

par´a•nor´mal adj. outside the realm of normal knowledge

par´a•pher•na´lia n. implements; equipment

para•ple´gi•a n. paralysis of the lower body

par´a•psy•chol´o•gy n. the study of paranormal activity

par´a•site n. an organism supported by another; one who relies on others

par´cel n. a package; a section of land —vt. portion out

parch vt., vt. to dry or shrivel; make or become thirsty

par´don n. foregiveness —vt. deliver from punishment; forgive

pare vt. to trim

par´ent n. an ancestor; a mother or father a source

par´ent•age a one's lineage

pa•ri´ah n. an outcast

par´ish n. a church congregation; a civil district similar to a township or county

par´i•ty n. equality

park n. a recreation area; a designated area: industrial park —vt. to place and leave temporarily

par´lance n. style of speech; jargon

par´lia•ment n. a legislative body

par´lor n a formal room

pa•ro´chi•al adj. of a local parish; local or conservative; provincial

par´o•dy n. a comic work that ridicules; something so bad as to be a mockery —vt. to ridicule; make a travesty of

par´ox•ysm n. a sudden outburst; sudden attack of a disease —**par´ox•ys´mal** adj.

par´quet´ n. a floor of inlaid wood

par´ri•cide n. murder of a relative, esp. of parents

parry n. evasion —vi., vt. ward off or avoid

parse vt. to break down and examine

par•si•mo´ni•ous adj. frugal

par•take´ vt., vi. receive a share in —**par•tak´er** n.

par´tial adj. incomplete; prejudiced or biased

par•tial´i•ty n. fondness or preference; bias

par•tic´i•pate vi. engage or share in

par•ti•cle n. tiny piece, least possible amount

par•tic´u•lar adj. fussy, attentive to detail; of a specific thing; noteworthy —n. a detail or specific

par´ti•san adj. based —n. an ardent supporter

par•ti´tion n. a separation —vt. divide or separate

part´ner n. one allied with another; an associate

par´ty adj. of a group; of a social gathering —n. a group or gathering; a participant, party to the action —vi. carouse —**party line** the standards or ideals of a group —**party pooper** one who shuns or avoids involvement —**par•ty•er** n.

pass n. a passageway; ticket or permit; a throw; sexual overture —vi., vt. move by; transfer; be satisfactory

pass´a•ble adj. navigable; acceptable; adequate

pas´sage n. a journey; path or road; movement, transition, or progress; an excerpt; enactment, as of a law

pas•sé´ adj. no longer fashionable

pas´sen•ger n. a rider

pas´sion n. intense emotion

pas´sive adj. without reaction; complacent

past adj. former or prior; gone by —n. a former time or event —prep beyond

paste n. a thick smooth adhesive —vt. fasten with paste

pas•tel´ n. a pale color; a chalk-like artist's medium

pas´teur•ize vt. process food so as to retard spoilage

pas´time n. amusement or diversion

pas´to•ral adj. of the country; rustic —n. an artistic work emulating country life, in music called a pas´to•rale´

pas´ture n. vegetation for grazing animals —vt. put an animal out to graze

pat adj. to the point —n. light tap or caress; a small bit of food —vt. lightly tap or caress; flatten or compress

patch n. a small piece or part —vt. mend or decorate

pat´ent adj. obvious, apparent —n. right granted to protect work for a time —vt. apply for or grant a patent

pa•ter´nal adj. of fatherhood —**pa•ter´nal•ism, pa•ter´ni•ty** n.

path n. a route for travel

pa•thet´ic adj. deserving of pity; inspiring contempt

path•o•log´i•cal adj. of habitual or obsessive behavior

pa•thol´o•gy n. the study of diseases

pa´thos n. sympathy, sorrow

pa´tience n. ability to accept without complaint

pa´tient adj. accepting delay or difficulty; tolerant —n. one under care

pat´i•na, pat•i´na n. change or color by age and exposure

pa´tio n. outdoor living space adjacent to a dwelling

pa´tois n. a provincial dialect

pa´tri•arch n. man heading a family or group; an elder

pa•tri´archy n. tracing of lineage through men

pa•tri´cian n. an aristocrat; one of refined manners and taste —adj.

pa´tri•ot n. supporter of one's country —**pa´tri•ot´ic** adj.

pa´tron n. a customer; one who supports a cause —**pa´tron•ize** vt.

pat´tern n. a model or drawing used as a guide; a reoccurring characteristic —vt. make according to a model

pau´ci•ty n. a lack or scarcity

pau´per n. an impoverished person

pause n. temporary halt; hesitation for effect —vi.

pave´ment (US) n. durable covering for a path or road

pa•vil´ion n. an open shelter

pawn n. security; one held hostage —vt. use or give as security —**pawn´shop** n.

pay vt. give value for goods or services; reward or punish; render, as a compliment — vi. make payment; be profitable —n. compensation

peace n. freedom from hostility; serenity —**peace´ful** adj.

peak adj. at or near the upper limit —n. a pointed top; height of development bring to a climax

peaked adj. pointed

peak´ed adj. appearing sickly

peal n. a ringing —vi., vt.

peas´ant n. a rustic

peb´ble n. small stone

pec´ca•ble adj. likely to sin

pec´u•late vt. wrongfully appropriate; embezzle

pe•cu´liar adj. odd or unusual; unique; characteristic to a person, group, etc

ped•a•gog´ics, ped´a•go•gy n. the teaching profession

ped´a•gogue n. an instructor; a narrow-minded teacher

ped´al adj. relating to the foot —n. pad for the foot —vt., vi. to operate with a pedal

pe•dan´tic adj. overly concerned with scholarship and formality

ped´dle vi., vt. to sell or offer for sale; promote, as an idea

ped´es•tal n. foundation; base

pe•des´tri•an adj. of travel by foot; ordinary or trite —n.

one moving on foot

pe•di•a•tri´cian n. doctor who treats infants

ped´i•gree n. a list of ancestors; lineage

pe•do•phile, pe•do•phil´i•ac n. an adult sexually attracted to children

peek n. momentary view —vi. view quickly; emerge gently

peel n. an outer covering —vi., vt. to strip off

peer vi. stare —n. an equal; one of noble birth

pe•jo´ra•tive adj. disparaging or derisive —n. a derisive word or phrase

pelt n. an animal skin —vt. to strike repeatedly

pen n. writing instrument; an enclosure —vt. write; confine

pe´nal adj. relating to punishment —**pe•nal•ize** vt.

pen´al•ty n. consequences

pen´ance n. an act of remorse

pen´chant n. an inclination or tendency; a predisposition

pen´cil n. a writing instrument —vt. to write

pen´dant n. a hanging ornament

pen´dent adj. hanging or projecting

pend´ing adj. awaiting settlement —prep.

pen´du•lum n. a hanging weight —**pen´du•lous** adj.

pen´e•trate vt. gain entrance; pierce; affect profoundly — **pen´e•tra•ble** adj.

pe•nin´su•la n. a point of land that projects into water

pen´i•tent adj. sorrowful or atoning for guilt —n. **pen´i•tence** n.

pen•i•ten´tia•ry (US) n. a prison

pen´nant n. a streamer

pe·nol´o·gy n. the study of prisons and rehabilitation

pen´sion n. money paid during retirement —vt.

pen´sive adj. inclined to thought —**pen´sive·ness** n.

pent´house n. a residence at or near the top of a building

pe·nu´ri·ous adj. frugal, miserly; unproductive, barren

pen´u·ry n. poverty

peo´ple n. humans in general —vt. to populate

per·ceive´ vt., vi. understand; become aware

per·cep´ti·ble adj. able to be discerned —**per·cep´tion** n.

per·cep´tive adj. observant

per´co·late vi., vt. to filter —n. a filtered liquid

pe·ren´ni·al adj. long-lasting or enduring; recurring often

per´fect adj. complete; free of fault, well-suited; capable - **per·fect´** vt. further develop or complete; make flawless

per·fid´i·ous adj. unfaithful or treacherous —**per´fi·dy** n.

per´fo·rate vt. pierce; mark with holes for separating

per·form´ vt., vi. act on; function; to entertain

per´fume n. an aromatic substance; a pleasant aroma

per·func´to·ry adj. indifferent; act mechanically, casually, or carelessly

per·haps´ adv. possibly

per´il n. exposure to danger

pe·rim´e·ter n. boundary

pe´ri·od n. span of time; (US) punctuation mark that ends a sentence

pe´ri·od´ic adj. cyclical; recurring at regular intervals —**pe·ri·od´i·cal** n.

per·i·pa·tet´ic adj. roaming about; itinerant —n. one

given to roaming

pe·riph´er·al adj. outer; minor

pe·riph´er·y n. outermost part

per´ish vi die; pass from existence —**per´ish·a·ble** adj.

per·jure´ vt. testify falsely; violate an oath —**per´jury** n.

per´ma·nent adj. durable; enduring; unchanging

per´me·ate vt., vi. spread throughout

per·mis´si·ble adj. allowed

per·mis´sion n. approval or authorization

per·mis´sive adj. lenient

per·mit´ vt. allow or authorize —**per´mit** n. a document that grants permission

per·ni´cious adj. harmful

per´o·rate vt. speak at length

per·pen·dic´u·lar adj. at right angles to the horizon

per´pe·trate vt. commit, as a crime — **per´pe·tra·tor** n.

per·pet´u·al adj. continuing indefinitely; recurrent

per·pet´u·ate vt. endure

per·plex´ vt. to confound or confuse —**per·plexed´** adj.

per´qui·site n. benefit associated with a position

per´se·cute vt. oppress or abuse —**per·se·cu´tion** n.

per·se·ver´ance n. patience and persistence; determination —**per´se·vere´** vi.

per´si·flage n. banter

per·sist´ vi. persevere, endure

per´son n. an individual; a living human body

per´son·a·ble adj. pleasant

per´son·al adj. relating to a particular person; intimate

per·son·al´i·ty n. qualities of a person; distinctive attributes; a famous person

per·son´i·fy vt. endow with human qualities

per•son•nel *n.* employees

per•spec´tive *n.* viewpoint; a panorama; a flat rendering of three dimensions

per•spi•ca´cious *adj.* demonstrating unusual insight — **per•spi•cac´i•ty** *n.*

per•suade´ *vt.* convince

per•sua´sion *n.* power to convince — **per•sua´sive** *adj.*

pert *adj.* vivacious; saucy

per•tain´ *vi.* to relate to

per´ti•nent *adj.* relevant

per•turb´ *vt.* disquiet or worry

pe•ruse´ *vt.* study thoroughly; scrutinize — **pe•rus´al** *n.*

per•vade´ *vt.* penetrate or permeate — **per•va´sive** *adj.*

per•verse´ *adj.* evil or wicked; obstinate — **per•ver´sion** *n.*

per•vert´ *vt.* use improperly; distort meaning; corrupt

per´vi•ous *adj.* permeable

pest *n.* a nuisance; something harmful, as a virus

pes´ter *vt.* harass or annoy

pes´ti•lence *n.* an epidemic; a dangerous or harmful agent

pes´tle *n.* a device for crushing or blending in a mortar

pet *n.* one treated affectionately —*adj.* regarded as a favorite —*vt.* indulge; caress

pe•tite´ *n.* small

pe•ti´tion *n.* an appeal —*vi.*, *vt.* make an appeal

pet´ri•fy *vt.* fossilize; paralyze with fright

pet´rol (*Brit.*) *n.* fuel for a motor vehicle

pe•tro´le•um (*US*) *n.* crude oil

pet´tish *adj.* irritable; peevish

pet´ty *adj.* trivial, unimportant; mean or miserly

pet´u•lant *adj.* ill-tempered; irritable

phan´tasm *n.* an apparition

phan´tom *adj.* illusory;

imaginary —*n.* an apparition

phar•ma•ceu´tics *pl. n.* preparation of medicinal compounds —**phar•ma•ceu´ti•cal** *adj.*—**phar•ma•ceu´tist** *n.*

phar•ma•col´o•gy *n.* study of drugs and their uses

phe•nom´e•nal *adj.* extraordinary or remarkable

phi•lan´thro•py *n.* charity; humanitarian endeavor

phi•lat´e•ly *n.* stamp collecting —**phi•lat´e•list** *n.*

phi•lol´o•gy *n.* classical studies —**phi•lol´o•gist** *n.*

phi•los´o•phy *n.* study of knowledge; a fundamental principle; a system of beliefs

pho´bia *n.* an irrational fear or aversion —**pho´bic** *adj.*

pho•net´ics *n.* the sounds of speech —**pho•net´ic** *adj.*

pho´ny *adj.* artificial; fake — *n.* an imitation; a fake

pho•to•syn´the•sis *n.* deriving nourishment using light as an energy source

phys´i•cal *adj.* of the body or tangible matter

phy•si´cian *n.* doctor of medicine; one devoted to healing

phys´ics *n.* study of matter and energy—**phys´i•cist** *n.*

phys•i•ol´o•gy *n.* the study of living organisms

phy•sique´ *n.* the structure and appearance of the body

pick *vt.* select or separate; to gather or pluck —**pick´er** *n.*

pic´nic *n.* an outdoor meal; something easy or enjoyable

pic´ture *n.* a visual or oral depiction; a mental image — *vt.* visualize; describe vividly

piece *n.* a part or portion; something of a type —*vt.* join together

pierce *vt.* penetrate

pi·e·ty *n.* devotion, reverence

pig´ment *n.* a dye or coloring

pile *n.* an accumulation —*vt.,* *vi.* to make or form a heap

pil´fer *vt., vi.* to steal

pil´grim *n.* a traveler, esp. on a sacred journey

pil´lage *vt.* plunder

pil´lar *n.* supporting column

pi´lot *n.* one who or that which operates or guides

pinch *n.* a sprinkling; a predicament —*vt.* squeeze so as to cause discomfort; arrest; steal —*vi.* squeeze; be stingy; become constricted

pin´na·cle *n.* crest or summit

pi·o·neer´ *adj.* early, experimental; adventurous —*n.* explorer of new territory —*vt., vi.* lead; prepare the way

pi´ous *adj.* devout, reverent

pipe *n.* a hollow tube; a smoking implement —*vt.* to convey through a pipe

pi´quant *adj.* spicy, interesting or charming

pique *n.* indignation or ire —*vt.* irritate; excite or arouse

pit *n.* hole in the ground; a small indentation; recessed area —*vt., vi.* mark with indentations; place in conflict

pit´e·ous *adj.* pitiful; deserving pity —**pit´e·ous·ly** *adv.*

pith *n.* core or essence

pith´y *adj.* meaningful; brief

pit´i·ful *adj.* arousing pity or contempt; pathetic

pit´tance *n.* a trifling sum

pit´y *n.* compassion

pix·i·lat·ed *adj* frivolous or whimsical —**pix·i·la´tion** *n.*

plac´a·ble *adj.* inclined to tolerance or acceptance

pla´cate *vt.* appease or pacify

place *n.* a position, space, or locality; one's status, job,

etc. —*vt.* situate; appoint; find a home or job for

pla·ce´bo *n.* a fake or phony medication; a sugar pill

plac´id *adj.* peaceful or calm

pla´gia·rism *n.* misappropriation of the works of another

plague *n.* sudden spread of disease; a sudden outbreak —*vt.* annoy; afflict

plain *adj.* unadorned; simple; open or obvious; ordinary

plain´tive *adj* mournful; lamenting

plan *n.* strategy; a diagram —*vt.* work out means for doing; have an intention

plan´et *n.* heavenly body revolving around a star

plan·ta´tion *n.* land under cultivation; an estate

plat *n.* a plot of land; a map of building lots, streets, etc. —*vt.* make a map

plate *n.* a flat piece; food service for one —*vt.* to overlay or coat —**plat´ed** *adj.*

pla·teau´ *n.* a flat-topped hill

plat´form *n.* a raised landing; statement of beliefs or goals

plat´i·tude *n.* a trite expression; a cliché

pla·ton´ic *adj.* spiritual; ideal

plau´si·ble *adj* probable; convincing

play *vi., vt.* act out; perform; participate in a game —*n.* a dramatic performance; looseness of a machine part

pla·za *n.* a public square

plea *n.* a request or appeal

plead *vi., vt.* beseech; offer an excuse or justification

pleas´ant *adj.* providing pleasure —**pleas´ant·ly** *adv.*

pleas´ant·ry *n.* a polite or humorous remark

please *vi., vt.* give pleasure

plea´sure n. delight; that brings happiness or enjoyment; a preference —**plea´sur•a•ble** adj.

pledge n. a binding promise; security for payment —vt.

plen´ty n. adequate amount; abundance —**plen´ti•ful** adj.

pleth´o•ra n. an excess

pli´a•ble adj. flexible

pli´ant adj. yielding; docile

plight n. predicament or difficulty; a condition or state; a promise —vt. a pledge

plod vi., vt. move or work steadily and painstakingly

plot n. parcel of land; story line; plan or conspiracy —vt. locate on a map; take part in conspiracy —vi. conspire

plug n. material that closes or obstructs; electrical connector; mention of a product —vt., vi. stop up or close off; advertise a product

plumb adj. precisely vertical —adv. vertical; squarely —n. a line used to establish a precise vertical —vt. make vertical;. check with a plumb

plum´met vi. fall rapidly

plump adj. full and rounded —vt., vi. become plump

plun´der n. stolen property —vt., vi. take by force

plunge vi., vt. to fall or thrust

plu´ral adj. more than one

plush adj. sumptuous; opulent —**plush´i•ness** n.

ply n. a thin layer —vt. to regularly practice, as a trade

po•di•a´try n. branch of medicine dealing with the feet

po´di•um n. a speaker's platform

po´em n. a work in verse

po´et•ry n. poetic works; the traits of a poem

poi´gnant adj. mentally intense; distressing or moving

point n. sharp end; a projection; a dot; a distinct element, quality, or condition —vi., vt. direct attention to

poise n. grace, dignity, and composure —vt., vi. to balance or hover

po´lar•ize vt. consolidate around differing views

po•lem´ics n. the art of debate

po´lice´ n. persons charged with law enforcement —vt.

pol´i•cy n. a plan or procedure; a contract

pol´ish n. luster or sheen; refinement —vt. make smooth and bright; make refined

po•lite´ adj. considerate, tactful; courteous

pol´i•tics n. science of government; tactics for gaining power —**po•lit´i•cal** adj.

pol´lute´ vt. contaminate —**pol•lu´tion** n.

pol´ter•geist n. a supernatural being creating disorder

pomp n. pageantry

pomp´ous adj. pretentious; boastful and arrogant

pond n. a small body of water

pon´der vt. consider carefully

pon´der•ous adj. weighty; dull or lifeless

pon•tif´i•cate vi. speak dogmatically

pool n. accumulation of liquid; small body of water; assemblage of persons or resources —vi., vt.

poor adj. lacking wealth; lacking basic needs; inferior

pop´u•lar adj. generally accepted; well-liked —**pop•u•lar´i•ty** n. —**pop´u•lar•ize** vt.

pop´u•late vt. to inhabit; furnish with inhabitants

pop•u•la´tion n. people of an area; a particular grouping

po´rous adj. having pores; absorbent; penetrable

por´ta•ble adj. easily carried or moved —**por•ta•bil´i•ty** n.

por´tal n. an entryway

por•tend´ vt. predict or foretell

por´tent n. a sign or omen

por•ten´tous adj. ominous or foreboding

port•fo´li•o n. a folder; a collection of documents

por´tion n. part or share; amount for one person —vt. separate; distribute

port´ly adj. stout

por•tray´ vt. to represent

pose n. a feigned attitude; an affectation —vi. assume a position; feign an attitude; misrepresent —vt. cause to sit for a portrait; put forth, as a question —**pos´er** n.

posh adj. comfortable

po•si´tion n. a specific place; a viewpoint; social or professional status —vt. to place

pos´i•tive adj. certain, absolutely sure; decisive; direct

pos•sess´ vt. have; dominate

pos•ses´sion n. thing owned or in one's custody

pos´si•ble adj. likely or able to be —**pos´si•bly** adv.

post n. a shaft or rod to support or connect; mail —vt. appoint or assign; (Brit.) send via the postal system

pos•te´ri•or adj. situated behind —n. buttocks

pos•ter´i•ty n. succeeding generations

post´hu•mous adj. after death

post•pone´ vt. to put off

pos´tu•late n. supposition -vt. presume without proof

pos´ture n. characteristic

bearing, manner, or attitude —vi. affect an attitude

po´ta•ble adj. suitable for drinking —n. a beverage

po´tent adj. strong; powerful

po•ten´tial adj. possible —n. unrealized capacity

po•tion n. a medicine or drug

pot´pour•ri´ n. a mixture or medley; a conglomeration

pot´sherd n. a fragment of pottery

pouch n. a hag or recepticle

pounce vi. attack or seize suddenly

pound n. unit of weight or currency; place of confinement —vt. strike repeatedly; tread heavily; confine

pour vi., vt. flow in a steady stream; rain profusely

pov´er•ty n. a state of want

pow´der n. fine particles —vi., vt. make granular; pulverize

pow´er n. strength, energy; authority —vt. provide with means of propulsion —adj. operated by motor or electricity —**pow´er•ful** adj.

prac´ti•cal adj. useful or usable; workable or sensible

prac´ti•cal•ly adv. almost

prac´tice n. repetition to improve; mode or manner. of functioning; a profession — **prac´tice** (US), **prac´tise** (Brit.) vt., vi. repeat an action to acquire skill; perform according to custom; work at a profession

prag•mat´ic adj. practical; concerning facts and logic

praise n. expression of approval —vt. express approval; honor or glorify

prank n. a practical joke

prate n. idle chatter —vi., vt. talk idly and frivolously

prayer *n.* an earnest appeal or supplication —**pray** *vi., vt.*

pre•am•ble *n.* a preface

pre•car•i•ous *adj.* uncertain or unstable

pre•cau´tion *n.* care taken

pre•cede´ *vt., vi.* come before

pre´cious *adj.* valuable; cherished; overly refined —*adv.*

pre•cip´i•tate *adj.* hasty or rash —*vi., vt.* fall, as rain; hasten occurrence

pre•cip•i•ta´tion *n.* haste or. rashness; falling moisture

pre•cip´i•tous *adj.* steep

pré•cis´ *n.* a summary

pre•cise´ *adj.* exact; well-defined —**pre•ci´sion** *n., adj.*

pre•clude´ *vt.* exclude or prohibit —**pre•clu´sion** *n.*

pre•co´cious *adj.* exhibiting early maturity

pre•cog•ni´tion *n.* foresight; prescience

pred´a•tor *n.* one preying on others —**pred´a•to•ry** *adj.*

pre•dic•a•ment *n.* difficult situation

pre•dict´ *vt.* assert or. foretell or prophesy —**pre•dict´able** *adj.* —**pre•dic´tion** *n.*

preen *vt., vi.* groom or primp; gloat

pref´ace *n.* an introduction —*vt.* furnish an opening message; serve as introduction

pre•fer´ *vt.* favor over another; like better —**pref´er•ence** *n.*

pref•er•a•ble *adj.* more desirable —**prefer•a•bly** *adv.*

pref•er•en´tial *adj.* favored; granting assistance

preg´na•ble *adj.* pervious; vulnerable

preg´nant *adj.* carrying a developing offspring; significant or meaningful

pre•hen´sile *adj.* adapted for grasping, as a monkey's tail

pre•his•tor´ic *adj.* of time before recorded history

prej´u•dice *n.* prejudgment; opinion founded on bias — *vt.* influence to prejudice; wrong by opinion or action

pre•lim´i•nar•y *adj.* introductory —*n.* an introduction; that which precedes

pre´mier´ *adj.* foremost —*n.* a chief administrative officer

pre•miere´ *n.* an introductory performance —*vt., vi.* present the first time

prem´ise *n.* an assumption that is the basis for debate

pre´mi•um *adj.* excellent; superior; —*n.* reward or bonus; excess over value

pre•mo•ni´tion *n.* foreboding; a sign or omen

pre•oc´cu•pied *adj.* distracted; troubled

prep•a•ra´tion *n.* readiness; organization; a mixture

pre•par´a•to•ry *adj.* introductory or preliminary — *adv.* in making ready for

pre•pare´ *vt.* arrange in advance; provide with needs; make complete

pre•pon´der•ant *adj.* superior; dominant

pre•pos´ter•ous *adj.* absurd; irrational

pre•rog´a•tive *n.* a right or privilege, as by rank or birth

pre´sci•ence *n.* foreknowledge

pre•scribe´ *vt.* direct or order

pre•scrip´tion *n.* directions or instructions; a formula

pres´ence *n.* attendance, proximity, or influence; appearance or bearing

pres´ent¹ *adj.* at this moment; current; existing; here; near at hand —*n.* now

pres·ent² n. a gift —**pre·sent´** vt. offer or give, as a gift

pre·sent´a·ble adj. suitable for offering or giving

pres´ent·ly adv. soon

pre·serv´a·tive n. a substance that prevents spoiling—adj.

pre·serve´ n. area kept in a natural state —vt. protect; save to a natural state; prepare so as to prevent spoilage —**pres·er·va´tion** n.

pre·side´ vi. officiate

pres´i·dent n. chief officer or executive; one who presides

press n. journalism or journalists; machine for printing; device to apply pressure; urgency —vt., vi. apply pressure

pres´sure n. constant application of force —vt. persuade

pres·tige´ n. distinction or renown; esteem

pre·sume´ vt. take for granted; undertake without authorization —vi. make excessive demands on

pre·tend´ vt., vi. feign or mimic.; make believe; be deceitful; attempt to deceive —**pre·tence´** (Brit.) **pre·tense´** (US) n.

pre·ten´tious adj. presumptuous or arrogant; pompous or showy—**pre·ten´sion** n.

pre´text n. subterfuge

pret´ty adj. attractive; considerable; insubstantial — adv. quite; somewhat

pre·vail´ vi. overcome; influence or effect

prev´a·lent adj. common or widespread

pre·var´i·cate vi. to lie

pre·vent´ vt. keep from happening; prohibit or hamper

pre·ven´tive adj. hindering; precautionary —n. a thing that prevents, as from disease —**pre·ven´tive·ly** adv.

pre·vi´ous adj. former; having occurred earlier

prey n. one hunted; a victim —vi. to hunt.; to victimize

price n. cost —vt. set value

pride n. self-esteem; haughtiness, disdain

pri´mal adj. primitive; original; primary

pri´mary adj. first; earliest; fundamental; principal

prime adj. of the finest quality; original —n. age of full perfection or vigor; best of anything —vt. prepare or make ready

pri·me´val adj. ancient; primitive

prim´i·tive adj. simple; ancient; uncivilized

primp vt., vi. groom with care

prin´ci·pal adj. first or leading —n. a person of importance

prin´ci·ple n. a fundamental rule or concept; an ideal

pri´or adj. preceding

pris´tine adj. unspoiled

pri´vate adj. not open to the public; not public; secluded

pri·va´tion n. abject poverty

priv´i·lege n. a special right

prize n. award; a thing desired —adj. valued —vt. to value highly

prob´a·ble adj. likely; worth believing —**prob·a·bil´i·ty** n.

pro·bi´ty n. honesty; integrity

prob´lem adj. difficult to manage a. something to be considered; a puzzle or dilemma

pro·ce´dure n. manner or system of doing

pro·ceed´ vi. move forward

proc'ess n. a system

pro•ces'sion n. an orderly progression; a parade

pro•claim' vt. to announce; praise

proc•la•ma'tion n. a formal announcement or edict

pro•cliv'i•ty n. an inherent inclination or tendency

pro•cras'ti•nate vi. to put off —vt. postpone or delay

pro•cure' vt. acquire

prod vt. goad or provoke —n. that incites to action

prod'i•gal adj. wasteful

pro•di'gious adj. extraordinary or impressive

prod'i•gy n. one with exceptional talent; a genius

prod•uce' n. farm products — **pro•duce'** vt. to make or manufacture; create

pro•duc'tive adj. fruitful or prolific; effective

pro•fane' adj. sacrilegious or irreverent; vulgar or base — vt. desecrate or debase

pro•fan'i•ty n. irreverence; abusive or vulgar language

pro•fess' vt. claim or declare; pretend or feign

pro•fes'sion n. an occupation; a declaration of faith

pro•fes'sion•al adj. skillful — n. one specially trained

pro•fes'sor n. (Brit.) a distinguished college or university teacher; (US) an educator, esp. at a college or university —**pro•fes•so'ri•al** adj.

prof'fer vt. to offer

pro•fi'cient adj. competent

pro'file n. a summary; a side view

prof'it n. gain from a business —vt., vi. realize gain or benefit; be of benefit to

prof'li•gate adj. extravagant

or wasteful

pro•found' adj. deep or penetrating; scholarly

pro•fuse' adj. abundant

pro•fu'sion n. an abundance

prog'e•ny n. offspring

prog•nos'ti•cate vt. to predict

program (US) n. schedule, agenda; radio or television show; computer instructions —vt prepare a schedule or agenda; write computer instructions

pro'gramme (Brit.) n. a schedule or agenda; radio or television show —vt. prepare a schedule or agenda

prog'ress n. advancement, development, or improvement —**pro•gress'** vi. move forward; grow or improve

pro•gres'sive adj. receptive to fresh ideas or concepts

pro•hib'it vt. forbid or ban

pro•hib'i•tive adj. forbidding

proj'ect n. a plan; a serious undertaking —**pro•ject'** vt. extend or thrust forward

pro•jec'tion n. a bulge; an extended part; a forecast

pro•lif'er•ate vi., vt. increase rapidly —**pro•lif•er•a'tion** n.

pro•lif'ic adj. producing in abundance

pro•lix' adj. excessively wordy

pro'logue n. introductory text

pro•long' vt. extend or lengthen

prom'i•nent adj. clearly discernable; well-known, celebrated —**prom'i•nence** n.

pro•mis'cu•ous adj. tending to casual relationships; indiscriminate; random

prom'ise n. a pledge or vow — vt. —**prom'is•so•ry** adj.

prom'on•to•ry n. high point of land extending into water

pro•mote´ vt. advance to a higher level; attempt to make popular or prominent

prompt adj. punctual; timely —vt. arouse or provoke; remind —**prompt´ly** adv.

prom•ul•gate vt. announce publicly or officially

prone adj. lying face downward; disposed to, likely

prong n. a pointed extension; (US) contact points for a connection

pro´noun n. designation that substitutes for a noun

pro•nounce´ vt., vi. speak clearly; announce officially

pro•nun•ci•a´tion n. accepted sound of a spoken word

proof n. evidence; demonstration of authenticity

prop•a•gan´da n. information to promote a point of view

prop´a•gate vt. breed or multiply; to spread or extend

pro•pel´ vt. drive forward

pro•pen´si•ty n. an inclination or tendency

prop´er adj. appropriate; fitting; conventional

prop´er•ty n. belongings or possessions; section of land; a characteristic or quality

proph´e•cy n. a prediction

proph´e•sy vt. to predict

proph´et n. one who pronounces or interprets by divine inspiration

pro•pi´ti•ate vt. appease

pro•pi´tious adj. promising or favorable; kindly disposed

pro•po´nent n. an advocate or defender; a supporter

pro•por´tion n. a share; relative magnitude; symmetry

pro•pos´al n. an offer; a plan

pro•pose´ vt. recommend; put forth for consideration;

intend—vi. make an offer

pro•pri´e•tor n. an owner; one having exclusive right to — **pro•pri´e•tar•y** adj.

pro•pri´e•ty n. good breeding; conformity to society

pro•sa´ic adj. commonplace; mundane, humdrum, or dull

pro•scribe´ vt. to condemn or forbid —**pro•scrip´tion** n.

prose n. the style of ordinary speech

pros´pect n. expectation —vt., vi. to search or explore

pros´per vi. to thrive —**pros´per•ous** adj.

pros•per´i•ty it. affluence or well-being

pros´trate adj. prone; submissive; overcome —vt. bow down or lie flat; be overcome

pro•tag´o•nist n. the principal character in a story

pro•tect´ vt. safeguard

pro´té•gé n. one endorsed by a person of influence

pro•test´ n. declaration or display of disapproval —**pro•test´** vt. object strongly

pro´to•col n. code of conduct; proper etiquette; ceremony

pro´to•type n. a model

pro•tract´ vt. prolong

pro•trude´ vt., vi. jut or thrust outward —**pro•tru´sion** n.

proud adj. full of self-esteem; vain or arrogant; dignified

prove vt. establish by argument or evidence —**prov´en** adj.

prov´en•der n. supplies; pro visions

prov´erb n. a saying or adage —**pro•ver´bi•al** adj.

pro•vide´ vt. to supply or furnish; stipulate

prov´i•dence n. advance preparation; divine guidance

prov´ince n. an outlying area

pro•vin´cial adj. crude or unsophisticated

pro•vi´sion n. supplies; a requirement —vt. to supply

pro•vi´sion•al adj. temporary

pro•vi´so n. a stipulation

pro•voke´ vt. induce, as to action or anger —**pro•voca´tion** n. —**pro•voc´a•tive** adj.

prow´ess n. skill or daring

prowl vt., vi. move stealthily

prox•im´i•ty n. nearness

prox´y n. an agent; authority to act as agent

prudence n. caution in the conduct of one's business

pru´ri•ent adj. overly interested in sexual matters

pry vi. snoop —vt. force open —n. a lever or bar for prying

pseu•do•nym n. an alias

psy´che n. the subconscious mind, the soul

psych•e•del´ic adj. marked by hallucination —n. a substance that alters awareness

pay•chi•a•try n. diagnosis and treatment of mental disorders —**psy•chi´a•trist** n.

psy´chic adj. mental; of exceptional mental processes —n a spiritualist

psy•cho•log´i•cal adj. of the mind or emotions

psy•cho•path´ic adj. antisocial, aggressive, or perverted

psy•cho•ther´a•py n. treatment for a mental or emotional disorder

pub n. a public house, a tavern

pub´lic adj common or shared, of a community

publication n. printed material; communication

public house (Brit.) a tavern

pub•lic´i•ty n. information of

a promotional nature

pu´er•ile adj. childish or juvenile

puff´er•y n. exaggerated praise; promotion

pu´gi•lism n. the sport of boxing —**pu´gi•list** n.

pug•na´cious adj. belligerent

pul´chri•tude n. great beauty

pule vi. to whine or whimper

pull n. allure; influence —vt. draw toward; tug; attract — vi. use force in hauling

pul´ley n. a simple machine

pul´sate vi. vibrate rhythmically —**pul•sa´tion** n.

pulse n. a rhythmic beating

pul´ver•ize vt. crush; reduce to powder

pump n. a device for moving liquid —vi., vt. move with a pump; move up and down

pun n. a play on words —vi.

punch n. a piercing tool; a fruit beverage —vt. strike

punc•til´i•ous adj. attentive to detail; precise

punc´tu•al adj. on time, prompt —**punc•tu•al´i•ty** n.

punc•tu•a´tion n. written marks to indicate pauses, separations, etc

punc´ture vt. to pierce —n a hole

pun´dit n. a critic or scholar

pun´gent adj. sharp or biting

pun´ish vt. penalize

pup´pet n. a figure moved by strings, hands, etc.; one controlled by another

pur´chase n. a thing bought —vt. to buy —**pur´chas•er** n.

pure adj. free of pollutants; without fault —**pu´ri•ty** n.

pu•rée´ n. a smooth paste — vt. reduce to a smooth paste

pur´ga•tive adj. tending to cleanse —n. a medication for

purging bowels: a laxative — **pur·ga´tion** n.

purge vt. cleanse or purify; rid of impurities —n. act of purification; action to rid of undesirable elements

pu·ri·fi·ca´tion n. an act of cleansing

pu´ri·fy vt. free of impurities or defilement —**pu´ri·fi·er** n.

pur·loin´ vi., vt. steal

pur·port´ vt. claim or have intention —**pur·port´ed** adj.

pur´pose n. aim; an Intention

pur´pose·ful adj. having intent —**pur´pose·ful·ly** adv.

purse n. (Brit.) a small tote used by women for currency, etc.; (US) a woman's handbag; award of money— vt. to gather in small folds

pur·sue´ vt. chase or hunt; aspire or strive for — **pur·suit´** n.

pur´view n. extent of ability, authority, etc.; range of understanding

push vt., vi. apply force to press —n. energy; drive

put vt. to place; cause to be placed —vi. to proceed

pu´ta·tive adj. supposed

pu·tre·fac´tion n. decomposed organic matter

pu´trid adj. decaying; corrupt; vile or offensive

put´ter n. a golf club —vt. poke about —vi. waste time

puz´zle n. a mystery —vt. baffle or bewilder

pyre n. a formation of material for burning a dead body

q. Q seventeenth letter of the alphabet

quad·ran·gle n. a plane figure with four sides; an area enclosed by buildings

quad´rant n. a 90° arc; one fourth of a circle

quaff vt., vi. to drink

quag´mire n. a slough or swamp; a difficult situation

quaint adj. curious or uncommon; picturesque

quake n. an earthquake —vi. to tremble or shake

qual´i·fied adj. capable; limited: a qualified success

qual´i·fy vi., vt. to be eligible; describe; limit

qual´i·ty n. a characteristic or trait, excellence

qualm n. uncertainty

quan´da·ry n. a dilemma

quan´ti·ty n. an amount; a considerable volume

quar·an·tine n. isolation, esp. to prevent spread of disease —vt. place in isolation

quar´rel n. disagreement; an argument —vi.

quar´ry n. something pursued; an excavation —vt. to dig up, as stone

quar´ter n. one-fourth —vt. divide into four; furnish lodging

quash vt. to suppress

qua´ver vi. to tremble

quea´sy adj. nauseated, uneasy or troubled

queer adj. strange, unusual; unconventional

quell vt. suppress; ease, calm

quench vt. extinguish; drench

quer´u·lous adj. complaining; peevish; disgruntled

quer´y n. a question or inquiry —vt. to question

quest n. search; journey of exploration —vi.

ques´tion n. inquiry; that open to discussion —vi., vt. interrogate; doubt; challenge

queue n. a waiting line

quib´ble n. a petty argument —vi. fret over trivial matters

quick adj. swift and abrupt; alert, intelligent —**quick´en** vi., vt.

qui•es•cent adj. still; inactive

qui´et adj. silent; calm; tranquil —vi., vt. to make or become still; make serene

quin•tes´sence n. essential quality

quip n. witty remark

quirk n. an idiosyncrasy

quit vi., vt. resign or relinquish; discontinue; to leave

quite adv. totally; absolutely; to a great extent: quite nice

quiv´er n. vibration —vi. shudder or tremble

quix•ot´ic adj. Idealistic

quiz n. a short test —vt. to question —**quiz´zi•cal** adj.

quote vt. repeat another's words; cite; state a price

quo•tid´i•an adj. commonplace; daily

r, R eighteenth letter of the alphabet

rab´bi n. a Jewish scholar

rab´ble n. unruly mob; riffraff

rab´id adj. fanatical; frenzied

race[1] n. people linked by appearance, location, etc.

race[2] n. a contest of speed; a rivalry —vi. take part in a race; proceed at great speed

rack n. framework for holding, etc.; an instrument of torture; a cut of meat —vt. cause severe distress

rac•on´teur n. a storyteller

rac´y adj. spirited; risque or suggestive; lewd

ra´di•ant adj. emitting heat or light; bright, glowing

ra´di•ate vi., vt. extend from a central point; emit

rad´i•cal adj. deviating; extreme -n. an advocate of extreme change

ra•di•ol´o•gy n. use of radioactive materials to diagnose and treat disease

raf´ter n. a supporting beam

rage n. violent anger; passion —vi. to speak or act violently

rag´ged adj. tattered; worn or frayed; rough or uneven

rag´time n. an American music form

raid n. an unexpected assault —vi., vt. invade —**raid´er** n.

rai´ment n. clothing

raise vt. move or make higher; increase; build —**rais´er** n.

rai´ly n. an assemblage —vi. assemble; recover

ram´ble n. leisurely stroll —vi. wander aimlessly

ram•i•fi•ca´tion n. a consequence

ramp re a sloping surface

ram´pant adj. uncontrolled; without restraint

ran´cid adj. stale or tainted

ran´cor n. harsh resentment; animosity —**ran´cor•ous** adj.

ran´dom adj. lacking order; haphazard

rand´y adj. lascivious

range n. reach or scope; area or extent; a limit —vi. wander; vary within limits

rank adj. of an offensive odor; utter or complete: rank amateur —n. station or position —vt. arrange in position

ran´kle vt. to irritate

ran´sack vt. to search or seek aggressively

rant vi., vt. speak wildly or incoherently —**rant´er** n.

ra•pa´cious adj. avaricious or greedy; ravenous

rap´id adj. swift; occurring

with unusual speed — **ra·pid´i·ty** n.

rap·port´ n. understanding

rapt adj. enthralled or engrossed; spellbound

rap´ture n. joy, ecstasy —**rap´tur·ous** adj.

rare adj. uncommon, unusual; excellent, incomparable —**rar´i·ty** n.

rash adj. impulsive or impetuous; reckless

rasp n. a coarse file; a harsh sound —vt., vt. abrade; speak in a hoarse voice

rate n. relative value; charge per unit —vt. set a value on

rath´er adv. preferably; to some extent; more accurately

rat´i·fy vt. approve; sanction

rat´io n. a proportion

ra´tion n. an assigned measure —vt. allot or distribute

ra´tio·nal adj. sane; able to reason —**ra´tio·nal·ize** vt.

ra´tio·nale´ n. grounds for reasoning; interpretation

rau´cous adj. loud and rowdy; boisterous

rav´age vi., vt. destroy

rave vi., vt. babble incoherently; to praise

rav´en·ous adj. hungry; insatiable; greedy

raw adj. not processed; inexperienced; exposed

reach n. extent or range—vi., vt. extend to; arrive

re·act´ vi. to respond or reply

re·ac´tion·ar·y adj. in opposition to progress

read vi., vt. study and understand —**read´a·ble** adj.

read´y adj. prepared and available; eager

re´al adj. genuine; not imaginary

re´al·is´tic adj. practical; truly representative

re´al·ize vt. recognize as true; make true

re´al·ly adv. truly; exceptionally

realm n. one's domain

re´al·ty n, real estate

reap vi., vt harvest; to gain

rea´son n. an explanation; intellect; a cause to believe — vi., vt consider logically; persuade by logic

rea´son·a·ble adj. able to reason; governed by reason

re·as·sure´ at. encourage; restore confidence

rebel n. one who defies authority —**re·bel´** vt. to resist authority

re·bel´lion n. show of defiance

re·buke´ n. a reprimand —vt.

re·cal´ci·trant adj. stubbornly defiant —**re·cal´ci·trance** n.

re·cant´ vt. retract or disavow

re·ca·pit´u·late vt. summarize

re·cede´ vi. move back

re·ceiv´a·ble adj. unpaid —n. an outstanding account

re·ceive´ vt. get, take possession of; experience or undergo; make welcome

re´cent adj. at a time just earlier than now

re·cep´ta·cle n. a container

re·cep´tion n. a greeting; a social gathering; acceptance

re·cep´tive adj. able or willing to receive; open-minded

re´cess n. a hollow; intermission —vi. take a break

re·ces´sion n. a receding; an economic downturn

re·cid´i·vism n. reversion to earlier conduct

re·cip´i·ent n. receiver

re·cip´ro·cal adj. complementary; interdependent

re•cip´ro•cate *vi.*, *vt.* give or take in return; move back and forth

re•cit´al *n.* a public performance; a detailed chronicling

re•cite´ *vt.* repeat a memorized text; recount in detail

reck´less *adj.* rash; heedless of consequences

reck´on *vt.* calculate, consider

rec´luse *n.* one in seclusion

rec´og•nize *vt.* distinguish; identify; acknowledge

re•coil´ *vi.* draw back

rec•ol•lect´ *vi.*, *vt.* remember

rec•om•mend´ *vt.* endorse

rec´om•pense *n.* compensation —*vt.* to repay

rec´on•cile *vt.* resolve differences —**rec´on•cil•a•ble** *adj.*

rec´ord *n.* document, registry, etc.; information —**re•cord´** *vt.* set down information

re•coup´ *vt.* regain

re•cov´er *vt.* regain; return to a former state

rec•re•a´tion *n.* diversion or amusement

re•crim•i•na´tion *n.* countering one charge with another

rec´ti•fy *vt.* to correct

rec´ti•tude *n.* righteousness

re•cum´bent *adj.* reclining

re•cu´per•ate *vt.*, *vi.* recover from illness or adversity

re•cuse´ *vt.* seek disqualification

red´o•lent *adj.* suggesting or reminiscent. —**red´o•lence** *n.*

re•doubt´a•ble *adj.* formidable; awe-inspiring

re•duce´ *vt.* diminish or decrease —**re•duc´tion** *n.*

re•dun´dant *adj.* superfluous; unnecessary

reel *n.* device for flexible material, as tape or rope; (*Brit.*) a device to hold cotton or thread; a lively dance —*vt.* wind —*vi.* lurch or stagger

re•fer´ *vt.* direct to; assign or attribute to —*vi.* mention; make reference

ref´eren´dum *n.* submission to popular vote

re•fine´ *vt.*, *vi.* make or become pure; rid of unsuitable elements; make or become more elegant or polished

re•flect´ *vt.* mirror; cast an image —*vi.* ponder

re•flec´tive *adj.* given to deep thought

re´flex *adj.* instinctive —*n.* involuntary response

re•form´ *adj.* advocating change —*n.* correction or improvement —*vt.* correct or improve —**re•form´er** *n.*

re•frain´ *vi.* abstain; hold back from

re•fresh´ *vt.* revive or restore

ref´uge *n.* place of safety or shelter

re•ful´gent *adj.* radiant; glorious —**re•ful´gence** *n.*

re•fur´bish *vt.* to restore or renovate

re•fuse´ *vt.*, *vi.* decline or deny —**ref´use** *n.* trash, waste

re•fute´ *vt.* disprove; contradict —**ref•u•ta´tion** *n.*

re´gal *adj.* befitting royalty; stately; splendid

re•gale´ *vt.* entertain lavishly

re•ga´lia *n.* trappings of royalty; impressive array

re•gard´ *n.* respect or admiration; heed —*vt.* admire; observe carefully; deem to be —*vi.* heed; gaze

re•gime´ *n.* a government, management, order, etc.

reg•is•tra´tion *n.* official recording —**reg´is•try** *n.*

re•gress´ *vi.* move backward;

degenerate —**re•gres´sion** n.

re•gret´ n. sorrow or remorse —vt. feel remorse

reg´u•lar adj. normal or usual; methodical; periodic; conforming to expectations

reg u•late vt. control, or direct; adjust

re•ha•bil´i•tate vt. restore to health

re•hearse´ vt. to practice

re•im•burse´ vt. pay back

re•it´er•ate vt. repeat

re•ject n. that discarded —**re•ject´** vt. refuse; discard

re•join´der n. a response

re•ju´ve•nate vt. refresh and revitalize

re•late´ vt. recount or describe; connect or associate

rel´a•tive adj. connected or affiliated; comparable —n. a family member

re•lax´ vi., vt. ease tension; make less intense

re´lay, re•lay´ vt. transmit; send forward

re•lease´ n. liberation; a catch —vt. set free; publish

rel´e•gate vt. assign, as a task or position

re•lent´ vi. surrender; soften

rel´e•vant adj. pertinent to the matter at hand

re•li´a•ble adj. dependable

re•li´ance n. confidence or trust —**re•li´ant** adj.

rel´ic n. an artifact; a thing of historical value

re•lief´ n. aid or assistance; alleviation from distress, etc.

re•li´gion n. a system of belief; order of worship

re•lin´quish vt. give up

re•luc´tant adj. hesitant or unwilling —**re•luc´tance** n.

re•ly´ vi. trust completely; depend on for help or support

re•main´ vi. continue unchanged; to stay

re•mark´ n. a comment —vt. comment briefly; to notice

re•mark´a•ble adj. noteworthy; striking or exceptional

re•me´di•al adj. intended to correct

rem´e•dy n. something that corrects —vt. make right

re•mem´ber vt. keep in the mind; retain —vt. recall

rem•i•nisce´ vi. dwell on the past —**rem•i•nis´cent** adj.

re•miss´ adj. negligent or careless

re•mis´sion n. a lessening

re•mit´ vt. transfer for deposit or payment

rem´nant n. a scrap; a trace or indication

re•mon´strate vi. protest —vt. argue against

re•morse´ n. repentance; sorrow for misconduct

re•mote´ adj. distant; secluded

re•move´ vt. take away —vi. relocate —**re•mov´a•ble** adj.

re•mu´ner•ate vt. compensate

ren´ais•sance n. revival or rebirth

rend vt. tear apart

ren´der vt. provide for payment or approval; depict by drawing; express by performing —**ren´der•ing** n.

ren´dez•vous n. a meeting —vi., vt. to meet at a specific place and time

ren•di´tion n. performance or interpretation, as of music

ren´e•gade n. rebel; traitor, defector

re•nege´ vi. fail to honor a commitment —**re•neg´er** n.

re•new´ vt. restore; make new; reaffirm or extend

re•nounce´ *vt.* repudiate or deny; forsake, as a right

re•nowned´ *adj.* celebrated; distinguished —**re•nown´** *n.*

rent *n.* payment. for occupancy or use —*vi.* hire out —*vt.* grant or gain use for payment —**rent´al** *n.*

re•pair´ *vt.* restore to useable condition; rectify, make up for —*n.* an assessment of condition; *in good repair*

rep•a•ra´tion *n.* compensation for loss; atonement

re•pay´ *vt.* reimburse, pay back; refund

re•peal´ *vt.* revoke, as a law

re•peat´ *vt.*, *vi.* say or do again

re•pel´ *vt.* repulse or ward off; disgust or offend

re•pent´ *vi.*, *vt.* feel remorse or regret; to change

re•per•cus´sion *n.* backlash; unexpected consequence

rep´er•toire *n.* works adopted by a performer or group of performers

rep•e•ti´tion *n.* reiteration; process of repeating

re•place´ *vt.* put back; substitute or supplant; return or restore

re•plete´ *adj.* abundant; lavish

rep´li•ca *n.* a copy

rep´li•cate *vt.* duplicate, as an experiment; make copies

re•ply´ *n.* a response —*vi.* give an answer; respond

re•port´ *n.* an account; a rumor —*vt.* inform; present an account of

re•pose´ *n.* sleep; calm; peacefulness —*vi.* lie prone

re•pos´i•to•ry *n.* place for safekeeping; a container

re•pos•sess´ *vt.* reclaim

rep•re•hen´si•ble *adj.* deserving blame; wicked

rep•re•sent´ *vt.* present a likeness of; stand in place of

rep•re•sent´a•tive *adj.* typical; characteristic —*n.* an example; an agent or delegate

re•press´ *vt.* restrain, control; quell, curb

re•prieve´ *n.* relief; deferment or repeal of punishment —*vi.* to suspend temporarily

rep´ri•nand *n.* censure; condemnation —*vt.* admonish or censure

re•pri´sal *n.* retaliation

re•proach´ *n.* condemnation; disgrace —*vt.* criticize or rebuke —**re•proach´ful** *adj.*

rep´ro•bate *adj.* perverted —*n.* an immoral person

re´pro•duce´ *vt.* copy or duplicate; propagate

re•proof´ *n.* disapproval

re•prove´ *vt.* criticize; admonish —**re•prov´al** *n.*

re•pub´lic *n.* government controlled by citizens or their representatives

re•pu´di•ate *vt.* reject or disavow; disown

re•pug´nant *adj.* offensive; revolting —**re•pug´nance** *n.*

re•pulse´ *vt.* fend off or repel; spurn by insolence or indifference —**re•pul´sive** *adj.*

rep•u•ta´tion *n.* one's standing; the way in which one is regarded by others; prominence or notoriety

re•quest´ *n.* entreaty; something desired —*vt.* express a desire for

re•quire´ *vt.* need; demand or request —**require´ment** *n.*

req´ui•site *adj.* required —*n.* that necessary or obligatory

re•quite´ *vt.* compensate;

repay; return in kind

re•scind´ *vt.* repeal; nullify

res´cue *vt.* liberate; set free

re•search´ *n.* scientific examination; deliberate study

re•sem´blance *n.* similarity

re•sent´ *vt.* take offense, as at insult or slight

re•serve´ *n.* restraint; caution; a thing set aside —*vt.* set aside —**re•serv´ed** *adj.*

res´er•voir *n.* a reserve supply

re•side´ *vi.* inhabit; live in

res´i•dence *n.* one's home

res´i•due *n.* remainder

re•sign´ *vt.* renounce, give up; accept as unavoidable

re•sign´ed *adj.* complacent; submissive

re•sil´ience, re•sil´ien•cy *n.* flexibility —**re•sil´ient** *adj.*

re•sist´ *vt.* defy or oppose; withstand

re•sis´tance *n.* force that hinders or opposes; capacity to ward off harm

res´o•lute *adj.* determined

res•o•lu´tion *n.* determination; outcome; a formal pronouncement; visual clarity

re•solve´ *n.* sense of purpose; determination —*vt.* decide; solve; end successfully

res´o•nant *adj.* vibrant; loud

re•sort´ *n.* a vacation retreat; a resource —*vt.* fall back on

re•sound´ *vi.* echo; reverberate

re´source *n.* that available for use, as equipment or property

re•source´ful *adj.* clever or imaginative

re•spect´ *n.* esteem or admiration; consideration; a feature or detail —*vt.* admire

re•spect´a•ble *adj.* worthy of esteem; conventional

re•spec´tive *adj.* specific or distinct

res•pi•ra´tion *n.* breathing

res´pite *n.* a short rest

re•splen´dent *adj.* brilliant, sparkling

re•spond´ *vi.* answer; react

re•sponse´ *n.* reply or reaction

re•spon´si•ble *adj.* accountable; capable of acting alone

re•spon´sive *adj.* tending to respond or react

rest *n.* relaxation; pause; remainder —*vi., vt.* relax; lie against or on —**rest´ful** *adj.*

res´tau•rant *n.* a public eating place —**res•tau•ra•teur´** *n.*

res•ti•tu´tion *n.* restoration; compensation

res´tive *adj.* impatient

rest´less *adj.* uneasy; impatient —**restlessness** *n.*

re•stor´a•tive *adj.* having power to restore; corrective —*n.* medication for health or well-being: a tonic

re•store´ *vt.* return to former condition, position, etc.; make amends

re•strain´ *vt.* check, hold back; confine

re•strict´ *vt.* limit —**re•stric´tive** *adj.*

re•sult´ *n.* an effect —*vi.* follow as an outcome

re•sume´ *vt.* begin again

ré´su•mé *n.* (*Brit.*) a summing up; (*US*), description of one's qualifications for employment

re•sur´gence *n.* renewal or reawakening

res•ur•rect´ *vt.* restore or revive

re•sus´ci•tate *vt., vi.* revive

re•tain´ *vt.* keep possession; remember; hire for a fee

re•tain´er *n.* a fee paid to

engage or reserve services; a servant

re•tal´iate *vi.*, *vt.* repay in kind; avenge

re•tard´ *n.* a slowing —*vt.* impede the course of

re•ten´tion *n.* memory; ability to keep and hold

ret´i•cent *adj.* restrained or reserved; hesitant

ret´i•nue *n.* followers

re•tire´ *vi.*, *vt.* withdraw or be removed, as from an occupation, or at the end of a day

re•tir´ing *adj.* withdrawn

re•tort´ *n.* a sharp reply —*vt.*, *vi.* to respond

re•tract´ *vt.*, *vi.* take back, as a claim —**re•trac´tion** *n.*

ret•ri•bu´tion *n.* compensation; reward or punishment

re•trieve´ *vt.* regain

ret•ro•ac´tive *adj.* applying to a prior period

ret´ro•grade *adj.* opposite; regressing to a prior state

ret´ro•gress *vi.* revert to an earlier state

ret´ro•spect *n.* reflection of things past, a look back

re•turn´ *adj.* of a coming back —*n.* that brought or sent bark; a prolit —*vi.*, *vt.* go or send back; yield, as profit; revert to a former owner

re•un´ion *n.* a gathering of former members

re•vamp´ *vt.* reorganize or renovate

re•veal´ *vt.* expose; disclose

rev´el *vi.* delight in; carouse —*n.* celebration

rev•e•la´tion *n.* a thing revealed; sudden inspiration

re•venge´ *n.* reprisal or retribution —*vt.* retaliate

rev´e•nue *n.* income; receipts

re•ver´ber•ate *vt.* resound or

echo repeatedly

re•vere´ *vt.* regard with awe; venerate —**rev´er•ence** *n.*

rev´er•ie *n.* idle contemplation; daydreaming

re•verse´ *adj.* backward; opposite an opposite side, condition, etc.; misfortune —*vt.* change to the opposite

re•vert´ *vi.* return to previous condition —**re•ver´sion** *n.*

re•view´ *n.* reexamination; critique, criticism —*vt.* reconsider, restudy

re•vile´ *vt.* berate

re•vise´ *vt.* change or modify

re•vive´ *vt.*, *vi.* restore to consciousness or life; to bring hack into use

re•voke´ *vt.* nullify or repeal

re•vol´ *n.* rebellion —*vi.* oppose; rebel; disgust

rev•o•lu´tion *n.* rotation; radical change

re•volve´ *vi.* rotate; turn on an axis

re•vue´ *n.* a musical comedy show

re•vul´sion *n.* sudden aversion or abhorrence

reward´ *n.* compensation —*vt.* recompense

rhap´so•dy *n.* state of ecstasy; excessive enthusiasm; an elegant literary or musical work

rhet´o•ric *n.* effective speaking or writing; pretentious, vacuous speech

rhyme *n.* verse with lines ending in similar sounds

rhythm *n.* regular cadence or accent; harmonious pattern

rib´ald *adj.* of vulgar humor

rib´bon *n.* a thin strip for tying, decoration, etc.

rich *adj.* wealthy; plentiful; elegant or lavish —**rich´es** *n.*

rick′et•y adj. wobbly

rid vt. release or free from

rid′dle n. a puzzle —vt. to perforate

ride vi. be conveyed; transported: riding on a cloud — **rid′er** n.

rid′i•cule n. that intended to mock; derision —vt. make fun of —**ri•dic′u•lous** adj.

rife adj. abundant

ri′fle n. a firearm —vt. search through; plunder

rift n. a fracture or tear

right adj. fitting and proper; equitable; accurate; lawful —adv. exactly, quite —n. that which is proper; privilege —vt. correct

right′eous adj. moral; virtuous —**righ′teous•ness** n.

rig′id adj. stiff; inflexible

rig′or (US), **rig′our** (Brit.) n. harshness; hardship

rile vt. anger; irritate or vex

rim n. border or edge

ring n. a circular object, area, shape, etc.; a group or gang

rinse n. liquid used rn washing, etc. at. to wash lightly

ri′ot n. public disturbance by a large group; an eruption, as of revelry —vi.

ripe adj. mature; fully developed —**rip′en** vt., vi.

rip′ple n. a small wave or wave-like motion —vi.

rise vi. move upward; increase, as in price, get up, as from a chair; emerge or originate

risk n. possible hazard; probability for loss —**risk′y** adj.

ris•qué′ adj. lewd; suggestive

rite n. a ritual or ceremony

rit′u•al n. observance; formality; an orderly procedure —adj. —**rit′u•al•is′tic** adj.

ri′val n. one in competition — vt. equal or exceed —adj. competing

riv′er n. a large body of naturally flowing water; an abundant flow

riv′et n. a metal fastener —vt. join with a rivet; fasten firmly; attract and hold attention —**riv′et•er** n.

roam vt., vi. wander or move about

roar n. a deep, prolonged cry; a burst of laughter —vt., vi.

roast vt. cook with dry heat; subject to excessive heat; deride —n. (US) a cut of meat; derision —adj.

robe n. a loose flowing garment; a dressing gown

ro′bot n. a device programmed to perform tasks; one who functions mechanically —**ro•bot′ic** adj.

ro•bot′ics n. the study or creation of robots

ro•bust′ adj. strong and healthy

rock n. a hard formation; firm support —vi., vt. wobble or sway —**rock′y** adj.

ro•co′co n. an ornate style

rod n. a thin straight shaft

rogue n. a scoundrel; a mischievous person; an abnormal plant or animal

roil vt. to disturb or stir up

role n. part for an actor; expected behavior

roll n. a cylinder; small baked bread; a registry; rocking motion —vi., vt. move by turning; suggest movement

rol′lick′ing adj. playful; boisterous

ro•mance′ n. passionate fondness; fascination; fantasy or fictional account

ro•man´tic *adj.* marked by infatuation, idealism, etc.; visionary; impractical —*n.*

romp *vi.* frolic or play —*n.* noisy frolic; an easy victory

room *n.* adequate space; an area within a structure —*vi.* to lodge —**room´y** *adj.*

root *n.* base of a plant; a base, source, or core; mental or emotional attachment

ros´ter *n.* a list

ros´trum *n.* speaker's platform

rot *n.* decomposition; silliness —*vi.* decay or disintegrate

ro´tate *vt., vi.* revolve; proceed by turns —**ro•ta´tion** *n.*

rote *n.* learning by repetition

rough *adj.* coarse or irregular; crude or impolite; difficult; disorderly —**rough´en** *vt.*

round *adj.* curved; of a curved shape; full-toned; approximate

rouse *vt., vt.* awaken; excite to action

rout *n.* defeat; disorderly light —*vt.* defeat or put to flight

route *n.* road or course; an itinerary —*vt.* direct by a certain course

rou•tine´ *adj.* usual or customary —*n.* a regular prpcedure.

row *n.* a continuous line; a disturbance —*vt.*

row´dy *adj.* clamorous; disorderly —*n.* a ruffian

rub *vi., vt.* stroke —*n.* a pitfall

rub´bish *n.* trash; nonense

rub´ble *n.* stone fragments

rub´down *n.* a massage

rude *adj.* ill-mannered; unrefined; crude, primitive

ru´di•ment *n.* a basic component —**ru•di•men´ta•ry** *adj.*

ruf´fle *n.* frilled trim —*vi.* rumple or wrinkle; irritate or annoy

rug´ged *adj.* sturdy; strong; tempestuous

ru´in *n.* total destruction —*vt.* destroy utterly

rule *n.* governing authority; regulation; generally accepted condition or course of action —*vi., vt.* direct and control; judge or decree

rum´ble *n.* a deep undulating sound —*vi.* —**rum´bly** *adj.*

ru´mi•nate *vi., vt.* ponder; consider intently

ru´mor *n.* gossip; unconfirmed news

rum´ple *vt.* wrinkle

run *n.* an indefinite period: *run of a play* —*vi.* move swiftly; operate; to flow, as liquid from a container; extend —**run´ning** *adj., n.*

rup´ture *n.* break —*vt., vi.* break apart

ru´ral *adj.* of the country

ruse *n.* a ploy or stratagem

rush *n.* abrupt motion; haste; a swell of emotion —*vi.* move quickly

rus´tic *adj.* rural; unsophisticated

rut *n.* a groove worn into a path or roadway

ruth´less *adj.* lacking pity or compassion

s, S nineteenth letter of the alphabet

sab•bat´i•cal *n.* a leave of absence

sa•bot´ *n.* a wooden shoe

sab´o•tage *n.* action to obstruct or defeat an enemy —*vi., vt.* —**sab´o•teur** *n.*

sa•chet´ *n.* a small perfumed parcel

sack *n.* a bag; dismissal from

a job —*vt.* plunder; dismiss

sac´ra•ment *n.* a religious rite

sa´cred *adj.* deserving of reverence or respect

sac´ri•fice *n.* an offering —*vt.* give up something of value

sac´ri•lege *n.* desecration or disrespect of that considered sacred —**sac•ri•le´gious** *adj.*

sac´ro•sanct *adj.* sacred or hallowed

sad *adj.* unhappy; sorrowful; downhearted; somber; dire, unfortunate

sa•fa´ri *n.* a journey

safe *adj.* free from risk or danger —*n.* a repository

sag *vi.* droop or slump

sa•ga´cious *adj.* discerning; wise —**sa•gac´i•ty** *n.*

sage *adj.* wise and discerning

sake *n.* reason or purpose; advantage or self-interest

sa•la´cious *adj.* arousing desire; lascivious

sal´a•ry *n.* fixed wages

sale *n.* exchange of goods or services for money

sa•li´ent *adj.* important or conspicuous; protruding

sa´line *adj.* consisting or or characteristic of salt; salty

sal´low *adj.* of a sickly or pasty complexion

sal´ly *n.* a sudden assault; an excursion; a witty remark —*vi.* rush out suddenly or energetically

sa•lon´ *n.* a large room or gallery; a fashionable gathering

sa•lu´bri•ous *adj.* healthy or wholesome

sal´u•tary *adj.* beneficial

sal•u•ta´tion *n.* a greeting

sa•lute´ *n.* a greeting; a gesture of welcome or honor —*vt.* greet

sal´vage *n.* property saved

from destruction —*vt.* retrieve for future use

salve *n.* ointment —*vt.* alleviate or remedy

same *adj.* identical

sam´ple *n.* a representative part; an example —*vt.* test

san•a•tar´i•um, san•a•to´ri•um *n.* a hospital or retreat

sanc•ti•mo´ni•ous *adj.* pretentiously pious

sanc´tion *n.* authorization; permission; penalty for nonconformity —*vt.* approve; punish for violation

sanc´tu•ar•y *n.* a sacred place; an asylum

sane *adj.* of sound mind

san´guine *adj.* optimistic; confident; red or ruddy

san•i•tar´i•um *n.* sanatorium

san´i•tar•y *adj.* uncontaminated; free of germs

san•i•ta´tion *n.* sanitary conditions; a local agency responsible for trash removal

san´i•ty *n.* soundness of mind

sap´i•ent *adj.* wise

sar´casm *n.* a caustic rejoinder —**sar•cas´tic** *adj.*

sar•coph´a•gus *n.* stone coffin

sar•don´ic *adj.* sarcastic

sar•to´ri•al *adj.* of a clothier or clothing

sash *n.* a cloth band; window frame

sas´sy *adj.* insolent, disrespectful; spirited, jaunty

sa•tan´ic *adj.* wicked; diabolic

sate *vt.* satiate

sat´el•lite *n.* an orbiting body; a dependency

sa´ti•ate *vt.* satisfy completely

sat´ire *n.* literary work using mockery or ridicule

sat•is•fac´tion *n.* gratification; fulfillment of obligation

sat´is•fy *vt.* fulfill a desire or

promise; convince or persuade; pacify —*vi.* be sufficient —**sat'is•fied** *adj.*

sa'trap *n.* a petty official

sat'u•rate *vt.* soak or fill completely —**sat•u•ra'tion** *n.*

sa'tyr *n.* a mythical creature, part man and part goat

sauce *n.* a seasoned liquid or condiment

sau'cy *adj.* impudent; pert

saunt'er *vi.* stroll leisurely

sav'age *adj.* uncivilized; vicious, ferocious —*n.* a rude or unruly person —*vt.* attack

save *vt.* rescue from danger or destruction; set aside for the future; conserve

sa'vor *n.* characteristic flavor or quality —*vt.* season; taste; relish, enjoy

say *vt.* speak; express in words; allege —*vi.* to speak

scab'rous *adj.* roughened; difficult to handle; salacious

scaf'fold *n.* a raised platform; a temporary structure

scal'a•wag *n.* a worthless person; a rascal

scald *vt.*, *vi.* to burn; clean with hot liquid or steam —*n.*

scale *vt.*, *vi.* ascend; climb

scal'lop *n.* a hinged-shell mollusk; ornamental edging

scalp *n.* skin of the head —*vt.* resell tickets for profit

scal'pel *n.* a surgical knife

scamp *n.* rogue or rascal; scalawag; an impish child

scam'per *vi.* run quickly

scan *vt.* examine closely; glance at

scan'dal *n.* injury to one's reputation; malicious gossip

scan'dal•ize *vt.* shock; outrage morally

scant *adj.* meager; less than

scant'y *adj.* insufficient; less

than necessary

scar *n.* mark left after healing

scarce *adj.* rare, unusual; insufficient —**scar'ci•ty** *n.*

scare *vt.* frighten —**scar'y** *adj.*

scarp *n.* a steep slope

scathe *vt.* criticize severely; denounce —**scath'ing** *adj.*

scat'ter *vt.* throw about; disperse —*vi.* separate

scav'enge *vt.* forage; scrounge

scene *n.* a locality or area; setting for a drama

sce'nic *adj.* of a beautiful natural vista

scent *n.* an odor or aroma; a fragrance —**scent'ed** *adj.*

scep'ter *n.* a staff of authority

sched'ule *n.* (*US*) timetable; (*Brit.*) a list of appointments, social activities, etc.; a detailed plan —*vt.* plan for a specified time

sche•mat'ic *n.* a diagram

scheme *n.* a plan or program; a plot —*vt.*, *vi.* plan or plot

schism *n.* division

schol'ar *n.* a learned person; an authority

schol'ar•ship *n.* learning; aid to a student

school *n.* an educational institution; a congregation of fish —*vi.* come together in a school —**scho•las'tic** *adj.*

school'ing *n.* formal education; classroom instruction

sci'ence *n.* knowledge from observation and experiment

scin•til'la *n.* a trace

scin'til•late *vi.* be witty

sci'on *n.* a descendant

scoff *vi.* address scornfully

scold *vt.*, *vi.* find fault; nag

sconce *n.* ornamental bracket

scope *n.* range of view

scorch *vt.* burn slightly —*n.* the mark of a burn

score n. points in a game or test; written music; a group of 20

scorn n. contempt —vt. treat with contempt

scoun´drel n. unscrupulous person; a villain

scour vt. clean thoroughly; brighten by rubbing

scourge n. a whip; severe punishment; a cause of suffering —vt. flog; punish

scout n. one sent ahead for information —vt. spy on

scowl n. a gloomy aspect —vi. wrinkle the brow; look threatening or angry

scrag´gly adj. uneven

scram´ble vi. move in a disorderly manner —vt. mix hurriedly or haphazardly —n. a struggle

scrap n. a fragment; a quarrel —vt. discard —vi. quarrel — adj. waste; fragmentary

scrape vt. rub so as to abrade; gather with effort —n. act, effect, or noise of scraping; a difficult situation; a fight

scratch vt. to mark; scrape lightly; write hurriedly; cancel or withdraw, as an entry —vi. manage with difficulty —n. a mark or sound of scraping —adj. hasty or haphazard —**scratch´y** adj.

scrawl n. irregular or illegible writing —vt., vi. write hastily

scrawn´y adj. lean and bony

scream n. a piercing cry —vt., vi. to cry out —**scream´er** n.

screech n. a shrill sound

screed n. prolonged tirade; harangue

screen n. a light partition; fine mesh; that conceals or protects; a panel for projecting images —vt. conceal; sift; classify

scrib´ble vt. write hastily —n.

scribe n. a clerk; public writer

scrim n. a lightweight fabric

scrip n. writing; an instrument of entitlement

script n. cursive writing; text of a play —**script´er** n.

scrip´ture n. sacred writings

scriv´en•er n. scribe or notary

scroll n. a parchment roll

scrounge vt., vi. scavenge

scrub vt., vi. rub vigorously

scruff n. nape of the neck

scruff´y adj. shabby, seedy

scrump´tious adj. delicious; elegant

scru´ple n. reluctance fostered by disapproval

scru´ti•nize vt. examine carefully; observe

sculp´ture n. three-dimensional art —vt. to fashion

scur´ril•ous adj. grossly offensive; abusive

scur´ry vi. move hurriedly

scut´tle n. a covered opening —vt. wreck or destroy

sea n. great body of salt water; the ocean; anything vast

seal n. impression attesting to authenticity; a decorative stamp —vt. close securely or permanently —**seal´able** adj.

seam n. a visible joint

seam´y adj. unpleasant; depraved or base; squalid

sear vi. dry up or wither; to scorch —adj. withered

search vt. look for thoroughly; seek out —n. —**search´er** n.

sea´son n. a part of the year; time of special activity —vt. add spices, etc. to food; improve by aging

sea´son•a•ble adj. usual for the time; practical for the season —**sea´son•a•bly** adv.

seat n. a place to sit —vt. place in a sitting position; accommodate: *seat 30 people*; set firmly in a place

se•cede´ vt. formally withdraw

se•clude´ vt. set apart; isolate

sec´ond n. a unit of time; an angular measure; a formal attendant; thing of inferior quality —adj. of a brief time; next in order; of lesser value —vt. formally support

se´cret adj. kept hidden; esoteric; not revealed; mysterious —n. a mystery; that known to only a few

sec´re•tary n. an office worker; an official responsible for record keeping; head of a government department; a writing desk

se•crete´ vt. conceal; hide away; to form and release a substance —**se•cre´tion** n.

sec´tion n. a part —vt. divide into parts

sec´u•lar adj. worldly; temporal; not religious

se•cure´ adj. unlikely to be threatened; confident —vt. protect; make certain; obtain

se•cur´i•ty n. being secure; those responsible for protection; measures providing protection; a pledge

se•date´ adj. composed; dignified —vt. to calm

sed´a•tive n. medicine that serves to calm

sed´en•tary adj. inactive

sed´i•ment n. matter that settles in a liquid; material deposited by water, ice, etc.

se•di´tion n. resistance or action against lawful authority

se•duce´ vt. lead astray; tempt or entice into a wrong —

sed´u•lous adj. industrious

see vt. view with the eyes; perceive in the mind; encounter; be certain: *see that you go* —vi. exercise power of sight; comprehend; be attentive

seed n. ovule that produces a plant; origin; a small granular fruit —vt. plant; scatter; remove seeds from

seek vt. search or strive for

seem vi. appear to be

seem´ly adj. proper; decorous

seep vi. gradually diffuse; penetrate through

se´er n. a prophet

seethe vi. boil; be agitated

seg´ment n. a distinct part —vt., vi. cut or separate

seg´re•gate vt. isolate; separate —adj. set apart

se´gue vi. move smoothly from one element to another

seis•mol´o•gy n. the study of earthquakes and related phenomena —**seis´mic** adj. —**seis•mol´o•gist** n.

seize vt. grasp suddenly and forcefully; take possession; take immediate advantage

sel´dom adv. infrequently — adj. infrequent or rare

se•lect´ vt., vi. choose —adj. superior; careful in choosing

self n. distinct identity and individuality

self´ish adj. motivated by personal gain

sell vt. transfer property for a consideration —vi.

se•man´tics pl. n. study of structure, meaning, shift, etc. of speech forms; deliberate distortion of meaning

sem´blance n. likeness or resemblance; the barest trace

sem´i- prefix partly; exactly half; occurring twice in the period: *semiannual*

sen´ate *n.* a legislative body

send *vt.* transmit; cause or enable to go; drive or impel

se´nile *adj.* of old age

sen´ior *adj.* older in years, time of *service,* etc. —*n.* an elderly person; one advanced in rank, dignity, etc.

sen´sate *adj.* having physical sensation; perceived by the senses

sen•sa´tion *n.* stimulation; response to stimulation

sen•sa´tion•al *adj.* causing excitement

sense *n.* faculty to respond to stimuli; special capacity to appreciate; vague perception; power to reason —*vt.* perceive; become aware

sen´si•ble *adj.* having mental perception; perceptible — **sen•si•bil´i•ty** *n.*

sen´si•tive *adj.* acutely responsive to sensation or to others; appreciative of aesthetic or intellectual qualities; easily offended

sen´su•al *adj.* indulgent to the appetites or senses

sen´su•ous *adj.* appealing to the senses

sen´tence *n.* determination or judgement; a penalty; words that express a thought

sen´tient *adj.* possessing powers of perception

sen´ti•ment *n.* delicate sensibility; a complex of feelings

sen´ti•nel, sen´try *n.* a guard

sep´a•rate *vt.* set apart or divide —*vi.* become divided; draw apart —*adj.* distinct; detached —**sep•a•ra´tion** *n.*

sep´ul•cher *n.* a burial place

se´quel *n.* an ongoing narrative; a consequence

se´quence *n.* following in or der —**se•quen´tial** *adj.*

se•ques´ter *vt.* place apart or seclude; property held in custody pending a claim

ser´e•nade´ *n.* a love song —*vi., vt.* to sing, especially to one's love

se•rene´ *adj.* untroubled; tranquil —**se•ren´i•ty** *n.*

se´ries *n.* an arrangement of related things —**se´ri•al** *adj.*

se´ri•ous *adj.* thoughtful, sober; involving much work; of grave importance

ser´mon *n.* a lecture; a serious talk; a discourse

ser´pent *n.* a snake

ser´pen•tine *adj.* winding

ser´rate, ser´rat•ed *adj.* of a sawlike edge or structure

se´rum *n.* fluid constituent of blood; a fluid that confers immunity

ser´vant *n.* one employed to assist in domestic matters

serve *vi., vt.* work as a servant; be of service; satisfy a requirement; perform duties of an office

serv´ice *n.* an act or manner of serving; maintenance and repair; public worship —*vt.* maintain or repair —*adj.* of the act of serving; designated for those who serve

serv´ice•a•ble *adj.* useful; beneficial; durable

ser´vile *adj.* submissive; abject —**ser•vil´i•ty** *n.*

ses´sion *n.* a meeting

set *vt.* place; fix in place; bring to a specified condition; establish; mount a gem —*vi.* wane; solidify; begin —*n.* an allied group; things belonging together

set´tle *vt.* put in order; set to

rights; establish in place; calm.; sink; determine finally; pay a debt —vi. come to rest; sink gradually; become established; pay a bill

set´tle·ment n. an area newly colonized; an agreement or adjustment

sev´er vt. separate; break off —vi.break or come apart

sev´eral adj. a few; individually different, diverse

se·vere´ adj. harsh; extremely strict, austere; plain and simple —**se·ver´i·ty** n.

sew vt., vi. make, mend, or fasten with thread

sex n. division of organisms for reproductive functions; activity concerned with reproduction —**sex´u·al** adj.

sex´ism n. discrimination against the opposite sex

sex´ton n. a church officer

shab´by adj. threadbare

shack n. a crude dwelling

shade vt. to screen; represent by gradation of color —n. relative darkness; darkened color; a minute variation; a screen that partly obscures

shad´ow n. image produced by interruption of light; a trace —vt. cast a shadow; follow —**shad´ow·y** adj.

shad´y adj. dark; sheltered; morally or legally suspect

shake vt., vi. vibrate; agitate or rouse —**shak´y** adj.

shal´low adj. lacking depth or extent; superficial

sham adj. false; pretended — n. a hoax; a counterfeit; artificiality or pretension

sham´ble vi. walk with a shuffling or unsteady gait

shame n. guilt; disgrace or humiliation; disappointment

—vt. humiliate; dishonor

shame´ful adj. disgraceful; scandalous; indecent

shame´less adj. brazen; immodest; done without shame

shan´ty n. a shack

shape n. outward form; final form —vt. give form to; adapt or modify; put in final form —vi. develop

shard n. a pottery fragment

share n. a portion; stock in a company —vt., vi. participate in; divide into parts

sharp adj. having a keen edge; capable of cutting or piercing; abrupt; well-defined; quick to perceive; shrewd; intense —**sharp´en** vt., vi.

shat´ter vt. damage or demolish —vi. burst

shave vt. remove hair; trim closely; slice thinly —n. a cutting; a thin slice

shawl n. a cloth wrap

shed vt. pour forth; radiate; repel; cast off; get rid of —vi. cast off by natural. process —n. a small storage building

sheen vi. glisten —n. luster

sheep´ish adj. .embarrassed; meek or timid

shelf n. a platform or ledge

shell n. hard outer covering; framework; a hollow pastry; an explosive projectile —vt. remove an outer covering; bombard

shel´ter n. that which protects —vt. provide cover

shift vt., vi. change position — n. a change in attitude, loyalty, etc.; an unbelted dress

shift´y adj. marked by deceit or trickery; resourceful

shim´mer vi. shine faintly; glimmer —n. a gleaming

shine vi. emit light; glow:

excel —vt. brighten by rubbing —n. radiance; sheen

ship n. a deep-water vessel; an aircraft —vt. transport

ship´ment n. goods transported

shirk vt., vi. avoid obligation

shiv´er vi. tremble with cold or fear —**shiv´er•y** adj.

shock n. a violent blow; trauma associated with injury —vt. horrify or disgust

shod´dy adj. poorly made

shoot vt. wound; fire a weapon; send forth; pass over swiftly; photograph —vi. discharge; move swiftly; put forth buds —n. the act of shooting; early growth

shop n. place where goods are sold, manufactured, or repaired —vi. inspect and purchase goods —**shop assis•tant** (Brit.) one who works in a retail store —**shop´per** n.

shore n. land adjoining water

short adj. less than usual extent; of brief duration; of a limited distance; less than required —**short´en** vt., vi.

short´ly adv. soon

shove vt., vi push; press forcibly against —**shov´er** n.

show vt. present to view; explain or prove; lead —vi. become visible —n. a movie or stage production; exhibition; a competition; ostentation

show´er n. a brief rain; a sudden outpouring; a party; a cleansing with a fine spray of water —vt., vi. honor; make wet; bathe

show´y adj. flamboyant; ostentatious —**show´i•ness** n.

shred n. a fragment —vt. cut or tear into fragments

shrewd adj. having keen insight; calculating

shriek n. a shrill cry —vi.

shrill adj. high-pitched and piercing —vi., vt.

shrine n. sacred place; site or structure respected for importance; a memorial

shrink vi., vt. contract; diminish; recoil, as in disgust

shriv´el vt., vi. contract into wrinkles; become helpless

shroud n. cloth to wrap a corpse; that which conceals —vt. cover or conceal

shud´der vi. tremble

shuf´fle vt., vi. move with a dragging gait; mix; move, change, or rearrange —n. a trick or deception

shunt vt., vi. turn aside; divert —n. a connector that diverts

shut vt. close, as a door; collapse, as an umbrella

shut´-in n. an invalid; one unable to leave —adj.

shy adj. uneasy with others; timid; easily startled; expressing reserve —vt. draw back: shy away

shy´ster n. an unscrupulous businessman

sib´i•lant adj. hissing; of the consonants s, z, sh, and zh

sib´ling n. a brother or sister

sick adj. ill; diseased; weak; nauseated; emotionally upset —**sick´ly** adj., adv.

side n. boundry; the lateral half of a surface; aspect, point of view; a group competing together

si•de´re•al adj. of the stars

si´dle vi. move sideways —n. sideways movement

siege n. surrounding so as to sieze; a prolonged bout —vt. besiege or assault

sift vt. examine carefully;

separate out; filter: sift fact from fiction

sigh *n.* deep audible breath — *vi.* express sorrow,weariness, etc.

sight *n.* vision; an image; mental perception; device for aiming; observation with a telescope — *vt.* catch a view of; observe — *vi.* take aim; make an observation — *adj.*

sign *n.* telltale indication; action used to communicate; a symbol; a device for advertising — *vt., vi.* write a signature; indicate or signal

sig·nal *n.* a sign to convey information — *adj.* notable — *vt.* communicate by a sign

sig·na·to·ry *n.* bound by a signed document — *adj.* being a signer

sig·na·ture *n.* a person's name written by himself; a part of a book; symbols that show time and key for music

sig·nif·i·cant *adj.* rich in meaning; important

sig·ni·fy *vt.* represent; make known — *vi.* have meaning or importance

si·lent *adj.* soundless; mute; taciturn, disinclined to talk; not audible; free from disturbance; absence of comment — **si·lence** *n.*

sil·hou·ette´ *n.* a profile

sil´ly *adj.* foolish; frivolous

sim·i·lar *adj.* having resemblance or like characteristics

sim·i·le *n.* a figure of speech expressing likeness

si·mil·i·tude *n.* similarity

si·mo·ny *n.* buying or selling of that which is sacred

sim´per *vi.* smirk — *vt.* utter with a smirk — *n.* a silly, self-conscious smile

sim´ple *adj.* easy; plain, unadorned; free from affectation; silly or foolish; ordinary

sim´pli·fy *vt.* make easy

sim´u·late *vt.* make pretense of; assume appearance of

si·mul·ta·ne´ous *adj.* occurring at the same time

sin *n.* transgression against moral or religious law — *vi.* do wrong

since *adv.* from past to present; at a time before the present — *prep.* from a time in the past — *conj.* inasmuch as

sin·cere´ *adj.* genuine; free from hypocrisy or deceit

sin·e·cure *n.* a profitable position requiring little effort

sing *vi.* produce music with the voice — *vt.* perform vocally; chant

singe *vt.* burn slightly — *n.* a superficial burn

sin´gle *adj.* consisting of one; solitary; unmarried

sin´gu·lar *adj.* unique; remarkable; uncommon

sin·is·ter *adj.* of the left; evil; ominous; threatening misfortune

sink *vi.,vt.* descend; slope gradually; approach death; lessen; defeat — *n.* a wash basin; a depression; device that absorbs or dissipates energy: *a heat sink*

sin·u·ous *adj.* winding or undulating; devious

sip *vt., vi.* drink in small quantities — *n.* a small drink

si´phon *n.* a device for transferring liquid — *vt.* draw off

sir *n.* respectful address to a man; a title

sire *n.* male parent

si´ren *n.* an enticing woman; a device that warns

—adj. seductive

sis´sy *n.* a weakling

sis´ter *n.* a female sibling

sit *vi.* rest on the buttocks; perch or roost; pose; hold a session; be situated or located *—vt.* seat oneself

site *n.* a specific location

sit´u•ate *vt.* to place or locate

sit•u•a´tion *n.* way in which a thing rests; condition as modified or determined by circumstance a salaried post; a state of affairs

size *n.* dimensions; one of a set of standard measures

skel´e•ton *n.* supporting framework of a structure; a sketch or outline

ske´pti•cal *adj.* doubtful, suspicious *—***skep´ti•cism** *n.*

sketch *n.* a rough drawing; a preliminary study; a brief description; a short play

sketch´y *adj.* lacking detail; superficial

skiff *n.* a light boat

skill *n.* proficiency; a craft or trade

skim *vt., vi.* remove from a surface; move lightly over; cover with a thin film; read hastily *—* *n.* a thin coating

skimp *vi., vt.* do poorly or carelessly; provide too little

skin *n.* an outer covering; a container made from the hide of an animal

skir´mish *n.* a minor encounter *—vi.* battle

skirt *n.* a garment that hangs from the waist; border of an area *—vt., vi.* form or pass along a border; avoid

skit *n.* a short play

skit´tish *adj.* easily frightened; playful

skulk *vi.* move about furtively

sky *n.* heaven; upper atmosphere

slab *n.* a thick, flat slice

slack *adj.* hanging loosely; listless; careless

slake *vt.* to quench

slam *vt.* shut violently; dash; criticize *—vi.* shut with force *—n.* severe criticism

slan´der *vt., vi.* utter falsely; defame *—n.* false statement *—***slan´der•ous** *adj.*

slang *n.* unconventional use of standard vocabulary

slant *vt.* to slope; promote a biased view *—adj.* sloping *— n.* an incline; an opinion

slap *vt.* strike with the open hand; insult *—n.* a blow; an insult

slash *vt.* cut violently; strike with a whip; reduce sharply *—vi.* make a long sweeping stroke *—n.* a cut or gash; an ornamental slit; a forest clearing covered with debris

slat *n.* a thin strip of wood

slaugh´ter *vt.* kill for food; murder savagely *—n.* a savage killing

slave *n.* one owned by another; one controlled by another, a habit, or influence *—vi.* toil ceaselessly

slay *vt.* kill violently

slea´zy *adj.* shoddy or shabby; vulgar or tawdry

sleek *adj.* smooth and glossy; well-groomed; slick

sleep *n.* period of complete rest *—vt., vi.* rest; fall asleep

sleep´er *n.* one sleeping; a railway car; something that unexpectedly excels; *(Brit.) a* section that separates and supports railway tracks

sleet *n.* frozen rain *—vi.* fall as frozen rain *—***sleet´y** *adj.*

sleeve n. part that covers the arm; a covering or wrapper

sleigh n. a horse-drawn vehicle with runners for travel over snow or ice

slen´der adj. long and thin; attractively slim

sleuth n. a detective

slice n. a thin piece; a portion —vt. in. cut divide into parts

slick adj. smooth, sleek; deceptively clever —n. a film

slight adj. of small importance; slender; frail —vt. do carelessly or thoughtlessly; treat as trivial —n. an act of disrespect

slim adj. lacking girth; meager —vt., vi. make or become slimmer

sling n. a strap for hurling; a device to support or lift —vt. throw or fling

slink vi. move furtively

slink´y adj. stealthy; graceful; serpentine —slink´i•ness n.

slip v. put on or off easily; convey slyly; pass unobserved —vi. to slide; fall into error; escape; move stealthily; overlook —n. a sudden slide; an error; woman's undergarment; a pillowcase; undesired motion

slit n. a long, narrow opening —vt. cut lengthwise

slith´er vi. glide like a snake - —n. a sinuous gliding

slob n. an ill-kempt person

slog vt., vi. to plod

slo´gan n. a motto

sloop n. a small sailboat

slop vi., vt. cause to splash or spill —n. waste food; swill

slope vi. slant —n. a slanting surface; degree of inclination

slosh vi. to splash; flounder

slot n. a narrow groove or opening: coin slot; a narrow cut to receive a corresponding part; an opening, as for a job —vt. cut a slot; assign

sloth n. a slow-moving mammal; laziness

slouch n. drooping appearance; an incompetent person —vi. sit or move in an ungraceful, drooping manner

slough n. a stagnant swamp or backwater

slov´en•ly adj. untidy and careless —adv.

slow adj. taking time; dull in comprehending; tedious; not brisk —vt., vi. make slow or slower; delay —adv. at less than normal speed

slug´gard n. a slow or lazy person; an idler

slug´gish adj. inactive; habitually slow and lazy

sluice n. a channel for water; a device for controlling flow

slum n. a squalid living area

slum´ber vi. sleep lightly —n. quiet sleep -**slum´ber•ous** adj.

slur vt. slight or disparage; to pronounce indistinctly -n. a disparaging remark

sly adj. stealthy; roguish

smack n. a quick, sharp sound; a noisy kiss; a slap

small adj. unimportant; having little body or volume; mean-spirited -n. a petite or slender part

smart n. a stinging sensation - vi., vt. feel a stinging pain; feel remorse or anguish — adj. intelligent; clever or shrewd; impertinent; brisk: a smart pace; fashionable

smash vt. break into pieces; crush; strike —n. an outstanding success

smat´ter•ing n. a little bit; superficial knowledge

smear vt. soil; apply thickly; slander

smell vt. perceive, examine, or discover by odor —n. an unpleasant odor

smirk n. a sarcastic or derisive grin —vi. to grin

smock n. a loose garment

smog n. a noxious mist

smoke n. vaporous byproduct of combustion; a tobacco product —vi. give off smoke; use tobacco products — vt. flavor by treating with smoke; force out

smol´der vi. burn slowly; have suppressed emotions

smooth adj. even; without lumps; sauve and flattering —vt., vi. make even; make free of lumps

smoth´er vt. prevent breathing; suffocate; stifle or overwhelm

smudge vt., vi, smear or become smeared —n. a stain; heavy smoke

smug adj. self-satisfied; complacent

smug´gle vt. take in or out of a country illegally

smut n. blackening from soot; something obscene; a fungal disease of plants

snag n. a jagged bulge; an obstacle or difficulty —vt. to catch on a protrusion

snap n. a sharp sound; a quick, sharp closing of jaws; sudden breaking or release; a fastener; busk energy; an easy task —adj. done suddenly —vi., vt. grasp suddenly; speak sharply; move quickly and smartly

snare n. a trap; something

that misleads —vt. trap; entrap by trickery

snatch vt. seize suddenly or eagerly; obtain as opportunity allows

sneak vi., vt. move stealthily —n. a stealthy movement; a dishonest person —adj. stealthy —**sneak´y** adj.

sneak´er (US) n. a flexible sports shoe

sneer n. scornful grimace—vi. show or express contempt

snif´ter n. a brandy goblet

snip vt., vi. cut with short, quick strokes —n. small cut

snip´py adj. abrupt; insolent

snitch vt. steal —vi. inform on

sniv´el vi. whine tearfully —n.

snob n. one preoccupied with wealth and station

snoop vi. to pry —n.

snub vt. treat with disdain — n. a deliberate slight

snug adj. cozy; close-fitting

snug´gle vt, vi. nestle, cuddle

soak vt. saturate; drench

soap n. a cleansing agent

soar vi. float aloft; glide through air

sob vi., vt. weep audibly

so´ber adj. unaffected by drugs or alcohol; temperate, rational; solemn or serious —vt., vi. make or become sober —**so•bri´e•ty** n.

so´bri•quet n. a nickname

so´cia•ble adj. preferring company; friendly

so´cial adj. of society or its mores; friendly; pertaining to public welfare; existing in communities —n. an informal gathering

so´cial•ite n. one prominent in fashionable society

so•ci´e•ty n. persons sharing certain attributes as

303

language or customs; -fashionable members of a community;- association based on common purpose, shared interest, etc.

so•ci•ol•o•gy n. study of the evolution of society —**so•ci•ol•o•gist** n.

so•ci•o•path n. one who is antisocial

sodden adj. saturated; drenched; dull from drink

soft adj. yielding; easily worked; smooth and delicate; expressing sympathy

soi•rée n. an evening reception

so•journ vi. stay temporarily —n. a short stay

sol•ace vt. comfort; alleviate; soothe —n. that which furnishes comfort

so•lar adj. of the sun

sol•e•cism n. grammatical error; an incongruity

sol•emn adj. sacred; marked by ceremony or majesty

so•lem•ni•ty n. a solemn rite

so•lic•it vt. ask earnestly; entice to an immoral act

so•lic•i•tous adj. concerned

sol•id adj. having shape and volume; having resistance to pressure; filling space; of the same substance throughout; well-built; financially sound; reliable —n. a three-dimensional object

so•lil•o•quy n. a speech by a lone actor

sol•ip•sism n. the concept that self knowledge is the only reality

sol•i•tar•y adj. alone; remote or excluded

sol•i•tude n. seclusion; loneliness

sol•stice n. semiannual event

when the sun is farthest from the celestial equator

sol•u•ble adj. able to be solved; able to be dissolved

so•lu•tion n. a mixture; answer to a problem

solve vt. work out a solution or answer —**solv•a•ble** adj.

sol•vent adj. financially sound; able to be dissolved —n. substance capable of dissolving other substances

som´ber adj. dark, gloomy; melancholy

some adj. of an indeterminate number —pron. an undetermined number —adv.

son´ic adj. relating to sound

son´net n. a poem of 14 lines

so•no´rous adj. of a deep rich sound; lofty sounding

soon adv. in the near future;

soothe vt. calm; relieve, as pain —vi. afford relief

sooth´say•er n. one who claims to foretell the future

soph´ism n. a misleading argument; a fallacy

so•phis´ti•cate n. one presumed to be worldly-wise

soph´o•more (US) n. a second-year student —adj. of the second year of school

soph•o•mor´ic (US) adj. of a sophomore; shallow, pretentious; immature

sop•o•rif´ic adj. sleepy

so•pra´no n. music of the highest range

sor´cer•er n. a wizard

sor´cer•y n. magic; witchcraft

sordid adj. degrading; vile; squalid —**sor´did•ness** n.

sore n. a bruise, inflammation, etc.; thing causing pain or trouble —adj. tender; pained, distressed

sor´row n. pain or sadness of

loss; event that causes distress; expression of grief

sor´ry *adj.* feeling regret or remorse; affected by sorrow; paltry or worthless

sort *vt.* arrange —*n.* a particular kind

soul *n.* moral or spiritual part of man; emotional or spiritual depth or vitality; essence; the disembodied spirit of one who has died

sound *n.* that perceptible by hearing; noise of a particular quality; significance: a sinister *sound* —*vi., vt.* give forth a noise —*adj.* healthy; free from flaw, decay, etc.; correct or logical; financially solvent; thorough

soup•con´ *n.* small quantity; a taste

source *n.* origin or derivation

souse *vt., vi.* steep in liquid; pickle —*n.* pickled meat; a drunkard

south *n.* direction to the right of sunrise —*adj.* in a southerly direction

sou•venir´ *n.* a memento

space *n.* expanse of the universe; a specific distance or area; area designed for particular use —*adj.*

spa´cious *adj.* roomy

span *vt.* measure; extend across or over —*n.* distance between two points; a part that extends over

spare *vt.* treat mercifully; relieve; use frugally —*adj.* held in reserve; lean; scanty —*n.* thing saved for future use

sparse *adj.* scattered; not dense —**spar´si•ty** *n.*

spasm *n.* sudden, involuntary muscular contraction; sudden action or effort

spas•mod´ic, spas•mod´i•cal *adj.* temporary; transitory

spas´tic *adj.* marked by spasms —**spas´ti•cal•ly** *adv.*

spate *n.* overflow; sudden outpouring, as of words

spa´tial *adj.* relating to space

speak *vi.* utter; express or convey; deliver an address; converse —*vt.* make known; utter; be able to converse, esp. in a foreign language

spe´cial *adj.* out of the ordinary; designed for specific purpose; notable —*n.* thing designated —**spe´cial•ist** *n.*

spe´ci•al•ize *vi.* to focus on an activity, branch of learning; etc. —*vt.* adapt for particular use or purpose

spe´cie *n.* coined money

spe´cies *n.* a category of animals or plants

spe•cif´ic *adj.* distinct; explicit —*n.* medicine; a particular item or detail

spec•i•fi•ca´tion *n.* a detailed description

spec´i•fy *vt.* state in full and explicit detail

spec´i•men *n.* that regarded as representative; a sample for laboratory anyalsis

spe´cious *adj.* plausible, but without merit

spec´ta•cle *n.* a grand display; a deplorable exhibition

spec•tac´u•lar *adj.* wonderfully exciting; lavish

spec´ter *n.* an apparition

spec´u•late *vi.* ponder, theorize; involve in endeavor or investment entailing risk

speech *n.* power to speak; that spoken; a public address or lecture

speed *n.* rapid motion; rate of movement —*vi.* move or go rapidly —*vt.* promote forward progress

spell˙bind *vt.* to enthrall

spe•lunk˙er *n.* one who explores and studies caves

spend *vt.* pay out; use up; use wastefully or squander

spew *vi.* come or issue forth — *vt.* eject or send forth

sphere *n.* a perfectly round body; field of activity, influence, etc. —**spher˙i•cal** *adj.*

sphinx *n.* a mythical monster; a mysterious person

spice *n.* aromatic flavoring; that which gives zest or adds interest —*vi.*

spill *vi.*, *vt.* run over or cause to run over —*n.* that spilled

spin *vt.* twist fiber into thread, yarn, etc.; produce a web; tell a story —*vi.* make thread or yarn; whirl rapidly —*n.* a pleasure jaunt; uncontrolled spiral descent of an airplane

spin˙et *n.* a small harpsichord or upright piano

spin˙ster *n.* a woman who has never married

spi˙ral *n.* a winding curve — *vt.*, *vt.* take or cause to take a spiral form or course

spir˙it *n.* animating element; a supernatural being; mood or disposition; vivacity or energy; unspecified intent — *vt.* carry off mysteriously — *adj.* of ghosts

spir˙it•ed *adj.* lively, animated; of a characteristic

spir˙i•tu•al *adj.* of moral or intellectual qualities; sacred or religious; supernatural

spite *n.* malicious bitterness or resentment —*vt.* vex maliciously

splen˙did *adj.* magnificent, imposing; conspicuously

illustrious **splen˙dor** *n.*

split *vt.* separate Into parts; divide and distribute —*vi.* divide lengthwise; share with others —*n.* separation into factions; a share —*adj.* divided or separated

spoil *vt.* damage or destory; overindulge another —*vi.* become tainted or decayed

spoils *n.* plunder; jobs for faithful supporters

spo˙ken *adj.* uttered aloud

sponge *n.* a plantlike marine animal; an absorbent substance; leavened dough —*vt.* wipe with a sponge; impose on others

spon˙sor *n.* one acting as surety; a person or group that establishes or finances —*vt.* act as sponsor

spon•ta˙ne•ous *adj.* arising naturally; produced without human involvement

spoof *vt.*, *vi.* deceive; satirize —*n.* a hoax; a playful parody

spoor *n.* footprints or other traces of a wild animal

spo•rad˙ic *adj.* infrequent; not widely diffused

spore *n.* reproductive body in plants; a minute organism

sport *n.* a diversion; spirit of raillery; a laughingstock — *vi.* jest —*adj.* pertaining to sports; of casual wear

spouse *n.* partner in marriage

spout *vi.*, *vt.* pour out under pressure; utter angrily

sprawl *vi.* sit or lie ungracefully; to spread out

spread *vt.* open or unfold; force apart; disperse widely —*vi.* be extended or expanded; be dispersed

spree *n.* a period of heavy drinking; boisterous fun

sprig n. a shoot or sprout

spring vi. jump; occur suddenly; proceed from a source —vt. cause to move or occur suddenly —n. a device that yields under stress and recovers; a flow of water; season preceding summer

spring´y adj. elastic; resiliant

sprint n. a short race —vi. run fast

sprite n. a fairy; an elflike person

sprout vi. put forth shoots; develop or grow rapidly —n. a new shoot on a plant

spruce adj. smart and neat in appearance —n. a type of pine tree

spry adj. quick; agile

spume n. froth or foam —vi. to foam

spur n. a thing that incites or urges; a lateral mountain ridge; a railroad branch —vt. urge, as with a spur

spu·ri·ous adj. not genuine or authenticated

spurn vt., vi. reject

spurt n. a sudden gush —vi. gush forth; make a sudden, forceful effort

squab´ble vi. quarrel —n. a petty argument

squal´id´ adj. dirty, neglected, or poverty-stricken

squall n. screaming outcry; brief commotion; burst of wind and rain or snow

squan´der vt. spend wastefully —n. wastefulness

square n. a plane figure of four equal sides; a device to lay out a right angle; a park bordered by intersecting streets —adj. perfectly adjusted; honest, fair —vt. make square; test for squareness —vi. be at right angles; conform, harmonize

squash vt. crush; suppress —vi. he crushed —n. crush; sound made by walking through muck; an indoor game played with rackets and ball; an edible gourd

squat vi. crouch or cower; settle on land illegally; settle on government land according to regulation —adj. short and thick —n. a crouch

squeam´ish adj. easily shocked; overly scrupulous

squeeze vt. extract by pressure; embrace —vi. apply pressure; yield to pressure —n. pressure an embrace; time of difficulty

squelch vt. squash; silence with a retort —n. a crushing reply —**squelch´er** n.

squire n. (Brit.) a prominent landowner; (US) a lawyer or justice of the peace; an escort or suitor

squirt vi., vt. come forth or eject in a thin stream —n. a jet of liquid

stab vt., vi. thrust with a pointed weapon; a wound; sharp pain; an effort

sta´ble adj. standing firm; having permanence; resistant to change —n. lodging for livestock; performers, writers, etc. under the same agency —**sta´bly** adv.

sta·di·um n. a large structure for sporting events

staff n. a stick or rod; a cudgel; emblem of authority; pole that supports; group of assistants or advisors

stage n. a platform; step or level in a process; portion of a journey —*vt.* exhibit on stage; plan and carry out, simulate —**the stage** any activity or profession associated with theater or drama

stag´ger *vi., vt.* move unsteadily; overwhelm; place alternately —*n.* an unsteady walk

stag´nant *adj.* not flowing; foul from standing; sluggish

staid *adj.* sedate; serious

stake *n.* a sharpened stick; something wagered; share in an enterprise —*vt.* mark a boundary; wager; back with money, equipment, etc.

stale *adj.* no longer fresh; deteriorated; lacking effectiveness, spontaneity, etc.

stale´mate *n.* a deadlock —*vt.* bring to a standstill

stalk *n.* a supporting part, a plant stem —*vi., vt.* approach stealthily

stal´wart *adj.* strong and robust; determined; courageous —*n.* an uncompromising partisan

stam´i•na *n.* endurance

stam•pede´ *n.* a sudden, impulsive rush; a spontaneous trend —*vt., vi.*

stance *n.* a mode of standing; a point of view

stanch *vt.* stop or check; end

stand *vi.* take or have position; assume an attitude —*vt.* place upright; endure —*n.* a designated place; an opinion or attitude; structure similar to a stage; a stall where merchandise is traded; a growth of trees

stan´dard *n.* flag or banner; an emblem or symbol; a model; an established reference —*adj.* of recognized

excellence, popularity, etc.; not special; typical —**stan´dard•ise** (*Brit.*), **stan´dard•ize** (*US*) *vt.*

stare *vt., vi.* gaze fixedly —*n.* a steady, fixed gaze

stark *adj.* barren, bleak; severe; lacking ornamentation; grim, pitiless —*adv.* utterly

start *vt., vi.* make a quick, involuntary movement; begin; set in motion; establish —*n.* a quick movement; beginning or commencement

star´tle *vt., vi.* arouse or be aroused; excite suddenly

starve *vi.* perish from lack of food; suffer extreme hunger; suffer lack —*vt.* cause to die of hunger; to deprive

state *n.* a condition; status; a grand, ceremonious, or luxurious style; a sovereign political unit —*adj.* of government; intended for ceremonial use —*vt.* set forth in speech or writing

state´ly *adj.* dignified; majestic —*adv.* loftily

atat´ic *adj.* of bodies at rest or forces in equilibrium; at rest; not active —*n.* electrical noise

sta´tion *n.* an assigned place; headquarters; stop for a conveyance; social rank or standing —*vt.* assign a place; set in position

sta´tion•ar•y *adj.* remaining in one place; fixed

sta´tion•er•y *n.* office supplies

sta•tis´tic *n.* a value based on sampling

stat´ue *n.* a three-dimensional representation

stat´ure *n.* natural height; status or reputation

sta´tus *n.* state or condition;

relative position or rank

stat´ute n. an established law or regulation

stay vi. stop, halt; remain —vt. bring to a halt; hinder; postpone —n. suspension

stead n. in place of another

stead´fast adj. firmly fixed

stead´y adj. stable; unfaltering, constant; regular —vt., vi. make or become steady

steal vt. take unlawfully; obtain subtly —vi. move quietly and stealthily; commit theft —n. a bargain

steep[1] adj. sloping sharply; precipitous; costly

steep[2] vt. soak in liquid

stee´ple n. the lofty structure above the roof of a church

steer vt., vi. direct the course

stench n. an offensive odor

sten´cil n. an openwork pattern for copying a design

stere n. a cubic meter

ster´ile adj. having no reproductive power; free of microorganisms; lacking vigor

stern adj. severe or harsh; austere; resolute

stick´ler n. one with exacting standards; a baffling issue

stiff adj. rigid; resistant; unnatural; strong and steady; stiff *breeze*; thick, viscous, harsh; stubborn, unyielding; difficult, arduous —n. an awkward or unresponsive person —**stiff´ness** n.

sti´fle vt. kill by suffocating; suppress, as tears —vi. die of suffocation

stig´ma n. mark of disgrace; spot or scar on the skin

still adj. motionless; free of disturbance; silent; soft, subdued —adv. up to now; in spite of; in increasing

degree —conj. nevertheless —vt. silence; allay —vi. become still —**still´ness** n.

stim´u•late vt. rouse to activity; affect by intoxicants —vi. act as stimulus or stimulant

stim´u•lus n. anything that rouses to activity

sting vt., vi. prick painfully; suffer sharp, smarting pain

stin´gy adj. miserly; meager

stink n. a foul odor —vi., vt. give forth a foul odor

stint vt. limit —vi. be frugal or sparing —n. a restriction or limit; specified task or time

sti´pend n. a regular fixed allowance

stip´u•late vt. specify —vi. demand as a requirement n.

sto•chas´tic adj. characterized by conjecture; involving probability

stock n. goods on hand; original from which others are descended; main stem of a plant; shares in a corporation; raw material; broth —vt. supply; keep on hand to sell; put aside for future use —adj. commonplace

stodg´y adj. dull, boring; heavy or indigestible

sto´ic n. one unaffected by emotion —**sto´ic, sto´i•cal** adj. impassive or indifferent

stol´id adj. without feeling; impassive —**stol´id•ly** adv.

stomp vt., vi. to tread heavily upon —n. a jazz dance

stone n. a small rock; shaped rock; something small and hard; pit of a fruit —adj. made of stone —vt. hurl stones at; remove pits from

stooge n. a dupe

stool n. a seat; a low bench

stoop vi. lean forward and

down; lower or degrade one-self —vt. bend forward —n. habitual inclination of head and shoulders; small porch

stop vt. bring to a halt; prevent completion; cease doing; check or stanch; close, as with a cork —vi. come to a halt —n. an obstruction

stor´age n. placing for safekeeping; charge for storing

store vt. put away for future use —n. a business that sells merchandise

sto´rey (Brit.) n. level of a building

sto´ried adj. having a notable history

storm n. heavy prolonged winds and precipitation; a violent outburst; political or social disturbance -vi. blow or rage —vt. attack

sto´ry n. a narrative; an anecdote; plot of a fictional account; a falsehood; (US) level of a building

stout adj. thick-set; courageous—n. strong dark beer

stow vt. pack; store

stow´age n. space or charge for storing; goods stored

strad´dle vt. stand or sit with legs on either side; favor both sides of an issue

strag´gle vi. stray or wander; fall behind

straight adj. without curve or bend; erect; fair and honest; correctly arranged; accepted as normal or conventional —adv. in a direct course; at once; without qualification

strain vt. exert; injure by overexertion; remove with a filter —vi. make an effort; become wrenched or twisted; filter —n. taxing demand on

resources; a violent effort; injury from excessive effort

strait n. a narrow passage of water

strange adj. unfamiliar; peculiar, out of the ordinary; out of place

stran´ger n. one unfamiliar; one ignorant of

stran´gle vt. choke to death; suppress

stra•te´gic adj. vital, essential

strat´e•gy n. a broad-based plan; the use of artifice

strat´i•fy vt., vi. arrange or form in layers

stray vi. wander; to deviate from right or goodness —adj. wandering; out of place —n. a domestic animal that has wandered —**stray´er** n.

stream n. a flow of water; an uninterrupted flow —vi. pour forth or issue; proceed without interruption

strength n. ability to apply or withstand force; intensity

stren´u•ous adj. marked by effort or exertion

stress n. physical or emotional tension; emphasis; pressure —vt. subject to stress; give emphasis to

stretch vt. draw out; strain to the utmost; adapt to circumstances —vi. extend; —n. continuous space or time —adj. able to he distended

stri´ate vt. mark with grooves, stripes, etc. —**stri•a´tion** n.

strick´en adj. affected by injury, disease, sorrow, etc.

strict adj. harsh, stern, exacting; absolute

stric´ture n. that which restricts; narrowing or closure

stri´dent adj. loud and harsh

strife n. angry contention

strike vt. hit; affect suddenly; cease work in protest; make a bargain —vi. come into violent contact; cease work —n. a blow; sudden success; work stoppage

strin´gent adj. rigid or severe; convincing —**strin´gen•cy** n.

strip n. a narrow piece; set of cartoon drawings —vt. lay bare; deprive; damage gears or threads —vi. undress

stripe n. a contrasting band; a distinctive quality; blow struck with a whip or rod —vt. mark with a band

strip´ling n. a lad

strive vi. make an effort; fight

stroll vi. walk casually —n. a leisurely walk —**stroll´er** n.

strong adj. physically powerful; healthy, robust; especially competent or able; firm, tenacious —adv. in a firm manner

struc´ture n. a fabrication; founded on a plan —vt. build; conceive as a whole

strug´gle n. arduous effort; a war —vt. contend; strive

strut n. pompous walk; a supporting member —vi. walk pompously —vt. support or separate with a brace

stub´born adj. inflexible; not easily overcome

stu´dent n. one engaged in a course of study

stu´dio n. working area for an artist, photographer, etc.

stud´y n. the process of acquiring knowledge; a branch of knowledge; a room for reading or studying —vt. acquire knowledge; examine thoroughly —vi. apply the mind to learning

stuff vt. fill completely; plug or stop up —n. fundamental element; personal possessions; unspecified matter; a miscellaneous collection

stuff´y adj. poorly ventilated, impeding respiration; straitlaced, stodgy

stum´ble vi. miss one's step; speak in a halting manner; happen upon by chance; do wrong

stump n. portion left when a part is cut off; a place for political speeches —adj. of political campaigning —vt. make a political speech

stun vt. render incapable of action; astound, overwhelm

stu•pen´dous adj. astonishing; immense

stu´por n. abnormal lethargy; intellectual dullness

stur´dy adj. robust and powerful; firm and resolute

style n. fashionable appearance; distinctive fashion, manner, etc. —vt. give a name or title; alter

suave adj. pleasant and courteous

sub•con´scious adj. not attended by full awareness

subdue´ vt. gain dominion over; repress —**sub•du´er** n.

sub´ject adj. under power of; having a tendency —n. one under power of another; a theme or topic; a branch of learning —**sub•ject´** vt. bring under control; make liable

sub•jec´tive adj. of personal feeling or opinion; influenced by emotion or prejudice —**sub•jec•tiv´i•ty** n.

sub•ju•gate vt. conquer; make subservient

sub´li•mate vt. convert to that which is socially acceptable

sub•lime´ *adj.* characterized by grandeur

sub•lim´in•al *adj.* below the threshold of consciousness; too slight to be perceived

sub•merge´ *vt.* place under water —*vi.* sink beneath the surface

sub•merse´ *vt.* submerge

sub•mers´i•ble *adj.* that may be submerged —*n.* a craft for operation on the surface of or under water; an underwater craft used for observation, rescue, etc.

sub•mis´sion *n.* yielding; presenting for consideration; something submitted, as a manuscript

sub•mis´sive *adj.* inclined to submit

submit´ *vt.* to yield; present for consideration —*vi.* surrender; obey

sub•or´di•nate *adj.* lower in rank; secondary —*n.* one of lower rank; a helper or assistant —*vt.* assign a lower rank; make subservient

sub•orn´ *vt.* bribe to commit perjury; incite to an unlawful act

sub•poe´na *n.* writ requiring a court appearance

sub´ro•gate *vt.* substitute one for another, esp. a creditor

sub•scribe´ *vt.* sign one's name to express assent; promise to pay; give approval; agree; pay in advance, as for a periodical

sub´se•quent *adj.* following in time, order, etc. —**sub´se•quent•ly** *adv.*

sub•ser´vi•ent *adj.* servile or obsequious —**sub•ser´vi•ence** *n.*

sub•side´ *vi.* lower; calm

sub•sid´i•ar•y *adj.* supplementary or auxiliary —*n.* a business with over half its assets owned by another

sub´si•dize *vt.* aid

sub´si•dy *n.* a financial grant

sub•sist´ *vi.* continue to exist; to maintain life

sub•sist´ence *n.* that by which one subsists, as food or earnings

sub´stance *n.* material of which a thing is made; essential component; wealth or property; the quality of being constant or solid

sub•stan´tial *adj.* firm and solid; tangible; of significant worth or importance —**sub•stan´tial•ly** *adv.*

sub•stan´ti•ate *vt.* prove

sub•stan•tive *n.* a noun or pronoun, or a verbal form replacing a noun —*adj.* that can be used as a noun; denoting existence; having substance —**sub´stan•tive•ly** *adv.*

sub´sti´tute *vt.* put in place of; take the place of —*vi.* act as substitute —*n.* an alternate or replacement —*adj.* alternative; temporary

sub•sti•tu´tion *n.* replacing; being a replacement; a substitute

sub´ter•fuge *n.* deception

sub´ter•ra´ne•an *adj.* below the surface of the earth

sub´tle *adj.* not easily detected; not obvious; skillful or ingenious

sub´tle•ty *n.* the quality of being subtle; a small differentiation

sub•tract´ *vt., vi.* take away or deduct —**sub•trac´tive** *adj.*

sub´urb *n,* an area *adjacent* to

a city; an outlying distnct

sub•ur´ban•ite n. resident of a suburb

sub•ur´bi•a n. the suburbs or suburbanites collectively; the cultural world of suburbanites

sub•ver´sive n. one trying to weaken or overthrow —adj. tending to undermine or weaken

sub•vert´ vt. corrupt; destroy utterly

sub´way n. an underpass; an underground railway

suc•ceed´ vt. accomplish or turn out as intended; come next in order —et. to come after in time or order

suc•cess´ n. a favorable termination; gaining of fame, wealth, etc.; the scale or level of gain

suc•cess´ful adj. ending in success

suc•ces´sion n. following in order; right to office, possessions, etc.

suc•ces´sive adj. following in order

suc•cinct´ adj. clear and concise; marked by brevity

suc´cu•lent adj. juicy; having thick fleshy leaves; interesting —n. a succulent plant —**suc´cu•lence** n.

suc•cumb´ vi. to yield; to die

such adj. being the same or similar: times such as these; extreme: such art uproar —pron. the same as implied or indicated —adv. especially; in such good spirits

suck vt. draw in by partial vacuum; to pull or draw in: lure of profit sucked him in —vi. draw in by suction; suckle

suc´tion n. a partial vacuum —adj. created or operated by suction

sud´den adj. happening quickly without warning; Macy, rash

suds pl. n. froth, foam —**suds•y** adj.

sue vt. take legal action to n-dress a wrong; prosecute —vi. start legal proceedings; seek to persuade by entreaty: sue for peace

suede n. hide or fabric having a napped surface

suf´fer vi. feel pain or distress; sustain loss or injury; undergo punishment —vt. have inflicted on one; endure; allow

suf•fer•ance n. permission granted or implied; capacity for suffering

suf•fice´ vi. be sufficient or adequate

suf•fi´cient adj. all that is needed; enough —**suf•fi´cient•ly** adv.

suf´fix n. addition to a word that modifies —vt. to add

suf´fo•cate vi., vi. distress or kill by depriving of oxygen; smother, as a fire; stifle: suffocate with affection

suf´frage n. voting; a vote

suf•fuse´ vt. spread through or over; suffuse with light —**suf•fu´sion** n.

sug•gest´ et. present for consideration; associate: gold suggests wealth; imply

sug•ges´ti•ble adj. that can be recommended; easily lead

sug•ges´tion n. something offered for consideration; small amount, a trace

sug•ges´tive adj. stimulating reflection or thought; hinting of something improper

su·i·cide n. taking of one's own life; ruin brought on by one's own actions — **su·i·ci´dal** adj.

suit n. a garment or set of garments; a grouping of compatible things: *bedroom suit*; a court proceeding; the courting of a woman —vt. meet requirements; satisfy; adapt; furnish with clothes —vi. prove satisfactory — **suit´a·ble** adj.

suite n. things intended for use together, as connecting rooms; a set of matched furniture, a suit

sulk vi. be sullen and withdrawn —n. a sullen mood

sulk´y n. a light, horse-drawn vehicle —adj. sullen and withdrawn

sul´len adj. ill-humored; glum; depressing; slow or sluggish

sul´ly vt. soil; shame or defile

sul´try adj. hot and humid; arousing passion; sensual — **sul´tri·ness** n.

sum n. entire amount; a summary

sum´ma·rize vt. present a summary

sum´ma·ry n. a brief account —adj. containing essential details; performed without ceremony or delay

sum·ma´tion n. adding numbers; a final review of main points

sum´mit n. the highest point or part; the highest level or office

sum´mon vt. send for; call together; rouse to action — **sum´mon·er** n.

sum´mons n. a notice to

appear in court

sump´tu·ous adj. lavish; luxurious

sunk´en adj. at the bottom; lower than the surrounding area

sun n. a star, as at the center of the solar system vt. expose to the sun —vi. bask in the sun

sun´ny adj. filled with sunlight, bright, cheerful — **sun´ni·ly** adv.

sun´set n. time at which sun tails below the horizon; a final period

su´per adj. surpassing others of its kind; outstanding —n. a superintendent

su´per·a·ble adj. that can be overcome

su·perb´ adj. extraordinarily good

su·per·cil´i·ous adj. haughtily disdainful; arrogant

su·per·fi´cial adj. on or near the surface; trivial, not profound; hasty; apparent: *superficial resemblance* — **su·per·fi´cial·ly** adv.

su·per´flu·ous adj. surplus; exceeding what is needed; unnecessary or irrelevant

su·per·in·tend´ vt. direct or survise

su·per·in·tend´ence n.

su·per·in·tend´ent n. one in charge; one responsible for maintenance and repair

su·pe´ri·or adj. higher in rank, quality, etc.; affecting an attitude of indifference or disdain —n. one who is higher in rank

su·per´la·tive adj. of the highest degree; most excellent; exaggerated —n. thing of the highest grade

su•per•nat´u•ral *adj.* existing outside of nature; miraculous or divine; of ghosts, demons, etc. —*n.* unnatural phenomena

su•per•sede´ *vt.* replace with something newer or better; take the place of —**su•per•sed´er** *n.*

su•per•son´ic *adj.* moving faster than the speed of sound

su•per•sti´tion *n.* an irrational belief; any practice inspired by such belief

su•per•sti´tious *adj.* influenced by superstition; based on superstition

su´per•vise´ *vt.* have charge of; oversee or manage —**su´per•vi•sor** *n.*

su•pine´ *adj.* lying face up

sup´per *n.* the evening meal; last meal of the day

sup•plant´ *vt.* displace, as something outdated; displace by treachery

sup´ple *adj.* flexible; agile or graceful; yielding readily, compliant; adaptable —*vt., vi.* make supple

sup´ple•ment *n.* that added to correct or augment —*vt.* make an addition to —**sup•ple•men´tal** *adj.*

sup´pli•cate *vt., vi.* ask humbly or by earnest prayer —**sup•pli•ca´tion** *n.*

sup•ply´ *vt.* make available; furnish —*vi.* take the place of temporarily —*n.* quantity on hand or available

sup•port´ *vt.* bear the weight of; hold in position; provide with necessities; substantiate or defend; provide with means to endure —*n.* person or thing that supports

sup•port´er *n.* one who provides with necessities; a brace

sup•port´ive *adj.* contributing significantly —**sup•port´ive•ness** *n.*

sup•pose´ *vt.* believe to be possible; expect; imply —**sup•pos´a•bly** *adv.*

sup•posed´ *adj.* accepted as genuine; imagined —**sup•pos•ed´ly** *adv.*

sup•po•si´tion *n.* conjecture or assumption —**sup•po•si´tion•al** *adj.*

sup•press´ *vt.* end or stop; hold back or repress; check

sup•pres´sion *n.* instance of suppressing; exclusion of unpleasant memories, etc. from consciousness

su•prem´a•cy *n.* supreme power or authority

su•preme´ *adj.* dominant; highest in degree, etc.; ultimate

sur•cease´ *n.* a cessation —*vt., vi.* to end

sure *adj.* without doubt; postive

sur´e•ty *n* security against loss

surf *n.* swelling of the sea breaking on the shore —*vi.* ride a surfboard

sur´face *n.* exterior; a superficial aspect —*vt.* apply or improve an exterior; cause to rise —*vi.* rise; come to public notice

sur´feit *vt.* supply to excess —*vi.* overindulge tit food or drink —*n.* an excessive amount

surge *vi.* move with a swelling motion; increase suddenly —*n.* a great swelling or rolling; a sudden increase

sur´ger•y n. medical treatment by operative means; branch of medicine concerned with treatment by surgery; an operating room

sur•ly adj. ill-humored; gruff or insolent —**sur´li•ness** n.

sur•mise´ vt., vi. infer on slight evidence —n. a supposition

sur•mount´ vt. overcome; mount or pass over, as an obstacle; place above —**sur•mount´a•ble** adj.

sur´name n. a family name; a cognomen or nickname —vt. furnish with a nickname

sur•pass´ vt. to go beyond or past

sur´plus n. that over what is required —adj. excess

sur•prise´ vt. feel wonder or astonishment; take unawares —n. astonishment; that causing astonishment —**sur•pris´ing** adj.

sur•re´al adj. having a dreamlike quality —**sur•re´al•ly** adv.

sur•re´al•ism n. art characterized by use of dreamlike elements

sur•ren´der vt. yield; give up in favor of another; give oneself over to —vi. to give oneself up —n. the act of surrendering

sur•rep•ti´tious adj. accomplished by secret means; acting with stealth —**sur•rep•ti´tious•ly** adv.

sur´ro•gate n. one acting in place of another; a probate court judge —vt. deputize or substitute

sur•round´ vt. encircle

sur•round´ings n. one's environment

sur•veil´lance n. discreet observation of someone or something

sur•vey´, sur´vey vt. look at carefully; scrutinize; determine accurately the area, boundaries, etc. of land —n. surveying land; systematic collection and analysis of data; a general or overall view

sur•viv´a•ble adj. that can be survived

sur•vive´ vi. remain in existence; live past the death of another —vt. outlast; go on living in spite of

sus•cep´ti•ble adj. readily affected; vulnerable; able to be influenced

sus•pect´ vt. think guilty without proof; distrust or doubt —vi. have suspicions —**sus•pect´, sus´pect** adj. inspiring suspicion —**sus´pect** n. one who may be guilty

sus•pend´ vt. bar, cease, or interrupt for a time; defer action; move freely while hanging from a support

sus•pense´ n. anxiety caused by uncertainty —**sus•pense´ful** adj.

sus•pen´sion n. temporary removal, withholding of privilege, etc.; cessation or deferment; hanging freely; dispersion in liquid or gas

sus•pi´cion n. uncertain belief in another's guilt; a slight amount

sus•pi´cious adj. questionable; disposed to doubt

sus•tain´ vt. keep up or maintain; provide with necessities; endure or withstand; suffer or undergo;

uphold or prove as bring true or just

sus´te·nance n. maintenance of life or health; that which sustains

svelte adj. slender; smart or chic

swab n. a soft, absorbent substance on a short stick for applying medication, etc.; specimen for medical examination; a mop for cleaning —vt. clean or apply with a swab

swad´dle vt. wrap in strips of cloth —n. bands or cloth for swaddling

swag n. a decorative hanging, as a gathered drape at the top of a window; a similar carved motif; stolen property; (Austral.) a bundle of personal belongings

swag´ger vi. walk with an air of self-confidence; behave or boast in a self-satisfied manner —n. a self-confident gait —adj. showy

swal´low vt. cause to pass from the mouth into the stomach; take in or engulf; submit to, as insults; suppress: swallow one´s pride —n. amount taken in at one time; mouthful; small bird

swamp n. low land saturated with water —vt. drench with water; overwhelm —vi. sink in water

swank n. ostentatious display; stylishness —adj. stylish or smart

swank´y adj. ostentatiously fashionable

swap vt., vi. exchange or trade —n. something traded — **swap meet** a gathering for trading goods

swarm n. a large crowd or mass —vi. come together or move in great numbers; be overrun

swarth´y adj. dark complected

swat vt. strike with a quick blow

swath n. a strip or row, as cut grain

swathe vt. bind or wrap, as with bandages —n. .a bandage

sway vi. swing from side to side; incline in opinion, sympathies, etc.; to control —vt. cause to swing or lean; influence —n. power or influence; a turning from side to side

smear vi. make a solemn affirmation; make a vow; use profanity —vt. assert solemnly; vow; declare emphatically

sweat vi. exude salty moisture from pores; condense moisture on a surface; work hard; suffer from anxiety —vt. join metal with solder; subject to rigorous interrogation —n. —**sweat´y** adj.

sweep vt. clear or clean; pass over swiftly; win overwhelmingly —vi. clean a surface with a broom, etc.; move quickly; extend: the road sweeps along the lake —n. a long stroke or movement; the act of clearing; an unbroken stretch; an overwhelming victory; one who cleans chimneys, streets, etc.; a flowing contour

sweet adj. flavored like sugar; pleasing to the senses —n. something agreeable or pleasing

sweet′en n. make agreeable or pleasing—**sweet′en•er** n.

swell vi. increase in size or volume, as by inflation or absorption; to increase in amount, etc.; arise in waves; bulge —vt. cause to increase; cause to bulge; puff with pride —n. expansion; a rise or undulation; a bulge; a long continuous wave — adj. fashionable, elegant — **swell′ing** n., adj.

swel′ter vi., vt. suffer oppressive heat —n. oppressive heat

swerve vi., vt. turn or cause to turn aside —n. a sudden turning

swift adj. capable of moving with great speed; happening without delay —**swift′ly** adv.

swill vt., vi. drink greedily —n. semiliquid food for animals; unappetizing food; garbage

swim vi. move through water with the limbs; move with a flowing motion; to be flooded —vt. traverse by swimming; cause to swim —n. swimmung; the distance swum

swin′dle vt. cheat or defraud; obtain by fraud —vi. practice fraud —n. the act of defrauding

swing vi., vt. move to and fro rhythmically; pivot; be suspended; be contemporary and sophisticated; conclude successfully: swing a deal— n. a free swaying motion; a hanging seat; a trip or tour: swing through the low country; a type of jazz

swirl vi., vt. to move or cause to move with a whirling race tion —n.

switch n. a flexible rod or whip; a mechanism for shifting or changing —vt. whip or lash; turn aside or divert; exchange —vt. turn aside; change —**switch′er** n.

swiv′el n. a pivot that permits independent rotation; anything that turns on a pivot — vt., vi. to turn

swoon vi. faint —n. a fainting spell

swoop vi. descend suddenly; pounce —vt. seize suddenly —n. a sudden violent descent

sword n. a long blade fixed in a hilt

syc′o•phant n. a servile flatterer

syl•lab′ic adj. pertaining to syllables; having every syllable distinctly pronounced

syl•lab′i•cate, syl•lab′i•fy vt. divide into syllables

syl′la•ble n. a word or part of a word uttered in a single vocal impulse

syl′la•bus n. a concise description

syl′lo•gism n. a conclusion derived from communality of two premises

syl′van adj. of a wooded area; of a creature living in woods

sym•bi•o•sis n. a mutually advantageous relationship between dissimilar organisms

sym′bol n. a mark, emblem, etc. representing something

sym′bol•ism n. investing with symbolic meaning; system of symbolic developments

sym′bol•ize vt. represent symbolically; to use symbols

sym′metry n. balancing of parts or elements; beauty

and harmony resulting from balance

sym•pa•thet´ic *adj.* having compassion for others; in accord or harmony; of sounds produced by responsive vibrations

sym´pa•thize *vi.* understand sentiments of another; feel or express compassion; be in harmony or agreement

sym´pa•thy *n.* agreement of feeling; compassion for another; agreement, accord; support or approval

sym•pho´ni•ous *adj.* in accord; harmonious

sym´pho•ny *n.* agreeable mingling of sounds, color, etc; composition for orchestra —**sym•phon´ic** *adj.*

sym•po´si•um *n.* meeting for discussion of a particular subject; writing on a particular subject

symp´tom *n.* condition indicating presence of disease; an indication: *a symptom of civil unrest*

syn´a•gogue *n.* a place of meeting for Jewish worship and religious instruction; a Jewish congregation

syn´apse *n.* junction of two neurons across which nerve impulses pass

syn•chron´ic *adj.* of the events of a particular time

syn´chro•nism *n.* concurrence; grouping of historic persons or events by date

syn´chro•nize *vt.* occur at the same time; operate in unison —*vt.* cause to operate together; assign the same date or period

syn´chro•nous *adj.* occurring at the same time

syn•co•pa´tion *n.* suppression of an expected rhythmic accent in music

syn´di•cate *n.* an association united to engage in an enterprise —*vt.* to combine into a syndicate

syn´drome *n.* combined symptoms characteristic of a disease; traits regarded as characteristic of a condition, etc. —**syn´drom•ic** *adj.*

syn´er•gism *n.* the reinforcing action of separate organs, agents, etc.

syn´er•gy *n.* synergism

syn´od *n.* an ecclesiastical council

syn´o•nym *n.* a word having almost the same meaning as another

syn•on´y•mous *adj.* being equivalent or similar in meaning

syn•op´sis *n.* condensation of a story, book,. etc.; a summary

syn•op´tic *adj.* giving a general view; offering a similar point of view

syn´tax *n.* arrangement of words in grammatical construction

syn´the•sis *n.*, *pl.* **syn´the•ses** the assembly of subordinate parts into a new form; the resulting complex form created

syn´the•size *vt.* to produce by synthesis

syn´the•siz•er *n.* an electronic device used to create musical tones

syn•thet´ic *adj.* produced artificially, as by chemical synthesis; artificial

sy•ringe´ *n.* a device to remove or inject fluids

sys´tem n. an arrangement of parts, facts, etc. that interact with each other; a group of logically related facts, beliefs, etc.; a method of classification, arrangement, etc.

sys´tem•a•tize vt. organize methodically

sys´tem´ic adj. of a system; affecting the entire body: systemic poison

t, T n. 20th letter of the alphabet —**to a T** perfectly, precisely

tab n. a flap, projection, etc. as on a garment or file card —vt. provide with a tab

tab´er•na•cle n. a house of worship; receptacle for the eucharistic elements; a portable sanctuary used by the Israelites

ta´ble n. an article of furniture with a flat top and legs; surface for serving food; food served; elements arranged in rows and columns for easy reference; a listing: table of contents; a tablet or slab — vt. to postpone discussion

tab´leau n., pl. **tab´leaux** or **tab´leaus** a picturesque representation

table d´hôte a complete meal served at a fixed price

ta´ble•spoon n. a measure equal to three teaspoons; a tablespoonful

ta´ble•spoon´ful n. amount a tablespoon will hold

tab´let n. a pill; a pad of paper; a flat surface intended for an inscription or design

ta´ble•ware n. dishes and implements for dining

tab´loid n. a newspaper in which news is presented

concisely and often sensationally

ta•boo´, ta•bu´ n. restriction or ban based on religious belief, custom, etc. —adj. restricted or prohibited —vt. place under taboo

tab´u•lar adj. arranged in a table or list

tab´u•late vt. arrange in a table or list —**tab•u•la´tion** n.

ta•chom´e•ter n. a device indicating speed of rotation, as for an engine

tach´y•car´di•a n. abnormally rapid heartbeat

tac´it adj. not, spoken; inferred or implied —**tac´it•ly** adv.

tac´i•turn adj. habitually re served

tack n. small nail with a broad flat head; policy or course of action; a temporary fastening —vt. fasten with a tack; secure temporarily—vi. change one's course of action

tack´le n. combination of ropes and pulleys for hoisting; rigging of a ship; sport or work gear —vt. undertake: tackle a problem; seize suddenly and forcefully

tack´y adj. slightly sticky; in poor taste —**tack´i•ness** n.

tact n. ability to say or do the proper thing —**tact´ful** adj.

tac´ti•cal adj. pertaining to tactics; adept at planning and maneuvering —**tac•ti´cian** n.

tac´tics n. strategy; the art of maneuvering to gain an end

tac´tile adj. of the sense of touch; that may be perceived by touch

tact´less adj. lacking tact

taf′fe•ta *n.* a fine, stiff fabric —*adj.* made of taffeta

taf′fy *n.* a chewy confection

tag *n.* an attachment that identifies, prices, etc.; a children's game —*vt.* fit with a tag; follow closely; touch

ta•hi′ni *n.* sesame seed butter

tail *n.* flexible appendage of an animal; an extension: *tail of a comet*; hind or back portion —*vt.* be at the end of; follow stealthily —*vi.* follow closely; diminish gradually —*adj.* rearmost; coming from behind

tail′gate *n.* hinged gate on a motor vehicle —*vt., vi.* follow too closely

tai′lor *n.* one who makes or repairs garments —*vi.* do a tailor's work —*vt.* fit with garments; adapt to meet a need —**tai′lor•ing** *n.*

tai′lored *adj.* custom-made; severe or tight-fitting

tai′lor-made′ *adj.* made by a tailor; perfectly suited to a need

taint *vt., vi.* be affected by contamination or corruption —*n.* a cause or result of contamination

take *vt.* lay hold or gain possession of; choose; steal; undergo or submit to; accept; charm or captivate; perform: *take action*; to feel —*vi.* acquire; be captivated: *taken with her beauty*; require; enter upon: *take a job*; assume: *take blame*; have intended effect —*n.* something taken or received; amount received —**tak′er** *n.*

tale *n.* a story; a narrative of events; idle or malicious gossip; a lie

tale′bear•er *n.* one who gossips or spreads rumors

tal′ent *n.* natural ability; aptitude; those with special abilities

tal′is•man *n.* an object to ward off evil or bring good luck; anything with seeming magical power

talk *vi.* express audibly; convey a message: *money talks*; make sounds suggesting speech —*vt.* express in words —*n.* conversation or speech; conference or discussion; sounds suggesting speech

talk′a•tive *adj.* given to much talk

talk′y *adj.* talkative; given overly to talk: *a talky movie* —**talk′i•ness** *n.*

tall *adj.* of more than average height; of a specified height; exaggerated: *a tall story*; extensive: *a tall order* —*adv.* proudly: *walk tall*

tal′low *n.* rendered animal fat

tal′ly *n.* score or mark; a reckoning; mark indicating a number —*vt.* to score; reckon; to make correspond —*vi.* keep score; agree precisely

tal′on *n.* claw of an animal

ta•ma′le *n.* seasoned meat rolled in corn meal, then wrapped in leaves and steamed

tame *adj.* domesticated; docile, subdued; lacking spirit, uninteresting —*vt.* domesticate; tone down

tamp *vt.* pack down

tam′per *vt.* meddle or interfere with, make potentially harmful changes; use improper measures

tan *vt.* convert into leather; darken by exposure to sunlight —*vi.* become darkened —*n.* a yellow-brown color; dark skin coloring

tan´dem *adv.* one behind the other —*n.* a team of horses harnessed one behind the other; the carriage they pull; a bicycle with two or more seats —*adj.*

tang *n.* a sharp, penetrating taste or odor —**tang´y** *adj.*

tan´gent *adj.* touching without intersecting —**tan´gen•cy** *n.*

tan•gen´tial *adj.* touching lightly

tan´ger•ine´ *n.* a variety of orange

tan´gi•ble *adj.* perceptible by touch; real or concrete —*n.* assets having value that can be appraised

tan´gle *vt.* twist into a mass; ensnare or enmesh; involve so as to confuse —*vi.* become tangled —*n.* a confused intertwining

tan´go *n.* a Latin American dance, the music for such a dance —*vi*

tank *n.* a large receptacle; an armored combat vehicle —*vt.* store in a tank

tan´kard *n.* a large, handled drinking cup, often with a cover

tan´ner•y *n.* place for curing leather

tan´ta•lize *vt.* torment by withholding —**tan´ta•liz•ing•ly** *adv.*

tan´ta•mount *adj.* equivalent to

tan´trum *n.* a fit of temper

tap *n.* act or sound of striking gently; a spout for drawing

liquid; a plug or stopper —*vt.* touch or strike gently; open or provide with a spigot; draw upon

tape *n.* a narrow strip for measuring or binding —*vt.* secure with tape

ta´per *n.* a slender candle; a wick for lighting candles; a cone —*vt., vi.* make or become thin toward one end; lessen gradually —*adj.*

tap´es•try *n.* a heavy woven textile with a pictorial design

tape´worm *n.* a parasitic worm

tap•i•o•ca *n.* a starchy food obtained from cassava

tar•an•tel´la *n.* a lively dance

ta•ran´tu•la *n.* a large hairy spider

tar´dy *adj.* not happening as anticipated; moving ahead slowly

tar´get *n.* object of an action —*vt.* establish as a goal

tar´iff *n.* duties imposed on imports and exports; a price schedule —*vt.* fix a price on

tarn *n.* a small mountain lake

tar´nish *vt.* dim the luster of, sully or debase —*vi.* become tarnished

ta´ro *n* tropical plant having a starchy edible rootstock

ta´rot *n.* cards used mainly for fortunetelling

tar•pau´lin *n* a waterproof material used as a protective covering

tar´pon *n.* a large game fish

tar´ra•gon *n.* a European plant with leaves used for seasoning

tar´ry *vi.* put off going; linger; remain temporarily

tar´sal *adj.* pertaining to the ankle

tar·sus n.. the ankle

tart n. a small filled pastry — adj. having a sharp sour taste; caustic, as a remark —**tart´ly** adv.

tar´tan n. woolen fabric, esp. one distinctive to a Scottish clan

task n.a designated job; a difficult assignment —vi. assign a task; overburden

task´mas·ter n. one who assigns tasks, esp. burdensome ones

tas´sel n. an ornamental tuft of loose hanging cords —vt. adorn with tassels —vi. put forth tassels, as on corn

taste vt., vi. perceive flavor; consume a small amount; experience: *taste victory*; have a specific flavor —n. stimulation of the taste buds; a small quantity; special fondness: *taste for music*; respect for propriety and refinement

taste buds receptors on the tongue

taste´ful adj. conforming to good taste —**taste´ful·ly** adv.

taste´less adj. without flavor; lacking taste or quality

tast´y adj. having a fine flavor

tat´ter n. a torn shred — vt., vi. make or become ragged —**tat´tern** ragged clothing

tat·ter·de·ma´lion n. one wearing ragged clothing; a ragamuffin

tat´ter·sall n. a pattern of intersecting dark lines on a light background; cloth of this design —adj.

tat´tle vi., vt. gossip —n. idle chatter

tat´tle·tale n. an informer

—adj. revealing: tattletale signs

tat·too´ vt. mark skin with patterns —n. pattern or design on the skin; a drumbeat; sounding of drum or bugle to signal return to quarters

tat´ty adj. worn or shabby

taunt n. a sarcastic remark; a jibe —vt. provoke with derision or insults

taupe n. a brownish gray color

taut adj. stretched tight; tidy

tau·tol´o·gy n. needless repetition in speaking —**tau·to·log´i·cal** adj.

tav´ern n. an inn; a place licensed to sell alcoholic beverages

taw´dry adj. cheap and showy; lacking taste or quality

tawn´y adj. tan-colored —n. tan

tax n. charge levied for support of government; heavy demand —vt. levy a tax; Impose a burden on —**tax shelter** a financial manipulation designed to reduce tax liability

tax·a´tion n. process of taxing; amount levied; revenue raised

tax´i n. a taxicab —vi. ride in a taxicab; move along the surface

tax´i·cab a passenger vehicle for hire

tax·i·der·my n. the art of stuffing and mounting animals

tax´ing adj. difficult, trying

tax·on´o·my n. principles for classification of plant and animal life

T cell *n.* a type of white blood cell essential to the immune system

tea *n.* leaves of an Asian plant used to prepare a beverage; a beverage; a social gathering —**tea service** a set of matching cups, saucers, creamer, etc. for serving tea

teach *vt.* provide instruction; instruct in: *teach French*; train —**teach´er** *n.*

teaching machine a computer that presents material for learning and provides corrective feedback

teak *n.* an extremely durable wood

team *n.* a group working together as a unit —*vi.* work as a unit —**team player** one who works cooperatively — **team´work** harmony of action among members of a group

team´ster *n.* one who drives a team of horses or a motor vehicle

tear *n.* fluid from the eye; a break or rip; a violent outburst —*vt.* pull apart; wound or lacerate; distress or disrupt —*vi.* become torn; move with haste or energy

tear´ful *adj.* causing tears; accompanied by tears — **tear´ful•ly** *adv.*

tear´ing *adj.* with great haste

tear´jerk•er *n.* a book, play, etc. designed to evoke tears

tear´y *adj.* filled or wet with tears; sentimental; over-emotional

tease *vt.* annoy or vex; coax or beg; comb —*vi.* annoy in a petty way —*n.* one who teases —**teas´er** *n.*

tea´spoon *n.* a small spoon

tea´spoon, tea´spoon•ful *n.* the amount a teaspoon will hold

tech´ni•cal *adj.* relating to a particular art, trade, etc.; exhibiting technique; according to accepted rules — **tech´ni•cal•ly** *adv.*

tech•ni•cal´i•ty *n.* method peculiar to an art, trade, etc.; a petty detail

tech•ni´cian *n.* one skilled in a particular field

tech´nics *n.* the study or principles of an art, trade, etc.

tech•nique´ *n.* a way of working; degree of skill exhibited; a method of accomplishing

tech•noc´ra•cy *n.* government dominated by technicians

tech•nol´o•gy *n.* technical means for meeting needs of a society; technical terms

tec•ton´ics *n.* the art of construction; study of the movements of the earth´s crust —**tec•ton´ic** *adj.*

te´di•ous *adj.* boring or repetitious

te´di•um *n.* the quality of being boring, monotonous, etc.

teem *vi.* be full or overflowing

teen´age, teen´-age, teen´-aged, teen´-aged *adj.* of the ages from 13 to 19 —**teen, teen´ager, teen´-ag´er** *n.*

tee´ter *vi.* walk unsteadily; vacillate or waver

teethe *vi.* develop teeth

tee•to´tal *adj.* advocating abstention from alchohohc beverages

tel´e•cast *vt., vi.* broadcast by television —*n.*

tel•e•com•mu•ni•ca´tion *n.* communicating by radio,

television, telephone, etc.

tel·e·com·mut·ing *n.* working from home through a computer link

tel·e·com´fer·ence *n.* a meeting conducted by telephone or closed circuit television —*vi.* participate in a teleconference

tel´e·graph *n.* a system for transmitting messages over a distance

tel·e·ki·ne´sis *n.* unexplained movement of objects, as by occult power

tel·e·mar·ket·ing *n.* the selling of products by telephone or television

te·lem´e·try *n.* automatic measurement and transmission of data

tel·e·ol´o·gy *n.* study of final causes; explanation of natural phenomenon in terms of design and purpose —**tel·e·ol´o·gist** *n.*

te·lep´a·thy *n.* extrasensory communication —**tel·e·path´ic** *adj.*

tel´e·phone *n.* a device for transmitting speech —*vt., vi.* communicate by telephone

te·leph´o·ny *n.* the technology of telephone communication

tel·e·pho´to *adj.* of a lens which produces a near view of far objects

tel·e·pho·tog´raphy *n.* technique for producing magnified photographs of distant objects

tel´e·scope *n.* an instrument for viewing distant objects

tel´e·thon *n.* a television show intended to raise funds

tel·e·van´ge·lism *n.* the broadcasting of religious shows

tel´e·vise *vt., vi.* transmit a television signal

tel·e·vi´sion *n.* a system for transmission and reception of visual images and sound

tell *vt.* narrate or relate in detail; express in words; as certain or distinguish: *tell who is taller*—*vi.* give an account; serve as an indication: *their rags fell of their poverty*

tell´er *n.* one who narrates; (US) a bank employee

tell´ing *adj.* producing a marked effect —**tell´ing·ly** *adv.*

tell´tale *adj.* revealing —*n.* a tattler; an outward sign or indication

tem·er·ar´i·ous *adj.* daring or reckless —**tem·er·ar´i·ous·ly** *adv.*

te·mer´i·ty *n.* disregard for danger

tem´peh *n.* a high-protein food made from fermented soybeans

tem´per *n.* a fit of anger; a tendency to anger; temperament; hardness of a metal —*vt.* moderate, as by adding; toughen, as by hardship —*vi.* be or become tempered

tem´per·a *n.* a type of paint

tem´per·a·ment *n.* nature or disposition; a moody disposition

tem·per·a·men´tal *adj.* overly excitable, capricious, etc.; unpredictable — **tem·per·a·men´tal·ly** *adv.*

tem´per·ance *n.* moderation, self-control -*adj.* restraint

tem´per·ate *adj.* marked by moderation; not extreme; calm, restrained

tem´per·a·ture n. relative heat or cold; an excess of heat. in a body

tem´pered adj. of a particular temperament: *quick-tempered*; modified: *discipline tempered with love*

tem´pest n. a violent wind; violent disturbance

tem·pes´tu·ous adj. stormy, turbulent —**tem·pes´tu·ous·ly** adv.

tem´plate n. a pattern

tem´ple n. a place of worship; a structure dedicated to a special purpose: *a temple of learning*

tem´po n. relative speed and rhythm

tem´po·ral adj. worldly; material as contrasted to spiritual; transitory; of time — **tem´po·ral·ness** n.

tem´po·rar·y adj. lasting for a time only; not permanent — n. a seasonal or substitute employee

tem´po·rize vi. act evasively to gain time or defer commitment; give in to a situation, circumstances, etc.; compromise

tempt vt. try to persuade; risk provoking: tempt fate; influence: *tempted by profit*

temp·ta´tion n. that which tempts; the state of being tempted

tempt´ing adj. attractive; seductive

tem´pu·ra n. vegetables or seafood fried in a light batter

ten´a·ble adj. capable of being maintained or defended

te·na´cious adj. obstinate or persistent; adhesive or sticky; strongly retentive — **te·nac´i·ty** n.

ten´an·cy n. the holding of property; the period of possession

ten´ant n. one who rents or has title to property belonging to another; an occupant - vt., vi.

tend vi. have an aptitude or inclination; attend; serve; give attention or care —vt. care for; watch over

tend´en·cy n. an inclination; movement toward an end or result

ten·den´tious, ten·den´cious adj. disposed to a particular view

ten´der[1] adj. delicate, fragile; youthful: *a tender age*; marked by gentleness and consideration; expressing affection; sensitive

tend´er[2] vt. present for acceptance —n. an offer; that offered, esp. of money; boat that ferries passengers or supplies; railway car that carries fuel and water; person who tends or ministers

ten´der·foot n. a newcomer or beginner —adj. inexperienced

ten´der·heart·ed adj. responsive to another's troubles; compassionate; sympathetic

ten´der·loin n. cut of meat; a district known for crime and corruption

ten·di·ni´tis, ten·do·ni´tis n. inflammation of a tendon

ten´don n. tough, fibrous tissue that attaches muscle to bone

ten´dril n. a delicate, curling extension by which certain plants attach themselves

ten´e·ment n. rented rooms; a low-rent run-down building;

property held by a renter

ten´et n. a principle or doctrine

ten´on n. a projection for insertion into a mortise to form ajoint

ten´or n. character or nature; a general course or tendency; male voice higher than a baritone —adj. of a voice, singing part, or musical instrument in the upper range

tense adj. stretched tight; under mental stress; providing suspense. —vt., vi. make or become tense —n. quality of a verb that denotes time or state of being

ten´sile adj. of tension; capable of being stretched

tensile strength resistance of material to force that tends to rupture

ten´sion n. a stretching or being stretched; mental strain, anxiety; device on a machine that regulates stress —**ten´sion•al** adj.

ten´sor n. a muscle that tenses or stretches —**ten•so´ri•al** adj.

tent n. a portable shelter —vi. pitch a tent; camp

ten•ta•cle n. a long, flexible appendage for touching, grasping, etc.

ten´ta•tive adj. not finalized, subject to change; somewhat uncertain

ten´ter n. a drying frame for cloth

ten´ter•hook a pin for holding cloth on a tenter — **be on tenterhooks** be in a state of anxiety

ten´u•ous adj. weak, lacking substance, as of evidence;

thin: lacking density

ten´ure n. right or condition, etc. of holding property, office, etc.

tep´id adj. moderately warm; unenthusiastic —**tep´id•ly** adv.

te•qui´la n. an alcoholic beverage of Mexican origin

te•rat´o•gen n. an agent that causes malformation in a developing fetus —**te•rat•o•gen´ic** adj.

ter´i•ya´ki n. a Japanese dish of broiled marinated fish or meat

term n. word or expression to name, convey a concept, etc.; conditions of an agreement; a fixed period; a prescribed period —vt. to designate

term insurance life insurance active for a specific period

ter´ma´gant n. a scolding woman — adj. abusive or quarrelsome

ter´mi•na•ble adj. that may be terminated —**ter´mi•na•bly** adv.

ter´mi•nal adj. of an end to action, life, etc.; at or forming an end or limit —n. an intermediate or terminating point; an electrical junction; a computer work station

ter´mi•nate vt., vi. end; bound or limit —**ter´mi•na•tive** adj.

ter´mi•na´tion n. ending, outcome, or conclusion; being terminated; that which bounds or limits

ter´mi•na•tor n. one who or that which terminates

ter´mi•nol´o•gy n. terms relating to a discipline, as art, science, etc.

ter·mi·nus *n.* final point or end; a terminal

ter·mi·tar´i·um *n.* a termite nest

ter´mite´ *n.* an insect resembling the ant, noted for boring into wood

terp´si·cho·re´an *adj.* of dancing

ter´race *n.* a raised level area; a raised street fronting row houses; paved area connected to a house —*vt.* provide with a terrace —**terrace house** (*Brit.*) one of a row of dwellings that share common walls with those adjoining

ter´ra cot´ta clay pottery; a reddish-brown color —**ter´ra-cot´ta** *adj.*

ter´ra fir´ma solid ground

ter·rain´ *n.* land area described by a particular characteristic

ter·rane´ *n.* a series of similar rock formations

ter´ra·pin *n.* a type of tortoise

ter·rar´i·um *n.* a glass enclosure for growing small plants

ter·raz´zo *n.* flooring of stone chips set in mortar

ter·res´tri·al *adj.* belonging to the planet Earth; pertaining to earth; of land as distinct from water

ter´ri·ble *adj.* causing fear or dread; severe or extreme: *a terrible headache*; dreadful: *a terrible meal*

ter´ri·er *n.* a breed of small dogs

ter·rif´ic *adj.* arousing fear or terror; unusually good

ter´ri·fy *vt.* fill with terror

ter·rine´ *n.* a dish for cooking and serving food

ter·ri·to´ri·al *adj.* of a territory; restricted to a particular territory

territorial waters coastal waters under government jurisdiction

ter·ri·to´ri·al·ize *vt.* create or extend a territory

ter´ri·to·ry *n.* a governed domain; a distinctive area: *sales territory*; a region self-governed but lacking the status of a state or province

ter´ror *n.* great fear; that which causes fear; a difficult child

ter´ror·ism *n.* violence to achieve political end —**ter´ror·ist** *n.*

ter´ror·ize *vt.* terrify or intimidate, esp. by acts of violence

ter´ry, ter´ry·cloth *n.* an absorbent pile fabric

terse *adj.* short and to the point

ter´ti·ar·y *adj.* third in importance

test *vt.* subject to examination —*vi.* undergo examination —*n.* an examination; a criterion or standard

tes´ta·ment *n.* a will; a statement testifying to some belief; proof

tes´tate *adj.* having a will

tes´ter *n.* one who administers tests; a canopy, as over a bed

tes´ti·cle *n.* one of the two sex glands of the male

tes´ti·fy *vi.* make a solemn declaration; bear witness; serve as evidence

tes·ti·mo´ni·al *n.* an endorsement of character, value, etc.; public acknowledgment

tes·ti·mo·ny *n.* a statement under oath; public acknowledgment; evidence or proof

tes'ty *adj.* irritable —**tes'ti·ness** *n.*

tet·a·nus *n.* an often fatal bacterial disease marked by spasmodic muscular contractions

tête'-à-tête' *adj.* confidential —*n.* a private conversation

teth'er *n.* line for restraining an animal; limit of one's power, etc.

te·tral'o·gy *n.* a series of four novels, plays, etc.

text *n.* words of an author or speaker; main body of matter in a book; words of a song, opera, etc.

text'book *n.* a book used as a standard or basis of instruction

tex'tile *n.* a fabric —*adj.* of weaving or woven fabric

tex'tu·al *adj.* of or relating to a text

tex'tu·al·ism *n.* strict religious interpretation of a text

tex'ture *n.* characteristic appearance or tactile qualities: *texture of bread*; structure, form, etc. of a work: *the tightly-knit texture of his prose*; basic nature

thal'a·mus *n.* matter at the base of the brain involved in sensory transmission

than·a·tol'o·gy *n.* the study of death and dying —**than·a·tol'o·gist** *n.*

thane *n.* in Anglo-Saxon England, one granted land for military service; chief of a Scottish clan

thank *vt.* express gratitude

thank'ful *adj.* feeling or expressing gratitude

thank'less *adj.* unlikely to elicit approval; unappreciated

thanks'giv'ing *n.* giving of thanks; a means of expressing thanks

that *adj.* of something previously mentioned, understood, or pointed out; denoting something remote —*pron.* a thing mentioned, understood, etc.; the thing more remote —*adv.* to the extent required: *I can't see that far* —*conj.*

thatch *n.* a covering of leaves, reeds, etc. made to shed water; material used for such covering —*vt.* cover with a thatch —**thatch'er** *n.*

thaw *vi.* melt; rise in temperature; become less aloof —*vt.* cause to thaw —*n.* warmth of temperature; progression toward sociability

the·a·ter *n.* structure or area for presentation of entertainment, lectures, etc.; the legitimate stage; scene of an action: *theater of war*

the·at'ric, the·at'ri·cal *adj.* pertaining to any aspect of the theater; dramatically compelling; pretentious —**the·at'ri·cal'i·ty** *n.*

the·at'rics *n.* undue dramatization

theft *n.* stealing; that which is stolen

the'ism *n.* belief in a god or gods

theme *n.* main subject or topic of art, speech, etc.; a short essay

the·oc'ra·cy *n.* government by religious authority

the·od'o·lite *n.* a surveying instrument

the·og'o·ny n. chronicle of the genealogy of gods — **the·o·gon'ic** adj.

the·o·lo'gi·an n. one trained or engaged in study of religious belief

the·o·log'ic, the·o·log'i·cal adj. relating to religious matters

the·ol'o·gy n. the study of religion and religious doctrine

the'o·rem n. a proposition demonstrably true or considered to be so

the·o·ret'ic, the·o·ret'i·cal adj. relating to theory; existing in theory only, disposed to speculation

the'o·rize vt. speculate; put forth as a theory —**the'o·rist** n.

the'o·ry n. conjecture or speculation; fundamental or abstract. principles; a proposed explanation

the·os'o·phy n. religious philosophy based on mystical insight

ther·a·peu'tic adj. having curative powers —**ther'a·peu'ti·cal·ly** adv.

ther·a·peu'tics n. study of treatment for illness and disease

ther'a·py n. treatment of illness and disease; a type of treatment: *physical therapy* —**ther'a·pist** n.

there adv. in or at that place; yonder; in that respect —n. a position removed from that of the speaker

there'a·bout, there'a·bouts adv. approximately

there'af'ter adv. from that time on

there'by' adv. through the agency of

there'fore' adv., conj. for that reason; consequently

there'in' adv. in that respect

there'in·af'ter adv. in a subsequent part

ther'e·min n. an electronic instrument for producing musical tones

there·upon' adv. following or in consequence of

there·with' adv. thereupon

ther'mal, ther'mic adj. relating to or caused by heat; warm — n. a rising current of warm air

ther·mo·dy·nam'ics n. the relationship between heat and other energy sources

ther'mo·gram n. the record made by a thermograph

ther'mo·graph n. device that records temperature as it is registered

ther·mog'ra·phy n. use of heat to produce raised letters on paper; the recording of temperature with a thermograph

ther·mom'eter n. device for measuring temperature

ther'mo·nu·cle·ar adj. fusion of atomic particles by heat

ther·mo·plas'tic adj. soft when heated —n. a thermoplastic resin

ther'mo·stat n. a device to control temperature indoors

ther·mo·trop'ic adj. tending to grow or move toward heat

the·sau'rus n. a collection of words with their synonyms; words relating to a specific subject

the'sis n., pl. **the'ses** n. a proposition advanced and defended by argumentation; an unproved premise; a formal treatise

thes´pi•an adj. relating to drama —n. an actor or actress

they pron. persons or things previously mentioned; people in general

thi•am´in, thi•am´ine n. vi. tamin ß₁

thick adj. relatively large in depth or extent; being a specified dimension; closely packed: a field thick with flowers; viscous: thick sauce; dense: thick fog, noticeable: thick accent —n. most dense or intense part: thick of battle—adv.

thick´en vt., vi. make or become thick or thicker

thick´et n. a dense growth

thick´set´ adj. short and stocky; closely planted

thick´-skinned´ adj. slow to anger; indifferent to insults

thief n. one who takes without permission

thieve vt. steal —vi. be a thief

thiev´er•y it stealing

thigh n. part of the leg between the hip and knee

thin adj. of little depth or width; lean and slender; lacking density: thin sauce —vt., vi. make or become thin or thinner —adv.

thing n. a separate entity; circumstance: things have changed; an act: the right thing to do; an idea or notion: don't put things in her head; an unexplainable or mysterious quality or attraction: he has a thing for tall women

think vt. conceive mentally; determine by reasoning; believe to be true; remember or recall; intend —vi. engage in thought; weigh in the mind; have an opinion, feeling, etc.; recall —**think better of** reconsider —**think little of** consider inconsequential —**think the world of** venerate or admire

think´a•ble adj. possible; worth considering —**think´a•bly** adv.

think´ing adj. intellectually active —n. result of thought; one's opinion or bias

think tank n. a group of scientists, executives, etc., joined to study a particular problem

thin´—skinned´ adj. easily offended

third adj., adv. next in order after the second; being one of three parts —n.

third´-rate´ adj. of poor quality

third world underdeveloped nations

thirst n. a need for water; any craving: thirst for glory —vi. have a desire or craving

thirst´y adj. lacking moisture; parched; eagerly desirous

this adj. that near or present, understood, or just mentioned —pron. a person or thing near or present, etc.—adv.

thong n. a narrow strip, as for fastening; a lash of a whip; a type of sandal; a type of beach wear

tho•rac´ic adj. relating to the thorax

tho´rax n.the body between the neck and abdomen, enclosed by ribs; middle segment of an insect

thorn n. a sharp outgrowth; a source of discomfort

thorn´y adj. full of thorns; difficult or perplexing -- **thorn´i·ness** n.

thor´ough adj. attentive to detail; complete, exhaustive: a *thorough search* —**thor´ough·ness** n.

thor´ough·bred adj. bred from pure stock; possessing excellence —n. a horse bred for racing

thor´ough·fare [US] n. a main road

thor´ough·go·ing adj. characterized by thoroughness

though conj. notwithstanding; even if; and yet —adv.

thought n. process or product of thinking; concepts identified with a time, place, discipline, etc.: *modern political thought*; consideration or attention; preoccupation

thought´ful. adj. contemplative, reflective; attentive or considerate; preoccupied —**thought´ful·ness** n.

thought´less adj. marked by lack of care or regard; inconsiderate; flighty —**thought·less·ness** it

thrall n.one held in bondage

thrash vt. to thresh grain; beat; defeat utterly —vi. move about violently

thread n. slender cord or line; filament; that runs through: the thread of a plot —vt., vi.

threadbare adj. worn; commonplace

threat n. declaration of intent to harm; danger

threat´en vt., vi. utter threats; appear menacing —**threat´en·ing** adj.

thresh vt. beat to separate grain from husks —vi. to thrash about

thresh´old n. a doorsill; an entering point or beginning

thrift n. care in the management of resources —**thrift´y** adj.

thrift´shop a shop for used goods

thrill vi., vt. feel excitement — n. a feeling of excitement

thrill´er n. an exciting story

thrive vi. be succesful; prosper; flourish —**thriv´ing·ly** adv.

throat n. front part of the neck; passage at the back of the mouth; any narrow passage

throat´y adj. guttural or husky

throb vi. pulsate rhythmically; show emotion by trembling —n. a pulsation —**throb´bing·ly** adv.

throe n. violent pain, as in death or childbirth

throm·bo´sis n. formation of a blood clot, as in the heart or an artery

throm´bus n. a clot

throne n. authority of a ruler; a seat symbolizing authority

throng n. a closely packed group —vi., vt. gather or crowd together

throt´tle n. a valve controlled flow —vt. choke or strangle; silence or suppress; change speed by means of a throttle

through prep. from end to end, side to side, etc.; permeating; by way of —adv.

through·out´ adv. in every part —prep. all through

throw vt. hurl; place carelessly; direct or project —vi. cast or fling —n. casting or flinging; distance flung; a scarf or light covering

thrust *vt.* push or shove with force; pierce ⁻*vi.* make a sudden push; force oneself through —*n.* sudden forceful push; vigorous attack; force that drives or propels; a salient force: the thrust *of his remarks*

thud *n.* a dull, heavy sound; a blow or fall —*vi.*

thug *n.* a hoodlum or ruffian; formerly, a professional assassin

thumb *n.* a digit of the human hand; similar part on animals

thumb index indentations along the edge of a book to indicate sections

thumb´screw *n.* a screw turned with the fingers; instrument of torture

thumb´tack *n.* a broadheaded tack

thump *n.* a blow with a blunt object; the sound of a blow — *vt., vi.* beat or strike

thun´der *n.* sound accompanying lightning; a similar noise —*vi., vt.* make a noise like thunder

thun´der•bolt *n.* lightning attended by thunder; a forceful person

thun´der•clap *n.* sound of thunder

thun´der•cloud *n.* large, dark cloud

thun´der•ous *adj.* of a loud sound

thun´der•show•er *n.* rain accompanied by thunder and lightning

thun´der•storm *n.* a heavy blowing rain accompanied by thunder

thun´der•strick•en,   thun´der•struck *adj.* astonished

thwart *vt.* frustrate or foil; extend across —*n.* seat or brace extending across a small boat or canoe —*adj.* extending or passing across

thyme *n.* a plant of the mint family; the leaves, used for seasoning

thy´mus *n.* a ductless glendlike structure at the base of the neck

thy´roid *n.* cartilage of the larynx which form the Adam's apple; a large, ductless gland located near the larynx —*adj.*

ti•ar´a *n.* a jeweled head ornament

tib´ia *n.* the larger of two leg bones extending below the knee; the shinbone —**tib´i•al** *adj.*

tic *n.* involuntary muscular spasm

tick´et *n.* thing showing entitlement to transportation, a show, etc.; a tag or label; candidates on a ballot; a court summons —*vt.* attach a label; furnish with a ticket

tick´le *vt.* cause to laugh by touching; amuse or entertain —*vi.* have or cause a tingling sensation —*n.*

tick´ler *n.* a file, note, etc. that serves as reminder

tick´lish *adj.* responsive to tickling; easily offended; requiring tact

tid´al *adj.* pertaining to or influenced by tides; dependent on tides

tidal wave a great incoming rise of water; a surge, as of public opinion

tid´bit *n.* a delicacy

tide *n.* periodic rise and fall of the ocean's water

tide´land n. land periodically covered by a rising tide

tide´wa•ter n. water near a coast affected by the tides

ti´dings n, news

ti´dy adj. neat and orderly —vt., vi. put in order —**ti´di•ness** n.

tie vt. make a knot; fasten or join; equal another —vi. make a connection; make the same score —n. fastener; a bond or connection; (US) timber that supports tracks

tier n. one arranged above another

tiff n. a spat; a small argument —vi. take part in a spat

ti´ger n. a large striped carnivorous feline; a fiercely determined person

ti´ger-eye n. yellow and brown semiprecious stone

tight adj. firmly fixed or secure; fully stretched; difficult or demanding; closely fitted; scarce; stingy; intoxicated —adv. securely

tight´en vt., vi. make tight or tighter

tight´-fist´ed adj. stingy

tight´-lipped adj. uncommunicative; secretive

tights n. close-fitting garment, worn by dancers, gymnasts, etc.

tight´wad n. a miser

til´de n. diacritical mark (-) used to indicate a change in pronunciation

tile n. a thin ornamental piece for covering roofs, floors, walls, etc. —vt. cover with tiles

till vt., vi. work soil for cultivation —n. a money drawer; available cash

till´age n. cultivation of land

tilt vi., vt. incline at an angle

tim´bal n. a kettledrum

tim´bale n. baked custard with cheese, fish, etc.

tim´ber n. (Brit.) wood dressed for use in construction; standing trees

tim´ber•land n. land covered with trees

tim´ber•line n. an imaginary line beyond which trees do not grow, as on a mountainside

tim´bre n. quality of a sound

time n. the concept of continuous existence; a moment or period; system for measuring duration; musical tempo —adj. relating to time; payable in the future —vt. record speed or duration; mark rhythm

time´-hon´ored adj. accepted as customary or traditional

time´less adj. eternal; not limited to a specific time —**time´less•ness** n.

time´ly adj. occurring at a proper or convenient time —**time´li•ness** n.

time´ous adj. timely

time shar•ing n. access to a central computer; use of vacation property by several owners in turn

time´ta•ble n. a schedule; a plan for completion of parts of a project

tlme´worn adj. ineffective by time or overuse, as a motto or maxim

tim´id adj. fearful; lacking self-confidence —**ti•mid´i•ty** n.

tim´ing n. regulating occurance to insure maximum effect

tim·o·rous *adj.* fearful; anxious

tlm·o·thy *n.* a perennial grass

tim·pa·ni *n.* kettledrums

tin *n.* metallic element used alloys

tinc·ture *n.* a medicinal solution; a coloring substance; a slight trace

tin·der *n.* dry substance that ignites easily —**tin·der·y** *adj.*

tin·der·box *n.* container of material for starting a fire; highly flammable material; an excitable person

tine *n.* a prong, as on a fork

tinge *n.* a faint trace, as of color —*vt.* to tint or color lightly

tin·gle *vi., vt.* experience a prickly, stinging sensation —*n.* a stinging sensation —**tin·gly** *adv.*

tin·kle *vi., vt.* produce light metallic sounds, as of a bell

tin·ni·tus *n.* a ringing or buzzing in the ears

tin·ny *adj.* of or containing tin; flimsy; of a flat sound

tin·sel *n.* thin glittering bits of ornamentation; something showy, but of little value —*adj.* decorated with tinsel; gaudy or showy *vt.* hang with tinsel —**tin·sel·ry** *n.*

tin·smith *n.* one who works with tin

tint *n.* a pale color; shading or gradation of color —*vt.* apply color

tin·tin·nab·u·la·tion *n.* the ringing of bells

ti·ny *adj.* very small

tip *n.* a light tap; gift of money for service; a helpful hint; confidential information; an extremity; an end or cap —*vt.* lean; overturn; strike lightly; adorn the tip of —*vi.* become tilted; overturn

tip·off *n.* a warning

tip·ple *vt., vi.* drink frequently and habitually

tip·sy *adj.* unsteady; intoxicated

ti·rade´ *n.* a prolonged denunciation

tire *vt.* reduce the strength of by exertion; make weary or impatient —*vi.* become weary; lose patience —*n.* (US) covering for a wheel

tired *adj.* weary; fatigued

tire·less *adj.* not easily fatigued; energetic

tire·some *adj.* tedious or boring; mundane

tis·sue *n.* an aggregate of organic cells and associated matter; a light fabric; light disposable paper

tissue culture tissue kept alive and growing in a culture medium

tissue paper thin wrapping paper

ti·tan *n.* a giant

tithe *n.* one tenth; contribution for support of the clergy and church; a tax or levy —*vt.* pay a tithe

tit·il·late *vt.* cause a tickling sensation; stimulate or excite erotically

ti·tle *n.* a descriptive name; name of a book, song, etc.; a designation of rank, profession, etc.; legal right to property —*vt.* give a name or designation; entitle to

ti·tled *adj.* having a title

tit·ter *n.* a suppressed laugh

tit·tle *n.*. the tiniest amount

tit·u·lar *adj.* existing in name only

tiz´zy n. a bewildered state of mind

toad a. a jumping amphibian resembling a frog; loathsome person

toad´y adj. an obsequious flatterer; one acting without scruples to gain favor —vt., vi. flatter or serve without question —**toad´y·ism** n.

toast vt., vi. make warm or browned; drink to one's health —n. a tribute followed by a drink; one well-known and greatly admired

toast´mas·ter n. host at a public banquet

toast´y adj. comfortably warm

to·bog´gan n. a sledlike vehicle for traveling over snow or Ice —vi. ride on a toboggan

tod´dle vi. walk unsteadily —n. a shaky walk

tod´dy n. spirits mixed with hot water, spices, and sugar

toe n. a digit of the foot

to´fu n. a cheese-like food made from soybeans

to´ga n. a loose flowing robe

to·geth´er adv. in the company of others; collectively, as one unit

tog´ger·y n. clothing

toil n. strenuous labor —vt. work hard —vt. accomplish with great effort —**toil´er** n.

toi´let n. a bathroom fixture; the process of grooming —adj. used in grooming: toilet articles

toi´let·ry n. soap, cologne, etc. for personal grooming

toil´some adj. involving hard work; difficult

to´ken n. tangible evidence of affection, authority, etc.; a metal piece issued in place of currency —adj. nominal

or minimal; partial

to´ken·ism n. attempting to fulfill an obligation with a symbolic gesture

tol´er·a·ble adj. endurable; barely satisfactory —**tol´er·a·bly** adv.

tol´er·ance n. freedom from prejudice; ability to bear hardship; allowance for variation; resistance

tol´er·ant adj. long-suffering; indulgent

tol´er·ate vt. allow or concede; bear

toll n. a charge, as for passage; sound of a bell rung slowly and regularly —vi., vt. take or exact a charge; to sound, as a bell

tomb n. a burial place —vt. entomb or bury

tomb´stone n. marker on a grave

tome n. a large heavy book

tom·fool´er·y adj. nonsensical behavior; foolishness

to·mor´row n. the day after today

ton´al adj. pertaining to tone or tonality —**to´nal·ly** adv. **to´nal·i·ty** n. a system or scheme of tones as in music or visual art

tone n. musical sound or its quality; characteristic tendency or quality: mode of writing or speech; style or elegance; effect of light and color —vt. impart a desired sound or color —**tone down** quiet or soften

tongue n. muscular organ of the mouth; manner of speaking; language or dialect; anything resembling a tongue —**tongue twister** a phrase difficult to repeat

ton´ic n. that promoting health or well-being; quinine water —adj. of tone; stimulating or refreshing

ton´sil n. either of two lymphoid masses located in the opening between the mouth and larynx

ton•sil•lec´to•my n. surgical removal of the tonsils

ton•sil•li´tis n. inflammation of the tonsils

ton•so´ri•al adj. of a barber or barbering

ton´sure n. shaving of the head —vt.

ton´tine n. an agreement by which an investment held in trust reverts to the survivor or survivors

too adv. also; excessive; extremely

tool n. an implement used to accomplish: books are tools of learning; one used for the designs of another —vt. form or shape with a tool; to scribe a motif or design

tool´mak•er n. a machinist who makes or repairs tools

tooth n. hard structure for seizing and chewing food; small projection on a saw, gear, etc.; a rough surface; appetite or taste

tooth´ache n. pain in a tooth

tooth´less adj. lacking teeth; lacking effectiveness — **tooth´less•ly** adv.

tooth´some adj. pleasant tasting

top n. uppermost part; upper surface; a lid; highest degree; the best —adj. relating to the top; most important, best —vt. remove the uppermost part; provide a top; surmount or surpass

top´coat n. a light overcoat

top´-heavy adj. unstable due to excess weight at the top; of an organization with an overly large executive staff

to´pi•ar•y n. bushes or trees, formed in decorative shapes —adj. pertaining to the art of topiary

top´ic n. subject matter, as for a speech

top´i•cal adj. relating to matters of local or current interest; pertaining to a topic

top´knot n. a tuft, knot of hair, etc.; an ornament worn as a headdress

top´less adj. lacking a top; nude above the waist

top´lev´el adj. of the highest rank or importance

to•pog´ra•phy n. physical features of a region topographic surveying

top´o•nym n. a place name — **top•o•nym´ic** adj.

to•pon´y•my n. study of place names

top´ple vi. to fall —vt..cause to fall; to overthrow

top´soil n. the surface soil of land

top´sy•tur´vy adj., adv. upside down; in utter disarray —n. a state of disorder

tor n. a rocky peak

torch n. a flaming stick or rod; anything that brightens; a device producing an intense flame

torch´bear•er n. one who carries a torch; one who conveys truth or knowledge; leader of a cause

to´re•a•dor n. a bullfighter -

tor´ment n. intense pain or anguish, or its source — **tor•ment´** vt. torture; harass

tor•na´do n. a whirling wind - of exceptional force

tor´pid adj. dormant; sluggish; apathetic —**tor´pid•• ness** n.

tor´por n. loss of sensibility or power of motion; apathy, listlessness

torque n. turning or twisting force; measure of tendency to rotation

tor´rent n. rapid, turbulent stream; a violent flow: tor- rent of abuse

tor´rid adj. intensely hot and dry; passionate—**tor-rid•• ness** n.

tor´so n. trunk of the human body

tort n. a civil wrong not involving breach of contract — **tor´tious** adj.

tor´te n. a rich cake

tor•tel•li´ni n. ring-shaped pasta stuffed with cheese, spinach, etc.

tor•ti´lla n. a small, flat bread made of corn meal and baked on a skillet

tor´toise n. a land turtle

tor´tu•ous adj. twisting, as a road; devious: tortuous logic

tor´ture n. intence suffering; something that causes pain —vt. inflict pain upon; cause to suffer

tor•tur•ous adj. pertaining to torture

toss vt. throw or cast; pitch or fling about; interject casu- ally; turn over and mix —vi. be thrown about; roll about restlessly, as in sleep —n. a throw; a quick movement

toss´pot n. a drunkard

to´tal n. entire amount —adj. complete —vt. ascertain the amount

to•tal´i•tar´i•an adj. of an op- pressive government with absolute power

to•tal´i•ty n. total amount; the state of being whole

tote vt. to carry —n. some- thrng carried —**tot´a•ble** adj.

to´tem n. an object or repre- sentation that serves as em- blem for a group, tribe, etc.

tot´ter vi. tremble or waver: seem near to collapse; walk unsteadily —n. an unsteady or wobbly walk

tou´can n. a tropical bird with colorful plumage and large beak

touch vt. perceive by feel; be or come into contact with; to affect; impress emotionally — vi. come into contact —n. contact; sensation conveyed by contact; a distinctive manner or style: master's touch; a trace —**touch on** concern or relate to —**touch up** correct or correction

touched adj. effected emo- tionally; mentally unbal- anced; peculiar or eccentric

touch´ing adj. appealing to emotion —prep. with regard to; concerning

touch´y adj. apt to take of- fense; liable to cause offense or contention

tough adj. able to bear stress or strain; difficult to chew; requiring intense effort; un- yielding; severe or harsh — n. a rowdy

tough´en vt., vi. make or be- come tough or tougher — **tough´en•er** n.

tough´-mind´ed adj. facing difficulty with resolve; un- sentimental

tou•pee´ n. a small wig

tour n. a journey or excursion; fixed period of service —vi., vt. go on a trip; take a show on the road

tour´ist n. one traveling for pleasure —adj. suitable for recreational travelers

tour´ist•y adj.

tour´na•ment n. competitive events

tour´ni•quet n. a device to control severe external bleeding

tou´sle vt. dishevel—n. mussed hair

tout vt. solicit; praise highly; sell information —vt. solicit customers, patronage, etc.; sell information —n. one who sells Information

tow vt. pull or drag n. something towed —**in tow** drawn or brought along

to´ward prep. in the direction of; for the purpose of; near, approaching

tow´el n. material for wiping or polishing

tow el´ing n. material for making towels

tow´er n. a tall structure; a place of security —vi. extend to great height

tow´er•ing adj. very tall; very great

town (US) n. an incorporated area larger than a village and smaller than a city; a city; inhabitants or government of a town —adj. of a town or its population

town house (US) a house sharing a common wall with those adjoining

tow´path n. road along a waterway, used by those towing boats

tox•e´mi•a n. presence of toxins in the blood

tox´ic adj. poisonous; caused by poison or a toxin —**tox´ic´i•ty** a.

tox´i•cant n. a poison —adj. poisonous

tox•i•col´o•gy n. the study of poisons **tox•i•col´o•gist** n.

tox´in n. a poisonous substance

toy n. that serving as a plaything; something trifling or ineffectual —vt. consider: toy with an idea; use for one's amusement —adj. designed as ur resembling a toy

trace n. a vestige or mark; a barely detectable quality, characteristic, etc. —vt. find by investigation; copy onto an overlay —vi. follow a track, course of development, etc.

trac´er•y n. delicate ornamentation

tra´chea n. the windpipe; an air passage —**tra´che•al** adj.

tra•che•ot´o•my, tra•che•os´to•my n. surgical incision of the trachea

tra•cho´ma n. a contagious viral disease of the eye

track n. mark left by passage; a path beaten down by use, a trail or roadway; a following or tracing; a continuous belt on which some vehicles ride; metal rails —vt. follow the course of, trail; make tracks —vi. leave tracks; be in agreement: on the saute track

track record history of achievement

tract n. an extended area; a short discourse or pamphlet

trac´ta•ble adj. easily led; malleable

trac′tion n. the act of pulling; pulling power; rolling friction, as of tires on the road

trac′tor n. a farm machine; a motor vehicle used to haul a trailer of freight

trade n. a business or craft; those engaged in a particular business; buying, selling, or exchange; customers —vt. give in exchange; barter —vi. engage in commerce

trade′mark n. that used to distinguish a product; a distinctive feature —vt. to legally protect

tra•di′tion n. body of knowledge transmitted through generations

tra•di′tion•al•ism n. adherence to tradition —**tra•di′tion•al•ist** n.

tra•duce′ vt. willfully harm through misrepresentation; to defame or slander —**tra•duc′er** n.

traf′fic n. passage of people, messages, etc.; those moving; business of buying and selling; transit

tra•ge′di•an n. a dramatic actor or writer

trag′e•dy n. drama which ends unhappily; a calamitous incident

trag′ic adj. of the nature of a tragedy; causing suffering

trag•i•com′e•dy n. a drama having characteristics of both comedy and tragedy; an incident of this nature

trail vt. draw lightly over a surface; follow the track of; follow behind —vi. to hang or extend loosely; grow along the ground; lag behind —n. traces left by passage; something that follows; (US) a worn path, as through a wilderness area

trail′blaz•er n. one who breaks a new trail; an innovator or pioneer

trail′er (US) n. drawn vehicle

train n. a series of rail cars; a thing drawn along or following behind; a connected set —vt. make skillful or proficient; teach; to point —vi. undergo a course of instruction

train′er n. one who coaches; a device to improve physical fitness or skill; (Brit.) a flexible sports shoe

train′ing n. systematic instruction

traipse vi. walk or wander about

trait n. distinguishing quality

trai′tor n. one who betrays a trust; a person found guilty of treason

trai′tor•ous adj. constituting treason; characteristic of a traitor

tra•jec′to•ry n. the path described by a body moving in space

tramp vi., vt. wander; walk heavily —n. one who lives by odd jobs or charity; a long walk; a heavy tread

tram′ple vi., vt. tread heavily; injure or crush by treading

trance n. a dreamlike state as induced by hypnosis, etc.; profound concentration —**trance′like** adj.

tran′quil adj. calm; peaceful —**tran′quil′ness** n.

tran′quil•ize vt., vi. make tranquil

tran′quil•iz•er n. a drug that calms without impairing consciousness

tran·quil'li·ty *n.* the state of being tranquil

trans·act' *vt.* accomplish —*vi.* conduct business —**trans'·ac'tion** *n.*

tran·scend' *vt.* go beyond limits; rise above —*vi.* excel

tran·scen·den'tal *adj.* beyond ordinary limits; supernatural; pertaining to transcendentalism

tran·scen·den'tal·ism *n.* belief that one can attain knowledge that surpasses sensory phenomena

trans·cribe' *vt.* copy or record

tran'script *n.* a copy; a thing recorded, as from notes

tran·sect' *vt.* to divide by cutting across —**tran·sec'·tion** *n.*

trans'fer, trans·fer' *vt.* convey from one person or place to another —**trans'fer** *n.* that conveyed; assignment of title or property

trans·fig·u·ra'tion *n.* a change in appearance

trans·fig'ure *vt.* change appearance of; make splendid

trans·fix' *vt.* pierce through; impale; render motionless

trans·form' *vt.* change form or appearance of; change the nature or character of

trans·fuse' *vt.* cause to flow from one to another; pass into, permeate —**trans·fu'sion** *n.*

trans·gress' *vt.* overstep bounds of propriety or good taste —*vt.* break a law; sin —**trans·gres'sion** *n.*

tran'sient *adj.* not permanent; transitory; residing temporarily —*n.* a temporary resident; a visitor; a tramp —**tran'sience** *n.*

tran'sit *n.* passing over or through; change; carrying across; transportation; a surveying instrument

tran·si'tion *n.* passage from one place, condition, etc. to another

tran'si·to·ry *adj.* existing briefly; ephemeral

trans·late' *vt.* convert to another language; explain in other words

trans·lu'cent *adj.* allowing the passage of light, but not transparent

trans·mi'grate *vi.* move from one place to another; pass into another body, as of the soul at death

trans·mis'si·ble *adj.* able to be transmitted

trans·mit' *vt.* send or pass from one to another; serve as a medium of passage —**trans·mis'sion** *n.*

trans·mog'ri·fy *vt.* transform radically; make into something different

tran'som *n.* a horizontal piece over an opening; a lintel; a small window over a door

trans·par'en·cy *n.* the quality of being transparent; a section of photographic film

trans·par'ent *adj.* that can be seen through; easy to understand; obvious —**trans·par'ent·ness** *n.*

trans·plant' *vt.* uproot and replant; move for resettlement; implant living tissue —*n.* that which is relocated —**trans·plant·ta'tion** *n.*

trans·port' *vt.* carry or convey; seize by emotion —**trans'port** *n.* means or system of conveyance; a state of emotional bliss

trans·por·ta´tion n. a means of transport or travel; conveyance of passengers or freight

trans·pose´ vt. reverse

trans·sex´u·al n. one identifying with the opposite sex

tran·sub·stan´ti·ate vt. transform from one substance into another

trans·verse´ adj. lying across —n. a thing that lies across, from side to side, as a beam

trans·ves´tite n. one who wears the clothing of the opposite sex

trap n. a device for catching; a plan for catching one unawares; device that prevents a return flow —vt. to catch —vi. to set traps for game

tra·peze´ n. a suspended bar for exercise or acrobatics

trap´e·zoid n. a four-sided plane figure with two parallel sides

trap´pings n. adornment or ornamentation; goods or privilege: the trappings of wealth

trash n. (US) waste material; foolish talk; anything worthless

trat·to·ri´a n. an Italian restaurant

trau´ma n. physical or emotional injury; shock — **traumat´ic** adj.

travail´ n. pain or anguish; labor in childbirth —vi. suffer the pangs of childbirth; to toil

trav´el vi. make a journey; proceed; go from place to place —vt. move or journey across or through —n. passage to or over a certain place; a distance moved

trav´eled adj. having made many journeys; frequented by travelers

trav´el·og, trav´el·ogue n. a film or illustrated lecture on travel

tra·verse´ vt. pass over, across, or through —vi. move across; move back and forth —**trav´erse** n. a crosspiece; a screen or barrier —adj. lying across

trav´es·ty n. an absurd rendering, as if in mockery —vt. to parody

trawl n. a large fishing net; an anchored line from which many lines are strung —vi. fish with a trawl —vt. drag to catch fish —**trawl´er** n.

treach´er·ous adj. likely to betray; potentially dangerous or unreliable

treach´er·y n. violation of confidence; treason

trea´cle n. molasses; overly sentimental speech — **trea´cly** adj.

tread vt. step or walk; trample; oppress —vi. walk; press beneath the feet —n. act or sound of treading or trampling; part of a wheel that contacts the surface; impression made by a tire, foot, etc.; a step

trea´dle n. a foot-operated lever — vi.

tread´mill n. mechanism rotated by a walking animal; a monotonous routine

trea´son n. betrayal; a breech of faith —**trea´son·ous** adj.

trea´son·a·ble adj. involving betrayal

trea´sure n. accumulated riches; something precious —vt. set a high value on

treas·ur·er n. one responsible for funds of an organization

trea'sure·trove n. hidden treasure; a rich or rewarding discovery

trea'sur·y n. a department of finance; place where funds are received and disbursed

treat vt., vi. look upon or regard; provide medical attention; deal with; buy for another —**treat'er** n.

treat'a·ble adj. responsive to treatment

trea'tise n. a formal critique

treat'ment n. an act, manner, or process; measures designed to heal or alleviate

trea'ty n. a formal agreement

treb'u·chet n., a medieval catapult

tree n. a woody perennial; something resembling a tree —vt. force to take refuge; to corner or trap

trek vi. move along slowly or with effort; to journey —n. a journey

trel'lis n. a lattice used to support plants, etc.

trem'ble vi. shake involuntarily; vibrate —n. a perceptible shaking

tre·men'dous adj. extraordinarily large; awe-inspiring; marvelous

trem'or n. sudden shaking or vibration; agitation or excitement

trem'u·lous adj. characterized by trembling; showing timidity

trench n. long, narrow ditch; a deep section, as on the ocean floor —vt., vi. dig a ditch

tren'chant adj. clear and effective; cutting or caustic

trench'er·man n. a hearty eater

trend n. prevailing tendency; probable course; popular preference —vi. follow a general course; exhibit a tendency

trend'y adj. of the latest style; fashionable; inclined to current fashion

trep'id adj. timid; timorous; trembling —**trep'id·ly** adv.

trep'i·da'tion n. agitation from fear or apprehension

tres'pass vt. violate the rights of another; go beyond the hounds of what is right or proper —n. transgression of law or moral duty; an intrusion —**tres'pass·er** n.

tress n. a lock of hair

tres'tle n. framework for a table, platform, etc.; a framework bridge

tri'ad n. a group of three

tri·age' n. allocation of a scarce commodity; selection for medical treatment based on immediacy

tri'al n. examination in a court; the process of testing; hardship

tri·an'gle n. a three-sided figure; something involving three persons

tri·an·gu·la'tion n. a method of positioning using trigonometry

tri·ath'lon n. an athletic contest comprising three events

tribe n. people united by ancestry, language, or culture —**trib'al** adj.

trib·u·la'tion n. distress or suffering; cause for distress

tri·bu'nal n. a judicial body; a seat for magistrates, etc.

trib´u·tar·y *adj.* flowing into a larger body; owing tribute

trib´ute *n.* that paid for peace or protection; any obligatory payment

tri·chi´na *n.* a roundworm which carries trichinosis

trich·i·no´sis *n.* an affliction caused by eating under-cooked meat

trick *a.* a deception or practical joke; a malicious act; a peculiar trait or skill —*vt., vi.* to practice deceit

trick´le *vi.* flow or cause to flow in a thin stream —*n.* a thin stream

trick´y *adj.* deceitful; requiring dexterity or skill

tri´dent *n.* a three-pronged spear

tried *adj.* tested; freed of impurities

tri·en´nial *adj.* every third year; lasting three years

tri´fle *vi.* treat as of no value or importance; toy with —*vt.* spend idly and purposelessly —*n.* a thing of little value or importance; a small amount

tri´fling *adj.* frivolous; insignificant

tri·fo´li·ate *adj.* having three leaves

tri·fur´cate, tri·fur´cat·ed *adj.* having three forks or branches

trig·o·nom´e·try *n.* science of the relationships between the sides and angles of a triangle

tri·lat´er·al *adj.* having three sides

trill *vt.* sing or play in a quavering tone —*n.* successive quavering tones; a warble

tril´o·gy *n.* a work in three parts

trim *vt.* remove by cutting; ornament; smooth or make neat —*n.* good physical condition; molding or ornamentation

tri·mes´ter *n.* a three-month period

trin´ket *n.* a small ornament; a trifle

tri´o *n.* a group of three

trip *n.* a journey; a misstep; a nimble step; a blunder —*vi., vt.* stumble or cause to stumble; move quickly and lightly; make an error

tri´ple *vt., vi.* make or become three times as many or as large

trip´let *n.* any of three children from one birth

trip´li·cate *n.* one of three —*vt.* make a set of three

tri´pod *n.* three-legged stand

trip´tych *n.* a work of art on three adjacent panels

tri´reme *n.* ancient warship with three banks of oars

tri·sect´ *vt.* divide into three

trite *adj.* commonplace or hackneyed —**trite´ness** *n.*

trit´u·rate *vt.* reduce to a powder; pulverize —*n.* a powdered pharmaceutical —**trit·u·ra´tion** *n.*

tri´umph *vi.* win a victory; be successful —*n.* an important success

tri·um´phant *adj.* victorious; exultant in victory

tri·um´vi·rate *n.* a coalition of three

triv´et *n.* a three-legged stand for holding a cooking vessel

triv´ia *a.* insignificant matters

triv´i·al *adj.* of little importance; insignificant

triv´i·al·ize *vt.* regard as unimportant; make trivial

tro´che *n.* a medicated lozenge

trog´lo•dyte *n.* a prehistoric man; a person considered primitive

troop *n.* a gathering; a flock or herd; a unit of cavalry —*vi.* move as a group

trope *n.* a figure of speech

tro´phy *n.* proof of victory

trot *n.* a slow running gait —*vi., vt.* go at a slow run

trou´ba•dour *n.* a wandering minstrel

trou´ble *n.* distress or worry; that which causes difficulty; a difficult situation; disease or ailment; effort; general unrest —*vt.* distress or worry; inconvenience or annoy; cause physical pain or discomfort —*vi.* take pains

trou´ble•mak•er *n.* one who habitually causes distress

trou´ble•shoot•er *is.* one assigned to resolve problems, mediate disputes

trou´ble•some *adj.* difficult or trying; of a source of difficulty

trough *n.* a food or water container for animals; a long, narrow depression, as between waves

trounce *vt.* beat or thrash severely

troupe *n.* a company of performers —*vi,* travel as a performer

trous´seau *n.* clothing and linens assembled by a bride

trove *n.* collection of valuable items

trow´el *n.* an implement for digging, applying, smoothing, etc.—*vt,* dig or smooth with a trowel

tru´ant *n.* one absent without

permission; one who shirks a responsibility —*adj.* a juvenile offender; a loafer —*vi.* shirk responsibility

truce *n.* agreement to suspend hostilities; a respite

truck *n.* (US) a vehicle for transporting heavy loads —*vt.* carry goods; drive a truck

truck´ing (US) *n.* the business of operating trucks

truck´le *vi., vt.* yield or submit weakly; move or cause to move on rollers or casters —*n.* small wheel

truc´u•lent *adj.* savage; inclined to ferocity —**truc´u•lence** *n.*

trudge *vi.* walk wearily or laboriously —*n.* tiresome walk

true *adj.* real or genuine; faithful or dependable to friends, promises, etc. —*vt.* bring to conformity with a standard —*adv.* in truth, truly; within tolerance

truf´fle *n.* an edible fungus, similar to a mushroom; a chocolate

tru´ly *adv.* conforming to fact; with accuracy; with loyalty

trump *is.* a card or suit of the highest rank; a hidden advantage —*vt.* take with a trump; surpass or beat; outdo or outmaneuver —*vi.* play a trump —**trump up** invent for fraudulent purposes

trump´er•y *n.* worthless finery; nonsense

trum´pet *n.* brass wind instrument; resembling the flaring bell of a trumpet; a loud penetrating sound —*vt.* sound or publish abroad —*vi.* play a trumpet; sound forth

trun´cate *n.* cut the top from —*adj.* ending abruptly

trun´cheon *n.* a short, thick stick or club; a mark of office or authority; *(Brit.)* a policeman's nightstick —*vt.* beat; cudgel

trunk *n.* main stem of a tree; central part of the body; a passage for blood, transportation, communication, etc; a large container

truss *n.* supporting framework, as for a roof or bridge —*vt.* support or brace; bind

trust *n.* reliance on the integrity of another; that committed to urtc's care; confident expectation; an affiliation to control output; prices, etc. —*vt.* rely on, commit to the care of another; expect or believe —*vi* place confidence in —*adj.* held in trust

trust•ee´ *n.* one entrusted with the property or affairs of another

trust´ful *adj.* inclined to believe; showing trust

trust fund assets held in trust

trust´ing *adj.* showing trust —**trust´ing•ly** *adv.*

trust´wor•thy *adj.* deserving of cuandence; reliable

trust´y *adj.* faithful to duty

truth *n.* conformity to fact; that which is true

truth´ful *adj.* conforming to fact; telling the truth

try *vt.* attempt; experiment with; subject to a test; subject to stress; extract by rendering —*vi.* make an attempt; put forth effort; make a test *n.* an attempt; a test

try´ing *adj.* difficult to endure

tryst *n.* an appointment; a meeting

tsu•nam´i *n.* immense wave generated by an earthquake

tub *n.* a large flat-bottomed container; *(US)* a bathtub

tub´by *adj.* round and fat; resembling a tub

tube *n.* a long, hollow cylinder

tu´ber *n.* short, thickened portion of a root; a tubercle

tu´ber•cle *n.* a small rounded eminence

tu•ber´cu•lar *adj.* affected with tubercles; tuberculosis

tu•ber•cu•lo´sis *it* a disease marked by tubercles in the lungs

tu´ber•ous *adj.* bearing projections or prominences

tu´bu•lar *adj.* having the form of a tube; consisting of tubes

tuft *n.* a clump of hair, feathers, etc. —*vt.* provide with tightly drawn buttons, as on upholstery; cover or adorn with tufts — *vi.* form or grow in tufts — **tuft´ed** *adj.* — **tuft´er** *n.*

tug *vt.*, *vi.* pull with effort —*n.* a violent pull; a strenuous effort

tu•i•tion *n.* payment for instruction

tum´ble *vt.* toss about; perform acrobatics —*vt.* cause to tall

tum´bler *n.* a drinking glass; an acrobat; a revolving cage or cylinder as on a clothes dryer

tum´brel *n.* a rude cart

tu´me•fy *vi.*, *vt.* to swell

tu•mes´cent *adj.* swelling; timid

tu´mor *n.* a growth or swelling on or in the body —**tu´mor•ous** *adj.*

tu′mult *n.* commotion or disturbance; agitation

tu•mul′tu•ous *adj.* greatly disturbed; stormy, tempestuous

tun *n.* a large cask

tu′na *n.* a large food fish

tun′dra *n.* a rolling treeless plain

tune *n.* a coherent succession of musical tones; correct pitch; harmony; fine adjustment —*vt.* adjust

tune′ful *adj.* melodic

tu′nic *n.* a loose outer garment gathered at the waist; a short coat

tun′nel *n.* underground passageway —*vt.* dig; make a passageway under

tun′ny *n.* tuna

tur′ban *n.* a head covering

tur′bid *adj.* muddy, dense or opaque; confused

tur′bine *n.* a rotary engine

tur′bot *n.* a large European flatfish

tur•bu′lent *adj.* violently disturhed or agitated; tending to disturb

tu•reen′ *n.* a covered serving bowl

turf *n.* a section of grass; an area regarded possessively —*vt.* cover with sod

tur•ges′cent *adj.* swollen; pompous

tur•gid *adj.* unnaturally distended; swollen

tur′key *n.* a large North American bird; something lacking quality

tur′moil *n.* disturbance; tumult

turn *vi., vt.* revolve or cause to revolve; change direction; give finished form; to bend, curve, twist, etc.; transform —*n.* a change of direction

turn′ing *n.* art of shaping on a lathe

turn′pike *n.* a toll road

tur•pi•tude *n.* depravity

tur′ret *n.* a small projecting tower

tur′tle *n.* a four-limbed reptile with a soft body encased in a shell

tusk *n.* a long projecting tooth —*vt.* to gore, root, etc. with a tusk

tus′sle *vt., vi.* scuffle or struggle —*n.* a scuffle

tu•te•lage *n.* being under care of a tutor or guardian; the office of a guardian; the act of tutoring

tu′tor *n.* a private teacher —*vt., vi.* to act as a tutor — **tu•to′ri•al** *adj.*

tu′tu *n.* a ballet skirt

tux•e′do *n.* formal attire

twad′dle *n.* it pretentious, silly talk

twang *vt., vi.* make a sharp, vibrant sound; speak with a nasal sound —*n.* a vibrating or nasal sound

tweak *vt.* pinch or twist sharply; fine-tune —*n.* a pinch

tweed *n.* a woolen fabric

tweez′ers *n.* small pincers

twig *n.* a small shoot or branch

twi′light *n.* the period after sunset and before sunrise; any faint light; waning glory

twin *n.* either of two young from the same birth; one greatly similar

twine *vt.* twist together; coil *vi.* interlace; proceed on a winding course —*n.* string; act of entwining

twinge *n.* sudden sharp pain;

a mental pang —*vi.*, *vt.* feel
or cause to feel sudden pain
vi. shine intermittently; sparkle; move lightly and rapidly
—*vt.* cause to flicker; quick
movement of the eyelids *n.*

twin'kling *n.* an instant, a
moment; a wink

twirl *vt.*, *vi.* whirl or rotate
rapidly; twist or curl —*n.* a
whirling motion; a curl or
twist

twist *vt.* wind around; form by
winding; deform or distort —
vi. become wound; move in a
winding course; squirm or
writhe —*n.* a curve or bend;
strain of a joint; unnatural
inclination; unexpected turn
or development

twist'er *n.* one or that which
twists; a tornado or cyclone

twit *vt.* taunt —*n.* a reproach
or taunt; a foolish person

twitch *vt.*, *vi.* move with a quick
spasmodic jerk —*n.* a
sudden involuntary muscle
contraction

two'-faced *adj.* double-deal-
ing; insincere

tycoon' *n.* a wealthy, powerful businessman or financier

tyke *n.* a small child

type' *n.* traits in common; a
standard; raised characters
used for printing —*vt.* represent; typify; classify

typhoid fever an infectious
disease contracted from
contaminated water or food

typhoon' *n.* a violent tropical
storm

ty'phus *n.* a contagious disease spread by fleas or lice

typ'i·cal *adj.* characteristic of
a group or type —**typ'i·cal·
ly** *adv.*

typ'i·fy *vt.*, serve as example

ty'po *n.* error in typing or
printing

ty·pog'ra·pher *n.* one who
sets material into type suitable for printing

**typo·graph'ic, ty·po·graph'-
i·cal** *adj.* relating to typeset-
ting or printing —**ty·pog'
ra·phy** *n.*

ty·ran'nic, ty·ran'ni·cal *adj.*
of or like a tyrant; despotic
or arbitrary

tyr'an·nize *vi.* exercise power
cruelly; rule as a tyrant — *vt.*
treat cruelly; domineer

tyr'an·nous *adj.* despotic; cruel

ty'rant *n.* one ruling oppres-
sively or cruelly; one exercising power or authority in
a harsh, cruel manner

tyre (*Brit.*) *n.* covering for a
wheel

ty'ro *n.* a novice or beginner

u, U twenty-first letter of the
alphabet

u·biq'ui·tous *adj.* seeming
everywhere at once; omni-
present

ug'ly *adj.* distasteful; repulsive; morally revolting

ul'cer *n.* an open sore; a corrupt condition —**ul'cer·ous**
adj.

ul'na *n.* larger bone of the
forearm

ul'ster *n.* a long, loose overcoat

ul·te'ri·or *adj.* intentionally
unrevealed; secondary in
importance

ul'ti·ma *n.* the last syllable of
a word

ul'ti·mate *adj.* last or final;
beyond all others; funda-
mental —*n.* best, latest,

most fundamental, etc. —**ul′ti•mate•ly** adv.

ul•ti•ma′tum n. final terms

u′ltra adj. extreme

ul′tra•light n. a lightweight airplane

ul•tra•mod′ern adj. extremely fresh and new

ul•tra•son′ic n. adj. of inaudible sound

ul′tra•sound′ n. the use of ultrasonic waves for medical diagnosis

ul•tra•vi′o•let adj. of a wavelength between visible violet and X-rays

ul′u•late vi. to howl or wail

um′ber n. brown iron oxide; color made from umber —adj. pertaining to umber or its color

um•bil′i•cal adj. of or situated near the naval —a. a tube that links an astronaut or aquanaut to a craft

um•bil′i•cus n. the naval

um′brage n. anger or resentment; shade or shadow

um•brel′la n. a portable canopy to protect from sun or rain; something serving as a cover or shield

um′laut n. an altered vowel sound; two dots over a vowel, as ä, ë, etc., used to mark a change in sound

um′pire n. one who settles disagreements or disputes; one who enforces rules of certain games

un•a•bat′ed adj. maintaining original force or intensity

un•a•bridged′ adj. containing all; complete

un•a•dorned′ adj. plain; lacking embellishment

un•a•dul′ter•at•ed adj. pure; not dilute; complete, utter

un•af•fect′ed adj. natural or sincere; not influenced or changed

u•nan′i•mous adj. in full agreement; without dissent —**u•na•nim′i•ty** n.

un•a•vail′ing adj. ineffective; futile

un•a•wares′ adv. unexpectedly; without preparation

un•be•liev′a•ble adj. incredible; too astonishing to be believed

un′bend′ing adj. resolute; firm; not relaxed or able to relax

un•bi′ased adj. impartial; not prejudiced

un•bid′den adj. spontaneous, without asking; not ordered or invited

un•blink′ing adj. without emotion; fearless

un•break′a•ble adj. impossible or difficult to break

un′bri′dled adj. unrestrained; uncontrolled

un•bro′ken adj. uninterrupted; continuous

un•bur′den vt. relieve from cares or worries; confess

un•can′ny adj. unnatural; weird; seeming to be supernatural

un•car′ing adj. lacking concern or sympathy

un•ceas′ing adj. continuous; without stopping; eternal

un•cen′sored adj. not examined for inappropriate material; complete

un•cer•e•mo′ni•ous adj. casual, informal; without preamble; rude or discourteous

un•char•ac•ter•is′tic adj. unusual; strange or exceptional: *uncharacteristic generosity*

un•chart'ed *adj.* unknown; unexplored

un•civ'il•ized *adj.* barbarous; rude and uncouth; remote

un•com'mon *adj.* remarkable; strange

un•con'scion•a•ble *adj.* unscrupulous; unbelievably bad or wrong

un•couth' *adj.* boorish or unrefined

unc'tion *n.* an anointing; substance for anointing; something that soothes; excessive or affected sincerity

unc'tu•ous *adj.* greasy to the touch; marked by excessive or affected sincerity; overly smooth or suave

un'der *prep.* beneath; covered by; lower than; less in value, amount, etc.; inferior to; subordinate to; being subject to; by virtue of; having regard to —*adv.* underneath; in an inferior position; less in amount, value, etc. —*adj.*

un'der•brush *n.* small trees, shrubs, etc. growing beneath forest trees

un'der•cur'rent *n.* air or water flowing beneath another layer; concealed or secret force or tendency

un'der•growth *n.* underbrush

un'der•hand'ed *adj., adv.* in a sly or treacherous manner

un•der•stand' *vt., vi.* come to know the meaning or import of; perceive the nature or character of; comprehend; suppose or believe; accept as a condition; have sympathy of tolerance for—**un•der•stand'a•ble** *adj.*

un•der•stand'ing *n.* comprehension; capacity to think; an agreement; a viewpoint or opinion; sympathy or tolerance for others —*adj.* marked by comprehension, sympathy, tolerance, etc.

un•der•stat'ed *adj.* marked by restraint; showing good taste

un•der•take' *vt.,* agree to attempt; contract to do

un•der•write' *vt.* sign; assume liability; guarantee —*vi.* act as a guarantor

un•doubt'ed *adj.* assured or certain; unsuspected

un•du'ly *adv.* excessively; improperly or unjustly

un•earth' *vt.* dig up; discover

un•earth'ly *adj.* seemingly not of this world; supernatural; terrifying

un•eas'y *adj.* disturbed; disquieted; causing discomfort; not stable or secure

un•ex•pect'ed *adj.* without warning; not foreseen

un•feigned' *adj.* sincere

un•flap'pa•ble *adj.* impassive; imperturbable

un•for'tu•nate *adj.* unlucky; resulting from misfortune; regrettable —*n.* a victim

un•gain'ly *adj.* awkward; clumsy; poorly proportioned

un'guent *n.* an ointment or salve

un•gu'late *adj.* having hoofs — *n.* a hoofed animal

u•ni•cel'lu•lar *adj.* consisting of a single cell

u'ni•corn *n.* a mythical horned creature resembling a horse

u'ni•fy *vt.* bring together or unite; make alike —**u•ni•fi•ca'tion** *n.*

u•ni•lat'er•al *adj.* affecting one only; having only one side; recognizing only one aspect

un•im•peach´a•ble *adj.* beyond question; blameless

un´ion *n.* a joining; that formed by joining or combining; a device for joining mechanical parts —*adj.* pertaining to a union

u•nique´ *adj.* being the only one of its kind; without equal; very unusual or remarkable

u´ni•son *n.* perfect agreement; speaking or singing together

u´nit *n.* a standard of comparison; a measure of requirements for a scholastic degree; a quantity required for a desired effect; persons or things considered as constituent parts of a whole —*adj.* being a distinct part — **u´ni•tar•y** *adj.*

unite´ *vt., vi.* to join; bring into close connection; possess in combination; to combine —**u´ni•ty** *n.*

u•ni•ver´sal *adj.* common everywhere; including all, without exception; adapted to a variety of uses —*n.* a general notion or idea; a trait common to all

u´ni•verse *n.* aggregate of all existing things; a field of thought or activity

u•ni•ver´si•ty *n.* an institute of higher learning including buildings, *faculty,* etc.

un•just´ *adj.* not fair; wrongful

un•kempt´ *adj.* not neat or tidy

un•less´ *conj.* except that prep. excepting

un•men´tion•a•ble *adj.* not fit for discussion; embarrassing

un•nerve´ *vt.* deprive of resolve, courage, etc.; make nervous

un•or•tho•dox *adj.* contrary to convention or tradition

un•plumbed´ *adj.* not fully measured or explored

un•prec´e•dent•ed *adj.* without precedent; new or novel

un•read´ *adj.* uninformed; un learned; not yet examined

un•re•gen´er•ate *adj.* not changed; sinful; stubbornly recalcitrant

un•ru´ly *adj.* tending to resist regulation; difficult to to control

un•scathed´ *adj.* not injured

un•ten´a•ble *adj.* impossible to defend, preserve, etc.

un•til´ *prep.* up to the time of —*conj.* to the time when; to the place or degree that

un•u´su•al *adj.* odd, rare, or extraordinary

un•writ´ten *adj.* based on tradition; understood

up *adv.* toward a higher place; in or on a higher place; to or at that deemed higher —*adj.* moving or directed upward; at or to a high level, condition, etc. —*prep.* toward or at a point higher or farther above or along —*n.* an ascent; a state of prosperity

up´beat *n.* an unaccented beat in music —*adj.* optimistic; confident

up´braid´ *vt.* reproach

up•hol´ster *vt.* fit with covering, cushions, etc.

up•hol´ster•y *n.* cover or repair of furniture; material fot covering

up´keep *n.* the act, state, or cost of maintaining in good condition

up´per *adj.* higher in position, rank, etc. —*n.* something above another

up′per•most *adj.* highest to rank, authority, etc.; foremost —*adv.*

up′right *adj.* erect; righteous —*n.* being erect; something erect —*adv.* to an upright or vertical position

up•stand′ing *adj.* honest, straightforward; upright; placed erect

up′start *n.* one who attains sudden power or importance

up′tight *adj.* anxious or nervous; angry; conventional, conservative

up′ward *adv.* toward a higher place; in the upper parts; toward a better condition —*adj.* directed toward or located in a higher place

ur′ban *adj.* pertaining to a city or city life; living or located in a city

ur•bane′ *adj.* refined; suave

ur′ban•ism *n.* life in a city; study of city life

ur•ban•ol′o•gy *n.* study of cities and city problems —**ur•ban•ol′o•gist** *n.*

urban renewal revitalization of cities

urban sprawl spread of population, shopping centers, etc. into rural or undeveloped areas

u•re′mi•a *n.* a toxic condition caused by failure of the kidneys to filter waste products from the blood

urge *vt.* drive or force forward; entreat earnestly —*vi.* present arguments, claims, etc. —*n.* strong impulse; the act of urging

ur′gent *adj.* requiring prompt action; insistent —**ur′gen•cy** *n.*

urn *n.* a footed receptacle

u•rol′o•gy *n.* study of the urinary system —**urol′o•gist** *n.*

us′a•ble, use′a•ble *adj.* that can be used; that may be useful

us′age *n.* act or manner of using; customary or habitual practice; accepted manner of using words

use *vt.* put into service; take advantage of —*n.* act of using or state of being used; function; advantage or usefulness; purpose for which something is employed

use′ful *adj.* serviceable; helpful

use′less *adj.* having no use; serving no function

ush′er *n.* one who escorts patrons to their seats; an official doorkeeper; male attendant in a wedding party —*vi., vt.* serve as an usher

u′su•al *adj.* customary or common

u•su′ri•ous *adj.* practicing usury; of or pertaining to usury

u•surp′ *vt.* seize without authority; take possession by force

u′su•ry *n.* lending money at excessive or unlawful interest rates; excessive or unlawful interest

uten′sil *n.* an implement that serves a useful purpose

u′tile *adj.* useful

u•til′i•ty *n.* fitness, suitability

u•ti•lize *vt.* make use of

ut′most *adj.* of the highest or greatest degree; at the furthest limit; extreme —*n.* most or best possible

ut′ter *vt.* say, express, give out, or send forth; put in circulation —*adj.* complete;

unqualified

ut'ter•ance n. a manner of speaking; a thing uttered

v, V twenty-second letter of the alphabet; in Roman characters, the symbol for 5

va'cant adj. containing nothing; empty; not being used; having no incumbent, officer —**va'can•cy** n.

va'cate vt. make vacant; set aside, as a ruling —vi. to leave

va•ca'tion (us) n. time for recreation or rest; a holiday —vi. take a holiday

vac'ci•nate vt. innoculate as a preventive measure

vac•cine n. a preparation used to provide immunity

vac'il•late vi. waver; be irresolute

va•cu'i•ty n. emptiness; vacant space; lack of intelligence; something inane or stupid

vac'u•um adj. empty; lacking intelligence; lacking substance; devoid of meaning or expression

vac'u•um n. space nearly devoid of matter; reduction of pressure below that of surroundings

vag'a•bond n. a wanderer without visible means of support; shiftless, irresponsible person —adj. wandering; aimless; irresponsible

va'gar•y n. a wild fancy or extravagant notion

va'grant n. one without a home or job; a tramp —adj. wandering aimlessly; wayward

vague n. lacking definition; indistinct; not clearly stated

vain adj. excessively proud; unproductive or useless —**in vain'** to no purpose

vain'glo•ry n. excessive vanity; ostentation —**vain•glo'ri•ous** adj.

val'ance (US) n. decorative drapery edging a canopy or the top of a window; a decorative panel that covers fixtures above a window

val•e•dic'tion n. a farewell

val•e•dic•to'ri•an n. student who delivers the farewell address at a graduation ceremony

val'e•dic'to•ry adj. of a leave-taking —n. parting address

va'lence n. capacity of an atom or radical to combine with another

val'et n. a personal servant; one who performs personal services for hotel guests —vt. vi. serve as valet

val•e•tu•di•nar'i•an n. chronic invalid —adj. infirm or ailing; overly concerned about one's health

val'iant adj. strong and courageous; performed with valor

val'id adj. based on facts or evidence; well-founded; effective; legally binding —**va'lid•i•ty** n.

val'i•date vt. confirm as true; declare to be legally binding; mark or stamp to give sanction or make official —**val•i•da'tion** n.

va•lise' n. a traveling bag

val'ley n. area drained by a river; low land; a hollow

val'or n. remarkable courage; bravery —**val'or•ous** adj.

val'u•a•ble adj. having significant worth or value; costly

—**val′u•a•bles** *n.* expensive or treasured articles

val•u•a′tion *n.* an estimate of worth; an estimated value

val′ue *n.* worth; that regarded as desirable or worthy; market price; a bargain; number represented by a symbol; relative lightness or darkness of a color — *vt.* assess or appraise; regard highly; consider relatively important

val′ued *adj.* highly esteemed: *a valued friend;* of specific worth

val′ue•less *adj.* worthless

valve *n.* a device that controls movement or flow

vam′pire *n.* in folklore, a reanimated corpse that feeds on human blood; one who preys on those of the opposite sex; a bat that feeds on the blood of mammals

van *n.* a large, enclosed wagon or truck; (*Brit.*) a railroad car for freight or baggage; (*Brit.*) a caravan; (*US*) a passenger vehicle somewhat like a small bus

van′dal•ism *n.* willful defacement of property

van′dal•ize *vt.* willfully deface or destroy property

vane *n.* a thin plate on a pivot to indicate wind direction; an arm or plate of a wind mill, propeller, etc.

van′guard *n.* forward part of an advancing army; foremost position; leaders of a movement, trend, etc.

va•nil′la *n.* an orchid of tropical America; a flavoring extract; vanilla flavoring made synthetically

van′ish *vi.* disappear; pass out of existence

van′i•ty *n.* excessive pride in one's talents, etc.; something worthless or futile; a dressing table —**vanity case** a case for cosmetics

van′quish *vt.* defeat in battle; suppress, or overcome, as fear

van′tage *n.* superiority or advantage; position or condition that offers advantage; an overall view

vap′id *adj.* flat or dull; lacking flavor or attraction

va′por *n.* moisture in the air; cloudy substance; something insubstantial and fleeting —*vt.* vaporize —*vi.* emit or pass off in vapor

va′por•ize *vt.,* vi. convert or be converted into vapor

va′por•ous *adj.* misty; emitting or forming vapor; whimsical

var′i•a•ble *adj.* having capacity to change; likely to change; of no fixed size, amount, etc. —*n.* that liable or able to change

var′i•ance *n.* discrepancy or difference; license or permission to do that contrary to local ordinance

var′i•ant *adj.* differing from a standard or type —*n.* an alternative, as in spelling or pronunciation

var•i•a′tion *n.* difference or modification; extent of difference; that which differs from others of the same type

var′ied *adj.* diverse; modified or altered —**var′ied•ly** *adv.*

var′i•e•gat•ed *adj.* varied in color

va•ri′e•tal *adj.* describing a variety —*n.* wane named for a grape variety

va·ri·e·ty n. diversity, difference; sort or kind; collection, assortment

var·i·ous adj. different from one another; several; separate; multifaceted

var·nish n. a finish for wood; outward show —vt. coat with varnish; hide or gloss over: varnish the truth

var·y vt. change or modify; diversify deviate; become changed

vas·cu·lar adj. pertaining to body vessels or ducts

vast adj. immense; great in quantity, importance, etc.; extensive

vat n. a large open vessel or tub

vaude·ville n. theatrical entertainment of short sketches, songs, dances, etc.; a variety show

vault n. an arched roof or ceiling; a room or compartment for storage or safekeeping; a burial chamber —vi., vt. to leap

vault·ing n. construction that forms a vault

vaunt vi., vt. to boast

veer vi. turn; shift from an opinion, belief, etc. —vt. change direction of

veg·an n. a vegetarian whose diet is limited to food derived from plants

veg·e·ta·ble n. a plant cultivated for food; edible part of a plant —adj. relating to or derived from plants; made from edible plants

veg·e·tal adj. of plants or vegetables

veg·e·tar·i·an n. one who does not eat meat; one who advocates a diet that excludes meat and sometimes seafood or animal products as well —adj. of vegetarians or vegetarianism; consisting only of vegetables, grains, fruit, nuts, and seeds

veg·e·tate vi. grow, as a plant; exist in a monotonous, passive state

veg·e·ta·tion n. plant life

ve·he·ment adj. marked by strong feeling or passion; acting with great force

ve·hi·cle n. any conveyance for people or freight — **ve·hic·u·lar** vdj.

veil n. a thin fabric for covering; anything that conceals or covers —vt. to cover, con-ceal, disguise, etc.

veil·ing n. covering; material for making a veil

vein n. a tubular vessel that conveys blood; a branching structure such as ribs in a leaf or the wing of an insect; a colored streak in wood, stone, etc.; a distinctive tendency or disposition —it extend or mark throughout like veins

veld, veldt n. a South African plain

vel·lum n. fine parchment

veloc·i·ty n. speed; quickness of motion

ve·lour n. a soft fabric having a short, thick pile

vel·vet n. fabric with short, smooth pile on one side and a plain underside —adj. made of velvet; smooth and soft to the touch

ve·nal adj. characterized by corruption or brihery

vend vt. to sell —vi. be em-ployed in selling

ven•det´ta *n.* private feud in which relatives of a wronged person seek revenge; any bitter quarrel

ve•neer´ *n.* thin layer; surface or show: *veneer of civility* — *vt.* cover with veneer; to conceal something

ven´er•a•ble *adj.* worthy of respect because of dignity, age, etc.

ven´er•ate *vt.* to regard with respect or awe —**ven•er•a´tion** *n.*

ve•ne´re•al *adj.* of or proceeding from sexual intercourse

ve•ne•re•ol´o•gy *n.* study of sexually transmitted disease

ven´geance *n.* a deserved penalty; retribution

venge´ful *adj.* seeking revenge; unforgiving

ve´ni•al *adj.* slight or trivial, as a fault —**ve•ni•al´i•ty** *n.*

ven´i•son *n.* flesh of a wild animal used for food

ven´om *n.* poison secreted by certain reptiles, insects, etc.; ill will

ve´nous *adj.* pertaining to or carried by veins; of blood returning to the heart and lungs; having veins

vent *n.* an outlet or opening; a slit In a garment —*vt.* give expression to; permit escape, as of a gas; make a vent in

ven•ti•la´tion *n.* free circulation of air; exposure to examination and discussion; oxygenation blood

ven´tral *adj.* toward, at, or near the abdomen

ven´tri•cle *n.* small cavity in the body —**ven•tric´u•lar** *adj.*

ven´ture *vt.* expose to risk — *vi.* take risk —*n.* an undertaking marked by risk

venture capital investment in an untried business

ven´ture´some *adj.* bold or daring; involving risk

ven´tur•ous *adj.* adventurous; risky

ven´ue *n.* place or setting of action or event; in law, location of a crime or cause of action, or where a trial must be held

ve•ra´cious *adj.* truthful; accurate

ve•rac´i•ty *n.* honesty; accuracy

ve•ran´da *n.* an open porch

verb *n.* a word that expresses action, existence, or occurence

ver´bal *adj.* referring to words: *verbal image;* of words rather than ideas: literal —*n.* in grammar, a noun derived from a verb

ver´bal•ize *vt.* express in words —*vi.* speak or write in a wordy fashion

ver•ba´tim *adj., adv.* exactly, word for word

ver´bi•age *n.* use of too many words; manner of expression

ver•bose´ *adj.* overly wordy; repetitive, redundant; containing unnecessary words

ver´dant *adj.* covered with vegetation; inexperienced

ver´dict *n.* decision of a jury; conclusion or opinion

ver´dure *n.* fresh greenness of growing vegetation; lush vegetation

verge *n.* extreme edge; a boundary —*vi.* be contiguous or adjacent; approach or come close to

ver·i·fi·ca·tion n. proof, confirmation

ver·i·fi·a·ble adj. that can be confirmed or proven

ver·i·fy vt. prove; test the accuracy or truth of

ver·i·si·mil·i·tude n. the appearance of truth or reality; that which has the appearance of truth or reality

ver·i·ta·ble adj. genuine or real; actual

ver·i·ty n. truth; the quality of being true or real

ver·mi·form adj. shaped like a worm

ver·min n. destructive animals or insects; a repulsive person

ver·mouth´ n. a fortified wine

ver·nac·u·lar n. language peculiar to a locality; common daily speech; specialized vocabulary of a trade or profession —adj. of a particular language or argot; relating to a locality

ver´nal adj. appropriate to spring; fresh or youthful — **ver´nal·ly** adv.

ver´sa·tile adj. having many talents; having many uses

verse n. poetry; a line or group of lines of poetry, scripture, etc.

versed adj. skilled; knowledgeable

ver´si·fy vt. to convert into poetry —vi. write poetry

ver´sion n. translation, or rendition; an adaptation: film version of a novel: a personal account

ver´so n. a left-handed page; the reverse of a coin or medallion

ver´sus prep. against; alternative of

ver´te·bra n., pl. **ver´te·brae** a bone of the spinal column

ver´te·brate adj. having a backbone

ver´tical adj. upright or erect; directly overhead; at right angles to the horizon — n. something upright

ver·tig´i·nous adj. affected by vertigo; spinning

ver·ti·go n. dizziness; disorientation; a disorder in which a person or surroundings seem to whirl about

verve n. energy; enthusiasm

ver´y adv. to a high degree; exactly —adj. suitable; identical; a thing itself: the very thing I wanted

ves·i·cle n. a small cavity or cyst; a blister —**ve·sic´u·lar** adj.

ves´pers n. evening worship

ves´sel n. an open container; a physical process for fluid: blood vessel; a ship or aircraft

vest n. (Brit.) a garment worn under a shirt; (US) a short, sleeveless outer garment — vt. confer, as ownership or authority

vest´ed adj. inalienable or absolute

ves´ti·bule n. an entryway or antechamber; enclosed passageway between cars of a passenger tram

ves´tige n. a discernible trace; a remnant —**ves·tig´ial** adj.

vest´ment n. an article of clothing; a ritual garment

ves´try n. a church room for storing vestments, conducting meetings, etc.; church's administrative body

vet´er·an n. one experienced

vet´er·i·nar·y *adj.* of prevention and treatment of diseases and injuries of animals —**vet·er·i·nar´i·an** *n.*

ve´to *vt.* refuse, as approval or consent —*n.* right to cancel, prohibit, or postpone; exercising such right

vex *vt.* annoy; trouble, afflict; baffle or confuse —**vex·a´tion** *n.*

vexed *adj.* annoyed or disturbed; baffled

vex·a´tious *adj.* annoying; disturbing

vi´a *prep.* by way of; by means of

vi·a·ble *adj.* capable of living and developing normally; workable —**vi·a·bil´i·ty** *n.*

vi´a·duct *a.* a bridgehke structure of arched masonry

vi´al *n.* a small bottle

vi´brant *adj.* vigorous, enthusiastic; energetic; powerful

vi´brate *vt., vi.* move back and forth rapidly —**vi·bra´tion** *n.*

vi·bra´to *n.* cyclical variation in the pitch of a tone

vic´ar *n.* one authorized to act in the stead of another; a church representative

vi·car´i·ous *adj.* suffered or done in place of another; identifying with experience of another; delegated

vice *n.* moral depravity; an immoral action, trait, etc.; habitual failing or shortcoming; (*Brit.*) a clamping device, as for woodworking

vice´roy *n.* one who acts by authority of a sovereign

vi·chys·soise´ *n.* a cream soup of potato and leeks

vi·cin´i·ty *n.* nearness; proximity; a nearby area, region, etc.

vi´cious *adj.* dangerous; marked by evil intent: vicious rumor, depraved or immoral; forceful or intense

vi·cis´si·tude *n.* change or alteration —**vi·cis´si·tudes** *pl. n.* irregular changes of conditions, fortune, etc.

vlc´tim *n.* one harmed, as by injury, disease, fraud, trickery, etc.

vic´tim·ize *vt.* cause to suffer: cheat or dupe

vic´tor *n.* une who wins —**vic·to´ri·ous** *adj.*

vie *vi.* put forth effort; compete; contend for superiority

view *n.* range of vision; something seen; an opinion or belief — *of.* look at; examine; consider; regard in a certain way

vig´il *n.* time of keeping watch

vig´i·lant *adj.* alert to danger; wary

vig·i·lan´te *n.* an advocate for preempting the law

vi·gnette´ *n.* a picture shading off into the background; a brief literary sketch; a decorative design

vig´or *n.* energy; vital or natural growth; intensity —**vig´-or·ous** *adj.*

vile *adj.* morally base; corrupt; loathsome; very bad: *vile tasting*

vil´i·fy *vt.* speak of abusively; defame —**vil·i·fi·ca´tion** *n.*

vil´lage *n.* (*US*) residential area smaller than a town but larger than a hamlet; inhabitants of a village collectively —**vil´lag·er** *n.*

vil´lain *n.* a scoundrel

vil´lain·ous *adj.* wicked; evil

vin´ci·ble *adj.* easily overcome; that can be conquered

vin´di·cate vt. clear of suspicion; maintain a right or claim; justify

vin·dic´tive adj. having a vengeful spirit

vine n. a climbing plant

vin´e·gar n. a variously flavored condiment and preservative; acerbity, as of speech

vine´yard n. an area devoted to the cultivation of grapes

vin´i·cul·ture n. cultivation of wine grapes

vin´i·fy vt. convert into wine

vi´nous adj. pertaining to or characteristic of wine

vin´tage n. yield of grapes or wine for a season; region and year in which a wine is produced —adj. of a fine wine; of a good year for wine

vint´ner n. wine maker or merchant

vi´nyl n. a type of plastic

vi·o´la n. a musical instrument similar to a violin

vi´o·la·ble adj. that can be or is likely to be violated

vi´o·late vt. break a law, agreement, etc.; ravish or rape; offend

vi´o·lence n. physical force used to injure, damage, or destroy; intensity, severity; injury or damage

vi´o·lent adj. marked by physical force or intense emotional excitement; characterized by intensity

vi´o·let n. a bluish-purple color; a plant bearing violet-colored flowers

vi·o·lin´ n. a stringed instrument of the highest register; a violinist

vi·o·lin´ist n. one who plays violin

vi´ol·ist n. one who plays viola

vi·o·lon·cel´lo n. a cello

vi´per n. kind of snake; a treacherous or spiteful person — **vi´per·ish** adj.

vi´per·ous adj. pertaining to vipers or snakes; treacherous or spiteful

vi·ra´go n. an ill-tempered woman; a shrew

vi´ral adj. pertaining to or caused by a virus —**vi´ral·ly** adv.

vi·res´cent adj. greenish

vir´gin n. one who has never had sexual intercourse; an unmarried woman —adj. being a virgin; pertaining or suited to a virgin; uncorrupted, pure; not hitherto used or processed; virgin wool

vir´gule n. a diagonal mark (/)

vir·i·des´cent adj. greenish; turning green

vir´ile adj. having vigor or strength of manhood; able to procreate

vi·rol´o·gy n. the study of viruses

vir´tu·al adj. existing in essence or effect, but not in actual form

vir´tue a. moral excellence; an admirable quality

vir·tu·os´i·ty n. technical mastery

vir·tu·o´so n. a master of technique, esp. in the arts — adj. capable of or displaying extraordinary skill

vir´tu·ous adj. righteous; pure and chaste —**vir´tu·ous·ly** adv.

vir´u·lent adj. extremely harmful; infectious; full of hatred

vi´rus n. a parasite able to re-produce only in living cells; disease caused by a para-site; an evil influence

vi´sa n. endorsement on a passport that permits entrance to a country

vis´age n. appearance; aspect

vis´cer•a n. internal organs

vis´cer•al adj. pertaining to the viscera; instinctive or emotional

vis•cos´i•ty n. property by which fluids resist flow or change

vis´cous adj. resistant to flow; of high viscosity —**vis´cous•ness** n.

vise (US) n. a clamping tool, as for woodworking —vt. hold or squeeze

vis´i•ble adj. capable of being seen; that can be perceived

vi´sion n. sight; that seen; something beautiful; a mental image; foresight; imagination

vi´sion•ar•y adj. existing in imagination; speculative; impractical —n. one who has visions; one whose plans or projects are impractical or unrealistic

vis´it vt. call on; go or come to a place; be a guest of; inflict upon —vi. pay a call; stay with temporarily —n. a so-cial call; a short stay

vis•it•a´tion n. a visit; official inspection or examination

vi´sor n. projection to shield the eyes

vis´ta n. a view; mental image

vi´su•al adj. pertaining to sight; perceptible by sight —n. pictures, charts, etc. that enhance a presentation —**vis´u•al•ly** adv.

vis•u•al•ize vt., vi. form a mental image; picture in the mind

vi´tal adj. pertaining to life; essential to or supporting life; of utmost importance; dynamic; full of life

vi•tal´i•ty n. power to live and develop; physical or mental energy

vi´tal•ize vt. endow with life or energy; make spirited or energetic

vi´ta•min n. a naturally oc-curring substance essential to health

vi´ti•ate vt. impair use or value; render weak or inef-fective; make legally invalid —**vi•ti•a´tion** n.

vit´i•cul•ture n. cultivation of grapes

vit´re•ous adj. glassy; ob-tained from glass; of the vit-reous humor

vitreous humor the clear jelly-like substance that fills the eyeball

vit´ri•fy vt., vi. change into glass or a glass-like subs-tance

vit´ri•ol n. a sulfate of metal; sulfuric acid; harshness or bitterness of thought or ex-pression; reproach

vit•ri•ol´ic adj., acrimonious; harsh or bitter

vi•tu´per•ate vt. fault abu-sively; berate or scold

vi•tu•per•a´tion n. harsh or abusive language; use of such language

vi•va´cious adj. full of life and spirit

viv´id adj. strong or intense, as of color; suggesting life-like images; producing a sharp impression

viv´i•fy *vt.* give life to; animate; make more vivid or striking

vl•vip´a•rous *adj.* bringing forth live young grown in the mother's body

viv•i•sec´tion *n.* cutting or dissection on a living animal

vix´en *n.* female fox; quarrelsome or malevolent woman

vo•cab´u•lar•y *n.* words of a language; the words one understands

vo´cal *adj.* of the voice; able to speak or utter sounds; speaking freely —**vo´cal•ise** (*Brit*), **vo´cal1ize** (*us*) *vt., vi.*

vo´cal•ist *n.* a singer; one who sings as a profession

vo•ca´tion *n.* a regular job or profession; a career

vo•ca´tion•al *adj.* pertaining to a job or profession; of training designed to provide specific useful skills

vo•cif´er•ate *vi. vi.* to cry out; protest boisterously —**vo•cif•er•ous** *ad*..

vogue *n.* fashion or style; popularity

voice *n.* sound produced by vocal organs; quality of sound; the right to expression; an agency for expressing, as a newspaper — *vt.* put into speech; give expression to

void *adj.* containing nothing; completely lacking; having no legal force; useless

voile *n.* a fine, sheer fabric

vol´a•tile *adj.* evaporating rapidly; prone to change suddenly and sharply; fleeting —**vol•a•til´i•ty** *n.*

vol•a•til•ize *vi., vt.* pass off as vapor; become or make volatile

vol•can´ic *adj.* of, produced by, or like a volcano; explosive or violent

vol•ca´no *n.* opening in the earth where hot matter is ejected; a mound formed by ejected material

vol•can•ol´o•gy *n.* study of volcanoes

vo•li´tion *n.* exercise of the will; willpower; power to make a choice

volt *n.* a unit of electric and electromotive potential

volt´age *n.* electromotive force expressed in volts

vol´u•ble *adj.* fluent; talkative

vol´ume *n.* a book, esp. one of a set; bound periodicals; an amount; capacity; space occupied —**vo•lu´mi•nous** *adj.*

vol•un•ta•rism *n.* the use of volunteer labor; willing participation; belief that free will is fundamental to individual action or experience

vol´un•tar•y *adj.* of one's own free will; acting without constraint; intentional; able to choose or elect; optional; supported by charitable donations —**vol´un•tar´i•ly** *adv.*

vol•un•teer´ *n.* an unpaid worker; one who performs of his own free will —*adj.* pertaining ·to or composed of volunteers—*vt.* offer or give voluntarily —*vi.* enter into service without pay

vo•lup´tu•ar•y *n.* one inclined to luxury and indulgence — *adj.* of luxury and extravagance

vo•lup´tu•ous *adj.* pertaining to sensual gratification; suggesting satisfaction *of* sensual desire

voo´doo *n.* a religion marked by belief in sorcery, use of charms, etc.; a charm or spell —*vt.* to bewitch —*adj.*

vo·ra´cious *n.* eager, insatiable; eating greedily

vo´ta·ry *n.* one bound by vows; one intensely devoted

vor´tex *n.*, *pl.* **vor´tex·es, vor´ti·ces** a mass of rotating or whirling fluid; something resembling a vortex

vote *n.* a means for expressing choice; ballots cast; right to choose —*vt., vi.* determine by vote; cast one's vote

vo´tive *adj.* performed in fulfillment of a vow

vouch *vi.* give assurance or guarantee; support or justify —*vt.* bear witness; declare; provide support or justification —**vouch´er** *n.*

vouch·safe´ *vt.* permit; grant —*vi.* condescend or deign

vow *n.* solemn promise; emphatic affirmation —*vt.* make a solemn promise or threat —*vi.* make a vow

voy´age *n.* a long journey —*vi.* take a journey

vo·yeur´ *n.* one gratified by observing objects or acts; one obsessed with viewing sensational or sordid events —**voy·eur·is´tic** *adj.*

vul´can·ize *vt., vi.* process in order to increase strength and elasticity

vul´gar *adj.* lacking manners, taste, etc.; offensive or obscene; pertaining to the common people; of a common language or dialect

vul´gar·ism *n.* word or expression in poor taste

vul´gar·ize *vt.* make common or coarse; popularize

vul´ner·a·ble *adj.* open to attack or injury; susceptible to temptation

vul´ture *n.* a large bird that feeds on carrion; one who preys on others

vy´ing *adj.* that vies or competes

w, W twenty-third letter of the alphabet

wad *n.* a small, compact mass; a large amount: a wad *of cash* —*vt.* press, roll, fold, etc. into a mass

wad´dle *vi.* a clumsy, rocking walk —*vi.* move awkwardly

wade *vi.* walk through something that offers resistance, as water or brush; proceed slowly or laboriously: *wade through paperwork* —*vt.* walk through; cross by walking on the bottom

wader, wading bird a long-legged bird that feeds in shallow water

wa´fer *n.* thin, crisp cookie, cracker, etc.; a disk of material for sealing or attaching

waf´fle *n.* a crisp batter cake —*vi.* be evasive

waft *vt.* bear gently through air or over water —*vi.* float on the wind; blow gently, as a breeze —*n.* lightly passing air, sound, or aroma

wag *vi., vt.* move or cause to move rapidly —*n.* a wagging motion; a droll person; a wit

wage *n.* payment for service; reward or consequence: *wages of sin* —*vt.* engage in: *wage war*

wa´ger *vt., vi.* gamble —*n.* a bet; amount at stake

wag´gish *adj.* humorous; said or done as a joke

waif *n.* a homeless child

wail *vi.* make a mournful, crying sound —*vt.* mourn or lament; cry out in sorrow

wain´scot, wain´scot•ing *n.* paneling for inside walls

wain´wright *n.* a maker of wagons

waist *n.* middle of the body; middle of a thing

waist´coat (Brit.) *n.* a short, sleeveless garment worn over a shirt; (US) a vest

wait *vi., vt.* anticipate: wait to be called; pause; delay or postpone; remain expectant or in readiness; serve as waiter or waitress —*n.* (Brit.) musicians employed to play at a public function; street carolers —**wait´ing** *n.*

waive *vt.* relinquish or forego a claim; put off temporarily

waiv´er *n.* voluntary relinquishment; an instrument which evidences relinquishment

wake[1] *vi.* emerge from sleep; become aware or alert —*vt.* rouse from sleep; make aware —*n.* a watch or vigil over the deceased; (Brit.) an annual parish festival; (Brit.) an annual vacation

wake[2] *n.* trail left by a vessel moving through water; turbulence left by anything that has passed

wake´ful *adj.* not sleepy; watchful, alert; restless — **wake´ful•ness** *n.*

wak´en *vt.* rouse from sleep; stir up: waken patriotic fervor —*vi.* cease sleeping; wake up; become active or animated —**wak´en•er** *n.*

wak´ing *adj.* characterized by consciousness or awareness

wale *n.* a ridge or rib on cloth —*vt.* raise welts by striking; manufacture cloth with ridges

walk *vi.* move or progress on foot; behave a certain way: walk *in peace;* leave abruptly —*vt.* pass through at a walk; force or help to walk: walk a bicycle uphill; accompany or escort on a walk; move: walk a refrigerator away from a wall —*n.* act of walking; a distinctive manner of walking; a place for walking; status or position: *people of all walks* — **walk all over** mistreat or use badly —**walk off with** steal —**walk on air** feel exhilarated or euphoric — **walk out on** abandon

walk´out *n.* a labor strike

walk´-up *n.* dwelling above the first floor in a building with no elevator

wall *n.* a structure that encloses or divides; something like a wall: wall of water, wall of silence —*vt.* provide a wall; enclose or separate with a wall —*adj.* attached to or built into a wall — **drive up a wall** frustrate or distress —**off the wall** unconventional; eccentric

wal´la•by *n.* a small kangaroo

wall´eye *n.* an *eye* with a light-colored iris; a condition in which the eyes diverge; a type of fish

wall´flow•er *n.* one who is shy or unpopular

wal´lop *vt.* beat soundly; strike a blow —*n.* a hard blow

wal´lop•ing *adj.* very large — *n.* beating; a crushing defeat

wal'low vi. roll about in mud, snow, etc.; enjoy: wallow in profits; indulge oneself: wallow in self-pity —n. the act of wallowing; a depression or hollow

waltz n. a ballroom dance — vi. dance; move quickly

wan adj. pale from illness; faint or feeble —**wan'ly** adv.

wand n. the rod of a conjurer; a staff of authority; a musician's baton

wan'der vi. roam; go casually or indirectly; twist, meander; stray —vt. meander across or through

wan'der·lust n. an impulse to travel; restlessness

wane vi. diminish; decline or decrease gradually —n. a decreasing; a period of decline

wan'gle vt. obtain indirectly or dishonestly —vi. resort to indirect or irregular methods

want vt. desire; lack or be deficient in; request —vi. have need; be destitute —n. a lack, scarcity, or shortage; poverty or destitution

want'ing adj. missing or lacking; not up to standard, need, or expectation

wan'ton adj licentious, lewd; heartless, malicious; unrestrained; capricious, unprovoked —vi. act in a wanton manner —vt. waste or squander —n. a lewd or licentious person

wap'i·ti n. the American elk

war n. armed strife; any conflict or struggle; warfare—vt. wage war; fight or take part in war; be in opposition or contention —adj. pertaining to war or its aftermath

war'ble vi., vt. sing with trills, tremulo, etc. —n. the act or sound of warbling

war chest a special fund, as for a political campaign

ward n. section of a hospital; administrative division of a city; one in the care of a guardian; the act of guarding or being guarded —vt. repel or turn aside

war'den n. supervisor or custodian; (Brit.) an executive or administrator, as a crown officer, college official, or church trustee; (US) chief administrative officer of a prison

ward'er n. one who guards or protects; (Brit.) a prison guard

ward'robe n. a cabinet or closet for wearing apparel; costumes belonging to a theater group; collectively, all of one's garments or those suited to a season

ware n. articles of a type; dishes or pottery; merchandise displayed for sale

ware'house n. storage for goods awaiting sale or use; (Brit.) a large cut-rate or retail store —vt. place or keep in a warehouse

war'fare n. waging of war; struggle or strife

war horse a veteran of many struggles, as a politician

war'like adj. fond of war; threatening war

war'lock n. a male witch; a sorcerer

war'lord n. a military commander who governs; a militaristic head of state

warm adj. moderately hot; imparting or preserving

warmth; heated from exertion; cordial, friendly; recently made: *warm from the oven*; suggesting warmth, as of a color —*vt.,* *vi.* make or become heated, interested, excited: *warmed to the idea*; become friendly; feel pleasure: *warm the heart* — **warm′ly** *adv.*

warm′-blood′ed *adj.* having nearly constant, warm body temperature; ardent or passionate

warmed′-o′ver *adj.* reheated; ineffectual from overuse

warm′-heart•ed *adj.* kind; sympathetic; generous

warmth *n.* a feeling of comfort; ardor or excitement; friendliness

warn *vt.* alert; advise; give notice —*vi.* give warning

warn′ing *n.* an act of giving notice or being alerted; a sign or signal —*adj.* serving as notice: *warning bell*

warp *vt.* twist; corrupt or pervert; divert; arrange strands for weaving —*vi.* become twisted or distorted; turn aside from a proper course; go astray —*n.* a distortion; an abnormality; mental or moral aberration; woven strands running the length of a fabric

war′rant *n.* legal authorization for arrest, search, etc.; a guarantee or warrantee; sanction or justification —*vt.* assure or guarantee quality or condition; guarantee against loss; give legal authority; guarantee clear title to property

war′rant•ee *n.* recipient of a warrant or warranty

war′ran•tor′ , **war′rant•er** *n.* one who issues a warrant or warrnty

war′ran•ty *n.* guarantee by a seller; official authorization or warrant; justification for action

war′ren *n.* an enclosure for small animals; overcrowded living space

war′ri•or *n.* one engaged or experienced in warfare

wart *n.* a small, hard growth on the skin; natural growth on plants and animals

war′y *adj.* watchful; marked by caution; shrewd or wily

wash *vt.* cleanse or remove; cover with liquid; soak or rinse; flow against or over; coat with a thin layer of pigment —*vi.* bathe or launder; be removed or drawn off by liquid —*n.* a wetting or cleaning; clothes to be laundered; a surge of water; removal or deposit of topsoil by water; a preparation for cleaning or coating; a thin coating of pigment: a tint

washed′-out′ *adj.* lacking intensity: faded; exhausted

washed′-up′ *adj.* finished; no longer capable or needed

wash′out *n.* erosion by the action of water; a failure

wash′room *n.* a lavatory

wash′stand *n.* cabinet for a pitcher, washbowl, etc.; a bathroom sink

wasp *n.* a flying insect with a slender segmented body

wasp′ish *adj.* slender; irritable or bad-tempered

was′sail *n.* an ancient toast; a spiced drink of ale and wine; a celebration —*vi.* revel or carouse

waste vt. use thoughtlessly; squander; make weak or feeble; fail to use or take advantage of; devastate—vi. lose vigor, bulk, etc.; diminish; pass gradually —n. unnecessary consumption; failure to benefit; a desolate place; gradual wearing away; something discarded

wast′ed adj. squandered; useless, excessive: *wasted effort;* frail or feeble from illness; inebriated or under influence of a narcotic

waste′ful adj. prone to or causing waste; extravagant

waste′land n. barren or desolate land

was′trel n. a spendthrift; an idler

watch vt. observe closely; be alert; wait expectantly; work as a guard; keep a religious vigil —vt. look at attentively; keep informed; be alert for; guard —n. careful observation; attitude of alertness; a time of guard duty; a small timepiece; a religious vigil

watch′dog n.; one who oversees waste, unlawful or prohibited acts, etc.

watch′ful adj. vigilant; alert

watch′word n. a password; a slogan

wa′ter n. colorless liquid essential to all organisms; a supply of water; preparation holding a substance in solution —vt. provide with water; dilute with water —vi. secrete or discharge water —

keep one′s head above water stay out of difficulty

water down reduce or dilute

—water under the bridge a bygone event

wa′ter•bed n. bed with a water-filled mattress

wa′ter•borne adj. floating on water; transported by ship

water clock a timepiece operated by water

water closet (Brit.) a toilet

wa′ter•col•or n. a water-soluble pigment; a painting rendered in watercolors —adj. painted with watercolors —**wa′ter•col•or•ist** n.

wa′ter•course n. a flow of water, as a river, etc.; a channel for water

wa′ter•front n. property close to or overlooking a body of water; an area of docks, warehouses, etc.

water gap a deep ravine permitting passage of a river or stream

wa′ter-glass n. a drinking vessel; a gauge for indicating water level; a bucket-like device with glass bottom, used to see under water

watering hole pond or pool frequented by wildlife; a tavern or pub

wa′ter•logged adj. soaked with water; so saturated as to be unmanageable and barely able to float

water main conduit for water

wa′ter•mark n. a waterline; a design impressed into paper —vt. impress on paper

water mill a mill operated by water

water nymph a mythical being that dwells in a stream, lake, etc.

water pipe conduit for water; a tobacco pipe filtered by water

wa′ter•pow•er n. energy derived from flowing water

wa´ter•shed n. an area draining into a river; a decisive turning point

wa´ter•spout a. a moving, whirling column of water; a pipe for discharging water

water table the upper level of saturated subterranean rock

wa´ter•tight adj. so closely made as not to leak; that cannot be misunderstood, found illegal, or in error

water tower a reservoir used to maintain water pressure

water vapor moisture mixed in air

wa´ter•way n. a river, channel, etc.

water wheel a wheel turned by flowing water

wa´ter•works n. a system of pumps, pipes, etc. for supplying water

wa´ter•worn adj. worn smooth or eroded by run-ning or falling water

wa´ter•y adj. like water; diluted; insipid

watt n. unit of electrical power

watt´age n. a measure of electrical power

wat´tle n. woven framework of poles and twigs; a fold of skin hanging from the throat of a bird or lizard

wave vi. move or flap in the wind; greet or signal with the hand; become curved or curled —vt. move freely; flourish; signal by waving; form into curves or curls — n. a ridge or undulation; a motion of the hand; a series of curves: a hair wave; an upsurge: a wave of nausea; a prolonged condition: heat wave; a pattern formed by energy: a sound wave

wave´form n. the curve produced by the movement of a wave of energy

wave´length n. the distance between crests or troughs in cycles of an energy wave.

wa´ver vi. move back and forth; be uncertain; falter — n. a wavering

wav´y adj. full of curves: wavy hair, undulating

wax n. a pliable substance insoluble in water and that burns in the air; waxlike product, as paraffin or furniture polish —adj. made with or from wax —vt.. coat or polish with wax —vi. gradually increase; express oneself: wax poetic

wax´en adj. consisting of or covered with wax; pale or pallid; malleable or pliant

wax museum a place that exhibits life-size wax figures

wax paper paper coated with wax, used in food preparation

wax´works n. an exhibit of wax sculptures

wax´y adj. resembling or abounding in wax; pale or pallid

way n. a direction; course or passage; space: make way; process or means: a way to succeed; customary manner: the way we live; condition : in a bad way —in a way to some extent —adv.

waybill n. a document that accompanies a shipment

way´far•er n. one who travels, usually aimlessly

way´lay vt. lie in ambush; meet on the way

ways and means methods for defraying costs

way´ward *adj.* willful, head-strong; not predictable

weak *adj.* lacking strength, vigor, etc.; not effective or forceful; lacking skill or experience; deficient

weak´en *vt., vi.* make or become weak or weaker

weak´ling *n.* feeble person or animal

weak´ly *adj.* sick or feeble — *adv.* in a weak manner

weak´ness *n.* the quality of being fragile or delicate; a slight failing or fault; a strong liking

weal *n.* a welt, as from a blow

wealth *n.* riches; the state of being rich; great abundance

wealth´y *adj.* possessing riches; characterized by abundance

wean *vt.* end dependence on mother's milk; withdraw from a detrimental habit or association

weap´on *n.* anything for use against an adversary — **weap´on•ry** *n.*

wear *vt.* have on, as a garment or ornament; display; damage by use; exhaust — *vi.* be gradually diminished by use; withstand the effects of use, time, etc.; have a tiring effect — *n.* act of wearing or being worn; articles of dress; destruction from use or time; durability

wear´a•ble *adj.* suitable for wear

wear•a•bil´i•ty *n.* ability to withstand use or time

wear´ing *adj.* tiresome; exhausting

wea´ry *adj.* tired; fatigued; discontented or bored; indicating fatigue —*vt., vi.* make or become weary

wea´ri•some *adj.* causing fatigue; tiresome **wea´sel** *n.* a small, slender carnivorous animal; a sly or treacherous person —*vi.* renege on a promise: *weasel out of a deal;* equivocate

weath´er *n.* general atmospheric conditions; unpleasant conditions — *vt.* expose to the elements; show effects of exposure; pass through and survive —*vi.* undergo change from exposure; resist the action of weather —*adj.* facing the wind

weath´er-beat´en *adj.* showing effects of exposure

weath´ered *adj.* worn or damaged; visibly improved by or intended to emulate exposure: *weathered* brick

weath´er•ing *n.* process by which exposure causes change; alteration by exposure, esp. for effect

weath´er•proof *adj.* capable of withstanding harsh weather —*vt.* make weatherproof

weath´er•strip•ping *n.* material in or over crevices to exclude drafts, rain, etc. —*vt.* attach or apply weatherstripping

weave *vt.* interlace; make by interlacing thread, cane, reeds, etc.; produce by linking parts: *weave* a tale; move from side to side —*vi.* make by weaving; become interlaced; make one's way by weaving

web *n.* network spun by a spider; an artfully contrived trap; entanglement: *web of deceit;* a complex network: *world-wide* web; membrane

— *vt.* create a web; trap

webbed *adj.* of or pertaining to a web: *webbed feet*

wed *vi., vt.* marry

wed'ding *n.* the rite of marriage; anniversary of a marriage

wedge *n.* a taper of metal, wood, etc. used to split a log, tighten a joint, etc.; something that facilitates entry, intrusion, etc. —*vt.* force apart or fix in place with a wedge; crowd or squeeze —*vi.* force oneself in

wed'lock *n.* marriage

wee *adj.* very small

weed *n.* an unwanted or unsightly plant —*vt., vi.* remove unwanted growth; remove that considered undesirable: *weed out useless data*

week *n.* seven calendar days; period described by an event: *Christmas week*; portion of a week dedicated to business: a *five-day week*

week'ly *adj., adv.* occurring every week; once a week; pertaining to a week —*n.* periodical issued once a week

weep *vt.* shed tears; form liquid on, as by condensation —*vt.* weep for; shed liquid   *n.* the act of weeping; an exhudation of liquid, as from a sore —**weep'y** *adj.* weeping or inclined to weep

wee'vil *n.* a small destructive beetle

weigh *vt.* determine the weight of; measure by weight; consider —*vi.* have a specified weight; have importance: *weigh heavy on the mind*; be burdensome: *weigh down with guilt*

weight *n.* heaviness; measure of heaviness; a piece used as a standard in weighing; a unit of heaviness; burden or pressure: weight of responsibility; importance or consequence; a heavy object used in competition or for exercise; an object used to hold down: paperweight —*vt.* make heavy; oppress or burden

weight'ed *adj.* having weight; adjusted to reflect the importance of elements: *weighted average*

weight'y *adj.* of great importance; effectual: a *weighty argument*; oppressive; heavy

weir *n.* a dam to raise or divert the water; a fence in a stream, used to catch or hold back fish

weird *adj.* odd or bizarre; of the supernatural or a supernatural occurrence — **weird'ness** *n.*

wel'come *vt.* greet pleasantly or hospitably; receive with pleasure —*n.* a warm reception —*adj.* received cordially; producing satisfaction or pleasure; free to use or enjoy

weld *vt.* unite, as metal by the application of heat; bring into close association —*n.* a joining; a joint

wel'fare *n.* well-being; prosperity; assistance to those in need

welfare state a system by which a government assumes responsibility for health care, retirement, etc.

well *n.* a shaft sunk into the earth; a source of continued supply; a depression to hold or collect water; a vertical opening through a building for light, ventilation, stairs, etc. —*vi.* rise to the surface —*vt.* gush or pour forth —*adv.* satisfactorily; in a correct manner; to a considerable extent; quite, positively —*adj.* suitable or proper; fortunate; in good health; prosperous

well´ad·just·ed *adj.* mentally sound

well´-be´ing *a.* health, happiness, or prosperity

well´born *adj.* of good family; titled; aristocratic

well´-nigh´ *adv.* almost

well´spring *n.* a source

well´-timed´ *adj.* happening at a propitious time

well´-wish·er *n.* a supporter

welt *n.* raised mark on the skin from a blow; material used to cover. or strengthen a seam —*vt.* decorate with awell; whip or flog

wen *n.* a cyst

wend *vt.* go on; proceed

west *n.* the general direction in which the sun sets —*adj.*

west´er·ly *add., adv.* in, toward, or of the west

west´ern *adj.* of, in, directed toward, or facing the west; from the west

west´ern·ize *vt.* adapt to customs of a western nation; adopt trappings of the American west

wet *adj.* moistened or covered with liquid; marked by rainfall; riot yet dry, as paint —*n.* moisture. rainy weather —*vt., vi.* make or become wet —**all wet** completely wrong —**wet behind the ears** inexperienced

wet´land *n.* land area saturated or partly under water

whack *vt., vi.* strike sharply — *n.* a resounding blow

whale *n.* a large marine mammal; a thing very good, large, or impressive: whale *of a party*

wharf *n., pl.* **wharfs, wharves** a place for docking and loading or unloading ships; a pier or dock

what *pron.* which specific thing, amount, circumstance, etc.; that which; whatever situation or contingency: take *what comes* — *adj.* which one; —*adv.* how much: *what does it matter?* —**what for** strong reproof or denunciation

what´not *n.* shelving designed to hold and display small objects; a small decorative object

wheal *n.* a small pimple on the skin

wheat *n.* a cereal grass

wheat germ the nutricious embryo of the wheat kernel

wheedle *vt.* persuade or ob-tain by flattery, cajolery, or coaxing —*vi.* use flattery or cajolery

wheel *n.* a disk or rim on a central axis; a turning or rotating movement; a person of influence —*vt.* move or convey on wheels; cause to turn; provide with wheels — *vi.* turn, as on an axis; change one's course; move on wheels

wheel´bar·row *n.* one -wheeled vehicle with opposing handles —*vt.* convey in a wheelbarrow

wheel´chair *n.* a wheeled seat for the use of one unable to walk

wheel′er-deal′er *n.* one who acts freely, aggressively, and often unscrupulously

wheel′wright *n.* a man whose business is making or repairing wheels

wheeze *vt., vi.* breathe with a husky, whistling sound —*n.* the sound of wheezing — **wheez′y** *adj.*

whelp re young of a dog, wolf, etc.; a worthless young fellow —*vt., vi.* give birth

when *adv.* at what or which time, at an earlier time; under what circumstances —*conj.*

whence *adv.* from what place or source —*conj.*

where *adv.* at or in what place or situation; to or from what place

where′with•al *n.* necessary means or resources

whet *vt.* sharpen, as a knife; excite or stimulate: *whet the appetite*

whet′stone *n.* a fine stone for sharpening knives, etc.

whey *n.* clear liquid produced from curdled milk

which *pron.* what thing; that previously indicated —*adj.* what specific one

whiff *n.* gust of air; an aroma; a pull

while *vt.* pass time pleasantly —*n.* a span of time —*conj.* during the time that; at the same time; whereas

whim *a.* a sudden, capricious idea or notion

whim′per *vi., vt.* cry or utter a plaintive sound

whim′si•cal *adj.* capricious; marked by erratic or unpredictable conduct; odd or quaint

whim′sy *n.* whim or caprice; odd or quaint humor

whine *vi.* utter a high, plaintive, nasal sound; complain in a fretful or childish way; make a steady high-pitched sound, as of a machine —*vt.* utter with a whine —*n.*

whip *vt.* strike with a lash, rod, etc.; buffet; heat to a froth; seize, jerk, throw, etc. with a sudden motion —*vi.* move or turn suddenly; thrash about —*n.* a lash; a whipping or thrashing motion; a legislator appointed to enforce discipline, attendance, etc.; a dessert containing whipped cream or beaten egg whites

whip′lash *n.* end of a whip; neck injury caused by a sudden snap of the head

whipping boy one who receives undeserved blame or punishment

whir *vt., vi.* fly or move with a buzzing sound —*n.* a whizzing sound; confusion or bustle

whirl vi, *vt.* turn or cause to turn or revolve rapidly; move or go swiftly; feel a spinning sensation —*n.* swift rotating motion; state of confusion; round of activities: social *whirl*

whirl′pool *n.* an eddy or vortex of rapidly whirling water

whirl′wind *n.* a rapidly spinning column of air; a destructive force —*adj.* extremely swift or impetuous: *a whirl wind* tour

whisk *vt.* brush or sweep lightly; beat with quick movements — *vi.* move quickly and lightly —*n.* light sweeping motion; a kitchen untensil for whipping or blending

whisk´er n. the hair of a beard; long bristly face hair on an animal

whis´key, whis´ky n. an alcoholic beverage —adj. pertaining to or made with whiskey

whis´per n. hushed speech; a secret communication; low, rustling noise —vi. speak in hushed tones; speak furtively; make a low, rustling sound —vt. utter in a low tone

whist n. a card game similar to bridge

whis´tle vi. make a sharp, shrill sound; sound a whistle produce a sound by whistling —n. a sharp, shrill sound; device for making such a sound

whis´tle-blow´er n. one who exposes wrongdoing

whistle stop town along the course of a railway where a train stops only when signaled; a small town, one of little importance; a brief stop by a political candidate

whit n. the smallest bit

white n. color produced by reflection of all visible colors of the spectrum; the condition of being white; anything white or nearly white; the white part of something, as an egg; light-colored pieces, as of chess men —adj. lacking hue; relatively light in color; relatively unmarked or clean; harmless or innocuous

white blood cell blood cells that help stave off infection and disease

white´-col´lar adj. designating salaried or office workers

white dwarf a small, faint, extremely dense star

white elephant a burden; expensive to maintain; of uncertain value

whit´en vt., vi. make or become white, as by bleaching

white paper an authoritative report on an important topic

white´wash n. a thin mixture of lime, water, sizing, etc. for coating walls, fences, etc.; a suppressing or concealing of faults or failure —t.n. coat with whitewash; suppress or gloss over wrongdoing

whit´tle vt. make or shape by cutting; reduce or wear away a little at a time: *whittle away an inheritance* —vi. cut or shape wood

whiz vi., vt. make or cause a hissing, humming sound — n. a whizzing sound; one of extraordinary ability

whiz kid a relatively young person who is extremely clever, talented, or successful

who•dun´it n. a mystery story

whole adj. complete or entire; not broken or defective; being the full amount —n. all the parts or elements that make up a thing

whole´heart•ed adj. complete and unreserved enthusiasm, energy, dedication, etc.

whole´sale n. sale of goods in bulk, usually for resale — adj. of the buying or selling of goods in bulk; made or done on a large scale —adv. in bulk or quantity; extensively or indiscriminately

whole´some *adj.* tending to promote health; advocating mental or moral righteousness

whol´ly *adv.* completely, totally; exclusively, only

whoop *vi.* utter loud cries — *vt.* call or chase with loud cries — *n.* shout of excitement, joy, decision, etc.

whop´per *n.* something large or remarkable; an outrageous lie **—whop´ping** *adj.*

why *adv.* for what cause, purpose, or reason — *n.* a cause or reason

wick *n.* a cord or strand conveying fuel to a flame — *vt.*, *vi.* to convey or be conveyed by capillary action

wick´ed *adj.* evil; mischievous or roguish; mean or troublesome

wide *adj.* broad or spacious; off a desired point: *wide of the mark*; having great scope — *adv.* extensively **—wide´ly** *adv.*

wid´en make or become wide or wider **—wid´en•er** *n.*

wide´spread´ *adj.* extending over a large area; extensive

wid´ow *n.* a woman whose husband has died

wid´ow•er *n.* a man whose wife has died

width *n.* dimension from side to side

wield *vt.* to use, as a weapon or tool; exercise authority, power, influence. etc. — **wield´a•ble** *adj.*

wield´y *adj.* easily handled or managed

wie´ner, wie´ner•wurst *n.* a kind of smoked sausage

wife *n.* a woman joined in marriage **—wife´ly** *adj.*

wig *n.* a head covering that replaces or augments hair — *vt.* furnish with a wig

wig´gle *vt.*, *vi.* move from side to side —*n.* **—wig´gly** *adj.*

wild *adj.* to a natural state; uncivilized; undisciplined; reckless, imprudent; extremely odd, strange, or bizarre; disorderly or disarranged; off the mark: *a wild throw* —*n.* an uninhabited or uncultivated place —*adv.* in a wild manner **—wild´ly** *adv.* **—wild´ness** *n.*

wild´cat *n.* a feral cat, as the lynx, cougar, etc.; an aggressive, quick-tempered person; a tricky or unsound business venture —*adj.* unsound or risky; unofficial or unauthorized — *vt.*, *vi.* drill for oil

wildcat strike an unauthorized walkout or labor stoppage

wil´der•ness *n.* an uncultivated or uninhabited area

wild´fire *n.* a raging fire

wild´fowl *n.* a wild game bird

wild´goose chase pursuit of the unknown or unattainable

wild´life *n.* wild animals collectively

wild rice an aquatic grass of North America or its edible grain

wild´wood *n.* natural forest land

wile *n.* a trick or artifice —*vt.* lure, beguile, or mislead

will *n.* power to choose; a specific purpose, choice, etc.; strong determination; self-control —*vt.* choose; resolve as an action or course; decree —*vi.* wish or desire

will´ful *adj.* deliberate, intentional; stubborn or headstrong

will´ing *adj.* favorably disposed; readily acting, responding, giving, etc.

wil´low *n.* a tree or shrub with flexible shoots often used in basketry —*adj.* made of willow wood

wil´low•y *adj.* tall and graceful; lithe or flexible; supple; abounding in willow trees

will´pow•er *n.* control of one's actions or desires; determination

wilt *vi., vt.* lose or cause to lose freshness, energy, etc.; droop

wil´y *adj.* sly or cunning

wimp *n.* one regarded as a weakling; one who whimpers

win *vi.* be victorious — *vt.* be successful in; gain victory; Influence — *n.* a victory

wince *vt.* shrink back; be startled; recoil, as in pain — *n.* a startled motion

wind *n.* movement of air; breath; idle chatter —*vt.* exhaust the breath of

wind *vt., vi.* coil or twine

wind´break *n.* that protecting from the wind

wind´ed *adj.* out of breath

wind´fall *n.* something, as ripened fruit, brought down by the wind; unexpected good fortune

wind´ing *adj.* turning about an axis or core; having bends or turns

wind´jam•mer *n.* a sailing vessel

wind´lass *n.* a device for hoisting or hauling

win´dow *n.* opening to admit light or air

window dressing arrangement in a store window; means for making something seem more attractive

win´dow•sill *n.* ledge beneath a window opening

wind´shear *n.* a strong rapid change in wind direction

wind´swept *adj.* exposed to or brushed by wind

wind´tunnel a device that artificially produces wind for the study of effects on design, materials, etc.

wind´up *a.* a conclusion

wind´ward *adj.* toward the wind; on the side exposed to the wind —*n.* direction facing the wind —*adv.* against the wind

wind´y *adj.* stormy; tempestuous; boastful or talkative

wine *n.* fermented fruit juice; color of red wine —*vt.* entertain or treat with wine

wine cellar a storage area for wines

wine´press *n.* an apparatus for extracting juice; place where juice is extracted

win´er•y *n.* an establishment where wine is made

wing *n.* organ of flight; anything resembling or suggesting a bird's wing; an attachment or extension, as of a building or stage —*vt.* pass over in flight; accomplish by flying; disable by wounding —*vt.* fly **winged** *adj.*

wink *vi., vt.* blink or cause to blink; signal by closing the lid of one eye; twinkle —*n.* fleeting time, twinkle; a hint conveyed by winking —**forty winks** a short nap

win´ner *n.* one who prevails; a victor; one likely to succeed

win´ning *adj.* successful; charming

win´now *vt.* separate, as grain from chaff; eliminate that which is bad —*vi.* separate grain from chaff —*n.* a device to separate grain

win´some *adj.* charming; attractive

win´ter *n.* the coldest season, between autumn and spring; *a year: a man of ninety winters* —*vi.* pass the winter —*vt.* protect during the winter —*adj.* suitable for or characteristic of winter

win´ter·green *n.* a small evergreen plant or flavoring oil extracted from its leaves

win´ter·y, win´try *adj.* of or like winter: cold, stormy, bleak, etc.

win´y *adj.* having the taste, color, etc. of wine

wipe *vt.* to rub —*n.* —**wipe out** destroy utterly

wire *n.* a slender strand of metal; something made of wire; telegram —*vt.* fasten with wire; equip with wire, as for providing electricity; send a telegram

wired *adj.* fitted out for electricity, telephones, etc.; keyed up; excited

wire´less *adj.* not requiring wires —*n.* device operating without wires; (*Brit.*) a radio

wire´tap *n.* a device for listening in on a telephone conversation —*vt.* connect or listen with a wiretap —*vi.* to use a wiretap

wir´ing *n.* wires installed in a building to provide electricity, telephone service, etc.; the process of connecting or installing wires

wir´y *adj.* lean; tough and sinewy; stiff or bristly

wis´dom *n.* ability to make sound judgements; insight or intuition; extensive knowledge; an accumulated body of knowledge

wise *adj.* having insight, common sense, or knowledge; shrewd and calculating —**wise´ly** *adv.*

wise´crack *n.* an insolent or supercilious remark

wish *n.* desire or longing; something desired —*vt.* have a desire or longing for; request or entreat —*vi.* feel a desire; express a desire

wish´ful *adj.* having or indicating a desire

wishful thinking believing that what one wants to be true is true

wish´y-wash´y *adj.* lacking in purpose; indecisive or ineffective

wisp *n.* a small bunch of straw, hair, etc.; an indication: *wisp of perfume*; slight, delicate thing: *wisp of a child* —**wisp´y** *adj.*

wist´ful *adj.* wishful, yearning; musing, pensive —**wist´ful·ly** *adv.*

wit *n.* intelligence; mental acuity; guile: *live by one's wits*; a clever or amusing person

witch *n.* woman who practices sorcery; an ugly or cruel old woman; a fascinating woman —*vt.* work a spell upon; fascinate or charm ,

witch´craft *n.* black magic, sorcery; extraordinary influence or charm

witch hunt investigation or harassment of dissenters

with·draw' vt. take away or remove; take back or rescind; prevent from using, selling, etc. —vi. retreat; remove oneself

with·draw·al n. a taking back, removing, retreating, etc.; process or effects of overcoming an addiction

with·drawn' adj. not responsive; introverted; isolated

with·er vi. become limp or dry; to waste, as flesh —vt. cause to become limp or dry; disconcert or humble, as by a scornful glance

with·hold' vt. hold back; refuse to grant, permit, etc. —in. refrain

with·stand' vt., vi. resist, oppose, or endure

wit·less adj. lacking intelligence; silly or foolish

wit'ness n. one competent to testify by virtue of having seen or learned something; one who attests to authenticity —vt. see or know personally; give testimony; subscribe to the authenticity of a document, signature, etc. — vi. testify

wit·ti·cism n. a clever or humorous remark

wit'ty adj. clever or humorous —**wit'ti·ness** n.

wiz'ard n. a sorcerer; one exceptionally skillful or clever –adj. (Brit.) extraordinary: a wizard pianist

wiz'ard·ry n. practice or methods of a wizard

wiz'ened adj. shriveled; dried up

wob'ble is. sway unsteadily; show indecision —vt. cause to wobble—n. unsteadiness; instability

woe n. overwhelming sorrow; suffering

woe'be·gone adj. mournful; sorrowful

woe'ful adj. causing sorrow; paltry —**woe'ful·ly** adv.

wolf n. a wild, carnivorous mammal related to the dog; a cruel or rapacious person; a man who flirts

wom'an n. an adult human female; a female attendant or servant —adj. of a woman or women; female

wom'an·ly adj. having qualities suited to a woman

womb n. a place where a thing is engendered or brought into life; a sheltering space or area

wom'bat n. a burrowing marsupial of Australia

won'der n. feeling of mingled surprise, admiration, and astonishment; that causing wonder —vt. have curiosity or doubt —vi. to marvel; be curious or doubtful —adj. spectacularly successful

won'der·ful adj. astonishing; very good —**won'der·ful·ly** adv.

won'der·ment a. astonishment or awe; something marvelous; puzzlement

won'drous adj. wonderful; marvelous; extraordinary —adv. surprisingly

wont adj. accustomed

wont'ed adj. commonly used or done; accustomed

woo vt. seek affection or approval; entreat earnestly —vi. pay court

wood n. hard fibrous material that constitutes the bulk of a tree; a forest — adj. pertaining to or using wood

wood´craft *n.* survival in the wild; the art of fashioning wooden articles

wood´cut *n.* engraved block or prints from the block

wood´ed *adj.* abounding with trees

wood´en *adj.* made of wood; stiff or awkward

wood´land *n.* land covered with trees; timberland —*adj.* belonging to or dwelling in the woods

wood nymph a forest sprite

wood´wind *n.* musical instrument that uses a wood or woodlike reed

wood´work *n.* things made of wood; interior trim, as door and window frames

wood´y *adj.* made of or containing wood; resembling wood; wooded

wool *n.* a soft, durable fiber from the fleece of animals; yarn, fabric, etc. made from animal fibers —**wool, wool´en** *adj.*

wool´ly, wool´y *adj.* resembling wool; not clear

word *n.* smallest meaningful unit of a language; speech; a brief remark, message, comment, etc.; a promise

word´ing *n.* style or arrangement of words; phraseology

word´play *n.* clever repartee

word´y *adj.* in too many words —**word´i•ness** *n.*

work *n.* physical or mental exertion; employment; one's profession or trade; place of employment —*vi.* perform work; be employed; prove effective —*vt.* cause or bring about; make or shape by toil or skill; cause to be productive; achieve by effort

work´able *adj.* capable of being worked or developed; practicable

work´ing *adj.* employed; occupied by work; functional; sufficient for use or action: working agreement

working capital finances available for operation of a business

working class those who work for wages

work´man•like *adj.* like or befitting a skilled workman; skillfully done

work´man•ship *n.* art or skill of a workman; quality of work; work accomplished

work of art a thing of beauty; fine art; anything done with great skill

work´out *n.* activity to improve skill, physical fitness, etc.; strenuous or intense activity

work sheet record of an employee's work times; preliminary notes or calculations; a spreadsheet

work´shop *n.* an area set aside for projects, a hobby, etc.; a seminar for training or discussion

world *n.* the earth; the universe; a celestial body; part of the earth: *Third World;* division of time, etc.: *ancient world, animal world;* large amount: *world of knowledge*

world´ly *adj.* of a world; devoted to secular, earthly things; sophisticated— **world´li•ness** *n.*

world´ly-wise *adj.* schooled in the ways of the world; sophisticated

world´-wea•ry *adj.* discontented with life

worm *n.* an elongated, limbless, soft-bodied creature; despicable person —*vt.* proceed like a worm; draw forth by artful means: *worm in. formation;* rid of intestinal worms *vi.* progress slowly and stealthily

worn *adj.* damaged by wear; showing effects of anxiety, etc., hackneyed

worn-out *adj.* having lost value or effectiveness; tired, exhausted

wor′ri•some *adj.* causing concern or anxiety

wor′ry *vi.* be uneasy; feel anxiety —*vt.* cause to feel uneasy; bother or pester; bite, pull, or shake with the teeth —*n.* anxiety or uneasiness; something causing such a state

worse *adj.* bad or ill to a greater degree; less favorable —*adv.* in a less favorable manner; with greater intensity, severity, etc.

wors′en *vt., vi.* make or be come less favorable

wor′ship *n.* adoration, homage; rituals, prayers, etc. in tribute to a dirty; excessive or ardent admiration —*vt.* venerate; have intense admiration or love for —*vi.* perform acts of veneration

wor′ship•ful *adj.* feeling or showing love, reverence, etc.

worst *adj.* extremely bad or ill; least favorable —*adv.* to the extreme degree of inferiority, badness, etc. —*vt.* defeat, vanquish

wor′sted *a.* a woolen yarn, or fabric made from such yarn —*adj.* made from worsted

worth *n.* value; a quality that makes estimable or desirable; amount obtainable for a sum: *two dollars worth;* wealth —*adj.* equal in value to; deserving of

worth′less *adj.* having no value —**worth′less•ness** *n.*

worth′while′ *adj.* sufficiently important to occupy; of sufficient value to repay effort

wor′thy *adj.* having valuable or useful qualitites; deserv-ing —*n.* a person of eminent worth

would′-be *adj.* desiring, professing, or intending

wound *n.* an injury; a cause of pain or grief- *vt., vi.* inflict a wound; injure feelings or pride of

wraith *n.* an apparition seen shortly before or after death; a specter

wren′gle *vi.* argue noisily and angrily —*vt.* argue, debate; get by arguing stubbornly; herd livestock —*n.* an angry dispute —**wran′gler** *n.*

wrap *vt.* surround and cover; to fold or wind about something —*n.* an outer garment

wrap′per *n.* material for enclosing; a dressing gown; one who wraps

wrap′ping *n.* a covering

wrath *n.* violent rage or fury

wrath′ful *adj.* full of wrath; extremely angry; expressing or resulting from rage

wreak *vt.* inflict or exact, as vengeance; give free expression to

wreath *n.* a circular band of flowers, leaves, etc.; curling or spiral band

wreathe *vt.* form into a wreath, as by twisting or twining; adorn or encircle

—*vi.* take the form of a wreath; twist, turn, or coil

wreck *vt.* cause destruction of; bring ruin upon — *vi.* suffer destruction; engage in destroying —*n.* the act of destroying; that ruined or destroyed; remnants, remains

wreck´age *n.* a broken remnant; fragments from a wreck

wreck´er *n.* one causing destruction; one employed in tearing down and removing structures; person or machine that clears disabled or damaged automobiles

wrench *n.* a violent twist; a sprain, twist, or pull of a part of the body; (US) a tool for turning, twisting, etc. — *vt.* twist violently; twist forcibly so as to injure —*vi.* give a twist

wrest *vt.* pull away by violent twisting; seize forcibly; gain by great effort

wres´tle *n.* engage in wrestling; struggle or contend — *vt.* contend in wrestling —*n.* a difficult struggle

wres´tling *n.* a sport in which unarmed contestants endeavor to force each other to the ground

wretch *n.* a vile person; miserable or unhappy person

wretch´ed *adj.* profoundly unhappy; marked by misery or poverty; despicable or contemptible

wrig´gle *vi.* twist in a sinuous manner; make one's way by evasive or indirect means — *vt.-* cause to wriggle; advance by evasive or sly means —*n.* the motion of one who or that wriggles —**wrig´gly** *adj.*

wrig´gler *n.* something that wriggles; a mosquito larva

wring *vt.* squeeze or compress by twisting; force out by twisting; acquire forcibly; distress —*n.* a twisting or forcing —**wring´er** *n.*

wrin´kle *n.* a small fold or crease; modification: *a new wrinkle* —*vt.*, *vi.* make or become creased

wrist *n.* the arm between forearm and hand; part of a garment covering the wrist

write *vt.* inscribe on a surface; communicate by letter; be author or composer of; leave evidence of —*vi.* inscribe; communicate in writing; work as an author

writhe *vi.* twist or distort the body in pain; suffer from embarrassment, sorrow, etc. —*vt.* cause to be twisted or distorted —**writh´er** *n.*

wrong *adj-* mistaken; inappropriate; not moral or legal; not working properly; unintentional —*adv.* incorrectly or improperly; erroneously —*n.* injury or injustice; a violation of rights —*vt.* violate rights of; impute evil unjustly; treat dishonorably

wrong´do•er *n.* one who does wrong; one acting unlawfully

wrong´ful *adj.* characterized by wrong or injustice; unlawful, illegal

wroth *adj.* angry

wrought *adj.* hammered into shape; formed delicately or elaborately

wrought up disturbed, excited

wry *adj.* bent to one side; contorted or askew; somewhat perverse or ironic: *wry humor*—**wry´ly** *adv.*

wurst *n.* sausage

x, X twenty-fourth letter of the alphabet

xan´thous *adj.* yellow

X chromosome a sex chromosome paired in the female and coupled with a Y chromosome in the male

xen•o•pho´bi•a *n.* fear of strangers or foreigners — **xen•o•pho•bic** *adj.*

x ray, x-ray *n.* a wavelength shorter than ultraviolet and longer than a gamma ray; an image made with x-rays — *adj. of,* made by, or producing x-rays —*vt.* examine or treat with x-rays

xy´lo•phone *n.* a percussion instrument of graduated bars, played by striking with small mallets

y, Y twenty-fifth letter of the alphabet

yacht *n.* a relatively small ship for pleasure or racing

ya´hoo *n.* a crude or awkward person; a bumpkin

yak *n.* a large, shaggy wild ox; idle chatter —*vi.* talk a great deal

ya´ku•za *n.* a Japanese gangster

yam *n.* a fleshy, edible tuberous root; a variety of sweet potato

yam´mer *vi.* whine or complain —*vt.* utter in a peevish manner

yank *vt., vi.* jerk or pull suddenly —*n.* a sudden sharp jerk

yap *vi.* talk or jabber; to yelp, as a dog —*n.* a yelp; worthless talk; the mouth

yard *n.* a plot of ground enclosed or set apart; (*Brit.*) paved area adjacent to a building; (*US*) grounds adjacent to a building; a slender spar set across a ship's mast; (*US*) a unit of length equal to three feet

yard´age *it,* length in yards; something dispensed in yards, as cloth

yard´stick *n.* a measuring stick one yard in length; a standard

yarn *n.* spun fiber for use in weaving, knitting, etc.; tale of adventure

yaw *vi.* move erratically, as a ship in heavy seas —*vt.* cause to yaw

yawl *n.* a small sailboat

yawn *vi.* open the mouth wide with a full inhalation from boredom, drowsiness, etc.; stand wide open —*vt.* express with a yawn — *n.* a wide opening —**yawn´er** *n.*

yaws *n. pl.* a contagious tropical disease marked by skin lesions

yea *adv.* yes —*n.* an affirmative vote; one casting an affirmative vote

year *n.* time Earth takes for one revolution around the sun; a period of 12 months; time a planet takes to revolve around its sun; a distinct period: *school year*

year´book *n.* a book documenting events of the previous year

year´ly *adj.* of a year; occurring once a year; continuing for a year —*adv.* once a year; annually

yearn *vi.* desire earnestly

yearn´ing *n.* strong emotional longing or desire

yeast *n.* a preparation used to leaven bread, make, beer, etc.; froth or spume —*vi.* to foam

yeast´y *adj.* of or resembling yeast; causing fermentation; covered with froth or bam .

yell *vt., vi.* shout, scream, or cheer —*n.* a sharp cry, of terror, pain, etc.; a rhythmic cheer

yel´low *adj.* colored by age, illness, etc.; of a light brown or yellowish complexion; offensively sensational: *yellow* journalism; cowardly —*n.* between green and orange in the color spectrum; the color of ripe lemons; yolk of an egg —*vt., vi.* become colored with age

yelp *vt.* utter a sharp or shrill cry —*vt.* express with a yelp

yen *n.* basic monetary unit of Japan; an ardent longing or desire —*vi.* yearn

yen´ta *n.* a gossip or meddler

yeo´man *n.* a petty officer in the U.S. Navy or Coast Guard; a yeoman of the guard; an attendant to noblility or royalty; a diligent worker

yeo´man•ly *adj.* of the attributes of a yeoman; brave or rugged —*adv.* like a yeoman; bravely

yes *n.* an affirmative response — *vt.* give an affirmative response —*adv.* as you say; truly

yes man one who invariably agrees with his superiors

yes´ter•day *n.* the day before today; the near past —*adv.*

yes´ter•year *n.* last year; time past: songs *of yesteryear* — *adv.*

yield *vt.* produce by natural process　or by cultivation; give in return as profit; surrender or relinquish —*vi.* provide a return; give up, surrender; give way; comply —*n.* amount produced; result of cultivation, investment, etc. —**yield´er** *n.*

yield´ing *adj.* productive; flexible or pliant; obedient

yip *n.* a yelp, as from a dog — *vi.* yelp

yo´del *vt., vi.* sing by alternating between low notes and falsetto

yoga *n.* Hindu discipline directed to spiritual illumination; exercises based on yoga techniques

yo´gi *n.* one who practices yoga

yo´gurt *n.* a soft food of milk curdled with bacteria cultures

yoke re a curved frame for coupling draft animals; a similar contrivance; animals joined　by a yoke; a thing that binds or connects; servitude —*vt.* attach with a yoke; join, as with a yoke — *vt.* be joined or linked

yo´kel *n.* a country bumpkin

yon´der *adj.* at a distance — *adv.* in that place; there

yore *a.* time long past

young *adj.* of or in an early stage of life or growth; newly formed; fresh and vigorous; immature —*n.* young people as a group; offspring of animals —**young´ster** *n.*

youth *n.* condition of being young; period when one is young; early period of being or development; young people as a group

youth´ful *adj.* fresh or vigorous; having youth

yowl *vi.* howl —*n.* prolonged wailing

z, Z twenty-sixth letter of the alphabet

za´ny *adj.* absurdly funny; ludicrous

zap *tn.* strike; kill; confront suddenly and forcefully

zeal *n.* ardor or enthusiasm

zeal´ot *n.* a fanatic

zeal´ous *adj.* filled with or showing exceptional enthusiasm

ze´bra *n.* a striped African mammal allied to the horse

ze´nith *n.* point of the celestial sphere exactly overhead; highest or culminating point

zeph´yr *n.* gentle wind; light woolen or worsted yarn

ze´ro *n.* the numeral or symbol 0; nothing; lowest or starting point — *vt.* adjust to an arbitrary zero point

zero gravity a condition of apparent weightlessness

zero hour a critical time

zero population growth a condition to which deaths and births in a population are closely matched

zero-sum a situation in which gains and losses offset

zest *n.* agreeable excitement; keen enjoyment; a quality that imparts emotion; piquant flavoring

zig´zag *n..* a path or pattern marked by sharp turns or angles — *vt.*, *vi.* to move in zigzags —*adj.*, *ads*

zilch *n.* nothing; zero

zil´lion *a.* a large, indeterminate number

zing *n.* a sharp buzzing or humming sound; energy, vitality, a verbal attack —*vi.* make a shrill humming sound ,—*vt.* criticize sharply

zip *n.* a sharp, hissing sound; energy vitality —*vt.* close with a zipper; give speed and energy,—*vi.* move with speed and energy

zip´py *adj.* brisk, energetic

zith´er *i.* a multi-stringed instrument played by plucking

zi´ti *n.* a tubular pasta

zo´di•a *n.* an imaginary belt of twive parts, encircling the movens

zom´bie *n.* a snake diety in voodo cults; a reanimated corpse; one who behaves mechanically

zone *n.* region or area set off by a special characteristic — *vt.* divide into zones, esp. of a municipality where activity is restricted by zone

zoo *n.* place for wild animal exhibits; a chaotic place or situation

zo•o•ge•og´ra•phy *n.* study of the distribution of animals and their environment —**zo•o•ge•og´ra•pher** *n.*

zo•og´ra•phy *n.* the branch of zoology dealing with descriptions of animals **zo´og´ra•pher** *n.*

zo•ol´o•gy *n.* study of animals and their structure, development, etc.; the animal life of an area

zo´a•phyte *n.* an invertebrate animal resembling a plant

zy•mol´o•gy *n.* the science of fermentation

zy´mur•gy *n.* the chemistry of fermentation as applied to brewing, making yeast, and making wine